SCHAUM'S OUTLINE

THEORY AND PROBLEMS

OF

INTRODUCTION
to
MATHEMATICAL
ECONOMICS

Second Edition

340101

•

EDWARD T. DOWLING, Ph.D.

Chairman and Professor
Department of Economics
Fordham University

SCHAUM'S OUTLINE SERIES

McGRAW-HILL, INC.

New York   St. Louis   San Francisco   Auckland   Bogotá   Caracas
Hamburg   Lisbon   London   Madrid   Mexico   Milan   Montreal
New Delhi   Paris   San Juan   São Paulo   Singapore
Sydney   Tokyo   Toronto

To my aunt and second mother,

Madeline Barnes

EDWARD T. DOWLING is professor of Economics at Fordham University and currently Chairman of the Department. He was Chairman of the Economics Department from 1979 to 1982 and Dean of Fordham College from 1982 to 1986. His Ph.D. is from Cornell University, and his main areas of professional interest are mathematical economics and economic development. In addition to journal articles, he is the author of *Schaum's Outline of Calculus for Business, Economics, and the Social Sciences* and coauthor with Dominick Salvatore of *Schaum's Outline of Development Economics*. A Jesuit priest, he is a member of the Jesuit Community at Fordham.

Schaum's Outline of Theory and Problems of
INTRODUCTION TO MATHEMATICAL ECONOMICS

4 5 6 7 8 9 10 11 12 13 14 15 16 17 18 19 20 SHP SHP 9 4

ISBN 0-07-017674-4

Sponsoring Editor; John Aliano
Production Supervisor; Leroy Young
Editing Supervisors; Meg Tobin, Maureen Walker
Cover design by Amy E. Becker.

 This book is printed on recycled paper containing 10% post consumer waste.

Library of Congress Cataloging-in-Publication Data

Dowling, Edward Thomas
    Schaum's outline of theory and problems of introduction to
mathematical economics/Edward T. Dowling.—2nd ed.
        p.   cm.—(Schaum's outline series)
    Rev. ed. of: Schaum's outline of theory and problems of
mathematics for economists. c1980.
    Includes index.
    ISBN 0-07-017674-4
    1. Economics, Mathematical. 2. Mathematics. I. Dowling, Edward
Thomas   Schaum's outline of theory and problems of
mathematics for economists. II. Title. III. Title: Theory and
problems of introduction to mathematical economics. IV. Title:
Introduction to mathematical economics.
HB135.D68   1992
510′.2433—dc20   90-49771
                                                  CIP

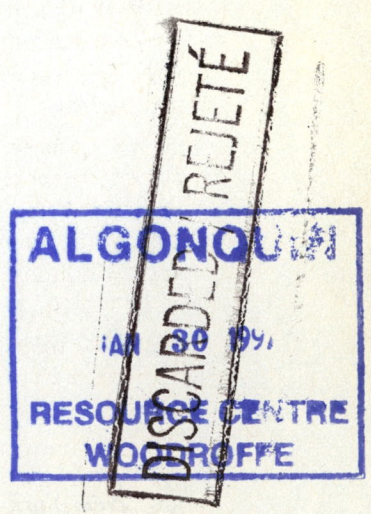

Preface

Introduction to Mathematical Economics, 2/e evolved from an earlier work, *Mathematics for Economists* and incorporates many of its strengths. It also offers something new for the advanced student and something new for the beginner. For the advanced student, a concluding chapter on the calculus of variations has been added. The increased emphasis on dynamic optimization in advanced macroeconomic theory today has made knowledge of the calculus of variations essential, yet heretofore no succinct treatment of the subject has been available to the economist. For the beginner or someone away from mathematics for a while, a new introductory review chapter has been added to refresh basic tools and concepts needed for later work.

Presentation of the derivative in the current edition is strengthened by the addition of sections on limits, continuity, and the relationship between continuity and differentiability. The current volume is also enhanced by timely, systematic references to connections between individual topics and their corresponding examples and related problems. A more thorough system of cross-referencing similar topics and problems has also been introduced.

The objectives of the book have not changed since the successful introduction of *Mathematics for Economists* ten years ago; only the scope has been broadened. People in business, economics, and the social sciences must be familiar with an increasingly wide variety of mathematical tools. *Introduction to Mathematical Economics, 2/e* is designed to fill this need by presenting a thorough, easily understood introduction to such varied and important topics as differential and integral calculus, linear algebra, linear programming, differential equations, difference equations, and the calculus of variations—all with direct, frequent, and practical applications to economic problems and everyday situations.

The theory-and-solved-problem format of each chapter provides concise explanations illustrated by examples, plus numerous problems with fully worked-out solutions. The topics and related problems range in difficulty from simpler mathematical operations to sophisticated applications. No mathematical proficiency beyond the high school level is assumed at the start. The learning-by-doing pedagogy will enable students to progress at their own rates and adapt the book to their own needs.

Introduction to Mathematical Economics, 2/e can be used by itself or as a supplement to other texts for undergraduate and graduate students in economics, business, and the social sciences. It is largely self-contained. Starting with a basic review of high school algebra in Chapter 1, the book consistently explains all the concepts and techniques needed for the material in subsequent chapters.

Since there is no universal agreement on the order in which differential calculus and linear algebra should be presented, the book is designed so that Chapters 10 and 11 on linear algebra can be covered immediately after Chapter 2, if so desired, without loss of continuity.

This book contains over 1,600 problems, all solved in considerable detail. To get the most from the book, students should strive as soon as possible to work independently of the solutions. This can be done by solving problems on individual sheets of paper with the book closed. If difficulties arise, the solution can then be checked in the book.

For best results, students should never be satisfied with passive knowledge—the capacity merely to follow or comprehend the various steps presented in the book. Mastery of the subject and doing well on exams require active knowledge—the ability to solve any problem, in any order, without the aid of the book.

Experience has proved that students of very different backgrounds and abilities can be successful in handling the subject matter of this text when the material is presented in the current format.

In closing, I would like to thank two of my colleagues at Fordham for invaluable support: Dr. Dominick Salvatore and Dr. Timothy Weithers. Without the latter's prompting, the chapter on the calculus of variations might not have been included. I am also indebted to Maria Cristina Cacdac, and Lisa Angeline, graduate students at Fordham, for proofreading the manuscript and offering insightful suggestions, and to the entire staff at McGraw-Hill, especially John Carleo, John Aliano, Meg Tobin, Maureen Walker, Pat Koch, and Patty Andrews.

EDWARD T. DOWLING

Contents

Chapter 1

Review

1.1 EXPONENTS

Given n a positive integer, x^n signifies that x is multiplied by itself n times. Here x is referred to as the *base*; n is termed an *exponent*. By convention an exponent of 1 is not expressed: $x^1 = x$, $8^1 = 8$. By definition any nonzero number or variable raised to the zero power is equal to 1: $x^0 = 1$, $3^0 = 1$. And 0^0 is undefined. Assuming a and b are positive integers and x and y are real numbers for which the following exist, the *rules of exponents* are outlined below and illustrated in Examples 1 and 2 and Problem 1.1.

1. $x^a(x^b) = x^{a+b}$ 6. $\dfrac{1}{x^a} = x^{-a}$

2. $\dfrac{x^a}{x^b} = x^{a-b}$ 7. $\sqrt{x} = x^{1/2}$

3. $(x^a)^b = x^{ab}$ 8. $\sqrt[a]{x} = x^{1/a}$

4. $(xy)^a = x^a y^a$ 9. $\sqrt[b]{x^a} = x^{a/b} = (x^{1/b})^a$

5. $\left(\dfrac{x}{y}\right)^a = \dfrac{x^a}{y^a}$ 10. $x^{-(a/b)} = \dfrac{1}{x^{a/b}}$

EXAMPLE 1. From Rule 2, it can easily be seen why any variable or nonzero number raised to the zero power equals 1. For example, $x^3/x^3 = x^{3-3} = x^0 = 1$; $8^5/8^5 = 8^{5-5} = 8^0 = 1$.

EXAMPLE 2. In multiplication, exponents of the same variable are added; in division, the exponents are subtracted; when raised to a power, the exponents are multiplied, as indicated by the rules above and shown in the examples below followed by illustrations in brackets.

(a) $x^2(x^3) = x^{2+3} = x^5 \neq x^6$ Rule 1

$$[x^2(x^3) = (x \cdot x)(x \cdot x \cdot x) = x \cdot x \cdot x \cdot x \cdot x = x^5]$$

(b) $\dfrac{x^6}{x^3} = x^{6-3} = x^3 \neq x^2$ Rule 2

$$\left[\frac{x^6}{x^3} = \frac{x \cdot x \cdot x \cdot x \cdot x \cdot x}{x \cdot x \cdot x} = x \cdot x \cdot x = x^3\right]$$

(c) $(x^4)^2 = x^{4 \cdot 2} = x^8 \neq x^{16}$ or x^6 Rule 3

$$[(x^4)^2 = (x \cdot x \cdot x \cdot x)(x \cdot x \cdot x \cdot x) = x^8]$$

(d) $(xy)^4 = x^4 y^4 \neq xy^4$ Rule 4

$$[(xy)^4 = (xy)(xy)(xy)(xy) = (x \cdot x \cdot x \cdot x)(y \cdot y \cdot y \cdot y) = x^4 y^4]$$

(e) $\left(\dfrac{x}{y}\right)^5 = \dfrac{x^5}{y^5} \neq \dfrac{x^5}{y}$ or $\dfrac{x}{y^5}$ Rule 5

$$\left[\left(\frac{x}{y}\right)^5 = \frac{(x)}{(y)}\frac{(x)}{(y)}\frac{(x)}{(y)}\frac{(x)}{(y)}\frac{(x)}{(y)} = \frac{x^5}{y^5}\right]$$

(f) $\dfrac{x^3}{x^4} = x^{3-4} = x^{-1} = \dfrac{1}{x} \neq x^{3/4}$ Rules 2 and 6

$$\left[\frac{x^3}{x^4} = \frac{x \cdot x \cdot x}{x \cdot x \cdot x \cdot x} = \frac{1}{x}\right]$$

(g) $\sqrt{x} = x^{1/2}$ Rule 7

Since $\sqrt{x} \cdot \sqrt{x} = x$ and from Rule 1 exponents of a common base are added in multiplication, the exponent of $\sqrt{x}$, when added to itself, must equal 1. With $\frac{1}{2} + \frac{1}{2} = 1$, the exponent of $\sqrt{x}$ is $\frac{1}{2}$. Thus, $\sqrt{x} \cdot \sqrt{x} = x^{1/2} \cdot x^{1/2} = x^{1/2 + 1/2} = x^1 = x$.

(h) $\sqrt[3]{x} = x^{1/3}$ Rule 8

Just as $\sqrt[3]{x} \cdot \sqrt[3]{x} \cdot \sqrt[3]{x} = x$, so $x^{1/3} \cdot x^{1/3} \cdot x^{1/3} = x^{1/3 + 1/3 + 1/3} = x^1 = x$.

(i) $x^{3/2} = (x^{1/2})^3$ or $(x^3)^{1/2}$ Rule 9

$$[4^{3/2} = (4^{1/2})^3 = (\sqrt{4})^3 = (\pm 2)^3 = \pm 8, \text{ or equally valid, } 4^{3/2} = (4^3)^{1/2} = (64)^{1/2} = \sqrt{64} = \pm 8]$$

(j) $x^{-2/3} = \dfrac{1}{x^{2/3}} = \dfrac{1}{(x^{1/3})^2}$ or $\dfrac{1}{(x^2)^{1/3}}$ Rule 10

$$\left[27^{-2/3} = \frac{1}{(27^{1/3})^2} = \frac{1}{(3)^2} = \frac{1}{9}, \text{ or equally valid, } 27^{-2/3} = \frac{1}{(27^2)^{1/3}} = \frac{1}{(729)^{1/3}} = \frac{1}{9}\right]$$

See Problem 1.1.

1.2 POLYNOMIALS

Given an expression such as $5x^3$, x is called a *variable* because it can assume any number of different values, and 5 is referred to as the *coefficient* of x. Expressions consisting simply of a real number or of a coefficient times one or more variables raised to the power of a positive integer are called *monomials*. Monomials can be added or subtracted to form *polynomials*. Each of the monomials comprising a polynomial is called a *term*. Terms that have the same variables and exponents are called *like terms*. Rules for adding, subtracting, multiplying, and dividing polynomials are explained in Examples 3 through 5 and treated in Problems 1.2 to 1.4.

EXAMPLE 3. Like terms in polynomials can be added or subtracted by adding or subtracting their coefficients. Unlike terms cannot be so added or subtracted. See Problems 1.2 and 1.3.

(a) $4x^5 + 9x^5 = 13x^5$ (b) $12xy - 3xy = 9xy$

(c) $(7x^3 + 5x^2 - 8x) + (11x^3 - 9x^2 - 2x) = 18x^3 - 4x^2 - 10x$

(d) $(24x - 17y) + (6x + 5z) = 30x - 17y + 5z$

EXAMPLE 4. Like and unlike terms can be multiplied or divided by multiplying or dividing both the coefficients and variables.

(a) $(5x)(13y^2) = 65xy^2$ (b) $(7x^3y^5)(4x^2y^4) = 28x^5y^9$

(c) $(2x^3y)(17y^4z^2) = 34x^3y^5z^2$ (d) $\dfrac{15x^4y^3z^6}{3x^2y^2z^3} = 5x^2yz^3$

(e) $\dfrac{4x^2y^5z^3}{8x^5y^3z^4} = \dfrac{y^2}{2x^3z}$

EXAMPLE 5. In multiplying two polynomials, each term in the first polynomial must be multiplied by each term in the second and their products added. See Problem 1.4.

$$(6x + 7y)(4x + 9y) = 24x^2 + 54xy + 28xy + 63y^2$$
$$= 24x^2 + 82xy + 63y^2$$
$$(2x + 3y)(8x - 5y - 7z) = 16x^2 - 10xy - 14xz + 24xy - 15y^2 - 21yz$$
$$= 16x^2 + 14xy - 14xz - 21yz - 15y^2$$

1.3 FACTORING

Factoring reverses the process of polynomial multiplication in order to express a given polynomial as a product of simpler polynomials called *factors*. A monomial such as the number 15 is easily factored by expressing it as a product of its integer factors $1 \cdot 15$ or $3 \cdot 5$. A *binomial* such as $8x^3 - 24x^2$ is easily factored by dividing or *factoring out* the *greatest common factor*, here $8x^2$, to obtain $8x^2(x - 3)$. Factoring a *trinomial* such as $mx^2 + nx + p$, however, requires the help of the following rules:

1. The factors of $mx^2 + nx + p$ are $(ax + b)(cx + d)$, where (1) $ac = m$, (2) $bd = p$, and (3) $ad + bc = n$.
2. The factors of $mx^2 + nxy + py^2$ are $(ax + by)(cx + dy)$, with the same three conditions as above.

See Example 6 and Problems 1.5 to 1.7.

EXAMPLE 6. To factor $x^2 + 13x + 30$, where in terms of Rule 1 above $m = 1$, $n = 13$, and $p = 30$, we seek integer factors such that:

1) $a \cdot c = 1$.   Integer factors: 1×1
2) $b \cdot d = 30$.   Integer factors: $1 \times 30, 2 \times 15, 3 \times 10, 5 \times 6$
3) $ad + bc = 13$.   With $a = c = 1$, $b + d$ must equal 13.

Adding the different combinations of factors from step 2, we have $1 + 30 = 31$, $2 + 15 = 17$, $3 + 10 = 13$, $5 + 6 = 11$. Since only $3 + 10 = 13$ in step 3, 3 and 10 are the only candidates for b and d from step 2 which, when used with $a = c = 1$ from step 1, fulfill all the above requirements. Hence,

$$x^2 + 13x + 30 = (x + 3)(x + 10) \tag{1.1}$$

See Problems 1.5 to 1.7 and 1.9.

1.4 EQUATIONS: LINEAR AND QUADRATIC

A mathematical statement setting two algebraic expressions equal to each other is called an *equation*. An equation in which all variables are raised to the first power is known as a *linear equation*. A linear equation can be solved by moving the unknown variable to the left-hand side of the equal sign and all the other terms to the right-hand side. A *quadratic equation* of the form $ax^2 + bx + c$, where a, b, and c are constants and $a \neq 0$, can be solved by factoring, *completing the square*, or using the *quadratic formula*:

$$x = \frac{-b \pm \sqrt{b^2 - 4ac}}{2a} \tag{1.2}$$

Solving quadratic equations by factoring is explained in Example 8 and Problem 1.9, by the quadratic formula in Example 9 and Problem 1.10, and by completing the square in Section 1.5.

EXAMPLE 7. The linear equation given below is solved in three easy steps.

$$\frac{x}{4} - 3 = \frac{x}{5} + 1$$

1. Move all terms with the unknown variable x to the left, here by subtracting $x/5$ from both sides of the equation.

$$\frac{x}{4} - 3 - \frac{x}{5} = 1$$

2. Move any term without the unknown variable to the right, here by adding 3 to both sides of the equation.

$$\frac{x}{4} - \frac{x}{5} = 1 + 3 = 4$$

3. Simplify both sides of the equation until the unknown variable is by itself on the left and the solution is on the right, here by multiplying both sides of the equation by 20 and subtracting.

$$20 \cdot \left(\frac{x}{4} - \frac{x}{5}\right) = 4 \cdot 20$$
$$5x - 4x = 80$$
$$x = 80$$

EXAMPLE 8. Factoring is used below to solve the quadratic equation

$$x^2 + 13x + 30 = 0$$

Substituting from *(1.1)* in Example 6, we have

$$(x + 3)(x + 10) = 0$$

For $(x + 3)(x + 10)$ to equal 0, $x + 3$ or $x + 10$ must equal 0. Setting each in turn equal to 0 and solving for x, we have

$$x + 3 = 0 \qquad x + 10 = 0$$
$$x = -3 \qquad x = -10$$

EXAMPLE 9. The quadratic formula is used below to solve the quadratic equation

$$5x^2 - 55x + 140 = 0$$

Substituting $a = 5$, $b = -55$, $c = 140$ from the given equation in *(1.2)* gives

$$x = \frac{-(-55) \pm \sqrt{(-55)^2 - 4(5)(140)}}{2(5)}$$

$$= \frac{55 \pm \sqrt{3025 - 2800}}{10} = \frac{55 \pm \sqrt{225}}{10} = \frac{55 \pm 15}{10}$$

Adding $+15$ and then -15 to find each of the two solutions, we get

$$x = \frac{55 + 15}{10} = 7 \qquad x = \frac{55 - 15}{10} = 4$$

See Problem 1.10.

1.5 COMPLETING THE SQUARE

An expression in the form $x^2 + bx$, where the coefficient of the squared term is $+1$, can be converted to a perfect square by taking $\frac{1}{2}$ the coefficient of x, here $b/2$, squaring it $[(b/2)^2]$, and adding the latter to the original expression, to obtain:

$$x^2 + bx + \frac{b^2}{4} = \left(x + \frac{b}{2}\right)^2$$

To solve a quadratic equation such as

$$x^2 - 18x + 45 = 0$$

by completing the square, (1) move the constant to the right:

$$x^2 - 18x = -45$$

(2) Apply the technique given above to the left-hand side of the equation: $b = -18$, $b/2 = -9$, and $(b/2)^2 = (-9)^2 = 81$. (3) Add $(b/2)^2$, here 81, to both sides of the equation and simplify by factoring.

$$x^2 - 18x + 81 = -45 + 81$$
$$(x - 9)^2 = 36$$

(4) Then take the square root of both sides and solve for x.

$$x - 9 = \pm\sqrt{36}$$
$$x = 9 \pm \sqrt{36} = 9 \pm 6 \qquad x = 15, x = 3$$

See Problem 1.11. For expressions in which the coefficient of the squared term is not $+1$, see Problem 1.12.

1.6 SIMULTANEOUS EQUATIONS

To solve a system of two or more equations simultaneously, (1) the equations must be *consistent* (noncontradictory), (2) they must be *independent* (not multiples of each other), and (3) there must be as many consistent and independent equations as variables. A system of simultaneous linear equations can be solved by either the *substitution* or *elimination* method, explained in Example 10 and Problems 2.11 to 2.16, as well as by methods developed later in linear algebra in Sections 10.12, 11.8, and 11.9.

EXAMPLE 10.   The equilibrium conditions for two markets, butter and margarine, where P_b and P_m are the prices of butter and margarine, respectively, are given in (1.3) and (1.4):

$$8P_b - 3P_m = 7 \qquad\qquad (1.3)$$
$$-P_b + 7P_m = 19 \qquad\qquad (1.4)$$

The prices that will bring equilibrium to the model are found below by using the substitution and elimination methods.

Substitution Method

1. Solve one of the equations for one variable in terms of the other. Solving (1.4) for P_b gives

$$P_b = 7P_m - 19$$

2. Substitute the value of that term in the *other* equation, here (1.3), and solve for P_m.

$$8P_b - 3P_m = 7$$
$$8(7P_m - 19) - 3P_m = 7$$
$$56P_m - 152 - 3P_m = 7$$
$$53P_m = 159$$
$$P_m = 3$$

3.   Then substitute $P_m = 3$ in either (1.3) or (1.4) to find P_b.

$$8P_b - 3(3) = 7$$
$$8P_b = 16$$
$$P_b = 2$$

Elimination Method

1.   Multiply (1.3) by the coefficient of P_b (or P_m) in (1.4) and (1.4) by the coefficient of P_b (or P_m) in (1.3). Picking P_m, we get

$$7(8P_b - 3P_m = 7) \qquad 56P_b - 21P_m = 49 \qquad\qquad (1.5)$$
$$-3(-P_b + 7P_m = 19) \qquad 3P_b - 21P_m = -57 \qquad\qquad (1.6)$$

2.   Subtract (1.6) from (1.5) to eliminate the selected variable.

$$53P_b = 106$$
$$P_b = 2$$

3.   Substitute $P_b = 2$ in (1.5) or (1.6) to find P_m as in step 3 of the substitution method.

1.7   FUNCTIONS

A *function f* is a *rule* which assigns to each value of a variable (x), called the *argument* of the function, one and only one value [$f(x)$], referred to as the *value of the function at x*. The *domain* of a function refers to the set of all possible values of x; the *range* is the set of all possible values for $f(x)$. Functions are generally defined by algebraic formulas as illustrated in Example 11. Other letters, such as g, h, or the Greek letter ϕ, are also used to express functions. Functions encountered frequently in economics are listed below.

Linear function:

$$f(x) = mx + b$$

Quadratic function:

$$f(x) = ax^2 + bx + c \qquad (a \neq 0)$$

Polynomial function of degree n:

$$f(x) = a_n x^n + a_{n-1} x^{n-1} + \cdots + a_0 \qquad (n = \text{nonnegative integer}; a_n \neq 0)$$

Rational function:

$$f(x) = \frac{g(x)}{h(x)}$$

where $g(x)$ and $h(x)$ are both polynomials and $h(x) \neq 0$. (*Note*: Rational comes from *ratio*.)

Power function:

$$f(x) = ax^n \qquad (n = \text{any real number})$$

EXAMPLE 11.   The function $f(x) = 8x - 5$ is the rule that takes a number, multiplies it by 8, and then subtracts 5 from the product. If a value is given for x, the value is substituted for x in the formula and the equation solved for $f(x)$. For example, if $x = 3$,

$$f(x) = 8(3) - 5 = 19$$

If $x = 4$,
$$f(x) = 8(4) - 5 = 27$$

See Problems 1.13-1.15.

EXAMPLE 12. Given below are examples of different functions:

Linear: $\qquad\qquad f(x) = 7x - 4 \qquad g(x) = -3x \qquad h(x) = 9$

Quadratic: $\qquad\quad f(x) = 5x^2 + 8x - 2 \qquad g(x) = x^2 - 6x \qquad h(x) = 6x^2$

Polynomial: $\qquad f(x) = 4x^3 + 2x^2 - 9x + 5 \qquad g(x) = 2x^5 - x^3 + 7$

Rational: $\qquad\quad f(x) = \dfrac{x^2 - 9}{x + 4} \quad (x \ne -4) \qquad g(x) = \dfrac{5x}{x - 2} \quad (x \ne 2)$

Power: $\qquad\qquad f(x) = 2x^6 \qquad g(x) = x^{1/2} \qquad h(x) = 4x^{-3}$

1.8 GRAPHS, SLOPES, AND INTERCEPTS

In graphing a function such as $y = f(x)$, x is placed on the horizontal axis and is known as the *independent variable*; y is placed on the vertical axis and is called the *dependent variable*. The graph of a linear function is a straight line. The *slope* of a line measures the *change in y* (Δy) divided by a *change in x* (Δx). The slope indicates the steepness and direction of a line. The greater the absolute value of the slope, the steeper the line. A positively sloped line moves up from left to right; a negatively sloped line moves down. The slope of a horizontal line, for which $\Delta y = 0$, is zero. The slope of a vertical line, for which $\Delta x = 0$, is undefined, i.e., does not exist because division by zero is impossible. The *y intercept* is the point where the graph crosses the y axis; it occurs when $x = 0$. The *x intercept* is the point where the line intersects the x axis; it occurs when $y = 0$. See Problem 1.16.

EXAMPLE 13. To graph a linear equation such as

$$y = -\tfrac{1}{4}x + 3$$

one need only find two points which satisfy the equation and connect them by a straight line. Since the graph of a linear function is a straight line, all the points satisfying the equation must lie on the line.

To find the y intercept, set $x = 0$ and solve for y, getting $y = -\tfrac{1}{4}(0) + 3$, $y = 3$. The y intercept is the point $(x, y) = (0, 3)$. To find the x intercept, set $y = 0$ and solve for x. Thus, $0 = -\tfrac{1}{4}x + 3$, $\tfrac{1}{4}x = 3$, $x = 12$. The x intercept is the point $(x, y) = (12, 0)$. Then plot the points $(0, 3)$ and $(12, 0)$ and connect them by a straight line, as in Fig. 1-1, to complete the graph of $y = -\tfrac{1}{4}x + 3$. See Examples 14 and 15 and Problems 1.16 to 1.19.

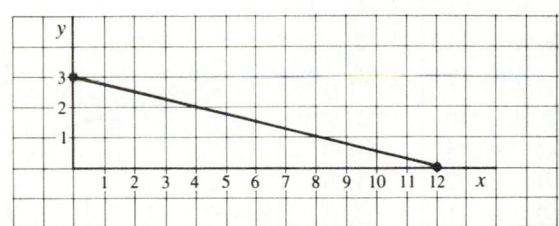

Fig. 1-1

EXAMPLE 14. For a line passing through points (x_1, y_1) and (x_2, y_2), the slope m is calculated as follows:

$$m = \frac{\Delta y}{\Delta x} = \frac{y_2 - y_1}{x_2 - x_1} \qquad x_1 \ne x_2$$

For the line in Fig. 1-1 passing through $(0, 3)$ and $(12, 0)$,

$$m = \frac{\Delta y}{\Delta x} = \frac{0 - 3}{12 - 0} = -\frac{1}{4}$$

and the vertical intercept can be seen to be the point $(0, 3)$.

EXAMPLE 15. For a linear equation in the *slope-intercept form*

$$y = mx + b \qquad m, b = \text{constants}$$

the slope and intercepts of the line can be read directly from the equation. For such an equation, m is the slope of the line; $(0, b)$ is the y intercept; and, as seen in Problem 1.16, $(-b/m, 0)$ is the x intercept. One can tell immediately from the equation in Example 13, therefore, that the slope of the line is $-\frac{1}{4}$, the y intercept is $(0, 3)$, and the x intercept is $(12, 0)$.

1.9 GRAPHS OF NONLINEAR FUNCTIONS

The graph of a *quadratic function* of the form $f(x) = ax^2 + bx + c$, where $a \neq 0$, is a *parabola*. In Fig. 1-2(a), $y = 2x^2$, where $a = 2$, $b = 0$, and $c = 0$, is graphed. The graph of a parabola is symmetric about a line called the *axis of symmetry*. The point of intersection of the parabola and its axis is called the *vertex*. In Fig. 1-2(a), the axis coincides with the y axis; the vertex is $(0, 0)$.

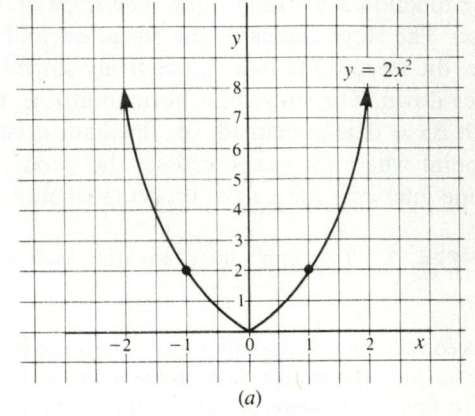

(a)	x	$f(x) = 2x^2 = y$	Points
	-2	$f(-2) = 2(-2)^2 = 8$	$(-2, 8)$
	-1	$f(-1) = 2(-1)^2 = 2$	$(-1, 2)$
	0	$f(0) = 2(0)^2 = 0$	$(0, 0)$
	1	$f(1) = 2(1)^2 = 2$	$(1, 2)$
	2	$f(2) = 2(2)^2 = 8$	$(2, 8)$
	3	$f(3) = 2(3)^2 = 18$	$(3, 18)$

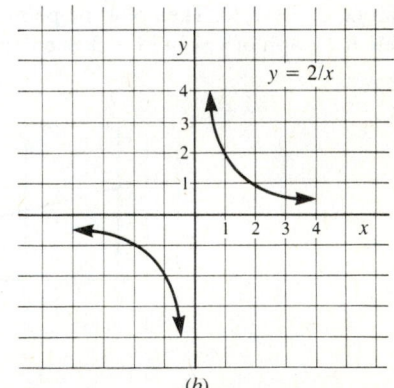

(b)	x	$f(x) = 2/x = y$	Points
	-4	$f(-4) = 2/(-4) = -\frac{1}{2}$	$(-4, -\frac{1}{2})$
	-2	$f(-2) = 2/(-2) = -1$	$(-2, -1)$
	-1	$f(-1) = 2/(-1) = -2$	$(-1, -2)$
	$-\frac{1}{2}$	$f(-\frac{1}{2}) = 2/(-\frac{1}{2}) = -4$	$(-\frac{1}{2}, -4)$
	$\frac{1}{2}$	$f(\frac{1}{2}) = 2/\frac{1}{2} = 4$	$(\frac{1}{2}, 4)$
	1	$f(1) = 2/1 = 2$	$(1, 2)$
	2	$f(2) = 2/2 = 1$	$(2, 1)$
	4	$f(4) = 2/4 = \frac{1}{2}$	$(4, \frac{1}{2})$

Fig. 1-2

For a quadratic function expressed in the form

$$y = a(x - h)^2 + k \tag{1.7}$$

the axis is $x - h = 0$, $x = h$; the vertex is (h, k). If $a > 0$, the parabola opens up; if $a < 0$, it opens down. See Problem 1.19, Section 2.5, and Problem 2.25.

The graph of $y = 2/x$, a *rational function*, is seen in Fig. 1-2(b). As $x \to 0$, the graph approaches the y axis. The y axis in this instance is called the *vertical asymptote*. As $x \to \infty$, the graph approaches the x axis, in this case called the *horizontal asymptote*. See Problem 2.26.

Solved Problems

EXPONENTS

1.1. Simplify the following, using the rules of exponents:

(a) $x^4 \cdot x^5$

$$x^4 \cdot x^5 = x^{4+5} = x^9$$

(b) $x^7 \cdot x^{-3}$

$$x^7 \cdot x^{-3} = x^{7+(-3)} = x^4$$

$$\left[x^7 \cdot x^{-3} = x^7 \cdot \frac{1}{x^3} = x \cdot x \cdot x \cdot x \cdot x \cdot x \cdot x \cdot \frac{1}{x \cdot x \cdot x} = x^4 \right]$$

(c) $x^{-2} \cdot x^{-4}$

$$x^{-2} \cdot x^{-4} = x^{-2+(-4)} = x^{-6} = \frac{1}{x^6}$$

$$\left[x^{-2} \cdot x^{-4} = \frac{1}{x \cdot x} \cdot \frac{1}{x \cdot x \cdot x \cdot x} = \frac{1}{x^6} \right]$$

(d) $x^2 \cdot x^{1/2}$

$$x^2 \cdot x^{1/2} = x^{2+(1/2)} = x^{5/2} = \sqrt{x^5}$$

$$[x^2 \cdot x^{1/2} = (x \cdot x)(\sqrt{x})$$
$$= (\sqrt{x} \cdot \sqrt{x} \cdot \sqrt{x} \cdot \sqrt{x})(\sqrt{x}) = (x^{1/2})^5 = x^{5/2}]$$

(e) $\dfrac{x^9}{x^3}$

$$\frac{x^9}{x^3} = x^{9-3} = x^6$$

(f) $\dfrac{x^4}{x^7}$

$$\frac{x^4}{x^7} = x^{4-7} = x^{-3} = \frac{1}{x^3}$$

$$\left[\frac{x^4}{x^7} = \frac{x \cdot x \cdot x \cdot x}{x \cdot x \cdot x \cdot x \cdot x \cdot x \cdot x} = \frac{1}{x^3} \right]$$

(g) $\dfrac{x^3}{x^{-4}}$

$$\frac{x^3}{x^{-4}} = x^{3-(-4)} = x^{3+4} = x^7$$

$$\left[\frac{x^3}{x^{-4}} = \frac{x^3}{1/x^4} = x^3 \cdot x^4 = x^7 \right]$$

(h) $\dfrac{x^3}{\sqrt{x}}$

$$\frac{x^3}{\sqrt{x}} = \frac{x^3}{x^{1/2}} = x^{3-(1/2)} = x^{5/2} = \sqrt{x^5}$$

(i) $(x^2)^5$

$$(x^2)^5 = x^{2 \cdot 5} = x^{10}$$

(j) $(x^4)^{-2}$

$$(x^4)^{-2} = x^{4 \cdot (-2)} = x^{-8} = \frac{1}{x^8}$$

(k) $\dfrac{1}{x^5} \cdot \dfrac{1}{y^5}$

$$\frac{1}{x^5} \cdot \frac{1}{y^5} = x^{-5} \cdot y^{-5} = (xy)^{-5} = \frac{1}{(xy)^5}$$

(l) $\dfrac{x^3}{y^3}$

$$\frac{x^3}{y^3} = \left(\frac{x}{y}\right)^3$$

POLYNOMIALS

1.2.   Perform the indicated arithmetic operations on the following polynomials:

(a) $3xy + 5xy$ (b) $13yz^2 - 28yz^2$ (c) $36x^2y^3 - 25x^2y^3$

(d) $26x_1x_2 + 58x_1x_2$ (e) $16x^2y^3z^5 - 37x^2y^3z^5$

(a) $8xy$,   (b) $-15yz^2$,   (c) $11x^2y^3$,   (d) $84x_1x_2$,   (e) $-21x^2y^3z^5$

1.3.   Add or subtract the following polynomials as indicated. Note that in subtraction the sign of every term within the parentheses must be changed before corresponding elements are added.

(a) $(34x - 8y) + (13x + 12y)$

$$(34x - 8y) + (13x + 12y) = 47x + 4y$$

(b) $(26x - 19y) - (17x - 50y)$

$$(26x - 19y) - (17x - 50y) = 9x + 31y$$

(c) $(5x^2 - 8x - 23) - (2x^2 + 7x)$

$$(5x^2 - 8x - 23) - (2x^2 + 7x) = 3x^2 - 15x - 23$$

(d) $(13x^2 + 35x) - (4x^2 + 17x - 49)$

$$(13x^2 + 35x) - (4x^2 + 17x - 49) = 9x^2 + 18x + 49$$

1.4.   Perform the indicated operations, recalling that each term in the first polynomial must be multiplied by each term in the second and their products summed.

(a) $(2x + 9)(3x - 8)$

$$(2x + 9)(3x - 8) = 6x^2 - 16x + 27x - 72 = 6x^2 + 11x - 72$$

(b) $(6x - 4y)(3x - 5y)$

$$(6x - 4y)(3x - 5y) = 18x^2 - 30xy - 12xy + 20y^2 = 18x^2 - 42xy + 20y^2$$

(c) $(3x - 7)^2$

$$(3x - 7)^2 = (3x - 7)(3x - 7) = 9x^2 - 21x - 21x + 49 = 9x^2 - 42x + 49$$

(d) $(x + y)(x - y)$

$$(x + y)(x - y) = x^2 - xy + xy - y^2 = x^2 - y^2$$

FACTORING

1.5. Factor each of the following, using integer coefficients:

(a) $x^2 + 28x + 27$

Here, using the notation from Rule 1 in Section 1.3, $m = 1$, $n = 28$, and $p = 27$. We seek integers such that:

  (1) $a \cdot c = 1$ [1, 1]   Henceforth, when $a = c = 1$, this step will be omitted.
  (2) $b \cdot d = 27$ [1, 27; 3, 9]
  (3) $ad + bc = 28$. With $a = 1 = c$, $b + d$ must equal 28.   [$1 + 27 = 28$; $3 + 9 \neq 28$]

$$x^2 + 28x + 27 = (x + 1)(x + 27)$$

(b) $x^2 + 11x + 24$

  (1) $b \cdot d = 24$ [1, 24; 2, 12; 3, 8; 4, 6]
  (2) $b + d = 11$ [only $3 + 8 = 11$]

$$x^2 + 11x + 24 = (x + 3)(x + 8)$$

(c) $x^2 - 22x + 40$

With $b \cdot d$ positive and $b + d$ negative, the two integer factors must both be negative.

  (1) $b \cdot d = 40$ [$-1, -40; -2, -20; -4, -10; -5, -8$]
  (2) $b + d = -22$ [only $-2 + (-20) = -22$]

$$x^2 - 22x + 40 = (x - 2)(x - 20)$$

(d) $x^2 + 19x - 66$

With $b \cdot d$ negative, the two integer factors must be of opposite signs; for $b + d$ to be positive when one of the two factors is negative, the factor with the larger absolute value must be positive.

  (1) $b \cdot d = -66$ [$-1, 66; -2, 33; -3, 22; -6, 11$]
  (2) $b + d = 19$ [only $-3 + 22 = 19$]

$$x^2 + 19x - 66 = (x - 3)(x + 22)$$

(e) $x^2 - 14x - 32$

With $b \cdot d$ and $b + d$ both negative, the factors must be of different signs, and the factor with the larger absolute value must be negative.

  (1) $b \cdot d = -32$ [1, -32; 2, -16; 4, -8]
  (2) $b + d = -14$ [$2 + (-16) = -14$]

$$x^2 - 14x - 32 = (x + 2)(x - 16)$$

(f) $x^2 - 81$

Here $b \cdot d$ is negative and $b + d = 0$. For this to be true, the factors must be of different signs and of the same absolute value.

$$(1) \quad b \cdot d = -81 \qquad [9, -9]$$
$$(2) \quad b + d = 0 \qquad [9 + (-9) = 0]$$

$$x^2 - 81 = (x + 9)(x - 9)$$

1.6. Use the techniques and procedures developed in Problem 1.5 to factor the following expressions in which the coefficient of x^2 is no longer limited to 1.

(a) $5x^2 + 23x + 12$

(1) $a \cdot c = 5$ [Factors are 5, 1, giving $(5x + ?)(x + ?)$]

(2) $b \cdot d = 12$ [1, 12; 2, 6; 3, 4]

(3) $ad + bc = 23$. Here all the pairs of possible factors from step 2 must be tried in *both* orders in step 1, that is, [5, 1] with [1, 12; 12, 1; 2, 6; 6, 2; 3, 4; 4, 3]

Of all the possible combinations of factors above, only $(5 \cdot 4) + (1 \cdot 3) = 23$. Carefully arranging the factors, therefore, to ensure that 5 multiplies 4 and 1 multiplies 3, we have

$$5x^2 + 23x + 12 = (5x + 3)(x + 4)$$

(b) $3x^2 - 41x + 26$

(1) $a \cdot c = 3$ [3, 1]

(2) $b \cdot d = 26$ [$-1, -26; -26, -1; -2, -13; -13, -2$]

(3) $ad + bc = -41$ [$(3 \cdot -13) + (1 \cdot -2) = -41$]

Then arranging the factors to ensure that 3 multiplies -13 and 1 multiplies -2, we have

$$3x^2 - 41x + 26 = (3x - 2)(x - 13)$$

(c) $7x^2 - 100x + 28$

(1) $a \cdot c = 7$ [7, 1]

(2) $b \cdot d = 28$ [$-1, -28; -28, -1; -2, -14; -14, -2; -4, -7; -7, -4$]

(3) $ad + bc = -100$ [$(7 \cdot -14) + (1 \cdot -2) = -100$]

$$7x^2 - 100x + 28 = (7x - 2)(x - 14)$$

(d) $5x^2 + 18x - 56$

(1) $a \cdot c = 5$ [5, 1]

(2) $b \cdot d = -56$ [1, 56; 2, 28; 4, 14; 7, 8; each combination must be considered in both orders *and* with alternating signs.]

(3) $ad + bc = 18$ [$(5 \cdot -2) + (1 \cdot 28) = 18$]

$$5x^2 + 18x - 56 = (5x + 28)(x - 2)$$

(e) $11x^2 - 16x - 12$

(1) $a \cdot c = 11$ [11, 1]

(2) $b \cdot d = -12$ [1, 12; 2, 6; 3, 4; considered as in (d)]

(3) $ad + bc = -16$ [$(11 \cdot -2) + (1 \cdot 6) = -16$]

$$11x^2 - 16x - 12 = (11x + 6)(x - 2)$$

1.7. Using Rule 2 from Section 1.3 and the techniques developed in Problems 1.5 and 1.6, factor the following polynomials:

(a) $x^2 - 19xy + 60y^2$

(1) $b \cdot d = 60$ $[-1, -60; -2, -30; -3, -20; -4, -15; -5, -12; -6, -10]$

(2) $b + d = -19$ $[-4 + (-15) = -19]$

$$x^2 - 19xy + 60y^2 = (x - 4y)(x - 15y)$$

(b) $x^2 + 19xy - 42y^2$

(1) $b \cdot d = -42$ $[-1, 42; -2, 21; -3, 14; -6, 7]$

(2) $b + d = 19$ $[-2 + 21 = 19]$

$$x^2 + 19xy - 42y^2 = (x - 2y)(x + 21y)$$

(c) $7x^2 - 65xy + 18y^2$

(1) $a \cdot c = 7$ $[7, 1]$

(2) $b \cdot d = 18$ $[-1, -18; -18, -1; -2, -9; -9, -2; -3, -6; -6, -3]$

(3) $ad + bc = -65$ $[(7 \cdot -9) + (1 \cdot -2) = -65]$

$$7x^2 - 65xy + 18y^2 = (7x - 2y)(x - 9y)$$

(d) $5x^2 + 31xy - 28y^2$

(1) $a \cdot c = 5$ $[5, 1]$

(2) $b \cdot d = -28$ $[1, 28; 2, 14; 4, 7;$ each combination must be considered in both orders *and* with alternating signs as in Problem 1.6$(d)]$

(3) $ad + bc = 31$ $[(5 \cdot 7) + (1 \cdot -4) = 31]$

$$5x^2 + 31xy - 28y^2 = (5x - 4y)(x + 7y)$$

(e) $9x^2 - 25y^2$

(1) $a \cdot c = 9$ $[1, 9; 3, 3]$

(2) $b \cdot d = -25$ $[1, -25; -1, 25; 5, -5]$

(3) $ad + bc = 0$ $[(3 \cdot 5) + (3 \cdot -5) = 0]$

$$9x^2 - 25y^2 = (3x + 5y)(3x - 5y)$$

SOLVING EQUATIONS

1.8.   Solve each of the following linear equations by moving all terms with the unknown variable to the left, moving all other terms to the right, and then simplifying.

(a) $5x + 6 = 9x - 10$

$$5x + 6 = 9x - 10$$
$$5x - 9x = -10 - 6$$
$$-4x = -16$$
$$x = 4$$

(b) $26 - 2x = 8x - 44$

$$26 - 2x = 8x - 44$$
$$-2x - 8x = -44 - 26$$
$$-10x = -70$$
$$x = 7$$

(c) $9(3x + 4) - 2x = 11 + 5(4x - 1)$

$$9(3x + 4) - 2x = 11 + 5(4x - 1)$$
$$27x + 36 - 2x = 11 + 20x - 5$$
$$27x - 2x - 20x = 11 - 5 - 36$$
$$5x = -30$$
$$x = -6$$

(d) $\dfrac{x}{3} - 16 = \dfrac{x}{12} + 14$

$$\frac{x}{3} - 16 = \frac{x}{12} + 14$$
$$\frac{x}{3} - \frac{x}{12} = 14 + 16$$

Multiplying both sides of the equation by the least common denominator (LCD), here 12, gives

$$12 \cdot \left(\frac{x}{3} - \frac{x}{12}\right) = 30 \cdot 12$$
$$4x - x = 360$$
$$x = 120$$

(e) $\dfrac{5}{x} + \dfrac{3}{x+4} = \dfrac{7}{x}$ $[x \neq 0, -4]$

$$\frac{5}{x} + \frac{3}{x+4} = \frac{7}{x}$$

Multiplying both sides by the LCD, we get

$$x(x+4) \cdot \left(\frac{5}{x} + \frac{3}{x+4}\right) = \frac{7}{x} \cdot x(x+4)$$
$$5(x+4) + 3x = 7(x+4)$$
$$8x + 20 = 7x + 28$$
$$x = 8$$

1.9. Solve the following quadratic equations by factoring:

(a) $x^2 + 11x + 24 = 0$

From Problem 1.5(b),
$$x^2 + 11x + 24 = (x+3)(x+8) = 0$$

For $(x+3)(x+8)$ to equal 0, $x+3 = 0$ or $x+8 = 0$. Setting each in turn equal to 0 and solving for x, we have

$$x + 3 = 0 \qquad x + 8 = 0$$
$$x = -3 \qquad x = -8$$

(b) $x^2 - 22x + 40 = 0$

From Problem 1.5(c),
$$x^2 - 22x + 40 = (x-2)(x-20) = 0$$
$$x - 2 = 0 \qquad x - 20 = 0$$
$$x = 2 \qquad x = 20$$

(c) $x^2 + 19x - 66 = 0$

From Problem 1.5(d),
$$x^2 + 19x - 66 = (x-3)(x+22) = 0$$
$$x - 3 = 0 \qquad x + 22 = 0$$
$$x = 3 \qquad x = -22$$

1.10. Solve the following quadratic equations, using the quadratic formula:

(a) $5x^2 + 23x + 12 = 0$

Using (1.2) and substituting $a = 5$, $b = 23$, and $c = 12$, we get

$$x = \frac{-b \pm \sqrt{b^2 - 4ac}}{2a}$$
$$= \frac{-23 \pm \sqrt{(23)^2 - 4(5)(12)}}{2(5)} = \frac{-23 \pm \sqrt{529 - 240}}{10}$$
$$= \frac{-23 \pm \sqrt{289}}{10} = \frac{-23 \pm 17}{10}$$
$$x = \frac{-23 + 17}{10} = -0.6 \qquad x = \frac{-23 - 17}{10} = -4$$

(b) $3x^2 - 41x + 26 = 0$

$$x = \frac{-(-41) \pm \sqrt{(-41)^2 - 4(3)(26)}}{2(3)} = \frac{41 \pm \sqrt{1681 - 312}}{6}$$

$$= \frac{41 \pm \sqrt{1369}}{6} = \frac{41 \pm 37}{6}$$

$$x = \frac{41 + 37}{6} = 13 \qquad x = \frac{41 - 37}{6} = \frac{2}{3}$$

To see how the same solutions might be obtained through factoring, see Problem 1.6(a) and (b).

1.11.   Solve the following quadratic equations by completing the square.

(a) $x^2 + 14x + 45 = 0$

Move the constant to the right, as explained in Section 1.5.

$$x^2 + 14x = -45$$

Ignore the constant for the moment, and complete the square on the left-hand side where in terms of Section 1.5, $b = 14$, $b/2 = 7$, and $(b/2)^2 = 49$. Now add 49 to *both* sides of the equation to keep the equality.

$$x^2 + 14x + 49 = -45 + 49$$

Next factor the left-hand side to obtain the perfect square,

$$(x + 7)^2 = 4$$

then take the square root of *both* sides of the equation, and solve for x:

$$x + 7 = \pm\sqrt{4}$$
$$x = -7 \pm 2$$
$$x = -7 + 2 = -5 \qquad x = -7 - 2 = -9$$

(b) $x^2 - 8x - 240 = 0$

Move the constant to the right.

$$x^2 - 8x = 240$$

Here $b = -8$, $b/2 = -4$, and $(-4)^2 = 16$. Add 16 to both sides.

$$x^2 - 8x + 16 = 240 + 16$$

Factor the left-hand side to obtain the perfect square.

$$(x - 4)^2 = 256$$

Then take the square root of both sides and solve for x.

$$x - 4 = \pm\sqrt{256}$$
$$x = 4 \pm \sqrt{256} = 4 \pm 16$$
$$x = 4 + 16 = 20 \qquad x = 4 - 16 = -12$$

1.12.   Solve the following quadratic equations by completing the square, being sure to first factor out the coefficient of the squared term any time it differs from $+1$.

(a) $-x^2 + 6x + 112 = 0$

Factor out -1 and move the constant.

$$x^2 - 6x - 112 = 0$$
$$x^2 - 6x = 112$$

Here $b = -6$, $b/2 = -3$, and $(-3)^2 = 9$. Add 9 and solve for x.

$$x^2 - 6x + 9 = 112 + 9$$
$$(x - 3)^2 = 121$$

$$x - 3 = \pm\sqrt{121}$$
$$x = 3 \pm \sqrt{121} = 3 \pm 11$$
$$x = 3 + 11 = 14 \qquad x = 3 - 11 = -8$$

(b) $5x^2 + 120x + 675 = 0$

Factor out 5.	$x^2 + 24x + 135 = 0$
Move the constant.	$x^2 + 24x = -135$
Add $(24/2)^2 = 144$.	$x^2 + 24x + 144 = -135 + 144$
And solve for x.	$(x + 12)^2 = 9$

$$x + 12 = \pm\sqrt{9}$$
$$x = -12 \pm \sqrt{9} = -12 \pm 3$$
$$x = -12 + 3 = -9 \qquad x = -12 - 3 = -15$$

FUNCTIONS

1.13. (a)   Given $f(x) = x^2 + 4x - 5$, find $f(2)$ and $f(-3)$.

Substituting 2 for each occurrence of x in the function gives

$$f(2) = (2)^2 + 4(2) - 5 = 7$$

Now substituting -3 for each occurrence of x, we get

$$f(-3) = (-3)^2 + 4(-3) - 5 = -8$$

(b)   Given $f(x) = 2x^3 - 5x^2 + 8x - 20$, find $f(5)$ and $f(-4)$.

$$f(5) = 2(5)^3 - 5(5)^2 + 8(5) - 20 = 145$$
$$f(-4) = 2(-4)^3 - 5(-4)^2 + 8(-4) - 20 = -260$$

1.14. In the following graphs (Fig. 1-3), where y replaces $f(x)$ as the dependent variable in functions, indicate which graphs are graphs of functions and which are not.

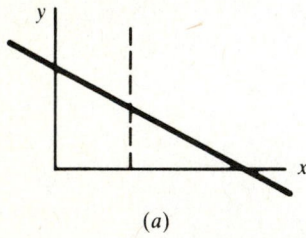

(a)

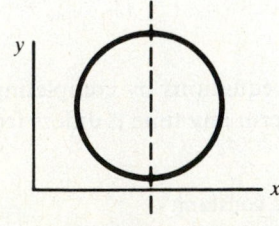

(b)

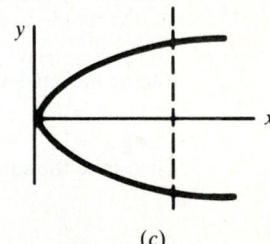

(c)

(d)

(e)

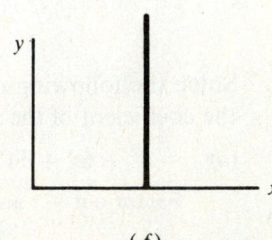

(f)

Fig. 1-3

For a graph to be the graph of a function, for each value of x, there can be one and only one value of y. If a vertical line can be drawn which intersects the graph at more than one point, then the graph is not the graph of a function. Applying this criterion, which is known as the *vertical-line test*, we see that (a), (b), and (d) are functions; (c), (e), and (f) are not.

1.15. Which of the following equations are functions and why?

(a) $y = -2x + 7$

$y = -2x + 7$ is a function because for each value of the independent variable x there is one and only one value of the dependent variable y. For example, if $x = 1$, $y = -2(1) + 7 = 5$. The graph would be similar to (a) in Fig. 1-3.

(b) $y^2 = x$

$y^2 = x$, which is equivalent to $y = \pm\sqrt{x}$, is not a function because for each positive value of x, there are two values of y. For example, if $y^2 = 9$, $y = \pm 3$. The graph would be similar to that of (c) in Fig. 1-3, illustrating that a parabola whose axis is parallel to the x axis cannot be a function.

(c) $y = x^2$

$y = x^2$ is a function. For each value of x there is only one value of y. For instance, if $x = -5$, $y = 25$. While it is also true that $y = 25$ when $x = 5$, it is irrelevant. The definition of a function simply demands that for each value of x there be one value of y, *not* that for each value of y there be only one value of x. The graph would be like (d) in Fig. 1-3, demonstrating that a parabola with axis parallel to the y axis is a function.

(d) $y = -x^2 + 6x + 15$

$y = -x^2 + 6x + 15$ is a function. For each value of x there is a unique value of y. The graph would be like (b) in Fig. 1-3.

(e) $x^2 + y^2 = 64$

$x^2 + y^2 = 64$ is not a function. If $x = 0$, $y^2 = 64$, and $y = \pm 8$. The graph would be a circle, similar to (e) in Fig. 1-3. A circle does not pass the vertical-line test.

(f) $x = 4$

$x = 4$ is not a function. The graph of $x = 4$ is a vertical line. This means that at $x = 4$, y has many values. The graph would look like (f) in Fig. 1-3.

GRAPHS, SLOPES, AND INTERCEPTS

1.16. Find the x intercept in terms of the parameters of the slope-intercept form of a linear equation $y = mx + b$.

Setting $y = 0$,

$$0 = mx + b$$
$$mx = -b$$
$$x = -\frac{b}{m}$$

Thus, the x intercept of the slope-intercept form is $(-b/m, 0)$.

1.17. Graph the following equations and indicate their respective slopes and intercepts:

(a) $3y + 15x = 30$ (b) $2y - 6x = 12$ (c) $8y - 2x + 16 = 0$ (d) $6y + 3x - 18 = 0$

To graph an equation, first set it in slope-intercept form by solving it for y in terms of x. From Example 15, the slope and two intercepts can then be read directly from the equation, providing three pieces of information whereas only two are needed to graph a straight line. See Fig. 1-4 and Problems 2.1 to 2.10.

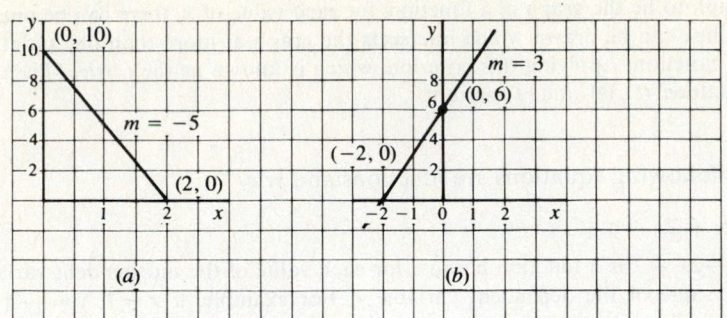

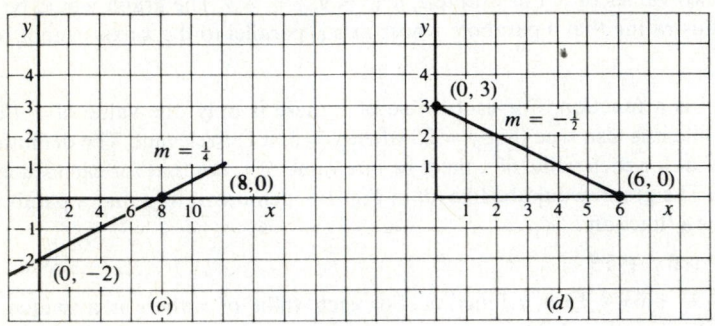

Fig. 1-4

(a) $3y + 15x = 30$

$\qquad 3y = -15x + 30$

$\qquad y = -5x + 10$

Slope $m = -5$

y intercept: $(0, 10)$

x intercept: $(2, 0)$

(b) $2y - 6x = 12$

$\qquad 2y = 6x + 12$

$\qquad y = 3x + 6$

Slope $m = 3$

y intercept: $(0, 6)$

x intercept: $(-2, 0)$

(c) $8y - 2x + 16 = 0$

$\qquad 8y = 2x - 16$

$\qquad y = \frac{1}{4}x - 2$

Slope $m = \frac{1}{4}$

y intercept: $(0, -2)$

x intercept: $(8, 0)$

(d) $6y + 3x - 18 = 0$

$\qquad 6y = -3x + 18$

$\qquad y = -\frac{1}{2}x + 3$

Slope $m = -\frac{1}{2}$

y intercept: $(0, 3)$

x intercept: $(6, 0)$

1.18. Find the slope m of the linear function passing through (a) $(4, 12)$, $(8, 2)$; (b) $(-1, 15)$, $(3, 6)$; (c) $(2, -3)$, $(5, 18)$.

(a) Substituting in the formula from Example 14, we get

$$m = \frac{y_2 - y_1}{x_2 - x_1} = \frac{2 - 12}{8 - 4} = \frac{-10}{4} = -2\frac{1}{2}$$

(b)

$$m = \frac{6 - 15}{3 - (-1)} = \frac{-9}{4} = -2\frac{1}{4}$$

(c)

$$m = \frac{18 - (-3)}{5 - 2} = \frac{21}{3} = 7$$

1.19. Convert the following quadratic functions to forms involving perfect squares, as in Equation (*1.7*), and draw a sketch of the graphs using the information from Sections 1.5 and 1.9.

(*a*) $y = x^2 + 6x + 13$

Here $b = 6$, $b/2 = 3$, and $3^2 = 9$. Adding and subtracting 9,

$$y = x^2 + 6x + 13 + 9 - 9$$

Then rearranging and factoring to find the perfect square, we find

$$y = (x^2 + 6x + 9) + (13 - 9)$$
$$= (x + 3)^2 + 4$$

From (*1.7*), when $y = a(x - h)^2 + k$, the axis is $x - h = 0$, $x = h$; and the vertex is (h, k). Here with $(x + 3)^2 + 4 = 0$, the axis is $x + 3 = 0$, $x = -3$; and the vertex is $(-3, 4)$. With $a = 1 > 0$, the parabola opens upward. See Fig. 1-5(*a*).

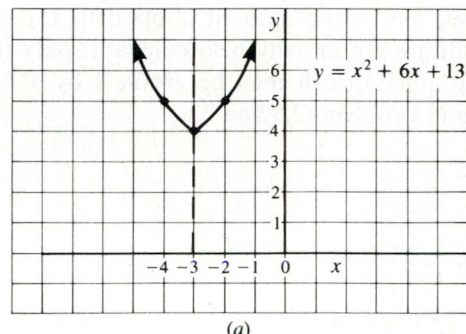

(*a*)

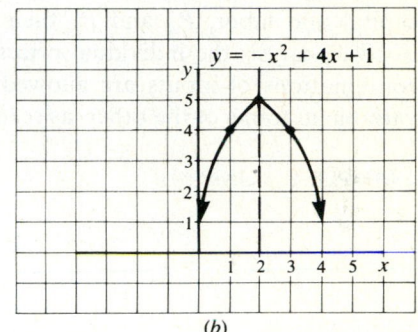

(*b*)

Fig. 1-5

(*b*) $y = -x^2 + 4x + 1$

If the coefficient of the squared term differs from $+1$, it must first be factored from all the terms involving x before we continue as above.

$$y = -1(x^2 - 4x) + 1$$

Now $b = -4$, $b/2 = -2$, $(-2)^2 = 4$. Add ± 4 *within* the parentheses.

$$y = -1(x^2 - 4x + 4 - 4) + 1$$

Note that $-1(-4) = 4$, rearrange, and factor.

$$y = -1(x^2 - 4x + 4) + 4 + 1$$
$$= -1(x - 2)^2 + 5$$

With $y = -1(x - 2)^2 + 5$, the axis is $x - 2 = 0$, $x = 2$; the vertex is $(2, 5)$. With $a = -1 < 0$, the parabola opens downward. See Fig. 1-5(*b*). (If desired, set $y = 0$ and solve for x to find that the x intercepts are $x = 2 + \sqrt{5}$ and $x = 2 - \sqrt{5}$.)

Chapter 2

Economic Applications of Graphs and Equations

2.1 ISOCOST LINES

An *isocost line* represents the different combinations of two inputs or factors of production that can be purchased with a given sum of money. The general formula is $P_K K + P_L L = E$, where K and L are capital and labor, P_K and P_L their respective prices, and E the amount allotted to expenditures. In isocost analysis the individual prices and the expenditure are initially held constant; only the different combinations of inputs are allowed to change. The function can then be graphed by expressing one variable in terms of the other, as seen in Example 1 and Problems 2.5 and 2.6.

EXAMPLE 1. Given:

$$P_K K + P_L L = E$$
$$P_K K = E - P_L L$$
$$K = \frac{E - P_L L}{P_K}$$
$$K = \frac{E}{P_K} - \left(\frac{P_L}{P_K}\right)L$$

This is the familiar linear function of the form $y = mx + b$, where $b = E/P_K =$ the vertical intercept and $m = -P_L/P_K =$ the slope. The graph is given by the solid line in Fig. 2-1.

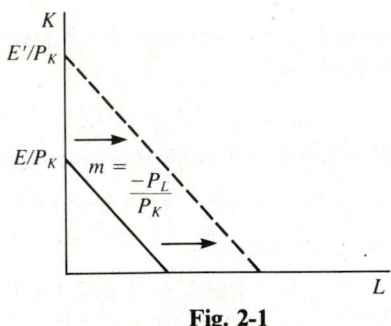

Fig. 2-1

From the equation and graph, the effects of a change in any one of the parameters are easily discernible. An increase in the expenditure from E to E' will increase the vertical intercept and cause the isocost line to shift out to the right (dashed line) parallel to the old line. The slope is unaffected because the slope depends on the relative prices $(-P_L/P_K)$ and prices are not affected by expenditure changes. A change in P_L will alter the slope of the line but leave the vertical intercept unchanged. A change in P_K will alter the slope and the vertical intercept. See Problems 2.5 and 2.6.

2.2 SUPPLY AND DEMAND ANALYSIS

Equilibrium in supply and demand analysis occurs when $Q_s = Q_d$. By equating the supply and demand functions, the equilibrium price and quantity can be determined. See Example 2 and Problems 2.1 to 2.4 and 2.11 to 2.16.

EXAMPLE 2. Given:

$$Q_s = -5 + 3P \qquad Q_d = 10 - 2P$$

In equilibrium,

$$Q_s = Q_d$$

Solving for P,

$$-5 + 3P = 10 - 2P$$
$$5P = 15 \qquad P = 3$$

Substituting $P = 3$ in either of the equations,

$$Q_s = -5 + 3P = -5 + 3(3) = 4 = Q_d$$

2.3 INCOME DETERMINATION MODELS

Income determination models generally express the equilibrium level of income in a four-sector economy as

$$Y = C + I + G + (X - Z)$$

where Y = income, C = consumption, I = investment, G = government expenditures, X = exports, and Z = imports. By substituting the information supplied in the problem, it is an easy matter to solve for the equilibrium level of income. *Aggregating* (summing) the variables on the right allows the equation to be graphed in two-dimensional space. See Example 3 and Problems 2.7 to 2.10 and 2.17 to 2.22.

EXAMPLE 3. Assume a simple two-sector economy where $Y = C + I$, $C = C_0 + bY$, and $I = I_0$. Assume further that $C_0 = 85$, $b = 0.9$, and $I_0 = 55$. The equilibrium level of income can be calculated in terms of (1) the general parameters and (2) the specific values assigned to these parameters.

1. The *equilibrium equation* is

$$Y = C + I$$

Substituting for C and I,

$$Y = C_0 + bY + I_0$$

Solving for Y,

$$Y - bY = C_0 + I_0$$
$$(1 - b)Y = C_0 + I_0$$
$$Y = \frac{C_0 + I_0}{1 - b}$$

The solution in this form is called the reduced form. The *reduced form* (or *solution equation*) expresses the endogenous variable (here Y) as an explicit function of the exogenous variables (C_0, I_0) and the parameters (b).

2. The specific equilibrium level of income can be calculated by substituting the numerical values for the parameters in either the original equation (a) or the reduced form (b):

$$(a) \quad Y = C_0 + bY + I_0 = 85 + 0.9Y + 55 \qquad\qquad (b) \quad Y = \frac{C_0 + I_0}{1 - b} = \frac{85 + 55}{1 - 0.9}$$

$$Y - 0.9Y = 140$$

$$0.1Y = 140 \qquad\qquad\qquad = \frac{140}{0.1} = 1400$$

$$Y = 1400$$

The term $1/(1 - b)$ is called the *autonomous expenditure multiplier* in economics. It measures the multiple effect each dollar of autonomous spending has on the equilibrium level of income. Since b = MPC in the income determination model, the multiplier = $1/(1 - \text{MPC})$.

Note: Decimals may be converted to fractions for ease in working with the income determination model. For example, $0.1 = \frac{1}{10}$, $0.9 = \frac{9}{10}$, $0.5 = \frac{1}{2}$, $0.2 = \frac{1}{5}$, etc.

2.4 *IS-LM* ANALYSIS

The *IS schedule* is a locus of points representing all the different combinations of interest rates and income levels consistent with equilibrium in the goods (commodity) market. The *LM schedule* is a locus of points representing all the different combinations of interest rates and income levels consistent with equilibrium in the money market. *IS-LM analysis* seeks to find the level of income and the rate of interest at which both the commodity market and the money market will be in equilibrium. This can be accomplished with the techniques used for solving simultaneous equations. Unlike the simple income determination model in Section 2.3, *IS-LM* analysis deals explicitly with the interest rate and incorporates its effect into the model. See Example 4 and Problems 2.23 and 2.24.

EXAMPLE 4. The commodity market for a simple two-sector economy is in equilibrium when $Y = C + I$. The money market is in equilibrium when the supply of money (M_s) equals the demand for money (M_d), which in turn is composed of the transaction-precautionary demand for money (M_t) and the speculative demand for money (M_z). Assume a two-sector economy where $C = 48 + 0.8Y$, $I = 98 - 75i$, $M_s = 250$, $M_t = 0.3Y$, and $M_z = 52 - 150i$.

Commodity equilibrium (*IS*) exists when $Y = C + I$. Substituting into the equation,

$$Y = 48 + 0.8Y + 98 - 75i$$
$$Y - 0.8Y = 146 - 75i$$
$$0.2Y + 75i - 146 = 0 \qquad (2.1)$$

Monetary equilibrium (*LM*) exists when $M_s = M_t + M_z$. Substituting into the equation,

$$250 = 0.3Y + 52 - 150i$$
$$0.3Y - 150i - 198 = 0 \qquad (2.2)$$

A condition of simultaneous equilibrium in both markets can be found, then, by solving (2.1) and (2.2) simultaneously:

$$0.2Y + 75i - 146 = 0 \qquad (2.1)$$

$$0.3Y - 150i - 198 = 0 \qquad (2.2)$$

Multiply (2.1) by 2, add the result (2.3) to (2.2) to eliminate i, and solve for Y.

$$0.4Y + 150i - 292 = 0 \qquad (2.3)$$
$$\underline{0.3Y - 150i - 198 = 0}$$
$$0.7Y \qquad - 490 = 0$$
$$Y = 700$$

Substitute $Y = 700$ in (2.1) or (2.2) to find i.

$$0.2Y + 75i - 146 = 0$$
$$0.2(700) + 75i - 146 = 0$$
$$140 + 75i - 146 = 0$$
$$75i = 6$$
$$i = \tfrac{6}{75} = 0.08$$

The commodity and money markets will be in simultaneous equilibrium when $Y = 700$ and $i = 0.08$. At that point $C = 48 + 0.8(700) = 608$, $I = 98 - 75(0.08) = 92$, $M_t = 0.3(700) = 210$,   and $M_z = 52 - 150(0.08) = 40$. $C + I = 608 + 92 = 700$ and $M_t + M_z = 210 + 40 = 250 = M_s$.

2.5 PRODUCTION-POSSIBILITIES FRONTIERS

A *production-possibilities frontier* (also called a *transformation curve*) depicts all the different combinations of goods a country or firm can produce while using all its resources efficiently with the best available technology. The curves are generally represented by quadratic functions as seen in Example 5 and Problem 2.25.

EXAMPLE 5.   A production-possibilities frontier such as

$$y = -\tfrac{1}{4}x^2 - \tfrac{1}{2}x + 42$$

for a country producing industrial goods (y) and agricultural goods (x) can be readily graphed by setting $y = 0$ and converting to a form involving a perfect square, such as in Equation (*1.7*) from Section 1.9.

$$y = -\tfrac{1}{4}x^2 - \tfrac{1}{2}x + 42 = 0$$

Factor out $-\tfrac{1}{4}$ from all the x terms as in Problem 1.19(*b*) and move the constant.

$$y = -\tfrac{1}{4}(x^2 + 2x) + 42 = 0$$

With $b = 2$, $b/2 = 1$, and $(1)^2 = 1$, add ± 1 *within* the parentheses.

$$y = -\tfrac{1}{4}(x^2 + 2x + 1 - 1) + 42 = 0$$

Noting that $-\tfrac{1}{4}(-1) = \tfrac{1}{4}$, rearrange and factor.

$$y = -\tfrac{1}{4}(x^2 + 2x + 1) + \tfrac{1}{4} + 42 = 0$$
$$= -\tfrac{1}{4}(x + 1)^2 + 42\tfrac{1}{4}$$

With $y = -\tfrac{1}{4}(x + 1)^2 + 42\tfrac{1}{4}$, the axis is $x + 1 = 0$, $x = -1$; and the vertex is $(-1, 42\tfrac{1}{4})$. With $a = -\tfrac{1}{4} < 0$, the parabola opens down. To find the x intercepts, set $y = 0$ and solve for x.

$$-\tfrac{1}{4}x^2 - \tfrac{1}{2}x + 42 = 0$$

Multiplying by -4 and factoring, we get

$$x^2 + 2x - 168 = 0$$
$$(x - 12)(x + 14) = 0$$
$$x = 12 \qquad x = -14$$

The x intercepts are $(-14, 0)$ and $(12, 0)$. To find the y intercept, if desired, we set $x = 0$ and solve for y, getting $y = 42$. The y intercept is $(0, 42)$. See Fig. 2-2 and note that in economics only the first quadrant with positive values for both x and y is relevant.

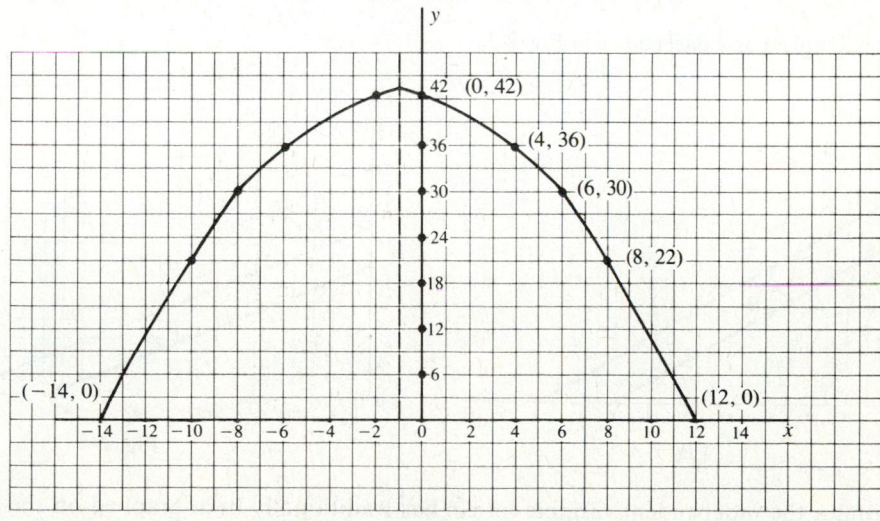

Fig. 2-2

Solved Problems

GRAPHS

2.1. A complete demand function is given by the equation

$$Q_d = -30P + 0.05Y + 2P_r + 4T$$

where P is the price of the good, Y is income, P_r is the price of a related good (here a substitute), and T is taste. Can the function be graphed?

Since the complete function contains five different variables, it cannot be graphed as is. In ordinary demand analysis, however, it is assumed that all the independent variables except price are held constant so that the effect of a change in price on the quantity demanded can be measured independently of the influence of other factors, or *ceteris paribus*. If the other variables (Y, P_r, T) are held constant, the function can be graphed.

2.2. (a) Draw the graph for the demand function in Problem 2.1, assuming $Y = 5000$, $P_r = 25$, and $T = 30$. (b) What does the typical demand function drawn in part (a) show? (c) What happens to the graph if the price of the good changes from 5 to 6? (d) What happens if any of the other variables change? For example, if income increases to 7400?

(a) By adding the new data to the equation in Problem 2.1, the function is easily graphable. See Fig. 2-3.

$$Q_d = -30P + 0.05Y + 2P_r + 4T = -30P + 0.05(5000) + 2(25) + 4(30) = -30P + 420$$

(b) The demand function graphed in part (a) shows all the different quantities of the good that will be demanded at different prices, assuming a given level of income, taste, and prices of substitutes (here 5000, 30, 25) which are not allowed to change.

(c) If nothing changes but the price of the good, the graph remains exactly the same since the graph indicates the different quantities that will be demanded at all the possible prices. A simple change in the price of the good occasions a movement along the curve which is called a *change in quantity demanded*. When the price goes from 5 to 6, the quantity demanded falls from 270 [420 − 30(5)] to 240 [420 − 30(6)], a movement from A to B on the curve.

(d) If any of the other variables change, there will be a shift in the curve. This is called a *change in demand* because it results in a totally new demand function (and curve) in response to the changed conditions. If income increases to 7400, the new demand function becomes

$$Q_d = -30P + 0.05(7400) + 2(25) + 4(30) = -30P + 540$$

This is graphed as a dashed line in Fig. 2-3.

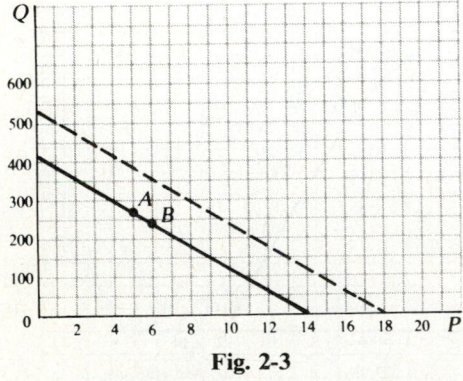

Fig. 2-3

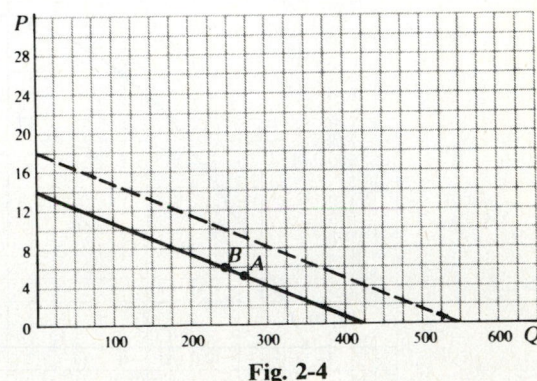

Fig. 2-4

2.3. In economics the independent variable (price) has traditionally been graphed on the vertical axis in supply and demand analysis, and the dependent variable (quantity) has been graphed on the horizontal. (a) Graph the demand function in Problem 2.2 according to the traditional method. (b) Show what happens if the price goes from 5 to 6 and income increases to 7400.

(a) The function $Q_d = 420 - 30P$ is graphed according to traditional economic practice by means of the *inverse function*, which is obtained by solving the original function for the independent variable in terms of the dependent variable. Solving algebraically for P in terms of Q_d, therefore, the inverse function of $Q_d = 420 - 30P$ is $P = 14 - \frac{1}{30}Q_d$. The graph appears as a solid line in Fig. 2-4.

(b) If P goes from 5 to 6, Q_d falls from 270 to 240.

$$P = 14 - \tfrac{1}{30}Q_d \qquad\qquad P = 14 - \tfrac{1}{30}Q_d$$
$$5 = 14 - \tfrac{1}{30}Q_d \qquad\qquad 6 = 14 - \tfrac{1}{30}Q_d$$
$$\tfrac{1}{30}Q_d = 9 \qquad\qquad\quad \tfrac{1}{30}Q_d = 8$$
$$Q_d = 270 \qquad\qquad\quad Q_d = 240$$

The change is represented by a movement from A to B in Fig. 2-4.

If $Y = 7400$, as in Problem 2.2(d), $Q_d = 540 - 30P$. Solving algebraically for P in terms of Q, the inverse function is $P = 18 - \frac{1}{30}Q_d$. It is graphed as a dashed line in Fig. 2-4.

2.4. (a) Graph the demand function

$$Q_d = -4P + 0.01Y - 5P_r + 10T$$

when $Y = 8000$, $P_r = 8$, and $T = 4$. (b) What type of good is the related good? (c) What happens if T increases to 8, indicating greater preference for the good? (d) Construct the graph along the traditional economic lines with P on the vertical axis and Q on the horizontal axis.

(a) $$Q_d = -4P + 0.01(8000) - 5(8) + 10(4) = -4P + 80$$

This is graphed as a solid line in Fig. 2-5(a).

(b) The related good has a negative coefficient. This means that a rise in the price of the related good will lead to a decrease in demand for the original good. The related good is, by definition, a complementary good.

(c) If $T = 8$, indicating greater preference, there will be a totally new demand.

$$Q_d = -4P + 0.01(8000) - 5(8) + 10(8) = -4P + 120$$

See the dashed line in Fig. 2-5(a).

(d) Graphing P on the vertical calls for the inverse function. Solving for P in terms of Q_d, the inverse of $Q_d = 80 - 4P$ is $P = 20 - \frac{1}{4}Q_d$ and is graphed as a solid line in Fig. 2-5(b). The inverse of $Q_d = 120 - 4P$ is $P = 30 - \frac{1}{4}Q_d$. It is the dashed line in Fig. 2-5(b).

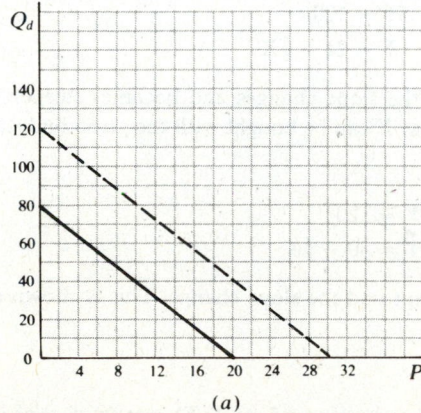
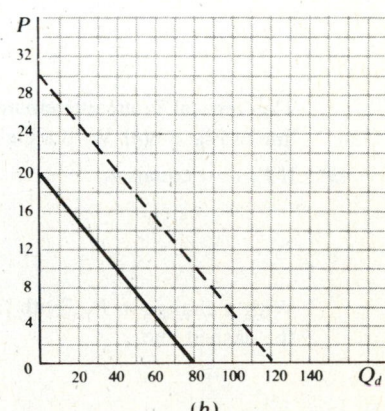

(a)   (b)

Fig. 2-5

2.5.   A person has $120 to spend on two goods (X, Y) whose respective prices are $3 and $5. (a) Draw a *budget line* showing all the different combinations of the two goods that can be bought with the given budget (B). What happens to the original budget line (b) if the budget falls by 25 percent, (c) if the price of X doubles, (d) if the price of Y falls to 4?

(a)   The general function for a budget line is $P_X X + P_Y Y = B$

If $P_X = 3$, $P_Y = 5$, and $B = 120$, $3X + 5Y = 120$

Solving for Y in terms of X in order to graph the function, $Y = 24 - \frac{3}{5}X$

The graph is given as a solid line in Fig. 2-6(a).

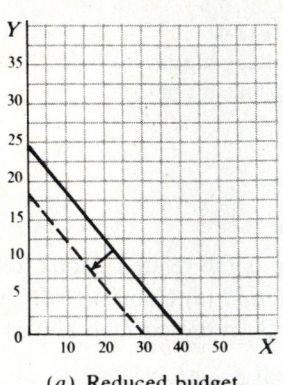 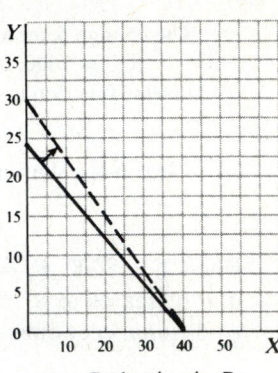

(a) Reduced budget   (b) Increase in P_X (c) Reduction in P_Y

Fig. 2-6

(b)   If the budget falls by 25 percent, the new budget is 90 [$120 - \frac{1}{4}(120) = 90$]. The equation for the new budget line is

$$3X + 5Y = 90$$
$$Y = 18 - \frac{3}{5}X$$

The graph is a dashed line in Fig. 2-6(a). Lowering the budget causes the budget line to shift parallel to the left.

(c)   If P_X doubles, the original equation becomes

$$6X + 5Y = 120$$
$$Y = 24 - \frac{6}{5}X$$

The vertical intercept remains the same, but the slope changes and becomes steeper. See the dashed line in Fig. 2-6(b). With a higher price for X, less X can be bought with the given budget.

(d)   If P_Y now equals 4,

$$3X + 4Y = 120$$
$$Y = 30 - \frac{3}{4}X$$

With a change in P_Y, both the vertical intercept and the slope change. This is shown in Fig. 2-6(c) by the dashed line.

2.6.   Either coal (C) or gas (G) can be used in the production of steel. The cost of coal is 100, the cost of gas 500. Draw an isocost curve showing the different combinations of gas and coal that can be purchased (a) with an initial expenditure (E) of 10 000, (b) if expenditures increase by 50 percent, (c) if the price of gas is reduced by 20 percent, (d) if the price of coal rises by 25 percent. Always start from the original equation.

(a)
$$P_C C + P_G G = E$$
$$100C + 500G = 10\,000$$
$$C = 100 - 5G$$

The graph is a solid line in Fig. 2-7(a).

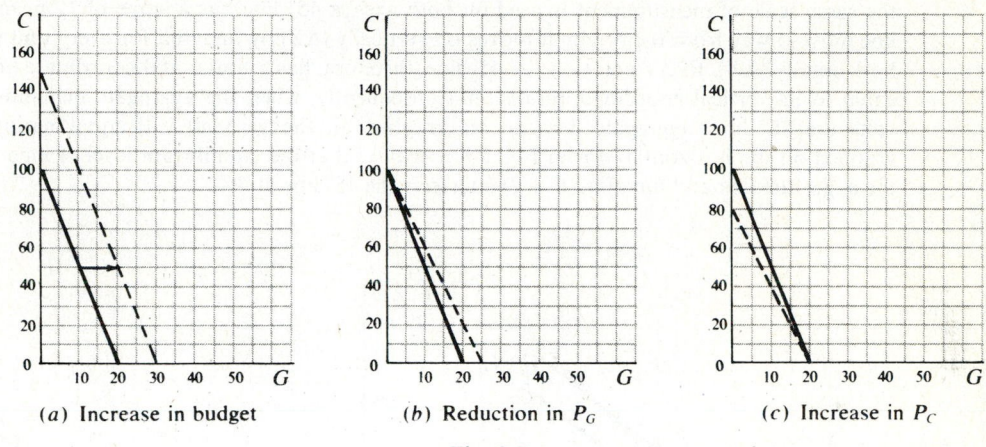

(a) Increase in budget   (b) Reduction in P_G (c) Increase in P_C

Fig. 2-7

(b) A 50 percent increase in expenditures makes the new outlay 15 000 [10 000 + 0.5(10 000)]. The new equation is

$$100C + 500G = 15\,000$$
$$C = 150 - 5G$$

The graph is the dashed line in Fig. 2-7(a).

(c) If the price of gas is reduced by 20 percent, the new price is 400 [500 − 0.2(500)], and the new equation is

$$100C + 400G = 10\,000$$
$$C = 100 - 4G$$

The graph is the dashed line in Fig. 2-7(b).

(d) A 25 percent rise in the price of coal makes the new price 125 [100 + 0.25(100)].

$$125C + 500G = 10\,000$$
$$C = 80 - 4G$$

The graph appears as a dashed line in Fig. 2-7(c).

GRAPHS IN THE INCOME DETERMINATION MODEL

2.7. Given: $Y = C + I$, $C = 50 + 0.8Y$, and $I_0 = 50$. (a) Graph the consumption function. (b) Graph the aggregate demand function, $C + I_0$. (c) Find the equilibrium level of income from the graph.

(a) Since consumption is a function of income, it is graphed on the vertical axis; income is graphed on the horizontal. See Fig. 2-8. When other components of aggregate demand such as I, G, and $X - Z$ are added to the model, they are also graphed on the vertical axis. It is easily determined from the linear form of the consumption function that the vertical intercept is 50 and the slope of the line (the MPC or $\Delta C / \Delta Y$) is 0.8.

(b) Investment in the model is *autonomous investment*. This means investment is independent of income and does not change in response to changes in income. When considered by itself, the graph of a constant is a horizontal line; when added to a linear function, it causes a parallel shift in the original function by an amount equal to its value. In Fig. 2-8, autonomous investment causes the aggregate demand function to shift up by 50 parallel to the initial consumption function.

(c) To obtain the equilibrium level of income from a graph, a 45° dashed line is drawn from the origin. If the same scale of measurement is used on both axes, a 45° line has a slope of 1, meaning that as the line moves away from the origin, it moves up vertically (ΔY) by one unit for every unit it moves across horizontally (ΔX). Every point on the 45° line, therefore, has a horizontal coordinate (*abscissa*) exactly equal to its vertical coordinate (*ordinate*). Consequently, when the aggregate demand function intersects the 45° line, aggregate demand (as graphed on the vertical) will equal national income (as graphed on the horizontal). From Fig. 2-8 it is clear that the equilibrium level of income is 500, since the aggregate demand function ($C + I$) intersects the 45° line at 500.

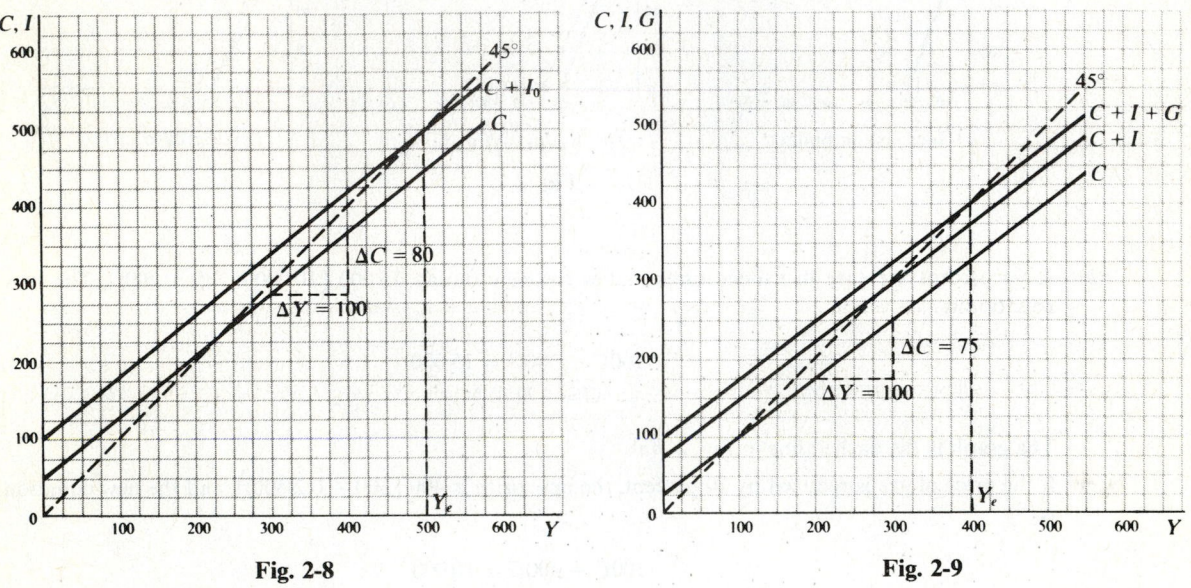

Fig. 2-8   Fig. 2-9

2.8. Given: $Y = C + I + G$, $C = 25 + 0.75Y$, $I = I_0 = 50$, and $G = G_0 = 25$. (a) Graph the aggregate demand function and show its individual components. (b) Find the equilibrium level of income. (c) How can the aggregate demand function be graphed directly, without having to graph each of the component parts?

(a) See Fig. 2-9.

(b) Equilibrium income = 400.

(c) To graph the aggregate demand function directly, sum up the individual components,

$$\text{Agg. } D = C + I + G = 25 + 0.75Y + 50 + 25 = 100 + 0.75Y$$

The direct graphing of the aggregate demand function coincides exactly with the graph of the summation of the individual graphs of C, I, and G above.

2.9. Use a graph to show how the addition of a lump-sum tax (a tax independent of income) influences the parameters of the income determination model. Graph the two systems individually, using a solid line for (*1*) and a dashed line for (*2*).

$$(1) \quad Y = C + I$$
$$C = 100 + 0.6Y$$
$$I_0 = 40$$

$$(2) \quad Y = C + I \qquad Yd = Y - T$$
$$C = 100 + 0.6Yd \qquad T = 50$$
$$I_0 = 40$$

The first system of equations presents no problems; the second requires that C first be converted from a function of Yd to a function of Y.

$$(1) \quad \text{Agg. } D = C + I$$
$$= 100 + 0.6Y + 40$$
$$= 140 + 0.6Y$$

$$(2) \quad \text{Agg. } D = C + I$$
$$= 100 + 0.6Yd + 40 = 140 + 0.6(Y - T)$$
$$= 140 + 0.6(Y - 50) = 110 + 0.6Y$$

A lump-sum tax has a negative effect on the vertical intercept of the aggregate demand function equal to $-\text{MPC}(T)$. Here $-0.6(50) = -30$. The slope is not affected (note the parallel lines for the two graphs in Fig. 2-10). Income falls from 350 to 275 as a result of the tax. See Fig. 2-10.

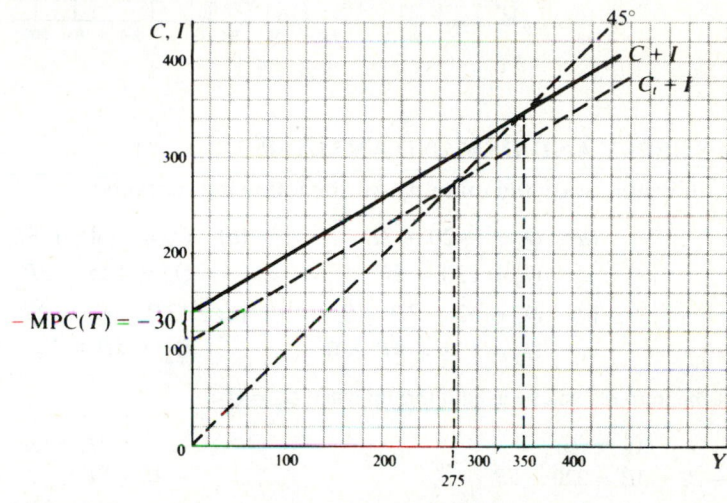

Fig. 2-10

2.10. Explain with the aid of a graph how the incorporation of a *proportional* tax (a tax depending on income) influences the parameters of the income determination model. Graph the model without the tax as a solid line and the model with the tax as a dashed line.

$$(1) \quad Y = C + I$$
$$C = 85 + 0.75Y$$
$$I_0 = 30$$

$$(2) \quad Y = C + I \qquad Yd = Y - T$$
$$C = 85 + 0.75Yd \qquad T = 20 + 0.2Y$$
$$I_0 = 30$$

$$(1) \quad \text{Agg. } D = C + I$$
$$= 85 + 0.75Y + 30$$
$$= 115 + 0.75Y$$

$$(2) \quad \text{Agg. } D = C + I$$
$$= 85 + 0.75Yd + 30 = 115 + 0.75(Y - T)$$
$$= 115 + 0.75(Y - 20 - 0.2Y)$$
$$= 115 + 0.75Y - 15 - 0.15Y = 100 + 0.6Y$$

Incorporation of a proportional income tax into the model affects the slope of the line, or the MPC. In this case it lowers it from 0.75 to 0.6. The vertical intercept is also lowered because the tax structure includes a lump-sum tax of 20. Because of the tax structure, the equilibrium level of income falls from 460 to 250. See Fig. 2-11.

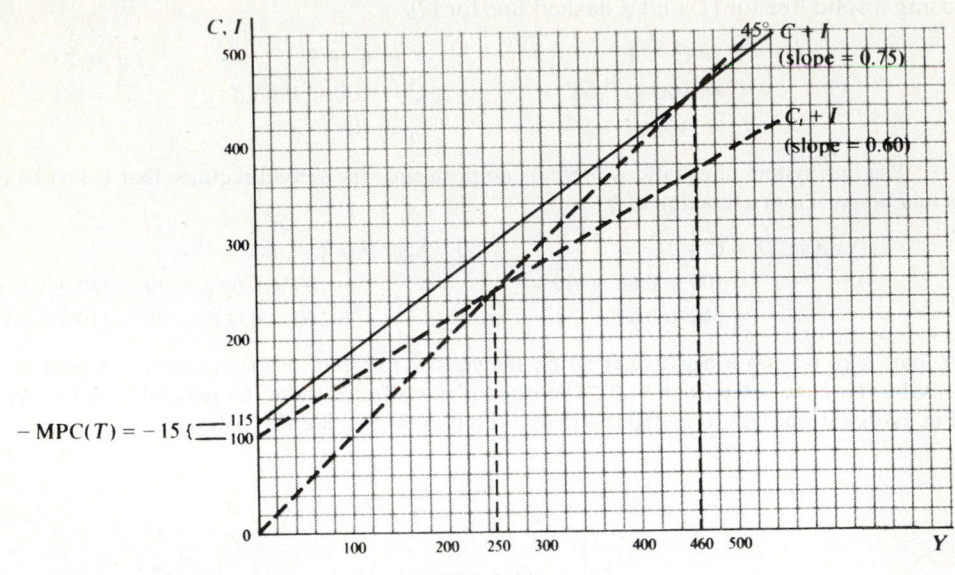

Fig. 2-11

EQUATIONS IN SUPPLY AND DEMAND ANALYSIS

2.11. Find the equilibrium price and quantity for the following markets:

$$
\begin{array}{ll}
(a) \quad Q_s = -20 + 3P & (b) \quad Q_s = -45 + 8P \\
\quad\ \ Q_d = 220 - 5P & \quad\ \ Q_d = 125 - 2P \\
(c) \quad Q_s + 32 - 7P = 0 & (d) \quad 13P - Q_s = 27 \\
\quad\ \ Q_d - 128 + 9P = 0 & \quad\ \ Q_d + 4P - 24 = 0
\end{array}
$$

Each of the markets will be in equilibrium when $Q_s = Q_d$.

(a)

$$
\begin{aligned}
Q_s &= Q_d \\
-20 + 3P &= 220 - 5P \\
8P &= 240 \\
P &= 30 \\
Q_s = -20 + 3P &= -20 + 3(30) \\
Q_s &= 70 = Q_d
\end{aligned}
$$

(b)

$$
\begin{aligned}
Q_s &= Q_d \\
-45 + 8P &= 125 - 2P \\
10P &= 170 \\
P &= 17 \\
Q_d = 125 - 2P &= 125 - 2(17) \\
Q_d &= 91 = Q_s
\end{aligned}
$$

(c)

$$
\begin{aligned}
Q_s &= 7P - 32 \\
Q_d &= 128 - 9P \\
7P - 32 &= 128 - 9P \\
16P &= 160 \\
P &= 10 \\
Q_s = 7P - 32 &= 7(10) - 32 \\
Q_s &= 38 = Q_d
\end{aligned}
$$

(d)

$$
\begin{aligned}
Q_s &= -27 + 13P \\
Q_d &= 24 - 4P \\
-27 + 13P &= 24 - 4P \\
17P &= 51 \\
P &= 3 \\
Q_d = 24 - 4P &= 24 - 4(3) \\
Q_d &= 12 = Q_s
\end{aligned}
$$

2.12. Given the following set of simultaneous equations for two related markets, beef (B) and pork (P), find the equilibrium conditions for each market, using the substitution method.

$$
\begin{array}{ll}
(1) \quad Q_{dB} = 82 - 3P_B + P_P & (2) \quad Q_{dP} = 92 + 2P_B - 4P_P \\
\quad\ \ Q_{sB} = -5 + 15P_B & \quad\ \ Q_{sP} = -6 + 32P_P
\end{array}
$$

Equilibrium requires that $Q_s = Q_d$ in each market.

(1)
$$Q_{sB} = Q_{dB}$$
$$-5 + 15P_B = 82 - 3P_B + P_P$$
$$18P_B - P_P = 87$$

(2)
$$Q_{sP} = Q_{dP}$$
$$-6 + 32P_P = 92 + 2P_B - 4P_P$$
$$36P_P - 2P_B = 98$$

This reduces the problem to two equations and two unknowns:

$$18P_B - P_P = 87 \tag{2.4}$$

$$-2P_B + 36P_P = 98 \tag{2.5}$$

Solving for P_P in (2.4) gives

$$P_P = 18P_B - 87$$

Substituting the value of this term in (2.5) gives

$$-2P_B + 36(18P_B - 87) = 98 \qquad -2P_B + 648P_B - 3132 = 98$$
$$646P_B = 3230 \qquad P_B = 5$$

Substituting $P_B = 5$ in (2.5), or (2.4),

$$-2(5) + 36P_P = 98$$
$$36P_P = 108 \qquad P_P = 3$$

Finally, substituting the values for P_B and P_P in either the supply or the demand function for each market,

(1) $Q_{dB} = 82 - 3P_B + P_P = 82 - 3(5) + (3)$
$\quad Q_{dB} = 70 = Q_{sB}$

(2) $Q_{dP} = 92 + 2P_B - 4P_P = 92 + 2(5) - 4(3)$
$\quad Q_{dP} = 90 = Q_{sP}$

2.13. Find the equilibrium price and quantity for two complementary goods, slacks (S) and jackets (J), using the elimination method.

(1) $Q_{dS} = 410 - 5P_S - 2P_J$
$\quad Q_{sS} = -60 + 3P_S$

(2) $Q_{dJ} = 295 - P_S - 3P_J$
$\quad Q_{sJ} = -120 + 2P_J$

In equilibrium,

(1)
$$Q_{dS} = Q_{sS}$$
$$410 - 5P_S - 2P_J = -60 + 3P_S$$
$$470 - 8P_S - 2P_J = 0$$

(2)
$$Q_{dJ} = Q_{sJ}$$
$$295 - P_S - 3P_J = -120 + 2P_J$$
$$415 - P_S - 5P_J = 0$$

This leaves two equations

$$470 - 8P_S - 2P_J = 0 \tag{2.6}$$

$$415 - P_S - 5P_J = 0 \tag{2.7}$$

Multiplying (2.7) by 8 gives (2.8). Subtract (2.6) from (2.8) to eliminate P_S, and solve for P_J.

$$3320 - 8P_S - 40P_J = 0 \tag{2.8}$$
$$\underline{-(+470 - 8P_S - 2P_J = 0)}$$
$$2850 - 38P_J = 0$$
$$P_J = 75$$

Substituting $P_J = 75$ in (2.6),

$$470 - 8P_S - 2(75) = 0$$
$$320 = 8P_S \qquad P_S = 40$$

Finally, substituting $P_J = 75$ and $P_S = 40$ into Q_d or Q_s for each market,

(1) $Q_{dS} = 410 - 5P_S - 2P_J = 410 - 5(40) - 2(75)$
$\quad Q_{dS} = 60 = Q_{sS}$

(2) $Q_{dJ} = 295 - P_S - 3P_J = 295 - 40 - 3(75)$
$\quad Q_{dJ} = 30 = Q_{sJ}$

2.14. Supply and demand conditions can also be expressed in quadratic form. Find the equilibrium price and quantity, given the demand function

$$P + Q^2 + 3Q - 20 = 0 \qquad (2.9)$$

and the supply function

$$P - 3Q^2 + 10Q = 5 \qquad (2.10)$$

Either the substitution method or the elimination method can be used, since this problem involves two equations and two unknowns. Using the substitution method, (2.10) is solved for P in terms of Q.

$$P - 3Q^2 + 10Q = 5$$
$$P = 3Q^2 - 10Q + 5$$

Substituting $P = 3Q^2 - 10Q + 5$ in (2.9),

$$(3Q^2 - 10Q + 5) + Q^2 + 3Q - 20 = 0$$
$$4Q^2 - 7Q - 15 = 0$$

Using the quadratic formula $Q_1, Q_2 = (-b \pm \sqrt{b^2 - 4ac})/(2a)$, where $a = 4$, $b = -7$, and $c = -15$, $Q_1 = 3$, and $Q_2 = -1.25$. Since neither price nor quantity can be negative, $Q = 3$. Substitute $Q = 3$ in (2.9) or (2.10) to find P.

$$P + (3)^2 + 3(3) - 20 = 0 \qquad P = 2$$

2.15. Use the elimination method to find the equilibrium price and quantity when the demand function is

$$3P + Q^2 + 5Q - 102 = 0 \qquad (2.11)$$

and the supply function is

$$P - 2Q^2 + 3Q + 71 = 0 \qquad (2.12)$$

Multiply (2.12) by 3 to get (2.13) and subtract it from (2.11) to eliminate P.

$$\begin{aligned} 3P + \ Q^2 + 5Q - 102 &= 0 \\ -(3P - 6Q^2 + 9Q + 213 &= 0) \\ \hline 7Q^2 - 4Q - 315 &= 0 \end{aligned} \qquad (2.13)$$

Use the quadratic formula (see Problem 2.14) to solve for Q, and substitute the result, $Q = 7$, in (2.12) or (2.11) to solve for P.

$$P - 2(7)^2 + 3(7) + 71 = 0 \qquad P = 6$$

2.16. Supply and demand analysis can also involve more than two markets. Find the equilibrium price and quantity for the three substitute goods below.

$$\begin{aligned} Q_{d1} &= 23 - 5P_1 + P_2 + P_3 & Q_{s1} &= -8 + 6P_1 \\ Q_{d2} &= 15 + P_1 - 3P_2 + 2P_3 & Q_{s2} &= -11 + 3P_2 \\ Q_{d3} &= 19 + P_1 + 2P_2 - 4P_3 & Q_{s3} &= -5 + 3P_3 \end{aligned}$$

For equilibrium in each market,

$Q_{d1} = Q_{s1}$	$Q_{d2} = Q_{s2}$	$Q_{d3} = Q_{s3}$
$23 - 5P_1 + P_2 + P_3 = -8 + 6P_1$	$15 + P_1 - 3P_2 + 2P_3 = -11 + 3P_2$	$19 + P_1 + 2P_2 - 4P_3 = -5 + 3P_3$
$31 - 11P_1 + P_2 + P_3 = 0$	$26 + P_1 - 6P_2 + 2P_3 = 0$	$24 + P_1 + 2P_2 - 7P_3 = 0$

This leaves three equations with three unknowns:

$$31 - 11P_1 + P_2 + P_3 = 0 \qquad (2.14)$$
$$26 + P_1 - 6P_2 + 2P_3 = 0 \qquad (2.15)$$
$$24 + P_1 + 2P_2 - 7P_3 = 0 \qquad (2.16)$$

Start by eliminating one of the variables (here P_2). Multiply (2.14) by 2 to get

$$62 - 22P_1 + 2P_2 + 2P_3 = 0$$

From this subtract (2.16).

$$\begin{array}{r} 62 - 22P_1 + 2P_2 + 2P_3 = 0 \\ -(24 + \quad P_1 + 2P_2 - 7P_3) = 0 \\ \hline 38 - 23P_1 \qquad\qquad + 9P_3 = 0 \end{array} \qquad (2.17)$$

Multiply (2.16) by 3.

$$72 + 3P_1 + 6P_2 - 21P_3 = 0$$

Add the result to (2.15).

$$\begin{array}{r} 26 + \quad P_1 - 6P_2 + \quad 2P_3 = 0 \\ 72 + 3P_1 + 6P_2 - 21P_3 = 0 \\ \hline 98 + 4P_1 \qquad\qquad - 19P_3 = 0 \end{array} \qquad (2.18)$$

Now there are two equations, (2.17) and (2.18), and two unknowns. Multiply (2.17) by 19 and (2.18) by 9; then add to eliminate P_3.

$$\begin{array}{r} 722 - 437P_1 + 171P_3 = 0 \\ 882 + \quad 36P_1 - 171P_3 = 0 \\ \hline 1604 - 401P_1 \qquad\qquad = 0 \\ P_1 = 4 \end{array}$$

Substitute $P_1 = 4$ in (2.18) to solve for P_3.

$$98 + 4(4) - 19P_3 = 0$$
$$19P_3 = 114 \qquad P_3 = 6$$

Substitute $P_1 = 4$ and $P_3 = 6$ into (2.14), (2.15), or (2.16), to solve for P_2.

$$31 - 11(4) + P_2 + (6) = 0 \qquad P_2 = 7$$

EQUATIONS IN THE INCOME DETERMINATION MODEL

2.17. Given: $Y = C + I + G$, $C = C_0 + bY$, $I = I_0$, and $G = G_0$, where $C_0 = 135$, $b = 0.8$, $I_0 = 75$, and $G_0 = 30$. (a) Find the equation for the equilibrium level of income in the reduced form. (b) Solve for the equilibrium level of income (1) directly and (2) with the reduced form.

(a)   From Section 2.3,
$$Y = C + I + G$$
$$= C_0 + bY + I_0 + G_0$$
$$Y - bY = C_0 + I_0 + G_0$$
$$(1 - b)Y = C_0 + I_0 + G_0$$
$$Y = \frac{C_0 + I_0 + G_0}{1 - b}$$

(b)   (1) $\qquad Y = C + I + G = 135 + 0.8Y + 75 + 30 \qquad$ (2) $\quad Y = \dfrac{C_0 + I_0 + G_0}{1 - b}$

$$Y - 0.8Y = 240$$
$$0.2Y = 240$$
$$Y = 1200$$

$$= \frac{135 + 75 + 30}{1 - 0.8}$$
$$= 5(240) = 1200$$

2.18. Find the equilibrium level of income $Y = C + I$, when $C = 89 + 0.8Y$ and $I_0 = 24$.

$$Y = \frac{C_0 + I_0}{1 - b} = 5(89 + 24) = 565$$

From Problem 2.17, the value of the multiplier $[1/(1 - b)]$ is already known for cases when $b = 0.8$. Use of the reduced form to solve the equation in this instance is faster, therefore, although the other method is also correct.

2.19. (a) Find the reduced form of the following income determination model where investment is not autonomous but is a function of income. (b) Find the numerical value of the equilibrium level of income (Y_e). (c) Show what happens to the multiplier.

$$Y = C + I \qquad C = C_0 + bY \qquad I = I_0 + aY$$

where $C_0 = 65$, $I_0 = 70$, $b = 0.6$, and $a = 0.2$.

(a)
$$Y = C + I$$
$$= C_0 + bY + I_0 + aY$$
$$Y - bY - aY = C_0 + I_0$$
$$(1 - b - a)Y = C_0 + I_0$$
$$Y = \frac{C_0 + I_0}{1 - b - a}$$

(b)
$$Y = C + I$$
$$= 65 + 0.6Y + 70 + 0.2Y$$
$$Y - 0.6Y - 0.2Y = 65 + 70$$
$$0.2Y = 135$$
$$Y = 675$$

(c) When investment is a function of income, and no longer autonomous, the multiplier changes from $1/(1 - b)$ to $1/(1 - b - a)$. This increases the value of the multiplier because it reduces the denominator of the fraction and makes the quotient larger, as substitution of the values of the parameters in the problem shows:

$$\frac{1}{1 - b} = \frac{1}{1 - 0.6} = \frac{1}{0.4} = 2.5 \qquad \frac{1}{1 - b - a} = \frac{1}{1 - 0.6 - 0.2} = \frac{1}{0.2} = 5$$

2.20. Find (a) the reduced form, (b) the numerical value of Y_e, and (c) the effect on the multiplier when a lump-sum tax is added to the model and consumption becomes a function of disposable income (Yd).

$$Y = C + I \qquad C = C_0 + bYd \qquad I = I_0 \qquad Yd = Y - T$$

where $C_0 = 100$, $b = 0.6$, $I_0 = 40$, and $T = 50$.

(a)
$$Y = C + I = C_0 + bYd + I_0 = C_0 + b(Y - T) + I_0 = C_0 + bY - bT + I_0$$
$$Y - bY = C_0 + I_0 - bT$$
$$Y = \frac{C_0 + I_0 - bT}{1 - b}$$

(b)
$$Y = 100 + 0.6Yd + 40 = 140 + 0.6(Y - T) \qquad \text{or} \qquad Y = \frac{100 + 40 - 0.6(50)}{1 - 0.6} = \frac{110}{0.4}$$

$$= 140 + 0.6(Y - 50) = 140 + 0.6Y - 30 \qquad\qquad\qquad = 275$$
$$Y - 0.6Y = 110$$
$$0.4Y = 110$$
$$Y = 275$$

The graph of this function is given in Problem 2.9.

(c) As seen in part (a), incorporation of a lump-sum tax into the model leaves the multiplier at $1/(1 - b)$. Only the aggregate value of the exogenous variables is reduced by an amount equal to $-bT$. Incorporation of other autonomous variables such as G_0, X_0, or Z_0 will not affect the value of the multiplier either.

2.21. Find (a) the reduced form, (b) the numerical value of Y_e, and (c) the effect on the multiplier if a proportional income tax (t) is incorporated into the model.

$$Y = C + I \qquad C = C_0 + bYd \qquad T = T_0 + tY \qquad Yd = Y - T$$

where $I = I_0 = 30$, $C_0 = 85$, $b = 0.75$, $t = 0.2$, and $T_0 = 20$.

(a)
$$
\begin{aligned}
Y = C + I &= C_0 + bYd + I_0 \\
&= C_0 + b(Y - T) + I_0 = C_0 + b(Y - T_0 - tY) + I_0 \\
&= C_0 + bY - bT_0 - btY + I_0 \\
Y - bY + btY &= C_0 + I_0 - bT_0 \\
(1 - b + bt)Y &= C_0 + I_0 - bT_0 \\
Y &= \frac{C_0 + I_0 - bT_0}{1 - b + bt}
\end{aligned}
$$

(b) Once the reduced form is found, its use speeds the solution. But sometimes the reduced form is not available, making it necessary to be familiar with the other method.

$$
\begin{aligned}
Y = C + I &= 85 + 0.75Yd + 30 = 115 + 0.75(Y - T) \\
&= 115 + 0.75(Y - 20 - 0.2Y) = 115 + 0.75Y - 15 - 0.15Y \\
Y - 0.75Y + 0.15Y &= 100 \\
0.4Y &= 100 \\
Y &= 250
\end{aligned}
$$

The graph of this function is given in Problem 2.10.

(c) The multiplier is changed from $1/(1 - b)$ to $1/(1 - b + bt)$. This reduces the size of the multiplier because it makes the denominator larger and the fraction smaller:

$$\frac{1}{1 - b} = \frac{1}{1 - 0.75} = \frac{1}{0.25} = 4$$

$$\frac{1}{1 - b + bt} = \frac{1}{1 - 0.75 + 0.75(0.2)} = \frac{1}{1 - 0.75 + 0.15} = \frac{1}{0.4} = 2.5$$

2.22. If the foreign sector is added to the model and there is a positive marginal propensity to import (z), find (a) the reduced form, (b) the equilibrium level of income, and (c) the effect on the multiplier.

$$Y = C + I + G + (X - Z) \qquad C = C_0 + bY \qquad Z = Z_0 + zY$$

where $I = I_0 = 90$, $G = G_0 = 65$, $X = X_0 = 80$, $C_0 = 70$, $Z_0 = 40$, $b = 0.9$, and $z = 0.15$.

(a)
$$
\begin{aligned}
Y = C + I + G + (X - Z) &= C_0 + bY + I_0 + G_0 + X_0 - Z_0 - zY \\
Y - bY + zY &= C_0 + I_0 + G_0 + X_0 - Z_0 \\
(1 - b + z)Y &= C_0 + I_0 + G_0 + X_0 - Z_0 \\
Y &= \frac{C_0 + I_0 + G_0 + X_0 - Z_0}{1 - b + z}
\end{aligned}
$$

(b) Using the reduced form above,

$$Y = \frac{70 + 90 + 65 + 80 - 40}{1 - 0.9 + 0.15} = \frac{265}{0.25} = 1060$$

(c) Introduction of the marginal propensity to import (z) into the model reduces the size of the multiplier. It makes the denominator larger and the fraction smaller:

$$\frac{1}{1-b} = \frac{1}{1-0.9} = \frac{1}{0.1} = 10$$

$$\frac{1}{1-b+z} = \frac{1}{1-0.9+0.15} = \frac{1}{0.25} = 4$$

IS-LM EQUATIONS

2.23. Given: $C = 102 + 0.7Y$, $I = 150 - 100i$, $M_s = 300$, $M_t = 0.25Y$, and $M_z = 124 - 200i$. Find (a) the equilibrium level of income and the equilibrium rate of interest and (b) the level of C, I, M_t, and M_z when the economy is in equilibrium.

(a) Commodity market equilibrium (IS) exists where

$$Y = C + I$$
$$= 102 + 0.7Y + 150 - 100i$$
$$Y - 0.7Y = 252 - 100i$$
$$0.3Y + 100i - 252 = 0$$

Monetary equilibrium (LM) exists where

$$M_s = M_t + M_z$$
$$300 = 0.25Y + 124 - 200i$$
$$0.25Y - 200i - 176 = 0$$

Simultaneous equilibrium in both markets requires that

$$0.3Y + 100i - 252 = 0 \tag{2.19}$$
$$0.25Y - 200i - 176 = 0 \tag{2.20}$$

Multiply (2.19) by 2, and add the result to (2.20) to eliminate i:

$$\begin{array}{r} 0.6Y + 200i - 504 = 0 \\ 0.25Y - 200i - 176 = 0 \\ \hline 0.85Y \qquad\qquad = 680 \\ Y = 800 \end{array}$$

Substitute $Y = 800$ in (2.19) or (2.20):

$$0.25Y - 200i - 176 = 0$$
$$0.25(800) - 200i - 176 = 0$$
$$-200i = -24$$
$$i = 0.12$$

(b) At $Y = 800$ and $i = 0.12$,

$$C = 102 + 0.7(800) = 662 \qquad M_t = 0.25(800) = 200$$
$$I = 150 - 100(0.12) = 138 \qquad M_z = 124 - 200(0.12) = 100$$

and

$$C + I = Y \qquad M_t + M_z = M_s$$
$$662 + 138 = 800 \qquad 200 + 100 = 300$$

2.24. Find (a) the equilibrium income level and interest rate and (b) the levels of C, I, M_t, and M_z in equilibrium when

$$C = 89 + 0.6Y \qquad I = 120 - 150i \qquad M_s = 275 \qquad M_t = 0.1Y \qquad M_z = 240 - 250i$$

(a)   For *IS*:

$$Y = 89 + 0.6Y + 120 - 150i$$
$$Y - 0.6Y = 209 - 150i$$
$$0.4Y + 150i - 209 = 0$$

For *LM*:

$$M_s = M_t + M_z$$
$$275 = 0.1Y + 240 - 250i$$
$$0.1Y - 250i - 35 = 0$$

In equilibrium,

$$0.4Y + 150i - 209 = 0 \qquad (2.21)$$
$$0.1Y - 250i - 35 = 0 \qquad (2.22)$$

Multiply (*2.22*) by 4, and subtract the result from (*2.21*) to eliminate *Y*.

$$\begin{array}{r} 0.4Y + 150i - 209 = 0 \\ -(0.4Y - 1000i - 140 = 0) \\ \hline 1150i \qquad\quad = 69 \\ i = 0.06 \end{array}$$

Substitute $i = 0.06$ in (*2.21*) or (*2.22*).

$$0.4Y + 150(0.06) - 209 = 0$$
$$0.4Y = 200$$
$$Y = 500$$

(b)   At $Y = 500$ and $i = 0.06$,

$$C = 89 + 0.6(500) = 389 \qquad M_t = 0.1(500) = 50$$
$$I = 120 - 150(0.06) = 111 \qquad M_z = 240 - 250(0.06) = 225$$

and

$$C + I = Y \qquad M_t + M_z = M_s$$
$$389 + 111 = 500 \qquad 50 + 225 = 275$$

PRODUCTION POSSIBILITIES FRONTIERS

2.25.   Graph the production-possibilities frontier given by

$$y = -\tfrac{1}{5}x^2 - \tfrac{3}{5}x + 26$$

for a country producing two goods *x* and *y*.

The production-possibilities frontier is readily graphed by setting $y = 0$ and completing the square as in Section 2.5.

$$-\tfrac{1}{5}x^2 - \tfrac{3}{5}x + 26 = 0$$

Factor out $-\tfrac{1}{5}$ from the *x* terms, as in Problem 1.19(*b*), and move the constant.

$$y = -\tfrac{1}{5}(x^2 + 3x) + 26$$

With $b = 3$, $b/2 = 1.5$, and $(1.5)^2 = 2.25$, add ± 2.25 *within* the parentheses.

$$y = -\tfrac{1}{5}(x^2 + 3x + 2.25 - 2.25) + 26$$

Note that $-\tfrac{1}{5}(-2.25) = 0.45$, rearrange, and factor.

$$y = -\tfrac{1}{5}(x^2 + 3x + 2.25) + 0.45 + 26$$
$$= -\tfrac{1}{5}(x + 1.5)^2 + 26.45$$

With $y = -\frac{1}{5}(x + 1.5)^2 + 26.45$, the axis is $x + 1.5 = 0$, $x = -1.5$; and the vertex is $(-1.5, 26.45)$. With $a = -\frac{1}{5} < 0$, the parabola opens down. Now set $y = 0$ and factor to find the x intercepts.

$$-\tfrac{1}{5}x^2 - \tfrac{3}{5}x + 26 = 0$$

Multiply by -5 and factor,

$$x^2 + 3x - 130 = 0$$
$$(x + 13)(x - 10) = 0$$
$$x = -13 \qquad x = 10$$

The x intercepts are $(-13, 0)$ and $(10, 0)$. See Fig. 2-12.

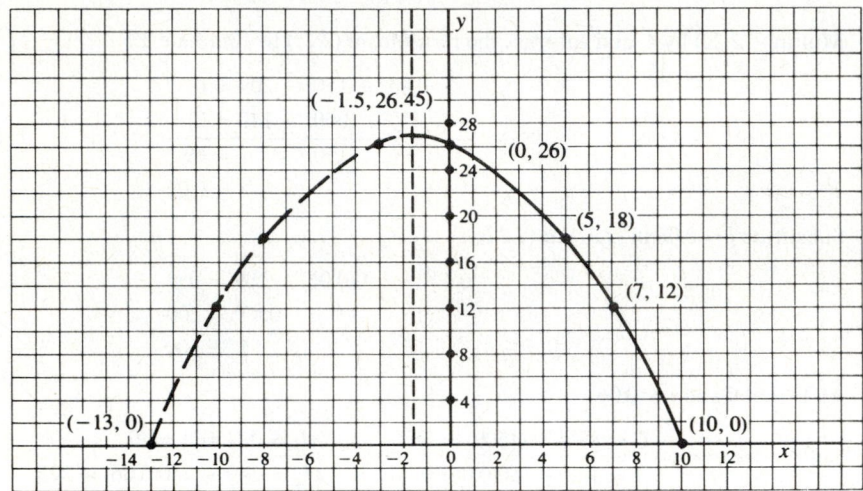

Fig. 2-12

2.26. The cost of cleaning a pollutant from the air is estimated by the rational function

$$C(x) = \frac{150x}{105 - x} \qquad (0 \le x \le 100)$$

where C is the cost in thousands of dollars of removing x percent of the pollutant. Graph the equation to show the sharply rising costs of cleaning up the last percentages of the pollutant.

Set up a schedule of representative values for x and y and graph as in Fig. 2-13.

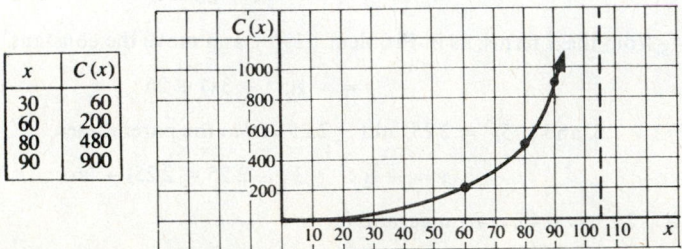

x	$C(x)$
30	60
60	200
80	480
90	900

Fig. 2-13

Chapter 3

The Derivative
and the Rules of Differentiation

3.1 LIMITS

If the functional values $f(x)$ of a function f draw closer to one and only one finite real number L for all values of x as x draws closer to but does not equal a, L is defined as the *limit* of $f(x)$ as x approaches a and is written

$$\lim_{x \to a} f(x) = L$$

Assuming that $\lim_{x \to a} f(x)$ and $\lim_{x \to a} g(x)$ both exist, the *rules of limits* are given below, explained in Example 2, and treated in Problems 3.1 to 3.4.

1. $\displaystyle\lim_{x \to a} k = k \qquad (k = \text{a constant})$

2. $\displaystyle\lim_{x \to a} x^n = a^n \qquad (n = \text{a positive integer})$

3. $\displaystyle\lim_{x \to a} kf(x) = k \lim_{x \to a} f(x) \qquad (k = \text{a constant})$

4. $\displaystyle\lim_{x \to a} [f(x) \pm g(x)] = \lim_{x \to a} f(x) \pm \lim_{x \to a} g(x)$

5. $\displaystyle\lim_{x \to a} [f(x) \cdot g(x)] = \lim_{x \to a} f(x) \cdot \lim_{x \to a} g(x)$

6. $\displaystyle\lim_{x \to a} [f(x) \div g(x)] = \lim_{x \to a} f(x) \div \lim_{x \to a} g(x) \qquad \left[\lim_{x \to a} g(x) \neq 0\right]$

7. $\displaystyle\lim_{x \to a} [f(x)]^n = \left[\lim_{x \to a} f(x)\right]^n \qquad (n > 0)$

EXAMPLE 1. (*a*) From the graph of the function $f(x)$ in Fig. 3-1, it is clear that as the value of x approaches 3 from either side, the value of $f(x)$ approaches 2. This means that the limit of $f(x)$ as x approaches 3 is the number 2, which is written

$$\lim_{x \to 3} f(x) = 2$$

As x approaches 7 from either side in Fig. 3-1, where the open circle in the graph of $f(x)$ signifies there is a gap in the function at that point, the value of $f(x)$ approaches 4 even though the function is not defined at that point.

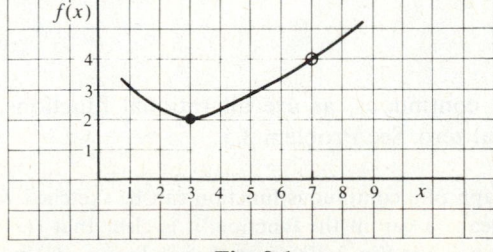

Fig. 3-1

39

Since the limit of a function as x approaches a number depends only on the values of x *close to* that number, the limit exists and is written

$$\lim_{x \to 7} f(x) = 4$$

(*b*) In Fig. 3-2, as x approaches 4 from the left (from values less than 4), written $x \to 4^-$, $g(x)$ approaches 3, called a *one-sided limit*; as x approaches 4 from the right (from values greater than 4), written $x \to 4^+$, $g(x)$ approaches 4. The limit does not exist, therefore, since $g(x)$ does not approach a *single* number as x approaches 4 from *both* sides.

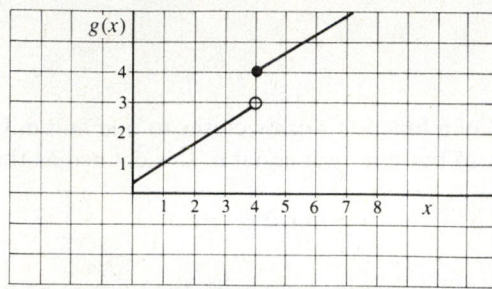

Fig. 3-2

EXAMPLE 2.   In the absence of a graph, limits can be found by using the rules of limits enumerated above.

(*a*) $\lim\limits_{x \to 5} 9 = 9$ Rule 1

(*b*) $\lim\limits_{x \to 6} x^2 = (6)^2 = 36$ Rule 2

(*c*) $\lim\limits_{x \to 3} 2x^3 = 2 \lim\limits_{x \to 3} x^3 = 2(3)^3 = 54$ Rules 2 and 3

(*d*) $\lim\limits_{x \to 2} (x^4 + 3x) = \lim\limits_{x \to 2} x^4 + 3 \lim\limits_{x \to 2} x$ Rule 4

$\qquad\qquad = (2)^4 + 3(2) = 22$

(*e*) $\lim\limits_{x \to 4} [(x + 8)(x - 5)] = \lim\limits_{x \to 4} (x + 8) \cdot \lim\limits_{x \to 4} (x - 5)$ Rule 5

$\qquad\qquad = (4 + 8) \cdot (4 - 5) = -12$

3.2   CONTINUITY

A *continuous* function is one which has no breaks in its curve. It can be drawn without lifting the pencil from the paper. A function f is continuous at $x = a$ if:

1. $f(x)$ is defined, i.e., exists, at $x = a$
2. $\lim\limits_{x \to a} f(x)$ exists, *and*
3. $\lim\limits_{x \to a} f(x) = f(a)$

All polynomial functions are continuous, as are all rational functions, except where undefined, i.e., where their denominators equal zero. See Problem 3.5.

EXAMPLE 3.   Given that the graph of a continuous function can be sketched without ever removing pencil from paper and that an open circle means a gap in the function, it is clear that $f(x)$ is discontinuous at $x = 4$ in Fig. 3-3(*a*) and $g(x)$ is discontinuous at $x = 5$ in Fig. 3-3(*b*), even though $\lim_{x \to 5} g(x)$ exists.

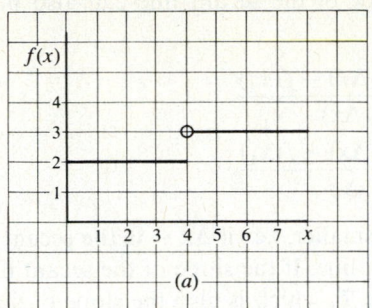 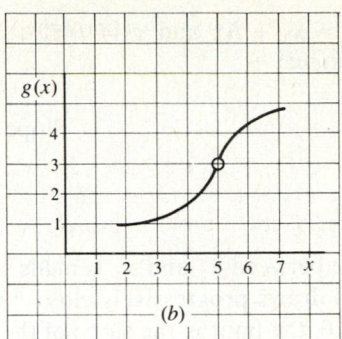

Fig. 3-3

3.3 THE SLOPE OF A CURVILINEAR FUNCTION

The slope of a curvilinear function is not constant. It differs at different points on the curve. In geometry, the slope of a curvilinear function at a given point is measured by the slope of a line drawn tangent to the function at that point. A *tangent line* is a straight line that touches a curve at only one point. Measuring the slope of a curvilinear function at different points requires separate tangent lines, as in Fig. 3-4(*a*).

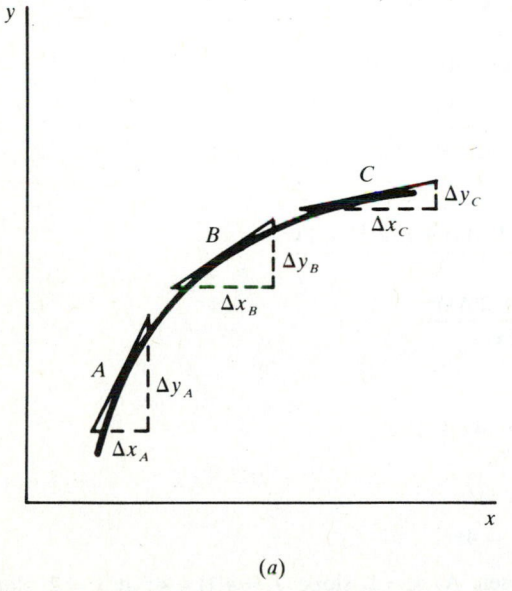 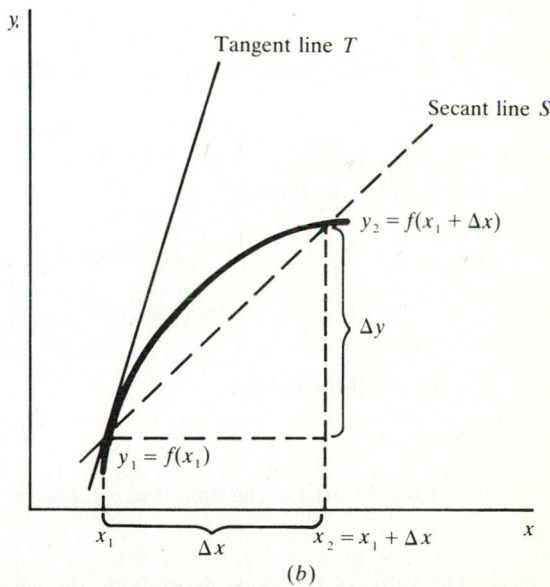

(*a*)   (*b*)

Fig. 3-4

The slope of a tangent line is derived from the slopes of a family of secant lines. A *secant line* S is a straight line that intersects a curve at two points, as in Fig. 3-4(*b*), where

$$\text{Slope } S = \frac{y_2 - y_1}{x_2 - x_1}$$

By letting $x_2 = x_1 + \Delta x$ and $y_2 = f(x_1 + \Delta x)$, the slope of the secant line can also be expressed by a *difference quotient*:

$$\text{Slope } S = \frac{f(x_1 + \Delta x) - f(x_1)}{(x_1 + \Delta x) - x_1}$$
$$= \frac{f(x_1 + \Delta x) - f(x_1)}{\Delta x}$$

If the distance between x_2 and x_1 is made smaller and smaller, i.e., if $\Delta x \to 0$, the secant line pivots back to the left and draws progressively closer to the tangent line. If the slope of the secant line approaches a limit as $\Delta x \to 0$, the limit is the slope of the tangent line T, which is also the slope of the function at the point. It is written

$$\text{Slope } T = \lim_{\Delta x \to 0} \frac{f(x_1 + \Delta x) - f(x_1)}{\Delta x} \tag{3.1}$$

Note: In many texts h is used in place of Δx, giving

$$\text{Slope } T = \lim_{h \to 0} \frac{f(x_1 + h) - f(x_1)}{h} \tag{3.1a}$$

EXAMPLE 4. To find the slope of a curvilinear function, such as $f(x) = 2x^2$, (1) employ the specific function in the algebraic formula (*3.1*) or (*3.1a*) and substitute the arguments $x_1 + \Delta x$ (or $x_1 + h$) and x_1, respectively, (2) simplify the function, and (3) evaluate the limit of the function in its simplified form. From (*3.1*),

$$\text{Slope } T = \lim_{\Delta x \to 0} \frac{f(x + \Delta x) - f(x)}{\Delta x}$$

(1)   Employ the function $f(x) = 2x^2$ and substitute the arguments.

$$\text{Slope } T = \lim_{\Delta x \to 0} \frac{2(x + \Delta x)^2 - 2x^2}{\Delta x}$$

(2)   Simplify the result.

$$\text{Slope } T = \lim_{\Delta x \to 0} \frac{2[x^2 + 2x(\Delta x) + (\Delta x)^2] - 2x^2}{\Delta x}$$
$$= \lim_{\Delta x \to 0} \frac{4x(\Delta x) + 2(\Delta x)^2}{\Delta x}$$

Divide through by Δx.

$$\text{Slope } T = \lim_{\Delta x \to 0} (4x + 2\Delta x)$$

(3)   Take the limit of the simplified expression.

$$\text{Slope } T = 4x$$

Note: The value of the slope depends on the value of x chosen. At $x = 1$, slope $T = 4(1) = 4$; at $x = 2$, slope $T = 4(2) = 8$.

3.4   THE DERIVATIVE

Given a function $y = f(x)$, the *derivative* of the function f at x, written $f'(x)$ or dy/dx, is defined as

$$f'(x) = \lim_{\Delta x \to 0} \frac{f(x + \Delta x) - f(x)}{\Delta x} \qquad \text{if the limit exists} \tag{3.2}$$

or from (*3.1a*),

$$f'(x) = \lim_{h \to 0} \frac{f(x_1 + h) - f(x_1)}{h}$$ (*3.2a*)

where $f'(x)$ is read "the derivative of f with respect to x" or "f prime of x."

The derivative of a function, $f'(x)$ or simply f', is itself a function which measures both the slope and the instantaneous rate of change of the original function $f(x)$ at a given point.

3.5 DIFFERENTIABILITY AND CONTINUITY

A function is *differentiable* at a point if the derivative exists (may be taken) at that point. To be differentiable at a point, a function must (1) be continuous at that point and (2) have a unique tangent at that point. In Fig. 3-5, $f(x)$ is not differentiable at a and c because gaps exist in the function at those points and the derivative cannot be taken at any point where the function is discontinuous.

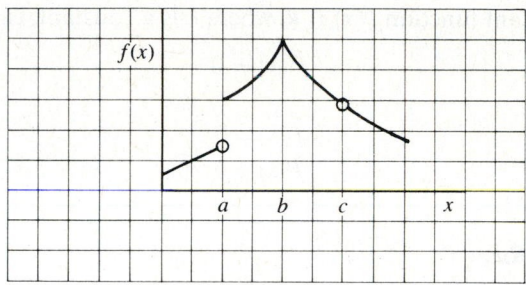

Fig. 3-5

Continuity alone, however, does not ensure (is not a sufficient condition for) differentiability. In Fig. 3-5, $f(x)$ is continuous at b, but it is not differentiable at b because at a sharp point or *cusp* an infinite number of tangent lines (and no one unique tangent line) can be drawn.

3.6 DERIVATIVE NOTATION

The derivative of a function can be written in many different ways. If $y = f(x)$, the derivative can be expressed as

$$f'(x) \qquad y' \qquad \frac{dy}{dx} \qquad \frac{df}{dx} \qquad \frac{d}{dx}[f(x)] \qquad \text{or} \qquad D_x[f(x)]$$

If $y = \phi(t)$, the derivative can be written

$$\phi'(t) \qquad y' \qquad \frac{dy}{dt} \qquad \frac{d\phi}{dt} \qquad \frac{d}{dt}[\phi(t)] \qquad \text{or} \qquad D_t[\phi(t)]$$

If the derivative of $y = f(x)$ is evaluated at $x = a$, proper notation includes $f'(a)$ and $\left.\dfrac{dy}{dx}\right|_a$.

EXAMPLE 5. If $y = 5x^2 + 7x + 12$, the derivative can be written

$$y' \qquad \frac{dy}{dx} \qquad \frac{d}{dx}(5x^2 + 7x + 12) \qquad \text{or} \qquad D_x(5x^2 + 7x + 12)$$

If $z = \sqrt{8t - 3}$, the derivative can be expressed as

$$z' \qquad \frac{dz}{dt} \qquad \frac{d}{dt}\left(\sqrt{8t - 3}\right) \qquad \text{or} \qquad D_t\left(\sqrt{8t - 3}\right)$$

See Problems 3.6 to 3.8.

3.7 RULES OF DIFFERENTIATION

Differentiation is the process of finding the derivative of a function. It involves nothing more complicated than applying a few basic rules or formulas to a given function. In explaining the rules of differentiation for a function such as $y = f(x)$, other functions such as $g(x)$ and $h(x)$ are commonly used, where g and h are both unspecified functions of x. The rules of differentiation are listed below and treated in Problems 3.6 to 3.21. Selected proofs are found in Problems 3.24 to 3.26.

3.7.1 The Constant Function Rule

The derivative of a constant function $f(x) = k$, where k is a constant, is zero.

Given $f(x) = k$, $\qquad\qquad\qquad\qquad\qquad f'(x) = 0$

EXAMPLE 6. Given $f(x) = 8$, $\qquad\qquad\qquad f'(x) = 0$
Given $f(x) = -6$, $\qquad\qquad\qquad\qquad f'(x) = 0$

3.7.2 The Linear Function Rule

The derivative of a linear function $f(x) = mx + b$ is equal to m, the coefficient of x. The derivative of a variable raised to the first power is always equal to the coefficient of the variable, while the derivative of a constant is simply zero.

Given $f(x) = mx + b$, $\qquad\qquad\qquad\qquad f'(x) = m$

EXAMPLE 7. Given $f(x) = 3x + 2$, $\qquad\qquad f'(x) = 3$
Given $f(x) = 5 - \frac{1}{4}x$, $\qquad\qquad\qquad\qquad f'(x) = -\frac{1}{4}$
Given $f(x) = 12x$, $\qquad\qquad\qquad\qquad\quad f'(x) = 12$

3.7.3 The Power Function Rule

The derivative of a power function $f(x) = kx^n$, where k is a constant and n is any real number, is equal to the coefficient k times the exponent n, multiplied by the variable x raised to the $n - 1$ power.

Given $f(x) = kx^n$, $\qquad\qquad\qquad\qquad f'(x) = k \cdot n \cdot x^{n-1}$

EXAMPLE 8. Given $f(x) = 4x^3$, $\qquad\qquad f'(x) = 4 \cdot 3 \cdot x^{3-1} = 12x^2$
Given $f(x) = 5x^2$, $\qquad\qquad\qquad\qquad f'(x) = 5 \cdot 2 \cdot x^{2-1} = 10x$
Given $f(x) = x^4$, $\qquad\qquad\qquad\qquad\quad f'(x) = 1 \cdot 4 \cdot x^{4-1} = 4x^3$

See also Problem 3.7.

3.7.4 The Rules for Sums and Differences

The derivative of a sum of two functions $f(x) = g(x) + h(x)$, where $g(x)$ and $h(x)$ are both differentiable functions, is equal to the sum of the derivatives of the individual functions. Similarly, the derivative

of the difference of two functions is equal to the difference of the derivatives of the two functions.
Given $f(x) = g(x) \pm h(x)$, $\qquad\qquad f'(x) = g'(x) \pm h'(x)$

EXAMPLE 9. Given $f(x) = 12x^5 - 4x^4$, $\qquad f'(x) = 60x^4 - 16x^3$
Given $f(x) = 9x^2 + 2x - 3$, $\qquad\qquad f'(x) = 18x + 2$

See Problem 3.8. For derivation of the rule, see Problem 3.24.

3.7.5   The Product Rule

The derivative of a product $f(x) = g(x) \cdot h(x)$, where $g(x)$ and $h(x)$ are both differentiable functions, is equal to the first function multiplied by the derivative of the second plus the second function multiplied by the derivative of the first. Given $f(x) = g(x) \cdot h(x)$,

$$f'(x) = g(x) \cdot h'(x) + h(x) \cdot g'(x) \qquad\qquad (3.3)$$

EXAMPLE 10. Given $f(x) = 3x^4(2x - 5)$, let $g(x) = 3x^4$ and $h(x) = 2x - 5$. Taking the individual derivatives, $g'(x) = 12x^3$ and $h'(x) = 2$. Then by substituting these values in the product-rule formula (3.3),

$$f'(x) = 3x^4(2) + (2x - 5)(12x^3)$$

and simplifying algebraically gives

$$f'(x) = 6x^4 + 24x^4 - 60x^3 = 30x^4 - 60x^3$$

See Problems 3.9 to 3.11; for the derivation of the rule, see Problem 3.25.

3.7.6   The Quotient Rule

The derivative of a quotient $f(x) = g(x) \div h(x)$, where $g(x)$ and $h(x)$ are both differentiable functions and $h(x) \neq 0$, is equal to the denominator times the derivative of the numerator, minus the numerator times the derivative of the denominator, all divided by the denominator squared. Given $f(x) = g(x)/h(x)$,

$$f'(x) = \frac{h(x) \cdot g'(x) - g(x) \cdot h'(x)}{[h(x)]^2} \qquad\qquad (3.4)$$

EXAMPLE 11. Given

$$f(x) = \frac{5x^3}{4x + 3}$$

where $g(x) = 5x^3$ and $h(x) = 4x + 3$, we know that $g'(x) = 15x^2$ and $h'(x) = 4$. Substituting these values in the quotient – rule formula (3.4),

$$f'(x) = \frac{(4x + 3)(15x^2) - 5x^3(4)}{(4x + 3)^2}$$

Simplifying algebraically,

$$f'(x) = \frac{60x^3 + 45x^2 - 20x^3}{(4x + 3)^2} = \frac{40x^3 + 45x^2}{(4x + 3)^2} = \frac{5x^2(8x + 9)}{(4x + 3)^2}$$

See Problems 3.12 and 3.13; for the derivation of the rule, see Problem 3.26.

3.7.7   The Generalized Power Function Rule

The derivative of a function raised to a power, $f(x) = [g(x)]^n$, where $g(x)$ is a differentiable function and n is any real number, is equal to the exponent n times the function $g(x)$ raised to the $n - 1$ power, multiplied in turn by the derivative of the function itself $g'(x)$. Given $f(x) = [g(x)]^n$,

$$f'(x) = n[g(x)]^{n-1} \cdot g'(x) \tag{3.5}$$

EXAMPLE 12. Given $f(x) = (x^3 + 6)^5$, let $g(x) = x^3 + 6$, then $g'(x) = 3x^2$. Substituting these values in the generalized power function formula (3.5) gives

$$f'(x) = 5(x^3 + 6)^{5-1} \cdot 3x^2$$

Simplifying algebraically,

$$f'(x) = 5(x^3 + 6)^4 \cdot 3x^2 = 15x^2(x^3 + 6)^4$$

Note: The generalized power function rule is derived from the chain rule which follows below. See Problems 3.14 and 3.15.

3.7.8 The Chain Rule

Given a *composite function*, also called a *function of a function*, in which y is a function of u and u in turn is a function of x, that is, $y = f(u)$ and $u = g(x)$, then $y = f[g(x)]$ and the derivative of y with respect to x is equal to the derivative of the first function with respect to u times the derivative of the second function with respect to x:

$$\frac{dy}{dx} = \frac{dy}{du} \cdot \frac{du}{dx} \tag{3.6}$$

See Problems 3.16 and 3.17.

EXAMPLE 13. Consider the function $y = (5x^2 + 3)^4$. To use the chain rule, let $y = u^4$ and $u = 5x^2 + 3$. Then $dy/du = 4u^3$ and $du/dx = 10x$. Substitute these values in (3.6):

$$\frac{dy}{dx} = 4u^3 \cdot 10x = 40xu^3$$

Then to express the derivative in terms of a single variable, substitute $5x^2 + 3$ for u.

$$\frac{dy}{dx} = 40x(5x^2 + 3)^3$$

For more complicated functions, different combinations of the basic rules must be used. See Problems 3.18 and 3.19.

3.8 HIGHER-ORDER DERIVATIVES

The second-order derivative, written $f''(x)$, measures the slope and the rate of change of the first derivative, just as the first derivative measures the slope and the rate of change of the original or *primitive function*. The third-order derivative $f'''(x)$ measures the slope and rate of change of the second-order derivative, etc. Higher-order derivatives are found by applying the rules of differentiation to lower-order derivatives, as illustrated in Example 14 and treated in Problems 3.20 and 3.21.

EXAMPLE 14. Given $y = f(x)$, common notation for the second-order derivative includes $f''(x)$, d^2y/dx^2, y'', and D^2y; for the third-order derivative, $f'''(x)$, d^3y/dx^3, y''', and D^3y; for the fourth-order derivative, $f^{(4)}(x)$, d^4y/dx^4, $y^{(4)}$, and D^4y; etc.

Higher-order derivatives are found by successively applying the rules of differentiation to derivatives of the previous order. Thus, if $f(x) = 2x^4 + 5x^3 + 3x^2$,

$$f'(x) = 8x^3 + 15x^2 + 6x$$
$$f''(x) = 24x^2 + 30x + 6$$
$$f'''(x) = 48x + 30$$
$$f^{(4)}(x) = 48 \qquad f^{(5)}(x) = 0$$

See Problems 3.20 and 3.21.

3.9 IMPLICIT DIFFERENTIATION

Economics deals most often with *explicit functions* in which the dependent variable is to the left of the equal sign and the independent variable to the right. Occasionally *implicit functions* are encountered in which both variables are on the same side of the equal sign. Some implicit functions can be easily converted to explicit functions by solving for the dependent variable in terms of the independent variable; others cannot. For those not readily convertible, the derivative may be found by *implicit differentiation*. See Example 16, Problems 3.22 and 3.23 and 4.38 and 4.39; also see Section 5.10 and Problems 5.20, 5.21, 6.55, and 6.56.

EXAMPLE 15. Samples of explicit and implicit functions include:

Explicit:
$$y = 4x \qquad y = x^2 + 6x - 7 \qquad y = \frac{x^4 - 9x^3}{x^2 - 13}$$

Implicit:
$$8x + 5y = 21 \qquad 3x^2 - 8xy - 5y = 49 \qquad 35x^3y^7 = 106$$

EXAMPLE 16. Given $3x^4 - 7y^5 = 86$, the derivative dy/dx is found by means of implicit differentiation in two easy steps.

(1) Differentiate both sides of the equation with respect to x while treating y as a function of x,

$$\frac{d}{dx}(3x^4 - 7y^5) = \frac{d}{dx}(86) \tag{3.7}$$

$$\frac{d}{dx}(3x^4) - \frac{d}{dx}(7y^5) = \frac{d}{dx}(86)$$

where $\dfrac{d}{dx}(3x^4) = 12x^3$ and $\dfrac{d}{dx}(86) = 0$. Using the generalized power function rule for $\dfrac{d}{dx}(7y^5)$ and noting that $\dfrac{d}{dx}(y) = \dfrac{dy}{dx}$, we get

$$\frac{d}{dx}(7y^5) = 7 \cdot 5 \cdot y^{5-1} \cdot \frac{d}{dx}(y) = 35y^4 \frac{dy}{dx}$$

Substitute the above values in (3.7).

$$12x^3 - 35y^4 \frac{dy}{dx} = 0 \tag{3.8}$$

(2) Now simply solve (3.8) algebraically for dy/dx:

$$-35y^4 \frac{dy}{dx} = -12x^3$$

$$\frac{dy}{dx} = \frac{12x^3}{35y^4}$$

Compare this answer to that in Example 16 of Chapter 5.

Solved Problems

LIMITS AND CONTINUITY

3.1. Use the rules of limits to find the limits for the following functions:

(a) $\lim\limits_{x \to 2} [x^3(x + 4)]$

$$\lim_{x \to 2} [x^3(x + 4)] = \lim_{x \to 2} x^3 \cdot \lim_{x \to 2} (x + 4) \qquad \text{(Rule 5)}$$
$$= (2)^3 \cdot (2 + 4) = 8 \cdot 6 = 48$$

(b) $\lim_{x \to 4} \dfrac{3x^2 - 5x}{x + 6}$

$$\lim_{x \to 4} \frac{3x^2 - 5x}{x + 6} = \frac{\lim_{x \to 4} (3x^2 - 5x)}{\lim_{x \to 4} (x + 6)} \qquad \text{(Rule 6)}$$

$$= \frac{3(4)^2 - 5(4)}{4 + 6} = \frac{48 - 20}{10}$$

$$= 2.8$$

(c) $\lim_{x \to 2} \sqrt{6x^3 + 1}$

$$\lim_{x \to 2} \sqrt{6x^3 + 1} = \lim_{x \to 2} (6x^3 + 1)^{1/2}$$

$$= [\lim_{x \to 2} (6x^3 + 1)]^{1/2} \qquad \text{(Rule 7)}$$

$$= [6(2)^3 + 1]^{1/2} = (49)^{1/2} = \pm 7$$

3.2. Find the limits for the following polynomial and rational functions.

(a) $\lim_{x \to 3} (5x^2 - 4x + 9)$

From the properties of limits it can be shown that for all polynomial functions and all rational functions, where defined, $\lim_{x \to a} f(x) = f(a)$. The limits can be taken, therefore, by simply evaluating the functions at the given level of a.

$$\lim_{x \to 3} (5x^2 - 4x + 9) = 5(3)^2 - 4(3) + 9 = 42$$

(b) $\lim_{x \to -4} (3x^2 + 7x - 12)$

$$\lim_{x \to -4} (3x^2 + 7x - 12) = 3(-4)^2 + 7(-4) - 12 = 8$$

(c) $\lim_{x \to 6} \dfrac{4x^2 - 2x - 8}{5x^2 + 6}$

$$\lim_{x \to 6} \frac{4x^2 - 2x - 8}{5x^2 + 6} = \frac{4(6)^2 - 2(6) - 8}{5(6)^2 + 6} = \frac{124}{186} = \frac{2}{3}$$

3.3. Find the limits of the following rational functions. If the limit of the denominator equals zero, neither Rule 6 nor the generalized rule for rational functions used above applies.

(a) $\lim_{x \to 7} \dfrac{x - 7}{x^2 - 49}$

The limit of the denominator is zero, so Rule 6 cannot be used. Since we are only interested in the function as x draws *near* to 7, however, the limit can be found if by factoring and canceling, the problem of zero in the denominator is removed.

$$\lim_{x \to 7} \frac{x - 7}{x^2 - 49} = \lim_{x \to 7} \frac{x - 7}{(x + 7)(x - 7)}$$

$$= \lim_{x \to 7} \frac{1}{x + 7} = \frac{1}{14}$$

(b) $\displaystyle\lim_{x \to -7} \frac{x - 7}{x^2 - 49}$

$$\lim_{x \to -7} \frac{x - 7}{x^2 - 49} = \lim_{x \to -7} \frac{x - 7}{(x + 7)(x - 7)}$$
$$= \lim_{x \to -7} \frac{1}{x + 7}$$

The limit does not exist.

(c) $\displaystyle\lim_{x \to 6} \frac{x^2 - 2x - 24}{x - 6}$

With the limit of the denominator equal to zero, factor.

$$\lim_{x \to 6} \frac{x^2 - 2x - 24}{x - 6} = \lim_{x \to 6} \frac{(x + 4)(x - 6)}{x - 6} = \lim_{x \to 6} (x + 4) = 10$$

3.4. Find the limits of the following functions, noting the role that infinity plays.

(a) $\displaystyle\lim_{x \to 0} \frac{2}{x}$ $(x \neq 0)$

As seen in Fig. 1-2(b), as x approaches 0 from the right $(x \to 0^+)$, $f(x)$ approaches positive infinity; as x approaches 0 from the left $(x \to 0^-)$, $f(x)$ approaches negative infinity. If a limit approaches either positive or negative infinity, the limit does *not* exist and is written

$$\lim_{x \to 0^+} \frac{2}{x} = \infty \qquad \lim_{x \to 0^-} \frac{2}{x} = -\infty \qquad \text{The limit does not exist.}$$

(b) $\displaystyle\lim_{x \to \infty} \frac{2}{x}$ $\displaystyle\lim_{x \to -\infty} \frac{2}{x}$

As also seen in Fig. 1-2(b), as x approaches ∞, $f(x)$ approaches 0; as x approaches $-\infty$, $f(x)$ also approaches 0. The limit exists in both cases and is written

$$\lim_{x \to \infty} \frac{2}{x} = 0 \qquad \lim_{x \to -\infty} \frac{2}{x} = 0$$

(c) $\displaystyle\lim_{x \to \infty} \frac{3x^2 - 7x}{4x^2 - 21}$

As $x \to \infty$, both numerator and denominator become infinite, leaving matters unclear. A trick in such circumstances is to divide all terms by the highest power of x which appears in the function. Here dividing all terms by x^2 leaves

$$\lim_{x \to \infty} \frac{3x^2 - 7x}{4x^2 - 21} = \lim_{x \to \infty} \frac{3 - (7/x)}{4 - (21/x^2)} = \frac{3 - 0}{4 - 0} = \frac{3}{4}$$

3.5. Indicate whether the following functions are continuous at the specified points by determining whether at the given point all the following conditions from Section 3.2 hold: (1) $f(x)$ is defined, (2) $\lim_{x \to a} f(x)$ exists, and (3) $\lim_{x \to a} f(x) = f(a)$.

(a) $f(x) = 5x^2 - 8x + 9$ at $x = 3$

(1) $f(3) = 5(3)^2 - 8(3) + 9 = 30$

(2) $\displaystyle\lim_{x \to 3} (5x^2 - 8x + 9) = 5(3)^2 - 8(3) + 9 = 30$

(3) $\displaystyle\lim_{x \to 3} f(x) = 30 = f(3)$ $f(x)$ is continuous.

(b) $f(x) = \dfrac{x^2 + 3x + 12}{x - 3}$ at $x = 4$

    (1) $f(4) = \dfrac{(4)^2 + 3(4) + 12}{4 - 3} = \dfrac{40}{1} = 40$

    (2) $\lim\limits_{x \to 4} \dfrac{x^2 + 3x + 12}{x - 3} = 40$

    (3) $\lim\limits_{x \to 4} f(x) = 40 = f(4)$ $f(x)$ is continuous.

(c) $f(x) = \dfrac{x - 3}{x^2 - 9}$ at $x = 3$

    (1) $f(3) = \dfrac{3 - 3}{(3)^2 - 9}$

With the denominator equal to zero, $f(x)$ is not defined at $x = 3$ and so cannot be continuous at $x = 3$ even though the limit exists at $x = 3$. See steps 2 and 3.

    (2) $\lim\limits_{x \to 3} \dfrac{x - 3}{x^2 - 9} = \lim\limits_{x \to 3} \dfrac{x - 3}{(x + 3)(x - 3)} = \lim\limits_{x \to 3} \dfrac{1}{x + 3} = \dfrac{1}{6}$

    (3) $\lim\limits_{x \to 3} f(x) = \frac{1}{6} \neq f(3)$. So $f(x)$ is discontinuous at $x = 3$.

DERIVATIVE NOTATION AND SIMPLE DERIVATIVES

3.6.   Differentiate each of the following functions and practice the use of the different notations for a derivative.

(a) $f(x) = 17$

    $f'(x) = 0$ (constant rule)

(b) $y = -12$

    $\dfrac{dy}{dx} = 0$

(c) $y = 5x + 12$

    $y' = 5$ (linear function rule)

(d) $f(x) = 9x - 6$

    $f' = 9$

3.7.   Differentiate each of the following functions, using the power function rule. Continue to use the different notations.

(a) $y = 8x^3$

    $\dfrac{d}{dx}(8x^3) = 24x^2$

(b) $f(x) = -6x^5$

    $f' = -30x^4$

(c) $f(x) = 5x^{-2}$

    $f'(x) = 5(-2) \cdot x^{[-2-(1)]} = -10x^{-3} = -\dfrac{10}{x^3}$

(d) $y = -9x^{-4}$

    $\dfrac{dy}{dx} = -9(-4) \cdot x^{[-4-(1)]} = 36x^{-5} = \dfrac{36}{x^5}$

(e) $y = \dfrac{7}{x} = 7x^{-1}$

    $D_x(7x^{-1}) = 7(-1)x^{-2} = -7x^{-2} = -\dfrac{7}{x^2}$

(f) $f(x) = 18\sqrt{x} = 18x^{1/2}$

$$\frac{df}{dx} = 18\left(\frac{1}{2}\right) \cdot x^{1/2-1} = 9x^{-1/2} = \frac{9}{\sqrt{x}}$$

3.8. Use the rule for sums and differences to differentiate the following functions. Treat the dependent variable on the left as y and the independent variable on the right as x.

(a) $R = 8t^2 + 5t - 6$

(b) $C = 4t^3 - 9t^2 + 28t - 68$

$$\frac{dR}{dt} = 16t + 5$$

$$C' = 12t^2 - 18t + 28$$

(c) $p = 6q^5 - 3q^3$

(d) $q = 7p^4 + 15p^{-3}$

$$\frac{dp}{dq} = 30q^4 - 9q^2$$

$$D_p(7p^4 + 15p^{-3}) = 28p^3 - 45p^{-4}$$

THE PRODUCT RULE

3.9. Given $y = f(x) = 5x^4(3x - 7)$, (a) use the product rule to find the derivative. (b) Simplify the original function first and then find the derivative. (c) Compare the two derivatives.

(a) Recalling the formula for the product rule from (3.3),

$$f'(x) = g(x) \cdot h'(x) + h(x) \cdot g'(x)$$

let $g(x) = 5x^4$ and $h(x) = 3x - 7$. Then $g'(x) = 20x^3$ and $h'(x) = 3$. Substitute these values in the product — rule formula.

$$y' = f'(x) = 5x^4(3) + (3x - 7)(20x^3)$$

Simplify algebraically.

$$y' = 15x^4 + 60x^4 - 140x^3 = 75x^4 - 140x^3$$

(b) Simplify the original function by multiplication.

$$y = 5x^4(3x - 7) = 15x^5 - 35x^4$$

Take the derivative.

$$y' = 75x^4 - 140x^3$$

(c) The derivatives found in parts (a) and (b) are identical. The derivative of a product can be found by either method, but as the functions grow more complicated, the product rule becomes more useful. Knowledge of another method helps to check answers.

3.10. Redo Problem 3.9, given $y = f(x) = (x^8 + 8)(x^6 + 11)$.

(a) Let $g(x) = x^8 + 8$ and $h(x) = x^6 + 11$. Then $g'(x) = 8x^7$ and $h'(x) = 6x^5$. Substituting these values in (3.3),

$$y' = f'(x) = (x^8 + 8)(6x^5) + (x^6 + 11)(8x^7)$$
$$= 6x^{13} + 48x^5 + 8x^{13} + 88x^7 = 14x^{13} + 88x^7 + 48x^5$$

(b) Simplifying first through multiplication,

$$y = (x^8 + 8)(x^6 + 11) = x^{14} + 11x^8 + 8x^6 + 88$$

Then

$$y' = 14x^{13} + 88x^7 + 48x^5$$

(c) The derivatives are identical.

3.11. Differentiate each of the following functions, using the product rule. *Note*: The choice of problems is purposely kept simple in this and other sections of the book to enable students to see how various rules work. While it is proper and often easier to simplify a function algebraically before taking the derivative, applying the rules to the problems as given in the long run will help the student to master the rules more efficiently.

(a) $y = (4x^2 - 3)(2x^5)$

$$\frac{dy}{dx} = (4x^2 - 3)(10x^4) + 2x^5(8x) = 40x^6 - 30x^4 + 16x^6 = 56x^6 - 30x^4$$

(b) $y = 7x^9(3x^2 - 12)$

$$\frac{dy}{dx} = 7x^9(6x) + (3x^2 - 12)(63x^8) = 42x^{10} + 189x^{10} - 756x^8 = 231x^{10} - 756x^8$$

(c) $y = (2x^4 + 5)(3x^5 - 8)$

$$\frac{dy}{dx} = (2x^4 + 5)(15x^4) + (3x^5 - 8)(8x^3) = 30x^8 + 75x^4 + 24x^8 - 64x^3 = 54x^8 + 75x^4 - 64x^3$$

(d) $z = (3 - 12t^3)(5 + 4t^6)$

$$\frac{dz}{dt} = (3 - 12t^3)(24t^5) + (5 + 4t^6)(-36t^2) = 72t^5 - 288t^8 - 180t^2 - 144t^8 = -432t^8 + 72t^5 - 180t^2$$

QUOTIENT RULE

3.12. Given

$$y = \frac{10x^8 - 6x^7}{2x}$$

(a) find the derivative directly, using the quotient rule. (b) Simplify the function by division and then take its derivative. (c) Compare the two derivatives.

(a)   From (*3.4*), the formula for the quotient rule is

$$f'(x) = \frac{h(x) \cdot g'(x) - g(x) \cdot h'(x)}{[h(x)]^2}$$

where $g(x) =$ the numerator $= 10x^8 - 6x^7$ and $h(x) =$ the denominator $= 2x$. Take the individual derivatives.

$$g'(x) = 80x^7 - 42x^6 \qquad h'(x) = 2$$

Substitute in the formula,

$$y' = \frac{2x(80x^7 - 42x^6) - (10x^8 - 6x^7)(2)}{(2x)^2}$$

$$= \frac{160x^8 - 84x^7 - 20x^8 + 12x^7}{4x^2} = \frac{140x^8 - 72x^7}{4x^2}$$

$$= 35x^6 - 18x^5$$

(b)   Simplifying the original function first by division,

$$y = \frac{10x^8 - 6x^7}{2x} = 5x^7 - 3x^6$$

$$y' = 35x^6 - 18x^5$$

(c)   The derivatives will always be the same if done correctly, but as functions grow in complexity, the quotient rule becomes more important. A second method is also a way to check answers.

3.13. Differentiate each of the following functions by means of the quotient rule. Continue to apply the rules to the functions as given. Later, when all the rules have been mastered, the functions can be simplified first and the easiest rule applied.

(a) $y = \dfrac{3x^8 - 4x^7}{4x^3}$

Here $g(x) = 3x^8 - 4x^7$ and $h(x) = 4x^3$. Thus, $g'(x) = 24x^7 - 28x^6$ and $h'(x) = 12x^2$. Substituting in the quotient formula,

$$y' = \frac{4x^3(24x^7 - 28x^6) - (3x^8 - 4x^7)(12x^2)}{(4x^3)^2}$$

$$= \frac{96x^{10} - 112x^9 - 36x^{10} + 48x^9}{16x^6} = \frac{60x^{10} - 64x^9}{16x^6} = 3.75x^4 - 4x^3$$

(b) $y = \dfrac{4x^5}{1 - 3x}$ $(x \neq \tfrac{1}{3})$

(*Note*: The qualifying statement is added because if $x = \tfrac{1}{3}$, the denominator would equal zero and the function would be undefined.)

$$\frac{dy}{dx} = \frac{(1 - 3x)(20x^4) - 4x^5(-3)}{(1 - 3x)^2} = \frac{20x^4 - 60x^5 + 12x^5}{(1 - 3x)^2} = \frac{20x^4 - 48x^5}{(1 - 3x)^2}$$

(c) $y = \dfrac{15x^2}{2x^2 + 7x - 3}$

$$\frac{dy}{dx} = \frac{(2x^2 + 7x - 3)(30x) - 15x^2(4x + 7)}{(2x^2 + 7x - 3)^2}$$

$$= \frac{60x^3 + 210x^2 - 90x - 60x^3 - 105x^2}{(2x^2 + 7x - 3)^2} = \frac{105x^2 - 90x}{(2x^2 + 7x - 3)^2}$$

(d) $y = \dfrac{6x - 7}{8x - 5}$ $(x \neq \tfrac{5}{8})$

$$\frac{dy}{dx} = \frac{(8x - 5)(6) - (6x - 7)(8)}{(8x - 5)^2} = \frac{48x - 30 - 48x + 56}{(8x - 5)^2} = \frac{26}{(8x - 5)^2}$$

(e) $y = \dfrac{5x^2 - 9x + 8}{x^2 + 1}$

$$\frac{dy}{dx} = \frac{(x^2 + 1)(10x - 9) - (5x^2 - 9x + 8)(2x)}{(x^2 + 1)^2}$$

$$= \frac{10x^3 - 9x^2 + 10x - 9 - 10x^3 + 18x^2 - 16x}{(x^2 + 1)^2} = \frac{9x^2 - 6x - 9}{(x^2 + 1)^2}$$

THE GENERALIZED POWER FUNCTION RULE

3.14. Given $y = (5x + 8)^2$, (a) use the generalized power function rule to find the derivative; (b) simplify the function first by squaring it and then take the derivative; (c) compare answers.

(a)   From the generalized power function rule in (3.5), if $f(x) = [g(x)]^n$,

$$f'(x) = n[g(x)]^{n-1} \cdot g'(x)$$

Here $g(x) = 5x + 8$, $g'(x) = 5$, and $n = 2$. Substitute these values in the generalized power function rule,

$$y' = 2(5x + 8)^{2-1} \cdot 5 = 10(5x + 8) = 50x + 80$$

(b) Square the function first and then take the derivative,

$$y = (5x + 8)(5x + 8) = 25x^2 + 80x + 64$$
$$y' = 50x + 80$$

(c) The derivatives are identical. But for higher, negative, and fractional values of n, the generalized power function rule is faster and more practical.

3.15. Find the derivative for each of the following functions with the help of the generalized power function rule.

(a) $y = (6x^3 + 9)^4$

Here $g(x) = 6x^3 + 9$, $g'(x) = 18x^2$, and $n = 4$. Substitute in the generalized power function rule,

$$y' = 4(6x^3 + 9)^{4-1} \cdot 18x^2$$
$$= 4(6x^3 + 9)^3 \cdot 18x^2 = 72x^2(6x^3 + 9)^3$$

(b) $y = (2x^2 - 5x + 7)^3$

$$y' = 3(2x^2 - 5x + 7)^2 \cdot (4x - 5)$$
$$= (12x - 15)(2x^2 - 5x + 7)^2$$

(c) $y = \dfrac{1}{7x^3 + 13x + 3}$

First convert the function to an easier equivalent form,

$$y = (7x^3 + 13x + 3)^{-1}$$

then use the generalized power function rule,

$$y' = -1(7x^3 + 13x + 3)^{-2} \cdot (21x^2 + 13)$$
$$= -(21x^2 + 13)(7x^3 + 13x + 3)^{-2}$$
$$= \frac{-(21x^2 + 13)}{(7x^3 + 13x + 3)^2}$$

(d) $y = \sqrt{34 - 6x^2}$

Convert the radical to a power function, then differentiate.

$$y = (34 - 6x^2)^{1/2}$$
$$y' = \tfrac{1}{2}(34 - 6x^2)^{-1/2} \cdot (-12x)$$
$$= -6x(34 - 6x^2)^{-1/2} = \frac{-6x}{\sqrt{34 - 6x^2}}$$

(e) $y = \dfrac{1}{\sqrt{4x^3 + 94}}$

Convert to an equivalent form; then take the derivative.

$$y = (4x^3 + 94)^{-1/2}$$
$$y' = -\tfrac{1}{2}(4x^3 + 94)^{-3/2} \cdot (12x^2) = -6x^2(4x^3 + 94)^{-3/2}$$
$$= \frac{-6x^2}{(4x^3 + 94)^{3/2}} = \frac{-6x^2}{\sqrt{(4x^3 + 94)^3}}$$

CHAIN RULE

3.16. Use the chain rule to find the derivative dy/dx for each of the following functions of a function. Check each answer on your own with the generalized power function rule, noting that the generalized power function rule is simply a specialized use of the chain rule.

(a) $y = (3x^4 + 5)^6$

Let $y = u^6$ and $u = 3x^4 + 5$. Then $dy/du = 6u^5$ and $du/dx = 12x^3$. From the chain rule in (3.6),

$$\frac{dy}{dx} = \frac{dy}{du}\frac{du}{dx}$$

Substituting, $$\frac{dy}{dx} = 6u^5 \cdot 12x^3 = 72x^3 u^5$$

But $u = 3x^4 + 5$. Substituting again,

$$\frac{dy}{dx} = 72x^3(3x^4 + 5)^5$$

(b) $y = (7x + 9)^2$

Let $y = u^2$ and $u = 7x + 9$, then $dy/du = 2u$ and $du/dx = 7$. Substitute these values in the chain rule,

$$\frac{dy}{dx} = 2u \cdot 7 = 14u$$

Then substitute $7x + 9$ for u.

$$\frac{dy}{dx} = 14(7x + 9) = 98x + 126$$

(c) $y = (4x^5 - 1)^7$

Let $y = u^7$ and $u = 4x^5 - 1$; then $dy/du = 7u^6$, $du/dx = 20x^4$, and

$$\frac{dy}{dx} = 7u^6 \cdot 20x^4 = 140x^4 u^6$$

Substitute $u = 4x^5 - 1$.

$$\frac{dy}{dx} = 140x^4(4x^5 - 1)^6$$

3.17.   Redo Problem 3.16, given:

(a) $y = (x^2 + 3x - 1)^5$

Let $y = u^5$ and $u = x^2 + 3x - 1$, then $dy/du = 5u^4$ and $du/dx = 2x + 3$. Substitute in (3.6).

$$\frac{dy}{dx} = 5u^4(2x + 3) = (10x + 15)u^4$$

But $u = x^2 + 3x - 1$. Therefore,

$$\frac{dy}{dx} = (10x + 15)(x^2 + 3x - 1)^4$$

(b) $y = -3(x^2 - 8x + 7)^4$

Let $y = -3u^4$ and $u = x^2 - 8x + 7$. Then $dy/du = -12u^3$, $du/dx = 2x - 8$, and

$$\frac{dy}{dx} = -12u^3(2x - 8) = (-24x + 96)u^3$$

$$= (-24x + 96)(x^2 - 8x + 7)^3$$

COMBINATION OF RULES

3.18. Use whatever combination of rules is necessary to find the derivatives of the following functions. Do not simplify the original functions first. They are deliberately kept simple to facilitate the practice of the rules.

(a) $y = \dfrac{3x(2x - 1)}{5x - 2}$

The function involves a quotient with a product in the numerator. Hence both the quotient rule and the product rule are required. Start with the quotient rule from (3.4).

$$y' = \frac{h(x) \cdot g'(x) - g(x) \cdot h'(x)}{[h(x)]^2}$$

where $g(x) = 3x(2x - 1)$, $h(x) = 5x - 2$, and $h'(x) = 5$. Then use the product rule from (3.3) for $g'(x)$.

$$g'(x) = 3x \cdot 2 + (2x - 1) \cdot 3 = 12x - 3$$

Substitute the appropriate values in the quotient rule.

$$y' = \frac{(5x - 2)(12x - 3) - [3x(2x - 1)] \cdot 5}{(5x - 2)^2}$$

Simplify algebraically.

$$y' = \frac{60x^2 - 15x - 24x + 6 - 30x^2 + 15x}{(5x - 2)^2} = \frac{30x^2 - 24x + 6}{(5x - 2)^2}$$

Note: To check this answer one could let

$$y = 3x \cdot \frac{2x - 1}{5x - 2} \quad \text{or} \quad y = \frac{3x}{5x - 2} \cdot (2x - 1)$$

and use the product rule involving a quotient.

(b) $y = 3x(4x - 5)^2$

The function involves a product in which one function is raised to a power. Both the product rule and the generalized power function rule are needed. Starting with the product rule,

$$y' = g(x) \cdot h'(x) + h(x) \cdot g'(x)$$

where $\qquad g(x) = 3x \qquad h(x) = (4x - 5)^2 \qquad \text{and} \qquad g'(x) = 3$

Use the generalized power function rule for $h'(x)$.

$$h'(x) = 2(4x - 5) \cdot 4 = 8(4x - 5) = 32x - 40$$

Substitute the appropriate values in the product rule,

$$y' = 3x \cdot (32x - 40) + (4x - 5)^2 \cdot 3$$

and simplify algebraically,

$$y' = 96x^2 - 120x + 3(16x^2 - 40x + 25) = 144x^2 - 240x + 75$$

(c) $y = (3x - 4) \cdot \dfrac{5x + 1}{2x + 7}$

Here we have a product involving a quotient. Both the product rule and the quotient rule are needed. Start with the product rule,

$$y' = g(x) \cdot h'(x) + h(x) \cdot g'(x)$$

where $\qquad g(x) = 3x - 4 \qquad h(x) = \dfrac{5x + 1}{2x + 7} \qquad \text{and} \qquad g'(x) = 3$

and use the quotient rule for $h'(x)$.

$$h'(x) = \frac{(2x+7)(5) - (5x+1)(2)}{(2x+7)^2} = \frac{33}{(2x+7)^2}$$

Substitute the appropriate values in the product rule,

$$y' = (3x-4) \cdot \frac{33}{(2x+7)^2} + \frac{5x+1}{2x+7} \cdot 3 = \frac{99x-132}{(2x+7)^2} + \frac{15x+3}{2x+7}$$

$$= \frac{99x-132 + (15x+3)(2x+7)}{(2x+7)^2} = \frac{30x^2 + 210x - 111}{(2x+7)^2}$$

One could check this answer by letting $y = (3x-4)(5x+1)/(2x+7)$ and using the quotient rule involving a product.

(d) $y = \dfrac{(8x-5)^3}{(7x+4)}$

Start with the quotient rule, where

$$g(x) = (8x-5)^3 \qquad h(x) = 7x+4 \qquad h'(x) = 7$$

and use the generalized power function rule for $g'(x)$,

$$g'(x) = 3(8x-5)^2 \cdot 8 = 24(8x-5)^2$$

Substitute these values in the quotient rule,

$$y' = \frac{(7x+4) \cdot 24(8x-5)^2 - (8x-5)^3 \cdot 7}{(7x+4)^2}$$

$$= \frac{(168x+96)(8x-5)^2 - 7(8x-5)^3}{(7x+4)^2}$$

To check this answer, one could let $y = (8x-5)^3 \cdot (7x+4)^{-1}$ and use the product rule involving the generalized power function rule twice.

(e) $y = \left(\dfrac{3x+4}{2x+5}\right)^2$

Start with the generalized power function rule,

$$y' = 2\left(\frac{3x+4}{2x+5}\right) \cdot \frac{d}{dx}\left(\frac{3x+4}{2x+5}\right) \qquad\qquad (3.9)$$

Then use the quotient rule,

$$\frac{d}{dx}\left(\frac{3x+4}{2x+5}\right) = \frac{(2x+5)(3) - (3x+4)(2)}{(2x+5)^2} = \frac{7}{(2x+5)^2}$$

and substitute this value in (3.9),

$$y' = 2\left(\frac{3x+4}{2x+5}\right) \cdot \frac{7}{(2x+5)^2} = \frac{14(3x+4)}{(2x+5)^3} = \frac{42x+56}{(2x+5)^3}$$

To check this answer, let $y = (3x+4)^2 \cdot (2x+5)^{-2}$, and use the product rule involving the generalized power function rule twice.

3.19. Differentiate each of the following, using whatever rules are necessary:

(a) $y = (5x-1)(3x+4)^3$

Using the product rule together with the generalized power function rule,

$$\frac{dy}{dx} = (5x-1)[3(3x+4)^2(3)] + (3x+4)^3(5)$$

Simplifying algebraically,

$$\frac{dy}{dx} = (5x - 1)(9)(3x + 4)^2 + 5(3x + 4)^3 = (45x - 9)(3x + 4)^2 + 5(3x + 4)^3$$

(b) $y = \dfrac{(9x^2 - 2)(7x + 3)}{5x}$

Using the quotient rule along with the product rule,

$$y' = \frac{5x[(9x^2 - 2)(7) + (7x + 3)(18x)] - (9x^2 - 2)(7x + 3)(5)}{(5x)^2}$$

Simplifying algebraically,

$$y' = \frac{5x(63x^2 - 14 + 126x^2 + 54x) - 5(63x^3 + 27x^2 - 14x - 6)}{25x^2} = \frac{630x^3 + 135x^2 + 30}{25x^2}$$

(c) $y = \dfrac{15x + 23}{(3x + 1)^2}$

Using the quotient rule plus the generalized power function rule,

$$y' = \frac{(3x + 1)^2(15) - (15x + 23)[2(3x + 1)(3)]}{(3x + 1)^4}$$

Simplifying algebraically,

$$y' = \frac{15(3x + 1)^2 - (15x + 23)(18x + 6)}{(3x + 1)^4} = \frac{-135x^2 - 414x - 123}{(3x + 1)^4}$$

(d) $y = (6x + 1)\dfrac{4x}{9x - 1}$

Using the product rule and the quotient rule,

$$D_x = (6x + 1)\frac{(9x - 1)(4) - 4x(9)}{(9x - 1)^2} + \frac{4x}{9x - 1}(6)$$

Simplifying algebraically,

$$D_x = \frac{(6x + 1)(36x - 4 - 36x)}{(9x - 1)^2} + \frac{24x}{9x - 1} = \frac{216x^2 - 48x - 4}{(9x - 1)^2}$$

(e) $y = \left(\dfrac{3x - 1}{2x + 5}\right)^3$

Using the generalized power function rule and the quotient rule,

$$y' = 3\left(\frac{3x - 1}{2x + 5}\right)^2 \frac{(2x + 5)(3) - (3x - 1)(2)}{(2x + 5)^2}$$

Simplifying algebraically,

$$y' = \frac{3(3x - 1)^2}{(2x + 5)^2} \frac{17}{(2x + 5)^2} = \frac{51(3x - 1)^2}{(2x + 5)^4}$$

HIGHER-ORDER DERIVATIVES

3.20.   For each of the following functions, (1) find the second-order derivative and (2) evaluate it at $x = 2$. Practice the use of the different second-order notations.

(a) $y = 7x^3 + 5x^2 + 12$

(1) $\dfrac{dy}{dx} = 21x^2 + 10x$

   $\dfrac{d^2y}{dx^2} = 42x + 10$

(2)   At $x = 2$, $\dfrac{d^2y}{dx^2} = 42(2) + 10$

   $= 94$

(b) $f(x) = x^6 + 3x^4 + x$

(1) $f'(x) = 6x^5 + 12x^3 + 1$

   $f''(x) = 30x^4 + 36x^2$

(2)   At $x = 2$, $f''(x) = 30(2)^4 + 36(2)^2$

   $= 624$

(c) $y = (2x + 3)(8x^2 - 6)$

(1) $Dy = (2x + 3)(16x) + (8x^2 - 6)(2)$

   $= 32x^2 + 48x + 16x^2 - 12$

   $= 48x^2 + 48x - 12$

   $D^2y = 96x + 48$

(2)   At $x = 2$, $D^2y = 96(2) + 48$

   $= 240$

(d) $f(x) = (x^4 - 3)(x^3 - 2)$

(1) $f' = (x^4 - 3)(3x^2) + (x^3 - 2)(4x^3)$

   $= 3x^6 - 9x^2 + 4x^6 - 8x^3$

   $= 7x^6 - 8x^3 - 9x^2$

   $f'' = 42x^5 - 24x^2 - 18x$

(2)   At $x = 2$, $f'' = 42(2)^5 - 24(2)^2 - 18(2)$

   $= 1212$

(e) $y = \dfrac{5x}{1 - 3x}$

(1) $y' = \dfrac{(1 - 3x)(5) - 5x(-3)}{(1 - 3x)^2}$

   $= \dfrac{5 - 15x + 15x}{(1 - 3x)^2} = \dfrac{5}{(1 - 3x)^2}$

   $y'' = \dfrac{(1 - 3x)^2(0) - 5[2(1 - 3x)(-3)]}{(1 - 3x)^4}$

   $= \dfrac{-5(-6 + 18x)}{(1 - 3x)^4} = \dfrac{30 - 90x}{(1 - 3x)^4} = \dfrac{30}{(1 - 3x)^3}$

(2)   At $x = 2$, $y'' = \dfrac{30 - 90(2)}{[1 - 3(2)]^4}$

   $= \dfrac{-150}{(-5)^4}$

   $= -\dfrac{6}{25}$

(f) $y = \dfrac{7x^2}{x - 1}$

(1) $y' = \dfrac{(x - 1)(14x) - 7x^2(1)}{(x - 1)^2}$

   $= \dfrac{14x^2 - 14x - 7x^2}{(x - 1)^2} = \dfrac{7x^2 - 14x}{(x - 1)^2}$

   $y'' = \dfrac{(x - 1)^2(14x - 14) - (7x^2 - 14x)[2(x - 1)(1)]}{(x - 1)^4}$

   $= \dfrac{(x^2 - 2x + 1)(14x - 14) - (7x^2 - 14x)(2x - 2)}{(x - 1)^4}$

   $= \dfrac{14(x - 1)}{(x - 1)^4} = \dfrac{14}{(x - 1)^3}$

(2)   At $x = 2$, $y'' = \dfrac{14}{(2 - 1)^3}$

   $= 14$

(g) $f(x) = (8x - 4)^3$

(1) $f' = 3(8x - 4)^2(8)$

   $= 24(8x - 4)^2$

   $f'' = 2(24)(8x - 4)(8)$

   $= 384(8x - 4)$

(2)   At $x = 2$, $f'' = 384[8(2) - 4]$

   $= 4608$

(h) $y = (5x^3 - 7x^2)^2$

   (1) $Dy = 2(5x^3 - 7x^2)(15x^2 - 14x)$ (2)   At $x = 2$, $D^2y = 750(2)^4 - 1400(2)^3 + 588(2)^2$
   $= 150x^5 - 350x^4 + 196x^3$ $= 3152$
   $D^2y = 750x^4 - 1400x^3 + 588x^2$

3.21. For each of the following functions, (1) investigate the successive derivatives and (2) evaluate them at $x = 3$.

(a) $y = x^3 + 3x^2 + 9x - 7$

   (1) $y' = 3x^2 + 6x + 9$ (2)   At $x = 3$, $y' = 3(3)^2 + 6(3) + 9 = 54$
   $y'' = 6x + 6$ $y'' = 6(3) + 6 = 24$
   $y''' = 6$ $y''' = 6$
   $y^{(4)} = 0$ $y^{(4)} = 0$

(b) $y = (4x - 7)(9x + 2)$

   (1) $y' = (4x - 7)(9) + (9x + 2)(4)$ (2)   At $x = 3$, $y' = 72(3) - 55 = 161$
   $= 36x - 63 + 36x + 8 = 72x - 55$ $y'' = 72$
   $y'' = 72$ $y''' = 0$
   $y''' = 0$

(c) $y = (5 - x)^4$

   (1) $D_x = 4(5 - x)^3(-1) = -4(5 - x)^3$ (2)   At $x = 3$, $D_x = -4(5 - 3)^3 = -32$
   $D_x^2 = -12(5 - x)^2(-1) = 12(5 - x)^2$ $D_x^2 = 12(5 - 3)^2 = 48$
   $D_x^3 = 24(5 - x)(-1)$ $D_x^3 = 24(3) - 120 = -48$
   $= -24(5 - x) = 24x - 120$ $D_x^4 = 24$
   $D_x^4 = 24$ $D_x^5 = 0$
   $D_x^5 = 0$

IMPLICIT DIFFERENTIATION

3.22. Use implicit differentiation to find the derivative dy/dx for each of the following equations.

(a) $4x^2 - y^3 = 97$

Take the derivative with respect to x of both sides,

$$\frac{d}{dx}(4x^2) - \frac{d}{dx}(y^3) = \frac{d}{dx}(97) \tag{3.10}$$

where $\dfrac{d}{dx}(4x^2) = 8x$, $\dfrac{d}{dx}(97) = 0$, and use the generalized power function rule because y is considered a function of x,

$$\frac{d}{dx}(y^3) = 3 \cdot y^2 \cdot \frac{d}{dx}(y)$$

Set these values in (3.10) and recall that $\dfrac{d}{dx}(y) = \dfrac{dy}{dx}$.

$$8x - 3y^2\left(\frac{dy}{dx}\right) = 0$$

$$-3y^2\left(\frac{dy}{dx}\right) = -8x$$

$$\frac{dy}{dx} = \frac{8x}{3y^2}$$

(b) $3y^5 - 6y^4 + 5x^6 = 243$

Take the derivative with respect to x of both sides,

$$\frac{d}{dx}(3y^5) - \frac{d}{dx}(6y^4) + \frac{d}{dx}(5x^6) = \frac{d}{dx}(243)$$

$$15y^4\left(\frac{dy}{dx}\right) - 24y^3\left(\frac{dy}{dx}\right) + 30x^5 = 0$$

Solve for dy/dx,

$$(15y^4 - 24y^3)\left(\frac{dy}{dx}\right) = -30x^5$$

$$\frac{dy}{dx} = \frac{-30x^5}{15y^4 - 24y^3}$$

(c) $2x^4 + 7x^3 + 8y^5 = 136$

$$\frac{d}{dx}(2x^4) + \frac{d}{dx}(7x^3) + \frac{d}{dx}(8y^5) = \frac{d}{dx}(136)$$

$$8x^3 + 21x^2 + 40y^4\left(\frac{dy}{dx}\right) = 0$$

$$40y^4\left(\frac{dy}{dx}\right) = -(8x^3 + 21x^2)$$

$$\frac{dy}{dx} = \frac{-(8x^3 + 21x^2)}{40y^4}$$

3.23. Use the different rules of differentiation in implicit differentiation to find dy/dx for each of the following:

(a) $x^4 y^6 = 89$

$$\frac{d}{dx}(x^4 y^6) = \frac{d}{dx}(89)$$

Use the product rule and the generalized power function rule.

$$x^4 \cdot \frac{d}{dx}(y^6) + y^6 \cdot \frac{d}{dx}(x^4) = \frac{d}{dx}(89)$$

$$x^4 \cdot 6y^5 \frac{dy}{dx} + y^6 \cdot 4x^3 = 0$$

Solve algebraically for dy/dx.

$$6x^4 y^5 \frac{dy}{dx} = -4x^3 y^6$$

$$\frac{dy}{dx} = \frac{-4x^3 y^6}{6x^4 y^5} = \frac{-2y}{3x}$$

(b) $2x^3 + 5xy + 6y^2 = 87$

$$\frac{d}{dx}(2x^3 + 5xy + 6y^2) = \frac{d}{dx}(87)$$

Note that the derivative of $5xy$ requires the product rule.

$$6x^2 + \left[5x \cdot \left(\frac{dy}{dx}\right) + y \cdot (5)\right] + 12y\left(\frac{dy}{dx}\right) = 0$$

Solving algebraically for dy/dx

$$(5x + 12y)\left(\frac{dy}{dx}\right) = -6x^2 - 5y$$

$$\frac{dy}{dx} = \frac{-(6x^2 + 5y)}{5x + 12y}$$

(c) $7x^4 + 3x^3y + 9xy^2 = 496$

$$28x^3 + \left[3x^3 \cdot \left(\frac{dy}{dx}\right) + y \cdot 9x^2\right] + \left[9x \cdot 2y\left(\frac{dy}{dx}\right) + y^2 \cdot 9\right] = 0$$

$$28x^3 + 3x^3\left(\frac{dy}{dx}\right) + 9x^2y + 18xy\left(\frac{dy}{dx}\right) + 9y^2 = 0$$

$$(3x^3 + 18xy)\left(\frac{dy}{dx}\right) = -28x^3 - 9x^2y - 9y^2$$

$$\frac{dy}{dx} = \frac{-(28x^3 + 9x^2y + 9y^2)}{3x^3 + 18xy}$$

(d) $(5y - 21)^3 = 6x^5$

$$\frac{d}{dx}[(5y - 21)^3] = \frac{d}{dx}(6x^5)$$

Use the generalized power function rule.

$$3(5y - 21)^2 \cdot 5\left(\frac{dy}{dx}\right) = 30x^4$$

$$15(5y - 21)^2\left(\frac{dy}{dx}\right) = 30x^4$$

$$\frac{dy}{dx} = \frac{30x^4}{15(5y - 21)^2}$$

(e) $(2x^3 + 7y)^2 = x^5$

$$\frac{d}{dx}(2x^3 + 7y)^2 = \frac{d}{dx}(x^5)$$

$$2(2x^3 + 7y) \cdot \frac{d}{dx}(2x^3 + 7y) = 5x^4$$

$$(4x^3 + 14y)\left[6x^2 + 7\left(\frac{dy}{dx}\right)\right] = 5x^4$$

$$24x^5 + 28x^3\left(\frac{dy}{dx}\right) + 84x^2y + 98y\left(\frac{dy}{dx}\right) = 5x^4$$

$$(28x^3 + 98y)\frac{dy}{dx} = 5x^4 - 24x^5 - 84x^2y$$

$$\frac{dy}{dx} = \frac{5x^4 - 24x^5 - 84x^2y}{28x^3 + 98y}$$

See also Problems 4.38, 4.39, 5.20, 5.21, 6.55, and 6.56.

DERIVATION OF THE RULES OF DIFFERENTIATION

3.24. Given $f(x) = g(x) + h(x)$, where $g(x)$ and $h(x)$ are both differentiable functions, prove the rule of sums by demonstrating that $f'(x) = g'(x) + h'(x)$.

From (3.2) the derivative of $f(x)$ is

$$f'(x) = \lim_{\Delta x \to 0} \frac{f(x + \Delta x) - f(x)}{\Delta x}$$

Substituting $f(x) = g(x) + h(x)$,

$$f'(x) = \lim_{\Delta x \to 0} \frac{[g(x + \Delta x) + h(x + \Delta x)] - [g(x) + h(x)]}{\Delta x}$$

Rearrange terms.

$$f'(x) = \lim_{\Delta x \to 0} \frac{g(x + \Delta x) - g(x) + h(x + \Delta x) - h(x)}{\Delta x}$$

Separate terms, and take the limits.

$$f'(x) = \lim_{\Delta x \to 0} \left[\frac{g(x + \Delta x) - g(x)}{\Delta x} + \frac{h(x + \Delta x) - h(x)}{\Delta x} \right]$$

$$= \lim_{\Delta x \to 0} \frac{g(x + \Delta x) - g(x)}{\Delta x} + \lim_{\Delta x \to 0} \frac{h(x + \Delta x) - h(x)}{\Delta x}$$

$$= g'(x) + h'(x)$$

3.25. Given $f(x) = g(x) \cdot h(x)$, where $g'(x)$ and $h'(x)$ both exist, prove the product rule by demonstrating that $f'(x) = g(x) \cdot h'(x) + h(x) \cdot g'(x)$.

$$f'(x) = \lim_{\Delta x \to 0} \frac{f(x + \Delta x) - f(x)}{\Delta x}$$

Substitute $f(x) = g(x) \cdot h(x)$.

$$f'(x) = \lim_{\Delta x \to 0} \frac{g(x + \Delta x) \cdot h(x + \Delta x) - g(x) \cdot h(x)}{\Delta x}$$

Add and subtract $g(x + \Delta x) \cdot h(x)$,

$$f'(x) = \lim_{\Delta x \to 0} \frac{g(x + \Delta x)h(x + \Delta x) - g(x + \Delta x)h(x) + g(x + \Delta x)h(x) - g(x)h(x)}{\Delta x}$$

Partially factor out $g(x + \Delta x)$ and $h(x)$.

$$f'(x) = \lim_{\Delta x \to 0} \frac{g(x + \Delta x)[h(x + \Delta x) - h(x)] + h(x)[g(x + \Delta x) - g(x)]}{\Delta x}$$

$$= \lim_{\Delta x \to 0} \frac{g(x + \Delta x)[h(x + \Delta x) - h(x)]}{\Delta x} + \lim_{\Delta x \to 0} \frac{h(x)[g(x + \Delta x) - g(x)]}{\Delta x}$$

$$= \lim_{\Delta x \to 0} g(x + \Delta x) \cdot \lim_{\Delta x \to 0} \frac{h(x + \Delta x) - h(x)}{\Delta x} + \lim_{\Delta x \to 0} h(x) \cdot \lim_{\Delta x \to 0} \frac{g(x + \Delta x) - g(x)}{\Delta x}$$

$$= g(x) \cdot h'(x) + h(x) \cdot g'(x)$$

3.26. Given $f(x) = g(x)/h(x)$, where $g'(x)$ and $h'(x)$ both exist and $h(x) \neq 0$, prove the quotient rule by demonstrating

$$f'(x) = \frac{h(x) \cdot g'(x) - g(x) \cdot h'(x)}{[h(x)]^2}$$

Start with $f(x) = g(x)/h(x)$ and solve for $g(x)$,

$$g(x) = f(x) \cdot h(x)$$

Then take the derivative of $g(x)$, using the product rule,

$$g'(x) = f(x) \cdot h'(x) + h(x) \cdot f'(x)$$

and solve algebraically for $f'(x)$.

$$h(x) \cdot f'(x) = g'(x) - f(x) \cdot h'(x)$$
$$f'(x) = \frac{g'(x) - f(x) \cdot h'(x)}{h(x)}$$

Substitute $g(x)/h(x)$ for $f(x)$.

$$f'(x) = \frac{g'(x) - \dfrac{g(x) \cdot h'(x)}{h(x)}}{h(x)}$$

Now multiply both numerator and denominator by $h(x)$,

$$f'(x) = \frac{h(x) \cdot g'(x) - g(x) \cdot h'(x)}{[h(x)]^2}$$

Chapter 4

Uses of the Derivative in Mathematics and Economics

4.1 INCREASING AND DECREASING FUNCTIONS

A function $f(x)$ is said to be *increasing* (*decreasing*) at $x = a$ if in the immediate vicinity of the point $[a, f(a)]$ the graph of the function rises (falls) as it moves from left to right. Since the first derivative measures the rate of change and slope of a function, a positive first derivative at $x = a$ indicates the function is increasing at a; a negative first derivative indicates it is decreasing. In short, as seen in Fig. 4-1,

$$f'(a) > 0: \quad \text{increasing function at } x = a$$
$$f'(a) < 0: \quad \text{decreasing function at } x = a$$

A function that increases (or decreases) over its entire domain is called a *monotonic function*. It is said to increase (decrease) *monotonically*. See Problems 4.1 to 4.3.

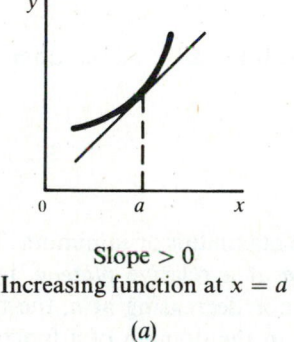

Slope > 0
Increasing function at $x = a$

(a)

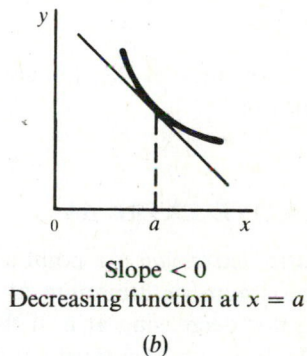

Slope < 0
Decreasing function at $x = a$

(b)

Fig. 4-1

4.2 CONCAVITY AND CONVEXITY

A function $f(x)$ is *concave* at $x = a$ if in some small region close to the point $[a, f(a)]$ the graph of the function lies completely below its tangent line. A function is *convex* at $x = a$ if in the area very close to $[a, f(a)]$ the graph of the function lies completely above its tangent line. A positive second derivative at $x = a$ denotes the function is convex at $x = a$; a negative second derivative at $x = a$ denotes the function is concave at a. The sign of the first derivative is irrelevant for concavity. In brief, as seen in Fig. 4-2 and Problems 4.1 to 4.4,

$$f''(a) > 0: \quad f(x) \text{ is convex at } x = a$$
$$f''(a) < 0: \quad f(x) \text{ is concave at } x = a$$

65

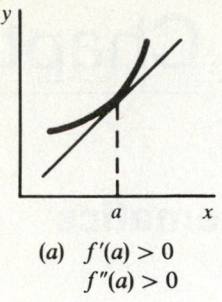

(a) $f'(a) > 0$
    $f''(a) > 0$

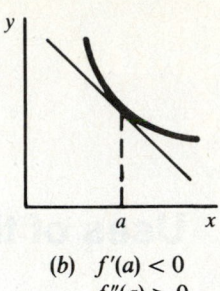

(b) $f'(a) < 0$
    $f''(a) > 0$

Convex at $x = a$

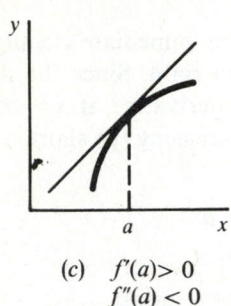

(c) $f'(a) > 0$
    $f''(a) < 0$

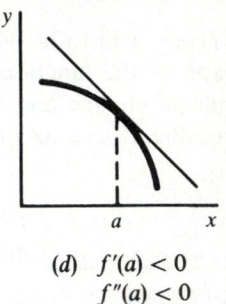

(d) $f'(a) < 0$
    $f''(a) < 0$

Concave at $x = a$

Fig. 4-2

If $f''(x) > 0$ for all x in the domain, $f(x)$ is *strictly convex.* If $f''(x) < 0$ for all x in the domain, $f(x)$ is *strictly concave.*

4.3   RELATIVE EXTREMA

A *relative extremum* is a point at which a function is at a relative maximum or minimum. To be at a relative maximum or minimum at a point a, the function must be at a relative *plateau*, i.e., neither increasing nor decreasing at a. If the function is neither increasing nor decreasing at a, the first derivative of the function at a must equal zero or be undefined. A point in the domain of a function where the derivative equals zero or is undefined is called a *critical point* or *value*.

To distinguish mathematically between a relative maximum and minimum, the *second-derivative test* is used. Assuming $f'(a) = 0$,

1. If $f''(a) > 0$, indicating that the function is convex and the graph of the function lies completely above its tangent line at $x = a$, the function is at a relative minimum at $x = a$.
2. If $f''(a) < 0$, denoting that the function is concave and the graph of the function lies completely below its tangent line at $x = a$, the function is at a relative maximum at $x = a$.
3. If $f''(a) = 0$, the test is inconclusive.

For functions which are differentiable at all values of x, called *differentiable or smooth functions*, one need only consider cases where $f'(x) = 0$ in looking for critical points. To summarize,

$$f'(a) = 0 \qquad f''(a) > 0: \qquad \text{relative minimum at } x = a$$
$$f'(a) = 0 \qquad f''(a) < 0: \qquad \text{relative maximum at } x = a$$

See Fig. 4-3 and Problems 4.5 and 4.6.

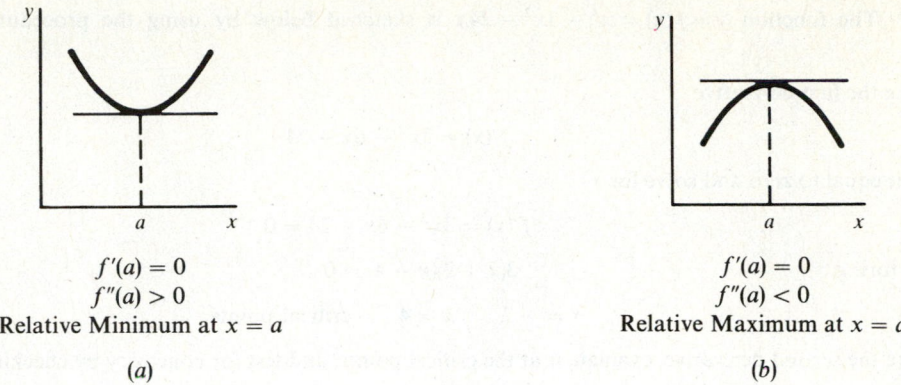

$f'(a) = 0$
$f''(a) > 0$
Relative Minimum at $x = a$

(a)

$f'(a) = 0$
$f''(a) < 0$
Relative Maximum at $x = a$

(b)

Fig. 4-3

4.4 INFLECTION POINTS

An *inflection point* is a point on the graph where the function crosses its tangent line and changes from concave to convex or vice versa. Inflection points occur only where the *second* derivative equals zero or is undefined. The sign of the first derivative is immaterial. In sum, for an inflection point at a, as seen in Fig. 4-4, Example 1, and Problems 4.6 and 4.8(c),

1. $f''(a) = 0$ or is undefined.
2. Concavity changes at $x = a$.
3. Graph crosses its tangent line at $x = a$.

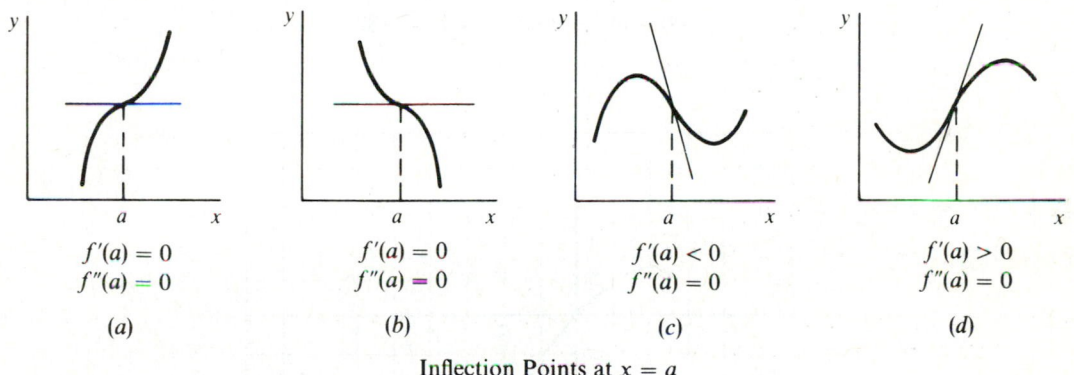

$f'(a) = 0$
$f''(a) = 0$

(a)

$f'(a) = 0$
$f''(a) = 0$

(b)

$f'(a) < 0$
$f''(a) = 0$

(c)

$f'(a) > 0$
$f''(a) = 0$

(d)

Inflection Points at $x = a$

Fig. 4-4

4.5 CURVE SKETCHING

The first and second derivatives provide useful information about the general shape of a curve and facilitate graphing. A relatively complicated function can be roughly sketched in a few easy steps. For a given $f(x)$:

1. Seek out any relative extremum by looking for points where the first derivative equals zero: $f'(x) = 0$.
2. Determine concavity at the critical point(s) by testing the sign of the second derivative to distinguish between a relative maximum $[f''(x) < 0]$ and a relative minimum $[f''(x) > 0]$.
3. Check for inflection points where $f''(x) = 0$ and concavity changes.

See Example 1 and Problems 4.7 and 4.8.

EXAMPLE 1. The function $y = f(x) = x^3 - 3x^2 - 24x$ is sketched below by using the procedure outlined in Section 4.5.

(a) Take the first derivative

$$f'(x) = 3x^2 - 6x - 24$$

set it equal to zero and solve for x:

$$f'(x) = 3x^2 - 6x - 24 = 0$$

Factoring, $$3(x + 2)(x - 4) = 0$$

$$x = -2 \qquad x = 4 \qquad \text{critical points}$$

(b) Take the second derivative, evaluate it at the critical points, and test for concavity by checking the signs.

$$f''(x) = 6x - 6$$
$$f''(-2) = 6(-2) - 6 = -18 < 0 \qquad \text{concave, relative maximum}$$
$$f''(4) = 6(4) - 6 = 18 > 0 \qquad \text{convex, relative minimum}$$

(c) Look for inflection points where $f''(x) = 0$ and concavity changes.

$$f''(x) = 6x - 6 = 0$$
$$x = 1$$

With $f''(x) = 0$ at $x = 1$ and $f(x)$ changing from concave at $x = -2$ to convex at $x = 4$, an inflection point exists at $x = 1$.

(d) Evaluate $f(x)$ at $x = -2, 1,$ and 4 and graph as in Fig. 4-5.

$$f(-2) = (-2)^3 - 3(-2)^2 - 24(-2) = 28$$
$$f(1) = (1)^3 - 3(1)^2 - 24(1) = -26$$
$$f(4) = (4)^3 - 3(4)^2 - 24(4) = -80$$

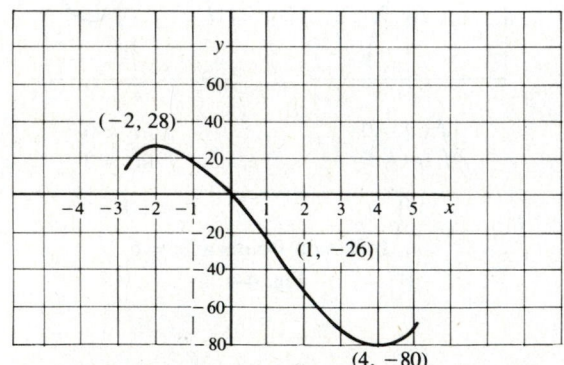

Fig. 4-5

4.6 OPTIMIZATION OF FUNCTIONS

Optimization is the process of finding the relative maximum or minimum of a function. Without the aid of a graph, this is done with the techniques developed in Sections 4.3 through 4.5 and outlined below. Given the usual differentiable function,

1. Take the first derivative, set it equal to zero, and solve for the critical point(s). This step is known as the *first-order condition*.

2. Take the second derivative, evaluate it at the critical point(s), and check the sign(s). If at a critical point a,

$$f''(a) > 0: \quad \text{convex, relative minimum}$$
$$f''(a) < 0: \quad \text{concave, relative maximum}$$
$$f''(a) = 0: \quad \text{The test is inconclusive.}$$

This step, the *second-derivative test*, is also called the *second-order condition*. In sum,

Relative maximum	Relative minimum
$f'(a) = 0$	$f'(a) = 0$
$f''(a) < 0$	$f''(a) > 0$

See Examples 2 and 3 and Problems 4.9 and 4.10.

EXAMPLE 2.   Optimize $f(x) = 2x^3 - 30x^2 + 126x + 59$.

(a) Find the critical points by taking the first derivative, setting it equal to zero, and solving for x.

$$f'(x) = 6x^2 - 60x + 126 = 0$$
$$6(x - 3)(x - 7) = 0$$
$$x = 3 \quad x = 7 \quad \text{critical points}$$

(b) Test for concavity by taking the second derivative, evaluating it at the critical points, and checking the signs to distinguish between a relative maximum and minimum.

$$f''(x) = 12x - 60$$
$$f''(3) = 12(3) - 60 = -24 < 0 \quad \text{concave, relative maximum}$$
$$f''(7) = 12(7) - 60 = 24 > 0 \quad \text{convex, relative minimum}$$

The function is maximized at $x = 3$ and minimized at $x = 7$.

EXAMPLE 3.   The second-derivative test would be inconclusive for functions such as those illustrated in Fig. 4-4(a) and (b) where inflection points occur at the critical values. In the event that $f''(a) = 0$ and without a graph for guidance, apply the *successive-derivative test*:

1. If, when evaluated at a critical point, the first nonzero value of a higher-order derivative is an odd-numbered derivative (third, fifth, etc.), the function is at an inflection point. See Problem 4.8(c).
2. If, when evaluated at a critical value, the first nonzero value of a higher-order derivative is an even-numbered derivative, the function is at a relative extremum, with a positive value of the derivative signifying a relative minimum and a negative value indicating a relative maximum. See Problems 4.6, 4.8(c) and (d), and 4.10(c) and (d).

4.7   MARGINAL CONCEPTS

Marginal cost in economics is defined as the change in total cost incurred from the production of an additional unit. *Marginal revenue* is defined as the change in total revenue brought about by the sale of an extra good. Since total cost (TC) and total revenue (TR) are both functions of the level of output (Q), marginal cost (MC) and marginal revenue (MR) can each be expressed mathematically as derivatives of their respective total functions. Thus,

if   TC $= \text{TC}(Q)$,   then $$\text{MC} = \frac{d\text{TC}}{dQ}$$

and if   TR $= \text{TR}(Q)$,   then $$\text{MR} = \frac{d\text{TR}}{dQ}$$

In short, the marginal concept of any economic function can be expressed as the derivative of its total function.

EXAMPLE 4.

1. If $TR = 75Q - 4Q^2$, then $MR = dTR/dQ = 75 - 8Q$.
2. If $TC = Q^2 + 7Q + 23$, then $MC = dTC/dQ = 2Q + 7$.

EXAMPLE 5. Given the demand function $P = 30 - 2Q$, the marginal revenue function can be found by first finding the total revenue function and then taking the derivative of that function with respect to Q. Thus,

$$TR = PQ = (30 - 2Q)Q = 30Q - 2Q^2$$

Then

$$MR = \frac{dTR}{dQ} = 30 - 4Q$$

If $Q = 4$, $MR = 30 - 4(4) = 14$; if $Q = 5$, $MR = 30 - 4(5) = 10$. See Problems 4.11 — 4.17.

4.8 OPTIMIZING ECONOMIC FUNCTIONS

The economist is frequently called upon to help a firm maximize profits and levels of physical output and productivity, as well as to minimize costs, levels of pollution, and the use of scarce natural resources. This is done with the help of techniques developed earlier and illustrated in Example 6 and Problems 4.18 to 4.24.

EXAMPLE 6. Maximize profits π for a firm, given total revenue $R = 4000Q - 33Q^2$ and total cost $C = 2Q^3 - 3Q^2 + 400Q + 5000$, assuming $Q > 0$.

(a) Set up the profit function: $\pi = R - C$.

$$\pi = 4000Q - 33Q^2 - (2Q^3 - 3Q^2 + 400Q + 5000)$$
$$= -2Q^3 - 30Q^2 + 3600Q - 5000$$

(b) Take the first derivative, set it equal to zero, and solve for Q to find the critical points.

$$\pi' = -6Q^2 - 60Q + 3600 = 0$$
$$= -6(Q^2 + 10Q - 600) = 0$$
$$= -6(Q + 30)(Q - 20) = 0$$
$$Q = -30 \qquad Q = 20 \qquad \text{critical points}$$

(c) Take the second derivative; evaluate it at the positive critical point and ignore the negative critical point, which has no economic significance and will prove mathematically to be a relative minimum. Then check the sign for concavity to be sure of a relative maximum.

$$\pi'' = -12Q - 60$$
$$\pi''(20) = -12(20) - 60 = -300 < 0 \qquad \text{concave, relative maximum}$$

Profit is maximized at $Q = 20$ where

$$\pi(20) = -2(20)^3 - 30(20)^2 + 3600(20) - 5000 = 39\,000$$

4.9 PRICE ELASTICITY OF DEMAND AND SUPPLY

In economics, *price elasticity ε of demand (supply)* measures the percentage change in quantity demanded (supplied) divided by the percentage change in price. Mathematically,

$$\varepsilon = \frac{dQ/Q}{dP/P} = \frac{dQ}{Q}\frac{P}{dP} = \frac{dQ}{dP}\frac{P}{Q} \tag{4.1a}$$

Since $dQ/dP = 1/(dP/dQ)$, for ease in computation when $P = f(Q)$, as is common in economics, ε is expressed alternately as

$$\varepsilon = \frac{1}{dP/dQ}\frac{P}{Q} \qquad (4.1b)$$

Or, as a geometric aid, assuming $Q = F(P)$,

$$\varepsilon = \frac{dQ}{dP}\frac{P}{Q} = \frac{dQ/dP}{Q/P} = \frac{\text{marginal function}}{\text{average function}} \qquad (4.1c)$$

and if $P = f(Q)$,

$$\varepsilon = \frac{1}{dP/dQ}\frac{P}{Q} = \frac{P/Q}{dP/dQ} = \frac{\text{average function}}{\text{marginal function}} \qquad (4.1d)$$

See Examples 7 through 9 and Problems 4.25 to 4.37.

EXAMPLE 7. The price elasticity of demand at $P = 20$ is determined below for the demand function $Q = 1400 - P^2$.

From (4.1a),
$$\varepsilon = \frac{dQ}{dP}\frac{P}{Q}$$

Take the derivative of Q,
$$\frac{dQ}{dP} = -2P$$

and evaluate it at $P = 20$.
$$\frac{dQ}{dP}(20) = -2(20) = -40$$

Evaluate Q at $P = 20$,
$$Q(20) = 1400 - (20)^2 = 1000$$

and substitute the appropriate values in ε.

$$\varepsilon = -40\left(\frac{20}{1000}\right) = \frac{-800}{1000} = -0.8$$

[For contrast, see Problem 4.27 for the elasticity of a function along traditional economic lines where $P = f(Q)$.]

EXAMPLE 8. By using the formula in (4.1c), the elasticity of demand (supply) can be calculated visually at a particular point, as in Fig. 4-6, by estimating the marginal and average functions at the point. The marginal function is estimated by the slope of the tangent to the curve at the point; the average function, by the slope of a straight line from the origin to the point.

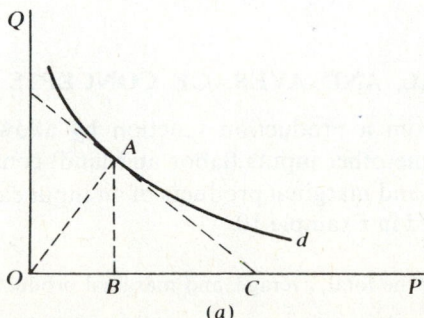
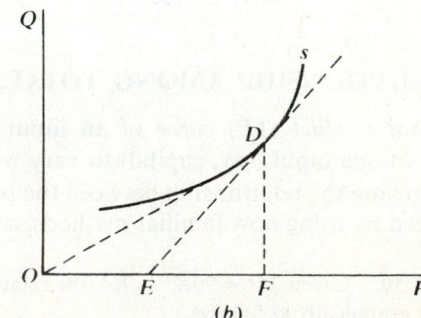

(a)   (b)

Fig. 4-6

For the demand function in Fig. 4-6(a): The slope of the marginal function at A is $-AB/BC$. The slope of the average function at A is AB/OB. Therefore

$$\varepsilon_d = \frac{-AB/BC}{AB/OB} = -\frac{AB}{BC}\frac{OB}{AB} = -\frac{OB}{BC}$$

For the supply function in Fig. 4-6(b): The slope of the marginal function at D is DF/EF. The slope of the average function at D is DF/OF. Therefore

$$\varepsilon_s = \frac{DF/EF}{DF/OF} = \frac{DF}{EF}\frac{OF}{DF} = \frac{OF}{EF}$$

When $Q = F(P)$, the price elasticity of demand $|\varepsilon_d|$ at a particular point equals the horizontal distance of the point from the origin (OB) divided by the horizontal distance of the point from the point at which the tangent to the demand curve crosses the horizontal axis (BC). The price elasticity of supply ϵ_s at a given point, when $Q = F(P)$, equals the horizontal distance of the point from the origin (OF) divided by the horizontal distance of the point from the point at which the tangent to the supply curve crosses the horizontal axis (EF). For adaptation of these relationships when $P = f(Q)$ and measurement of elasticities in terms of segments of the demand and supply curves, see Problems 4.25 to 4.37.

EXAMPLE 9.   Using the techniques from Example 8, the elasticities of demand and supply at the designated points in Fig. 4-7 are calculated below.

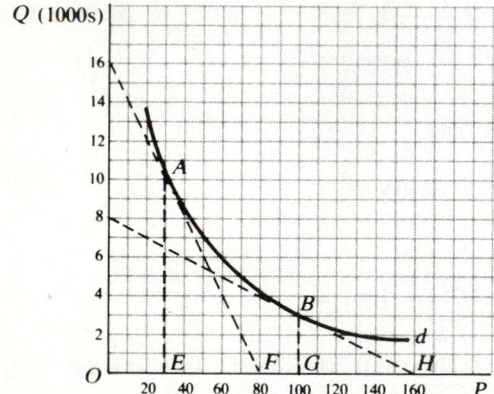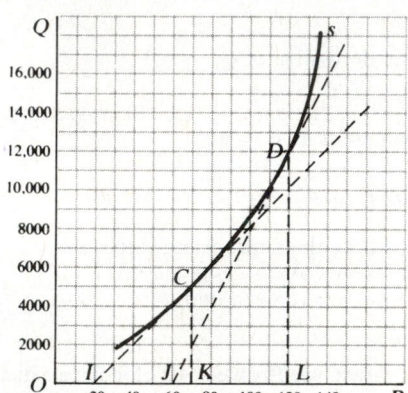

Fig. 4-7

Elasticity of demand:

At point A, $\varepsilon_d = -\dfrac{OE}{EF} = -\dfrac{30}{50} = -0.6$

At point B, $\varepsilon_d = -\dfrac{OG}{GH} = -\dfrac{100}{60} = -1.67$

Elasticity of supply:

At point C, $\varepsilon_s = \dfrac{OK}{IK} = \dfrac{70}{50} = 1.4$

At point D, $\varepsilon_s = \dfrac{OL}{JL} = \dfrac{120}{60} = 2$

4.10   RELATIONSHIP AMONG TOTAL, MARGINAL, AND AVERAGE CONCEPTS

A *total product* (TP) *curve* of an input is derived from a production function by allowing the amounts of one input (say, capital) to vary while holding the other inputs (labor and land) constant. A graph showing the relationship between the total, average, and marginal products of an input can easily be sketched by using now familiar methods, as demonstrated in Example 10.

EXAMPLE 10.   Given TP $= 90K^2 - K^3$, the relationship among the total, average, and marginal products can be illustrated graphically as follows.

1.   Test the first-order condition to find the critical values.

$$TP' = 180K - 3K^2 = 0$$
$$3K(60 - K) = 0$$
$$K = 0 \qquad K = 60 \qquad \text{critical values}$$

Check the second-order conditions.

$$TP'' = 180 - 6K$$
$$TP''(0) = 180 > 0 \qquad \text{convex, relative minimum}$$
$$TP''(60) = -180 < 0 \qquad \text{concave, relative maximum}$$

Check for inflection points.

$$TP'' = 180 - 6K = 0$$
$$K = 30$$
$$K < 30 \qquad TP'' > 0 \qquad \text{convex}$$
$$K > 30 \qquad TP'' < 0 \qquad \text{concave}$$

Since, at $K = 30$, $TP'' = 0$ and concavity changes, there is an inflection point at $K = 30$.

2. Find and maximize the average product of capital AP_K.

$$AP_K = \frac{TP}{K} = 90K - K^2$$
$$AP_K' = 90 - 2K = 0$$
$$K = 45 \qquad \text{critical value}$$
$$AP_K'' = -2 < 0 \qquad \text{concave, relative maximum}$$

3. Find and maximize the marginal product of capital MP_K, recalling that $MP_K = TP' = 180K - 3K^2$:

$$MP_K' = 180 - 6K = 0$$
$$K = 30 \qquad \text{critical value}$$
$$MP_K'' = -6 < 0 \qquad \text{concave, relative maximum}$$

4. Sketch the graphs, as in Fig. 4-8.

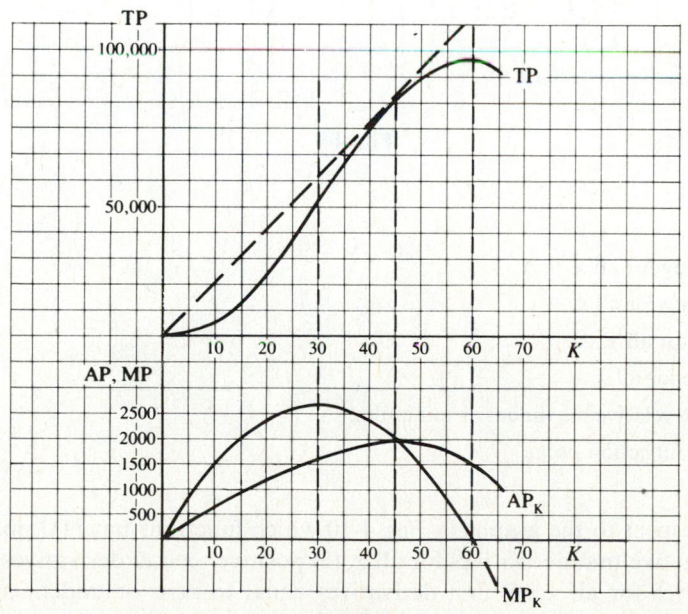

Fig. 4-8

Note that (a) MP_K increases when TP is convex and increasing at an increasing rate, is at a maximum where TP is at an inflection point, and decreases when TP is concave and increasing at a decreasing rate; (b) TP increases over the whole range where MP_K is positive, is at a maximum where $\text{MP}_K = 0$, and declines when MP_K is negative; (c) AP_K is at a maximum where the slope of a line from the origin to the TP curve is tangent to the TP curve, i.e., where $\text{MP}_K = \text{AP}_K$; (d) $\text{MP}_K > \text{AP}_K$ when AP_K is increasing, $\text{MP}_K = \text{AP}_K$ when AP_K is at a maximum, and $\text{MP}_K < \text{AP}_K$ when AP_K decreases; and (e) MP_K is negative when TP declines. See also Problem 4.40.

Solved Problems

INCREASING AND DECREASING FUNCTIONS, CONCAVITY AND CONVEXITY

4.1. From the graphs in Fig. 4-9, indicate which graphs (1) are increasing for all x, (2) are decreasing for all x, (3) are convex for all x, (4) are concave for all x, (5) have relative maxima or minima, and (6) have inflection points.

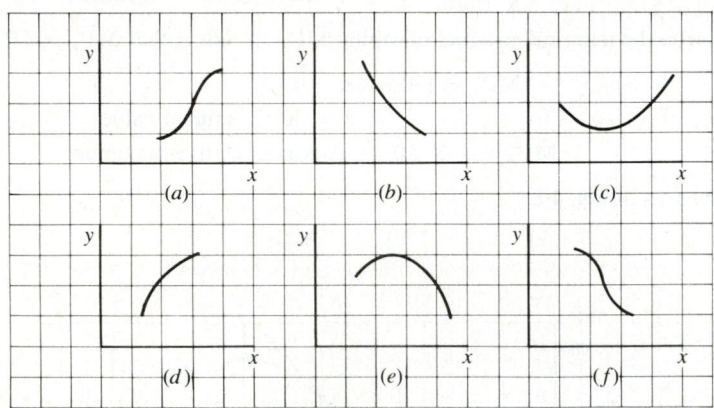

Fig. 4-9

(1) a, d: increasing for all x.

(2) b, f: decreasing for all x.

(3) b, c: convex for all x.

(4) d, e: concave for all x.

(5) c, e: exhibit a relative maximum or minimum.

(6) a, f: have an inflection point.

4.2. Indicate with respect to the graphs in Fig. 4-10 which functions have (1) positive first derivatives for all x, (2) negative first derivatives for all x, (3) positive second derivatives for all x, (4) negative second derivatives for all x, (5) first derivatives equal to zero or undefined at some point, and (6) second derivatives equal to zero or undefined at some point.

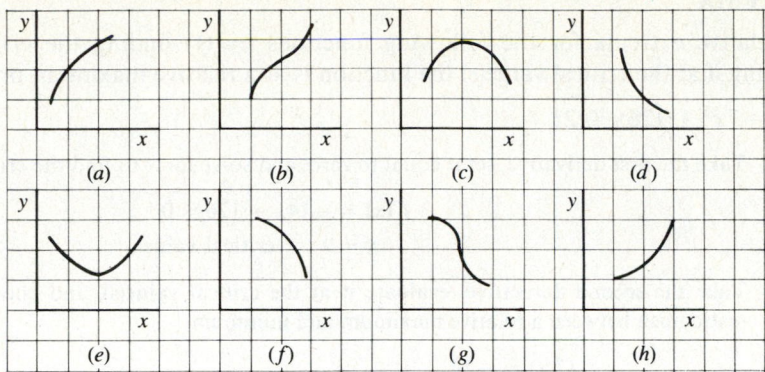

Fig. 4-10

(1) a, b, h: the graphs all move up from left to right.

(2) d, f, g: the graphs all move down from left to right.

(3) d, e, h: the graphs are all convex.

(4) a, c, f: the graphs are all concave.

(5) c, e: the graphs reach a plateau (at an extreme point).

(6) b, g: the graphs have inflection points.

4.3. Test to see whether the following functions are increasing, decreasing, or stationary at $x = 4$.

(a) $y = 3x^2 - 14x + 5$

$$y' = 6x - 14$$
$$y'(4) = 6(4) - 14 = 10 > 0 \qquad \text{Function is increasing.}$$

(b) $y = x^3 - 7x^2 + 6x - 2$

$$y' = 3x^2 - 14x + 6$$
$$y'(4) = 3(4)^2 - 14(4) + 6 = -2 < 0 \qquad \text{Function is decreasing.}$$

(c) $y = x^4 - 6x^3 + 4x^2 - 13$

$$y' = 4x^3 - 18x^2 + 8x$$
$$y'(4) = 4(4)^3 - 18(4)^2 + 8(4) = 0 \qquad \text{Function is stationary.}$$

4.4. Test to see if the following functions are concave or convex at $x = 3$.

(a) $y = -2x^3 + 4x^2 + 9x - 15$

$$y' = -6x^2 + 8x + 9$$
$$y'' = -12x + 8$$
$$y''(3) = -12(3) + 8 = -28 < 0 \qquad \text{concave}$$

(b) $y = (5x^2 - 8)^2$

$$y' = 2(5x^2 - 8)(10x) = 20x(5x^2 - 8) = 100x^3 - 160x$$
$$y'' = 300x^2 - 160$$
$$y''(3) = 300(3)^2 - 160 = 2540 > 0 \qquad \text{convex}$$

RELATIVE EXTREMA

4.5.   Find the relative extrema for the following functions by (1) finding the critical value(s) and (2) determining if at the critical value(s) the function is at a relative maximum or minimum.

(a) $f(x) = -7x^2 + 126x - 23$

        (1)   Take the first derivative, set it equal to zero, and solve for x to find the critical value(s).

$$f'(x) = -14x + 126 = 0$$
$$x = 9 \qquad \text{critical value}$$

        (2)   Take the second derivative, evaluate it at the critical value(s), and check for concavity to distinguish between a relative maximum and minimum.

$$f''(x) = -14$$
$$f''(9) = -14 < 0 \qquad \text{concave, relative maximum}$$

(b) $f(x) = 3x^3 - 36x^2 + 135x - 13$

        (1)

$$f'(x) = 9x^2 - 72x + 135 = 0$$
$$= 9(x^2 - 8x + 15) = 0$$
$$= 9(x - 3)(x - 5) = 0$$
$$x = 3 \qquad x = 5 \qquad \text{critical values}$$

        (2)

$$f''(x) = 18x - 72$$
$$f''(3) = 18(3) - 72 = -18 < 0 \qquad \text{concave, relative maximum}$$
$$f''(5) = 18(5) - 72 = 18 > 0 \qquad \text{convex, relative minimum}$$

(c) $f(x) = 2x^4 - 16x^3 + 32x^2 + 5$

        (1)

$$f'(x) = 8x^3 - 48x^2 + 64x = 0$$
$$= 8x(x^2 - 6x + 8) = 0$$
$$= 8x(x - 2)(x - 4) = 0$$
$$x = 0 \qquad x = 2 \qquad x = 4 \qquad \text{critical values}$$

        (2)

$$f''(x) = 24x^2 - 96x + 64$$
$$f''(0) = 24(0)^2 - 96(0) + 64 = 64 > 0 \qquad \text{convex, relative minimum}$$
$$f''(2) = 24(2)^2 - 96(2) + 64 = -32 < 0 \qquad \text{concave, relative maximum}$$
$$f''(4) = 24(4)^2 - 96(4) + 64 = 64 > 0 \qquad \text{convex, relative minimum}$$

4.6.   For the following functions, (1) find the critical values and (2) test to see if at the critical values the function is at a relative maximum, minimum, or possible inflection point.

(a) $y = -(x - 8)^4$

        (1)   Take the first derivative, set it equal to zero, and solve for x to obtain the critical value(s).

$$y' = -4(x - 8)^3 = 0$$
$$x - 8 = 0$$
$$x = 8 \qquad \text{critical value}$$

        (2)   Take the second derivative, evaluate it at the critical value(s), and check the sign for concavity to distinguish between a relative maximum, minimum, or inflection point.

$$y'' = -12(x - 8)^2$$
$$y''(8) = -12(8 - 8)^2 = 0 \qquad \text{test inconclusive}$$

If the second-derivative test is inconclusive, continue to take successively higher derivatives and evaluate them at the critical values until you come to the first higher-order derivative that is nonzero:

$$y''' = -24(x - 8)$$
$$y'''(8) = -24(8 - 8) = 0 \qquad \text{test inconclusive}$$
$$y^{(4)} = -24$$
$$y^{(4)}(8) = -24 < 0$$

As explained in Example 3, with the first nonzero higher-order derivative an even-numbered derivative, y is at a relative extremum. With that derivative negative, y is concave and at a relative maximum. See Fig. 4-11(a).

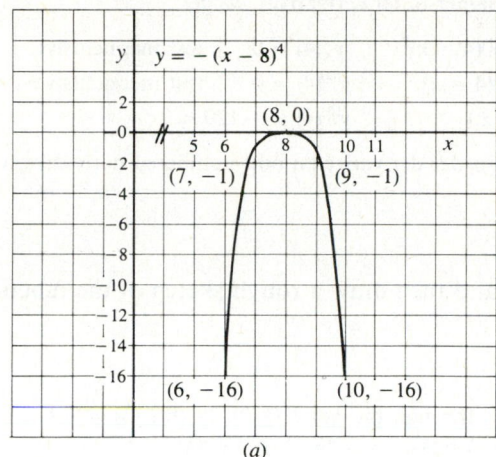
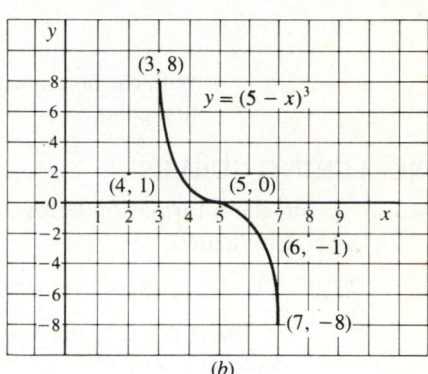

(a) (b)

Fig. 4-11

(b) $y = (5 - x)^3$

(1)
$$y' = 3(5 - x)^2(-1) = -3(5 - x)^2 = 0$$
$$x = 5 \qquad \text{critical value}$$

(2)
$$y'' = 6(5 - x)$$
$$y''(5) = 6(5 - 5) = 0 \qquad \text{test inconclusive}$$

Continuing to take successively higher-order derivatives and evaluating them at the critical value(s) in search of the first higher-order derivative that does not equal zero, we get

$$y''' = -6$$
$$y'''(5) = -6 < 0$$

As explained in Example 3, with the first nonzero higher-order derivative an odd-numbered derivative, y is at an inflection point and not at an extreme point. See Fig. 4-11(b).

(c) $y = -2(x - 6)^6$

(1)
$$y' = -12(x - 6)^5 = 0$$
$$x = 6 \qquad \text{critical value}$$

(2)
$$y'' = -60(x - 6)^4$$
$$y''(6) = -60(0)^4 = 0 \qquad \text{test inconclusive}$$

Continuing, we get

$$y''' = -240(x - 6)^3 \qquad y'''(6) = 0 \qquad \text{test inconclusive}$$
$$y^{(4)} = -720(x - 6)^2 \qquad y^{(4)}(6) = 0 \qquad \text{test inconclusive}$$
$$y^{(5)} = -1440(x - 6) \qquad y^{(5)}(6) = 0 \qquad \text{test inconclusive}$$
$$y^{(6)} = -1440 \qquad y^{(6)}(6) = -1440 < 0$$

With the first nonzero higher-order derivative an even-numbered derivative, y is at an extreme point; with $y^{(6)}(6) < 0$, y is concave and at a relative maximum.

(d) $y = (4 - x)^5$

(1)
$$y' = 5(4 - x)^4(-1) = -5(4 - x)^4 = 0$$
$$x = 4 \qquad \text{critical value}$$

(2)
$$y'' = 20(4 - x)^3$$
$$y''(4) = 20(0)^3 = 0 \qquad \text{test inconclusive}$$

Moving on to the third- and higher-order derivatives, we get

$$y''' = -60(4 - x)^2 \qquad y'''(4) = 0 \qquad \text{test inconclusive}$$
$$y^{(4)} = 120(4 - x) \qquad y^{(4)}(4) = 0 \qquad \text{test inconclusive}$$
$$y^{(5)} = -120 \qquad y^{(5)}(4) = -120 < 0$$

With the first nonzero higher-order derivative an odd-numbered derivative, y is at an inflection point.

SKETCHING CURVES

4.7. From the information below, describe and then draw a rough sketch of the function around the point indicated.

(a) $f(3) = 2$, $f'(3) = -1$, $f''(3) = 6$

With $f(3) = 2$, the function passes through the point (3, 2). With $f'(3) = -1 < 0$, the function is decreasing; with $f''(3) = 6 > 0$, the function is convex. See Fig. 4-12(a).

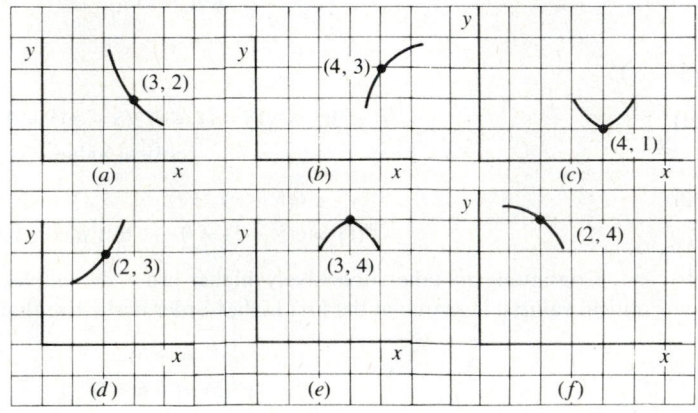

Fig. 4-12

(b) $f(4) = 3$, $f'(4) = 2$, $f''(4) = -4$

With $f(4) = 3$, the function passes through the point (4, 3). Since $f'(4) = 2$, the function is increasing; with $f''(4) = -4$, it is concave. See Fig. 4-12(b).

(c) $f(4) = 1$, $f'(4) = 0$, $f''(4) = 7$

The function passes through the point (4, 1). From $f'(4) = 0$, we know that the function is at a relative plateau at $x = 4$; and from $f''(4) = 7$, we know it is convex at $x = 4$. Hence it is at a relative minimum. See Fig. 4-12(c).

(d) $f(2) = 3$, $f'(2) = 1$, $f''(2) = 4$

The function passes through the point (2, 3) where it is increasing and convex. See Fig. 4-12(d).

(e) $f(3) = 4$, $f'(3) = 0$, $f''(3) = -6$

The function passes through the point (3, 4) where it is at a relative plateau and concave. The function, therefore, is at a relative maximum at (3, 4). See Fig. 4-12(e).

(f) $f(2) = 4$, $f'(2) = -2$, $f''(2) = -5$

The function passes through the point (2, 4) where it is decreasing and concave. See Fig. 4-12(f).

4.8. For the following functions, (1) find the critical values, (2) test for concavity to determine relative maxima or minima, (3) check for inflection points, (4) evaluate the function at critical values and inflection points, and (5) graph the function.

(a) $f(x) = x^3 - 18x^2 + 96x - 80$

(1)
$$f'(x) = 3x^2 - 36x + 96 = 0$$
$$= 3(x - 4)(x - 8) = 0$$
$$x = 4 \qquad x = 8 \qquad \text{critical values}$$

(2)
$$f''(x) = 6x - 36$$
$$f''(4) = 6(4) - 36 = -12 < 0 \qquad \text{concave, relative maximum}$$
$$f''(8) = 6(8) - 36 = 12 > 0 \qquad \text{convex, relative minimum}$$

(3)
$$f'' = 6x - 36 = 0$$
$$x = 6$$

With $f''(6) = 0$ and concavity changing between $x = 4$ and $x = 8$, as seen in step 2, there is an inflection point at $x = 6$.

(4)
$$f(4) = (4)^3 - 18(4)^2 + 96(4) - 80 = 80 \qquad (4, 80) \qquad \text{Relative maximum}$$
$$f(6) = (6)^3 - 18(6)^2 + 96(6) - 80 = 64 \qquad (6, 64) \qquad \text{Inflection point}$$
$$f(8) = (8)^3 - 18(8)^2 + 96(8) - 80 = 48 \qquad (8, 48) \qquad \text{Relative minimum}$$

(5) Cf. Fig. 4-13(a).

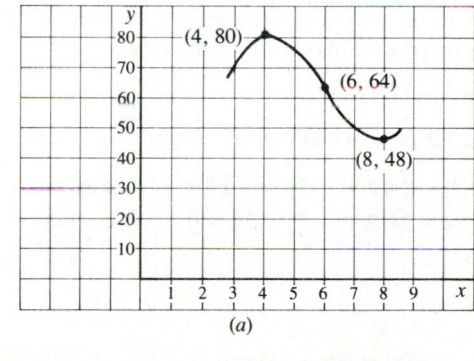

(a)

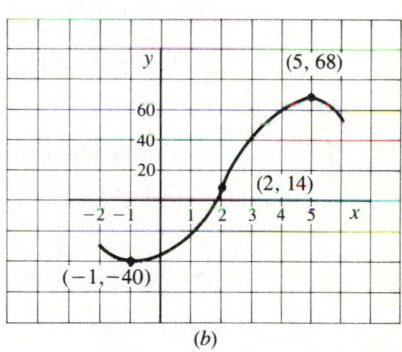

(b)

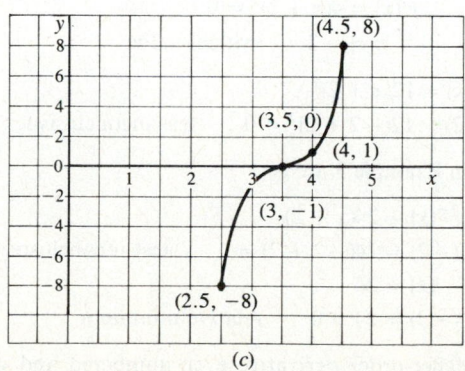

(c)

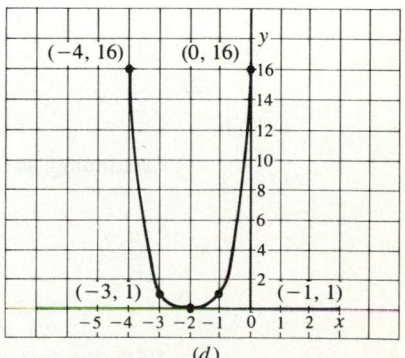

(d)

Fig. 4-13

(b) $f(x) = -x^3 + 6x^2 + 15x - 32$

(1)
$$f'(x) = -3x^2 + 12x + 15 = 0$$
$$= -3(x + 1)(x - 5) = 0$$
$$x = -1 \qquad x = 5 \qquad \text{critical values}$$

(2)
$$f''(x) = -6x + 12$$
$$f''(-1) = -6(-1) + 12 = 18 > 0 \qquad \text{convex, relative minimum}$$
$$f''(5) = -6(5) + 12 = -18 < 0 \qquad \text{concave, relative maximum}$$

(3)
$$f''(x) = -6x + 12 = 0$$
$$x = 2 \qquad \text{inflection point at } x = 2$$

(4)
$$f(-1) = -40 \qquad (-1, -40) \qquad \text{relative minimum}$$
$$f(2) = 14 \qquad (2, 14) \qquad \text{inflection point}$$
$$f(5) = 68 \qquad (5, 68) \qquad \text{relative maximum}$$

(5) See Fig. 4-13(b).

(c) $f(x) = (2x - 7)^3$

(1)
$$f'(x) = 3(2x - 7)^2(2) = 6(2x - 7)^2 = 0$$
$$x = 3.5 \qquad \text{critical value}$$

(2)
$$f''(x) = 12(2x - 7)(2) = 24(2x - 7)$$
$$f''(3.5) = 24[2(3.5) - 7] = 0 \qquad \text{test inconclusive}$$

Continuing on to successively higher-order derivatives, we find
$$f''' = 48$$
$$f'''(3.5) = 48 > 0$$

(3) As explained in Example 3, with the first nonzero higher-order derivative an odd-numbered derivative, the function is at an inflection point at $x = 3.5$. With an inflection point at the only critical value, there is no relative maximum or minimum.

(4)
$$f(3.5) = 0 \qquad (3.5, 0) \qquad \text{inflection point}$$

Testing for concavity to the left ($x = 3$) and right ($x = 4$) of $x = 3.5$ gives
$$f''(3) = 24[2(3) - 7] = -24 < 0 \qquad \text{concave}$$
$$f''(4) = 24[2(4) - 7] = 24 > 0 \qquad \text{convex}$$

(5) See Fig. 4-13(c).

(d) $f(x) = (x + 2)^4$

(1)
$$f'(x) = 4(x + 2)^3 = 0$$
$$x = -2 \qquad \text{critical value}$$

(2)
$$f''(x) = 12(x + 2)^2$$
$$f''(-2) = 12(-2 + 2)^2 = 0 \qquad \text{test inconclusive}$$

Continuing, as explained in Example 3, we get
$$f'''(x) = 24(x + 2)$$
$$f'''(-2) = 24(-2 + 2) = 0 \qquad \text{test inconclusive}$$
$$f^{(4)}(x) = 24$$
$$f^{(4)}(-2) = 24 > 0 \qquad \text{relative minimum}$$

With the first nonzero higher-order derivative even-numbered and greater than 0, $f(x)$ is minimized at $x = -2$.

(3)   There is no inflection point.

(4) $f(-2) = 0$ $(-2, 0)$ relative minimum

(5)   See Fig. 4-13(d).

OPTIMIZATION

4.9.   Optimize the following quadratic and cubic functions by (1) finding the critical value(s) at which the function is optimized and (2) testing the second-order condition to distinguish between a relative maximum or minimum.

(a) $y = 7x^2 + 112x - 54$

(1)   Take the first derivative, set it equal to zero, and solve for x to find the critical value(s).

$$y' = 14x + 112 = 0$$
$$x = -8 \quad \text{critical value}$$

(2)   Take the second derivative, evaluate it at the critical value, and check the sign for a relative maximum and minimum.

$$y'' = 14$$
$$y''(-8) = 14 > 0 \quad \text{convex, relative minimum}$$

(b) $y = -9x^2 + 72x - 13$

(1)
$$y' = -18x + 72 = 0$$
$$x = 4 \quad \text{critical value}$$

(2)
$$y'' = -18$$
$$y''(4) = -18 < 0 \quad \text{concave, relative maximum}$$

(c) $y = x^3 - 6x^2 - 135x + 4$

(1)
$$y' = 3x^2 - 12x - 135 = 0$$
$$= 3(x^2 - 4x - 45) = 0$$
$$= 3(x + 5)(x - 9) = 0$$
$$x = -5 \quad x = 9 \quad \text{critical values}$$

(2)
$$y'' = 6x - 12$$
$$y''(-5) = 6(-5) - 12 = -42 < 0 \quad \text{concave, relative maximum}$$
$$y''(9) = 6(9) - 12 = 42 > 0 \quad \text{convex, relative minimum}$$

(d) $y = -2x^3 + 15x^2 + 84x - 25$

(1)
$$y' = -6x^2 + 30x + 84 = 0$$
$$= -6(x + 2)(x - 7) = 0$$
$$x = -2 \quad x = 7 \quad \text{critical values}$$

(2)
$$y'' = -12x + 30$$
$$y''(-2) = -12(-2) + 30 = 54 > 0 \quad \text{convex, relative minimum}$$
$$y''(7) = -12(7) + 30 = -54 < 0 \quad \text{concave, relative maximum}$$

4.10.   Optimize the following higher-order polynomial functions, using the same procedure as in Problem 4.9.

(a) $y = x^4 - 8x^3 - 80x^2 + 15$

(1)
$$y' = 4x^3 - 24x^2 - 160x = 0$$
$$= 4x(x + 4)(x - 10) = 0$$
$$x = 0 \qquad x = -4 \qquad x = 10 \qquad \text{critical values}$$

(2)
$$y'' = 12x^2 - 48x - 160$$
$$y''(-4) = 12(-4)^2 - 48(-4) - 160 = 224 > 0 \qquad \text{convex, relative minimum}$$
$$y''(0) = 12(0)^2 - 48(0) - 160 = -160 < 0 \qquad \text{concave, relative maximum}$$
$$y''(10) = 12(10)^2 - 48(10) - 160 = 560 > 0 \qquad \text{convex, relative minimum}$$

(b) $y = -3x^4 - 20x^3 + 144x^2 + 17$

(1)
$$y' = -12x^3 - 60x^2 + 288x = 0$$
$$= -12x(x - 3)(x + 8) = 0$$
$$x = 0 \qquad x = 3 \qquad x = -8 \qquad \text{critical values}$$

(2)
$$y'' = -36x^2 - 120x + 288$$
$$y''(-8) = -36(-8)^2 - 120(-8) + 288 = -1056 < 0 \qquad \text{concave, relative maximum}$$
$$y''(0) = -36(0)^2 - 120(0) + 288 = 288 > 0 \qquad \text{convex, relative minimum}$$
$$y''(3) = -36(3)^2 - 120(3) + 288 = -396 < 0 \qquad \text{concave, relative maximum}$$

(c) $y = -(x + 13)^4$

(1)
$$y' = -4(x + 13)^3 = 0$$
$$x + 13 = 0 \qquad x = -13 \qquad \text{critical value}$$

(2)
$$y'' = -12(x + 13)^2$$
$$y''(-13) = -12(-13 + 13)^2 = 0 \qquad \text{test inconclusive}$$

Continuing as explained in Example 3 and Problem 4.6, we get

$$y''' = -24(x + 13)$$
$$y'''(-13) = -24(0) = 0 \qquad \text{test inconclusive}$$
$$y^{(4)} = -24$$
$$y^{(4)}(-13) = -24 < 0 \qquad \text{concave, relative maximum}$$

(d) $y = (9 - 4x)^4$

(1)
$$y' = 4(9 - 4x)^3(-4) = -16(9 - 4x)^3 = 0$$
$$9 - 4x = 0 \qquad x = 2\tfrac{1}{4} \qquad \text{critical value}$$

(2)
$$y'' = -48(9 - 4x)^2(-4) = 192(9 - 4x)^2$$
$$y''(2\tfrac{1}{4}) = 192(0)^2 = 0 \qquad \text{test inconclusive}$$
$$y''' = 384(9 - 4x)(-4) = -1536(9 - 4x)$$
$$y'''(2\tfrac{1}{4}) = -1536(0) = 0 \qquad \text{test inconclusive}$$
$$y^{(4)} = 6144$$
$$y^{(4)}(2\tfrac{1}{4}) = 6144 > 0 \qquad \text{convex, relative minimum}$$

MARGINAL, AVERAGE, AND TOTAL CONCEPTS

4.11. Find (1) the marginal and (2) the average functions for each of the following total functions. Evaluate them at $Q = 3$ and $Q = 5$.

(a) $\text{TC} = 3Q^2 + 7Q + 12$

(1) $\text{MC} = \dfrac{d\text{TC}}{dQ} = 6Q + 7$ (2) $\text{AC} = \dfrac{\text{TC}}{Q} = 3Q + 7 + \dfrac{12}{Q}$

    At $Q = 3$, $\text{MC} = 6(3) + 7 = 25$ At $Q = 3$, $\text{AC} = 3(3) + 7 + \tfrac{12}{3} = 20$

    At $Q = 5$, $\text{MC} = 6(5) + 7 = 37$ At $Q = 5$, $\text{AC} = 3(5) + 7 + \tfrac{12}{5} = 24.4$

Note: When finding the average function, be sure to divide the constant term by Q.

(b) $\pi = Q^2 - 13Q + 78$

(1) $\dfrac{d\pi}{dQ} = 2Q - 13$

   At $Q = 3$, $\dfrac{d\pi}{dQ} = 2(3) - 13 = -7$

   At $Q = 5$, $\dfrac{d\pi}{dQ} = 2(5) - 13 = -3$

(2) $A\pi = \dfrac{\pi}{Q} = Q - 13 + \dfrac{78}{Q}$

   At $Q = 3$, $A\pi = 3 - 13 + \frac{78}{3} = 16$
   At $Q = 5$, $A\pi = 5 - 13 + \frac{78}{5} = 7.6$

(c) $\text{TR} = 12Q - Q^2$

(1) $\text{MR} = \dfrac{d\text{TR}}{dQ} = 12 - 2Q$

   At $Q = 3$, $\text{MR} = 12 - 2(3) = 6$
   At $Q = 5$, $\text{MR} = 12 - 2(5) = 2$

(2) $\text{AR} = \dfrac{\text{TR}}{Q} = 12 - Q$

   At $Q = 3$, $\text{AR} = 12 - 3 = 9$
   At $Q = 5$, $\text{AR} = 12 - 5 = 7$

(d) $\text{TC} = 35 + 5Q - 2Q^2 + 2Q^3$

(1) $\text{MC} = \dfrac{d\text{TC}}{dQ} = 5 - 4Q + 6Q^2$

   At $Q = 3$, $\text{MC} = 5 - 4(3) + 6(3)^2 = 47$
   At $Q = 5$, $\text{MC} = 5 - 4(5) + 6(5)^2 = 135$

(2) $\text{AC} = \dfrac{\text{TC}}{Q} = \dfrac{35}{Q} + 5 - 2Q + 2Q^2$

   At $Q = 3$, $\text{AC} = \frac{35}{3} + 5 - 2(3) + 2(3)^2 = 28.67$
   At $Q = 5$, $\text{AC} = \frac{35}{5} + 5 - 2(5) + 2(5)^2 = 52$

4.12.   Find the marginal expense (ME) functions associated with each of the following supply functions. Evaluate them at $Q = 4$ and $Q = 10$.

(a) $P = Q^2 + 2Q + 1$

   To find the ME function, given a simple supply function, find the total expense (TE) function and take its derivative with respect to Q.

$$\text{TE} = PQ = (Q^2 + 2Q + 1)Q = Q^3 + 2Q^2 + Q$$

$$\text{ME} = \frac{d\text{TE}}{dQ} = 3Q^2 + 4Q + 1$$

At $Q = 4$, $\text{ME} = 3(4)^2 + 4(4) + 1 = 65$. At $Q = 10$, $\text{ME} = 3(10)^2 + 4(10) + 1 = 341$.

(b) $P = Q^2 + 0.5Q + 3$

$$\text{TE} = PQ = (Q^2 + 0.5Q + 3)Q = Q^3 + 0.5Q^2 + 3Q$$
$$\text{ME} = 3Q^2 + Q + 3$$

At $Q = 4$, $\text{ME} = 3(4)^2 + 4 + 3 = 55$. At $Q = 10$, $\text{ME} = 3(10)^2 + 10 + 3 = 313$.

4.13.   Find the MR functions for each of the following demand functions and evaluate them at $Q = 4$ and $Q = 10$.

(a) $Q = 36 - 2P$

   $P = 18 - 0.5Q$
   $\text{TR} = (18 - 0.5Q)Q = 18Q - 0.5Q^2$
   $\text{MR} = \dfrac{d\text{TR}}{dQ} = 18 - Q$

   At $Q = 4$, $\text{MR} = 18 - 4 = 14$
   At $Q = 10$, $\text{MR} = 18 - 10 = 8$

(b) $44 - 4P - Q = 0$

   $P = 11 - 0.25Q$
   $\text{TR} = (11 - 0.25Q)Q = 11Q - 0.25Q^2$
   $\text{MR} = \dfrac{d\text{TR}}{dQ} = 11 - 0.5Q$

   At $Q = 4$, $\text{MR} = 11 - 0.5(4) = 9$
   At $Q = 10$, $\text{MR} = 11 - 0.5(10) = 6$

4.14.   For each of the following consumption functions, use the derivative to find the marginal propensity to consume $\text{MPC} = dC/dY$.

(a) $C = C_0 + bY$ (b) $C = 1500 + 0.75Y$

$$\text{MPC} = \frac{dC}{dY} = b \qquad\qquad \text{MPC} = \frac{dC}{dY} = 0.75$$

4.15.   Given $C = 1200 + 0.8Yd$, where $Yd = Y - T$ and $T = 100$, use the derivative to find the MPC.

When $C = f(Yd)$, make $C = f(Y)$ before taking the derivative. Thus,

$$C = 1200 + 0.8(Y - 100) = 1120 + 0.8Y$$

$$\text{MPC} = \frac{dC}{dY} = 0.8$$

Note that the introduction of a lump-sum tax into the income determination model *does not* affect the value of the MPC (or the multiplier).

4.16.   Given $C = 2000 + 0.9Yd$, where $Yd = Y - T$ and $T = 300 + 0.2Y$, use the derivative to find the MPC.

$$C = 2000 + 0.9(Y - 300 - 0.2Y) = 2000 + 0.9Y - 270 - 0.18Y = 1730 + 0.72Y$$

$$\text{MPC} = \frac{dC}{dY} = 0.72$$

The introduction of a proportional tax into the income determination model *does* affect the value of the MPC and hence of the multiplier.

4.17.   Find the marginal cost functions for each of the following average cost functions.

(a) $\text{AC} = 1.5Q + 4 + \dfrac{46}{Q}$

Given the average cost function, the marginal cost function is determined by first finding the total cost function and then taking its derivative, as follows:

$$\text{TC} = (\text{AC})Q = \left(1.5Q + 4 + \frac{46}{Q}\right)Q = 1.5Q^2 + 4Q + 46$$

$$\text{MC} = \frac{d\text{TC}}{dQ} = 3Q + 4$$

(b) $\text{AC} = \dfrac{160}{Q} + 5 - 3Q + 2Q^2$

$$\text{TC} = \left(\frac{160}{Q} + 5 - 3Q + 2Q^2\right)Q = 160 + 5Q - 3Q^2 + 2Q^3$$

$$\text{MC} = \frac{d\text{TC}}{dQ} = 5 - 6Q + 6Q^2$$

OPTIMIZING ECONOMIC FUNCTIONS

4.18.   Maximize the following total revenue TR and total profit π functions by (1) finding the critical value(s), (2) testing the second-order conditions, and (3) calculating the maximum TR or π.

(a) $\text{TR} = 32Q - Q^2$

(1) $\text{TR}' = 32 - 2Q = 0$

$\qquad Q = 16 \qquad$ critical value

$\quad$ (2) $\mathrm{TR}'' = -2 < 0$ concave, relative maximum

$\quad$ (3) $\mathrm{TR} = 32(16) - (16)^2 = 256$

(b) $\pi = -Q^2 + 11Q - 24$

$\quad$ (1) $\pi' = -2Q + 11 = 0$

$$Q = 5.5 \quad \text{critical value}$$

$\quad$ (2) $\pi'' = -2 < 0$ concave, relative maximum

$\quad$ (3) $\pi = -(5.5)^2 + 11(5.5) - 24 = 6.25$

(c) $\pi = -\frac{1}{3}Q^3 - 5Q^2 + 2000Q - 326$

$\quad$ (1) $\pi' = -Q^2 - 10Q + 2000 = 0$ $\hfill (4.2)$

$$-1(Q^2 + 10Q - 2000) = 0 \hfill (4.3)$$

$$(Q + 50)(Q - 40) = 0$$

$$Q = -50 \quad Q = 40 \quad \text{critical values}$$

$\quad$ (2) $\qquad \pi'' = -2Q - 10$

$$\pi''(40) = -2(40) - 10 = -90 < 0 \quad \text{concave, relative maximum}$$

$$\pi''(-50) = -2(-50) - 10 = 90 > 0 \quad \text{convex, relative minimum}$$

Negative critical values will subsequently be ignored as having no economic significance.

$\quad$ (3) $\pi = -\frac{1}{3}(40)^3 - 5(40)^2 + 2000(40) - 326 = 50\,340.67$

Note: In testing the second-order conditions, as in step 2, always take the second derivative from the original first derivative (*4.2*) before any *negative* number has been factored out. Taking the second derivative from the first derivative after a negative has been factored out, as in (*4.3*), will reverse the second-order conditions and suggest that the function is maximized at $Q = -50$ and minimized at $Q = 40$. Test it yourself.

(d) $\pi = -Q^3 - 6Q^2 + 1440Q - 545$

$\quad$ (1) $\pi' = -3Q^2 - 12Q + 1440 = 0$

$$-3(Q - 20)(Q + 24) = 0$$

$$Q = 20 \quad Q = -24 \quad \text{critical values}$$

$\quad$ (2) $\qquad \pi'' = -6Q - 12$

$$\pi''(20) = -6(20) - 12 = -132 < 0 \quad \text{concave, relative maximum}$$

$\quad$ (3) $\pi = -(20)^3 - 6(20)^2 + 1440(20) - 545 = 17\,855$

4.19. From each of the following total cost TC functions, find (1) the average cost AC function, (2) the critical value at which AC is minimized, and (3) the minimum average cost.

(a) $\mathrm{TC} = Q^3 - 5Q^2 + 60Q$

$\quad$ (1) $\mathrm{AC} = \dfrac{\mathrm{TC}}{Q} = \dfrac{Q^3 - 5Q^2 + 60Q}{Q} = Q^2 - 5Q + 60$

$\quad$ (2) $\mathrm{AC}' = 2Q - 5 = 0 \qquad Q = 2.5$

$\qquad \mathrm{AC}'' = 2 > 0$ convex, relative minimum

$\quad$ (3) $\mathrm{AC}(2.5) = (2.5)^2 - 5(2.5) + 60 = 53.75$

(b) $\mathrm{TC} = Q^3 - 21Q^2 + 500Q$

$\quad$ (1) $\mathrm{AC} = \dfrac{Q^3 - 21Q^2 + 500Q}{Q} = Q^2 - 21Q + 500$

$\quad$ (2) $\mathrm{AC}' = 2Q - 21 = 0 \qquad Q = 10.5$

$\qquad \mathrm{AC}'' = 2 > 0$ convex, relative minimum

$\quad$ (3) $\mathrm{AC} = (10.5)^2 - 21(10.5) + 500 = 389.75$

4.20. Given the following total revenue and total cost functions for different firms, maximize profit π for the firms as follows: (1) Set up the profit function $\pi = TR - TC$, (2) find the critical value(s) where π is at a relative extremum and test the second-order condition, and (3) calculate the maximum profit.

(a) $TR = 1400Q - 6Q^2$ $TC = 1500 + 80Q$

     (1) $\pi = 1400Q - 6Q^2 - (1500 + 80Q)$

          $= -6Q^2 + 1320Q - 1500$

     (2) $\pi' = -12Q + 1320 = 0$

               $Q = 110$ critical value

         $\pi'' = -12 < 0$ concave, relative maximum

     (3) $\pi = -6(110)^2 + 1320(110) - 1500 = 71\,100$

(b) $TR = 1400Q - 7.5Q^2$ $TC = Q^3 - 6Q^2 + 140Q + 750$

     (1) $\pi = 1400Q - 7.5Q^2 - (Q^3 - 6Q^2 + 140Q + 750)$

          $= -Q^3 - 1.5Q^2 + 1260Q - 750$

     (2) $\pi' = -3Q^2 - 3Q + 1260 = 0$ (4.4)

          $= -3(Q^2 + Q - 420) = 0$

          $= -3(Q + 21)(Q - 20) = 0$

             $Q = -21$ $Q = 20$ critical values

        Take the second derivative directly from (4.4), as explained in Problem 4.18(c), and ignore all negative critical values.

                $\pi'' = -6Q - 3$

            $\pi''(20) = -6(20) - 3 = -123 < 0$ concave, relative maximum

     (3) $\pi = -(20)^3 - 1.5(20)^2 + 1260(20) - 750 = 15\,850$

(c) $TR = 4350Q - 13Q^2$ $TC = Q^3 - 5.5Q^2 + 150Q + 675$

     (1) $\pi = 4350Q - 13Q^2 - (Q^3 - 5.5Q^2 + 150Q + 675)$

          $= -Q^3 - 7.5Q^2 + 4200Q - 675$

     (2) $\pi' = -3Q^2 - 15Q + 4200 = 0$

            $= -3(Q^2 + 5Q - 1400) = 0$

            $= -3(Q + 40)(Q - 35) = 0$

               $Q = -40$ $Q = 35$ critical values

          $\pi'' = -6Q - 15$

       $\pi''(35) = -6(35) - 15 = -225 < 0$ concave, relative maximum

     (3) $\pi = -(35)^3 - 7.5(35)^2 + 4200(35) - 675 = 94\,262.50$

(d) $TR = 5900Q - 10Q^2$ $TC = 2Q^3 - 4Q^2 + 140Q + 845$

     (1) $\pi = 5900Q - 10Q^2 - (2Q^3 - 4Q^2 + 140Q + 845)$

          $= -2Q^3 - 6Q^2 + 5760Q - 845$

     (2) $\pi' = -6Q^2 - 12Q + 5760 = 0$

            $= -6(Q^2 + 2Q - 960) = 0$

            $= -6(Q + 32)(Q - 30) = 0$

               $Q = -32$ $Q = 30$ critical values

          $\pi'' = -12Q - 12$

       $\pi''(30) = -12(30) - 12 = -372 < 0$ concave, relative maximum

     (3) $\pi = -2(30)^3 - 6(30)^2 + 5760(30) - 845 = 112\,555$

4.21. Prove that marginal cost (MC) must equal marginal revenue (MR) at the profit-maximizing level of output.

$$\pi = \text{TR} - \text{TC}$$

To maximize π, $d\pi/dQ$ must equal zero.

$$\frac{d\pi}{dQ} = \frac{d\text{TR}}{dQ} - \frac{d\text{TC}}{dQ} = 0$$

$$\frac{d\text{TR}}{dQ} = \frac{d\text{TC}}{dQ}$$

$$\text{MR} = \text{MC} \quad \text{Q.E.D.}$$

4.22. A producer has the possibility of discriminating between the domestic and foreign markets for a product where the demands, respectively, are

$$Q_1 = 21 - 0.1P_1 \tag{4.5}$$

$$Q_2 = 50 - 0.4P_2 \tag{4.6}$$

Total cost $= 2000 + 10Q$ where $Q = Q_1 + Q_2$. What price will the producer charge in order to maximize profits (a) with discrimination between markets and (b) without discrimination? (c) Compare the profit differential between discrimination and nondiscrimination.

(a)   To maximize profits under price discrimination, the producer will set prices so that $\text{MC} = \text{MR}$ in each market. Thus, $\text{MC} = \text{MR}_1 = \text{MR}_2$. With $\text{TC} = 2000 + 10Q$,

$$\text{MC} = \frac{d\text{TC}}{dQ} = 10$$

Hence MC will be the same at all levels of output. In the domestic market,

$$Q_1 = 21 - 0.1P_1$$

Hence,
$$P_1 = 210 - 10Q_1$$

$$\text{TR}_1 = (210 - 10Q_1)Q_1 = 210Q_1 - 10Q_1^2$$

and
$$\text{MR}_1 = \frac{d\text{TR}_1}{dQ_1} = 210 - 20Q_1$$

When $\text{MR}_1 = \text{MC}$,
$$210 - 20Q_1 = 10 \qquad Q_1 = 10$$

When $Q_1 = 10$,
$$P_1 = 210 - 10(10) = 110$$

In the foreign market,

$$Q_2 = 50 - 0.4P_2$$

Hence,
$$P_2 = 125 - 2.5Q_2$$

$$\text{TR}_2 = (125 - 2.5Q_2)Q_2 = 125Q_2 - 2.5Q_2^2$$

Thus,
$$\text{MR}_2 = \frac{d\text{TR}_2}{dQ_2} = 125 - 5Q_2$$

When $\text{MR}_2 = \text{MC}$,
$$125 - 5Q_2 = 10 \qquad Q_2 = 23$$

When $Q_2 = 23$,
$$P_2 = 125 - 2.5(23) = 67.5$$

The discriminating producer charges a lower price in the foreign market where the demand is relatively more elastic and a higher price ($P_1 = 110$) in the domestic market where the demand is relatively less elastic.

(b) If the producer does not discriminate, $P_1 = P_2$ and the two demand functions (4.5) and (4.6) may simply be aggregated. Thus,

$$Q = Q_1 + Q_2 = 21 - 0.1P + 50 - 0.4P = 71 - 0.5P$$

Hence,
$$P = 142 - 2Q$$

$$\text{TR} = (142 - 2Q)Q = 142Q - 2Q^2$$

and
$$\text{MR} = \frac{d\text{TR}}{dQ} = 142 - 4Q$$

When $\text{MR} = \text{MC}$,
$$142 - 4Q = 10 \qquad Q = 33$$

When $Q = 33$,
$$P = 142 - 2(33) = 76$$

When no discrimination takes place, the price falls somewhere between the relatively high price of the domestic market and the relatively low price of the foreign market. Notice, however, that the quantity sold remains the same: at $P = 76$, $Q_1 = 13.4$, $Q_2 = 19.6$, and $Q = 33$.

(c) With discrimination,

$$\text{TR} = \text{TR}_1 + \text{TR}_2 = P_1Q_1 + P_2Q_2 = 110(10) + 67.5(23) = 2652.50$$

$\text{TC} = 2000 + 10Q$, where $Q = Q_1 + Q_2$.

$$\text{TC} = 2000 + 10(10 + 23) = 2330$$

Thus,
$$\pi = \text{TR} - \text{TC} = 2652.50 - 2330 = 322.50$$

Without discrimination,

$$\text{TR} = PQ = 76(33) = 2508$$

$\text{TC} = 2330$ since costs do not change with or without discrimination. Thus, $\pi = 2508 - 2330 = 178$. Profits are higher with discrimination (322.50) than without discrimination.

4.23. Faced with two distinct demand functions

$$Q_1 = 24 - 0.2P_1 \qquad Q_2 = 10 - 0.05P_2$$

where $\text{TC} = 35 + 40Q$, what price will the firm charge (a) with discrimination and (b) without discrimination?

(a) With $Q_1 = 24 - 0.2P_1$,

$$P_1 = 120 - 5Q_1$$
$$\text{TR}_1 = (120 - 5Q_1)Q_1 = 120Q_1 - 5Q_1^2$$
$$\text{MR}_1 = 120 - 10Q_1$$

The firm will maximize profits where $\text{MC} = \text{MR}_1 = \text{MR}_2$

$$\text{TC} = 35 + 40Q$$
$$\text{MC} = 40$$

When $\text{MC} = \text{MR}_1$,

$$40 = 120 - 10Q_1 \qquad Q_1 = 8$$

When $Q_1 = 8$,

$$P_1 = 120 - 5(8) = 80$$

In the second market, with $Q_2 = 10 - 0.05P_2$,

$$P_2 = 200 - 20Q_2$$
$$TR_2 = (200 - 20Q_2)Q_2 = 200Q_2 - 20Q_2^2$$
$$MR_2 = 200 - 40Q_2$$

When $MC = MR_2$,

$$40 = 200 - 40Q_2 \qquad Q_2 = 4$$

When $Q_2 = 4$,

$$P_2 = 200 - 20(4) = 120$$

(b) If the producer does not discriminate, $P_1 = P_2 = P$ and the two demand functions can be combined, as follows:

$$Q = Q_1 + Q_2 = 24 - 0.2P + 10 - 0.05P = 34 - 0.25P$$

Thus,

$$P = 136 - 4Q$$
$$TR = (136 - 4Q)Q = 136Q - 4Q^2$$
$$MR = 136 - 8Q$$

At the profit-maximizing level, $MC = MR$.

$$40 = 136 - 8Q \qquad Q = 12$$

At $Q = 12$,

$$P = 136 - 4(12) = 88$$

For more detailed treatment of price discrimination, see Problems 12.19 to 12.22.

4.24. Use the $MR = MC$ method to (a) maximize profit π and (b) check the second-order conditions, given

$$TR = 1400Q - 7.5Q^2 \qquad TC = Q^3 - 6Q^2 + 140Q + 750$$

(a) $MR = TR' = 1400 - 15Q$, $MC = TC' = 3Q^2 - 12Q + 140$

Equate $MR = MC$.

$$1400 - 15Q = 3Q^2 - 12Q + 140$$

Solve for Q by moving everything to the right.

$$3Q^2 + 3Q - 1260 = 0$$
$$3(Q + 21)(Q - 20) = 0$$
$$Q = -21 \qquad Q = 20 \qquad \text{critical values}$$

(b) $TR'' = -15 \qquad TC'' = 6Q - 12$

Since $\pi = TR - TC$ and the objective is to maximize π, be sure to *subtract* TC'' *from* TR'', or you will reverse the second-order conditions and select the wrong critical value.

$$\pi'' = TR'' - TC''$$
$$= -15 - 6Q + 12 = -6Q - 3$$
$$\pi''(20) = -6(20) - 3 = -123 < 0 \qquad \text{concave, relative maximum}$$

Compare these results with Problem 4.20(b).

ELASTICITY OF DEMAND

4.25. Using Fig. 4-14(a), prove that in traditional economic graphs where $P = f(Q)$, the price elasticity of a linear demand function ε_d at a point A is equal to both (a) the horizontal distance from point A to the point at which the demand curve crosses the horizontal axis (BC), divided by the horizontal distance of point A from the origin (OB) and (b) the length of the bottom segment of the demand curve (AC) divided by the length of the top segment of the curve (EA).

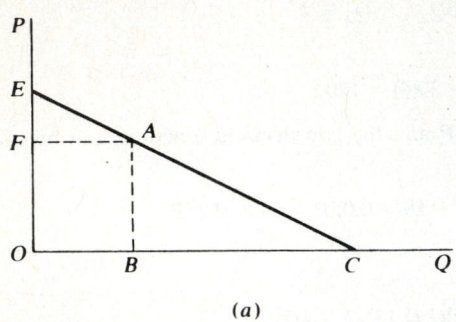 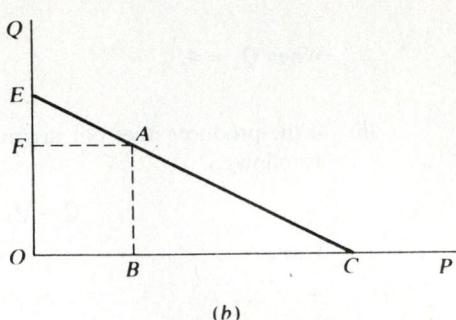

(a)   (b)

Fig. 4-14

(a) From (4.1b),
$$\varepsilon = \frac{1}{dP/dQ}\frac{P}{Q}$$

In Fig. 4-14(a),
$$\frac{dP}{dQ} = -\frac{AB}{BC}$$

At point A, $P = AB$, $Q = OB$. Substituting in the formula above gives
$$\varepsilon_d = \frac{1}{-AB/BC}\frac{AB}{OB} = -\frac{BC}{AB}\frac{AB}{OB}$$

$$\varepsilon_d = -\frac{BC}{OB} \tag{4.7}$$

(b) Since ABC and EFA are similar right triangles, and $FA = OB$, we can write
$$-\frac{AC}{BC} = -\frac{EA}{OB}$$

Multiplying each side by BC/EA gives
$$-\frac{AC}{EA} = -\frac{BC}{OB} = \varepsilon_d \qquad \text{Q.E.D.}$$

Note: In economics, elasticity of demand is frequently expressed in terms of absolute value $|\varepsilon_d|$, and the negative sign is not formally expressed. In terms of Fig. 4-14(b), prove for yourself that if $Q = F(P)$,
$$\varepsilon_d = -\frac{OB}{BC} \tag{4.7a}$$

4.26. Prove that for a linear demand function in the form $P = f(Q)$,

(a) $|\varepsilon_d| = 1$ in the middle of the demand curve

(b) $|\varepsilon_d| > 1$ above the middle of the demand curve

(c) $|\varepsilon_d| < 1$ below the middle of the demand curve.

Use Fig. 4-15 where A is in the middle of the demand curve.

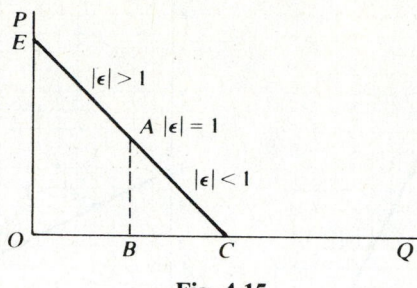

Fig. 4-15

(a) In Problem 4.25(a), it was demonstrated that elasticity of demand for a linear function is given by the length of the bottom segment of the demand curve divided by the length of the top segment. At point A, therefore,

$$|\varepsilon_d| = \frac{AC}{EA}$$

Since $AC = EA$ on the graph, at point $A, |\varepsilon_d| = 1$.

(b) For any point on the curve above A, hence to the left of A, $EA < AC$. With $EA < AC, |\varepsilon_d| > 1$ for any point on the line above A.

(c) For any point on the curve below A, hence to the right of A, $EA > AC$. With $EA > AC, |\varepsilon_d| < 1$ for any point on the line below A.

4.27. The demand function is $Q = 20 - 5P$. (a) Find the inverse function. (b) Estimate the elasticity of both functions at $P = 2$ and $P = 3$. (c) Graph the functions and indicate the estimated elasticities to show that the price elasticity of demand for both functions is the same and that only the relative positions on the curve differ.

(a) Solve $Q = 20 - 5P$ algebraically for P in terms of Q.

$$5P = 20 - Q$$
$$P = 4 - 0.2Q \qquad \text{inverse function}$$

(b) (1) $Q = 20 - 5P$

$$\frac{dQ}{dP} = -5$$

At $P = 2, Q = 20 - 5(2) = 10$.
Thus,

$$\varepsilon = \frac{dQ}{dP}\frac{P}{Q} = -5\left(\frac{2}{10}\right) = -1$$

At $P = 3, Q = 20 - 5(3) = 5$.

$$\varepsilon = -5(\tfrac{3}{5}) = -3$$

(2) $P = 4 - 0.2Q$

$$\frac{dP}{dQ} = -0.2$$

At $P = 2, 2 = 4 - 0.2Q$.

$$Q = 10$$

Thus,

$$\varepsilon = \frac{1}{dP/dQ}\frac{P}{Q} = \frac{1}{-0.2}\left(\frac{2}{10}\right) = -1$$

At $P = 3, 3 = 4 - 0.2Q$.

$$Q = 5$$

$$\varepsilon = \frac{1}{-0.2}\left(\frac{3}{5}\right) = -3$$

(c) The graphs for each function are given in Fig. 4-16. While the elasticities are the same at any given price level and $|\varepsilon| = 1$ always appears in the middle of the curve, Fig. 4-16 shows that $|\varepsilon| > 1$ appears in the bottom segment of the curve when $Q = F(P)$ and in the top segment of the curve when $P = f(Q)$.

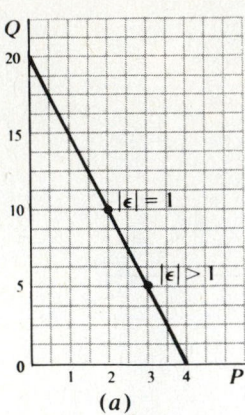 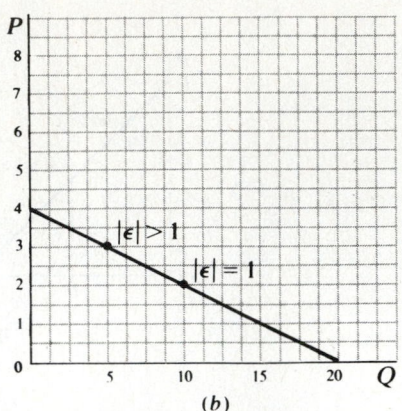

(a) (b)

Fig. 4-16

4.28. Given the graph of the demand function in Fig. 4-17 for $P = 16 - 2Q$, find the price elasticity graphically for points K, L, M, using the method demonstrated in Problem 4.25(a).

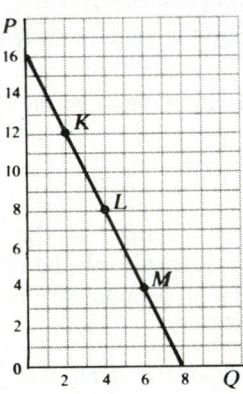

Fig. 4-17

From (4.7) and Fig. 4-14, we know that price elasticity of demand at a particular point equals the horizontal distance of the point from the point at which the demand curve crosses the horizontal axis (BC) divided by the horizontal distance of the point from the origin (OB). Thus,

At K, $|\varepsilon| = \dfrac{8 - 2}{2 - 0} = \dfrac{6}{2} = 3$

At L, $|\varepsilon| = \dfrac{8 - 4}{4 - 0} = \dfrac{4}{4} = 1$

At M, $|\varepsilon| = \dfrac{8 - 6}{6 - 0} = \dfrac{2}{6} = \dfrac{1}{3}$

4.29. Given the graph for $Q = 8 - 0.5P$, the inverse of the previous demand function, find the price elasticity at points K, L, M in Fig. 4-18.

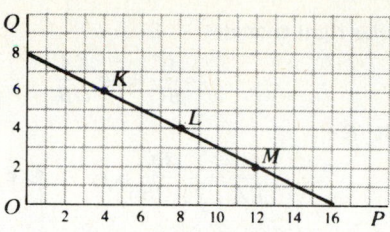

Fig. 4-18

From (4.7a) and Fig. 4-14(b) in Problem 4.25, price elasticity of demand at a particular point equals the horizontal distance of the point from the origin (OB) divided by the horizontal distance of the point from the point where the demand curve crosses the horizontal axis (BC). Thus,

At K,
$$|\varepsilon| = \frac{4-0}{16-4} = \frac{4}{12} = \frac{1}{3}$$

At L,
$$|\varepsilon| = \frac{8-0}{16-8} = \frac{8}{8} = 1$$

At M,
$$|\varepsilon| = \frac{12-0}{16-12} = \frac{12}{4} = 3$$

4.30. Using Fig. 4-19, where $P = f(Q)$, prove that price elasticity of demand for a curvilinear function at a point A is equal to both (a) the horizontal distance of the point from the point at which the tangent to the demand curve crosses the horizontal axis (BC), divided by the horizontal distance of the point from the origin (OB) and (b) the length of the bottom segment of the tangent to the demand curve at A (AC) divided by the length of the top segment of the tangent to the curve (EA).

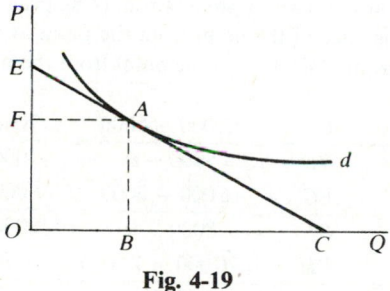

Fig. 4-19

(a)   From (4.1b),
$$\varepsilon = \frac{1}{dP/dQ}\frac{P}{Q}$$

The slope of the curvilinear function at A equals the slope of the tangent at A. Thus, in terms of Fig. 4-19,

$$\frac{dP}{dQ} = -\frac{AB}{BC}$$

At point A, $P = AB$, $Q = OB$. Substituting in the formula above yields

$$\varepsilon_d = \frac{1}{-AB/BC}\frac{AB}{OB} = -\frac{BC}{AB}\frac{AB}{OB} = -\frac{BC}{OB} \qquad (4.8)$$

(b)   From the properties of similar right triangles,

$$-\frac{AC}{BC} = -\frac{EA}{OB}$$

Multiplying each side by BC/EA,

$$-\frac{AC}{EA} = -\frac{BC}{OB} = \varepsilon_d \qquad \text{Q.E.D.}$$

4.31.   Find the price elasticity of demand at points K, L, and M on the curvilinear demand function given in Fig. 4-20.

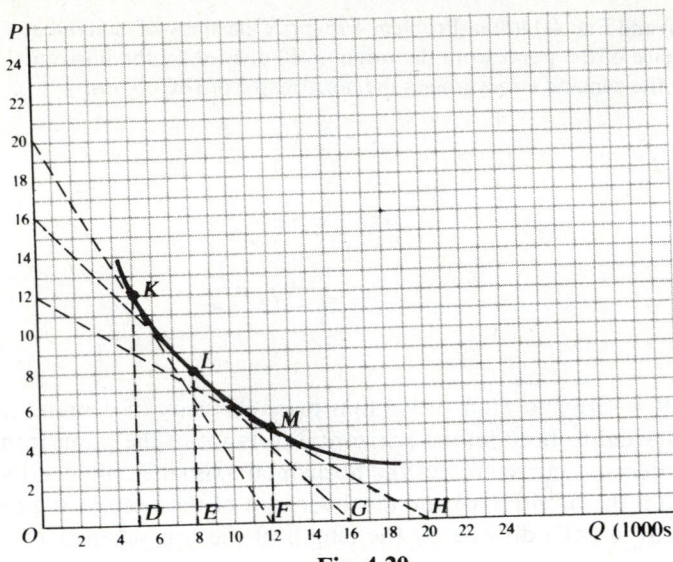

Fig. 4-20

Draw a tangent to the curve at the desired point. From (4.8), price elasticity of demand $|\varepsilon_d|$ at a particular point equals the horizontal distance of the point from the point at which the tangent crosses the horizontal axis (BC), divided by the horizontal distance of the point from the origin (OB). Thus,

At K, $\qquad \varepsilon = -\dfrac{DF}{OD} = -\dfrac{12\,000 - 5000}{5000 - 0} = -\dfrac{7000}{5000} = -1.4$

At L, $\qquad \varepsilon = -\dfrac{EG}{OE} = -\dfrac{16\,000 - 8000}{8000 - 0} = -\dfrac{8000}{8000} = -1$

At M, $\qquad \varepsilon = -\dfrac{FH}{OF} = -\dfrac{20\,000 - 12\,000}{12\,000 - 0} = -\dfrac{8000}{12\,000} = -0.67$

4.32.   In terms of the marginal and average concepts from (4.1c), find (a) the price elasticity of demand at point G in Fig. 4-21(a) and (b) the point where $|\varepsilon_d| = 1$ in Fig. 4-21(b). [Note that $Q = F(P)$.]

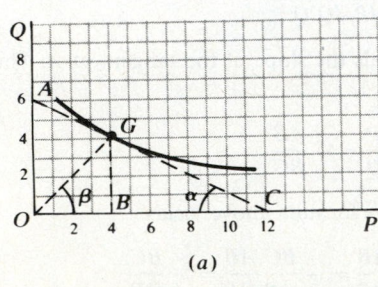

(a)

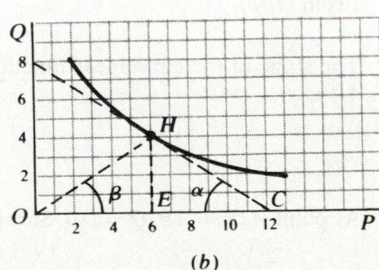

(b)

Fig. 4-21

(a) To get the marginal concept dQ/dP, draw a tangent to the curve at G. The slope of the curve (and the tangent of α) equals the marginal function. To get the average function Q/P, draw a straight line from the origin to G. The slope of OG (and the tangent of β) equals the average function since

$$\varepsilon = \frac{\text{marginal function}}{\text{average function}} = \frac{\text{tangent of } \alpha}{\text{tangent of } \beta} = \frac{-GB/BC}{GB/OB} = \frac{-OB}{BC} = \frac{-(4-0)}{12-4} = -\frac{1}{2}$$

(b) To find the point in Fig. 4-21(b) where $|\varepsilon| = 1$, simply find the point where the slope of the marginal function equals the slope of the average function, i.e., where $HE/EC = HE/OE$, or where $OE = EC$, or where tangent $\alpha = $ tangent β.

ELASTICITY OF SUPPLY

4.33. Using Fig. 4-22, prove that for a linear function $P = f(Q)$, the price elasticity of supply ε_s at a given point C equals the horizontal distance of the point from the point at which the supply curve intersects the horizontal axis (AB), divided by the horizontal distance of the point from the origin (OB).

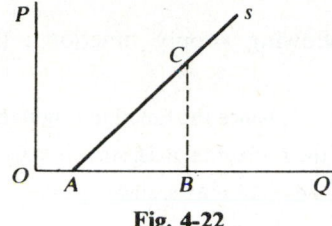

Fig. 4-22

From (4.1b),
$$\varepsilon_s = \frac{1}{dP/dQ} \frac{P}{Q}$$

where $dP/dQ = CB/AB$, $P = CB$, and $Q = OB$. Substituting,

$$\varepsilon_s = \frac{1}{CB/AB} \frac{CB}{OB} = \frac{AB}{CB} \frac{CB}{OB} = \frac{AB}{OB} \qquad \text{Q.E.D.}$$

4.34. Given Fig. 4-23, prove that for all positively sloped linear supply curves,

(a) $\varepsilon_s < 1$ if the supply curve intersects the horizontal axis (i.e., if the vertical intercept $a < 0$).

(b) $\varepsilon_s > 1$ if the supply curve intersects the vertical axis (if $a > 0$).

(c) $\varepsilon_s = 1$ if the supply curve originates from the origin (if $a = 0$).

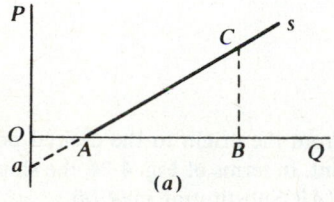 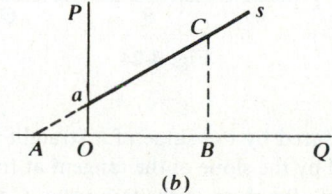 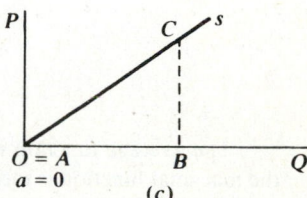

Fig. 4-23

(a) In Fig. 4-23(a),

$$\varepsilon = \frac{AB}{OB}$$

Since $AB < OB$, $\varepsilon < 1$. When $a < 0$, the supply curve intersects the horizontal axis. AB will be less than OB, and $\varepsilon_s < 1$.

(b) In Fig. 4-23(b) the graph is extended to A, a nonfeasible region, to provide the necessary measurement.

$$\varepsilon = \frac{AB}{OB} > 1$$

When $a > 0$, the supply curve intersects the vertical axis. AB will be greater than OB and $\varepsilon_s > 1$.

(c) In Fig. 4-23(c),

$$\varepsilon = \frac{AB}{OB} = 1$$

When $a = 0$, the supply curve starts from the origin. $AB = OB$, and $\varepsilon_s = 1$.

4.35. Tell whether the elasticity of supply

$$\varepsilon_s \gtreqless 1$$

by simply looking at the following supply functions: (a) $P = 3Q$, (b) $P = -2 + 5Q$, and (c) $P = 3 + 4Q$.

(a) $\varepsilon_s = 1$. The vertical intercept $a = 0$, hence the function originates from the origin.

(b) $\varepsilon_s < 1$. The function intersects the horizontal axis, since $a < 0$.

(c) $\varepsilon_s > 1$. The function intersects the vertical axis, since $a > 0$.

4.36. Given $P = f(Q)$, Fig. 4-24, and the formula from (4.1d)

$$\varepsilon = \frac{\text{average function}}{\text{marginal function}}$$

show that price elasticity of supply at a given point on a curvilinear function can be measured by drawing a tangent to the curve at that point and applying the rules of Problem 4.33 to the tangent.

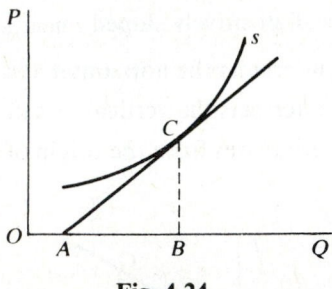

Fig. 4-24

The average function is measured by the slope of a straight line from the origin to the desired point; the marginal function is measured by the slope of the tangent at the point. In terms of Fig. 4-24, the slope of the average function at C is CB/OB; the slope of the tangent at C is CB/AB. Substituting in (4.1d),

$$\varepsilon_s = \frac{CB/OB}{CB/AB} = \frac{CB}{OB}\frac{AB}{CB} = \frac{AB}{OB}$$

where AB/OB is the horizontal distance of the given point C from the point at which the tangent to the supply curve intersects the horizontal axis, divided by the horizontal distance of the given point from the origin.

4.37. Given the supply curve in Fig. 4-25, find the elasticity of supply at points A, B, and C.

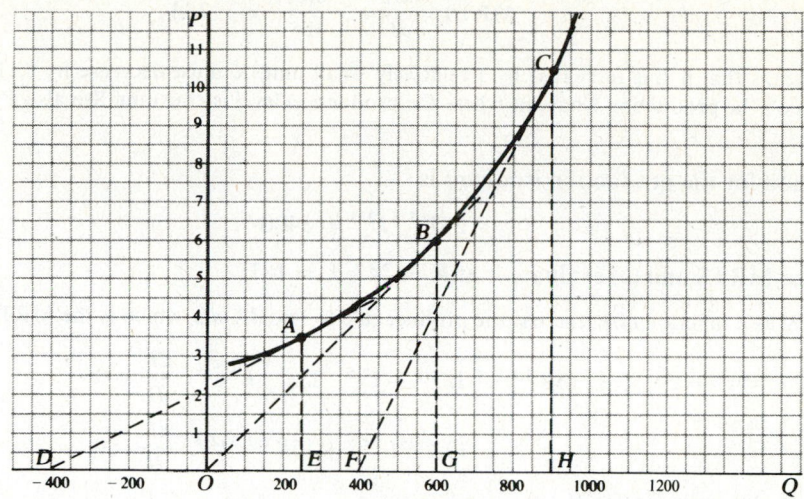

Fig. 4-25

At A,
$$\varepsilon_s = \frac{DE}{OE} = \frac{250 - (-400)}{250 - 0} = \frac{650}{250} = 2.6$$

At B,
$$\varepsilon_s = \frac{OG}{OG} = \frac{600 - 0}{600 - 0} = \frac{600}{600} = 1$$

At C,
$$\varepsilon_s = \frac{FH}{OH} = \frac{900 - 400}{900 - 0} = \frac{500}{900} = 0.56$$

THE MARGINAL RATE OF TECHNICAL SUBSTITUTION

4.38. The equation for a *production isoquant* which depicts the different combinations of inputs K and L that can be used to produce a specific level of output Q (here 2144 units) is

$$16K^{1/4}L^{3/4} = 2144$$

(a) Use implicit differentiation from Section 3.9 to find the slope of the isoquant dK/dL which in economics is called the *marginal rate of technical substitution* (MRTS). (b) Evaluate the marginal rate of technical substitution at $K = 256$, $L = 108$.

(a) Take the derivative of each term with respect to L and treat K as a function of L.

$$\frac{d}{dL}(16K^{1/4}L^{3/4}) = \frac{d}{dL}(2144)$$

Use the product rule since K is being treated as a function of L.

$$16K^{1/4} \cdot \frac{d}{dL}(L^{3/4}) + L^{3/4} \cdot \frac{d}{dL}(16K^{1/4}) = \frac{d}{dL}(2144)$$

$$\left(16K^{1/4} \cdot \frac{3}{4}L^{-1/4}\right) + \left(L^{3/4} \cdot 16 \cdot \frac{1}{4}K^{-3/4} \cdot \frac{dK}{dL}\right) = 0$$

$$12K^{1/4}L^{-1/4} + 4K^{-3/4}L^{3/4} \cdot \frac{dK}{dL} = 0$$

Solve algebraically for dK/dL.

$$\frac{dK}{dL} = \frac{-12K^{1/4}L^{-1/4}}{4K^{-3/4}L^{3/4}} = \frac{-3K}{L}$$

(b) At $K = 256$ and $L = 108$,

$$\text{MRTS} = \frac{dK}{dL} = \frac{-3(256)}{108} = -7.11$$

This means that if L is increased by 1 relatively small unit, K must decrease by 7.11 units in order to remain on the production isoquant where the production level is constant. See also Problem 6.55.

4.39. The equation for the production isoquant is

$$25K^{3/5}L^{2/5} = 5400$$

(a) Find the MRTS and (b) evaluate it at $K = 243$, $L = 181$.

(a) Treat K as a function of L and use the product rule to find dK/dL, which is the MRTS.

$$25K^{3/5} \cdot \frac{2}{5}L^{-3/5} + L^{2/5} \cdot 25 \cdot \frac{3}{5}K^{-2/5} \cdot \frac{dK}{dL} = 0$$

$$10K^{3/5}L^{-3/5} + 15K^{-2/5}L^{2/5} \cdot \frac{dK}{dL} = 0$$

Solve algebraically for dK/dL.

$$\frac{dK}{dL} = \frac{-10K^{3/5}L^{-3/5}}{15K^{-2/5}L^{2/5}} = \frac{-2K}{3L} = \text{MRTS}$$

(b) At $K = 243$ and $L = 181$,

$$\text{MRTS} = \frac{dK}{dL} = \frac{-2(243)}{3(181)} = -0.895$$

This means that if L is increased by 1 relatively small unit, K must decrease by 0.895 unit in order to remain on the production isoquant where the production level is constant. See Problem 6.56.

RELATIONSHIP BETWEEN FUNCTIONS AND GRAPHS

4.40. Given the total cost function $C = Q^3 - 18Q^2 + 750Q$, use your knowledge of calculus to help sketch a graph showing the relationship between total, average, and marginal costs.

(a) Take the first and second derivatives of the total cost function

$$C' = 3Q^2 - 36Q + 750$$
$$C'' = 6Q - 36$$

and check for (1) concavity and (2) inflection points.

(1) For $Q < 6$, $C'' < 0$ concave
     For $Q > 6$, $C'' > 0$ convex

(2) $6Q - 36 = 0$
           $Q = 6$

$$C(6) = (6)^3 - 18(6)^2 + 750(6) = 4068$$

With $C(Q)$ changing from concave to convex at $Q = 6$,

$$(6, 4068) \quad \text{inflection point}$$

(b) Find the average cost function AC and the relative extrema.

$$\text{AC} = \frac{\text{TC}}{Q} = Q^2 - 18Q + 750$$

$$\text{AC}' = 2Q - 18 = 0$$

$$Q = 9 \quad \text{critical value}$$

$$\text{AC}'' = 2 > 0 \quad \text{convex, relative minimum}$$

(c)   Do the same thing for the marginal cost function.

$$MC = C' = 3Q^2 - 36Q + 750$$
$$MC' = 6Q - 36 = 0$$
$$Q = 6 \qquad \text{critical value}$$
$$MC'' = 6 > 0 \qquad \text{convex, relative minimum}$$

(d)   Sketch the graph as in Fig. 4-26, noting that (1) MC decreases when TC is concave and increasing at a decreasing rate, increases when TC is convex and increasing at an increasing rate, and is at a minimum when TC is at an inflection point and changing concavity; and (2) AC decreases over the whole region where MC < AC, is at a minimum when MC = AC, and increases when MC > AC.

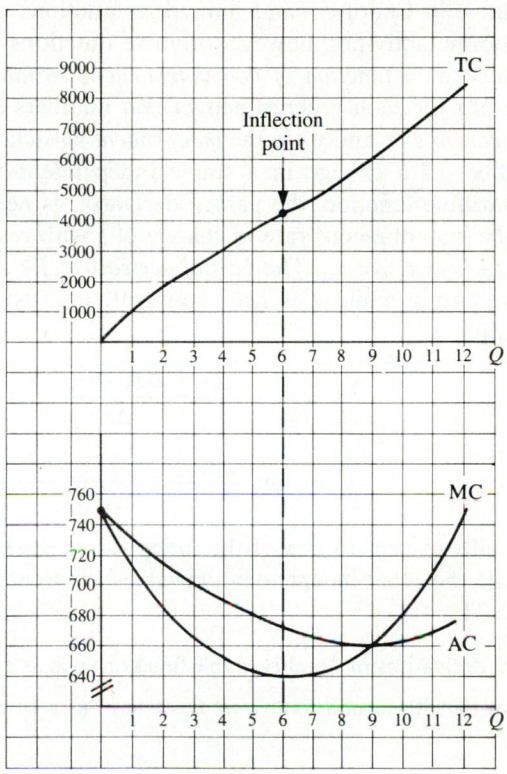

Fig. 4-26

Chapter 5

Calculus of Multivariable Functions

5.1 FUNCTIONS OF SEVERAL VARIABLES AND PARTIAL DERIVATIVES

Study of the derivative in Chapter 4 was limited to functions of a single independent variable such as $y = f(x)$. Many economic activities, however, involve functions of more than one independent variable. $z = f(x, y)$ is defined as a *function of two independent variables* if there exists one and only one value of z in the range of f for each ordered pair of real numbers (x, y) in the domain of f. By convention, z is the *dependent variable*; x and y are the *independent variables*.

To measure the effect of a change in a single independent variable (x or y) on the dependent variable (z) in a multivariable function, the partial derivative is needed. The *partial derivative of z with respect to x* measures the instantaneous rate of change of z with respect to x while y is held constant. It is written $\partial z/\partial x$, $\partial f/\partial x$, $f_x(x, y)$, f_x, or z_x. The *partial derivative of z with respect to y* measures the rate of change of z with respect to y while x is held constant. It is written $\partial z/\partial y$, $\partial f/\partial y$, $f_y(x, y)$, f_y, or z_y. Expressed mathematically,

$$\frac{\partial z}{\partial x} = \lim_{\Delta x \to 0} \frac{f(x + \Delta x, y) - f(x, y)}{\Delta x} \tag{5.1a}$$

$$\frac{\partial z}{\partial y} = \lim_{\Delta y \to 0} \frac{f(x, y + \Delta y) - f(x, y)}{\Delta y} \tag{5.1b}$$

Partial differentiation with respect to one of the independent variables follows the same rules as ordinary differentiation while the other independent variables are treated as constant. See Examples 1 and 2 and Problems 5.1 and 5.23.

EXAMPLE 1. The partial derivatives of a multivariable function such as $z = 3x^2 y^3$ are found as follows:

(a) When differentiating with respect to x, treat the y term as a constant by mentally bracketing it with the coefficient:

$$z = [3y^3] \cdot x^2$$

Then take the derivative of the x term, holding the y term constant,

$$\frac{\partial z}{\partial x} = z_x = [3y^3] \cdot \frac{d}{dx}(x^2)$$
$$= [3y^3] \cdot 2x$$

Recalling that a multiplicative constant remains in the process of differentiation, simply multiply and rearrange terms to obtain

$$\frac{\partial z}{\partial x} = z_x = 6xy^3$$

(b) When differentiating with respect to y, treat the x term as a constant by bracketing it with the coefficient; then take the derivative as was done above:

$$z = [3x^2] \cdot y^3$$
$$\frac{\partial z}{\partial y} = z_y = [3x^2] \cdot \frac{d}{dy}(y^3)$$
$$= [3x^2] \cdot 3y^2 = 9x^2 y^2$$

EXAMPLE 2. To find the partial derivatives for $z = 5x^3 - 3x^2y^2 + 7y^5$:

(a) When differentiating with respect to x, mentally bracket all y terms to remember to treat them as constants:

$$z = 5x^3 - [3y^2]x^2 + [7y^5]$$

Then take the derivative of each term, remembering that in differentiation multiplicative constants remain but additive constants drop out, because the derivative of a constant is zero.

$$\frac{\partial z}{\partial x} = \frac{d}{dx}(5x^3) - [3y^2] \cdot \frac{d}{dx}(x^2) + \frac{d}{dx}[7y^5]$$
$$= 15x^2 - [3y^2] \cdot 2x + 0$$
$$= 15x^2 - 6xy^2$$

(b) When differentiating with respect to y, block off all the x terms and differentiate as above.

$$z = [5x^3] - [3x^2]y^2 + 7y^5$$
$$\frac{\partial z}{\partial y} = \frac{d}{dy}[5x^3] - [3x^2] \cdot \frac{d}{dy}(y^2) + \frac{d}{dy}(7y^5)$$
$$= 0 - [3x^2] \cdot 2y + 35y^4$$
$$= -6x^2y + 35y^4$$

See Problem 5.1.

5.2 RULES OF PARTIAL DIFFERENTIATION

Partial derivatives follow the same basic patterns as the rules of differentiation in Section 3.7. A few key rules are given below, illustrated in Examples 3 to 5, treated in Problems 5.2 to 5.5, and verified in Problem 5.23.

5.2.1. Product Rule

Given $z = g(x, y) \cdot h(x, y)$,

$$\frac{\partial z}{\partial x} = g(x, y) \cdot \frac{\partial h}{\partial x} + h(x, y) \cdot \frac{\partial g}{\partial x} \tag{5.2a}$$

$$\frac{\partial z}{\partial y} = g(x, y) \cdot \frac{\partial h}{\partial y} + h(x, y) \cdot \frac{\partial g}{\partial y} \tag{5.2b}$$

EXAMPLE 3. Given $z = (3x + 5)(2x + 6y)$, by the product rule,

$$\frac{\partial z}{\partial x} = (3x + 5)(2) + (2x + 6y)(3) = 12x + 10 + 18y$$

$$\frac{\partial z}{\partial y} = (3x + 5)(6) + (2x + 6y)(0) = 18x + 30$$

5.2.2. Quotient Rule

Given $z = g(x, y)/h(x, y)$ and $h(x, y) \neq 0$,

$$\frac{\partial z}{\partial x} = \frac{h(x, y) \cdot \partial g/\partial x - g(x, y) \cdot \partial h/\partial x}{[h(x, y)]^2} \tag{5.3a}$$

$$\frac{\partial z}{\partial y} = \frac{h(x, y) \cdot \partial g/\partial y - g(x, y) \cdot \partial h/\partial y}{[h(x, y)]^2} \tag{5.3b}$$

EXAMPLE 4. Given $z = (6x + 7y)/(5x + 3y)$, by the quotient rule,

$$\frac{\partial z}{\partial x} = \frac{(5x + 3y)(6) - (6x + 7y)(5)}{(5x + 3y)^2}$$

$$= \frac{30x + 18y - 30x - 35y}{(5x + 3y)^2} = \frac{-17y}{(5x + 3y)^2}$$

$$\frac{\partial z}{\partial y} = \frac{(5x + 3y)(7) - (6x + 7y)(3)}{(5x + 3y)^2}$$

$$= \frac{35x + 21y - 18x - 21y}{(5x + 3y)^2} = \frac{17x}{(5x + 3y)^2}$$

5.2.3. Generalized Power Function Rule

Given $z = [g(x, y)]^n$,

$$\frac{\partial z}{\partial x} = n[g(x, y)]^{n-1} \cdot \frac{\partial g}{\partial x} \tag{5.4a}$$

$$\frac{\partial z}{\partial y} = n[g(x, y)]^{n-1} \cdot \frac{\partial g}{\partial y} \tag{5.4b}$$

EXAMPLE 5. Given $z = (x^3 + 7y^2)^4$, by the generalized power function rule,

$$\frac{\partial z}{\partial x} = 4(x^3 + 7y^2)^3 \cdot (3x^2) = 12x^2(x^3 + 7y^2)^3$$

$$\frac{\partial z}{\partial y} = 4(x^3 + 7y^2)^3 \cdot (14y) = 56y(x^3 + 7y^2)^3$$

5.3 SECOND-ORDER PARTIAL DERIVATIVES

Given a function $z = f(x, y)$, *the second-order (direct) partial derivative* signifies that the function has been differentiated partially with respect to one of the independent variables twice while the other independent variable has been held constant:

$$f_{xx} = (f_x)_x = \frac{\partial}{\partial x}\left(\frac{\partial z}{\partial x}\right) = \frac{\partial^2 z}{\partial x^2} \qquad f_{yy} = (f_y)_y = \frac{\partial}{\partial y}\left(\frac{\partial z}{\partial y}\right) = \frac{\partial^2 z}{\partial y^2}$$

In effect, f_{xx} measures the rate of change of the first-order partial derivative f_x with respect to x while y is held constant. And f_{yy} is exactly parallel. See Problems 5.6 and 5.8.

The *cross (or mixed) partial derivatives* f_{xy} and f_{yx} indicate that first the primitive function has been partially differentiated with respect to one independent variable and then that partial derivative has in turn been partially differentiated with respect to the other independent variable:

$$f_{xy} = (f_x)_y = \frac{\partial}{\partial y}\left(\frac{\partial z}{\partial x}\right) = \frac{\partial^2 z}{\partial y\,\partial x} \qquad f_{yx} = (f_y)_x = \frac{\partial}{\partial x}\left(\frac{\partial z}{\partial y}\right) = \frac{\partial^2 z}{\partial x\,\partial y}$$

In brief, a cross partial measures the rate of change of a first-order partial derivative with respect to the other independent variable. Notice how the order of independent variables changes in the different forms of notation. See Problems 5.7 and 5.9.

EXAMPLE 6. The (*a*) first, (*b*) second, and (*c*) cross partial derivatives for $z = 7x^3 + 9xy + 2y^5$ are taken as shown below.

(a) $\dfrac{\partial z}{\partial x} = z_x = 21x^2 + 9y$ $\dfrac{\partial z}{\partial y} = z_y = 9x + 10y^4$

(b) $\dfrac{\partial^2 z}{\partial x^2} = z_{xx} = 42x$ $\dfrac{\partial^2 z}{\partial y^2} = z_{yy} = 40y^3$

(c) $\dfrac{\partial^2 z}{\partial y\,\partial x} = \dfrac{\partial}{\partial y}\left(\dfrac{\partial z}{\partial x}\right) = \dfrac{\partial}{\partial y}(21x^2 + 9y) = z_{xy} = 9$

$\dfrac{\partial^2 z}{\partial x\,\partial y} = \dfrac{\partial}{\partial x}\left(\dfrac{\partial z}{\partial y}\right) = \dfrac{\partial}{\partial x}(9x + 10y^4) = z_{yx} = 9$

EXAMPLE 7. The (a) first, (b) second, and (c) cross partial derivatives for $z = 3x^2y^3$ are evaluated below at $x = 4$, $y = 1$.

(a) $z_x = 6xy^3$

$z_x(4, 1) = 6(4)(1)^3 = 24$ $z_y = 9x^2y^2$

$z_y(4, 1) = 9(4)^2(1)^2 = 144$

(b) $z_{xx} = 6y^3$

$z_{xx}(4, 1) = 6(1)^3 = 6$ $z_{yy} = 18x^2y$

$z_{yy}(4, 1) = 18(4)^2(1) = 288$

(c) $z_{xy} = \dfrac{\partial}{\partial y}(6xy^3) = 18xy^2$ $z_{yx} = \dfrac{\partial}{\partial x}(9x^2y^2) = 18xy^2$

$z_{xy}(4, 1) = 18(4)(1)^2 = 72$ $z_{yx}(4, 1) = 18(4)(1)^2 = 72$

By *Young's theorem*, if both cross partial derivatives are continuous, they will be identical. See Problems 5.7 to 5.9.

5.4   OPTIMIZATION OF MULTIVARIABLE FUNCTIONS

For a multivariable function such as $z = f(x, y)$ to be at a relative minimum or maximum, three conditions must be met:

1. The first-order partial derivatives must equal zero simultaneously. This indicates that at the given point (a, b), called a *critical point*, the function is neither increasing nor decreasing with respect to the principal axes but is at a relative plateau.
2. The second-order direct partial derivatives, when evaluated at the critical point (a, b), must both be positive for a minimum and negative for a maximum. This ensures that from a relative plateau at (a, b) the function is moving upward in relation to the principal axes in the case of a minimum and downward in relation to the principal axes in the case of a maximum.
3. The product of the second-order direct partials evaluated at the critical point must exceed the product of the cross partials evaluated at the critical point.

In sum, as seen in Fig. 5-1, when evaluated at a critical point (a, b),

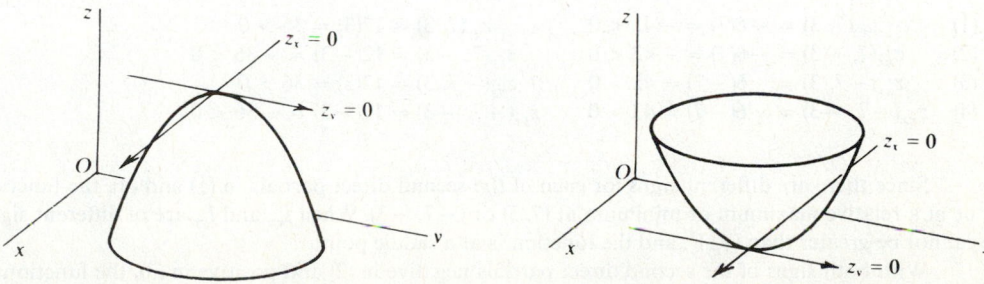

Fig. 5-1

Relative maximum	Relative minimum
1. $f_x, f_y = 0$	1. $f_x, f_y = 0$
2. $f_{xx}, f_{yy} < 0$	2. $f_{xx}, f_{yy} > 0$
3. $f_{xx} \cdot f_{yy} > (f_{xy})^2$	3. $f_{xx} \cdot f_{yy} > (f_{xy})^2$

Note the following:

(1) Since $f_{xy} = f_{yx}$ by Young's theorem, $f_{xy} \cdot f_{yx} = (f_{xy})^2$. Step 3 can also be written $f_{xx} \cdot f_{yy} - (f_{xy})^2 > 0$.

(2) If $f_{xx} \cdot f_{yy} < (f_{xy})^2$, when f_{xx} and f_{yy} have the same signs, the function is at an *inflection point*; when f_{xx} and f_{yy} have different signs, the function is at a *saddle point*, as seen in Fig. 5-2, where the function is at a maximum when viewed from one axis but at a minimum when viewed from the other axis.

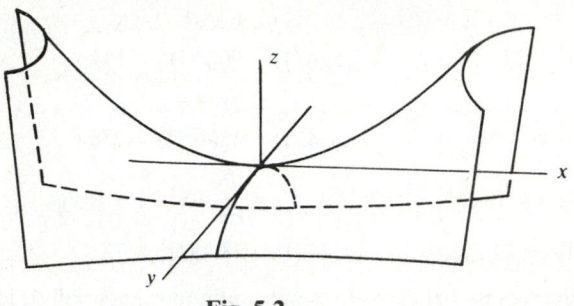

Fig. 5-2

(3) If $f_{xx} \cdot f_{yy} = (f_{xy})^2$, the test is inconclusive. See Example 8 and Problems 5.10 and 5.11; for inflection points, see Problems 5.10(c) and 5.11(b) and (c); for saddle points see Problems 5.10(d) and 5.11(a) and (d).

EXAMPLE 8. (a) Find the critical points. (b) Test whether the function is at a relative maximum or minimum, given

$$z = 2y^3 - x^3 + 147x - 54y + 12$$

(a) Take the first-order partial derivatives, set them equal to zero, and solve for x and y:

$$
\begin{array}{lll}
z_x = -3x^2 + 147 = 0 & \quad z_y = 6y^2 - 54 = 0 & \qquad (5.5)\\
x^2 = 49 & \quad y^2 = 9 \\
x = \pm 7 & \quad y = \pm 3
\end{array}
$$

With $x = \pm 7$, $y = \pm 3$, there are four distinct sets of critical points: $(7, 3)$, $(7, -3)$, $(-7, 3)$, and $(-7, -3)$.

(b) Take the second-order direct partials from (5.5), evaluate them at each of the critical points, and check the signs:

$$z_{xx} = -6x \qquad\qquad z_{yy} = 12y$$

(1) $z_{xx}(7, 3) = -6(7) = -42 < 0$ $z_{yy}(7, 3) = 12(3) = 36 > 0$

(2) $z_{xx}(7, -3) = -6(7) = -42 < 0$ $z_{yy}(7, -3) = 12(-3) = -36 < 0$

(3) $z_{xx}(-7, 3) = -6(-7) = 42 > 0$ $z_{yy}(-7, 3) = 12(3) = 36 > 0$

(4) $z_{xx}(-7, -3) = -6(-7) = 42 > 0$ $z_{yy}(-7, -3) = 12(-3) = -36 < 0$

Since there are different signs for each of the second direct partials in (1) and (4), the function cannot be at a relative maximum or minimum at $(7, 3)$ or $(-7, -3)$. When f_{xx} and f_{yy} are of different signs, $f_{xx} \cdot f_{yy}$ cannot be greater than $(f_{xy})^2$, and the function is at a saddle point.

With both signs of the second direct partials negative in (2) and positive in (3), the function *may be* at a relative maximum at $(7, -3)$ and at a relative minimum at $(-7, 3)$, but the third condition must be tested first to ensure against the possibility of an inflection point.

(c)   From (5.5), take the cross partial derivatives and check to make sure that $z_{xx}(a, b) \cdot z_{yy}(a, b) > [z_{xy}(a, b)]^2$.

$$z_{xy} = 0 \qquad z_{yx} = 0$$
$$z_{xx}(a, b) \cdot z_{yy}(a, b) \qquad > [z_{xy}(a, b)]^2$$

From (2),
$$(-42) \cdot (-36) \qquad > \qquad (0)^2$$
$$1512 > 0$$

From (3),
$$(42) \cdot (36) \qquad > \qquad (0)^2$$
$$1512 > 0$$

The function is maximized at $(7, -3)$ and minimized at $(-7, 3)$; for inflection points, see Problems 5.10(c) and 5.11(b) and (c).

5.5   CONSTRAINED OPTIMIZATION WITH LAGRANGE MULTIPLIERS

Differential calculus is also used to maximize or minimize a function subject to constraint. Given a function $f(x, y)$ subject to a constraint $g(x, y) = k$ (a constant), a new function F can be formed by (1) setting the constraint equal to zero, (2) multiplying it by λ (the *Lagrange multiplier*), and (3) adding the product to the original function:

$$F(x, y, \lambda) = f(x, y) + \lambda[k - g(x, y)] \tag{5.6}$$

Here $F(x, y, \lambda)$ is the *Lagrangian function*, $f(x, y)$ is the original or *objective function*, and $g(x, y)$ is the *constraint*. Since the constraint is always set equal to zero, the product $\lambda[k - g(x, y)]$ also equals zero, and the addition of the term does not change the value of the objective function. Critical values x_0, y_0, and λ_0, at which the function is optimized, are found by taking the partial derivatives of F with respect to *all three* independent variables, setting them equal to zero, and solving simultaneously:

$$F_x(x, y, \lambda) = 0 \qquad F_y(x, y, \lambda) = 0 \qquad F_\lambda(x, y, \lambda) = 0$$

Second-order conditions differ from those of unconstrained optimization and are treated in Section 12.5. See Example 9; Problems 5.12 to 5.14; Sections 6.6, 6.10, and 6.11; and Problems 6.28 to 6.43 and 6.45 to 6.48.

EXAMPLE 9.   Optimize the function

$$z = 4x^2 + 3xy + 6y^2$$

subject to the constraint $x + y = 56$.

1.   Set the constraint equal to zero,

$$56 - x - y = 0$$

Multiply it by λ and add it to the objective function to form the Lagrangian function Z.

$$Z = 4x^2 + 3xy + 6y^2 + \lambda(56 - x - y) \tag{5.7}$$

2.   Take the first-order partials, set them equal to zero, and solve simultaneously.

$$Z_x = 8x + 3y - \lambda = 0 \tag{5.8}$$
$$Z_y = 3x + 12y - \lambda = 0 \tag{5.9}$$
$$Z_\lambda = 56 - x - y = 0 \tag{5.10}$$

Subtracting (5.9) from (5.8) to eliminate λ gives

$$5x - 9y = 0 \qquad x = 1.8y$$

Substitute $x = 1.8y$ in (5.10),

$$56 - 1.8y - y = 0 \qquad y_0 = 20$$

From which we find

$$x_0 = 36 \qquad \lambda_0 = 348$$

Substitute the critical values in (5.7),

$$Z = 4(36)^2 + 3(36)(20) + 6(20)^2 + (348)(56 - 36 - 20)$$
$$= 4(1296) + 3(720) + 6(400) + 348(0) = 9744$$

In Chapter 12, Example 5, it will be shown that Z is at a minimum. Notice that at the critical values, the Lagrangian function Z equals the objective function z because the constraint equals zero. See Problems 5.12 to 5.14 and Sections 6.6, 6.10, and 6.11.

5.6 SIGNIFICANCE OF THE LAGRANGE MULTIPLIER

The Lagrange multiplier λ *approximates* the marginal impact on the objective function caused by a small change in the constant of the constraint. With $\lambda = 348$ in Example 9, for instance, a 1-unit increase (decrease) in the constant of the constraint would cause Z to increase (decrease) by approximately 348 units, as is demonstrated in Example 10. In this the Lagrange multiplier is akin to a shadow price (Sections 14.2 and 15.6). In utility maximization subject to a budget constraint, for example, λ will estimate the marginal utility of an extra dollar of income. See Problem 6.36.

Note: Since in (5.6) above $\lambda[k - g(x, y)] = \lambda[g(x, y) - k] = 0$, either form can be added to *or* subtracted from the objective function without changing the critical values of x and y. Only the sign of λ will be affected. For the interpretation of λ given in Section 5.6 to be valid, however, the precise form used in Equation (5.6) should be adhered to. See Problems 5.12 to 5.14.

EXAMPLE 10.   To verify that a 1-unit change in the constant of the constraint will cause a change of approximately 348 units in Z from Example 9, take the original objective function $z = 4x^2 + 3xy + 6y^2$ and optimize it subject to a new constraint $x + y = 57$ in which the constant of the constraint is 1 unit larger.

$$Z = 4x^2 + 3xy + 6y^2 + \lambda(57 - x - y)$$
$$Z_x = 8x + 3y - \lambda = 0$$
$$Z_y = 3x + 12y - \lambda = 0$$
$$Z_\lambda = 57 - x - y = 0$$

When solved simultaneously this gives

$$x_0 = 36.64 \qquad y_0 = 20.36 \qquad \lambda_0 = 354.2$$

Substituting these values in the Lagrangian function gives $Z = 10\,095$ which is 351 larger than the old constrained optimum of 9744, close to the approximation of the 348 increment suggested by λ.

5.7 DIFFERENTIALS

In Section 3.4 the derivative dy/dx was presented as a single symbol denoting the limit of $\Delta y/\Delta x$ as Δx approaches zero. The derivative dy/dx may also be treated as a ratio of differentials in which dy is the differential of y and dx the differential of x. Given a function of a single independent variable $y = f(x)$, the *differential of y, dy*, measures the change in y resulting from a small change in x, written dx.

Given $y = 2x^2 + 5x + 4$, the differential of y is found by first taking the derivative, which is a *rate of change*,

$$\frac{dy}{dx} = 4x + 5 \qquad \text{(a derivative)}$$

and then mentally multiplying both sides of the equation by dx, which signifies a small change in the independent variable, to obtain

$$dy = (4x + 5)\, dx \qquad \text{(a differential)}$$

EXAMPLE 11.

1. If $y = 4x^3 + 5x^2 - 7$, then $dy/dx = 12x^2 + 10x$ and the differential is

$$dy = (12x^2 + 10x)\,dx$$

2. If $y = (2x - 5)^2$, then $dy/dx = 2(2x - 5)(2) = 8x - 20$ and the differential is

$$dy = (8x - 20)\,dx$$

See Problem 5.15.

5.8 TOTAL AND PARTIAL DIFFERENTIALS

For a function of two or more independent variables, the *total differential* measures the change in the dependent variable brought about by a small change in each of the independent variables. If $z = f(x, y)$, the total differential dz is expressed mathematically as

$$dz = z_x\,dx + z_y\,dy \qquad (5.11)$$

where z_x and z_y are the partial derivatives of z with respect to x and y respectively, and dx and dy are small changes in x and y. The total differential can thus be found by taking the partial derivatives of the function with respect to each independent variable and substituting these values in the formula above.

EXAMPLE 12. The total differential is found as follows:

1. Given: $z = x^4 + 8xy + 3y^3$

$$z_x = 4x^3 + 8y \qquad z_y = 8x + 9y^2$$

which, when substituted in the total differential formula, gives

$$dz = (4x^3 + 8y)\,dx + (8x + 9y^2)\,dy$$

2. Given: $z = (x - y)/(x + 1)$

$$z_x = \frac{(x+1)(1) - (x-y)(1)}{(x+1)^2} = \frac{y+1}{(x+1)^2}$$

$$z_y = \frac{(x+1)(-1) - (x-y)(0)}{(x+1)^2} = \frac{-1(x+1)}{(x+1)^2} = \frac{-1}{x+1}$$

The total differential is
$$dz = \frac{y+1}{(x+1)^2}\,dx - \left(\frac{1}{x+1}\right)dy$$

If one of the independent variables is held constant, for example, $dy = 0$, we then have a partial differential:

$$dz = z_x\,dx$$

A *partial differential* measures the change in the dependent variable of a multivariate function resulting from a small change in one of the independent variables and assumes the other independent variables are constant. See Problems 5.16 and 5.17 and 6.49 to 6.56.

5.9 TOTAL DERIVATIVES

Given a case where $z = f(x, y)$ and $y = g(x)$, that is, when x and y are not independent, a change in x will affect z directly through the function f and indirectly through the function g. This is illustrated in the channel map in Fig. 5-3. To measure the effect of a change in x on z when x and y are not independent, the total derivative must be found. The *total derivative* measures the *direct* effect of x on z,

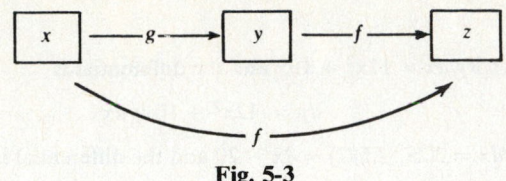

Fig. 5-3

$\partial z/\partial x$, *plus* the *indirect* effect of x on z through y, $\dfrac{\partial z}{\partial y}\dfrac{dy}{dx}$. In brief, the total derivative is

$$\frac{dz}{dx} = z_x + z_y \frac{dy}{dx} \qquad (5.12)$$

See Examples 13 to 15 and Problems 5.18 and 5.19.

EXAMPLE 13. An alternate method of finding the total derivative is to take the total differential of z

$$dz = z_x\, dx + z_y\, dy$$

and divide through mentally by dx. Thus,

$$\frac{dz}{dx} = z_x \frac{dx}{dx} + z_y \frac{dy}{dx}$$

Since $dx/dx = 1$, $\qquad\qquad\qquad\qquad \dfrac{dz}{dx} = z_x + z_y \dfrac{dy}{dx}$

EXAMPLE 14. Given

$$z = f(x,\, y) = 6x^3 + 7y$$

where $y = g(x) = 4x^2 + 3x + 8$, the total derivative dz/dx with respect to x is

$$\frac{dz}{dx} = z_x + z_y \frac{dy}{dx}$$

where $z_x = 18x^2$, $z_y = 7$, and $dy/dx = 8x + 3$. Substituting above,

$$\frac{dz}{dx} = 18x^2 + 7(8x + 3) = 18x^2 + 56x + 21$$

To check the answer, substitute $y = 4x^2 + 3x + 8$ in the original function to make z a function of x alone and then take the derivative as follows:

$$z = 6x^3 + 7(4x^2 + 3x + 8) = 6x^3 + 28x^2 + 21x + 56$$

$$\frac{dz}{dx} = 18x^2 + 56x + 21$$

Thus,

EXAMPLE 15. The total derivative can be expanded to accommodate other interconnections as well. Given

$$z = 8x^2 + 3y^2 \qquad x = 4t \qquad y = 5t$$

the total derivative of z with respect to t then becomes

$$\frac{dz}{dt} = z_x \frac{dx}{dt} + z_y \frac{dy}{dt}$$

where $z_x = 16x$, $z_y = 6y$, $dx/dt = 4$, and $dy/dt = 5$. Substituting above,

$$\frac{dz}{dt} = 16x(4) + 6y(5) = 64x + 30y$$

Then substituting $x = 4t$ and $y = 5t$ immediately above,

$$\frac{dz}{dt} = 64(4t) + 30(5t) = 406t$$

5.10 IMPLICIT AND INVERSE FUNCTION RULES

As seen in Section 3.9, functions of the form $y = f(x)$ express y explicitly in terms of x and are called *explicit functions*. Functions of the form $f(x, y) = 0$ do not express y explicitly in terms of x and are called *implicit functions*. If an implicit function $f(x, y) = 0$ exists and $f_y \neq 0$ at the point around which the implicit function is defined, the total differential is simply $f_x \, dx + f_y \, dy = 0$.

Recalling that a derivative is a ratio of differentials, we can then rearrange the terms to get the *implicit function rule*:

$$\frac{dy}{dx} = \frac{-f_x}{f_y} \tag{5.13}$$

Notice that the derivative dy/dx is the *negative* of the *reciprocal* of the corresponding partials.

$$\frac{dy}{dx} = \frac{-f_x}{f_y} = -\frac{1}{f_y/f_x}$$

Given a function $y = f(x)$, an *inverse function* $x = f^{-1}(y)$ exists if each value of y yields one and only one value of x. Most economic functions have inverse functions. Assuming the inverse function exists, the *inverse function rule* states that the derivative of the inverse function is the reciprocal of the derivative of the original function. Thus, if $Q = f(P)$ is the original function, the derivative of the original function is dQ/dP, the derivative of the inverse function $[P = f^{-1}(Q)]$ is dP/dQ, and

$$\frac{dP}{dQ} = \frac{1}{dQ/dP} \qquad \text{provided } \frac{dQ}{dP} \neq 0 \tag{5.14}$$

See Examples 16 and 17 and Problems 5.20 to 5.22, 6.55, and 6.56.

EXAMPLE 16. Given the implicit functions:

(a) $7x^2 - y = 0$ (b) $3x^4 - 7y^5 - 86 = 0$

the derivative dy/dx is found as follows:

(a) From (5.13),
$$\frac{dy}{dx} = -\frac{f_x}{f_y}$$

Here $f_x = 14x$ and $f_y = -1$. Substituting above,

$$\frac{dy}{dx} = -\frac{14x}{(-1)} = 14x$$

The function in this case was deliberately kept simple so the answer could easily be checked by solving for y in terms of x and then taking the derivative directly. Since $y = 7x^2$, $dy/dx = 14x$.

(b)
$$\frac{dy}{dx} = -\frac{f_x}{f_y} = -\frac{12x^3}{-35y^4} = \frac{12x^3}{35y^4}$$

Compare this answer with that in Example 16 of Chapter 3.

EXAMPLE 17. Find the derivative for the inverse of the following functions:

1. Given $Q = 20 - 2P$,

$$\frac{dP}{dQ} = \frac{1}{dQ/dP}$$

where $dQ/dP = -2$. Thus,

$$\frac{dP}{dQ} = \frac{1}{-2} = -\frac{1}{2}$$

2. Given $Q = 25 + 3P^3$,

$$\frac{dP}{dQ} = \frac{1}{dQ/dP} = \frac{1}{9P^2} \qquad (P \neq 0)$$

Solved Problems

FIRST-ORDER PARTIAL DERIVATIVES

5.1. Find the first-order partial derivatives for each of the following functions:

(a) $z = 8x^2 + 14xy + 5y^2$

$z_x = 16x + 14y$
$z_y = 14x + 10y$

(b) $z = 4x^3 + 2x^2 y - 7y^5$

$z_x = 12x^2 + 4xy$
$z_y = 2x^2 - 35y^4$

(c) $z = 6w^3 + 4wx + 3x^2 - 7xy - 8y^2$

$z_w = 18w^2 + 4x$
$z_x = 4w + 6x - 7y$
$z_y = -7x - 16y$

(d) $z = 2w^2 + 8wxy - x^2 + y^3$

$z_w = 4w + 8xy$
$z_x = 8wy - 2x$
$z_y = 8wx + 3y^2$

5.2. Use the product rule from Equation (5.2) to find the first-order partials for each of the following functions:

(a) $z = 3x^2(5x + 7y)$

$z_x = 3x^2(5) + (5x + 7y)(6x)$
$\quad = 45x^2 + 42xy$

and $z_y = 3x^2(7) + (5x + 7y)(0)$
$\quad = 21x^2$

(b) $z = (9x - 4y)(12x + 2y)$

$z_x = (9x - 4y)(12) + (12x + 2y)(9)$
$\quad = 108x - 48y + 108x + 18y = 216x - 30y$

and $z_y = (9x - 4y)(2) + (12x + 2y)(-4)$
$\quad = 18x - 8y - 48x - 8y = -30x - 16y$

(c) $z = (2x^2 + 6y)(5x - 3y^3)$

$z_x = (2x^2 + 6y)(5) + (5x - 3y^3)(4x)$
$\quad = 10x^2 + 30y + 20x^2 - 12xy^3$
$\quad = 30x^2 + 30y - 12xy^3$

and $z_y = (2x^2 + 6y)(-9y^2) + (5x - 3y^3)(6)$
$\quad = -18x^2 y^2 - 54y^3 + 30x - 18y^3$
$\quad = -72y^3 - 18x^2 y^2 + 30x$

(d) $z = (w - x - y)(3w + 2x - 4y)$

$z_w = (w - x - y)(3) + (3w + 2x - 4y)(1)$
$\quad = 6w - x - 7y$
$z_x = (w - x - y)(2) + (3w + 2x - 4y)(-1)$
$\quad = -w - 4x + 2y$

and $z_y = (w - x - y)(-4) + (3w + 2x - 4y)(-1)$
$\quad = -7w + 2x + 8y$

5.3. Use the quotient rule from Equation (5.3) to find the first-order partials of the following functions:

(a) $z = \dfrac{5x}{6x - 7y}$

$$z_x = \frac{(6x - 7y)(5) - (5x)(6)}{(6x - 7y)^2}$$

$$= \frac{-35y}{(6x - 7y)^2}$$

and $z_y = \dfrac{(6x - 7y)(0) - (5x)(-7)}{(6x - 7y)^2}$

$$= \frac{35x}{(6x - 7y)^2}$$

(b) $z = \dfrac{x + y}{3y}$

$$z_x = \frac{3y(1) - (x + y)(0)}{(3y)^2}$$

$$= \frac{1}{3y}$$

and $z_y = \dfrac{3y(1) - (x + y)(3)}{(3y)^2}$

$$= \frac{-3x}{(3y)^2} = \frac{-x}{3y^2}$$

(c) $z = \dfrac{4x - 9y}{5x + 2y}$

$$z_x = \frac{(5x + 2y)(4) - (4x - 9y)(5)}{(5x + 2y)^2}$$

$$= \frac{53y}{(5x + 2y)^2}$$

and $z_y = \dfrac{(5x + 2y)(-9) - (4x - 9y)(2)}{(5x + 2y)^2}$

$$= \frac{-53x}{(5x + 2y)^2}$$

(d) $z = \dfrac{x^2 - y^2}{3x + 2y}$

$$z_x = \frac{(3x + 2y)(2x) - (x^2 - y^2)(3)}{(3x + 2y)^2}$$

$$= \frac{3x^2 + 4xy + 3y^2}{(3x + 2y)^2}$$

and $z_y = \dfrac{(3x + 2y)(-2y) - (x^2 - y^2)(2)}{(3x + 2y)^2}$

$$= \frac{-2x^2 - 6xy - 2y^2}{(3x + 2y)^2}$$

5.4. Find the first-order partial derivatives for each of the following functions by using the generalized power function rule from Equation (5.4):

(a) $z = (x + y)^2$

$$z_x = 2(x + y)(1)$$
$$= 2(x + y)$$
and $z_y = 2(x + y)(1)$
$$= 2(x + y)$$

(b) $z = (2x - 5y)^3$

$$z_x = 3(2x - 5y)^2(2)$$
$$= 6(2x - 5y)^2$$
and $z_y = 3(2x - 5y)^2(-5)$
$$= -15(2x - 5y)^2$$

(c) $z = (7x^2 + 4y^3)^5$

$$z_x = 5(7x^2 + 4y^3)^4(14x)$$
$$= 70x(7x^2 + 4y^3)^4$$
and $z_y = 5(7x^2 + 4y^3)^4(12y^2)$
$$= 60y^2(7x^2 + 4y^3)^4$$

(d) $z = (5w + 4x + 7y)^3$

$$z_w = 3(5w + 4x + 7y)^2(5)$$
$$= 15(5w + 4x + 7y)^2$$
$$z_x = 3(5w + 4x + 7y)^2(4)$$
$$= 12(5w + 4x + 7y)^2$$
and $z_y = 3(5w + 4x + 7y)^2(7)$
$$= 21(5w + 4x + 7y)^2$$

5.5. Use whatever combination of rules is necessary to find the first-order partials for the following functions:

(a) $z = \dfrac{(5x^2 - 7y)(3x^2 + 8y)}{4x + 2y}$

Using the quotient rule and product rule,

$$z_x = \frac{(4x + 2y)[(5x^2 - 7y)(6x) + (3x^2 + 8y)(10x)] - (5x^2 - 7y)(3x^2 + 8y)(4)}{(4x + 2y)^2}$$

$$= \frac{(4x + 2y)(30x^3 - 42xy + 30x^3 + 80xy) - (5x^2 - 7y)(12x^2 + 32y)}{(4x + 2y)^2}$$

$$= \frac{(4x + 2y)(60x^3 + 38xy) - (5x^2 - 7y)(12x^2 + 32y)}{(4x + 2y)^2}$$

and

$$z_y = \frac{(4x + 2y)[(5x^2 - 7y)(8) + (3x^2 + 8y)(-7)] - (5x^2 - 7y)(3x^2 + 8y)(2)}{(4x + 2y)^2}$$

$$= \frac{(4x + 2y)(40x^2 - 56y - 21x^2 - 56y) - (5x^2 - 7y)(6x^2 + 16y)}{(4x + 2y)^2}$$

$$= \frac{(4x + 2y)(19x^2 - 112y) - (5x^2 - 7y)(6x^2 + 16y)}{(4x + 2y)^2}$$

(b) $z = (5x^2 - 4y)^2(2x + 7y^3)$

Using the product rule and the generalized power function rule,

$$z_x = (5x^2 - 4y)^2(2) + (2x + 7y^3)[2(5x^2 - 4y)(10x)]$$
$$= 2(5x^2 - 4y)^2 + (2x + 7y^3)(100x^3 - 80xy)$$

and

$$z_y = (5x^2 - 4y)^2(21y^2) + (2x + 7y^3)[2(5x^2 - 4y)(-4)]$$
$$= 21y^2(5x^2 - 4y)^2 + (2x + 7y^3)(-40x^2 + 32y)$$

(c) $z = \dfrac{(3x + 11y)^3}{2x + 6y}$

Using the quotient rule and the generalized power function rule,

$$z_x = \frac{(2x + 6y)[3(3x + 11y)^2(3)] - (3x + 11y)^3(2)}{(2x + 6y)^2}$$

$$= \frac{(18x + 54y)(3x + 11y)^2 - 2(3x + 11y)^3}{(2x + 6y)^2}$$

and

$$z_y = \frac{(2x + 6y)[3(3x + 11y)^2(11)] - (3x + 11y)^3(6)}{(2x + 6y)^2}$$

$$= \frac{(66x + 198y)(3x + 11y)^2 - 6(3x + 11y)^3}{(2x + 6y)^2}$$

(d) $z = \left(\dfrac{8x + 7y}{5x + 2y}\right)^2$

Using the generalized power function rule and the quotient rule,

$$z_x = 2\left(\frac{8x + 7y}{5x + 2y}\right)\left[\frac{(5x + 2y)(8) - (8x + 7y)(5)}{(5x + 2y)^2}\right]$$

$$= \frac{16x + 14y}{5x + 2y}\left[\frac{-19y}{(5x + 2y)^2}\right] = \frac{-(266y^2 + 304xy)}{(5x + 2y)^3}$$

and

$$z_y = 2\left(\frac{8x + 7y}{5x + 2y}\right)\left[\frac{(5x + 2y)(7) - (8x + 7y)(2)}{(5x + 2y)^2}\right]$$

$$= \frac{16x + 14y}{5x + 2y}\left[\frac{19x}{(5x + 2y)^2}\right] = \frac{304x^2 + 266xy}{(5x + 2y)^3}$$

SECOND-ORDER PARTIAL DERIVATIVES

5.6. Find the second-order direct partial derivatives z_{xx} and z_{yy} for each of the following functions:

(a) $z = x^2 + 2xy + y^2$

$$z_x = 2x + 2y \qquad z_y = 2x + 2y$$
$$z_{xx} = 2 \qquad z_{yy} = 2$$

(b) $z = x^3 - 9xy - 3y^3$

$$z_x = 3x^2 - 9y \qquad z_y = -9x - 9y^2$$
$$z_{xx} = 6x \qquad z_{yy} = -18y$$

(c) $z = 2xy^4 + 7x^3y$

$$z_x = 2y^4 + 21x^2y \qquad z_y = 8xy^3 + 7x^3$$
$$z_{xx} = 42xy \qquad z_{yy} = 24xy^2$$

(d) $z = x^4 + x^3y^2 - 3xy^3 - 2y^3$

$$z_x = 4x^3 + 3x^2y^2 - 3y^3 \qquad z_y = 2x^3y - 9xy^2 - 6y^2$$
$$z_{xx} = 12x^2 + 6xy^2 \qquad z_{yy} = 2x^3 - 18xy - 12y$$

(e) $z = (12x - 7y)^2$

$$z_x = 2(12x - 7y)(12) \qquad z_y = 2(12x - 7y)(-7)$$
$$= 288x - 168y \qquad = -168x + 98y$$
$$z_{xx} = 288 \qquad z_{yy} = 98$$

(f) $z = (7x + 3y)^3$

$$z_x = 3(7x + 3y)^2(7) \qquad z_y = 3(7x + 3y)^2(3)$$
$$= 21(7x + 3y)^2 \qquad = 9(7x + 3y)^2$$
$$z_{xx} = 42(7x + 3y)(7) \qquad z_{yy} = 18(7x + 3y)(3)$$
$$= 2058x + 882y \qquad = 378x + 162y$$

(g) $z = (x^2 + 2y)^4$

$$z_x = 4(x^2 + 2y)^3(2x) = 8x(x^2 + 2y)^3 \qquad z_y = 4(x^2 + 2y)^3(2) = 8(x^2 + 2y)^3$$
$$*z_{xx} = 8x[3(x^2 + 2y)^2(2x)] + (x^2 + 2y)^3(8) \qquad z_{yy} = 24(x^2 + 2y)^2(2) = 48(x^2 + 2y)^2$$
$$= 48x^2(x^2 + 2y)^2 + 8(x^2 + 2y)^3$$

5.7. Find the cross partial derivatives z_{xy} and z_{yx} for each of the following functions:

(a) $z = 3x^2 + 12xy + 5y^2$

$$z_x = 6x + 12y \qquad z_y = 12x + 10y$$
$$z_{xy} = 12 \qquad z_{yx} = 12$$

(b) $z = x^3 - xy - 2y^3$

$$z_x = 3x^2 - y \qquad z_y = -x - 6y^2$$
$$z_{xy} = -1 \qquad z_{yx} = -1$$

(c) $z = 8x^2y - 11xy^3$

$$z_x = 16xy - 11y^3 \qquad z_y = 8x^2 - 33xy^2$$
$$z_{xy} = 16x - 33y^2 \qquad z_{yx} = 16x - 33y^2$$

* By the product rule.

(d) $z = (8x - 4y)^5$

$$z_x = 5(8x - 4y)^4(8) \qquad z_y = 5(8x - 4y)^4(-4)$$
$$= 40(8x - 4y)^4 \qquad = -20(8x - 4y)^4$$
$$z_{xy} = 160(8x - 4y)^3(-4) \qquad z_{yx} = -80(8x - 4y)^3(8)$$
$$= -640(8x - 4y)^3 \qquad = -640(8x - 4y)^3$$

In items (a) through (d) above, notice how, in accord with Young's theorem, $z_{xy} = z_{yx}$ no matter which first partial is taken initially.

5.8. Find the first-order and second-order direct partial derivatives for the following functions:

(a) $z = x^{0.4}y^{0.6}$

$$z_x = 0.4x^{-0.6}y^{0.6} \qquad z_y = 0.6x^{0.4}y^{-0.4}$$
$$z_{xx} = -0.24x^{-1.6}y^{0.6} \qquad z_{yy} = -0.24x^{0.4}y^{-1.4}$$

(b) $f(x, y) = x^{0.7}y^{0.2}$

$$f_x = 0.7x^{-0.3}y^{0.2} \qquad f_y = 0.2x^{0.7}y^{-0.8}$$
$$f_{xx} = -0.21x^{-1.3}y^{0.2} \qquad f_{yy} = -0.16x^{0.7}y^{-1.8}$$

(c) $z = 2w^6x^5y^3$

$$z_w = 12w^5x^5y^3 \qquad z_x = 10w^6x^4y^3 \qquad z_y = 6w^6x^5y^2$$
$$z_{ww} = 60w^4x^5y^3 \qquad z_{xx} = 40w^6x^3y^3 \qquad z_{yy} = 12w^6x^5y$$

(d) $f(x, y, z) = 10x^3y^2z^4$

$$f_x = 30x^2y^2z^4 \qquad f_y = 20x^3yz^4 \qquad f_z = 40x^3y^2z^3$$
$$f_{xx} = 60xy^2z^4 \qquad f_{yy} = 20x^3z^4 \qquad f_{zz} = 120x^3y^2z^2$$

5.9. Find the cross partials for each of the following functions:

(a) $z = x^{0.3}y^{0.5}$

$$z_x = 0.3x^{-0.7}y^{0.5} \qquad z_y = 0.5x^{0.3}y^{-0.5}$$
$$z_{xy} = 0.15x^{-0.7}y^{-0.5} \qquad z_{yx} = 0.15x^{-0.7}y^{-0.5}$$

(b) $f(x, y) = x^{0.1}y^{0.8}$

$$f_x = 0.1x^{-0.9}y^{0.8} \qquad f_y = 0.8x^{0.1}y^{-0.2}$$
$$f_{xy} = 0.08x^{-0.9}y^{-0.2} \qquad f_{yx} = 0.08x^{-0.9}y^{-0.2}$$

(c) $z = w^3x^4y^3$

$$z_w = 3w^2x^4y^3 \qquad z_x = 4w^3x^3y^3 \qquad z_y = 3w^3x^4y^2$$
$$z_{wx} = 12w^2x^3y^3 \qquad z_{xw} = 12w^2x^3y^3 \qquad z_{yw} = 9w^2x^4y^2$$
$$z_{wy} = 9w^2x^4y^2 \qquad z_{xy} = 12w^3x^3y^2 \qquad z_{yx} = 12w^3x^3y^2$$

(d) $f(x, y, z) = x^3y^{-4}z^{-5}$

$$f_x = 3x^2y^{-4}z^{-5} \qquad f_y = -4x^3y^{-5}z^{-5} \qquad f_z = -5x^3y^{-4}z^{-6}$$
$$f_{xy} = -12x^2y^{-5}z^{-5} \qquad f_{yx} = -12x^2y^{-5}z^{-5} \qquad f_{zx} = -15x^2y^{-4}z^{-6}$$
$$f_{xz} = -15x^2y^{-4}z^{-6} \qquad f_{yz} = 20x^3y^{-5}z^{-6} \qquad f_{zy} = 20x^3y^{-5}z^{-6}$$

Note how by Young's theorem in (c) $z_{wx} = z_{xw}$, $z_{yw} = z_{wy}$, and $z_{xy} = z_{yx}$ and in (d) $f_{xy} = f_{yx}$, $f_{xz} = f_{zx}$, and $f_{yz} = f_{zy}$.

OPTIMIZING MULTIVARIABLE FUNCTIONS

5.10 For each of the following quadratic functions, (1) find the critical points at which the function may be optimized and (2) determine whether at these points the function is maximized, is minimized, is at an inflection point, or is at a saddle point.

(a) $z = 3x^2 - xy + 2y^2 - 4x - 7y + 12$

(1) Take the first-order partial derivatives, set them equal to zero, and solve simultaneously, using the methods of Section 1.6.

$$z_x = 6x - y - 4 = 0 \qquad (5.15)$$
$$z_y = -x + 4y - 7 = 0 \qquad (5.16)$$
$$x = 1 \qquad y = 2 \qquad (1, 2) \qquad \text{critical point}$$

(2) Take the second-order direct partial derivatives from (5.15) and (5.16), evaluate them at the critical point, and check signs.

$$z_{xx} = 6 \qquad\qquad z_{yy} = 4$$
$$z_{xx}(1, 2) = 6 > 0 \qquad z_{yy}(1, 2) = 4 > 0$$

With both second-order direct partial derivatives positive, the function is possibly at a relative minimum. Now take the cross partial from (5.15) or (5.16),

$$z_{xy} = -1 = z_{yx}$$

evaluate it at the critical point and test the third condition:

$$z_{xy}(1, 2) = -1 = z_{yx}(1, 2)$$
$$z_{xx}(1, 2) \quad \cdot \quad z_{yy}(1, 2) > [z_{xy}(1, 2)]^2$$
$$6 \quad \cdot \quad 4 \ > \ (-1)^2$$

With $z_{xx} z_{yy} > (z_{xy})^2$ and $z_{xx}, z_{yy} > 0$, the function is at a relative minimum at $(1, 2)$.

(b) $f(x, y) = 60x + 34y - 4xy - 6x^2 - 3y^2 + 5$

(1) Take the first-order partials, set them equal to zero, and solve.

$$f_x = 60 - 4y - 12x = 0 \qquad (5.17)$$
$$f_y = 34 - 6y - 4x = 0 \qquad (5.18)$$
$$x = 4 \qquad y = 3 \qquad (4, 3) \qquad \text{critical point}$$

(2) Take the second-order direct partials, evaluate them at the critical point, and check their signs.

$$f_{xx} = -12 \qquad\qquad f_{yy} = -6$$
$$f_{xx}(4, 3) = -12 < 0 \qquad f_{yy}(4, 3) = -6 < 0$$

Take the cross partial from (5.17) or (5.18),

$$f_{xy} = -4 = f_{yx}$$

evaluate it at the critical point and test the third condition:

$$f_{xy}(4, 3) = -4 = f_{yx}(4, 3)$$
$$f_{xx}(4, 3) \cdot f_{yy}(4, 3) > [f_{xy}(4, 3)]^2$$
$$-12 \quad \cdot \quad -6 \ > \ (-4)^2$$

With $f_{xx} f_{yy} > (f_{xy})^2$ and $f_{xx}, f_{yy} < 0$, the function is at a relative maximum at $(4, 3)$.

(c) $z = 48y - 3x^2 - 6xy - 2y^2 + 72x$

(1)
$$z_x = -6x - 6y + 72 = 0$$
$$z_y = -6x - 4y + 48 = 0$$
$$x = 0 \quad y = 12 \quad (0, 12) \quad \text{critical point}$$

(2) Test the second-order direct partials at the critical point.

$$z_{xx} = -6 \qquad\qquad z_{yy} = -4$$
$$z_{xx}(0, 12) = -6 < 0 \qquad z_{yy}(0, 12) = -4 < 0$$

With z_{xx} and $z_{yy} < 0$ at the critical point, the function may be at a relative maximum. Test the cross partials to be sure.

$$z_{xy} = -6 = z_{yx}$$
$$z_{xy}(0, 12) = -6 = z_{yx}(0, 12)$$
$$z_{xx}(0, 12) \cdot z_{yy}(0, 12) > [z_{xy}(0, 12)]^2$$
$$-6 \quad \cdot \quad -4 \quad \ngtr \quad (-6)^2$$

With z_{xx} and z_{yy} of the same sign and $z_{xx}z_{yy} < (z_{xy})^2$, the function is at an inflection point at $(0, 12)$.

(d) $f(x, y) = 5x^2 - 3y^2 - 30x + 7y + 4xy$

(1)
$$f_x = 10x + 4y - 30 = 0$$
$$f_y = 4x - 6y + 7 = 0$$
$$x = 2 \quad y = 2.5 \quad (2, 2.5) \quad \text{critical point}$$

(2)
$$f_{xx} = 10 \qquad\qquad f_{yy} = -6$$
$$f_{xx}(2, 2.5) = 10 > 0 \qquad f_{yy}(2, 2.5) = -6 < 0$$

Testing the cross partials,

$$f_{xy} = 4 = f_{yx}$$
$$f_{xx}(2, 2.5) \quad \cdot \quad f_{yy}(2, 2.5) > [f_{xy}(2, 2.5)]^2$$
$$10 \quad \cdot \quad -6 \quad \ngtr \quad 4^2$$

Whenever f_{xx} and f_{yy} are of different signs, $f_{xx}f_{yy}$ cannot be greater than $(f_{xy})^2$, and the function will be at a saddle point.

5.11. For the following cubic functions, (1) find the critical points and (2) determine if at these points the function is at a relative maximum, relative minimum, inflection point, or saddle point.

(a) $z(x, y) = 3x^3 - 5y^2 - 225x + 70y + 23$

(1) Take the first-order partials and set them equal to zero.

$$z_x = 9x^2 - 225 = 0 \qquad\qquad (5.19)$$
$$z_y = -10y + 70 = 0 \qquad\qquad (5.20)$$

Solve for the critical points.

$$9x^2 = 225 \qquad -10y = -70$$
$$x^2 = 25 \qquad\qquad y = 7$$
$$x = \pm 5$$
$$(5, 7) \quad (-5, 7) \quad \text{critical points}$$

(2) From (5.19) and (5.20), take the second-order direct partials,

$$z_{xx} = 18x \qquad z_{yy} = -10$$

evaluate them at the critical points and note the signs.

$$z_{xx}(5, 7) = 18(5) = 90 > 0 \qquad z_{yy}(5, 7) = -10 < 0$$
$$z_{xx}(-5, 7) = 18(-5) = -90 < 0 \qquad z_{yy}(-5, 7) = -10 < 0$$

Then take the cross partial from (5.19) or (5.20),

$$z_{xy} = 0 = z_{yx}$$

evaluate it at the critical points and test the third condition.

	$z_{xx}(a, b) \cdot z_{yy}(a, b)$		$> [z_{xy}(a, b)]^2$
At (5, 7),	90 $\cdot$ -10	$<$	0
At (−5, 7),	-90 $\cdot$ -10	$>$	0

With $z_{xx} z_{yy} > (z_{xy})^2$ and $z_{xx}, z_{yy} < 0$ at $(-5, 7)$, $z(-5, 7)$ is a relative maximum. With $z_{xx} z_{yy} < (z_{xy})^2$ and z_{xx} and z_{yy} of different signs at $(5, 7)$, $z(5, 7)$ is a saddle point.

(b) $f(x, y) = 3x^3 + 1.5y^2 - 18xy + 17$

(1) Set the first-order partial derivatives equal to zero,

$$f_x = 9x^2 - 18y = 0 \qquad\qquad (5.21)$$

$$f_y = 3y - 18x = 0 \qquad\qquad (5.22)$$

and solve for the critical values:

$$18y = 9x^2 \qquad 3y = 18x$$
$$y = \tfrac{1}{2}x^2 \qquad y = 6x \qquad\qquad (5.23)$$

Setting y equal to y,

$$\tfrac{1}{2}x^2 = 6x$$
$$x^2 - 12x = 0$$
$$x(x - 12) = 0$$
$$x = 0 \qquad x = 12$$

Substituting $x = 0$ and $x = 12$ in $y = 6x$ from (5.23),

$$y = 6(0) = 0$$
$$y = 6(12) = 72$$

Therefore,   (0, 0)   (12, 72)   critical points

(2) Take the second-order direct partials from (5.21) and (5.22),

$$f_{xx} = 18x \qquad f_{yy} = 3$$

evaluate them at the critical points and note the signs.

$$f_{xx}(0, 0) = 18(0) = 0 \qquad\qquad f_{yy}(0, 0) = 3 > 0$$
$$f_{xx}(12, 72) = 18(12) = 216 > 0 \qquad f_{yy}(12, 72) = 3 > 0$$

Then take the cross partial from (5.21) or (5.22),

$$f_{xy} = -18 = f_{yx}$$

evaluate it at the critical points and test the third condition.

	$f_{xx}(a, b) \cdot f_{yy}(a, b) > [f_{xy}(a, b)]^2$		
At (0, 0),	0 $\cdot$ 3	$<$	$(-18)^2$
At (12, 72),	216 $\cdot$ 3	$>$	$(-18)^2$
	648 $>$ 324		

With $f_{xx} f_{yy} > (f_{xy})^2$ and $f_{xx}, f_{yy} > 0$ at $(12, 72)$, $f(12, 72)$ is a relative minimum. With $f_{xx} f_{yy} < (f_{xy})^2$ and f_{xx} and f_{yy} of the same sign at $(0, 0)$, $f(0, 0)$ is an inflection point.

(c) $f = 3x^3 - 9xy + 3y^3$

(1)
$$f_x = 9x^2 - 9y = 0 \qquad (5.24)$$
$$f_y = 9y^2 - 9x = 0 \qquad (5.25)$$

From (5.24), $9y = 9x^2 \qquad y = x^2$

Substitute $y = x^2$ in (5.25),

$$9(x^2)^2 - 9x = 0$$
$$9x^4 - 9x = 0$$
$$9x(x^3 - 1) = 0$$
$$9x = 0 \quad \text{or} \quad x^3 - 1 = 0$$
$$x = 0 \qquad\qquad x^3 = 1$$
$$x = 1$$

Substituting these values in (5.24), we find that if $x = 0$, $y = 0$, and if $x = 1$, $y = 1$. Therefore,

$$(0, 0) \qquad (1, 1) \qquad \text{critical points}$$

(2)   Test the second-order conditions from (5.24) and (5.25).

$$f_{xx} = 18x \qquad\qquad f_{yy} = 18y$$
$$f_{xx}(0, 0) = 18(0) = 0 \qquad f_{yy}(0, 0) = 18(0) = 0$$
$$f_{xx}(1, 1) = 18(1) = 18 > 0 \qquad f_{yy}(1, 1) = 18(1) = 18 > 0$$
$$f_{xy} = -9 = f_{yx}$$

$$f_{xx}(a, b) \;\cdot\; f_{yy}(a, b) > [f_{xy}(a, b)]^2$$

At (0, 0), $0 \quad\cdot\quad 0 \quad < \quad (-9)^2$

At (1, 1), $18 \quad\cdot\quad 18 \quad > \quad (-9)^2$

With f_{xx} and $f_{yy} > 0$ and $f_{xx} f_{yy} > (f_{xy})^2$ at (1, 1), the function is at a relative minimum at (1, 1). With f_{xx} and f_{yy} of the same sign at (0, 0) and $f_{xx} f_{yy} < (f_{xy})^2$, the function is at an inflection point at (0, 0).

(d) $f(x, y) = x^3 - 6x^2 + 2y^3 + 9y^2 - 63x - 60y$

(1)
$$f_x = 3x^2 - 12x - 63 = 0 \qquad f_y = 6y^2 + 18y - 60 = 0 \qquad (5.26)$$
$$3(x^2 - 4x - 21) = 0 \qquad 6(y^2 + 3y - 10) = 0$$
$$(x + 3)(x - 7) = 0 \qquad (y - 2)(y + 5) = 0$$
$$x = -3 \quad x = 7 \qquad\qquad y = 2 \quad y = -5$$

Hence $(-3, 2) \qquad (-3, -5) \qquad (7, 2) \qquad (7, -5) \qquad \text{critical points}$

(2)   Test the second-order direct partials at each of the critical points. From (5.26),

$$f_{xx} = 6x - 12 \qquad\qquad f_{yy} = 12y + 18$$

(i) $f_{xx}(-3, 2) = -30 < 0 \qquad f_{yy}(-3, 2) = 42 > 0$

(ii) $f_{xx}(-3, -5) = -30 < 0 \qquad f_{yy}(-3, -5) = -42 < 0$

(iii) $f_{xx}(7, 2) = 30 > 0 \qquad f_{yy}(7, 2) = 42 > 0$

(iv) $f_{xx}(7, -5) = 30 > 0 \qquad f_{yy}(7, -5) = -42 < 0$

With different signs in (i) and (iv), $(-3, 2)$ and $(7, -5)$ can be ignored, if desired, as saddle points. Now take the cross partial from (5.26) and test the third condition.

$$f_{xy} = 0 = f_{yx}$$

$$f_{xx}(a, b) \;\cdot\; f_{yy}(a, b) > [f_{xy}(a, b)]^2$$

From (ii), $(-30) \quad\cdot\quad (-42) \quad > \quad (0)^2$

From (iii), $(30) \quad\cdot\quad (42) \quad > \quad (0)^2$

The function is at a relative maximum at $(-3, -5)$, at a relative minimum at $(7, 2)$, and at a saddle point at $(-3, 2)$ and $(7, -5)$.

CONSTRAINED OPTIMIZATION AND LAGRANGE MULTIPLIERS

5.12. (1) Use Lagrange multipliers to optimize the following functions subject to the given constraint, and (2) estimate the effect on the value of the objective function from a 1-unit change in the constant of the constraint.

(*a*) $z = 4x^2 - 2xy + 6y^2$ subject to $x + y = 72$

(1) Set the constraint equal to zero, multiply it by λ, and add it to the objective function, to obtain

$$Z = 4x^2 - 2xy + 6y^2 + \lambda(72 - x - y)$$

The first-order conditions are

$$Z_x = 8x - 2y - \lambda = 0 \qquad (5.27)$$

$$Z_y = -2x + 12y - \lambda = 0 \qquad (5.28)$$

$$Z_\lambda = 72 - x - y = 0 \qquad (5.29)$$

Subtract (5.28) from (5.27) to eliminate λ.

$$10x - 14y = 0 \qquad x = 1.4y$$

Substitute $x = 1.4y$ in (5.29) and rearrange.

$$1.4y + y = 72 \qquad y_0 = 30$$

Substitute $y_0 = 30$ in the previous equations to find that at the critical point

$$x_0 = 42 \qquad y_0 = 30 \qquad \lambda_0 = 276$$

Thus, $Z = 4(42)^2 - 2(42)(30) + 6(30)^2 + 276(72 - 42 - 30) = 9936$.

(2) With $\lambda = 276$, a 1-unit increase in the constant of the constraint will lead to an increase of approximately 276 in the value of the objective function, and $Z \approx 10\,212$.

(*b*) $f(x, y) = 26x - 3x^2 + 5xy - 6y^2 + 12y$ subject to $3x + y = 170$

(1) The Lagrangian function is

$$F = 26x - 3x^2 + 5xy - 6y^2 + 12y + \lambda(170 - 3x - y)$$

Thus,
$$F_x = 26 - 6x + 5y - 3\lambda = 0 \qquad (5.30)$$

$$F_y = 5x - 12y + 12 - \lambda = 0 \qquad (5.31)$$

$$F_\lambda = 170 - 3x - y = 0 \qquad (5.32)$$

Multiply (5.31) by 3 and subtract from (5.30) to eliminate λ.

$$-21x + 41y - 10 = 0 \qquad (5.33)$$

Multiply (5.32) by 7 and subtract from (5.33) to eliminate x.

$$48y - 1200 = 0 \qquad y_0 = 25$$

Then substituting $y_0 = 25$ into the previous equations shows that at the critical point

$$x_0 = \frac{145}{3} = 48\frac{1}{3} \qquad y_0 = 25 \qquad \lambda_0 = \frac{-139}{3} = -46\frac{1}{3}$$

Using $x_0 = \frac{145}{3}$, $y_0 = 25$, and $\lambda_0 = \frac{-139}{3}$, $F = -3160$.

(2)   With $\lambda = -46\frac{1}{3}$, a 1-unit increase in the constant of the constraint will lead to a *decrease* of approximately $46\frac{1}{3}$ in the value of the objective function, and $F \approx -3206.33$.

(c) $f(x, y, z) = 4xyz^2$ subject to $x + y + z = 56$

(1) $F = 4xyz^2 + \lambda(56 - x - y - z)$

$$F_x = 4yz^2 - \lambda = 0 \tag{5.34}$$

$$F_y = 4xz^2 - \lambda = 0 \tag{5.35}$$

$$F_z = 8xyz - \lambda = 0 \tag{5.36}$$

$$F_\lambda = 56 - x - y - z = 0 \tag{5.37}$$

Equate λ's from (5.34) and (5.35).

$$4yz^2 = 4xz^2 \qquad y = x$$

Equate λ's from (5.34) and (5.36).

$$4yz^2 = 8xyz \qquad z = 2x$$

Substitute $y = x$ and $z = 2x$ in (5.37).

$$56 - x - x - 2x = 0 \qquad 4x = 56 \qquad x_0 = 14$$

Then substituting $x_0 = 14$ in the previous equations gives

$$x_0 = 14 \qquad y_0 = 14 \qquad z_0 = 28 \qquad \lambda_0 = 43\,904$$
$$F_0 = 614\,656$$

(2) $F_1 \approx F_0 + \lambda_0 \approx 614\,656 + 43\,904 \approx 658\,560$

See Problem 12.32 for the second-order conditions.

(d) $f(x, y, z) = 5xy + 8xz + 3yz$ subject to $2xyz = 1920$

(1) $F = 5xy + 8xz + 3yz + \lambda(1920 - 2xyz)$

$$F_x = 5y + 8z - 2\lambda yz = 0 \tag{5.38}$$

$$F_y = 5x + 3z - 2\lambda xz = 0 \tag{5.39}$$

$$F_z = 8x + 3y - 2\lambda xy = 0 \tag{5.40}$$

$$F_\lambda = 1920 - 2xyz = 0 \tag{5.41}$$

Solve (5.38), (5.39), and (5.40) for λ.

$$\lambda = \frac{5y + 8z}{2yz} = \frac{2.5}{z} + \frac{4}{y} \tag{5.42}$$

$$\lambda = \frac{5x + 3z}{2xz} = \frac{2.5}{z} + \frac{1.5}{x} \tag{5.43}$$

$$\lambda = \frac{8x + 3y}{2xy} = \frac{4}{y} + \frac{1.5}{x} \tag{5.44}$$

Equate λ's in (5.42) and (5.43) to eliminate $2.5/z$,

$$\frac{4}{y} = \frac{1.5}{x} \qquad 4x = 1.5y \qquad x = \frac{1.5}{4}\,y$$

and λ's in (5.43) and (5.44) to eliminate $1.5/x$.

$$\frac{2.5}{z} = \frac{4}{y} \qquad 4z = 2.5y \qquad z = \frac{2.5}{4}\,y$$

Then substitute $x = (1.5/4)y$ and $z = (2.5/4)y$ in (5.41).

$$1920 = 2 \cdot \left(\frac{1.5}{4}\,y\right) \cdot y \cdot \left(\frac{2.5}{4}\,y\right)$$

$$y^3 = 1920 \cdot \frac{16}{7.5} = 4096$$

$$y_0 = 16$$

and the critical values are $x_0 = 6$, $y_0 = 16$, $z_0 = 10$, and $\lambda_0 = 0.5$.

$$F_0 = 1440$$

(2) $$F_1 \approx F_0 + \lambda_0 \approx 1440 + 0.5 \approx 1440.5$$

5.13. In Problem 5.12(a) it was estimated that if the constant of the constraint were increased by 1 unit, the constrained optimum would increase by approximately 276, from 9936 to 10 212. Check the accuracy of the estimate by optimizing the original function $z = 4x^2 - 2xy + 6y^2$ subject to a new constraint $x + y = 73$.

$$Z = 4x^2 - 2xy + 6y^2 + \lambda(73 - x - y)$$
$$Z_x = 8x - 2y - \lambda = 0$$
$$Z_y = -2x + 12y - \lambda = 0$$
$$Z_\lambda = 73 - x - y = 0$$

Simultaneous solution gives $x_0 = 42.58$, $y_0 = 30.42$, $\lambda_0 = 279.8$. Thus, $Z_0 = 10\,213.9$, compared to the 10 212 estimate from the original λ, a difference of 1.9 units or 0.02 percent.

5.14. Constraints can also be used simply to ensure that the two independent variables will always be in constant proportion, for example, $x = 3y$. In this case measuring the effect of λ has no economic significance since a 1-unit increase in the constant of the constraint would alter the constant proportion between the independent variables. With this in mind, optimize the following functions subject to the constant proportion constraint:

(a) $z = 4x^2 - 3x + 5xy - 8y + 2y^2$ subject to $x = 2y$

With $x - 2y = 0$, the Lagrangian function is

$$Z = 4x^2 - 3x + 5xy - 8y + 2y^2 + \lambda(x - 2y)$$
$$Z_x = 8x - 3 + 5y + \lambda = 0$$
$$Z_y = 5x - 8 + 4y - 2\lambda = 0$$
$$Z_\lambda = x - 2y = 0$$

When solved simultaneously, $x_0 = 0.5$, $y_0 = 0.25$, and $\lambda_0 = -2.25$. Thus, $Z_0 = -1.75$.

(b) $z = -5x^2 + 7x + 10xy + 9y - 2y^2$ subject to $y = 5x$

The Lagrangian function is $Z = -5x^2 + 7x + 10xy + 9y - 2y^2 + \lambda(5x - y)$

$$Z_x = -10x + 7 + 10y + 5\lambda = 0$$
$$Z_y = 10x + 9 - 4y - \lambda = 0$$
$$Z_\lambda = 5x - y = 0$$

Solving simultaneously, $x_0 = 5.2$, $y_0 = 26$, and $\lambda_0 = -43$. Thus, $Z_0 = 135.2$.

See also Problems 12.23 to 12.32.

DIFFERENTIALS

5.15. Find the differential dy for each of the following functions:

(a) $y = 7x^3 - 5x^2 + 6x - 3$

$$\frac{dy}{dx} = 21x^2 - 10x + 6$$

Thus, $dy = (21x^2 - 10x + 6)\,dx$

(b) $y = (4x + 3)(3x - 8)$

$$\frac{dy}{dx} = (4x + 3)(3) + (3x - 8)(4) = 24x - 23$$

Thus, $dy = (24x - 23)\,dx$

(c) $y = \dfrac{9x - 4}{5x}$

$$\frac{dy}{dx} = \frac{5x(9) - (9x - 4)(5)}{(5x)^2} = \frac{20}{25x^2}$$

$$dy = \frac{4}{5x^2}\,dx$$

(d) $y = (11x + 9)^3$

$$\frac{dy}{dx} = 3(11x + 9)^2(11)$$

$$dy = 33(11x + 9)^2\,dx$$

5.16. Find the total differential $dz = z_x\,dx + z_y\,dy$ for each of the following functions:

(a) $z = 5x^3 - 12xy - 6y^5$

$$z_x = 15x^2 - 12y \qquad z_y = -12x - 30y^4$$
$$dz = (15x^2 - 12y)\,dx - (12x + 30y^4)\,dy$$

(b) $z = 7x^2y^3$

$$z_x = 14xy^3 \qquad z_y = 21x^2y^2$$
$$dz = 14xy^3\,dx + 21x^2y^2\,dy$$

(c) $z = 3x^2(8x - 7y)$

$$z_x = 3x^2(8) + (8x - 7y)(6x) \qquad z_y = 3x^2(-7) + (8x - 7y)(0)$$
$$dz = (72x^2 - 42xy)\,dx - 21x^2\,dy$$

(d) $z = (5x^2 + 7y)(2x - 4y^3)$

$$z_x = (5x^2 + 7y)(2) + (2x - 4y^3)(10x) \qquad z_y = (5x^2 + 7y)(-12y^2) + (2x - 4y^3)(7)$$
$$dz = (30x^2 - 40xy^3 + 14y)\,dx - (112y^3 + 60x^2y^2 - 14x)\,dy$$

(e) $z = \dfrac{9y^3}{x - y}$

$$z_x = \frac{(x - y)(0) - 9y^3(1)}{(x - y)^2} \qquad z_y = \frac{(x - y)(27y^2) - 9y^3(-1)}{(x - y)^2}$$
$$dz = \frac{-9y^3}{(x - y)^2}\,dx + \frac{27xy^2 - 18y^3}{(x - y)^2}\,dy$$

(f) $z = (x - 3y)^3$

$$z_x = 3(x - 3y)^2(1) \qquad z_y = 3(x - 3y)^2(-3)$$
$$dz = 3(x - 3y)^2\, dx - 9(x - 3y)^2\, dy$$

5.17. Find the partial differential for a small change in x for each of the functions given in Problem 5.16, assuming $dy = 0$.

(a) $dz = (15x^2 - 12y)\, dx$ (b) $dz = 14xy^3\, dx$ (c) $dz = (72x^2 - 42xy)\, dx$

(d) $dz = (30x^2 - 40xy^3 + 14y)\, dx$ (e) $dz = \dfrac{-9y^3}{(x - y)^2}\, dx$ (f) $dz = 3(x - 3y)^2\, dx$

TOTAL DERIVATIVES

5.18. Find the total derivative dz/dx for each of the following functions:

(a) $z = 6x^2 + 15xy + 3y^2$ where $y = 7x^2$

$$\frac{dz}{dx} = z_x + z_y \frac{dy}{dx}$$
$$= (12x + 15y) + (15x + 6y)(14x)$$
$$= 210x^2 + 84xy + 12x + 15y$$

(b) $z = (13x - 18y)^2$ where $y = x + 6$

$$\frac{dz}{dx} = z_x + z_y \frac{dy}{dx}$$
$$= 26(13x - 18y) - 36(13x - 18y)(1)$$
$$= -10(13x - 18y)$$

(c) $z = \dfrac{9x - 7y}{2x + 5y}$ where $y = 3x - 4$

$$\frac{dz}{dx} = z_x + z_y \frac{dy}{dx}$$
$$= \frac{59y}{(2x + 5y)^2} - \frac{59x}{(2x + 5y)^2}(3) = \frac{59(y - 3x)}{(2x + 5y)^2}$$

(d) $z = 8x - 12y$ where $y = (x + 1)/x^2$

$$\frac{dz}{dx} = z_x + z_y \frac{dy}{dx}$$
$$= 8 - \frac{12(-x^2 - 2x)}{x^4}$$
$$= 8 + \frac{12(x + 2)}{x^3}$$

5.19. Find the total derivative dz/dw for each of the following functions:

(a) $z = 7x^2 + 4y^2$ where $x = 5w$ and $y = 4w$

$$\frac{dz}{dw} = z_x \frac{dx}{dw} + z_y \frac{dy}{dw} = 14x(5) + 8y(4) = 70x + 32y$$

(b) $z = 10x^2 - 6xy - 12y^2$ where $x = 2w$ and $y = 3w$

$$\frac{dz}{dw} = z_x \frac{dx}{dw} + z_y \frac{dy}{dw} = (20x - 6y)(2) + (-6x - 24y)(3) = 22x - 84y$$

IMPLICIT AND INVERSE FUNCTION RULES

5.20.   Find the derivatives dy/dx and dx/dy for each of the following implicit functions:

(a) $y - 6x + 7 = 0$

$$\frac{dy}{dx} = \frac{-f_x}{f_y} = \frac{-(-6)}{1} = 6 \qquad \frac{dx}{dy} = \frac{-f_y}{f_x} = \frac{-(1)}{-6} = \frac{1}{6}$$

(b) $3y - 12x + 17 = 0$

$$\frac{dy}{dx} = \frac{-f_x}{f_y} = \frac{-(-12)}{3} = 4 \qquad \frac{dx}{dy} = \frac{-f_y}{f_x} = \frac{-(3)}{-12} = \frac{1}{4}$$

(c) $x^2 + 6x - 13 - y = 0$

$$\frac{dy}{dx} = \frac{-f_x}{f_y} = \frac{-(2x + 6)}{-1} = 2x + 6 \qquad \frac{dx}{dy} = \frac{-f_y}{f_x} = \frac{-(-1)}{2x + 6} = \frac{1}{2x + 6} \qquad (x \neq -3)$$

Notice that in each of the above cases, one derivative is the inverse of the other.

5.21.   Use the implicit function rule to find dy/dx and, where applicable, dy/dz.

(a) $f(x, y) = 3x^2 + 2xy + 4y^3$

$$\frac{dy}{dx} = \frac{-f_x}{f_y} = -\frac{6x + 2y}{12y^2 + 2x}$$

(b) $f(x, y) = 12x^5 - 2y$

$$\frac{dy}{dx} = \frac{-f_x}{f_y} = \frac{-60x^4}{-2} = 30x^4$$

(c) $f(x, y) = 7x^2 + 2xy^2 + 9y^4$

$$\frac{dy}{dx} = \frac{-f_x}{f_y} = -\frac{14x + 2y^2}{36y^3 + 4xy}$$

(d) $f(x, y) = 6x^3 - 5y$

$$\frac{dy}{dx} = \frac{-f_x}{f_y} = -\frac{18x^2}{-5} = 3.6x^2$$

(e) $f(x, y, z) = x^2y^3 + z^2 + xyz$

$$\frac{dy}{dx} = \frac{-f_x}{f_y} = -\frac{2xy^3 + yz}{3x^2y^2 + xz}$$

$$\frac{dy}{dz} = \frac{-f_z}{f_y} = -\frac{2z + xy}{3x^2y^2 + xz}$$

(f) $f(x, y, z) = x^3z^2 + y^3 + 4xyz$

$$\frac{dy}{dx} = \frac{-f_x}{f_y} = -\frac{3x^2z^2 + 4yz}{3y^2 + 4xz}$$

$$\frac{dy}{dz} = \frac{-f_z}{f_y} = -\frac{2x^3z + 4xy}{3y^2 + 4xz}$$

5.22.   Find the derivative for the inverse function dP/dQ.

(a) $Q = 210 - 3P$

$$\frac{dP}{dQ} = \frac{1}{dQ/dP} = -\frac{1}{3}$$

(b) $Q = 35 - 0.25P$

$$\frac{dP}{dQ} = \frac{1}{-0.25} = -4$$

(c) $Q = 14 + P^2$

$$\frac{dP}{dQ} = \frac{1}{2P} \qquad (P \neq 0)$$

(d) $Q = P^3 + 2P^2 + 7P$

$$\frac{dP}{dQ} = \frac{1}{3P^2 + 4P + 7}$$

VERIFICATION OF RULES

5.23. For each of the following functions, use (1) the definition in (5.1a) to find $\partial z/\partial x$ and (2) the definition in (5.1b) to find $\partial z/\partial y$ in order to confirm the rules of differentiation.

(a) $z = 38 + 7x - 4y$

(1)   From (5.1a),

$$\frac{\partial z}{\partial x} = \lim_{\Delta x \to 0} \frac{f(x + \Delta x, y) - f(x, y)}{\Delta x}$$

Substituting,

$$\frac{\partial z}{\partial x} = \lim_{\Delta x \to 0} \frac{[38 + 7(x + \Delta x) - 4y] - (38 + 7x - 4y)}{\Delta x}$$

$$= \lim_{\Delta x \to 0} \frac{38 + 7x + 7\Delta x - 4y - 38 - 7x + 4y}{\Delta x}$$

$$= \lim_{\Delta x \to 0} \frac{7\Delta x}{\Delta x} = \lim_{\Delta x \to 0} 7 = 7$$

(2)   From (5.1b),

$$\frac{\partial z}{\partial y} = \lim_{\Delta y \to 0} \frac{f(x, y + \Delta y) - f(x, y)}{\Delta y}$$

Substituting,

$$\frac{\partial z}{\partial y} = \lim_{\Delta y \to 0} \frac{[38 + 7x - 4(y + \Delta y)] - (38 + 7x - 4y)}{\Delta y}$$

$$= \lim_{\Delta y \to 0} \frac{38 + 7x - 4y - 4\Delta y - 38 - 7x + 4y}{\Delta y}$$

$$= \lim_{\Delta y \to 0} \frac{-4\Delta y}{\Delta y} = \lim_{\Delta y \to 0} (-4) = -4$$

(b) $z = 18x - 5xy + 14y$

(1)

$$\frac{\partial z}{\partial x} = \lim_{\Delta x \to 0} \frac{[18(x + \Delta x) - 5(x + \Delta x)y + 14y] - (18x - 5xy + 14y)}{\Delta x}$$

$$= \lim_{\Delta x \to 0} \frac{18x + 18\Delta x - 5xy - 5\Delta xy + 14y - 18x + 5xy - 14y}{\Delta x}$$

$$= \lim_{\Delta x \to 0} \frac{18\Delta x - 5\Delta xy}{\Delta x} = \lim_{\Delta x \to 0} (18 - 5y) = 18 - 5y$$

(2)

$$\frac{\partial z}{\partial y} = \lim_{\Delta y \to 0} \frac{[18x - 5x(y + \Delta y) + 14(y + \Delta y)] - (18x - 5xy + 14y)}{\Delta y}$$

$$= \lim_{\Delta y \to 0} \frac{18x - 5xy - 5x\,\Delta y + 14y + 14\Delta y - 18x + 5xy - 14y}{\Delta y}$$

$$= \lim_{\Delta y \to 0} \frac{-5x\,\Delta y + 14\Delta y}{\Delta y} = \lim_{\Delta y \to 0} (-5x + 14) = -5x + 14$$

(c) $z = 3x^2 y$

(1)
$$\frac{\partial z}{\partial x} = \lim_{\Delta x \to 0} \frac{[3(x + \Delta x)^2 y] - 3x^2 y}{\Delta x}$$
$$= \lim_{\Delta x \to 0} \frac{3x^2 y + 6x\,\Delta xy + 3(\Delta x)^2 y - 3x^2 y}{\Delta x}$$
$$= \lim_{\Delta x \to 0} \frac{6x\,\Delta xy + 3(\Delta x)^2 y}{\Delta x}$$
$$= \lim_{\Delta x \to 0} (6xy + 3\Delta xy) = 6xy$$

(2)
$$\frac{\partial z}{\partial y} = \lim_{\Delta y \to 0} \frac{[3x^2(y + \Delta y)] - 3x^2 y}{\Delta y}$$
$$= \lim_{\Delta y \to 0} \frac{3x^2 y + 3x^2\,\Delta y - 3x^2 y}{\Delta y} = \lim_{\Delta y \to 0} \frac{3x^2\,\Delta y}{\Delta y} = \lim_{\Delta y \to 0} 3x^2 = 3x^2$$

(d) $z = 4x^2 y^2$

(1)
$$\frac{\partial z}{\partial x} = \lim_{\Delta x \to 0} \frac{[4(x + \Delta x)^2 y^2] - 4x^2 y^2}{\Delta x}$$
$$= \lim_{\Delta x \to 0} \frac{4x^2 y^2 + 8x\,\Delta xy^2 + 4(\Delta x)^2 y^2 - 4x^2 y^2}{\Delta x}$$
$$= \lim_{\Delta x \to 0} \frac{8x\,\Delta xy^2 + 4(\Delta x)^2 y^2}{\Delta x}$$
$$= \lim_{\Delta x \to 0} (8xy^2 + 4\Delta xy^2) = 8xy^2$$

(2)
$$\frac{\partial z}{\partial y} = \lim_{\Delta y \to 0} \frac{[4x^2(y + \Delta y)^2] - 4x^2 y^2}{\Delta y}$$
$$= \lim_{\Delta y \to 0} \frac{4x^2 y^2 + 8x^2 y\,\Delta y + 4x^2(\Delta y)^2 - 4x^2 y^2}{\Delta y}$$
$$= \lim_{\Delta y \to 0} \frac{8x^2 y\,\Delta y + 4x^2(\Delta y)^2}{\Delta y} = \lim_{\Delta y \to 0} (8x^2 y + 4x^2\,\Delta y) = 8x^2 y$$

Chapter 6

Calculus of Multivariable Functions in Economics

6.1 MARGINAL PRODUCTIVITY

The *marginal physical product* of capital (MPP_K) is defined as the change in output brought about by a small change in capital when all the other factors of production are held constant. Given a production function such as

$$Q = 36KL - 2K^2 - 3L^2$$

the MPP_K is measured by taking the partial derivative $\partial Q/\partial K$. Thus,

$$MPP_K = \frac{\partial Q}{\partial K} = 36L - 4K$$

Similarly, for labor, $MPP_L = \partial Q/\partial L = 36K - 6L$. See Problems 6.1 to 6.3.

6.2 INCOME DETERMINATION MULTIPLIERS

The partial derivative can also be used to derive the various multipliers of an income determination model. Given

$$Y = C + I + G + (X - Z)$$

where

$$C = C_0 + bY \qquad G = G_0 \qquad Z = Z_0$$
$$I = I_0 + aY \qquad X = X_0$$

from a problem such as Problem 2.19, it is clear that the equilibrium level of income is

$$\bar{Y} = \frac{1}{1 - b - a}(C_0 + I_0 + G_0 + X_0 - Z_0) \tag{6.1}$$

Taking the partial derivative of (6.1) with respect to any of the variables or parameters gives the multiplier for that variable or parameter. Thus, the government multiplier is given by

$$\frac{\partial \bar{Y}}{\partial G_0} = \frac{1}{1 - b - a}$$

The import multiplier is given by

$$\frac{\partial \bar{Y}}{\partial Z_0} = -\frac{1}{1 - b - a}$$

And the multiplier for a change in the marginal propensity to invest is given by $\partial \bar{Y}/\partial a$, where, by means of the quotient rule,

$$\frac{\partial \bar{Y}}{\partial a} = \frac{(1 - b - a)(0) - (C_0 + I_0 + G_0 + X_0 - Z_0)(-1)}{(1 - b - a)^2} = \frac{C_0 + I_0 + G_0 + X_0 - Z_0}{(1 - b - a)^2}$$

This can alternately be expressed as

$$\frac{\partial \bar{Y}}{\partial a} = \frac{1}{1-b-a}(C_0 + I_0 + G_0 + X_0 - Z_0)\left(\frac{1}{1-b-a}\right)$$

which from (6.1) reduces to

$$\frac{\partial \bar{Y}}{\partial a} = \frac{\bar{Y}}{1-b-a}$$

See Problems 6.4 to 6.8.

6.3 PARTIAL ELASTICITIES

Income elasticity of demand ϵ_Y measures the percentage change in the demand for a good resulting from a small percentage change in income, when all other variables are held constant. *Cross elasticity of demand* ϵ_c measures the relative responsiveness of the demand for one product to changes in the price of another, when all other variables are held constant. Given the demand function

$$Q_1 = a - bP_1 + cP_2 + mY$$

where Y = income and P_2 = the price of a substitute good, the income elasticity of demand is

$$\epsilon_Y = \frac{\partial Q_1}{Q_1} \div \frac{\partial Y}{Y} = \frac{\partial Q_1}{\partial Y}\left(\frac{Y}{Q_1}\right)$$

and the cross elasticity of demand is

$$\epsilon_c = \frac{\partial Q_1}{Q_1} \div \frac{\partial P_2}{P_2} = \frac{\partial Q_1}{\partial P_2}\left(\frac{P_2}{Q_1}\right)$$

Since a multivariate function has more than one elasticity, the various elasticities are called *partial elasticities*. See Examples 1 and 2 and Problems 6.18 to 6.21.

EXAMPLE 1.   Given the demand for beef

$$Q_b = 4850 - 5P_b + 1.5P_p + 0.1Y \tag{6.2}$$

with $Y = 10\,000$, $P_b = 200$, and the price of pork $P_p = 100$. The calculations for (1) the income elasticity and (2) the cross elasticity of demand for beef are given below.

(1)
$$\epsilon_Y = \frac{\partial Q_b}{Q_b} \div \frac{\partial Y}{Y} = \frac{\partial Q_b}{\partial Y}\left(\frac{Y}{Q_b}\right) \tag{6.3}$$

From (6.2),
$$\frac{\partial Q_b}{\partial Y} = 0.1$$

and
$$Q_b = 4850 - 5(200) + 1.5(100) + 0.1(10\,000) = 5000 \tag{6.4}$$

Substituting in (6.3), $\epsilon_Y = 0.1(10\,000/5000) = 0.2$.

With $\epsilon_Y < 1$, the good is income-inelastic. For any given percentage increase in national income, demand for the good will increase less than proportionately. Hence the relative market share of the good will decline as the economy expands. Since the income elasticity of demand suggests the growth potential of a market, the growth potential in this case is limited.

(2)
$$\epsilon_c = \frac{\partial Q_b}{Q_b} \div \frac{\partial P_p}{P_p} = \frac{\partial Q_b}{\partial P_p}\left(\frac{P_p}{Q_b}\right)$$

From (6.2), $\partial Q_b/\partial P_p = 1.5$; from (6.4), $Q_b = 5000$. Thus,

$$\epsilon_c = 1.5\left(\frac{100}{5000}\right) = 0.03$$

For *substitute goods*, such as beef and pork, $\partial Q_1/\partial P_2 > 0$ and the cross elasticity will be positive. For *complementary goods*, $\partial Q_1/\partial P_2 < 0$ and the cross elasticity will be negative. If $\partial Q_1/\partial P_2 = 0$, the goods are unrelated.

EXAMPLE 2.　Continuing with Example 1, the percentage change in the demand for beef resulting from a 10 percent increase in the price of pork is estimated as follows:

$$\epsilon_c = \frac{\partial Q_b}{Q_b} \div \frac{\partial P_p}{P_p}$$

Rearranging terms and substituting the known parameters,

$$\frac{\partial Q_b}{Q_b} = \epsilon_c \frac{\partial P_p}{P_p} = (0.03)(0.10) = 0.003$$

The percentage change in the demand for beef $\partial Q_b/Q_b$ will be 0.3 percent.

6.4　DIFFERENTIALS AND INCREMENTAL CHANGES

Frequently in economics we want to measure the effect on the dependent variable (costs, revenue, profit) of a change in an independent variable (labor hired, capital used, items sold). If the change is a relatively small one, the differential will measure the effect. Thus, if $z = f(x, y)$, the effect on z of a small change in x is given by the partial differential

$$dz = z_x \, dx$$

The effect of larger changes can be approximated by multiplying the partial derivative by the proposed change. Thus,

$$\Delta z \approx z_x \, \Delta x$$

If the original function $z = f(x, y)$ is linear,

$$\frac{dz}{dx} = \frac{\Delta z}{\Delta x}$$

and the effect of the change will be measured exactly:

$$\Delta z = z_x \, \Delta x$$

See Examples 3 and 4 and Problems 6.9 to 6.17.

EXAMPLE 3.　A firm's costs are related to its output of two goods x and y. The functional relationship is

$$TC = x^2 - 0.5xy + y^2$$

The additional cost of a slight increment in output x will be given by the differential

$$d\text{TC} = (2x - 0.5y) \, dx$$

The costs of larger increments can be approximated by multiplying the partial derivative with respect to x by the change in x. Mathematically,

$$\Delta \text{TC} \approx \frac{\partial \text{TC}}{\partial x} \, \Delta x \tag{6.5}$$

Since $\partial \text{TC}/\partial x =$ the marginal cost (MC_x) of x, we can also write (6.5) as

$$\Delta \text{TC} \approx \text{MC}_x \, \Delta x$$

If initially $x = 100$, $y = 60$, and $\Delta x = 3$, then

$$\Delta \text{TC} \approx [2(100) - 0.5(60)](3) \cong 510$$

EXAMPLE 4.   Assume in Section 6.2 that $b = 0.7$, $a = 0.1$, and $Y = 1200$. The differential can then be used to calculate the effect of an increase in any of the independent variables. Given the partial derivative

$$\frac{\partial \bar{Y}}{\partial G_0} = \frac{1}{1 - b - a}$$

the partial differential is

$$d\bar{Y} = \frac{1}{1 - b - a} dG_0$$

In a linear model such as this, where the slope is everywhere constant,

$$\frac{\partial \bar{Y}}{\partial G_0} = \frac{\Delta \bar{Y}}{\Delta G_0}$$

Hence

$$\Delta \bar{Y} = \frac{1}{1 - b - a} \Delta G_0$$

If the government increases expenditures by \$100,

$$\Delta \bar{Y} = \frac{1}{1 - 0.7 - 0.1}(100) = 500$$

6.5   OPTIMIZATION OF MULTIVARIABLE FUNCTIONS IN ECONOMICS

Food processors frequently sell different grades of the same product: quality, standard, economy; some, too, sell part of their output under their own brand name and part under the brand name of a large chain store. Clothing manufacturers and designers frequently have a top brand and cheaper imitations for discount department stores. Maximizing profits or minimizing costs under these conditions involves functions of more than one variable. Thus, the basic rules for optimization of multivariate functions (see Section 5.4) are required. See Examples 5 and 6 and Problems 6.22 to 6.27.

EXAMPLE 5.   A firm producing two goods x and y has the profit function

$$\pi = 64x - 2x^2 + 4xy - 4y^2 + 32y - 14$$

To find the profit-maximizing level of output for each of the two goods and test to be sure profits are maximized:

1. Take the first-order partial derivatives, set them equal to zero, and solve for x and y simultaneously.

$$\pi_x = 64 - 4x + 4y = 0 \qquad (6.6)$$

$$\pi_y = 4x - 8y + 32 = 0 \qquad (6.7)$$

   When solved simultaneously, $\bar{x} = 40$ and $\bar{y} = 24$.
2. Take the second-order direct partial derivatives since both must be negative for the function to be at a maximum. From (6.6) and (6.7),

$$\pi_{xx} = -4 \qquad \pi_{yy} = -8$$

3. Take the cross partials to make sure $\pi_{xx}\pi_{yy} > (\pi_{xy})^2$. From (6.6) and (6.7), $\pi_{xy} = 4 = \pi_{yx}$. Thus,

$$\pi_{xx}\pi_{yy} > (\pi_{xy})^2$$
$$(-4)(-8) > (4)^2$$
$$32 > 16$$

Profits are indeed maximized at $\bar{x} = 40$ and $\bar{y} = 24$. At that point, $\pi = 1650$.

EXAMPLE 6. In monopolistic competition producers must determine the price that will maximize their profit. Assume that a producer offers two different brands of a product, for which the demand functions are

$$Q_1 = 14 - 0.25P_1 \tag{6.8}$$

$$Q_2 = 24 - 0.5P_2 \tag{6.9}$$

and the joint cost function is

$$\text{TC} = Q_1^2 + 5Q_1Q_2 + Q_2^2 \tag{6.10}$$

The profit-maximizing level of output, the price that should be charged for each brand, and the profits are determined as follows:

First, establish the profit function π in terms of Q_1 and Q_2. Since π = total revenue (TR) minus total cost (TC) and the total revenue for the firm is $P_1Q_1 + P_2Q_2$, the firm's profit is

$$\pi = P_1Q_1 + P_2Q_2 - \text{TC}$$

Substituting from (6.10),

$$\pi = P_1Q_1 + P_2Q_2 - (Q_1^2 + 5Q_1Q_2 + Q_2^2) \tag{6.11}$$

Next find the inverse functions of (6.8) and (6.9) by solving for P in terms of Q. Thus, from (6.8),

$$P_1 = 56 - 4Q_1 \tag{6.12}$$

and from (6.9),

$$P_2 = 48 - 2Q_2 \tag{6.13}$$

Substituting in (6.11),

$$\pi = (56 - 4Q_1)Q_1 + (48 - 2Q_2)Q_2 - Q_1^2 - 5Q_1Q_2 - Q_2^2$$
$$= 56Q_1 - 5Q_1^2 + 48Q_2 - 3Q_2^2 - 5Q_1Q_2 \tag{6.14}$$

Then maximize (6.14) by the familiar rules:

$$\pi_1 = 56 - 10Q_1 - 5Q_2 = 0 \qquad \pi_2 = 48 - 6Q_2 - 5Q_1 = 0$$

which, when solved simultaneously, give $\bar{Q}_1 = 2.75$ and $\bar{Q}_2 = 5.7$.

Take the second derivatives to be sure π is maximized:

$$\pi_{11} = -10 \qquad \pi_{22} = -6 \qquad \pi_{12} = -5 = \pi_{21}$$

With both second direct partials negative and $\pi_{11}\pi_{22} > (\pi_{12})^2$, the function is maximized at the critical values.

Finally, substitute $\bar{Q}_1 = 2.75$ and $\bar{Q}_2 = 5.7$ in (6.12) and (6.13), respectively, to find the profit-maximizing price.

$$P_1 = 56 - 4(2.75) = 45 \qquad P_2 = 48 - 2(5.7) = 36.6$$

Prices should be set at $45 for brand 1 and $36.60 for brand 2, leading to sales of 2.75 of brand 1 and 5.7 of brand 2. From (6.11) or (6.14), maximum profit is

$$\pi = 45(2.75) + 36.6(5.7) - (2.75)^2 - 5(2.75)(5.7) - (5.7)^2 = 213.94$$

6.6 CONSTRAINED OPTIMIZATION OF MULTIVARIABLE FUNCTIONS IN ECONOMICS

Solutions to economic problems frequently have to be found under constraints (e.g., maximizing utility subject to a budget constraint or minimizing costs subject to some such minimal requirement of output as a production quota). Use of the Lagrangian function (see Section 5.5) greatly facilitates this task. See Example 7 and Problems 6.28 to 6.39.

EXAMPLE 7. Find the critical values for minimizing the costs of a firm producing two goods x and y when the total cost function is $c = 8x^2 - xy + 12y^2$ and the firm is bound by contract to produce a minimum combination of goods totaling 42, that is, subject to the constraint $x + y = 42$.

Set the constraint equal to zero, multiply it by λ, and form the Lagrangian function,

$$C = 8x^2 - xy + 12y^2 + \lambda(42 - x - y)$$

Take the first-order partials,

$$C_x = 16x - y - \lambda = 0$$
$$C_y = -x + 24y - \lambda = 0$$
$$C_\lambda = 42 - x - y = 0$$

Solving simultaneously, $\bar{x} = 25$, $\bar{y} = 17$, and $\bar{\lambda} = 383$. With $\bar{\lambda} = 383$, a 1-unit increase in the constraint or production quota will lead to an increase in cost of approximately \$383. For second-order conditions, see Section 12.5 and Problem 12.31(a).

6.7 INEQUALITY CONSTRAINTS

Several economic studies have suggested that large corporations maximize not profits, but rather sales revenue subject to some minimally acceptable level of profit. Given a function $f(x, y)$ subject to a constraint $g(x, y) \gtreqless 0$, the Lagrange multiplier method can be adapted to handle such inequalities. Simply assume the constraint is an equality, that is, $g(x, y) = 0$, and solve with the familiar Lagrange method (see Section 5.5). Then apply these simple rules:

Given $F(x, y, \lambda) = f(x, y) + \lambda[k - g(x, y)]$:

I. For maximization subject to $g(x, y) \geq 0$,
    1. If $\lambda < 0$, the constraint is functioning as a real limitation, and the desired constrained optimum has been determined.
    2. If $\lambda \geq 0$, the constraint is not a limitation. Ignore the equality constraint previously imposed and maximize the objective function by itself.

II. For maximization subject to $g(x, y) \leq 0$,
    1. If $\lambda < 0$, the constraint is not a limitation. Maximize the objective function independently of the constraint.
    2. If $\lambda \geq 0$, the constraint is operative and the desired constrained optimum has been found.

III. For minimization subject to $g(x, y) \geq 0$,
    1. If $\lambda < 0$, the constraint is not a limitation. Ignore the constraint and minimize the objective function.
    2. If $\lambda \geq 0$, the constraint is limiting the objective function and the constrained minimum has been found.

IV. For minimization subject to $g(x, y) \leq 0$,
    1. If $\lambda < 0$, the constraint is operative and the constrained minimum has been found.
    2. If $\lambda \geq 0$, the constraint is not a limitation. Minimize the objective function by itself.

See Examples 8 and 9 and Problems 6.40 to 6.43.

EXAMPLE 8. Given: $\pi = 64x - 2x^2 + 4xy - 4y^2 + 32y - 14$, subject to $x + y \leq 50$.
To maximize this function, assume the constraint is $x + y = 50$ and form the Lagrange expression

$$\Pi = 64x - 2x^2 + 4xy - 4y^2 + 32y - 14 + \lambda(50 - x - y)$$

Then
$$\Pi_x = 64 - 4x + 4y - \lambda = 0$$
$$\Pi_y = 4x - 8y + 32 - \lambda = 0$$
$$\Pi_\lambda = 50 - x - y = 0$$

from which $\bar{x} = 31.6$, $\bar{y} = 18.4$, $\bar{\lambda} = 11.2$, and $\pi = 1571.6$.

With λ positive when maximizing subject to $g(x, y) \leq 0$, the constraint is a limitation and the desired constrained maximum has been found. $\pi = 1571.6$ compared with $\pi = 1650$ for the unconstrained optimum of this function, as presented in Example 5.

EXAMPLE 9.   If the function given in Example 8 were subject to the constraint $x + y \leq 79$, it would be maximized as follows:

First, assume $x + y = 79$. Then, the Lagrangian function is

$$\Pi = 64x - 2x^2 + 4xy - 4y^2 + 32y - 14 + \lambda(79 - x - y)$$

and

$$\Pi_x = 64 - 4x + 4y - \lambda = 0$$
$$\Pi_y = 4x - 8y + 32 - \lambda = 0$$
$$\Pi_\lambda = 79 - x - y = 0$$

Hence, $\bar{x} = 49$, $\bar{y} = 30$, $\bar{\lambda} = -12$, and $\pi = 1560$.

With λ negative, the constraint is not a limitation. Maximum profits will be found by optimizing the objective function independently of the constraint. Unconstrained maximization in Example 5 led to $\pi = 1650$. Constrained optimization here leads to $\pi = 1560$.

6.8   HOMOGENEOUS PRODUCTION FUNCTIONS

A production function is said to be homogeneous if when each input factor is multiplied by a positive real constant k, the constant can be completely factored out. If the exponent of the factor is 1, the function is homogeneous of degree 1; if the exponent of the factor is greater than 1, the function is homogeneous of degree greater than 1; and if the exponent of the factor is less than 1, the function is homogeneous of degree less than 1. Mathematically, a function $z = f(x, y)$ is homogeneous of degree n if for all positive real values of k, $f(kx, ky) = k^n f(x, y)$. See Example 10 and Problem 6.44.

EXAMPLE 10.   The degree of homogeneity of a function is illustrated below.

1. $z = 8x + 9y$ is homogeneous of degree 1 because

$$f(kx, ky) = 8kx + 9ky = k(8x + 9y)$$

2. $z = x^2 + xy + y^2$ is homogeneous of degree 2 because

$$f(kx, ky) = (kx)^2 + (kx)(ky) + (ky)^2 = k^2(x^2 + xy + y^2)$$

3. $z = x^{0.3}y^{0.4}$ is homogeneous of degree less than 1 because

$$f(kx, ky) = (kx)^{0.3}(ky)^{0.4} = k^{0.3 + 0.4}(x^{0.3}y^{0.4}) = k^{0.7}(x^{0.3}y^{0.4})$$

4. $z = 2x/y$ is homogeneous of degree 0 because

$$f(kx, ky) = \frac{2kx}{ky} = 1\left(\frac{2x}{y}\right) \qquad \text{since} \quad \frac{k}{k} = k^0 = 1$$

5. $z = x^3 + 2xy + y^3$ is not homogeneous because k cannot be completely factored out:

$$f(kx, ky) = (kx)^3 + 2(kx)(ky) + (ky)^3$$
$$= k^3x^3 + 2k^2xy + k^3y^3 = k^2(kx^3 + 2xy + ky^3)$$

6.9   RETURNS TO SCALE

A production function exhibits *constant returns to scale* if when all inputs are increased by a given proportion k, output increases by the same proportion. If output increases by a proportion greater than k, there are *increasing returns to scale*; and if output increases by a proportion smaller than k, there are *diminishing returns to scale*. In other words, if the production function is homogeneous of degree greater than, equal to, or less than 1, returns to scale are increasing, constant, or diminishing. See Problems 6.44 and 6.57.

6.10   OPTIMIZATION OF COBB-DOUGLAS PRODUCTION FUNCTIONS

Economic analysis is frequently couched in terms of the *Cobb-Douglas production function* $q = AK^\alpha L^\beta$ $(A > 0; 0 < \alpha, \beta < 1)$, where q is the quantity of output in physical units, K the quantity of capital, and L the quantity of labor. Here α (the *output elasticity of capital*) measures the percentage change in q for a 1 percent change in K while L is held constant; β (the *output elasticity of labor*) is exactly parallel; and A is an *efficiency parameter* reflecting the level of technology.

A *strict* Cobb-Douglas function, in which $\alpha + \beta = 1$, exhibits *constant returns to scale*. A *generalized* Cobb-Douglas function, in which $\alpha + \beta \neq 1$, exhibits *increasing returns to scale* if $\alpha + \beta > 1$ and *decreasing returns to scale* if $\alpha + \beta < 1$. A Cobb-Douglas function is optimized subject to a budget constraint in Example 12 and Problems 6.45 and 6.46; second-order conditions are explained in Section 12.5. Selected properties of Cobb-Douglas functions are demonstrated and proved in Problems 6.57 to 6.62.

EXAMPLE 11.   The first and second partial derivatives for (a) $q = AK^\alpha L^\beta$ and (b) $q = 5K^{0.4}L^{0.6}$ are illustrated below.

(a)
$$q_K = \alpha AK^{\alpha-1}L^\beta \qquad\qquad q_L = \beta AK^\alpha L^{\beta-1}$$
$$q_{KK} = \alpha(\alpha-1)AK^{\alpha-2}L^\beta \qquad q_{LL} = \beta(\beta-1)AK^\alpha L^{\beta-2}$$
$$q_{KL} = \alpha\beta AK^{\alpha-1}L^{\beta-1} \qquad q_{LK} = \alpha\beta AK^{\alpha-1}L^{\beta-1}$$

(b)
$$q_K = 2K^{-0.6}L^{0.6} \qquad\qquad q_L = 3K^{0.4}L^{-0.4}$$
$$q_{KK} = -1.2K^{-1.6}L^{0.6} \qquad q_{LL} = -1.2K^{0.4}L^{-1.4}$$
$$q_{KL} = 1.2K^{-0.6}L^{-0.4} \qquad q_{LK} = 1.2K^{-0.6}L^{-0.4}$$

EXAMPLE 12.   Given a budget constraint of \$108 when $P_K = 3$ and $P_L = 4$, the generalized Cobb-Douglas production function $q = K^{0.4}L^{0.5}$ is optimized as follows:

1.   Set up the Lagrangian function.

$$Q = K^{0.4}L^{0.5} + \lambda(108 - 3K - 4L)$$

2.   Using the simple power function rule, take the first-order partial derivatives, set them equal to zero, and solve simultaneously for K_0 and L_0 (and λ_0, if desired).

$$\frac{\partial Q}{\partial K} = Q_K = 0.4K^{-0.6}L^{0.5} - 3\lambda = 0 \qquad\qquad (6.15)$$

$$\frac{\partial Q}{\partial L} = Q_L = 0.5K^{0.4}L^{-0.5} - 4\lambda = 0 \qquad\qquad (6.16)$$

$$\frac{\partial Q}{\partial \lambda} = Q_\lambda = 108 - 3K - 4L = 0 \qquad\qquad (6.17)$$

Rearrange, then divide (*6.15*) by (*6.16*) to eliminate λ.

$$\frac{0.4K^{-0.6}L^{0.5}}{0.5K^{0.4}L^{-0.5}} = \frac{3\lambda}{4\lambda}$$

Remembering to subtract exponents in division,

$$0.8K^{-1}L^1 = 0.75$$
$$\frac{L}{K} = \frac{0.75}{0.8} \qquad L = 0.9375K$$

Substitute $L = 0.9375K$ in (*6.17*).

$$108 - 3K - 4(0.9375K) = 0 \qquad K_0 = 16$$

Then by substituting $K_0 = 16$ in (*6.17*), $L_0 = 15$

6.11   OPTIMIZATION OF CONSTANT ELASTICITY OF SUBSTITUTION PRODUCTION FUNCTIONS

The *elasticity of substitution* σ measures the percentage change in the least-cost (K/L) input ratio resulting from a small percentage change in the input-price ratio (P_L/P_K).

$$\sigma = \frac{\dfrac{d(K/L)}{K/L}}{\dfrac{d(P_L/P_K)}{P_L/P_K}} = \frac{d(K/L)}{d(P_L/P_K)} \frac{K/L}{P_L/P_K} \tag{6.18}$$

where $0 \le \sigma \le \infty$. If $\sigma = 0$, there is no substitutability; the two inputs are complements and must be used together in fixed proportions. If $\sigma = \infty$, the two goods are perfect substitutes. A Cobb-Douglas production function, as shown in Problem 6.61, has a constant elasticity of substitution equal to 1. A *constant elasticity of substitution (CES) production function*, of which a Cobb-Douglas function is but one example, has an elasticity of substitution that is constant but not necessarily equal to 1.

A CES production function is typically expressed in the form

$$q = A[\alpha K^{-\beta} + (1 - \alpha)L^{-\beta}]^{-1/\beta} \tag{6.19}$$

where A is the efficiency parameter, α is the *distribution parameter* denoting relative factor shares, β is the *substitution parameter* determining the value of the elasticity of substitution, and the parameters are restricted so that $A > 0$, $0 < \alpha < 1$, and $\beta > -1$. CES production functions are optimized subject to budget constraints in Example 13 and Problems 6.47 and 6.48. Various important properties of the CES production function are demonstrated and proved in Problems 6.63 to 6.73.

EXAMPLE 13.   The CES production function

$$q = 75[0.3K^{-0.4} + (1 - 0.3)L^{-0.4}]^{-1/0.4}$$

is maximized subject to the constraint $4K + 3L = 120$ as follows:

1.   Set up the Lagrangian function.

$$Q = 75(0.3K^{-0.4} + 0.7L^{-0.4})^{-2.5} + \lambda(120 - 4K - 3L)$$

2.   Test the first-order conditions, using the generalized power function rule for Q_K and Q_L.

$$\begin{aligned}
Q_K &= -187.5(0.3K^{-0.4} + 0.7L^{-0.4})^{-3.5}(-0.12K^{-1.4}) - 4\lambda = 0 \\
&= 22.5K^{-1.4}(0.3K^{-0.4} + 0.7L^{-0.4})^{-3.5} - 4\lambda = 0
\end{aligned} \tag{6.20}$$

$$\begin{aligned}
Q_L &= -187.5(0.3K^{-0.4} + 0.7L^{-0.4})^{-3.5}(-0.28L^{-1.4}) - 3\lambda = 0 \\
&= 52.5L^{-1.4}(0.3K^{-0.4} + 0.7L^{-0.4})^{-3.5} - 3\lambda = 0
\end{aligned} \tag{6.21}$$

$$Q_\lambda = 120 - 4K - 3L = 0 \tag{6.22}$$

Rearrange, then divide *(6.20)* by *(6.21)* to eliminate λ.

$$\frac{22.5K^{-1.4}(0.3K^{-0.4} + 0.7L^{-0.4})^{-3.5}}{52.5L^{-1.4}(0.3K^{-0.4} + 0.7L^{-0.4})^{-3.5}} = \frac{4\lambda}{3\lambda}$$

$$\frac{22.5K^{-1.4}}{52.5L^{-1.4}} = \frac{4}{3}$$

Cross multiply.

$$67.5K^{-1.4} = 210L^{-1.4}$$
$$K^{-1.4} = 3.11L^{-1.4}$$

Take the -1.4 root,

$$K = (3.11)^{-1/1.4}L = (3.11)^{-0.71}L$$

and use a calculator.

$$K \approx 0.45L$$

Substitute in (6.22).

$$120 - 4(0.45L) - 3L = 0 \qquad L_0 = 25 \qquad K_0 = 11.25$$

Note: To find $(3.11)^{-0.71}$ with a calculator, enter 3.11, press the $\boxed{y^x}$ key, then enter 0.71 followed by the $\boxed{+/-}$ key to make it negative, and hit the $\boxed{=}$ key to find $(3.11)^{-0.71} = 0.44683$.

Solved Problems

MARGINAL CONCEPTS

6.1. Find the marginal physical productivity of the different inputs or factors of production for each of the following production functions Q:

(a) $Q = 6x^2 + 3xy + 2y^2$

$$\text{MPP}_x = \frac{\partial Q}{\partial x} = 12x + 3y$$

$$\text{MPP}_y = \frac{\partial Q}{\partial y} = 3x + 4y$$

(b) $Q = 0.5K^2 - 2KL + L^2$

$$\text{MPP}_K = K - 2L$$
$$\text{MPP}_L = 2L - 2K$$

(c) $Q = 20 + 8x + 3x^2 - 0.25x^3 + 5y + 2y^2 - 0.5y^3$

$$\text{MPP}_x = 8 + 6x - 0.75x^2$$
$$\text{MPP}_y = 5 + 4y - 1.5y^2$$

(d) $Q = x^2 + 2xy + 3y^2 + 1.5yz + 0.2z^2$

$$\text{MPP}_x = 2x + 2y$$
$$\text{MPP}_y = 2x + 6y + 1.5z$$
$$\text{MPP}_z = 1.5y + 0.4z$$

6.2. (a) Assume $\bar{y} = 4$ in Problem 6.1(a) and find the MPP_x for $x = 5$ and $x = 8$. (b) If the marginal revenue at $\bar{x} = 5$, $\bar{y} = 4$ is \$3, compute the marginal revenue product for the fifth unit of x.

(a) $\text{MPP}_x = 12x + 3y$ (b) $\text{MRP}_x = \text{MPP}_x(\text{MR})$

At $x = 5$, $\bar{y} = 4$, $\text{MPP}_x = 12(5) + 3(4) = 72$.   At $\bar{x} = 5$, $\bar{y} = 4$, $\text{MRP}_x = (72)(3) = 216$.

At $x = 8$, $\bar{y} = 4$, $\text{MPP}_x = 12(8) + 3(4) = 108$.

6.3. (a) Find the marginal cost of a firm's different products when the total cost function is $c = 3x^2 + 7x + 1.5xy + 6y + 2y^2$. (b) Determine the marginal cost of x when $x = 5$, $\bar{y} = 3$.

(a)
$$\text{MC}_x = 6x + 7 + 1.5y$$
$$\text{MC}_y = 1.5x + 6 + 4y$$

(b) The marginal cost of x when $x = 5$ and y is held constant at 3 is

$$\text{MC}_x = 6(5) + 7 + 1.5(3) = 41.5$$

INCOME DETERMINATION MULTIPLIERS

6.4.	Given a three-sector income determination model in which

$$Y = C + I_0 + G_0 \qquad Yd = Y - T \qquad C_0, I_0, G_0, T_0 > 0 \qquad 0 < b, t < 1$$
$$C = C_0 + bYd \qquad\qquad T = T_0 + tY$$

determine the magnitude and direction of a 1-unit change in (a) government spending, (b) lump-sum taxation, and (c) the tax rate on the equilibrium level of income. In short, calculate the *government multiplier*, the *autonomous tax multiplier*, and the *tax rate multiplier*.

To find the different multipliers, first solve for the equilibrium level of income, as follows:

$$Y = C_0 + bY - bT_0 - btY + I_0 + G_0$$
$$\bar{Y} = \frac{1}{1 - b + bt} (C_0 - bT_0 + I_0 + G_0) \tag{6.23}$$

Then take the appropriate partial derivatives.

(a)
$$\frac{\partial \bar{Y}}{\partial G_0} = \frac{1}{1 - b + bt}$$

Since $0 < b < 1$, $\partial \bar{Y}/\partial G_0 > 0$. A 1-unit increase in government spending will increase the equilibrium level of income by $1/(1 - b + bt)$.

(b)
$$\frac{\partial \bar{Y}}{\partial T_0} = \frac{-b}{1 - b + bt} < 0$$

A 1-unit increase in autonomous taxation will cause national income to fall by $b/(1 - b + bt)$.

(c)	Since t appears in the denominator in (6.23), the quotient rule is necessary.

$$\frac{\partial \bar{Y}}{\partial t} = \frac{(1 - b + bt)(0) - (C_0 - bT_0 + I_0 + G_0)(b)}{(1 - b + bt)^2}$$
$$= \frac{-b(C_0 - bT_0 + I_0 + G_0)}{(1 - b + bt)^2} = \frac{-b}{1 - b + bt} \left(\frac{C_0 - bT_0 + I_0 + G_0}{1 - b + bt} \right)$$

Thus, from (6.23),
$$\frac{\partial \bar{Y}}{\partial t} = \frac{-b\bar{Y}}{1 - b + bt} < 0$$

A 1-unit increase in the tax rate will cause national income to fall by an amount equal to the tax rate multiplier.

6.5.	Given a simple model

$$Y = C_0 + I_0 + G_0 \qquad Yd = Y - T$$
$$C = C_0 + bYd \qquad\qquad T = T_0$$

where taxation does *not* depend on income, calculate the effect on the equilibrium level of income of a 1-unit change in government expenditure exactly offset by a 1-unit change in taxation. That is, calculate the balanced-budget multiplier for an economy in which there is only autonomous taxation.

$$Y = C_0 + b(Y - T_0) + I_0 + G_0$$
$$\bar{Y} = \frac{1}{1 - b} (C_0 - bT_0 + I_0 + G_0)$$

Thus, the government multiplier is

$$\frac{\partial \bar{Y}}{\partial G_0} = \frac{1}{1 - b} \tag{6.24}$$

and the tax multiplier is

$$\frac{\partial \bar{Y}}{\partial T_0} = \frac{-b}{1 - b} \qquad (6.25)$$

The balanced-budget effect of a 1-unit increase in government spending matched by a 1-unit increase in taxation is the sum of (6.24) and (6.25). Therefore,

$$\Delta \bar{Y} = \frac{1}{1 - b} + \left(\frac{-b}{1 - b}\right) = \frac{1}{1 - b} - \frac{b}{1 - b} = \frac{1 - b}{1 - b} = 1$$

A change in government expenditure matched by an equal change in government taxation will have a *positive* effect on the equilibrium level of income exactly equal to the change in government expenditure and taxation. The multiplier in this case is $+1$.

6.6. Given

$$Y = C + I_0 + G_0 \qquad Yd = Y - T$$
$$C = C_0 + bYd \qquad T = T_0 + tY$$

where taxation is now a function of income, demonstrate the effect on the equilibrium level of income of a 1-unit change in government expenditure offset by a 1-unit change in *autonomous* taxation T_0. That is, demonstrate the effect of the *balanced-budget multiplier* in an economy in which taxes are a positive function of income.

From (6.23), $\bar{Y} = [1/(1 - b + bt)](C_0 - bT_0 + I_0 + G_0)$. Thus,

$$\frac{\partial \bar{Y}}{\partial G_0} = \frac{1}{1 - b + bt} \qquad (6.26)$$

and

$$\frac{\partial \bar{Y}}{\partial T_0} = \frac{-b}{1 - b + bt} \qquad (6.27)$$

The combined effect on $\bar{Y}$ of a 1-unit increase in government spending and an equal increase in autonomous taxation is the sum of (6.26) and (6.27). Thus,

$$\Delta \bar{Y} = \frac{1}{1 - b + bt} + \left(\frac{-b}{1 - b + bt}\right) = \frac{1 - b}{1 - b + bt}$$

which is positive but less than 1 because $1 - b < 1 - b + bt$. A change in government expenditures equaled by a change in autonomous taxes when taxes are positively related to income in the model, will have a positive effect on the equilibrium level of income, but the effect is smaller than the initial change in government expenditure. Here the multiplier is less than 1 because the total change in taxes ($\Delta T = \Delta T_0 + t \, \Delta Y$) is greater than the change in G_0.

6.7. Given

$$Y = C + I_0 + G_0 + X_0 - Z \qquad T = T_0 + tY$$
$$C = C_0 + bYd \qquad Z = Z_0 + zYd$$

where all the independent variables are positive and $0 < b, z, t < 1$. Determine the effect on the equilibrium level of income of a 1-unit change in (*a*) exports, (*b*) autonomous imports, and (*c*) autonomous taxation. In short, find the *export*, *autonomous import*, and *autonomous taxation multipliers*. [Note that $Z = f(Yd)$].

From the equilibrium level of income,

$$Y = C_0 + b(Y - T_0 - tY) + I_0 + G_0 + X_0 - Z_0 - z(Y - T_0 - tY)$$
$$\bar{Y} = \frac{1}{1 - b + bt + z - zt} (C_0 - bT_0 + I_0 + G_0 + X_0 - Z_0 + zT_0)$$

(*a*)

$$\frac{\partial \bar{Y}}{\partial X_0} = \frac{1}{1 - b + bt + z - zt} > 0$$

because $0 < b, z < 1$. A 1-unit increase in exports will have a positive effect on $\bar{Y}$, which is given by the multiplier.

(b)
$$\frac{\partial \bar{Y}}{\partial Z_0} = \frac{-1}{1 - b + bt + z - zt} < 0$$

An increase in autonomous imports will lead to a decrease in $\bar{Y}$.

(c)
$$\frac{\partial \bar{Y}}{\partial T_0} = \frac{z - b}{1 - b + bt + z - zt} < 0$$

because a country's marginal propensity to import z is usually smaller than its marginal propensity to consume b. With $z < b, z - b < 0$. An increase in autonomous taxes will lead to a decrease in national income, as in (6.27), but the presence of z in the numerator has a mitigating effect on the decrease in income. When there is a positive marginal propensity to import, increased taxes will reduce cash outflows for imports and thus reduce the negative effect of increased taxes on the equilibrium level of income.

6.8. Determine the effect on $\bar{Y}$ of a 1-unit change in the marginal propensity to import z in Problem 6.7.

$$\frac{\partial \bar{Y}}{\partial z} = \frac{(1 - b + bt + z - zt)(T_0) - (C_0 - bT_0 + I_0 + G_0 + X_0 - Z_0 + zT_0)(1 - t)}{(1 - b + bt + z - zt)^2}$$

$$= \frac{T_0}{1 - b + bt + z - zt} - \frac{\bar{Y}(1 - t)}{1 - b + bt + z - zt}$$

$$= \frac{-[\bar{Y} - (T_0 + t\bar{Y})]}{1 - b + bt + z - zt} = \frac{-\bar{Y}d}{1 - b + bt + z - zt} < 0$$

DIFFERENTIALS

6.9.
$$Y = C + I_0 + G_0 \qquad Yd = Y - T \qquad C_0 = 100 \qquad I_0 = 90 \qquad b = 0.75$$
$$C = C_0 + bYd \qquad T = T_0 + tY \qquad G_0 = 330 \qquad T_0 = 240 \qquad t = 0.20$$

(a) What is the equilibrium level of income $\bar{Y}$? What is the effect on $\bar{Y}$ of a \$50 increase in (b) government spending and (c) autonomous taxation T_0?

(a) From (6.23),
$$\bar{Y} = \frac{1}{1 - b + bt}(C_0 - bT_0 + I_0 + G_0)$$

$$= \frac{1}{1 - 0.75 + 0.75(0.20)}[100 - 0.75(240) + 90 + 330]$$

$$= \frac{1}{0.40}(100 - 180 + 90 + 330) = 2.5(340) = 850$$

(b) If government increases spending by 50,

$$\Delta\bar{Y} = \frac{\partial \bar{Y}}{\partial G_0}\Delta G_0 = \frac{1}{1 - b + bt}(50) = 2.5(50) = 125$$

(c) If autonomous taxation T_0 increases by 50,

$$\Delta\bar{Y} = \frac{\partial \bar{Y}}{\partial T_0}\Delta T_0 = \frac{-b}{1 - b + bt}(50) = \frac{-0.75}{1 - 0.75 + 0.75(0.20)}(50) = -1.875(50) = -93.75$$

6.10. If the full-employment level of income Y_{fe} in Problem 6.9(a) is 1000 and the government wishes to achieve it, by how much should it change (a) government spending or (b) autonomous taxation?

(a) The desired increase in economic activity is the difference between the full-employment level of income (1000) and the present level (850). Thus, the desired $\Delta\bar{Y} = 150$. Substituting in the formula from

Problem 6.9(b),

$$\Delta \bar{Y} = \frac{\partial \bar{Y}}{\partial G_0} \Delta G_0$$

$$150 = 2.5 \, \Delta G_0 \qquad \Delta G_0 = 60$$

Increased government expenditure of 60 will increase $\bar{Y}$ by 150.

(b)   If the government wishes to alter autonomous taxes to achieve full employment, from Problem 6.9(c),

$$\Delta \bar{Y} = \frac{\partial \bar{Y}}{\partial T_0} \Delta T_0$$

$$150 = -1.875 \, \Delta T_0 \qquad \Delta T_0 = -80$$

The government should cut autonomous taxes by 80.

6.11.   Explain the effect on the government deficit (a) if policy a in Problem 6.10 is adopted and (b) if policy b is adopted instead.

(a)   The government's financial condition is given by the difference between receipts T and expenditures G. At the initial 850 level of income,

$$T = 240 + 0.2(850) = 410 \qquad G_0 = 330 \qquad T - G_0 = 410 - 330 = 80$$

The government has a surplus of 80.

     If the government increases spending by 60, expenditures rise by 60. But tax revenues also increase as a result of the increase in income. With $\Delta \bar{Y} = 150$, $\Delta T = 0.2(150) = 30$. With expenditures rising by 60 and receipts increasing by 30, the net cost to the government of stimulating the economy to full employment is only \$30. At the new $\bar{Y} = 1000$,

$$T = 240 + 0.2(1000) = 440 \qquad G_0 = 330 + 60 = 390 \qquad T - G_0 = 440 - 390 = 50$$

The government surplus is reduced to \$50 from the previous \$80 surplus.

(b)   If the government reduces T_0 by 80, tax revenue falls initially by 80. But the \$150 stimulatory effect on income has a positive effect on total tax collections, since $\Delta T = 0.2(150) = 30$. Thus, the net cost of reducing autonomous taxation to stimulate the economy to full employment is \$50. The government surplus is reduced to \$30:

$$T = 160 + 0.2(1000) = 360 \qquad G_0 = 330 \qquad T - G_0 = 360 - 330 = 30$$

6.12.   (a) If the proportional tax in Problem 6.9 is increased by 10 percent, what is the effect on $\bar{Y}$? (b) If the government wants to alter the original marginal tax rate of 20 percent to achieve $Y_{fe} = 1000$, by how much should it change t?

(a)   If the proportional tax is increased by 10 percent,

$$\Delta t = 0.10(0.20) = 0.02$$

The resulting change in income is

$$\Delta \bar{Y} = \frac{\partial \bar{Y}}{\partial t} \Delta t$$

Substituting from Problem 6.4(c),

$$\Delta \bar{Y} \approx \frac{-b\bar{Y}}{1 - b + bt} (0.02)$$

Since a change in one of the parameters, unlike a change in one of the independent variables, will alter the value of the multiplier, the multiplier will only approximate the effect of the change.

$$\Delta \bar{Y} \approx \frac{-0.75(850)}{0.4} (0.02) = -31.88$$

(b) The government wants to raise $\bar{Y}$ by 150. Substituting $\Delta \bar{Y} = 150$ in the equation above,

$$150 \approx \frac{-0.75(850)}{0.4} \Delta t$$

$$\Delta t \approx -0.09$$

The tax rate should be reduced by approximately 0.09. The new tax rate should be around 11 percent $(0.20 - 0.09 = 0.11)$.

6.13. Given
$$Y = C + I_0 + G_0 + X_0 - Z \qquad T = T_0 + tY$$
$$C = C_0 + bYd \qquad\qquad Z = Z_0 + zYd$$

with
$$b = 0.9 \qquad t = 0.2 \qquad C_0 = 125$$
$$X_0 = 150 \qquad Z_0 = 55 \qquad I_0 = 92.5$$
$$z = 0.15 \qquad T_0 = 150 \qquad G_0 = 600$$

Calculate (a) the equilibrium level of income, (b) the effect on $\bar{Y}$ of an increase of 60 in autonomous exports X_0, and (c) the effect on $\bar{Y}$ of an increase of 30 in autonomous imports Z_0.

(a) From Problem 6.7,

$$\bar{Y} = \frac{1}{1 - b + bt + z - zt} (C_0 - bT_0 + I_0 + G_0 + X_0 - Z_0 + zT_0)$$

$$= \frac{1}{1 - 0.9 + 0.9(0.2) + 0.15 - 0.15(0.2)} [125 - 0.9(150) + 92.5 + 600 + 150 - 55 + 22.5]$$

$$= 2.5(800) = 2000$$

(b)
$$\Delta \bar{Y} = \frac{\partial \bar{Y}}{\partial X_0} \Delta X_0 = \frac{1}{1 - b + bt + z - zt} (60) = 2.5(60) = 150$$

(c)
$$\Delta \bar{Y} = \frac{\partial \bar{Y}}{\partial Z_0} \Delta Z_0 = \frac{-1}{1 - b + bt + z - zt} (30) = -2.5(30) = -75$$

6.14. If the full-employment level of income in Problem 6.13 is 2075, (a) by how much should the government increase expenditures to achieve it? (b) By how much should it cut autonomous taxes to have the same effect?

(a) The effect of government spending on national income is

$$\Delta \bar{Y} = \frac{\partial \bar{Y}}{\partial G_0} \Delta G_0$$

substituting $\Delta \bar{Y} = 75$,

$$75 = \frac{1}{1 - b + bt + z - zt} \Delta G_0 = 2.5 \, \Delta G_0 \qquad \Delta G_0 = 30$$

(b)
$$\Delta \bar{Y} = \frac{\partial \bar{Y}}{\partial T_0} \Delta T_0$$

$$75 = \frac{z - b}{1 - b + bt + z - zt} \Delta T_0 = -1.875 \, \Delta T_0 \qquad \Delta T_0 = -40$$

The government should cut autonomous taxation by 40.

6.15. Calculate the effect on the government deficit if the government in Problem 6.14 achieves full employment through (a) increased expenditure or (b) a tax cut.

(a) If the government increases expenditures by 30, the government deficit increases initially by 30. However, income is stimulated by 75. With $\Delta \bar{Y} = 75$, $\Delta T = 0.2(75) = 15$. Tax revenue increases by 15. Thus the net cost to the government from this policy, and the effect on the deficit, is \$15 $(30 - 15 = 15)$.

(b) If the government cuts autonomous taxation by 40, tax revenues fall initially by 40. But income increases by 75, causing tax revenues to increase by 15. Thus the net cost to the government of this policy is 25 $(40 - 15 = 25)$, and the government deficit worsens by 25.

6.16. Calculate the effect on the balance of payments (B/P) from (a) government spending and (b) the tax reduction in Problem 6.14.

(a) Since $B/P = X - Z$, substituting from Problem 6.13,

$$B/P = X_0 - (Z_0 + zYd) = X_0 - Z_0 - zY + zT_0 + ztY \tag{6.28}$$

With an increase of 30 in government spending, $\Delta \bar{Y} = 75$. Since Y is the only variable on the right-hand side of (6.28) to change,

$$\Delta(B/P) = -z(75) + zt(75)$$

Substituting $z = 0.15$, $zt = 0.03$, $\Delta(B/P) = -9$.

(b) When the government cuts autonomous taxes by 40, $\Delta \bar{Y} = 75$. Adjusting (6.28),

$$\Delta(B/P) = -z(75) + z(-40) + zt(75) = -15$$

The reduction in taxes leads to a greater increase in disposable income than the increased government spending, resulting in a higher level of imports and a more serious balance of payments deficit.

6.17. Estimate the effect on $\bar{Y}$ of a one-percentage-point decrease in the marginal propensity to import from Problem 6.13.

$$\Delta \bar{Y} \approx \frac{\partial \bar{Y}}{\partial z} \Delta z$$

Substituting from Problem 6.8,

$$\Delta \bar{Y} = \frac{-\bar{Y}d}{1 - b + bt + z - zt} \Delta z$$

where

$$\bar{Y}d = \bar{Y} - T_0 - t\bar{Y} = 2000 - 150 - 0.2(2000) = 1450$$

Thus,

$$\Delta \bar{Y} = \frac{-1450}{0.4}(-0.01) = +36.25$$

PARTIAL ELASTICITIES

6.18. Given $Q = 700 - 2P + 0.02Y$, where $P = 25$ and $Y = 5000$. Find (a) the price elasticity of demand and (b) the income elasticity of demand.

(a)

$$\epsilon_d = \frac{\partial Q}{\partial P}\left(\frac{P}{Q}\right)$$

where $\partial Q/\partial P = -2$ and $Q = 700 - 2(25) + 0.02(5000) = 750$. Thus,

$$\epsilon_d = -2\left(\frac{25}{750}\right) = -0.067$$

(b)
$$\epsilon_Y = \frac{\partial Q}{\partial Y}\left(\frac{Y}{Q}\right) = 0.02\left(\frac{5000}{750}\right) = 0.133$$

6.19. Given $Q = 400 - 8P + 0.05Y$, where $P = 15$ and $Y = 12\,000$. Find (a) the income elasticity of demand and (b) the growth potential of the product, if income is expanding by 5 percent a year. (c) Comment on the growth potential of the product.

(a) $Q = 400 - 8(15) + 0.05(12\,000) = 880$ and $\partial Q/\partial Y = 0.05$. Thus,

$$\epsilon_Y = \frac{\partial Q}{\partial Y}\left(\frac{Y}{Q}\right) = 0.05\left(\frac{12\,000}{880}\right) = 0.68$$

(b)
$$\epsilon_Y = \frac{\partial Q}{Q} \div \frac{\partial Y}{Y}$$

Rearranging terms and substituting the known parameters,

$$\frac{\partial Q}{Q} = \epsilon_Y \frac{\partial Y}{Y} = 0.68(0.05) = 0.034$$

The demand for the good will increase by 3.4 percent.

(c) Since $0 < \epsilon_Y < 1$, it can be expected that demand for the good will increase with national income, but the increase will be less than proportionate. Thus, while demand grows absolutely, the relative market share of the good will decline in an expanding economy. If $\epsilon_Y > 1$, the demand for the product would grow faster than the rate of expansion in the economy, and increase its relative market share. And if $\epsilon_Y < 0$, demand for the good would decline as income increases.

6.20. Given $Q_1 = 100 - P_1 + 0.75P_2 - 0.25P_3 + 0.0075Y$. At $P_1 = 10$, $P_2 = 20$, $P_3 = 40$, and $Y = 10\,000$, $Q_1 = 170$. Find the different cross elasticities of demand.

$$\epsilon_{12} = \frac{\partial Q_1}{\partial P_2}\left(\frac{P_2}{Q_1}\right) = 0.75\left(\frac{20}{170}\right) = 0.088$$

$$\epsilon_{13} = \frac{\partial Q_1}{\partial P_3}\left(\frac{P_3}{Q_1}\right) = -0.25\left(\frac{40}{170}\right) = -0.059$$

6.21. Given $Q_1 = 50 - 4P_1 - 3P_2 + 2P_3 + 0.001Y$. At $P_1 = 5$, $P_2 = 7$, $P_3 = 3$, and $Y = 11\,000$, $Q_1 = 26$. (a) Use cross elasticities to determine the relationship between good 1 and the other two goods. (b) Determine the effect on Q_1 of a 10 percent price increase for each of the other goods individually.

(a)
$$\epsilon_{12} = -3(\tfrac{7}{26}) = -0.81 \qquad \epsilon_{13} = 2(\tfrac{3}{26}) = 0.23$$

With ϵ_{12} negative, goods 1 and 2 are complements. An increase in P_2 will lead to a decrease in Q_1. With ϵ_{13} positive, goods 1 and 3 are substitutes. An increase in P_3 will increase Q_1.

(b)
$$\epsilon_{12} = \frac{\partial Q_1}{Q_1} \div \frac{\partial P_2}{P_2}$$

Rearranging terms and substituting the known parameters,

$$\frac{\partial Q_1}{Q_1} = \epsilon_{12} \frac{\partial P_2}{P_2} = -0.81(0.10) = -0.081$$

If P_2 increases by 10 percent, Q_1 decreases by 8.1 percent.

$$\epsilon_{13} = \frac{\partial Q_1}{Q_1} \div \frac{\partial P_3}{P_3}$$

$$\frac{\partial Q_1}{Q_1} = \epsilon_{13} \frac{\partial P_3}{P_3} = 0.23(0.10) = 0.023$$

If P_3 increases by 10 percent, Q_1 increases by 2.3 percent.

OPTIMIZING ECONOMIC FUNCTIONS

6.22. Given the profit function $\pi = 160x - 3x^2 - 2xy - 2y^2 + 120y - 18$ for a firm producing two goods x and y, (a) maximize profits, (b) test the second-order condition, and (c) evaluate the function at the critical values $\bar{x}$ and $\bar{y}$.

(a)
$$\pi_x = 160 - 6x - 2y = 0 \qquad \pi_y = -2x - 4y + 120 = 0$$

When solved simultaneously, $\bar{x} = 20$ and $\bar{y} = 20$.

(b) Taking the second partials,

$$\pi_{xx} = -6 \qquad \pi_{yy} = -4 \qquad \pi_{xy} = -2$$

With both direct second partials negative, and $\pi_{xx}\pi_{yy} > (\pi_{xy})^2$, π is maximized at $\bar{x} = \bar{y} = 20$.

(c)
$$\pi = 2782$$

6.23. Redo Problem 6.22, given $\pi = 25x - x^2 - xy - 2y^2 + 30y - 28$.

(a)
$$\pi_x = 25 - 2x - y = 0 \qquad \pi_y = -x - 4y + 30 = 0$$

Thus, $\bar{x} = 10$ and $\bar{y} = 5$.

(b)
$$\pi_{xx} = -2 \qquad \pi_{yy} = -4 \qquad \pi_{xy} = -1$$

With π_{xx} and π_{yy} both negative and $\pi_{xx}\pi_{yy} > (\pi_{xy})^2$, π is maximized.

(c)
$$\pi = 172$$

6.24. A monopolist sells two products x and y for which the demand functions are

$$x = 25 - 0.5P_x \tag{6.29}$$

$$y = 30 - P_y \tag{6.30}$$

and the combined cost function is

$$c = x^2 + 2xy + y^2 + 20 \tag{6.31}$$

Find (a) the profit-maximizing level of output for each product, (b) the profit-maximizing price for each product, and (c) the maximum profit.

(a) Since $\pi = \text{TR}_x + \text{TR}_y - \text{TC}$, in this case,

$$\pi = P_x x + P_y y - c \tag{6.32}$$

From (6.29) and (6.30),

$$P_x = 50 - 2x \tag{6.33}$$

$$P_y = 30 - y \tag{6.34}$$

Substituting in (6.32),

$$\pi = (50 - 2x)x + (30 - y)y - (x^2 + 2xy + y^2 + 20)$$
$$= 50x - 3x^2 + 30y - 2y^2 - 2xy - 20 \tag{6.35}$$

The first-order condition for maximizing (6.35) is

$$\pi_x = 50 - 6x - 2y = 0 \qquad \pi_y = 30 - 4y - 2x = 0$$

Solving simultaneously, $\bar{x} = 7$ and $\bar{y} = 4$. Testing the second-order condition, $\pi_{xx} = -6$, $\pi_{yy} = -4$, and $\pi_{xy} = -2$. With both direct partials negative and $\pi_{xx}\pi_{yy} > (\pi_{xy})^2$, π is maximized.

(b) Substituting $\bar{x} = 7$, $\bar{y} = 4$ in (6.33) and (6.34),

$$P_x = 50 - 2(7) = 36 \qquad P_y = 30 - 4 = 26$$

(c) Substituting $\bar{x} = 7$, $\bar{y} = 4$ in (6.35), $\pi = 215$.

6.25. Find the profit-maximizing level of (a) output, (b) price, and (c) profit for a monopolist with the demand functions

$$x = 50 - 0.5P_x \tag{6.36}$$

$$y = 76 - P_y \tag{6.37}$$

and the total cost function $c = 3x^2 + 2xy + 2y^2 + 55$.

(a) From (6.36) and (6.37),

$$P_x = 100 - 2x \tag{6.38}$$

$$P_y = 76 - y \tag{6.39}$$

Substituting in $\pi = P_x x + P_y y - c$,

$$\begin{aligned}
\pi &= (100 - 2x)x + (76 - y)y - (3x^2 + 2xy + 2y^2 + 55) \\
&= 100x - 5x^2 + 76y - 3y^2 - 2xy - 55 \tag{6.40}
\end{aligned}$$

Maximizing (6.40),

$$\pi_x = 100 - 10x - 2y = 0 \qquad \pi_y = 76 - 6y - 2x = 0$$

Thus, $\bar{x} = 8$ and $\bar{y} = 10$. Checking the second-order condition, $\pi_{xx} = -10$, $\pi_{yy} = -6$, and $\pi_{xy} = -2$. Since $\pi_{xx}, \pi_{yy} < 0$ and $\pi_{xx}\pi_{yy} > (\pi_{xy})^2$, π is maximized at the critical values.

(b) Substituting $\bar{x} = 8$, $\bar{y} = 10$ in (6.38) and (6.39),

$$P_x = 100 - 2(8) = 84 \qquad P_y = 76 - 10 = 66$$

(c) From (6.40), $\pi = 725$.

6.26. Find the profit-maximizing level of (a) output, (b) price, and (c) profit for the monopolistic producer with the demand functions

$$Q_1 = 49\tfrac{1}{3} - \tfrac{2}{3}P_1 \tag{6.41}$$

$$Q_2 = 36 - \tfrac{1}{2}P_2 \tag{6.42}$$

and the joint cost function $c = Q_1^2 + 2Q_1Q_2 + Q_2^2 + 120$.

(a) From (6.41) and (6.42),

$$P_1 = 74 - 1.5Q_1 \tag{6.43}$$

$$P_2 = 72 - 2Q_2 \tag{6.44}$$

Substituting in $\pi = P_1Q_1 + P_2Q_2 - c$,

$$\begin{aligned}
\pi &= (74 - 1.5Q_1)Q_1 + (72 - 2Q_2)Q_2 - (Q_1^2 + 2Q_1Q_2 + Q_2^2 + 120) \\
&= 74Q_1 - 2.5Q_1^2 + 72Q_2 - 3Q_2^2 - 2Q_1Q_2 - 120 \tag{6.45}
\end{aligned}$$

The first-order condition for maximizing (6.45) is

$$\pi_1 = 74 - 5Q_1 - 2Q_2 = 0 \qquad \pi_2 = 72 - 6Q_2 - 2Q_1 = 0$$

Thus, $\bar{Q}_1 = 11.54$ and $\bar{Q}_2 = 8.15$. Testing the second-order condition, $\pi_{11} = -5$, $\pi_{22} = -6$, and $\pi_{12} = -2$. Thus, $\pi_{11}, \pi_{22} < 0$; $\pi_{11}\pi_{22} > (\pi_{12})^2$, and π is maximized.

(b) Substituting the critical values in (6.43) and (6.44),

$$P_1 = 74 - 1.5(11.54) = 56.69 \qquad P_2 = 72 - 2(8.15) = 55.70$$

(c) $$\pi = 600.46$$

6.27. Find the profit-maximizing level of (a) output, (b) price, and (c) profit when

$$Q_1 = 5200 - 10P_1 \tag{6.46}$$

$$Q_2 = 8200 - 20P_2 \tag{6.47}$$

and $$c = 0.1Q_1^2 + 0.1Q_1Q_2 + 0.2Q_2^2 + 325$$

(a)   From (6.46) and (6.47),

$$P_1 = 520 - 0.1Q_1 \tag{6.48}$$

$$P_2 = 410 - 0.05Q_2 \tag{6.49}$$

Thus, $$\pi = (520 - 0.1Q_1)Q_1 + (410 - 0.05Q_2)Q_2 - (0.1Q_1^2 + 0.1Q_1Q_2 + 0.2Q_2^2 + 325)$$
$$= 520Q_1 - 0.2Q_1^2 + 410Q_2 - 0.25Q_2^2 - 0.1Q_1Q_2 - 325 \tag{6.50}$$

Maximizing (6.50),

$$\pi_1 = 520 - 0.4Q_1 - 0.1Q_2 = 0 \qquad \pi_2 = 410 - 0.5Q_2 - 0.1Q_1 = 0$$

Thus, $\bar{Q}_1 = 1152.63$ and $\bar{Q}_2 = 589.47$. Checking the second-order condition, $\pi_{11} = -0.4$, $\pi_{22} = -0.5$, and $\pi_{12} = -0.1 = \pi_{21}$. Since $\pi_{11}, \pi_{22} < 0$ and $\pi_{11}\pi_{22} > (\pi_{12})^2$, π is maximized at $\bar{Q}_1 = 1152.63$ and $\bar{Q}_2 = 589.47$.

(b)   Substituting in (6.48) and (6.49),

$$P_1 = 520 - 0.1(1152.63) = 404.74 \qquad P_2 = 410 - 0.05(589.47) = 380.53$$

(c) $$\pi = 420\,201.32$$

CONSTRAINED OPTIMIZATION IN ECONOMICS

6.28. (a) What combination of goods x and y should a firm produce to minimize costs when the joint cost function is $c = 6x^2 + 10y^2 - xy + 30$ and the firm has a production quota of $x + y = 34$? (b) Estimate the effect on costs if the production quota is reduced by 1 unit.

(a)   Form a new function by setting the constraint equal to zero, multiplying it by λ, and adding it to the original or objective function. Thus,

$$C = 6x^2 + 10y^2 - xy + 30 + \lambda(34 - x - y)$$
$$C_x = 12x - y - \lambda = 0$$
$$C_y = 20y - x - \lambda = 0$$
$$C_\lambda = 34 - x - y = 0$$

Solving simultaneously, $\bar{x} = 21$, $\bar{y} = 13$, and $\bar{\lambda} = 239$. Thus, $C = 4093$. Second-order conditions are discussed in Section 12.5.

(b)   With $\lambda = 239$, a decrease in the constant of the constraint (the production quota) will lead to a cost reduction of approximately 239.

6.29. (a) What output mix should a profit-maximizing firm produce when its total profit function is $\pi = 80x - 2x^2 - xy - 3y^2 + 100y$ and its maximum output capacity is $x + y = 12$? (b) Estimate the effect on profits if output capacity is expanded by 1 unit.

(a) $$\Pi = 80x - 2x^2 - xy - 3y^2 + 100y + \lambda(12 - x - y)$$
$$\Pi_x = 80 - 4x - y - \lambda = 0$$
$$\Pi_y = -x - 6y + 100 - \lambda = 0$$
$$\Pi_\lambda = 12 - x - y = 0$$

When solved simultaneously, $\bar{x} = 5$, $\bar{y} = 7$, and $\bar{\lambda} = 53$. Thus, $\pi = 868$.

(b)   With $\bar{\lambda} = 53$, an increase in output capacity should lead to increased profits of approximately 53.

6.30. A rancher faces the profit function

$$\pi = 110x - 3x^2 - 2xy - 2y^2 + 140y$$

where $x =$ sides of beef and $y =$ hides. Since there are two sides of beef for every hide, it follows that output must be in the proportion

$$\frac{x}{2} = y \qquad x = 2y$$

At what level of output will the rancher maximize profits?

$$\Pi = 110x - 3x^2 - 2xy - 2y^2 + 140y + \lambda(x - 2y)$$
$$\Pi_x = 110 - 6x - 2y + \lambda = 0$$
$$\Pi_y = -2x - 4y + 140 - 2\lambda = 0$$
$$\Pi_\lambda = x - 2y = 0$$

Solving simultaneously, $\bar{x} = 20$, $\bar{y} = 10$, $\bar{\lambda} = 30$, and $\pi = 1800$.

6.31. (a) Minimize costs for a firm with the cost function $c = 5x^2 + 2xy + 3y^2 + 800$ subject to the production quota $x + y = 39$. (b) Estimate additional costs if the production quota is increased to 40.

(a)
$$C = 5x^2 + 2xy + 3y^2 + 800 + \lambda(39 - x - y)$$
$$C_x = 10x + 2y - \lambda = 0$$
$$C_y = 2x + 6y - \lambda = 0$$
$$C_\lambda = 39 - x - y = 0$$

When solved simultaneously, $\bar{x} = 13$, $\bar{y} = 26$, $\bar{\lambda} = 182$, and $C = 4349$.

(b) Since $\bar{\lambda} = 182$, an increased production quota will lead to additional costs of approximately 182.

6.32. A monopolistic firm has the following demand functions for each of its products x and y:

$$x = 72 - 0.5P_x \qquad (6.51)$$
$$y = 120 - P_y \qquad (6.52)$$

The combined cost function is $c = x^2 + xy + y^2 + 35$, and maximum joint production is 40. Thus, $x + y = 40$. Find the profit-maximizing level of (a) output, (b) price, and (c) profit.

(a) From (6.51) and (6.52),

$$P_x = 144 - 2x \qquad (6.53)$$
$$P_y = 120 - y \qquad (6.54)$$

Thus, $\pi = (144 - 2x)x + (120 - y)y - (x^2 + xy + y^2 + 35) = 144x - 3x^2 - xy - 2y^2 + 120y - 35$. Incorporating the constraint,

$$\Pi = 144x - 3x^2 - xy - 2y^2 + 120y - 35 + \lambda(40 - x - y)$$

Thus,
$$\Pi_x = 144 - 6x - y - \lambda = 0$$
$$\Pi_y = -x - 4y + 120 - \lambda = 0$$
$$\Pi_\lambda = 40 - x - y = 0$$

and, $\bar{x} = 18$, $\bar{y} = 22$, and $\bar{\lambda} = 14$.

(b)   Substituting in (6.53) and (6.54),

$$P_x = 144 - 2(18) = 108 \qquad P_y = 120 - 22 = 98$$

(c) $\pi = 2861$

6.33.   A manufacturer of parts for the tricycle industry sells three tires (x) for every frame (y). Thus,

$$\frac{x}{3} = y \qquad x = 3y$$

If the demand functions are

$$x = 63 - 0.25P_x \tag{6.55}$$

$$y = 60 - \tfrac{1}{3}P_y \tag{6.56}$$

and costs are

$$c = x^2 + xy + y^2 + 190$$

find the profit-maximizing level of (a) output, (b) price, and (c) profit.

(a)   From (6.55) and (6.56),

$$P_x = 252 - 4x \tag{6.57}$$

$$P_y = 180 - 3y \tag{6.58}$$

Thus, $\pi = (252 - 4x)x + (180 - 3y)y - (x^2 + xy + y^2 + 190) = 252x - 5x^2 - xy + 180y - 190 - 4y^2$

Forming a new, constrained function,

$$\Pi = 252x - 5x^2 - xy - 4y^2 + 180y - 190 + \lambda(x - 3y)$$

Hence, $\Pi_x = 252 - 10x - y + \lambda = 0 \qquad \Pi_y = -x - 8y + 180 - 3\lambda = 0 \qquad \Pi_\lambda = x - 3y = 0$

and $\bar{x} = 27$, $\bar{y} = 9$, and $\bar{\lambda} = 27$.

(b)   From (6.57) and (6.58), $P_x = 144$ and $P_y = 153$.

(c) $\pi = 4022$

6.34.   Problem 4.22 dealt with the profit-maximizing level of output for a firm producing a single product that is sold in two distinct markets when it does and does not discriminate. The functions given were

$$Q_1 = 21 - 0.1P_1 \tag{6.59}$$

$$Q_2 = 50 - 0.4P_2 \tag{6.60}$$

$$c = 2000 + 10Q \qquad \text{where } Q = Q_1 + Q_2 \tag{6.61}$$

Use multivariable calculus to check your solution to Problem 4.22.

From (6.59), (6.60), and (6.61),

$$P_1 = 210 - 10Q_1 \tag{6.62}$$

$$P_2 = 125 - 2.5Q_2 \tag{6.63}$$

$$c = 2000 + 10Q_1 + 10Q_2$$

With discrimination $P_1 \neq P_2$ since different prices are charged in different markets, and therefore

$$\pi = (210 - 10Q_1)Q_1 + (125 - 2.5Q_2)Q_2 - (2000 + 10Q_1 + 10Q_2)$$
$$= 200Q_1 - 10Q_1^2 + 115Q_2 - 2.5Q_2^2 - 2000$$

Taking the first partials,

$$\pi_1 = 200 - 20Q_1 = 0 \qquad \pi_2 = 115 - 5Q_2 = 0$$

Thus, $\bar{Q}_1 = 10$ and $\bar{Q}_2 = 23$. Substituting in (6.62) and (6.63), $\bar{P}_1 = 110$ and $\bar{P}_2 = 67.5$.

If there is no discrimination, the same price must be charged in both markets. Hence $P_1 = P_2$. Substituting from (6.62) and (6.63),

$$210 - 10Q_1 = 125 - 2.5Q_2$$
$$2.5Q_2 - 10Q_1 = -85$$

Rearranging this as a constraint and forming a new function,

$$\Pi = 200Q_1 - 10Q_1^2 + 115Q_2 - 2.5Q_2^2 - 2000 + \lambda(85 - 10Q_1 + 2.5Q_2)$$

Thus, $\Pi_1 = 200 - 20Q_1 - 10\lambda = 0 \qquad \Pi_2 = 115 - 5Q_2 + 2.5\lambda = 0 \qquad \Pi_\lambda = 85 - 10Q_1 + 2.5Q_2 = 0$

and $\bar{Q}_1 = 13.4$, $\bar{Q}_2 = 19.6$, and $\bar{\lambda} = -6.8$. Substituting in (6.62) and (6.63),

$$P_1 = 210 - 10(13.4) = 76$$
$$P_2 = 125 - 2.5(19.6) = 76$$
$$Q = 13.4 + 19.6 = 33$$

6.35. Check your answers to Problem 4.23, given

$$Q_1 = 24 - 0.2P_1 \qquad Q_2 = 10 - 0.05P_2$$
$$c = 35 + 40Q \qquad \text{where} \quad Q = Q_1 + Q_2$$

From the information given,

$$P_1 = 120 - 5Q_1 \tag{6.64}$$
$$P_2 = 200 - 20Q_2 \tag{6.65}$$
$$c = 35 + 40Q_1 + 40Q_2$$

With price discrimination,

$$\pi = (120 - 5Q_1)Q_1 + (200 - 20Q_2)Q_2 - (35 + 40Q_1 + 40Q_2) = 80Q_1 - 5Q_1^2 + 160Q_2 - 20Q_2^2 - 35$$

Thus, $$\pi_1 = 80 - 10Q_1 = 0 \qquad \pi_2 = 160 - 40Q_2 = 0$$

and $\bar{Q}_1 = 8$, $\bar{Q}_2 = 4$, $P_1 = 80$, and $P_2 = 120$.

If there is no price discrimination, $P_1 = P_2$. Substituting from (6.64) and (6.65),

$$120 - 5Q_1 = 200 - 20Q_2$$
$$20Q_2 - 5Q_1 = 80 \tag{6.66}$$

Forming a new function with (6.66) as a constraint,

$$\Pi = 80Q_1 - 5Q_1^2 + 160Q_2 - 20Q_2^2 - 35 + \lambda(80 + 5Q_1 - 20Q_2)$$

Thus, $\Pi_1 = 80 - 10Q_1 + 5\lambda = 0 \qquad \Pi_2 = 160 - 40Q_2 - 20\lambda = 0 \qquad \Pi_\lambda = 80 + 5Q_1 - 20Q_2 = 0$

and $\bar{Q}_1 = 6.4$, $\bar{Q}_2 = 5.6$, and $\bar{\lambda} = -3.2$. Substituting in (6.64) and (6.65),

$$P_1 = 120 - 5(6.4) = 88$$
$$P_2 = 200 - 20(5.6) = 88$$
$$Q = 6.4 + 5.6 = 12$$

6.36. (a) Maximize utility $u = Q_1Q_2$ when $P_1 = 1$, $P_2 = 4$, and one's budget $B = 120$. (b) Estimate the effect of a 1-unit increase in the budget.

(a) The budget constraint is $Q_1 + 4Q_2 = 120$. Forming a new function to incorporate the constraint,

$$U = Q_1 Q_2 + \lambda(120 - Q_1 - 4Q_2)$$

Thus, $\quad U_1 = Q_2 - \lambda = 0 \qquad U_2 = Q_1 - 4\lambda = 0 \qquad U_\lambda = 120 - Q_1 - 4Q_2 = 0$

and $\bar{Q}_1 = 60, \bar{Q}_2 = 15$, and $\bar{\lambda} = 15$.

(b) With $\bar{\lambda} = 15$, a \$1 increase in the budget will lead to an increase in the utility function of approximately 15. Thus, the marginal utility of money (or income) at $\bar{Q}_1 = 60$ and $\bar{Q}_2 = 15$ is approximately 15.

6.37. (a) Maximize utility $u = Q_1 Q_2$, subject to $P_1 = 10$, $P_2 = 2$, and $B = 240$. (b) What is the marginal utility of money?

(a) Form the Lagrangian function $U = Q_1 Q_2 + \lambda(240 - 10Q_1 - 2Q_2)$.

$$U_1 = Q_2 - 10\lambda = 0 \qquad U_2 = Q_1 - 2\lambda = 0 \qquad U_\lambda = 240 - 10Q_1 - 2Q_2 = 0$$

Thus, $\bar{Q}_1 = 12, \bar{Q}_2 = 60$, and $\bar{\lambda} = 6$.

(b) The marginal utility of money at $\bar{Q}_1 = 12$ and $\bar{Q}_2 = 60$ is approximately 6.

6.38. Maximize utility $u = Q_1 Q_2 + Q_1 + 2Q_2$, subject to $P_1 = 2$, $P_2 = 5$, and $B = 51$.

Form the Lagrangian function $U = Q_1 Q_2 + Q_1 + 2Q_2 + \lambda(51 - 2Q_1 - 5Q_2)$.

$$U_1 = Q_2 + 1 - 2\lambda = 0 \qquad U_2 = Q_1 + 2 - 5\lambda = 0 \qquad U_\lambda = 51 - 2Q_1 - 5Q_2 = 0$$

Thus, $\bar{Q}_1 = 13, \bar{Q}_2 = 5$, and $\bar{\lambda} = 3$.

6.39. Maximize utility $u = xy + 3x + y$ subject to $P_x = 8$, $P_y = 12$, and $B = 212$.

The Lagrangian function is $U = xy + 3x + y + \lambda(212 - 8x - 12y)$.

$$U_x = y + 3 - 8\lambda = 0 \qquad U_y = x + 1 - 12\lambda = 0 \qquad U_\lambda = 212 - 8x - 12y = 0$$

Thus, $\bar{x} = 15, \bar{y} = 7\frac{2}{3}$, and $\bar{\lambda} = 1\frac{1}{3}$.

INEQUALITY CONSTRAINTS

6.40. Minimize $z = 3x^2 - xy + 2y^2 - 4x - 7y + 12$ subject to the constraint $x + y \geq 15$.

Assume initially that $x + y = 15$ and optimize the Lagrangian function.

$$Z = 3x^2 - xy + 2y^2 - 4x - 7y + 12 + \lambda(15 - x - y)$$
$$Z_x = 6x - y - 4 - \lambda = 0 \qquad Z_y = -x + 4y - 7 - \lambda = 0$$
$$Z_\lambda = 15 - x - y = 0$$

Thus, $\bar{x} = 6, \bar{y} = 9, \bar{\lambda} = 23$, and $\bar{Z} = 141$.

From rule III in Section 6.7, when minimizing subject to $g(x, y) \geq 0$, if $\lambda \geq 0$, the constraint is a limitation and the constrained minimum has been found. If there were no constraint, the function would be minimized at $x = 1$ and $y = 2$, as found in Problem 5.10(a), where $z = 3$.

6.41. Minimize the function in Problem 6.40 subject to $x + y \geq 2$.

$$Z = 3x^2 - xy + 2y^2 - 4x - 7y + 12 + \lambda(2 - x - y)$$
$$Z_x = 6x - y - 4 - \lambda = 0 \qquad Z_y = -x + 4y - 7 - \lambda = 0$$
$$Z_\lambda = 2 - x - y = 0$$

Here $\bar{x} \approx 0.58, \bar{y} \approx 1.42, \bar{\lambda} \approx -1.94$, and $\bar{Z} \approx 3.96$.

With $\lambda < 0$, the constraint is not a limitation. By minimizing the objective function without the constraint, the desired minimum will be found. From Problem 5.10(a), at $x = 1$ and $y = 2$, $z = 3$, which satisfies $x + y \geq 2$.

6.42. Maximize a firm's profit function $\pi = 160x - 3x^2 - 2xy - 2y^2 + 120y - 18$ given the fact that the firm's joint output cannot exceed 35, that is, $x + y \leq 35$.

The Lagrangian function is

$$\Pi = 160x - 3x^2 - 2xy - 2y^2 + 120y - 18 + \lambda(35 - x - y)$$

$$\Pi_x = 160 - 6x - 2y - \lambda = 0 \qquad \Pi_y = -2x - 4y + 120 - \lambda = 0 \qquad \Pi_\lambda = 35 - x - y = 0$$

Thus, $\bar{x} = 18.33$, $\bar{y} = 16.67$, $\bar{\lambda} = 16.67$, and $\pi = 2740.34$.

When maximizing subject to $g(x, y) \leq 0$, if $\bar{\lambda} > 0$, the constraint is a limitation and the constrained maximum has been found. From Problem 6.22, unconstrained profits are $\pi = 2782$ at $\bar{x} = 20$ and $\bar{y} = 20$.

6.43. Maximize the function in Problem 6.42 subject to $x + y \leq 50$.

Form the Lagrangian function $\Pi = 160x - 3x^2 - 2xy - 2y^2 + 120y - 18 + \lambda(50 - x - y)$.

$$\Pi_x = 160 - 6x - 2y - \lambda = 0 \qquad \Pi_y = -2x - 4y + 120 - \lambda = 0 \qquad \Pi_\lambda = 50 - x - y = 0$$

Thus, $\bar{x} = 23.33$, $\bar{y} = 26.67$, $\bar{\lambda} = -33.33$, and $\pi = 2615.33$.

With $\bar{\lambda} < 0$, the constraint is not a limitation. Ignore the constraint and simply maximize the objective function.

HOMOGENEITY AND RETURNS TO SCALE

6.44. Determine the level of homogeneity and returns to scale for each of the following production functions:

(a) $Q = x^2 + 6xy + 7y^2$

Q is homogeneous of degree 2, and returns to scale are increasing because

$$f(kx, ky) = (kx)^2 + 6(kx)(ky) + 7(ky)^2 = k^2(x^2 + 6xy + 7y^2)$$

(b) $Q = x^3 - xy^2 + 3y^3 + x^2y$

Q is homogeneous of degree 3, and returns to scale are increasing because

$$f(kx, ky) = (kx)^3 - (kx)(ky)^2 + 3(ky)^3 + (kx)^2(ky) = k^3(x^3 - xy^2 + 3y^3 + x^2y)$$

(c) $Q = \dfrac{3x^2}{5y^2}$

Q is homogeneous of degree 0, and returns to scale are decreasing because

$$f(kx, ky) = \frac{3(kx)^2}{5(ky)^2} = \frac{3x^2}{5y^2} \qquad \text{and} \qquad k^0 = 1$$

CONSTRAINED OPTIMIZATION OF COBB-DOUGLAS FUNCTIONS

6.45. Optimize the following Cobb-Douglas production functions subject to the given constraints by (1) forming the Lagrange function and (2) finding the critical values as in Example 12.

(a) $q = K^{0.3}L^{0.5}$ subject to $6K + 2L = 384$

(1) $$Q = K^{0.3}L^{0.5} + \lambda(384 - 6K - 2L)$$

(2) $$Q_K = 0.3K^{-0.7}L^{0.5} - 6\lambda = 0 \tag{6.67}$$

$$Q_L = 0.5K^{0.3}L^{-0.5} - 2\lambda = 0 \tag{6.68}$$

$$Q_\lambda = 384 - 6K - 2L = 0 \tag{6.69}$$

Rearrange, then divide (6.67) by (6.68) to eliminate λ.

$$\frac{0.3K^{-0.7}L^{0.5}}{0.5K^{0.3}L^{-0.5}} = \frac{6\lambda}{2\lambda}$$

Subtracting exponents in division,

$$0.6K^{-1}L^1 = 3$$

$$\frac{L}{K} = \frac{3}{0.6} \qquad L = 5K$$

Substitute $L = 5K$ in (6.69).

$$384 - 6K - 2(5K) = 0 \qquad K_0 = 24 \qquad L_0 = 120$$

Second-order conditions are tested in Problem 12.31(b).

(b) $q = 10K^{0.7}L^{0.1}$, given $P_K = 28$, $P_L = 10$, and $B = 4000$

(1) $$Q = 10K^{0.7}L^{0.1} + \lambda(4000 - 28K - 10L)$$

(2) $$Q_K = 7K^{-0.3}L^{0.1} - 28\lambda = 0 \tag{6.70}$$

$$Q_L = 1K^{0.7}L^{-0.9} - 10\lambda = 0 \tag{6.71}$$

$$Q_\lambda = 4000 - 28K - 10L = 0 \tag{6.72}$$

Divide (6.70) by (6.71) to eliminate λ.

$$\frac{7K^{-0.3}L^{0.1}}{1K^{0.7}L^{-0.9}} = \frac{28\lambda}{10\lambda}$$

$$7K^{-1}L^1 = 2.8$$

$$\frac{L}{K} = \frac{2.8}{7} \qquad L = 0.4K$$

Substituting in (6.72), $\qquad K_0 = 125 \qquad L_0 = 50$

See Problem 12.31(c) for the second-order conditions.

6.46. Maximize the following utility functions subject to the given budget constraints, using the same steps as above.

(a) $u = x^{0.6}y^{0.25}$, given $P_x = 8$, $P_y = 5$, and $B = 680$

(1) $$U = x^{0.6}y^{0.25} + \lambda(680 - 8x - 5y)$$

(2) $$U_x = 0.6x^{-0.4}y^{0.25} - 8\lambda = 0 \tag{6.73}$$

$$U_y = 0.25x^{0.6}y^{-0.75} - 5\lambda = 0 \tag{6.74}$$

$$U_\lambda = 680 - 8x - 5y = 0 \tag{6.75}$$

Divide (6.73) by (6.74).

$$\frac{0.6x^{-0.4}y^{0.25}}{0.25x^{0.6}y^{-0.75}} = \frac{8\lambda}{5\lambda}$$

$$2.4x^{-1}y^1 = 1.6$$

$$y = \tfrac{2}{3}x$$

Substitute in (6.75). $\qquad x_0 = 60 \qquad y_0 = 40$

(b) $u = x^{0.8}y^{0.2}$, given $P_x = 5$, $P_y = 3$, and $B = 75$

(1)
$$U = x^{0.8}y^{0.2} + \lambda(75 - 5x - 3y)$$

(2)
$$U_x = 0.8x^{-0.2}y^{0.2} - 5\lambda = 0 \tag{6.76}$$

$$U_y = 0.2x^{0.8}y^{-0.8} - 3\lambda = 0 \tag{6.77}$$

$$U_\lambda = 75 - 5x - 3y = 0 \tag{6.78}$$

Divide (6.76) by (6.77).

$$\frac{0.8x^{-0.2}y^{0.2}}{0.2x^{0.8}y^{-0.8}} = \frac{5\lambda}{3\lambda}$$

$$4x^{-1}y^1 = \tfrac{5}{3}$$

$$y = \tfrac{5}{12}x$$

Substitute in (6.78). $x_0 = 12 \qquad y_0 = 5$

CONSTRAINED OPTIMIZATION OF CES PRODUCTION FUNCTIONS

6.47. Optimize the following CES production function subject to the given constraint by (1) forming the Lagrange function and (2) finding the critical values as in Example 13:

$$q = 80[0.4K^{-0.25} + (1 - 0.4)L^{-0.25}]^{-1/0.25} \qquad \text{subject to } 5K + 2L = 150$$

(1)
$$Q = 80(0.4K^{-0.25} + 0.6L^{-0.25})^{-4} + \lambda(150 - 5K - 2L)$$

(2) Using the generalized power function rule for Q_K and Q_L,

$$\begin{aligned} Q_K &= -320(0.4K^{-0.25} + 0.6L^{-0.25})^{-5}(-0.1K^{-1.25}) - 5\lambda = 0 \\ &= 32K^{-1.25}(0.4K^{-0.25} + 0.6L^{-0.25})^{-5} - 5\lambda = 0 \end{aligned} \tag{6.79}$$

$$\begin{aligned} Q_L &= -320(0.4K^{-0.25} + 0.6L^{-0.25})^{-5}(-0.15L^{-1.25}) - 2\lambda = 0 \\ &= 48L^{-1.25}(0.4K^{-0.25} + 0.6L^{-0.25})^{-5} - 2\lambda = 0 \end{aligned} \tag{6.80}$$

$$Q_\lambda = 150 - 5K - 2L = 0 \tag{6.81}$$

Rearrange, then divide (6.79) by (6.80) to eliminate λ.

$$\frac{32K^{-1.25}(0.4K^{-0.25} + 0.6L^{-0.25})^{-5}}{48L^{-1.25}(0.4K^{-0.25} + 0.6L^{-0.25})^{-5}} = \frac{5\lambda}{2\lambda}$$

$$\frac{32K^{-1.25}}{48L^{-1.25}} = 2.5$$

$$K^{-1.25} = 3.75L^{-1.25}$$

Take the -1.25 root.

$$K = (3.75)^{-1/1.25}L = (3.75)^{-0.8}L$$

To find $(3.75)^{-0.8}$, enter 3.75 on a calculator, press the $\boxed{y^x}$ key, then enter 0.8 followed by the $\boxed{+/-}$ key to make it negative, and hit the $\boxed{=}$ key to find $(3.75)^{-0.8} = 0.34736$. Thus,

$$K \approx 0.35L$$

Substitute in (6.81).

$$150 - 5(0.35L) - 2L = 0 \qquad L_0 = 40 \qquad K_0 = 14$$

6.48. Optimize the CES production function

$$q = 100[0.2K^{-(-0.5)} + (1 - 0.2)L^{-(-0.5)}]^{-1/(-0.5)}$$

subject to the constraint $10K + 4L = 4100$, as in Problem 6.47.

$$(1) \qquad Q = 100(0.2K^{0.5} + 0.8L^{0.5})^2 + \lambda(4100 - 10K - 4L)$$

$$(2) \qquad Q_K = 200(0.2K^{0.5} + 0.8L^{0.5})(0.1K^{-0.5}) - 10\lambda = 0$$
$$= 20K^{-0.5}(0.2K^{0.5} + 0.8L^{0.5}) - 10\lambda = 0 \qquad (6.82)$$

$$Q_L = 200(0.2K^{0.5} + 0.8L^{0.5})(0.4L^{-0.5}) - 4\lambda = 0$$
$$= 80L^{-0.5}(0.2K^{0.5} + 0.8L^{0.5}) - 4\lambda = 0 \qquad (6.83)$$

$$Q_\lambda = 4100 - 10K - 4L = 0 \qquad (6.84)$$

Divide (6.82) by (6.83) to eliminate λ.

$$\frac{20K^{-0.5}(0.2K^{0.5} + 0.8L^{0.5})}{80L^{-0.5}(0.2K^{0.5} + 0.8L^{0.5})} = \frac{10\lambda}{4\lambda}$$

$$\frac{20K^{-0.5}}{80L^{-0.5}} = 2.5$$

$$K^{-0.5} = 10L^{-0.5}$$

Take the -0.5 root. $\qquad K = (10)^{-1/0.5}L = (10)^{-2}L$

$$K = 0.01L$$

Substitute in (6.84). $\qquad L_0 = 1000 \qquad K_0 = 10$

PARTIAL DERIVATIVES AND DIFFERENTIALS

6.49. Given $Q = 10K^{0.4}L^{0.6}$, (a) find the marginal productivity of capital and labor and (b) determine the effect on output of an additional unit of capital and labor at $K = 8$, $L = 20$.

(a) $\qquad \text{MP}_K = \dfrac{\partial Q}{\partial K} = 0.4(10)K^{-0.6}L^{0.6} = 4K^{-0.6}L^{0.6} \qquad \text{MP}_L = \dfrac{\partial Q}{\partial L} = 0.6(10)K^{0.4}L^{-0.4} = 6K^{0.4}L^{-0.4}$

(b) $\Delta Q \approx (\partial Q/\partial K)\,\Delta K$. For a 1-unit change in K, at $K = 8$, $L = 20$, $\Delta Q \approx 4K^{-0.6}L^{0.6} = 4(8)^{-0.6}(20)^{0.6}$. Using a calculator,

$$\Delta Q \approx 4K^{-0.6}L^{0.6} \approx 4(8)^{-0.6}(20)^{0.6} \approx 4(0.28717)(6.03418) \approx 6.93$$

Note: To find $(8)^{-0.6}$ on a calculator, enter 8, press the $\boxed{y^x}$ key, then enter 0.6 followed by the $\boxed{+/-}$ key to make it negative, and hit the $\boxed{=}$ key to find $(8)^{-0.6} = 0.28717$. To find $(20)^{0.6}$, enter 20, press the $\boxed{y^x}$ key, then enter 0.6, and hit the $\boxed{=}$ key to find $(20)^{0.6} = 6.03418$.

For a 1-unit change in L,

$$\Delta Q \approx 6K^{0.4}L^{-0.4} \approx 6(8)^{0.4}(20)^{-0.4} \approx 6(2.29740)(0.30171) \approx 4.16$$

6.50. Redo Problem 6.49, given $Q = 12K^{0.3}L^{0.5}$ at $K = 10$, $L = 15$.

(a) $\qquad \text{MP}_K = 3.6K^{-0.7}L^{0.5} \qquad \text{MP}_L = 6K^{0.3}L^{-0.5}$

(b) For a 1-unit change in K, at $K = 10$, $L = 15$, $\Delta Q \approx 3.6K^{-0.7}L^{0.5}$.

$$\Delta Q \approx 3.6(10)^{-0.7}(15)^{0.5} \approx 3.6(0.19953)(3.87298) \approx 2.78$$

For a 1-unit change in L,

$$\Delta Q \approx 6(10)^{0.3}(15)^{-0.5} \approx 6(1.99526)(0.25820) \approx 3.09$$

6.51. Given $Q = 4\sqrt{KL}$, find (a) MP_K and MP_L, and (b) determine the effect on Q of a 1-unit change in K and L, when $K = 50$ and $L = 600$.

(a) $Q = 4\sqrt{KL} = 4(KL)^{1/2}$. By the generalized power function rule,

$$\text{MP}_K = Q_K = 2(KL)^{-1/2}(L) = \frac{2L}{\sqrt{KL}} \qquad \text{MP}_L = Q_L = 2(KL)^{-1/2}(K) = \frac{2K}{\sqrt{KL}}$$

(b) For a 1-unit change in K at $K = 50$, $L = 600$,

$$\Delta Q \approx 2[50(600)]^{-1/2}(600) \approx 2(0.00577)(600) \approx 6.93$$

For a 1-unit change in L,

$$\Delta Q \approx 2[50(600)]^{-1/2}(50) \approx 2(0.00577)(50) \approx 0.58$$

6.52. Redo Problem 6.51, given $Q = 2\sqrt{KL}$, where $K = 100$ and $L = 1000$.

(a)
$$Q = 2(KL)^{1/2}$$

$$MP_K = (KL)^{-1/2}(L) = \frac{L}{\sqrt{KL}} \qquad MP_L = (KL)^{-1/2}(K) = \frac{K}{\sqrt{KL}}$$

(b) For a 1-unit change in K at $K = 100$, $L = 1000$,

$$\Delta Q \approx [100(1000)]^{-1/2}(1000) \approx (0.00316)(1000) \approx 3.16$$

For a 1-unit change in L,

$$\Delta Q \approx [100(1000)]^{-1/2}(100) \approx (0.00316)(100) \approx 0.316$$

6.53. A company's sales s have been found to depend on price P, advertising A, and the number of field representatives r it maintains.

$$s = (12\,000 - 900P)A^{1/2}r^{1/2}$$

Find the change in sales associated with (a) hiring another field representative, (b) an extra \$1 of advertising, (c) a \$0.10 reduction in price, at $P = \$6$, $r = 49$, and $A = \$8100$.

(a)
$$\Delta s \approx \frac{\partial s}{\partial r}\,\Delta r = \frac{1}{2}(12\,000 - 900P)A^{1/2}r^{-1/2}\,\Delta r$$
$$= \tfrac{1}{2}[12\,000 - 900(6)](8100)^{1/2}(49)^{-1/2}(1) = \tfrac{1}{2}(6600)(90)(\tfrac{1}{7}) = 42\,429$$

(b)
$$\Delta s \approx \frac{\partial s}{\partial A}\,\Delta A = \frac{1}{2}(12\,000 - 900P)A^{-1/2}r^{1/2}\,\Delta A = \frac{1}{2}(6600)\left(\frac{1}{90}\right)(7)(1) = 256.67$$

(c)
$$\Delta s \approx \frac{\partial s}{\partial P}\,\Delta P = -900A^{1/2}r^{1/2}\,\Delta P = -900(90)(7)(-0.10) = 56\,700$$

6.54. Given the sales function for a firm similar to the one in Problem 6.53: $s = (15\,000 - 1000P)A^{2/3}r^{1/4}$, estimate the change in sales from (a) hiring an extra field representative, (b) a \$1 increase in advertising, and (c) a \$0.01 reduction in price, when $P = 4$, $A = \$6000$, and $r = 24$.

(a)
$$\Delta s \approx \tfrac{1}{4}(15\,000 - 1000P)A^{2/3}r^{-3/4}\,\Delta r$$
$$\approx \tfrac{1}{4}(11\,000)(6000)^{2/3}(24)^{-3/4}(1)$$
$$\approx 2750(330.19)(0.09222) \approx 83\,740$$

(b)
$$\Delta s \approx \tfrac{2}{3}(15\,000 - 1000P)A^{-1/3}r^{1/4}\,\Delta A$$
$$\approx \tfrac{2}{3}(11\,000)(6000)^{-1/3}(24)^{1/4}(1)$$
$$\approx (7333.33)(0.05503)(2.21336) \approx 893$$

(c)
$$\Delta s \approx -1000A^{2/3}r^{1/4}\,\Delta P$$
$$\approx -1000(6000)^{2/3}(24)^{1/4}(-0.01)$$
$$\approx 10(330.19)(2.21336) \approx 7308$$

6.55. Given the equation for a *production isoquant*

$$16K^{1/4}L^{3/4} = 2144$$

use the implicit function rule from Section 5.10 to find the slope of the isoquant dK/dL which is the *marginal rate of technical substitution* (MRTS).

Set the equation equal to zero to get

$$F(K, L) = 16K^{1/4}L^{3/4} - 2144 = 0$$

Then from the implicit function rule in Equation (*5.13*),

$$\frac{dK}{dL} = \frac{-F_L}{F_K} = \frac{-12K^{1/4}L^{-1/4}}{4K^{-3/4}L^{3/4}} = \frac{-3K}{L} = \text{MRTS}$$

Compare this answer with that in Problem 4.38.

6.56. Given the equation for the production isoquant

$$25K^{3/5}L^{2/5} = 5400$$

find the MRTS, using the implicit function rule.

Set up the implicit function,

$$F(K, L) = 25K^{3/5}L^{2/5} - 5400 = 0$$

and use (*5.13*).

$$\frac{dK}{dL} = \frac{-F_L}{F_K} = \frac{-10K^{3/5}L^{-3/5}}{15K^{-2/5}L^{2/5}} = \frac{-2K}{3L} = \text{MRTS}$$

Compare this answer with that in Problem 4.39.

PROOFS

6.57. Use the properties of homogeneity to show that a strict Cobb-Douglas production function $q = AK^\alpha L^\beta$, where $\alpha + \beta = 1$, exhibits constant returns to scale.

Multiply each of the inputs by a constant k and factor.

$$\begin{aligned} q(kK, kL) &= A(kK)^\alpha(kL)^\beta = Ak^\alpha K^\alpha k^\beta L^\beta \\ &= k^{\alpha+\beta}(AK^\alpha L^\beta) = k^{\alpha+\beta}(q) \end{aligned}$$

As explained in Section 6.10, if $\alpha + \beta = 1$, returns to scale are constant; if $\alpha + \beta > 1$, returns to scale are increasing; and if $\alpha + \beta < 1$, returns to scale are decreasing.

6.58. Given the utility function $u = Ax^a y^b$ subject to the budget constraint $P_x x + P_y y = B$, prove that at the point of constrained utility maximization the ratio of prices P_x/P_y must equal the ratio of marginal utilities MU_x/MU_y.

$$U = Ax^a y^b + \lambda(B - P_x x - P_y y)$$

$$U_x = aAx^{a-1}y^b - \lambda P_x = 0 \tag{6.85}$$

$$U_y = bAx^a y^{b-1} - \lambda P_y = 0 \tag{6.86}$$

$$U_\lambda = B - P_x x - P_y y = 0$$

where in (*6.85*) $aAx^{a-1}y^b = u_x = \text{MU}_x$, and in (*6.86*) $bAx^a y^{b-1} = u_y = \text{MU}_y$.

From (*6.85*),

$$\lambda = \frac{aAx^{a-1}y^b}{P_x} = \frac{\text{MU}_x}{P_x}$$

From (*6.86*),

$$\lambda = \frac{bAx^a y^{b-1}}{P_y} = \frac{\text{MU}_y}{P_y}$$

Equating λ's,

$$\frac{\text{MU}_x}{P_x} = \frac{\text{MU}_y}{P_y} \qquad \frac{\text{MU}_x}{\text{MU}_y} = \frac{P_x}{P_y} \qquad \text{Q.E.D.}$$

6.59. Given a generalized Cobb-Douglas production function $q = AK^\alpha L^\beta$ subject to the budget constraint $P_K K + P_L L = B$, prove that for constrained optimization the least-cost input ratio is

$$\frac{K}{L} = \frac{\alpha P_L}{\beta P_K}$$

Using the Lagrangian method,

$$Q = AK^\alpha L^\beta + \lambda(B - P_K K - P_L L)$$

$$Q_K = \alpha AK^{\alpha-1}L^\beta - \lambda P_K = 0 \qquad (6.87)$$

$$Q_L = \beta AK^\alpha L^{\beta-1} - \lambda P_L = 0 \qquad (6.88)$$

$$Q_\lambda = B - P_K K - P_L L = 0$$

From (6.87) and (6.88),

$$\frac{\alpha AK^{\alpha-1}L^\beta}{P_K} = \lambda = \frac{\beta AK^\alpha L^{\beta-1}}{P_L}$$

Rearranging terms,

$$\frac{P_L}{P_K} = \frac{\beta AK^\alpha L^{\beta-1}}{\alpha AK^{\alpha-1}L^\beta}$$

where $L^{\beta-1} = L^\beta/L$ and $1/K^{\alpha-1} = K/K^\alpha$. Thus,

$$\frac{P_L}{P_K} = \frac{\beta K}{\alpha L} \qquad \frac{K}{L} = \frac{\alpha P_L}{\beta P_K} \qquad \text{Q.E.D.} \qquad (6.89)$$

6.60. Prove that for a linearly homogeneous Cobb-Douglas production function $Q = AK^\alpha L^\beta$, $\alpha = $ the output elasticity of capital (ϵ_{QK}) and $\beta = $ the output elasticity of labor (ϵ_{QL}).

From the definition of output elasticity,

$$\epsilon_{QK} = \frac{\delta Q/\delta K}{Q/K} \qquad \text{and} \qquad \epsilon_{QL} = \frac{\delta Q/\delta L}{Q/L}$$

Since $\alpha + \beta = 1$, let $\beta = 1 - \alpha$ and let $k = K/L$. Then

$$Q = AK^\alpha L^{1-\alpha} = A\left(\frac{K}{L}\right)^\alpha L = Ak^\alpha L$$

Find the marginal functions.

$$\frac{\delta Q}{\delta K} = \alpha AK^{\alpha-1}L^{1-\alpha} = \alpha AK^{\alpha-1}L^{-(\alpha-1)} = \alpha A\left(\frac{K}{L}\right)^{\alpha-1} = \alpha Ak^{\alpha-1}$$

$$\frac{\delta Q}{\delta L} = (1-\alpha)AK^\alpha L^{-\alpha} = (1-\alpha)A\left(\frac{K}{L}\right)^\alpha = (1-\alpha)Ak^\alpha$$

Find the average functions.

$$\frac{Q}{K} = \frac{Ak^\alpha L}{K} = \frac{Ak^\alpha}{k} = Ak^{\alpha-1}$$

$$\frac{Q}{L} = \frac{Ak^\alpha L}{L} = Ak^\alpha$$

Then divide the marginal functions by their respective average functions to obtain ϵ.

$$\epsilon_{QK} = \frac{\delta Q/\delta K}{Q/K} = \frac{\alpha Ak^{\alpha-1}}{Ak^{\alpha-1}} = \alpha \qquad \text{Q.E.D.}$$

$$\epsilon_{QL} = \frac{\delta Q/\delta L}{Q/L} = \frac{(1-\alpha)Ak^\alpha}{Ak^\alpha} = 1 - \alpha = \beta \qquad \text{Q.E.D.}$$

6.61. Equation (*6.89*) gave the least-cost input ratio for a generalized Cobb-Douglas production function. Prove that the elasticity of substitution σ of any generalized Cobb-Douglas production function is unitary, i.e., that $\sigma = 1$.

In Section 6.11, the elasticity of substitution is defined as the percentage change in the least-cost K/L ratio resulting from a small percentage change in the input-price ratio P_L/P_K.

$$\sigma = \frac{\dfrac{d(K/L)}{K/L}}{\dfrac{d(P_L/P_K)}{P_L/P_K}} = \frac{\dfrac{d(K/L)}{d(P_L/P_K)}}{\dfrac{K/L}{P_L/P_K}} \tag{6.90}$$

Since α and β are constants in (*6.89*) and P_K and P_L are independent variables, K/L can be considered a function of P_L/P_K. Noting that in the second ratio of (*6.90*), σ = the marginal function divided by the average function, first find the marginal function of (*6.89*).

$$\frac{d(K/L)}{d(P_L/P_K)} = \frac{\alpha}{\beta}$$

Then find the average function by dividing both sides of (*6.89*) by P_L/P_K.

$$\frac{K/L}{P_L/P_K} = \frac{\alpha}{\beta}$$

Substituting in (*6.90*),

$$\sigma = \frac{\dfrac{d(K/L)}{d(P_L/P_K)}}{\dfrac{K/L}{P_L/P_K}} = \frac{\alpha/\beta}{\alpha/\beta} = 1 \qquad \text{Q.E.D.}$$

6.62. Use the least-cost input ratio for a Cobb-Douglas function given in (*6.89*) to check the answer to Example 12, where $q = K^{0.4}L^{0.5}$, $P_K = 3$, and $P_L = 4$.

With $\alpha = 0.4$ and $\beta = 0.5$, from (*6.89*),

$$\frac{K}{L} = \frac{0.4(4)}{0.5(3)} = \frac{1.6}{1.5}$$

Capital and labor must be used in the ratio of $16K : 15L$. This confirms the answer found in Example 12 of $K_0 = 16$, $L_0 = 15$.

6.63. Given the CES production function

$$q = A[\alpha K^{-\beta} + (1 - \alpha)L^{-\beta}]^{-1/\beta} \tag{6.91}$$

and bearing in mind from Problem 6.58 that the ratio of prices must equal the ratios of marginal products if a function is to be optimized, (*a*) prove that the elasticity of substitution σ of a CES production is constant and (*b*) demonstrate the range that σ may assume.

(*a*) First-order conditions require that

$$\frac{\partial Q/\partial L}{\partial Q/\partial K} = \frac{P_L}{P_K} \tag{6.92}$$

Using the generalized power function rule to take the first-order partials of (*6.91*),

$$\frac{\partial Q}{\partial L} = -\frac{1}{\beta} A[\alpha K^{-\beta} + (1 - \alpha)L^{-\beta}]^{-(1/\beta)-1}(-\beta)(1 - \alpha)L^{-\beta-1}$$

Canceling $-\beta$'s, rearranging $1 - \alpha$, and adding the exponents $-(1/\beta) - 1$, we get

$$\frac{\partial Q}{\partial L} = (1 - \alpha)A[\alpha K^{-\beta} + (1 - \alpha)L^{-\beta}]^{-(1+\beta)/\beta}L^{-(1+\beta)}$$

Substituting $A^{1+\beta}/A^{\beta} = A$ for A,

$$\frac{\partial Q}{\partial L} = (1 - \alpha)\frac{A^{1+\beta}}{A^{\beta}}[\alpha K^{-\beta} + (1 - \alpha)L^{-\beta}]^{-(1+\beta)/\beta}L^{-(1+\beta)}$$

From (6.91), $A^{1+\beta}[\alpha K^{-\beta} + (1 - \alpha)L^{-\beta}]^{-(1+\beta)/\beta} = Q^{1+\beta}$ and $L^{-(1+\beta)} = 1/L^{1+\beta}$. Thus,

$$\frac{\partial Q}{\partial L} = \frac{1 - \alpha}{A^{\beta}}\left(\frac{Q}{L}\right)^{1+\beta} \tag{6.93}$$

Similarly,

$$\frac{\partial Q}{\partial K} = \frac{\alpha}{A^{\beta}}\left(\frac{Q}{K}\right)^{1+\beta} \tag{6.94}$$

Substituting (6.93) and (6.94) in (6.92), which leads to the cancellation of A^{β} and Q,

$$\frac{1 - \alpha}{\alpha}\left(\frac{K}{L}\right)^{1+\beta} = \frac{P_L}{P_K}$$

$$\left(\frac{K}{L}\right)^{1+\beta} = \frac{\alpha}{1 - \alpha}\frac{P_L}{P_K}$$

$$\frac{\bar{K}}{\bar{L}} = \left(\frac{\alpha}{1 - \alpha}\right)^{1/(1+\beta)}\left(\frac{P_L}{P_K}\right)^{1/(1+\beta)} \tag{6.95}$$

Since α and β are constants, by considering $\bar{K}/\bar{L}$ a function of P_L/P_K, as in Problem 6.61, we can find the elasticity of substitution as the ratio of the marginal and average functions. Simplifying first by letting

$$h = \left(\frac{\alpha}{1 - \alpha}\right)^{1/(1+\beta)}$$

$$\frac{\bar{K}}{\bar{L}} = h\left(\frac{P_L}{P_K}\right)^{1/(1+\beta)} \tag{6.96}$$

The marginal function is

$$\frac{d(\bar{K}/\bar{L})}{d(P_L/P_K)} = \frac{h}{1+\beta}\left(\frac{P_L}{P_K}\right)^{1/(1+\beta)-1} \tag{6.97}$$

and the average function is

$$\frac{\bar{K}/\bar{L}}{P_L/P_K} = \frac{h(P_L/P_K)^{1/(1+\beta)}}{P_L/P_K} = h\left(\frac{P_L}{P_K}\right)^{1/(1+\beta)-1} \tag{6.98}$$

By dividing the marginal function in (6.97) by the average function in (6.98), the elasticity of substitution is

$$\sigma = \frac{\dfrac{d(K/L)}{d(P_L/P_K)}}{\dfrac{K/L}{P_L/P_K}} = \frac{\dfrac{h}{1+\beta}(P_L/P_K)^{1/(1+\beta)-1}}{h(P_L/P_K)^{1/(1+\beta)-1}} = \frac{1}{1+\beta} \tag{6.99}$$

Since β is a given parameter, $\sigma = 1/(1+\beta)$ is a constant.

(b) If $-1 < \beta < 0, \sigma > 1$. If $\beta = 0, \sigma = 1$. If $0 < \beta < \infty, \sigma < 1$.

6.64. Prove that the CES production function is homogeneous of degree 1 and thus has constant returns to scale.

From (6.91),
$$Q = A[\alpha K^{-\beta} + (1 - \alpha)L^{-\beta}]^{-1/\beta}$$

Multiplying inputs K and L by k, as in Section 6.8,

$$\begin{aligned}
f(kK, kL) &= A[\alpha(kK)^{-\beta} + (1 - \alpha)(kL)^{-\beta}]^{-1/\beta} \\
&= A\{k^{-\beta}[\alpha K^{-\beta} + (1 - \alpha)L^{-\beta}]\}^{-1/\beta} \\
&= A(k^{-\beta})^{-1/\beta}[\alpha K^{-\beta} + (1 - \alpha)L^{-\beta}]^{-1/\beta} \\
&= kA[\alpha K^{-\beta} + (1 - \alpha)L^{-\beta}]^{-1/\beta} = kQ \qquad \text{Q.E.D.}
\end{aligned}$$

6.65. Find the elasticity of substitution for the CES production function, $q = 75(0.3K^{-0.4} + 0.7L^{-0.4})^{-2.5}$, given in Example 13.

From (6.99),
$$\sigma = \frac{1}{1 + \beta}$$

where $\beta = 0.4$. Thus, $\sigma = 1/(1 + 0.4) = 0.71$.

6.66. Use the optimal K/L ratio in (6.95) to check the answer in Example 13 where $q = 75(0.3K^{-0.4} + 0.7L^{-0.4})^{-2.5}$ was optimized under the constraint $4K + 3L = 120$, giving $\bar{K} = 11.25$ and $\bar{L} = 25$.

From (6.95),
$$\frac{\bar{K}}{\bar{L}} = \left(\frac{\alpha}{1 - \alpha}\frac{P_L}{P_K}\right)^{1/(1 + \beta)}$$

Substituting $\alpha = 0.3$, $1 - \alpha = 0.7$, and $\beta = 0.4$,

$$\frac{\bar{K}}{\bar{L}} = \left(\frac{0.3}{0.7}\frac{3}{4}\right)^{1/1.4} = \left(\frac{0.9}{2.8}\right)^{0.71} = (0.32)^{0.71} \approx 0.45$$

With $\bar{K} = 11.25$ and $\bar{L} = 25$, $\bar{K}/\bar{L} = 11.25/25 = 0.45$.

6.67. Use (6.95) to check the answer to Problem 6.47 where $q = 80(0.4K^{-0.25} + 0.6L^{-0.25})^{-4}$ was optimized subject to the constraint $5K + 2L = 150$ at $\bar{K} = 14$ and $\bar{L} = 40$.

Substituting $\alpha = 0.4$, $1 - \alpha = 0.6$, and $\beta = 0.25$ in (6.95),

$$\frac{\bar{K}}{\bar{L}} = \left(\frac{0.4}{0.6}\frac{2}{5}\right)^{1/1.25} = \left(\frac{0.8}{3}\right)^{0.8} \approx 0.35$$

Substituting $\bar{K} = 14$ and $\bar{L} = 40$, $\frac{14}{40} = 0.35$.

6.68. Find the elasticity of substitution from Problem 6.67.

From (6.99),
$$\sigma = \frac{1}{1 + \beta} = \frac{1}{1 + 0.25} = 0.8$$

6.69. Use (6.95) to check the answer to Problem 6.48 where $q = 100(0.2K^{0.5} + 0.8L^{0.5})^2$ was optimized subject to the constraint $10K + 4L = 4100$ at $\bar{K} = 10$ and $\bar{L} = 1000$.

With $\alpha = 0.2$, $1 - \alpha = 0.8$, and $\beta = -0.5$,

$$\frac{\bar{K}}{\bar{L}} = \left[\left(\frac{0.2}{0.8}\right)\left(\frac{4}{10}\right)\right]^{1/(1 - 0.5)} = \left(\frac{0.8}{8}\right)^2 = (0.1)^2 = 0.01$$

Substituting $\bar{K} = 10$ and $\bar{L} = 1000$, $\frac{10}{1000} = 0.01$.

6.70.   Find the elasticity of substitution from Problem 6.69.

From (6.99),
$$\sigma = \frac{1}{1+\beta} = \frac{1}{1-0.5} = 2$$

6.71.   (a) Use the elasticity of substitution found in Problem 6.68 to estimate the effect on the least-cost $(\bar{K}/\bar{L})$ ratio in Problem 6.47 if P_L increases by 25 percent. (b) Check your answer by substituting the new P_L in (6.95).

(a)   The elasticity of substitution measures the relative change in the $\bar{K}/\bar{L}$ ratio brought about by a relative change in the price ratio P_L/P_K. If P_L increases by 25 percent, $P_L = 1.25(2) = 2.5$. Thus, $P_L/P_K = 2.5/5 = 0.5$ vs. $\frac{2}{5} = 0.4$ in Problem 6.47.

The percentage increase in the price ratio, therefore, is $(0.5 - 0.4)/0.4 = 0.25$. With the elasticity of substitution $= 0.8$ from Problem 6.68, the expected percentage change in the $\bar{K}/\bar{L}$ ratio is

$$\frac{\Delta(\bar{K}/\bar{L})}{\bar{K}/\bar{L}} \approx 0.8(0.25) = 0.2 \quad \text{or} \quad 20\%$$

With $(\bar{K}/\bar{L})_1 = 0.35$, $(\bar{K}/\bar{L})_2 \approx 1.2(0.35) \approx 0.42$.

(b)   Substituting $P_L = 2.5$ in (6.95),

$$\frac{\bar{K}}{\bar{L}} = \left(\frac{0.4}{0.6}\frac{2.5}{5}\right)^{0.8} = \left(\frac{1}{3}\right)^{0.8} \approx 0.42$$

6.72.   (a) Use the elasticity of substitution to estimate the new $\bar{K}/\bar{L}$ ratio if the price of capital decreases by 20 percent. Assume the initial data of Problem 6.47. (b) Check your answer.

(a)   If P_K decreases by 20 percent, $P_K = 0.8(5) = 4$. Thus, $P_L/P_K = \frac{2}{4} = 0.5$ which is a 25 percent increase in the P_L/P_K ratio, as seen above. Therefore,

$$\frac{\Delta(\bar{K}/\bar{L})}{\bar{K}/\bar{L}} = 0.8(0.25) = 0.2 \quad \text{or} \quad 20\%$$

and $(\bar{K}/\bar{L})_2 \approx 1.2(0.35) = 0.42$.

(b)   Substituting $P_K = 4$ in (6.95),

$$\frac{\bar{K}}{\bar{L}} = \left(\frac{0.4}{0.6}\frac{2}{4}\right)^{0.8} = \left(\frac{0.8}{2.4}\right)^{0.8} = 0.42$$

6.73.   (a) If the price of labor decreases by 10 percent in Problem 6.48, use the elasticity of substitution to estimate the effect on the least-cost $\bar{K}/\bar{L}$ ratio. (b) Check your answer.

(a)   If P_L decreases by 10 percent, $P_L = 0.9(4) = 3.6$, and the P_L/P_K ratio also decreases by 10 percent. With a 10 percent decrease in P_L/P_K and an elasticity of substitution $= 2$,

$$\frac{\Delta(\bar{K}/\bar{L})}{\bar{K}/\bar{L}} \approx 2(-0.10) = -0.20 \quad \text{or} \quad -20\%$$

With the old $\bar{K}/\bar{L} = 0.01$, $(\bar{K}/\bar{L})_2 \approx (1 - 0.2)(0.01) = 0.8(0.01) = 0.008$.

(b)   Substituting $P_L = 3.6$ in (6.95),

$$\frac{\bar{K}}{\bar{L}} = \left(\frac{0.2}{0.8}\frac{3.6}{10}\right)^2 = \left(\frac{0.72}{8}\right)^2 = (0.09)^2 = 0.0081$$

Chapter 7

Exponential and Logarithmic Functions

7.1 EXPONENTIAL FUNCTIONS

Previous chapters dealt mainly with *power functions*, such as $y = x^a$, in which a variable base x is raised to a constant exponent a. In this chapter we introduce an important new function in which a constant base a is raised to a variable exponent x. It is called an *exponential function* and is defined as

$$y = a^x \qquad a > 0 \qquad \text{and} \qquad a \neq 1$$

Commonly used to express rates of growth and decay, such as interest compounding and depreciation, exponential functions have the following general properties. Given $y = a^x$, $a > 0$, and $a \neq 1$:

1. The domain of the function is the set of all real numbers; the range of the function is the set of all positive real numbers, i.e., for all x, even $x < 0$, $y > 0$.
2. For $a > 1$, the function is increasing and convex; for $0 < a < 1$, the function is decreasing and convex.
3. At $x = 0$, $y = 1$, independently of the base.

See Example 1 and Problems 7.1 and 7.2; for a review of exponents, see Section 1.1 and Problem 1.1.

EXAMPLE 1. Given (a) $y = 2^x$ and (b) $y = 2^{-x} = (\frac{1}{2})^x$, the above properties of exponential functions can readily be seen from the tables and graphs of the functions in Fig. 7-1. More complicated exponential functions are estimated with the help of the $\boxed{y^x}$ key on pocket calculators.

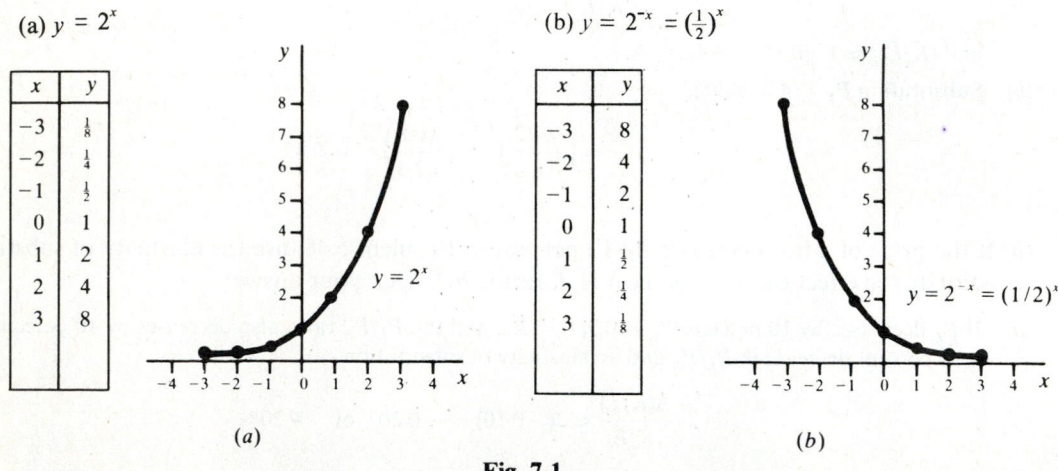

Fig. 7-1

7.2 LOGARITHMIC FUNCTIONS

Interchanging the variables of an exponential function f defined by $y = a^x$ gives rise to a new function g defined by $x = a^y$ such that any ordered pair of numbers in f will also be found in g in reverse order. For example, if $f(2) = 4$, then $g(4) = 2$; if $f(3) = 8$, then $g(8) = 3$. The new function g, the *inverse* of the exponential function f, is called a *logarithmic function with base a*. Instead of $x = a^y$, the logarithmic function with base a is more commonly written

$$y = \log_a x \qquad a > 0, a \neq 1$$

$\log_a x$ is the exponent to which a must be raised to get x. Any positive number except 1 may serve as the base for a logarithm. The *common logarithm of* x, written $\log_{10} x$ or simply $\log x$, is the exponent to which 10 must be raised to get x. Logarithms have the following properties. Given $y = \log_a x$, $a > 0$, $a \neq 1$:

1. The domain of the function is the set of all positive real numbers; the range is the set of all real numbers—the exact opposite of its inverse function, the exponential function.
2. For base $a > 1$, $f(x)$ is increasing and concave. For $0 < a < 1$, $f(x)$ is decreasing and convex.
3. At $x = 1$, $y = 0$ independent of the base.

See Examples 2 to 4 and Problems 7.5 and 7.6.

EXAMPLE 2. A graph of two functions f and g in which x and y are interchanged, such as $y = 2^x$ and $x = 2^y$ in Fig. 7-2, reveals that one function is a *mirror image* of the other along the 45° line $y = x$, such that if $f(x) = y$, then $g(y) = x$. Recall that $x = 2^y$ is equivalent to and more commonly expressed as $y = \log_2 x$.

(a) $y = 2^x$ (b) $y = \log_2 x \leftrightarrow x = 2^y$

x	y
-3	$\frac{1}{8}$
-2	$\frac{1}{4}$
-1	$\frac{1}{2}$
0	1
1	2
2	4
3	8

x	y
$\frac{1}{8}$	-3
$\frac{1}{4}$	-2
$\frac{1}{2}$	-1
1	0
2	1
4	2
8	3

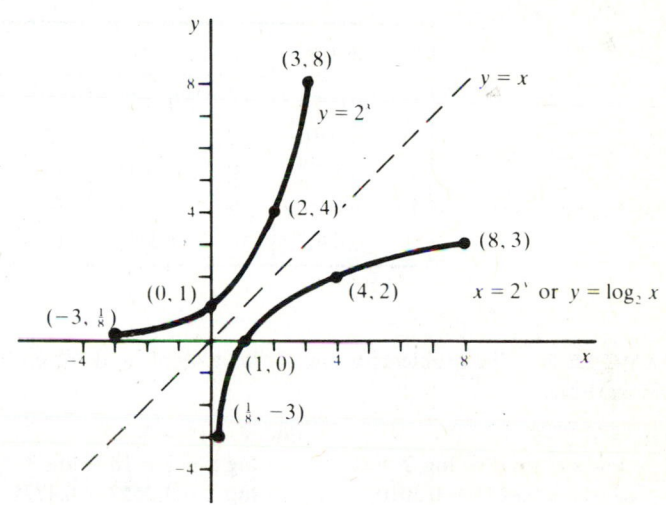

Fig. 7-2

EXAMPLE 3. Knowing that the common logarithm of x is the power to which 10 must be raised to get x, it follows that

$$\log 10 = 1 \quad \text{since } 10^1 = 10 \qquad \log 1 = 0 \quad \text{since } 10^0 = 1$$
$$\log 100 = 2 \quad \text{since } 10^2 = 100 \qquad \log 0.1 = -1 \quad \text{since } 10^{-1} = 0.1$$
$$\log 1000 = 3 \quad \text{since } 10^3 = 1000 \qquad \log 0.01 = -2 \quad \text{since } 10^{-2} = 0.01$$

EXAMPLE 4. For numbers that are exact powers of the base, logs are easily calculated without the aid of calculators.

$$\log_7 49 = 2 \quad \text{since } 7^2 = 49 \qquad \log_2 16 = 4 \quad \text{since } 2^4 = 16$$
$$\log_{36} 6 = \tfrac{1}{2} \quad \text{since } 36^{1/2} = 6 \qquad \log_{16} 2 = \tfrac{1}{4} \quad \text{since } 16^{1/4} = 2$$
$$\log_3 \tfrac{1}{9} = -2 \quad \text{since } 3^{-2} = \tfrac{1}{9} \qquad \log_2 \tfrac{1}{8} = -3 \quad \text{since } 2^{-3} = \tfrac{1}{8}$$

For numbers that are not exact powers of the base, log tables or calculators are needed.

7.3 PROPERTIES OF EXPONENTS AND LOGARITHMS

Assuming $a, b > 0$; $a, b \neq 1$; and x and y are any real numbers:

1. $a^x \cdot a^y = a^{x+y}$
2. $\dfrac{1}{a^x} = a^{-x}$
3. $\dfrac{a^x}{a^y} = a^{x-y}$
4. $(a^x)^y = a^{xy}$
5. $a^x \cdot b^x = (ab)^x$
6. $\dfrac{a^x}{b^x} = \left(\dfrac{a}{b}\right)^x$

For a, x, and y positive real numbers, n a real number, and $a \neq 1$:

1. $\log_a xy = \log_a x + \log_a y$
2. $\log_a \dfrac{x}{y} = \log_a x - \log_a y$
3. $\log_a x^n = n \log_a x$
4. $\log_a \sqrt[n]{x} = \dfrac{1}{n} \log_a x$

Properties of exponents were treated in Section 1.1 and Problem 1.1. Properties of logarithms are treated in Example 5 and Problems 7.12 to 7.16.

Table 7.1

x	$\log x$	x	$\log x$	x	$\log x$	x	$\log x$
1	0.0000	6	0.7782	11	1.0414	16	1.2041
2	0.3010	7	0.8451	12	1.0792	17	1.2304
3	0.4771	8	0.9031	13	1.1139	18	1.2553
4	0.6021	9	0.9542	14	1.1461	19	1.2788
5	0.6990	10	1.0000	15	1.1761	20	1.3010

EXAMPLE 5. The problems below are kept simple and solved by means of logarithms to illustrate the properties of logarithms.

(a) $x = 7 \cdot 2$
$\log x = \log 7 + \log 2$
$\log x = 0.8451 + 0.3010$
$\log x = 1.1461$
$x = 14$

(b) $x = 18 \div 3$
$\log x = \log 18 - \log 3$
$\log x = 1.2553 - 0.4771$
$\log x = 0.7782$
$x = 6$

(c) $x = 3^2$
$\log x = 2 \log 3$
$\log x = 2(0.4771)$
$\log x = 0.9542$
$x = 9$

(d) $x = \sqrt[3]{8}$
$\log x = \frac{1}{3} \log 8$
$\log x = \frac{1}{3}(0.9031)$
$\log x = 0.3010$
$x = 2$

7.4 NATURAL EXPONENTIAL AND LOGARITHMIC FUNCTIONS

The most commonly used base for exponential and logarithmic functions is the irrational number e. Expressed mathematically,

$$e = \lim_{n \to \infty} \left(1 + \frac{1}{n}\right)^n \approx 2.71828 \qquad (7.1)$$

Exponential functions to base e are called *natural exponential functions* and are written $y = e^x$; logarithmic functions to base e are termed *natural logarithmic functions* and are expressed as $y = \log_e x$ or, more commonly, $\ln x$. Thus $\ln x$ is simply the exponent or power to which e must be raised to get x.

As with other exponential and logarithmic functions to a common base, one function is the inverse of the other, such that the ordered pair (a, b) will belong to the set of e^x if and only if (b, a) belongs to the set of $\ln x$. Natural exponential and logarithmic functions follow the same rules as other exponential and logarithmic functions and are estimated with the help of tables or the $\boxed{e^x}$ and $\boxed{\ln x}$ keys on pocket calculators. See Problems 7.3, 7.4, and 7.6.

7.5 SOLVING NATURAL EXPONENTIAL AND LOGARITHMIC FUNCTIONS

Since natural exponential functions and natural logarithmic functions are inverses of each other, one is generally helpful in solving the other. Mindful that $\ln x$ signifies the power to which e must be raised to get x, it follows that:

1. e raised to the natural log of a constant $(a > 0)$, a variable $(x > 0)$, or a function of a variable $[f(x) > 0]$ must equal that constant, variable, or function of the variable:

$$e^{\ln a} = a \qquad e^{\ln x} = x \qquad e^{\ln f(x)} = f(x) \qquad (7.2)$$

2. Conversely, the natural log of e raised to the power of a constant, variable, or function of a variable must also equal that constant, variable, or function of the variable:

$$\ln e^a = a \qquad \ln e^x = x \qquad \ln e^{f(x)} = f(x) \qquad (7.3)$$

See Example 6 and Problems 7.18 to 7.22.

EXAMPLE 6. The principles of (7.2) and (7.3) are used below to solve the given equations for x.

(a) $5e^{x+2} = 120$

    (1) Solve algebraically for e^{x+2},

$$5e^{x+2} = 120$$
$$e^{x+2} = 24$$

    (2) Take the natural log of both sides to eliminate e.

$$\ln e^{x+2} = \ln 24$$

From (7.3),
$$x + 2 = \ln 24$$
$$x = \ln 24 - 2$$

    Enter 24 on your calculator and press the $\boxed{\ln x}$ key to find $\ln 24 = 3.17805$. Then substitute and solve.

$$x = 3.17805 - 2 = 1.17805$$

(b) $6 \ln x - 7 = 12.2$

    (1) Solve algebraically for $\ln x$,

$$6 \ln x = 19.2$$
$$\ln x = 3.2$$

    (2) Set both sides of the equation as exponents of e to eliminate the natural log expression,

$$e^{\ln x} = e^{3.2}$$

From (7.2),
$$x = e^{3.2}$$

    Enter 3.2 on your calculator and press the $\boxed{e^x}$ key to find $e^{3.2} = 24.53253$ and substitute.

$$x = 24.53253$$

Note: On many calculators the e^x key is the inverse (shift, or second function) of the $\ln x$ key, and to activate the e^x key, one must first press the **INV** (**Shift**, or **2ndF**) key followed by the $\ln x$ key.

7.6 LOGARITHMIC TRANSFORMATION OF NONLINEAR FUNCTIONS

Linear algebra and regression analysis using ordinary or two-stage least squares, common tools in economic analysis, assume linear functions or equations. Some nonlinear functions, such as Cobb-Douglas production functions, can easily be converted to linear functions through simple logarithmic transformation; others, such as CES production functions, cannot. For example, from the properties of logarithms, it is clear that given a generalized Cobb-Douglas production function

$$q = AK^{\alpha}L^{\beta}$$
$$\ln q = \ln A + \alpha \ln K + \beta \ln L \tag{7.4}$$

which is log-linear. But given the CES production function,

$$q = A[\alpha K^{-\beta} + (1-\alpha)L^{-\beta}]^{-1/\beta}$$
$$\ln q = \ln A - \frac{1}{\beta} \ln [\alpha K^{-\beta} + (1-\alpha)L^{-\beta}]$$

which is not linear even in logarithms because of $K^{-\beta}$ and $L^{-\beta}$. Ordinary least-square estimation of the coefficients in a log transformation of a Cobb-Douglas production function, such as in (7.4), has the nice added feature that estimates for α and β provide direct measures of the *output elasticity* of K and L respectively, as was proved in Problem 6.60.

Solved Problems

GRAPHS

7.1. Make a schedule for each of the following exponential functions with base $a > 1$ and then sketch them on the same graph to convince yourself that (1) the functions never equal zero; (2) they all pass through $(0, 1)$; and (3) they are all positively sloped and convex.

   (*a*) $y = 3^x$ (*b*) $y = 4^x$ (*c*) $y = 5^x$

(*a*)

x	y
-3	$\frac{1}{27}$
-2	$\frac{1}{9}$
-1	$\frac{1}{3}$
0	1
1	3
2	9
3	27

(*b*)

x	y
-3	$\frac{1}{64}$
-2	$\frac{1}{16}$
-1	$\frac{1}{4}$
0	1
1	4
2	16
3	64

(*c*)

x	y
-3	$\frac{1}{125}$
-2	$\frac{1}{25}$
-1	$\frac{1}{5}$
0	1
1	5
2	25
3	125

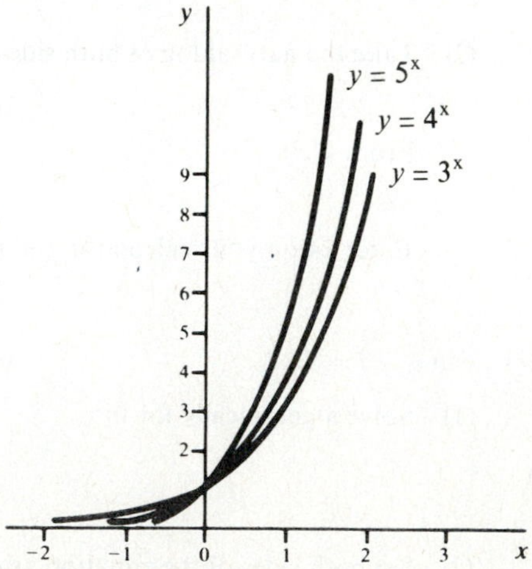

Fig. 7-3

7.2. Make a schedule for each of the following exponential functions with $0 < a < 1$ and then sketch them on the same graph to convince yourself that (1) the functions never equal zero; (2) they all pass through $(0, 1)$, and (3) they are all negatively sloped and convex.

(a) $y = (\frac{1}{3})^x = 3^{-x}$ (b) $y = (\frac{1}{4})^x = 4^{-x}$ (c) $y = (\frac{1}{5})^x = 5^{-x}$

(a)			(b)			(c)	
x	y		x	y		x	y
-3	27		-3	64		-3	125
-2	9		-2	16		-2	25
-1	3		-1	4		-1	5
0	1		0	1		0	1
1	$\frac{1}{3}$		1	$\frac{1}{4}$		1	$\frac{1}{5}$
2	$\frac{1}{9}$		2	$\frac{1}{16}$		2	$\frac{1}{25}$
3	$\frac{1}{27}$		3	$\frac{1}{64}$		3	$\frac{1}{125}$

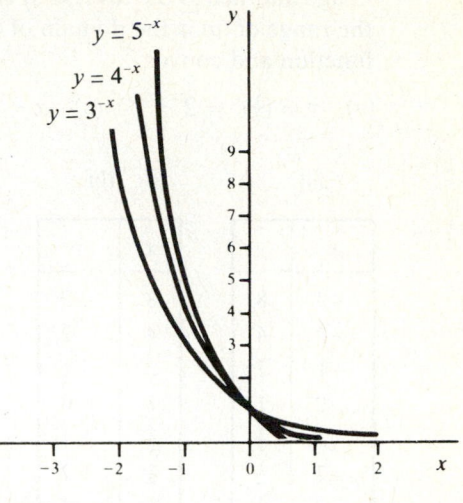

Fig. 7-4

7.3. Using a calculator or tables, set up a schedule for each of the following natural exponential functions $y = e^{kx}$ where $k > 0$, noting (1) the functions never equal zero; (2) they all pass through $(0, 1)$, and (3) they are all positively sloped and convex.

(a) $y = e^{0.5x}$ (b) $y = e^x$ (c) $y = e^{2x}$

(a)			(b)			(c)	
x	y		x	y		x	y
-2	0.37		-2	0.14		-2	0.02
-1	0.61		-1	0.37		-1	0.14
0	1.00		0	1.00		0	1.00
1	1.65		1	2.72		1	7.39
2	2.72		2	7.39		2	54.60

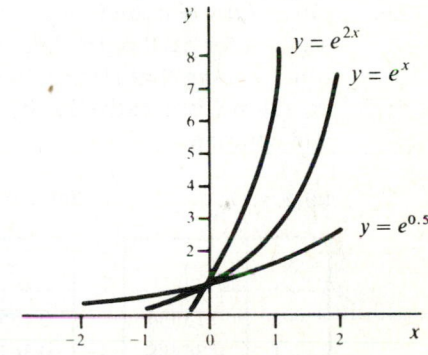

Fig. 7-5

7.4. Set up a schedule, rounding to two decimal places, for the following natural exponential functions $y = e^{kx}$ where $k < 0$, noting (1) the functions never equal zero; (2) they all pass through $(0, 1)$; and (3) they are all negatively sloped and convex.

(a) $y = e^{-0.5x}$ (b) $y = e^{-x}$ (c) $y = e^{-2x}$

(a)			(b)			(c)	
x	y		x	y		x	y
-2	2.72		-2	7.39		-2	54.60
-1	1.65		-1	2.72		-1	7.39
0	1.00		0	1.00		0	1.00
1	0.61		1	0.37		1	0.14
2	0.37		2	0.14		2	0.02

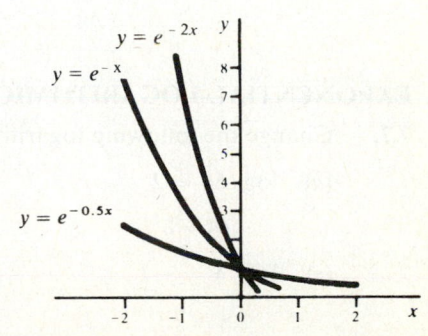

Fig. 7-6

7.5. Construct a schedule and draw a graph for the following functions to show that one is the mirror image and hence the inverse of the other, noting that (1) the domain of (a) is the range of (b) and the range of (a) is the domain of (b); and (2) a logarithmic function with $0 < a < 1$ is a decreasing function and convex.

(a) $y = (\frac{1}{2})^x = 2^{-x}$ (b) $x = (\frac{1}{2})^y$ or $y = \log_{1/2} x$

(a)

x	y
-3	8
-2	4
-1	2
0	1
1	$\frac{1}{2}$
2	$\frac{1}{4}$
3	$\frac{1}{8}$

(b)

x	y
8	-3
4	-2
2	-1
1	0
$\frac{1}{2}$	1
$\frac{1}{4}$	2
$\frac{1}{8}$	3

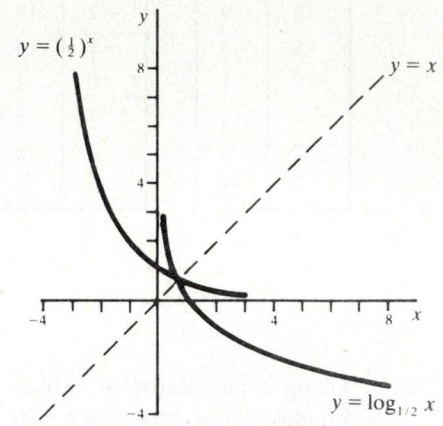

Fig. 7-7

7.6. Given (a) $y = e^x$ and (b) $y = \ln x$, and using a calculator or tables, construct a schedule and draw a graph for each of the functions to show that one function is the mirror image or inverse of the other, noting that (1) the domain of (a) is the range of (b) while the range of (a) is the domain of (b), (2) $\ln x$ is negative for $0 < x < 1$ and positive for $x > 1$; and (3) $\ln x$ is an increasing function and concave.

(a) $y = e^x$

x	y
-2	0.13534
-1	0.36788
0	1.00000
1	2.71828
2	7.38906

(b) $y = \ln x$

x	y
0.13534	-2
0.36788	-1
1.00000	0
2.71828	1
7.38906	2

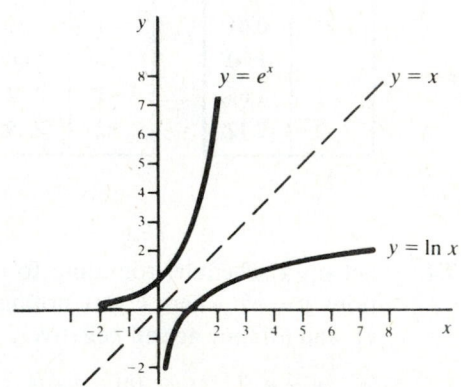

Fig. 7-8

EXPONENTIAL-LOGARITHMIC CONVERSION

7.7. Change the following logarithms to their equivalent exponential forms:

(a) $\log_8 64 = 2$

    $64 = 8^2$

(b) $\log_5 125 = 3$

    $125 = 5^3$

(c) $\log_7 \frac{1}{7} = -1$

    $\frac{1}{7} = 7^{-1}$

(d) $\log_3 \frac{1}{81} = -4$

    $\frac{1}{81} = 3^{-4}$

(e) $\log_{36} 6 = \frac{1}{2}$

$6 = 36^{1/2}$

(f) $\log_{16} 2 = \frac{1}{4}$

$2 = 16^{1/4}$

(g) $\log_a y = 6x$

$y = a^{6x}$

(h) $\log_2 y = 7x$

$y = 2^{7x}$

7.8. Convert the following natural logarithms to natural exponential functions:

(a) $\ln 32 = 3.46574$

$32 = e^{3.46574}$

(b) $\ln 0.8 = -0.22314$

$0.8 = e^{-0.22314}$

(c) $\ln 20 = 2.99573$

$20 = e^{2.99573}$

(d) $\ln 2.5 = 0.91629$

$2.5 = e^{0.91629}$

(e) $\ln y = -4x$

$y = e^{-4x}$

(f) $\ln y = 2t + 1$

$y = e^{2t+1}$

7.9. Change the following exponential forms to logarithmic forms:

(a) $81 = 9^2$

$\log_9 81 = 2$

(b) $32 = 2^5$

$\log_2 32 = 5$

(c) $\frac{1}{9} = 3^{-2}$

$\log_3 \frac{1}{9} = -2$

(d) $\frac{1}{16} = 2^{-4}$

$\log_2 \frac{1}{16} = -4$

(e) $5 = 125^{1/3}$

$\log_{125} 5 = \frac{1}{3}$

(f) $11 = 121^{1/2}$

$\log_{121} 11 = \frac{1}{2}$

(g) $27 = 9^{3/2}$

$\log_9 27 = \frac{3}{2}$

(h) $64 = 256^{3/4}$

$\log_{256} 64 = \frac{3}{4}$

7.10. Convert the following natural exponential expressions to equivalent natural logarithmic forms:

(a) $4.8 = e^{1.56862}$

$\ln 4.8 = 1.56862$

(b) $15 = e^{2.70805}$

$\ln 15 = 2.70805$

(c) $0.6 = e^{-0.51083}$

$\ln 0.6 = -0.51083$

(d) $130 = e^{4.86753}$

$\ln 130 = 4.86753$

(e) $y = e^{(1/2)t}$

$\ln y = \frac{1}{2}t$

(f) $y = e^{t-5}$

$\ln y = t - 5$

7.11. Solve the following for x, y, or a by finding the equivalent expression:

(a) $y = \log_{30} 900$

$900 = 30^y$

$y = 2$

(b) $y = \log_2 \frac{1}{32}$

$\frac{1}{32} = 2^y$

$y = -5$

(c) $\log_4 x = 3$

$x = 4^3$

$x = 64$

(d) $\log_{81} x = \frac{3}{4}$

$x = 81^{3/4}$

$x = 27$

(e) $\log_a 27 = 3$

$27 = a^3$

$a = 27^{1/3}$

$a = 3$

(f) $\log_a 4 = \frac{2}{3}$

$4 = a^{2/3}$

$a = 4^{3/2}$

$a = 8$

(g) $\log_a 125 = \frac{3}{2}$

$125 = a^{3/2}$

$a = 125^{2/3}$

$a = 25$

(h) $\log_a 8 = \frac{3}{4}$

$8 = a^{3/4}$

$a = 8^{4/3}$

$a = 16$

PROPERTIES OF LOGARITHMS AND EXPONENTS

7.12. Use the properties of logarithms to write the following expressions as sums, differences, or products:

(a) $\log_a 56x$

$\log_a 56x = \log_a 56 + \log_a x$

(b) $\log_a 33x^4$

$\log_a 33x^4 = \log_a 33 + 4\log_a x$

(c) $\log_a x^2 y^3$

$\log_a x^2 y^3 = 2\log_a x + 3\log_a y$

(d) $\log_a u^5 v^{-4}$

$\log_a u^5 v^{-4} = 5\log_a u - 4\log_a v$

(e) $\log_a \dfrac{6x}{7y}$

$\log_a \dfrac{6x}{7y} = \log_a 6x - \log_a 7y$

$= \log_a 6 + \log_a x - (\log_a 7 + \log_a y)$

$= \log_a 6 + \log_a x - \log_a 7 - \log_a y$

(f) $\log_a \dfrac{x^7}{y^4}$

$\log_a \dfrac{x^7}{y^4} = 7\log_a x - 4\log_a y$

(g) $\log_a \sqrt[3]{x}$

$\log_a \sqrt[3]{x} = \frac{1}{3}\log_a x$

7.13. Use the properties of logarithms to write the following natural logarithmic forms as sums, differences, or products:

(a) $\ln 76x^3$

$\ln 76x^3 = \ln 76 + 3\ln x$

(b) $\ln x^5 y^2$

$\ln x^5 y^2 = 5\ln x + 2\ln y$

(c) $\ln \dfrac{x^4}{y^6}$

$\ln \dfrac{x^4}{y^6} = 4\ln x - 6\ln y$

(d) $\ln \dfrac{8x}{9y}$

$\ln \dfrac{8x}{9y} = \ln 8x - \ln 9y$

$= \ln 8 + \ln x - (\ln 9 + \ln y)$

$= \ln 8 + \ln x - \ln 9 - \ln y$

(e) $\ln \sqrt[4]{x}$

$\ln \sqrt[4]{x} = \frac{1}{4}\ln x$

(f) $\ln (x^5 \sqrt{y})$

$\ln (x^5 \sqrt{y}) = 5\ln x + \frac{1}{2}\ln y$

(g) $\ln \dfrac{3\sqrt[5]{x}}{\sqrt{y}}$

$$\ln \frac{3\sqrt[5]{x}}{\sqrt{y}} = \ln 3 + \tfrac{1}{5}\ln x - \tfrac{1}{2}\ln y$$

(h) $\ln \sqrt{\dfrac{x^7}{y^4}}$

$$\ln \sqrt{\frac{x^7}{y^4}} = \tfrac{1}{2}(7\ln x - 4\ln y)$$

7.14. Use the properties of exponents to simplify the following exponential expressions, assuming a, $b > 0$ and $a \neq b$:

(a) $a^x \cdot a^y$

$$a^x \cdot a^y = a^{x+y}$$

(b) $a^{4x} \cdot a^{5y}$

$$a^{4x} \cdot a^{5y} = a^{4x+5y}$$

(c) $\dfrac{a^{2x}}{a^{3y}}$

$$\frac{a^{2x}}{a^{3y}} = a^{2x-3y}$$

(d) $\dfrac{a^x}{b^x}$

$$\frac{a^x}{b^x} = \left(\frac{a}{b}\right)^x$$

(e) $\sqrt{a^{7x}}$

$$\sqrt{a^{7x}} = (a^{7x})^{1/2} = a^{(7/2)x}$$

(f) $(a^x)^{4y}$

$$(a^x)^{4y} = a^{4xy}$$

7.15. Simplify the following natural exponential expressions:

(a) $e^{5x} \cdot e^{2y}$

$$e^{5x} \cdot e^{2y} = e^{5x+2y}$$

(b) $(e^{3x})^5$

$$(e^{3x})^5 = e^{15x}$$

(c) $\dfrac{e^{8x}}{e^{6x}}$

$$\frac{e^{8x}}{e^{6x}} = e^{8x-6x} = e^{2x}$$

(d) $\dfrac{e^{4x}}{e^{7x}}$

$$\frac{e^{4x}}{e^{7x}} = e^{4x-7x} = e^{-3x} = \frac{1}{e^{3x}}$$

7.16. Simplify the following natural logarithmic expressions:

(a) $\ln 8 + \ln x$

$$\ln 8 + \ln x = \ln 8x$$

(b) $\ln x^5 - \ln x^3$

$$\ln x^5 - \ln x^3 = \ln \frac{x^5}{x^3} = \ln x^2 = 2\ln x$$

(c) $\ln 12 + \ln 5 - \ln 6$

$$\ln 12 + \ln 5 - \ln 6 = \ln \frac{12 \cdot 5}{6} = \ln 10$$

(d) $\ln 7 - \ln x + \ln 9$

$$\ln 7 - \ln x + \ln 9 = \ln \frac{7 \cdot 9}{x} = \ln \frac{63}{x}$$

(e) $\tfrac{1}{2}\ln 81$

$$\tfrac{1}{2}\ln 81 = \ln 81^{1/2} = \ln 9$$

(f) $5\ln \tfrac{1}{2}$

$$5\ln \tfrac{1}{2} = \ln \left(\tfrac{1}{2}\right)^5 = \ln \tfrac{1}{32}$$

(g) $\tfrac{1}{3}\ln 27 + 4\ln 2$

$$\tfrac{1}{3}\ln 27 + 4\ln 2 = \ln 27^{1/3} + \ln 2^4 = \ln (3 \cdot 16) = \ln 48$$

(h) $2\ln 4 - \tfrac{1}{3}\ln 8$

$$2\ln 4 - \tfrac{1}{3}\ln 8 = \ln 4^2 - \ln 8^{1/3} = \ln \tfrac{16}{2} = \ln 8$$

7.17. Simplify each of the following exponential expressions:

(a) $e^{3 \ln x}$

$$e^{3 \ln x} = e^{\ln x^3} \qquad \text{But from } (7.2), e^{\ln f(x)} = f(x), \text{ so}$$
$$e^{3 \ln x} = x^3$$

(b) $e^{4 \ln x + 5 \ln y}$

$$e^{4 \ln x + 5 \ln y} = e^{\ln x^4} \cdot e^{\ln y^5} = x^4 y^5$$

(c) $e^{(1/2) \ln 6x}$

$$e^{(1/2) \ln 6x} = e^{\ln (6x)^{1/2}} = (6x)^{1/2} = \sqrt{6x}$$

(d) $e^{4 \ln x - 9 \ln y}$

$$e^{4 \ln x - 9 \ln y} = \frac{e^{\ln x^4}}{e^{\ln y^9}} = \frac{x^4}{y^9}$$

SOLVING EXPONENTIAL AND LOGARITHMIC FUNCTIONS

7.18. Use the techniques from Section 7.5 to solve the following natural exponential functions for x:

(a) $3e^{5x} = 8943$

    (1) Solve algebraically for e^{5x}.

$$e^{5x} = 2981$$

    (2) Then take the natural log of both sides to eliminate e.

$$\ln e^{5x} = \ln 2981$$

From (7.3), $\qquad\qquad\qquad\qquad 5x = \ln 2981$

To find the value of $\ln 2981$, enter 2981 on a calculator and press the $\boxed{\ln x}$ key to find $\ln 2981 = 8.00001 \approx 8$. Then substitute and solve algebraically.

$$5x = 8$$
$$x = 1.6$$

(b) $4e^{3x - 1.5} = 360$

    (1) Solve for $e^{3x - 1.5}$. $\qquad\qquad e^{3x - 1.5} = 90$

    (2) Take the natural log. $\qquad \ln e^{3x - 1.5} = \ln 90$

       From (7.3), $\qquad\qquad\quad 3x - 1.5 = \ln 90$

For $\ln 90$, enter 90 on a calculator and press the $\boxed{\ln x}$ key to find $\ln 90 = 4.49981 \approx 4.5$. Substitute and solve.

$$3x - 1.5 = 4.5 \qquad x = 2$$

(c) $\frac{1}{2}e^{x^2} = 259$

    (1) Solve for e^{x^2} $\qquad\qquad\qquad e^{x^2} = 518$

    (2) Take the natural log. $\qquad\quad \ln e^{x^2} = \ln 518$

       From (7.3), $\qquad\quad x^2 = 6.24998 \approx 6.25 \qquad x = \pm 2.5$

7.19. Using the techniques of Section 7.5, solve the following natural logarithmic functions for x:

(a) $5 \ln x + 8 = 14$

(1) Solve algebraically for $\ln x$.

$$5 \ln x = 6 \qquad \ln x = 1.2$$

(2) Set both sides of the equation as exponents of e to eliminate the natural log.

$$e^{\ln x} = e^{1.2}$$

From (7.2), $\qquad\qquad x = e^{1.2}$

To find the value of $e^{1.2}$, enter 1.2 on a calculator, press the $\boxed{e^x}$ key to find $e^{1.2} = 3.32012$, and substitute. If the $\boxed{e^x}$ key is the inverse of the $\boxed{\ln x}$ key, enter 1.2, then press the $\boxed{\text{INV}}$ key followed by the $\boxed{\ln x}$ key.

$$x = 3.32012 \approx 3.32$$

(b) $\ln (x + 4)^2 = 3$

(1) Simplify with the laws of logs, then solve for $\ln x$.

$$2 \ln (x + 4) = 3$$
$$\ln (x + 4) = 1.5$$

(2) $\qquad\qquad\qquad e^{\ln (x+4)} = e^{1.5}$

From (7.2), $\qquad\qquad x + 4 = e^{1.5}$

Using a calculator, $\qquad\quad x + 4 = 4.48169$

$$x = 4.48169 - 4 = 0.48169 \approx 0.5$$

(c) $\ln \sqrt{x + 34} = 2.55$

(1) Simplify and solve. $\qquad \frac{1}{2} \ln (x + 34) = 2.55$

$$\ln (x + 34) = 5.1$$

(2) From (7.2), $\qquad\qquad x + 34 = e^{5.1} \approx 164$

$$x = 130$$

7.20. Solve each of the following equations for x in terms of y:

(a) $\log_a x = y^3$ $\qquad$ (b) $\log_a x = \log_a 3 + \log_a y$

$\quad x = a^{y^3}$ $\qquad\qquad\quad x = 3y \qquad$ since addition in logs = multiplication in algebra.

(c) $\ln x = 3y$ $\qquad$ (d) $\ln x = \log_a y$ $\qquad$ (e) $\log_a x = \ln y$

$\quad x = e^{3y}$ $\qquad\qquad\quad x = e^{\log_a y}$ $\qquad\qquad\quad x = a^{\ln y}$

(f) $y = ge^{hx}$

To solve for x when x is an exponent in a natural exponential function, take the natural log of both sides and solve algebraically, as follows:

$$\ln y = \ln g + hx \ln e = \ln g + hx$$
$$x = \frac{\ln y - \ln g}{h}$$

(g) $y = ae^{x + 1}$

$$\ln y = \ln a + (x + 1) \ln e = \ln a + x + 1$$
$$x = \ln y - \ln a - 1$$

(h) $y = p(1 + i)^x$

When x is an exponent in an exponential function with a base other than e, take the common log of both sides and solve algebraically.

$$\log y = \log p + x \log(1 + i)$$
$$x = \frac{\log y - \log p}{\log(1 + i)}$$

7.21. Use common logs to solve each of the following equations:

(a) $y = 625(0.8)$

(1)   Take the common log of both sides of the equation, using the properties of logarithms from Section 7.3.

$$\log y = \log 625 + \log 0.8$$

To find the logs of 625 and 0.8, enter each number individually on the calculator, press the $\boxed{\log x}$ key to get the common log of each number, and perform the required arithmetic.

$$\log y = 2.79588 + (-0.09691) = 2.69897$$

(2)   Since $\log y = 2.69897$ indicates that 10 must be raised to the 2.69897 power to get y, to find the *antilogarithm* of 2.69897 and solve for y, enter 2.69897 on a calculator, press the $\boxed{10^x}$ key to find that $10^{2.69897} = 500$, and substitute. If the $\boxed{10^x}$ key is the inverse of the $\boxed{\log x}$ key, enter 2.69897 and press the $\boxed{\text{INV}}$ key followed by the $\boxed{\log x}$ key.

$$y = \text{antilog } 2.69897 = 10^{2.69897} = 500$$

(b) $y = \frac{40}{100}$

(1) $$\log y = \log 40 - \log 100$$

(2) $$\log y = 1.60206 - 2 = -0.39794$$
$$y = \text{antilog}(-0.39794) = 10^{-0.39794} = 0.4$$

(c) $y = \dfrac{130}{0.25}$

(1) $$\log y = \log 130 - \log 0.25$$

(2) $$\log y = 2.11394 - (-0.60206) = 2.71600$$
$$y = \text{antilog } 2.71600 = 10^{2.71600} = 519.996 \approx 520$$

(d) $y = (1.06)^{10}$

(1) $$\log y = 10 \log 1.06$$

(2) $$\log y = 10(0.02531) = 0.2531$$
$$y = \text{antilog } 0.2531 = 10^{0.2531} = 1.791$$

(e) $y = 1024^{0.2}$

(1) $$\log y = 0.2 \log 1024$$

(2) $$\log y = 0.2(3.0103) = 0.60206$$
$$y = \text{antilog } 0.60206 = 10^{0.60206} = 4$$

(f) $y = \sqrt[5]{1024}$

(1) $\log y = \frac{1}{5} \log 1024$

(2) $\log y = \frac{1}{5}(3.0103) = 0.60206$

$y = \text{antilog}\, 0.60206 = 10^{0.60206} = 4$

The answer is the same as in part (e) because $y = 1024^{1/5} = 1024^{0.2} = 4$. Taking the fifth root is the same thing as raising to the 0.2 or one-fifth power. In one case the log is divided by 5; in the other, it is multiplied by 0.2.

7.22.   Use natural logs to solve the following equations:

(a) $y = 12.5^3$

(1) $\ln y = 3 \ln 12.5$

To find the natural log of 12.5, enter 12.5 on a calculator and press the $\boxed{\ln x}$ key to find $\ln 12.5 = 2.52573$. Then substitute.

(2) $\ln y = 3(2.52573) = 7.57719$

Since $\ln y = 7.57719$ indicates that e must be raised to the 7.57719 power to get y, to find the *antilogarithm$_e$* of 7.57719 and solve for y, enter 7.57719 on a calculator, press the $\boxed{e^x}$ key to find that $e^{7.57719} \approx 1953.1$ and substitute. If the $\boxed{e^x}$ key is the inverse of the $\boxed{\ln x}$ key, enter 7.57719 and press the $\boxed{\text{INV}}$ key followed by the $\boxed{\ln x}$ key.

$y = \text{antilog}_e\, 7.57719 = e^{7.57719} \approx 1953.1$

(b) $y = \sqrt[4]{28\,561}$

(1) $\ln y = \frac{1}{4} \ln 28\,561$

(2) $\ln y = \frac{1}{4}(10.25980) = 2.56495$

$y = \text{antilog}_e\, 2.56495 = e^{2.56495} = 13$

Chapter 8

Exponential and Logarithmic
Functions in Economics

8.1 INTEREST COMPOUNDING

A given principal P compounded annually at an interest rate i for a given number of years t will have a value S at the end of that time given by the exponential function

$$S = P(1 + i)^t \qquad (8.1)$$

If compounded m times a year for t years,

$$S = P\left(1 + \frac{i}{m}\right)^{mt} \qquad (8.2)$$

If compounded continuously at 100 percent interest for 1 year,

$$S = P \lim_{m \to \infty} \left(1 + \frac{1}{m}\right)^m = P(2.71828) = Pe$$

For interest rates r other than 100 percent and time periods t other than 1 year,

$$S = Pe^{rt} \qquad (8.3)$$

For negative growth rates, such as depreciation or deflation, the same formulas apply, but i and r are negative. See Example 1 and Problems 8.1 to 8.6 and 8.9 to 8.17.

EXAMPLE 1. Find the value of \$100 at 10 percent interest for 2 years compounded:

1. Annually, $S = P(1 + i)^t$.

$$S = 100(1 + 0.10)^2 = 121$$

2. Semiannually, $S = P[1 + (i/m)]^{mt}$, where $m = 2$ and $t = 2$.

$$S = 100\left(1 + \frac{0.10}{2}\right)^{2(2)} = 100(1 + 0.05)^4$$

To find the value of $(1.05)^4$, enter 1.05 on a calculator, press the $\boxed{y^x}$ key, enter 4, and hit the $\boxed{=}$ key to find $(1.05)^4 = 1.2155$. Then substitute.

$$S = 100(1.2155) = 121.55$$

3. Continuously, $S = Pe^{rt}$.

$$S = 100e^{0.1(2)} = 100e^{0.2}$$

For $e^{0.2}$, enter 0.2 on a calculator, press the $\boxed{e^x}$ key to find that $e^{0.2} = 1.2214$, and substitute. If the $\boxed{e^x}$ key is the inverse (shift, or second function) of the $\boxed{\ln x}$ key, enter 0.2 and press the $\boxed{\text{INV}}$ (**Shift**, or **2ndF**) key followed by the $\boxed{\ln x}$ key.

$$S = 100(1.2214) = 122.14$$

8.2 EFFECTIVE VS. NOMINAL RATES OF INTEREST

As seen in Example 1, a given principal set out at the same *nominal rate of interest* will earn different *effective rates of interest* which depend on the type of compounding. When compounded annually for 2 years, \$100 will be worth \$121; when compounded semiannually, $S = \$121.55$; when compounded continuously, $S = \$122.14$.

To find the effective annual rate of interest i_e for multiple compounding:

$$P(1 + i_e)^t = P\left(1 + \frac{i}{m}\right)^{mt}$$

Dividing by P and taking the tth root of each side,

$$1 + i_e = \left(1 + \frac{i}{m}\right)^m$$

$$i_e = \left(1 + \frac{i}{m}\right)^m - 1 \tag{8.4}$$

To find the effective annual rate of interest for continuous compounding:

$$1 + i_e = e^r$$

$$i_e = e^r - 1 \tag{8.5}$$

See Example 2 and Problems 8.7 and 8.8.

EXAMPLE 2. Find the effective annual rate of interest for a nominal interest rate of 10 percent when compounded for 2 years (1) semiannually and (2) continuously.

1. Semiannually, $$i_e = \left(1 + \frac{i}{m}\right)^m - 1 = (1.05)^2 - 1$$

   For $(1.05)^2$, enter 1.05 on a calculator, press the $\boxed{x^2}$ key, or press the $\boxed{y^x}$ key, and then enter 2 followed by the $\boxed{=}$ key, to find $(1.05)^2 = 1.1025$, and substitute.

$$i_e = 1.1025 - 1 = 0.1025 = 10.25\%$$

2. Continuously, $$i_e = e^r - 1 = e^{0.1} - 1$$

   To find the value of $e^{0.1}$, enter 0.1 on a calculator, press the $\boxed{e^x}$ key to learn $e^{0.1} = 1.10517$, and substitute.

$$i_e = 1.10517 - 1 = 0.10517 \approx 10.52\%$$

8.3 DISCOUNTING

A sum of money to be received in the future is not worth as much as an equivalent amount of money in the present, because the money on hand can be lent at interest to grow to an even larger sum by the end of the year. If present market conditions will enable a person to earn 8 percent interest compounded annually, \$100 will grow to \$108 by the end of the year. And \$108 one year from now, therefore, is equivalently worth (has a *present value* of) only \$100 today.

Discounting is the process of determining the present value P of a future sum of money S. If under annual compounding

$$S = P(1 + i)^t$$

then

$$P = \frac{S}{(1 + i)^t} = S(1 + i)^{-t} \tag{8.6}$$

Similarly, under multiple compoundings $P = S[1 + (i/m)]^{-mt}$, and under continuous compounding $P = Se^{-rt}$. When finding the present value, the interest rate is called the *rate of discount*. See Example 3 and Problems 8.18 to 8.22.

EXAMPLE 3. The present value of a 5-year bond with a face value of $1000 and no coupons is calculated below. It is assumed that comparable opportunities offer interest rates of 9 percent under annual compounding.

$$P = S(1 + i)^{-t} = 1000(1 + 0.09)^{-5}$$

To find the value of $(1.09)^{-5}$, enter 1.09 on a calculator, press the $\boxed{y^x}$ key, and enter -5 by first entering 5 and then pressing the $\boxed{+/-}$ key followed by the $\boxed{=}$ key to find $(1.09)^{-5} = 0.64993$, and substitute.

$$P = 1000(0.64993) = 649.93$$

Thus, a bond with no coupons promising to pay $1000 five years from now is worth approximately $649.93 today since $649.93 at 9 percent interest will grow to $1000 in 5 years.

8.4 DISCOUNTING A FUTURE STREAM OF INCOME

Investment in plant or equipment normally returns a stream of income over a period of years. The present value of a stream of future income is the summation of each component discounted to its present value. If each component S is equal and interest is compounded annually, the discounting formula is

$$P = S\left(\frac{1}{i}\right)\left[1 - \frac{1}{(1 + i)^t}\right] \tag{8.7}$$

See Examples 4 and 5 and Problems 8.23 to 8.25.

EXAMPLE 4. The present value of $100 annually for 8 years when the rate of discount in society is 6 percent is determined as follows:

$$P = S\left(\frac{1}{i}\right)\left[1 - \frac{1}{(1 + i)^t}\right] = 100\left(\frac{1}{0.06}\right)\left[1 - \frac{1}{(1.06)^8}\right]$$

Using a calculator for $1/(1.06)^8 = (1.06)^{-8}$, enter 1.06, press the $\boxed{y^x}$ key and enter -8 by pressing 8 then hitting the $\boxed{+/-}$ key followed by the $\boxed{=}$ key, to find $(1.06)^{-8} = 0.62741$, and substitute.

$$P = 100\left(\frac{1}{0.06}\right)(1 - 0.62741) = 620.98$$

EXAMPLE 5. A firm can determine how much it should be willing to pay for a machine that will raise net revenues by $1000 a year for 10 years, with no scrap value, when the rate of discount is 2 percent, by using the formula illustrated in Example 4. In this case,

$$P = 1000\left(\frac{1}{0.02}\right)\left[1 - \frac{1}{(1.02)^{10}}\right]$$

Using a calculator for $(1.02)^{-10}$ and substituting, we have

$$P = 1000\left(\frac{1}{0.02}\right)(1 - 0.82035) = 8982.50$$

8.5 CONVERTING EXPONENTIAL TO NATURAL EXPONENTIAL FUNCTIONS

In Section 8.1 we saw that (1) exponential functions are used to measure rates of *discrete growth*, i.e., growth that takes place at discrete intervals of time, such as the end of the year or the end of the quarter as in ordinary interest compounding or discounting; and (2) natural exponential functions are used to measure rates of *continuous growth*, i.e., growth that takes place constantly rather than at discrete intervals, as in continuous compounding, animal development, or population growth. An exponential function $S = P(1 + i/m)^{mt}$ expressing discrete growth can be converted to an equivalent natural exponential function $S = Pe^{rt}$ measuring continuous growth, by setting the two expressions equal to each other and solving for r, as follows:

$$P\left(1 + \frac{i}{m}\right)^{mt} = Pe^{rt}$$

By canceling P's,

$$\left(1 + \frac{i}{m}\right)^{mt} = e^{rt}$$

Taking the natural log of each side,

$$\ln\left(1 + \frac{i}{m}\right)^{mt} = \ln e^{rt}$$

$$mt \ln\left(1 + \frac{i}{m}\right) = rt$$

Dividing both sides by t,

$$r = m \ln\left(1 + \frac{i}{m}\right)$$

Thus, $$S = P\left(1 + \frac{i}{m}\right)^{mt} = Pe^{m \ln (1 + i/m)t}$$ (8.8)

See Examples 6 and 7 and Problems 8.40 to 8.45.

EXAMPLE 6.   A natural exponential function can be used to determine the value of \$100 at 10 percent interest compounded semiannually for 2 years, as shown below.

$$S = Pe^{rt}$$

where $r = m \ln (1 + i/m)$. Thus,

$$r = 2 \ln\left(1 + \frac{0.10}{2}\right) = 2 \ln 1.05 = 2(0.04879) = 0.09758$$

Substituting above,

$$S = 100e^{(0.09758)2} = 100e^{0.19516}$$

Using a calculator here and throughout,

$$S = 100(1.2155) = 121.55$$

as was found in Example 1.

Note that with natural exponential functions, the continuous growth is given by r in Pe^{rt}. Thus, the continuous growth rate of \$100 at 10 percent interest compounded semiannually is 0.09758, or 9.758 percent a year. That is to say, 9.758 percent interest at continuous compounding is equivalent to 10 percent interest when compounded semiannually.

EXAMPLE 7.   A small firm with current annual sales of \$10 000 projects a 12 percent growth in sales annually. Its projected sales in 4 years are calculated below in terms of an *ordinary exponential function.*

$$S = 10\,000(1 + 0.12)^4$$
$$= 10\,000(1.5735) = 15\,735$$

EXAMPLE 8.   The sales projections specified in Example 7 are recalculated below, using a natural exponential function with $r = m \ln (1 + i/m)$ and $m = 1$.

$$r = \ln 1.12 = 0.11333$$
$$S = 10\,000e^{0.11333(4)} = 10\,000(1.5735) = 15\,735$$

8.6 ESTIMATING GROWTH RATES FROM DATA POINTS

Given two sets of data for a function—sales, costs, profits—growing consistently over time, annual growth rates can be measured and a natural exponential function estimated through a system of simultaneous equations. For example, if sales volume equals 2.74 million in 1986 and 4.19 million in 1991, let $t = 0$ for the base year 1986, then $t = 5$ for 1991. Express the two sets of data points in terms of a natural exponential function $S = Pe^{rt}$, recalling that $e^0 = 1$.

$$2.74 = Pe^{r(0)} = P \tag{8.9}$$

$$4.19 = Pe^{r(5)} \tag{8.10}$$

Substitute $P = 2.74$ from (8.9) in (8.10) and simplify algebraically.

$$4.19 = 2.74e^{5r}$$
$$1.53 = e^{5r}$$

Take the natural log of both sides.

$$\ln 1.53 = \ln e^{5r} = 5r$$
$$0.42527 = 5r$$
$$r = 0.08505 \approx 8.5\%$$

Substituting,
$$S = 2.74e^{0.085t}$$

With $r = 0.085$, the rate of continuous growth per year is 8.5 percent. To find the rate of discrete growth i, recall that

$$r = m \ln\left(1 + \frac{i}{m}\right)$$

Thus, for annual compounding with $m = 1$,

$$0.085 = \ln(1 + i)$$
$$1 + i = \text{antilog}_e \, 0.085 = e^{0.085} = 1.08872$$
$$i = 1.08872 - 1 = 0.08872 \approx 8.9\%$$

See Example 9 and Problems 8.46 to 8.48.

EXAMPLE 9. Given the original information above, an ordinary exponential function for growth in terms of $S = P(1 + i)^t$ can also be estimated directly from the data.

Set the data in ordinary exponential form.

$$2.74 = P(1 + i)^0 = P \tag{8.11}$$

$$4.19 = P(1 + i)^5 \tag{8.12}$$

Substitute $P = 2.74$ from (8.11) in (8.12) and simplify.

$$4.19 = 2.74(1 + i)^5$$
$$1.53 = (1 + i)^5$$

Take the common log of both sides.

$$\log 1.53 = 5 \log(1 + i)$$
$$\tfrac{1}{5}(0.18469) = \log(1 + i)$$
$$\log(1 + i) = 0.03694$$
$$1 + i = \text{antilog} \, 0.03694 = 10^{0.03694} = 1.08878$$
$$i = 1.08878 - 1 = 0.08878 \approx 8.9\%$$

Substituting,
$$S = 2.74(1 + 0.089)^t$$

Solved Problems

COMPOUNDING INTEREST

8.1   Given a principal P of \$1000 at 6 percent interest i for 3 years, find the future value S when the principal is compounded (a) annually, (b) semiannually, and (c) quarterly.

(a)   From (8.1), $S = P(1 + i)^t = 1000(1 + 0.06)^3$

For $(1.06)^3$, enter 1.06 on a calculator, press the $\boxed{y^x}$ key, enter 3 followed by the $\boxed{=}$ key to find $(1.06)^3 = 1.19102$, then substitute.

$$S = 1000(1.19102) \approx 1191.02$$

(b)   From (8.2), $S = P\left(1 + \dfrac{i}{m}\right)^{mt} = 1000\left(1 + \dfrac{0.06}{2}\right)^{2(3)} = 1000(1.03)^6$

For $(1.03)^6$, enter 1.03, hit the $\boxed{y^x}$ key and then 6, and substitute.

$$S = 1000(1.19405) \approx 1194.05$$

(c) $S = 1000\left(1 + \dfrac{0.06}{4}\right)^{4(3)} = 1000(1.015)^{12}$

Enter 1.015, hit the $\boxed{y^x}$ key then 12, and substitute.

$$S = 1000(1.19562) \approx 1195.62$$

8.2   Redo Problem 8.1, given a principal of \$100 at 8 percent for 5 years.

(a) $S = 100(1.08)^5$

$$= 100(1.46933) \approx 146.93$$

(b) $S = 100\left(1 + \dfrac{0.08}{2}\right)^{2(5)} = 100(1.04)^{10}$

$$= 100(1.48024) \approx 148.02$$

(c) $S = 100\left(1 + \dfrac{0.08}{4}\right)^{4(5)} = 100(1.02)^{20}$

$$= 100(1.48595) \approx 148.60$$

8.3.   Redo Problem 8.1, given a principal of \$1250 at 12 percent for 4 years.

(a) $S = 1250(1.12)^4 = 1250(1.57352) \approx 1966.90$

(b) $S = 1250(1.06)^8 = 1250(1.59385) \approx 1992.31$

(c) $S = 1250(1.03)^{16} = 1250(1.60471) \approx 2005.89$

8.4.   Find the future value of a principal of \$100 at 5 percent for 6 years when compounded (a) annually and (b) continually.

(a) $S = 100(1.05)^6 = 100(1.34010) \approx 134.01$

(b)   From (8.3), $S = Pe^{rt} = 100e^{0.05(6)} = 100e^{0.3}$

For $e^{0.3}$, enter 0.3, hit the $\boxed{e^x}$ key, and substitute.

$$S = 100(1.34986) \approx 134.99$$

8.5.   Redo Problem 8.4, given a principal of \$150 at 7 percent for 4 years.

(a) $S = 150(1.07)^4 = 150(1.31080) \approx 196.62$

(b) $S = 150e^{0.07(4)} = 150e^{0.28} = 150(1.32313) \approx 198.47$

8.6. From Problems 8.4 and 8.5, use natural logs to find (*a*) $S = 100e^{0.3}$ and (*b*) $S = 150e^{0.28}$.

(*a*)
$$\ln S = \ln 100 + 0.3 \ln e = 4.60517 + 0.3(1) = 4.90517$$
$$S = \text{antilog}_e 4.90517 = e^{4.90517} \approx 134.99$$

(*b*)
$$\ln S = \ln 150 + 0.28 \ln e = 5.01064 + 0.28 = 5.29064$$
$$S = \text{antilog}_e 5.29064 = e^{5.29064} \approx 198.47$$

8.7. Find the effective annual interest rate on \$100 at 6 percent compounded (*a*) semiannually and (*b*) continuously.

(*a*) From (*8.4*),
$$i_e = \left(1 + \frac{i}{m}\right)^m - 1$$
$$= 1.0609 - 1 = 0.06090 \approx 6.09\%$$

(*b*) From (*8.5*),
$$i_e = e^r - 1 = e^{0.06} - 1$$
$$= 1.06184 - 1 = 0.06184 \approx 6.18\%$$

8.8. Calculate the rate of effective annual interest on \$1000 at 12 percent compounded (*a*) quarterly and (*b*) continuously.

(*a*)
$$i_e = \left(1 + \frac{i}{m}\right)^m - 1 = (1.03)^4 - 1$$
$$= 1.12551 - 1 = 0.12551 \approx 12.55\%$$

(*b*)
$$i_e = e^r - 1 = e^{0.12} - 1$$
$$= 1.12750 - 1 = 0.12750 \approx 12.75\%$$

TIMING

8.9. Determine the interest rate needed to have money double in 10 years under annual compounding.

$$S = P(1 + i)^t$$

If money doubles, $S = 2P$. Thus, $2P = P(1 + i)^{10}$.

Dividing by P, and taking the tenth root of each side,

$$2 = (1 + i)^{10} \qquad (1 + i) = \sqrt[10]{2}$$

For $\sqrt[10]{2}$, enter 2, press the $\boxed{\sqrt[x]{y}}$ key, then 10 followed by the $\boxed{=}$ key, and substitute. If the $\boxed{\sqrt[x]{y}}$ is the inverse (shift, or second function) of the $\boxed{y^x}$ key, enter 2, hit the $\boxed{\text{INV}}$ (**Shift**, or **2ndF**) key followed by the $\boxed{y^x}$ key, and then enter 10 and hit the $\boxed{=}$ key.

$$1 + i = 1.07177$$
$$i = 1.07177 - 1 = 0.07177 \approx 7.18\%$$

Note that since $\sqrt[10]{2} = 2^{1/10} = 2^{0.1}$, $\sqrt[10]{2}$ or any root can also be found with the $\boxed{y^x}$ key.

8.10. Determine the interest rate needed to have money double in 6 years when compounded semiannually.

$$S = P\left(1 + \frac{i}{m}\right)^{mt}$$
$$2P = P\left(1 + \frac{i}{2}\right)^{2(6)}$$
$$2 = 1(1 + 0.5i)^{12}$$
$$1 + 0.5i = \sqrt[12]{2}$$

$$\ln(1 + 0.5i) = \tfrac{1}{12}\ln 2 = \tfrac{1}{12}(0.69315) = 0.05776$$
$$1 + 0.5i = e^{0.05776} = 1.05946$$
$$0.5i = 1.05946 - 1 = 0.05946$$
$$i = 0.11892 \approx 11.89\%$$

8.11. What interest rate is needed to have money treble in 10 years when compounded quarterly?

$$S = P\left(1 + \frac{i}{4}\right)^{4(10)}$$

If money trebles,

$$3P = P\left(1 + \frac{i}{4}\right)^{40}$$
$$3 = (1 + 0.25i)^{40}$$
$$1 + 0.25i = \sqrt[40]{3}$$
$$\ln(1 + 0.25i) = \frac{1}{40}\ln 3 = 0.02747$$
$$1 + 0.25i = e^{0.02747} = 1.02785$$
$$i = 0.1114 \approx 11.14\%$$

8.12. At what interest rate will money treble if compounded continuously for 8 years?

$$S = Pe^{rt}$$
$$3P = Pe^{r(8)}$$
$$\ln 3 = \ln e^{8r}$$
$$1.09861 = 8r \qquad r = 0.1373 = 13.73\%$$

8.13. At what interest rate will money quintuple if compounded continuously for 25 years?

$$S = Pe^{rt}$$
$$5 = e^{25r}$$
$$\ln 5 = 25r$$
$$1.60944 = 25r \qquad r = 0.0644 = 6.44\%$$

8.14. How long will it take money to double at 12 percent interest under annual compounding? Round answers to two decimal places.

$$S = P(1 + i)^t \qquad 2 = (1 + 0.12)^t$$
$$\ln 2 = t \ln 1.12 \qquad 0.69315 = 0.11333t$$
$$t \approx 6.12 \text{ years}$$

8.15. How long will it take money to increase to $2\tfrac{1}{2}$ times its present value when compounded semi-annually at 8 percent?

$$S = P\left(1 + \frac{0.08}{2}\right)^{2t} \qquad 2.5 = (1.04)^{2t}$$
$$\ln 2.5 = 2t \ln 1.04 \qquad 0.91629 = 2(0.03922)t$$
$$t \approx 11.68 \text{ years}$$

8.16. How long will it take money to double at 5 percent interest when compounded quarterly?

$$S = P\left(1 + \frac{0.05}{4}\right)^{4t} \qquad 2 = (1.0125)^{4t}$$
$$\ln 2 = 4t \ln 1.0125 \qquad 0.69315 = 4(0.01242)t$$
$$t \approx 13.95 \text{ years}$$

8.17. How long will it take money (a) to quadruple when compounded continuously at 9 percent and (b) to treble at 12 percent?

(a) $S = Pe^{rt}$ $4 = e^{0.09t}$ (b) $S = Pe^{rt}$ $3 = e^{0.12t}$

  $\ln 4 = 0.09t$ $1.38629 = 0.09t$ $\ln 3 = 0.12t$ $1.09861 = 0.12t$

  $t \approx 15.4$ years $t \approx 9.16$ years

DISCOUNTING

8.18. Find the present value of $750 to be paid 4 years from now when the prevailing interest rate is 10 percent if interest is compounded (a) annually and (b) semiannually.

(a) Using (8.6) and its modifications throughout,

$$P = S(1 + i)^{-t} = 750(1.10)^{-4}$$

For $(1.10)^{-4}$, enter 1.10, hit the $\boxed{y^x}$ key, enter 4, then press the $\boxed{+/-}$ key to find $(1.10)^{-4} = 0.68301$, and substitute.

$$P = 750(0.68301) \approx 512.26$$

(b)
$$P = S\left(1 + \frac{i}{m}\right)^{-mt} = 750(1.05)^{-8}$$
$$= 750(0.67684) \approx 507.63$$

8.19. Redo Problem 8.18, for $600 to be paid 7 years hence at a prevailing interest rate of 4 percent.

(a) $P = 600(1.04)^{-7}$ (b) $P = 600(1.02)^{-14}$

  $= 600(0.75992) \approx 455.95$ $= 600(0.75788) \approx 454.73$

8.20. Find the present value of $500 in 3 years at 8 percent when interest is compounded (a) annually and (b) continuously.

(a) $P = 500(1.08)^{-3}$ (b) $P = Se^{-rt} = 500e^{-0.08(3)} = 500e^{-0.24}$

  $= 500(0.79383) \approx 396.92$ $= 500(0.78663) \approx 393.32$

8.21. Redo Problem 8.20, for $120 in 5 years at 9 percent.

(a) $P = 120(1.09)^{-5}$ (b) $P = 120e^{-0.09(5)} = 120e^{-0.45}$

  $= 120(0.64993) \approx 77.99$ $= 120(0.63763) \approx 76.52$

8.22. Use natural logs to solve Problem 8.21(b).
$$P = 120e^{-0.45}$$
$$\ln P = \ln 120 + (-0.45) = 4.78749 - 0.45 = 4.33749$$
$$P = \text{antilog}_e\, 4.33749 = e^{4.33749} \approx 76.52$$

DISCOUNTING A FUTURE STREAM

8.23. Find the present value of $1000 to be received each year for 4 years when the rate of discount is 4 percent compounded annually.

$$P = S\left(\frac{1}{i}\right)\left[1 - \frac{1}{(1 + i)^t}\right] = 1000\left(\frac{1}{0.04}\right)\left[1 - \frac{1}{(1.04)^4}\right]$$

where $1/(1.04)^4 = (1.04)^{-4} = 0.85480$. Substituting,

$$P = 1000\left(\frac{1}{0.04}\right)(1 - 0.85480) = 25\,000(0.14520) \approx 3630.00$$

8.24. How much should a firm be willing to pay for a machine that will provide net savings of $600 a year for 8 years, with no scrap value, when the discount rate is 12 percent?

$$P = 600\left(\frac{1}{0.12}\right)\left[1 - \frac{1}{(1.12)^8}\right]$$
$$= 600\left(\frac{1}{0.12}\right)(1 - 0.40388) = 5000(0.59612) \approx 2980.60$$

8.25. A firm buys a machine for $6500. It expects an annual 10 percent rate of return over the machine's 11-year life span. Calculate the projected net savings each year from the machine.

$$6500 = S\left(\frac{1}{0.10}\right)\left[1 - \frac{1}{(1.10)^{11}}\right]$$
$$6500 = S\left(\frac{1}{0.10}\right)(1 - 0.35049) \qquad S = \frac{6500}{6.4951} \approx 1000.75$$

EXPONENTIAL GROWTH FUNCTIONS

8.26. A firm with sales of 150 000 a year expects to grow by 8 percent a year. Determine the expected level of sales in 6 years.

$$S = 150\,000(1.08)^6$$
$$= 150\,000(1.58687) \approx 238\,031$$

8.27. Profits are projected to rise by 9 percent a year over the decade. With current profits of 240 000, what will the level of profits be at the end of the decade?

$$\pi = 240\,000(1.09)^{10}$$
$$= 240\,000(2.36736) \approx 568\,166$$

8.28. The cost of food has been increasing by 3.6 percent a year. What can a family with current food expenditures of $200 a month be expected to pay for food each month in 5 years?

$$F = 200(1.036)^5$$
$$= 200(1.19344) \approx 238.69$$

8.29. If the cost of living had continued to increase by 12.5 percent a year from a base of 100 in 1983, what would the cost-of-living index be in 1990?

$$C = 100(1.125)^7$$
$$= 100(2.28070) \approx 228.07$$

8.30. A discount clothing store reduces prices by 10 percent each day until the goods are sold. What will a $175 suit sell for in 5 days?

$$P = 175(1 - 0.10)^5$$
$$= 175(0.9)^5 = 175(0.59049) \approx 103.34$$

8.31. A new car depreciates in value by 3 percent a month for the first year. What is the book value of a $6000 car at the end of the first year?

$$B = 6000(0.97)^{12}$$
$$= 6000(0.69384) \approx 4163.04$$

8.32. If the dollar depreciates at 2.6 percent a year, what will a dollar be worth in real terms 25 years from now?

$$D = 1.00(0.974)^{25}$$
$$= 1.00(0.51758) \approx 0.5176 \text{ or } 51.76¢$$

8.33. The cost of an average hospital stay was $500 at the end of 1979. The average cost in 1989 was $1500. What was the annual rate of increase?

$$1500 = 500(1 + i)^{10}$$
$$3 = (1 + i)^{10}$$
$$1 + i = \sqrt[10]{3}$$

For $\sqrt[10]{3}$, enter 3, press the $\boxed{\sqrt[x]{y}}$ key then 10, and substitute.

$$1 + i = 1.11612 \qquad i = 0.11612 \approx 11.6\%$$

8.34. A 5-year development plan calls for boosting investment from 2.6 million a year to 4.2 million. What average annual increase in investment is needed each year?

$$4.2 = 2.6(1 + i)^{5}$$
$$1.615 = (1 + i)^{5}$$
$$1 + i = \sqrt[5]{1.615} = 1.10061$$
$$i = 0.10061 \approx 10\%$$

8.35. A developing country wishes to increase savings from a present level of 5.6 million to 12 million. How long will it take if it can increase savings by 15 percent a year?

$$12 = 5.6(1.15)^{t}$$

To solve for an exponent, use a logarithmic transformation.

$$\ln 12 = \ln 5.6 + t \ln 1.15$$
$$2.48491 = 1.72277 + 0.13976t$$
$$0.13976t = 0.76214 \qquad t \approx 5.45 \text{ years}$$

8.36. Population in many third world countries is growing at 3.2 percent. Calculate the population 20 years from now for a country with 1 000 000 people.

Since population increases continually over time, a natural exponential function is needed.

$$P = 1\,000\,000e^{0.032(20)} = 1\,000\,000e^{0.64}$$
$$= 1\,000\,000(1.89648) \approx 1\,896\,480$$

8.37. If the country in Problem 8.36 reduces its population increase to 2.4 percent, what will the population be in 20 years?

$$P = 1\,000\,000e^{0.024(20)} = 1\,000\,000e^{0.48}$$
$$= 1\,000\,000(1.61607) \approx\ = 1\,616\,070$$

8.38. If world population grows at 2.6 percent, how long will it take to double?

$$2 = e^{0.026t}$$
$$\ln 2 = 0.026t$$
$$0.69315 = 0.026t \qquad t = 26.66 \text{ years}$$

8.39. If arable land in the Sahel is eroding by 3.5 percent a year because of climatic conditions, how much of the present arable land A will be left in 12 years?

$$P = Ae^{-0.035(12)} = Ae^{-0.42}$$
$$= 0.657047 A \quad \text{or} \quad 66\%$$

CONVERTING EXPONENTIAL FUNCTIONS

8.40. Find the future value of a principal of $2000 compounded semiannually at 12 percent for 3 years, using (a) an exponential function and (b) the equivalent natural exponential function.

(a)
$$S = P\left(1 + \frac{i}{m}\right)^{mt} = 2000\left(1 + \frac{0.12}{2}\right)^{2(3)} = 2000(1.06)^6 = 2000(1.41852) \approx 2837.04$$

(b)
$$S = Pe^{rt}$$

where $r = m\ln(1 + i/m) = 2\ln 1.06 = 2(0.05827) = 0.11654$.

Thus, $\qquad S = 2000e^{0.11654(3)} = 2000e^{0.34962} = 2000(1.41853) \approx 2837.06*$

8.41. Redo Problem 8.40 for a principal of $600 compounded annually at 9 percent for 5 years.

(a)
$$S = 600(1.09)^5 = 600(1.53862) \approx 923.17$$

(b) $S = Pe^{rt}$, where $r = \ln 1.09 = 0.08618$. Thus,

$$S = 600e^{0.08618(5)} = 600e^{0.4309} = 600(1.53864) \approx 923.18*$$

8.42. Redo Problem 8.40 for a principal of $1800 compounded quarterly at 8 percent interest for $2\frac{1}{2}$ years.

(a) $S = 1800(1.02)^{10}$
$\qquad = 1800(1.21899) \approx 2194.18$

(b) $r = 4\ln 1.02 = 4(0.01980) = 0.07920$
$\qquad S = 1800e^{0.07920(2.5)} = 1800e^{0.19800}$
$\qquad\qquad = 1800(1.21896) = 2194.13*$

8.43. Find the equivalent form under annual discrete compounding for $S = Pe^{0.07696\,t}$.

$$r = m\ln\left(1 + \frac{i}{m}\right)$$

Since compounding is annual, $m = 1$

$$0.07696 = \ln(1 + i)$$
$$1 + i = \text{antilog}_e\, 0.07696 = 1.08$$
$$i = 0.08$$

Thus, $\qquad\qquad\qquad S = P(1.08)^t$

---

* Slight discrepancy is due to earlier rounding.

8.44. Find the equivalent form under semiannual discrete compounding for $Pe^{0.09758\,t}$.

$$r = 2\ln(1 + 0.5i)$$
$$0.09758 = 2\ln(1 + 0.5i)$$
$$1 + 0.5i = \text{antilog}_e\, 0.04879 = 1.05$$
$$0.5i = 0.05 \quad i = 0.10$$

Thus,
$$S = P(1.05)^{2t}$$

8.45. Find the equivalent form for $S = Pe^{0.15688\,t}$ under quarterly compounding.

$$r = 4\ln(1 + 0.25i)$$
$$\tfrac{1}{4}(0.15688) = \ln(1 + 0.25i)$$
$$1 + 0.25i = \text{antilog}_e\, 0.03922 = 1.04$$
$$i = 0.16$$
$$S = P(1.04)^{4t}$$

ESTABLISHING EXPONENTIAL FUNCTIONS FROM DATA

8.46. An animal population goes from 3.5 million in 1987 to 4.97 million in 1991. Express population growth P in terms of a natural exponential function and determine the rate of growth.

$$3.50 = P_0\, e^{r(0)} = P_0 \qquad (8.13)$$
$$4.97 = P_0\, e^{r(4)} \qquad (8.14)$$

Substitute $P_0 = 3.50$ from (8.13) in (8.14) and simplify.

$$4.97 = 3.50e^{4r}$$
$$1.42 = e^{4r}$$

Take the natural log of both sides.

$$\ln 1.42 = \ln e^{4r} = 4r$$
$$0.35066 = 4r$$
$$r = 0.08767 \approx 8.8\%$$

Thus,
$$P = 3.50e^{0.088t} \qquad r = 8.8\%$$

8.47. Costs C of a government program escalate from 5.39 billion in 1985 to 10.64 billion in 1991. Express costs in terms of an ordinary exponential function, and find the annual rate of growth.

$$5.39 = C_0(1 + i)^0 = C_0 \qquad (8.15)$$
$$10.64 = C_0(1 + i)^6 \qquad (8.16)$$

Substitute $C_0 = 5.39$ from (8.15) in (8.16) and simplify.

$$10.64 = 5.39(1 + i)^6$$
$$1.974 = (1 + i)^6$$

Take the common log of both sides.

$$\log 1.974 = 6\log(1 + i)$$
$$\tfrac{1}{6}(0.29535) = \log(1 + i)$$
$$\log(1 + i) = 0.04923$$
$$1 + i = \text{antilog}\, 0.04923 = 10^{0.04923} = 1.12$$
$$i = 1.12 - 1 = 0.12 = 12\%$$

Hence,
$$C = 5.39(1 + 0.12)^t \qquad i = 12\%$$

8.48. Redo Problem 8.47, given $C = 2.80$ in 1981 and $C = 5.77$ in 1991.

$$2.80 = C_0(1 + i)^0 = C_0 \qquad (8.17)$$

$$5.77 = C_0(1 + i)^{10} \qquad (8.18)$$

Substitute $C_0 = 2.80$ in (8.18) and simplify.

$$5.77 = 2.80(1 + i)^{10}$$
$$2.06 = (1 + i)^{10}$$

Take the logs.
$$\log 2.06 = 10 \log(1 + i)$$
$$\tfrac{1}{10}(0.31387) = \log(1 + i)$$
$$\log(1 + i) = 0.03139$$
$$1 + i = \text{antilog}\, 0.03139 = 10^{0.03139} = 1.07495$$
$$i = 1.07495 - 1 = 0.07495 \approx 7.5\%$$

Hence,
$$C = 2.80(1 + 0.075)^t \qquad i = 7.5\%$$

Chapter 9

Differentiation of Exponential and Logarithmic Functions

9.1 RULES OF DIFFERENTIATION

The rules of exponential and logarithmic differentiation are presented below, illustrated in Examples 1 to 4, and treated in Problems 9.1 to 9.8. Selected proofs for the rules are offered in Problems 9.35 to 9.40.

9.1.1 The Natural Exponential Function Rule

Given $f(x) = e^{g(x)}$, where $g(x)$ is a differentiable function of x, the derivative is

$$f'(x) = e^{g(x)} \cdot g'(x) \tag{9.1}$$

In short, the derivative of a natural exponential function is equal to the original natural exponential function times the derivative of the exponent.

EXAMPLE 1. The derivatives of each of the natural exponential functions below are found as follows:

1. $f(x) = e^x$
   Let $g(x) = x$, then $g'(x) = 1$. Substituting in (9.1),
   $$f'(x) = e^x \cdot 1 = e^x$$
   The derivative of e^x is simply e^x, the original function itself.

2. $f(x) = e^{x^2}$
   Since $g(x) = x^2$, then $g'(x) = 2x$. Substituting in (9.1),
   $$f'(x) = e^{x^2} \cdot 2x = 2xe^{x^2}$$

3. $f(x) = 3e^{7-2x}$
   Here $g(x) = 7 - 2x$, so $g'(x) = -2$. From (9.1),
   $$f'(x) = 3e^{7-2x} \cdot -2 = -6e^{7-2x}$$
   Evaluating the slope of this function at $x = 4$,
   $$f'(4) = -6e^{7-2(4)} = -6e^{-1} = -6\left(\frac{1}{2.71828}\right) = -2.2$$
   See also Problem 9.1.

9.1.2 The Exponential Function Rule for Base a Other than e

Given $f(x) = a^{g(x)}$, where $a > 0$, $a \neq 1$, and $g(x)$ is a differentiable function of x, the derivative is

$$f'(x) = a^{g(x)} \cdot g'(x) \cdot \ln a \tag{9.2}$$

The derivative is simply the original function times the derivative of the exponent times the natural log of the base.

EXAMPLE 2.   The exponential function rule for base a is demonstrated in the following cases:

1. $f(x) = a^{1-2x}$. Let $g(x) = 1 - 2x$, then $g'(x) = -2$. Substituting in (9.2),

$$f'(x) = a^{1-2x} \cdot -2 \cdot \ln a = -2a^{1-2x} \ln a$$

2. $y = a^x$. Here $g(x) = x$ and $g'(x) = 1$. From (9.2),

$$y' = a^x \cdot 1 \cdot \ln a = a^x \ln a$$

Remember that a may also assume a numerical value. See Problem 9.2(c) through (g).

3. $y = x^2 a^{3x}$. With y a product of x^2 and a^{3x}, the product rule is necessary.

$$y' = x^2(a^{3x} \cdot 3 \cdot \ln a) + a^{3x}(2x)$$
$$= xa^{3x}(3x \ln a + 2)$$

See also Problem 9.2.

9.1.3   The Natural Logarithmic Function Rule

Given $f(x) = \ln g(x)$, where $g(x)$ is positive and differentiable, the derivative is

$$f'(x) = \frac{1}{g(x)} \cdot g'(x) = \frac{g'(x)}{g(x)} \tag{9.3}$$

See Example 3 and Problems 9.3 to 9.5.

EXAMPLE 3.   Finding the derivative of a natural logarithmic function is demonstrated below:

1. $f(x) = \ln 6x^2$. Let $g(x) = 6x^2$, then $g'(x) = 12x$. Substituting in (9.3),

$$f'(x) = \frac{1}{6x^2} \cdot 12x = \frac{2}{x}$$

2. $y = \ln x$. Since $g(x) = x$, $g'(x) = 1$. From (9.3),

$$y' = \frac{1}{x} \cdot 1 = \frac{1}{x}$$

3. $y = \ln(x^2 + 6x + 2)$. The derivative is

$$y' = \frac{1}{x^2 + 6x + 2} \cdot (2x + 6) = \frac{2x + 6}{x^2 + 6x + 2}$$

Evaluating the slope of this function at $x = 4$,

$$y'(4) = \tfrac{14}{42} = \tfrac{1}{3}$$

9.1.4   The Logarithmic Function Rule for Base a Other than e

Given $f(x) = \log_a g(x)$, where $a > 0$, $a \neq 1$, and $g(x)$ is positive and differentiable, the derivative is

$$f'(x) = \frac{1}{g(x)} \cdot g'(x) \cdot \log_a e \qquad \text{or} \qquad f'(x) = \frac{1}{g(x)} \cdot g'(x) \cdot \frac{1}{\ln a} \tag{9.4}$$

since $\log_a e = 1/\ln a$. See Example 4 and Problems 9.6 and 9.40.

EXAMPLE 4.   Derivatives of logarithmic functions to base a are found as shown below.

1. $f(x) = \log_a (2x^2 + 1)$. Let $g(x) = 2x^2 + 1$; then $g'(x) = 4x$. Substituting in (9.4),

$$f'(x) = \frac{1}{2x^2 + 1} \cdot 4x \cdot \log_a e = \frac{4x}{2x^2 + 1} \log_a e$$

or, from (9.4),

$$f'(x) = \frac{4x}{(2x^2 + 1)\ln a}$$

2. $y = \log_a x$. Here $g(x) = x$, and $g'(x) = 1$. From (9.4),

$$y' = \frac{1}{x} \cdot 1 \cdot \log_a e = \frac{\log_a e}{x}$$

or

$$y' = \frac{1}{x \ln a}$$

9.2 HIGHER-ORDER DERIVATIVES

Higher-order derivatives are found by taking the derivative of the previous derivative, as illustrated in Example 5 and Problems 9.9 and 9.10.

EXAMPLE 5.   Finding the first and second derivatives of exponential and logarithmic functions is illustrated below:

1. Given $y = e^{5x}$. The first and second derivatives are

$$\frac{dy}{dx} = e^{5x}(5) = 5e^{5x}$$

$$\frac{d^2 y}{dx^2} = 5e^{5x}(5) = 25e^{5x}$$

2. Given $y = a^x$. The first derivative is

$$\frac{dy}{dx} = a^x(1)\ln a = a^x \ln a$$

where $\ln a$ is a constant. Thus, the second derivative is

$$\frac{d^2 y}{dx^2} = a^x(\ln a)(1)(\ln a) = a^x(\ln a)^2 = a^x \ln^2 a$$

3. Given $y = \ln 2x$. The first derivative is

$$\frac{dy}{dx} = \frac{1}{2x}(2) = \frac{1}{x} \quad \text{or} \quad x^{-1}$$

By the simple power function rule,

$$\frac{d^2 y}{dx^2} = -x^{-2} \quad \text{or} \quad -\frac{1}{x^2}$$

4. Given $y = \log_a 3x$. The first derivative is

$$\frac{dy}{dx} = \frac{1}{3x}(3)\frac{1}{\ln a} = \frac{1}{x \ln a}$$

By the quotient rule, where $\ln a$ is a constant, the second derivative is

$$\frac{d^2 y}{dx^2} = \frac{x \ln a(0) - 1 \ln a}{(x \ln a)^2} = \frac{-\ln a}{x^2 \ln^2 a} = -\frac{1}{x^2 \ln a}$$

9.3   PARTIAL DERIVATIVES

Partial derivatives are found by differentiating the function with respect to one variable, while keeping the other independent variables constant. See Example 6 and Problem 9.11.

EXAMPLE 6.   Finding all the first and second partial derivatives for a function is illustrated below:

1.   Given $z = e^{(3x + 2y)}$. The first and second partials are

$$z_x = e^{(3x + 2y)}(3) = 3e^{(3x + 2y)} \qquad z_y = e^{(3x + 2y)}(2) = 2e^{(3x + 2y)}$$
$$z_{xx} = 3e^{(3x + 2y)}(3) = 9e^{(3x + 2y)} \qquad z_{yy} = 2e^{(3x + 2y)}(2) = 4e^{(3x + 2y)}$$

$$z_{xy} = 6e^{(3x + 2y)} = z_{yx}$$

2.   Given $z = \ln(5x + 9y)$, the partial derivatives are

$$z_x = \frac{5}{5x + 9y} \qquad z_y = \frac{9}{5x + 9y}$$

By the simple quotient rule,

$$z_{xx} = \frac{(5x + 9y)(0) - 5(5)}{(5x + 9y)^2} \qquad z_{yy} = \frac{(5x + 9y)(0) - 9(9)}{(5x + 9y)^2}$$
$$= \frac{-25}{(5x + 9y)^2} \qquad\qquad = \frac{-81}{(5x + 9y)^2}$$

$$z_{xy} = \frac{-45}{(5x + 9y)^2} = z_{yx}$$

9.4   OPTIMIZATION OF EXPONENTIAL AND LOGARITHMIC FUNCTIONS

Exponential and logarithmic functions follow the general rules for optimization presented in Sections 4.6 and 5.4. The method is demonstrated in Example 7 and treated in Problems 9.12 to 9.21.

EXAMPLE 7.   The procedure for finding critical values and determining whether exponential and logarithmic functions are maximized or minimized is illustrated below:

1.   Given $y = 2xe^{4x}$. Using the product rule and setting the derivative equal to zero, we get

$$\frac{dy}{dx} = 2x(4e^{4x}) + 2(e^{4x}) = 0$$
$$= 2e^{4x}(4x + 1) = 0$$

For the derivative to equal zero, either $2e^{4x} = 0$ or $4x + 1 = 0$. Since $2e^{4x} \neq 0$ for any value of x,

$$4x + 1 = 0 \qquad \bar{x} = -\tfrac{1}{4}$$

Testing the second-order condition,

$$\frac{d^2 y}{dx^2} = 2e^{4x}(4) + (4x + 1)(2e^{4x})(4) = 8e^{4x}(4x + 2)$$

Evaluated at the critical value, $\bar{x} = -\tfrac{1}{4}$, $d^2y/dx^2 = 8e^{-1}(-1 + 2) = 8/e > 0$. The function is thus at a minimum, since the second derivative is positive.

2.   Given $y = \ln(x^2 - 6x + 10)$. By the natural log rule,

$$\frac{dy}{dx} = \frac{2x - 6}{x^2 - 6x + 10} = 0$$

Multiplying both sides by the denominator $x^2 - 6x + 10$,

$$2x - 6 = 0 \qquad \bar{x} = 3$$

Using the simple quotient rule for the second derivative,

$$\frac{d^2 y}{dx^2} = \frac{(x^2 - 6x + 10)(2) - (2x - 6)(2x - 6)}{(x^2 - 6x + 10)^2}$$

Evaluating the second derivative at $\bar{x} = 3$, $d^2y/dx^2 = 2 > 0$. The function is minimized.

3. Given $z = e^{(x^2 - 2x + y^2 - 6y)}$.

$$z_x = (2x - 2)e^{(x^2 - 2x + y^2 - 6y)} = 0 \qquad z_y = (2y - 6)e^{(x^2 - 2x + y^2 - 6y)} = 0$$

Since $e^{(x^2 - 2x + y^2 - 6y)} \neq 0$ for any value of x or y,

$$2x - 2 = 0 \qquad 2y - 6 = 0$$
$$\bar{x} = 1 \qquad\quad \bar{y} = 3$$

Testing the second-order conditions, using the product rule,

$$z_{xx} = (2x - 2)(2x - 2)e^{(x^2 - 2x + y^2 - 6y)} + e^{(x^2 - 2x + y^2 - 6y)}(2)$$
$$z_{yy} = (2y - 6)(2y - 6)e^{(x^2 - 2x + y^2 - 6y)} + e^{(x^2 - 2x + y^2 - 6y)}(2)$$

When evaluated at $\bar{x} = 1$, $\bar{y} = 3$,

$$z_{xx} = 0 + 2e^{-10} > 0 \qquad z_{yy} = 0 + 2e^{-10} > 0$$

since e to any power is positive. Then testing the mixed partials,

$$z_{xy} = (2x - 2)(2y - 6)e^{(x^2 - 2x + y^2 - 6y)} = z_{yx}$$

Evaluated at $\bar{x} = 1$, $\bar{y} = 3$, $z_{xy} = 0 = z_{yx}$. Thus, the function is at a minimum at $\bar{x} = 1$ and $\bar{y} = 3$ since z_{xx} and $z_{yy} > 0$ and $z_{xx} z_{yy} > (z_{xy})^2$.

9.5 LOGARITHMIC DIFFERENTIATION

The natural logarithm function and its derivative are frequently used to facilitate the differentiation of products and quotients involving multiple terms. The process is called *logarithmic differentiation* and is demonstrated in Example 8 and Problem 9.22.

EXAMPLE 8. To find the derivative of a function such as

$$g(x) = \frac{(5x^3 - 8)(3x^4 + 7)}{(9x^5 - 2)} \tag{9.5}$$

use logarithmic differentiation as follows:

(a) Take the natural logarithm of both sides.

$$\ln g(x) = \ln \frac{(5x^3 - 8)(3x^4 + 7)}{(9x^5 - 2)}$$
$$= \ln(5x^3 - 8) + \ln(3x^4 + 7) - \ln(9x^5 - 2)$$

(b) Take the derivative of $\ln g(x)$.

$$\frac{d}{dx}[\ln g(x)] = \frac{g'(x)}{g(x)} = \frac{15x^2}{5x^3 - 8} + \frac{12x^3}{3x^4 + 7} - \frac{45x^4}{9x^5 - 2} \tag{9.6}$$

(c)   Solve algebraically for $g'(x)$ in (9.6).

$$g'(x) = \left(\frac{15x^2}{5x^3 - 8} + \frac{12x^3}{3x^4 + 7} - \frac{45x^4}{9x^5 - 2}\right) \cdot g(x) \qquad (9.7)$$

(d)   Then substitute (9.5) for $g(x)$ in (9.7).

$$g'(x) = \left(\frac{15x^2}{5x^3 - 8} + \frac{12x^3}{3x^4 + 7} - \frac{45x^4}{9x^5 - 2}\right) \cdot \frac{(5x^3 - 8)(3x^4 + 7)}{(9x^5 - 2)}$$

9.6   ALTERNATIVE MEASURES OF GROWTH

Growth G of a function $y = f(t)$ is defined as

$$G = \frac{dy/dt}{y} = \frac{f'(t)}{f(t)} = \frac{y'}{y}$$

From Section 9.1.3 this is exactly equivalent to the derivative of $\ln y$. The growth of a function, therefore, can be measured (1) by dividing the derivative of the function by the function itself or (2) by taking the natural log of the function and then simply differentiating the natural log function. This latter method is sometimes helpful with more complicated functions. See Example 9 and Problems 9.23 to 9.30.

EXAMPLE 9.   Finding the growth rate of $V = Pe^{rt}$, where P is a constant, is illustrated below by using the two methods outlined above.

1.   By the first method,

$$G = \frac{V'}{V}$$

where $V' = Pe^{rt}(r) = rPe^{rt}$. Thus,

$$G = \frac{rPe^{rt}}{Pe^{rt}} = r$$

2.   For the second method, take the natural log of the function.

$$\ln V = \ln P + \ln e^{rt} = \ln P + rt$$

and then take the derivative of the natural log function with respect to t.

$$G = \frac{1}{V}\frac{dV}{dt} = \frac{d}{dt}(\ln V) = \frac{d}{dt}(\ln P + rt) = 0 + r = r$$

9.7   OPTIMAL TIMING

Exponential functions are used to express the value of goods that appreciate or depreciate over time. Such goods include wine, cheese, and land. Since a dollar in the future is worth less than a dollar today, its future value must be discounted to a present value. Investors and speculators seek to maximize the present value of their assets, as is illustrated in Example 10 and Problems 9.31 to 9.34.

EXAMPLE 10.   The value of cheese that improves with age is given by $V = 1400(1.25)^{\sqrt{t}}$. If the cost of capital under continuous compounding is 9 percent a year and there is no storage cost for aging the cheese in company caves, how long should the company store the cheese?

The company wants to maximize the present value of the cheese: $P = Ve^{-rt}$. Substituting the given values of V and r, $P = 1400(1.25)^{\sqrt{t}}e^{-0.09t}$. Taking the natural log,

$$\ln P = \ln 1400 + t^{1/2}\ln 1.25 - 0.09t$$

Then taking the derivative and setting it equal to zero to maximize P,

$$\frac{1}{P}\frac{dP}{dt} = 0 + \frac{1}{2}(\ln 1.25)t^{-1/2} - 0.09 = 0$$

$$\frac{dP}{dt} = P\left[\frac{1}{2}(\ln 1.25)t^{-1/2} - 0.09\right] = 0 \qquad (9.8)$$

Since $P \neq 0$,
$$\tfrac{1}{2}(\ln 1.25)t^{-1/2} - 0.09 = 0$$

$$t^{-1/2} = \frac{0.18}{\ln 1.25}$$

$$t = \left(\frac{\ln 1.25}{0.18}\right)^2 = \left(\frac{0.22314}{0.18}\right)^2 \approx 1.54 \text{ years}$$

Using the product rule when taking the second derivative from (9.8), because $P = f(t)$, we get

$$\frac{d^2P}{dt^2} = P\left[-\frac{1}{4}(\ln 1.25)t^{-3/2}\right] + \left[\frac{1}{2}(\ln 1.25)t^{-1/2} - 0.09\right]\frac{dP}{dt}$$

Since $dP/dt = 0$ at the critical point,

$$\frac{d^2P}{dt^2} = P\left[-\frac{1}{4}(\ln 1.25)t^{-3/2}\right] = -P(0.05579\,t^{-3/2})$$

With $P, t > 0$, $d^2P/dt^2 < 0$ and the function is at a maximum.

9.8   DERIVATION OF A COBB-DOUGLAS DEMAND FUNCTION USING A LOGARITHMIC TRANSFORMATION

A demand function expresses the amount of a good a consumer will purchase as a function of commodity prices and consumer income. A Cobb-Douglas demand function is derived by maximizing a Cobb-Douglas utility function subject to the consumer's income. Given $u = x^\alpha y^\beta$ and the budget constraint $p_x x + p_y y = M$, begin with a logarithmic transformation of the utility function

$$\ln u = \alpha \ln x + \beta \ln y$$

Then set up the Lagrangian function and maximize.

$$U = \alpha \ln x + \beta \ln y + \lambda(M - p_x x - p_y y)$$

$$U_x = \alpha \cdot \frac{1}{x} - \lambda p_x = 0 \qquad\qquad \alpha = \lambda p_x x$$

$$U_y = \beta \cdot \frac{1}{y} - \lambda p_y = 0 \qquad\qquad \beta = \lambda p_y y$$

$$U_\lambda = M - p_x x - p_y y = 0$$

Add $\alpha + \beta$ from U_x and U_y, recalling that $p_x x + p_y y = M$.

$$\alpha + \beta = \lambda(p_x x + p_y y) = \lambda M$$

Thus,
$$\lambda = \frac{\alpha + \beta}{M}$$

Now substitute $\lambda = (\alpha + \beta)/M$ back in U_x and U_y to get

$$\frac{\alpha}{x} - \left(\frac{\alpha + \beta}{M}\right)p_x = 0 \qquad \bar{x} = \left(\frac{\alpha}{\alpha + \beta}\right)\left(\frac{M}{p_x}\right) \qquad (9.9a)$$

$$\frac{\beta}{y} - \left(\frac{\alpha + \beta}{M}\right)p_y = 0 \qquad \bar{y} = \left(\frac{\beta}{\alpha + \beta}\right)\left(\frac{M}{p_y}\right) \qquad (9.9b)$$

For a strict Cobb-Douglas function where $\alpha + \beta = 1$,

$$\bar{x} = \frac{\alpha M}{p_x} \quad \text{and} \quad \bar{y} = \frac{\beta M}{p_y} \tag{9.9c}$$

EXAMPLE 11.   Given the utility function $u = x^{0.3} y^{0.7}$ and the income constraint $M = 200$, from the information derived in Section 9.8, the demand functions for x and y are (a) derived and (b) evaluated at $p_x = 5$, $p_y = 8$ and $p_x = 6$, $p_y = 10$, as follows:

(a)   From (9.9c),
$$\bar{x} = \frac{\alpha M}{p_x} \quad \text{and} \quad \bar{y} = \frac{\beta M}{p_y}$$

(b)   At $p_x = 5$, $p_y = 8$,

$$\bar{x} = \frac{0.3(200)}{5} = 12 \quad \text{and} \quad \bar{y} = \frac{0.7(200)}{8} = 17.5$$

At $p_x = 6$, $p_y = 10$,

$$\bar{x} = \frac{0.3(200)}{6} = 10 \quad \text{and} \quad \bar{y} = \frac{0.7(200)}{10} = 14$$

Solved Problems

DERIVATIVES OF NATURAL EXPONENTIAL FUNCTIONS

9.1.   Differentiate each of the following natural exponential functions according to the rule $d/dx[e^{g(x)}] = e^{g(x)} \cdot g'(x)$:

(a) $y = e^{2x}$

Letting $g(x) = 2x$, then $g'(x) = 2$,
and $y' = e^{2x}(2) = 2e^{2x}$

(b) $y = e^{(-1/3)x}$

$g(x) = -\frac{1}{3}x$, $g'(x) = -\frac{1}{3}$, and
$y' = e^{-(1/3)x}(-\frac{1}{3}) = -\frac{1}{3}e^{(-1/3)x}$

(c) $y = e^{x^3}$

$y' = e^{x^3}(3x^2) = 3x^2 e^{x^3}$

(d) $y = 3e^{x^2}$

$y' = 3e^{x^2}(2x) = 6xe^{x^2}$

(e) $y = e^{2x+1}$

$y' = e^{2x+1}(2) = 2e^{2x+1}$

(f) $y = e^{1-4x}$

$y' = -4e^{1-4x}$

(g) $y = 5e^{1-x^2}$

$y' = -10xe^{1-x^2}$

(h) $y = 2xe^x$

By the product rule,
$y' = 2x(e^x) + e^x(2) = 2e^x(x + 1)$

(i) $y = 3xe^{2x}$

$y' = 3x(2e^{2x}) + e^{2x}(3) = 3e^{2x}(2x + 1)$

(j) $y = x^2 e^{5x}$

$y' = x^2(5e^{5x}) + e^{5x}(2x) = xe^{5x}(5x + 2)$

(k) $y = \dfrac{e^{5x} - 1}{e^{5x} + 1}$

By the quotient rule,

$$y' = \frac{(e^{5x} + 1)(5e^{5x}) - (e^{5x} - 1)(5e^{5x})}{(e^{5x} + 1)^2} = \frac{10e^{5x}}{(e^{5x} + 1)^2}$$

(*l*) $y = \dfrac{e^{2x} + 1}{e^{2x} - 1}$

$$y' = \frac{(e^{2x} - 1)(2e^{2x}) - (e^{2x} + 1)(2e^{2x})}{(e^{2x} - 1)^2} = \frac{-4e^{2x}}{(e^{2x} - 1)^2}$$

DIFFERENTIATION OF EXPONENTIAL FUNCTIONS WITH BASES OTHER THAN *e*

9.2.   Differentiate each of the following exponential functions according to the rule $d/dx[a^{g(x)}] = a^{g(x)} \cdot g'(x) \cdot \ln a$:

(*a*) $y = a^{2x}$

Letting $g(x) = 2x$, then $g'(x) = 2$, and

$$y' = a^{2x}(2)\ln a = 2a^{2x}\ln a$$

(*b*) $y = a^{5x^2}$

$$y' = a^{5x^2}(10x)\ln a = 10xa^{5x^2}\ln a$$

(*c*) $y = 4^{2x+7}$

$$y' = 4^{2x+7}(2)\ln 4 = 2(4)^{2x+7}\ln 4$$

Using a calculator, $y' = 2(1.38629)(4)^{2x+7} = 2.77258(4)^{2x+7}$

(*d*) $y = 2^x$

$$y' = 2^x(1)\ln 2 = 2^x\ln 2 = 0.69315(2)^x$$

(*e*) $y = 7^{x^2}$

$$y' = 7^{x^2}(2x)\ln 7 = 2x(7)^{x^2}\ln 7 = 2x(7)^{x^2}(1.94591) = 3.89182x(7)^{x^2}$$

(*f*) $y = x^3 2^x$

By the product rule, recalling that x^3 is a power function and 2^x is an exponential function,

$$y' = x^3[2^x(1)\ln 2] + 2^x(3x^2) = x^2 2^x(x\ln 2 + 3)$$

(*g*) $y = x^2 2^{5x}$

$$y' = x^2[2^{5x}(5)\ln 2] + 2^{5x}(2x) = x2^{5x}(5x\ln 2 + 2)$$

DERIVATIVES OF NATURAL LOGARITHMIC FUNCTIONS

9.3.   Differentiate each of the following natural log functions according to the rule $d/dx[\ln g(x)] = 1/[g(x)] \cdot g'(x)$:

(*a*) $y = \ln 2x^3$

Let $g(x) = 2x^3$, then $g'(x) = 6x^2$, and

$$y' = \frac{1}{2x^3}(6x^2) = \frac{3}{x}$$

(*b*) $y = \ln 7x^2$

$$y' = \frac{1}{7x^2}(14x) = \frac{2}{x}$$

(*c*) $y = \ln(1 + x)$

$$y' = \frac{1}{1 + x}$$

(*d*) $y = \ln(4x + 7)$

$$y' = \frac{1}{4x + 7}(4) = \frac{4}{4x + 7}$$

(*e*) $y = \ln 6x$

$$y' = \frac{1}{6x}(6) = \frac{1}{x}$$

(*f*) $y = 6\ln x$

$$y' = 6\left(\frac{1}{x}\right) = \frac{6}{x}$$

Notice how a multiplicative constant within the log expression in part (e) drops out in differentiation, whereas a multiplicative constant outside the log expression in part (f) remains.

9.4.   Redo Problem 9.3 for each of the following functions:

(a) $y = \ln^2 x = (\ln x)^2$

By the generalized power function rule,

$$y' = 2 \ln x \, \frac{d}{dx} (\ln x) = 2 \ln x \left(\frac{1}{x}\right) = \frac{2 \ln x}{x}$$

(b) $y = \ln^2 8x = (\ln 8x)^2$

$$y' = 2 \ln 8x \left(\frac{1}{8x}\right)(8) = \frac{2 \ln 8x}{x}$$

(c) $y = \ln^2(3x + 1) = [\ln (3x + 1)]^2$

$$y' = 2 \ln (3x + 1)\left(\frac{1}{3x + 1}\right)(3) = \frac{6 \ln (3x + 1)}{3x + 1}$$

(d) $y = \ln^2 (5x + 6)$

$$y' = 2 \ln (5x + 6)\left(\frac{1}{5x + 6}\right)(5) = \frac{10 \ln (5x + 6)}{5x + 6}$$

(e) $y = \ln^3(4x + 13)$

$$y' = 3[\ln (4x + 13)]^2\left(\frac{1}{4x + 13}\right)(4) = 3 \ln^2 (4x + 13)\left(\frac{4}{4x + 13}\right) = \frac{12}{4x + 13} \ln^2 (4x + 13)$$

(f) $y = \ln (x + 5)^2 \neq [\ln (x + 5)]^2$

Letting $g(x) = (x + 5)^2$, then $g'(x) = 2(x + 5)$, and

$$y' = \frac{1}{(x + 5)^2} \, [2(x + 5)] = \frac{2}{x + 5}$$

(g) $y = \ln (x - 8)^2$

$$y' = \frac{1}{(x - 8)^2} \, [2(x - 8)] = \frac{2}{x - 8}$$

(h) $y = 3 \ln (1 + x)^2$

$$y' = 3\left[\frac{1}{(1 + x)^2}\right][2(1 + x)] = \frac{6}{1 + x}$$

9.5.   Use the laws of logarithms in Section 7.3 to simplify the differentiation of each of the following natural log functions:

(a) $y = \ln (x + 5)^2$

From the rules for logs, $\ln (x + 5)^2 = 2 \ln (x + 5)$. Thus, as in Problem 9.4(f),

$$y' = 2\left(\frac{1}{x + 5}\right)(1) = \frac{2}{x + 5}$$

(b) $y = \ln(2x + 7)^2$

$$y = 2\ln(2x + 7)$$
$$y' = 2\left(\frac{1}{2x + 7}\right)(2) = \frac{4}{2x + 7}$$

(c) $y = \ln[(3x + 7)(4x + 2)]$

$$y = \ln(3x + 7) + \ln(4x + 2)$$
$$y' = \frac{3}{3x + 7} + \frac{4}{4x + 2}$$

(d) $y = \ln[5x^2(3x^3 - 7)]$

$$y = \ln 5x^2 + \ln(3x^3 - 7)$$
$$y' = \frac{10x}{5x^2} + \frac{9x^2}{3x^3 - 7}$$
$$= \frac{2}{x} + \frac{9x^2}{3x^3 - 7}$$

(e) $y = \ln \dfrac{3x^2}{x^2 - 1}$

$$y = \ln 3x^2 - \ln(x^2 - 1)$$
$$y' = \frac{2}{x} - \frac{2x}{x^2 - 1}$$

(f) $y = \ln \dfrac{x^3}{(2x + 5)^2}$

$$y = \ln x^3 - \ln(2x + 5)^2$$
$$y' = \frac{1}{x^3}(3x^2) - 2\left(\frac{1}{2x + 5}\right)(2)$$
$$= \frac{3}{x} - \frac{4}{2x + 5}$$

(g) $y = \ln \sqrt{\dfrac{2x^2 + 3}{x^2 + 9}}$

$$y = \tfrac{1}{2}[\ln(2x^2 + 3) - \ln(x^2 + 9)]$$
$$y' = \frac{1}{2}\left(\frac{4x}{2x^2 + 3} - \frac{2x}{x^2 + 9}\right)$$
$$= \frac{2x}{2x^2 + 3} - \frac{x}{x^2 + 9}$$

DERIVATIVES OF LOGARITHMIC FUNCTIONS WITH BASES OTHER THAN e

9.6.   Differentiate each of the following logarithmic functions according to the rule

$$\frac{d}{dx}[\log_a g(x)] = \frac{1}{g(x)} \cdot g'(x) \cdot \log_a e = \frac{1}{g(x)} \cdot g'(x) \cdot \frac{1}{\ln a}$$

(a) $y = \log_a(4x^2 - 3)$

$$y' = \frac{1}{4x^2 - 3}(8x)\left(\frac{1}{\ln a}\right)$$
$$= \frac{8x}{(4x^2 - 3)\ln a}$$

(b) $y = \log_4 9x^3$

$$y' = \frac{1}{9x^3}(27x^2)\left(\frac{1}{\ln 4}\right)$$
$$= \frac{3}{x \ln 4}$$

(c) $y = \log_2(8 - x)$

$$y' = \frac{1}{(8 - x)}(-1)\left(\frac{1}{\ln 2}\right)$$
$$= -\frac{1}{(8 - x)\ln 2}$$

(d) $y = x^3 \log_6 x$

By the product rule,

$$y' = x^3\left[\frac{1}{x}(1)\left(\frac{1}{\ln 6}\right)\right] + \log_6 x(3x^2)$$
$$= \frac{x^2}{\ln 6} + 3x^2 \log_6 x$$

(e) $y = \log_a \sqrt{x^2 - 7}$

From the law of logs, $y = \tfrac{1}{2}\log_a(x^2 - 7)$. Thus,

$$y' = \frac{1}{2}\left[\frac{1}{x^2 - 7}(2x)\left(\frac{1}{\ln a}\right)\right] = \frac{x}{(x^2 - 7)\ln a}$$

COMBINATION OF RULES

9.7.   Use whatever combinations of rules are necessary to differentiate the following functions:

(a) $y = x^2 \ln x^3$

By the product rule,

$$y' = x^2\left(\frac{1}{x^3}\right)(3x^2) + \ln x^3(2x) = 3x + 2x \ln x^3 = 3x + 6x \ln x = 3x(1 + 2\ln x)$$

(b) $y = x^3 \ln x^2$

$$y' = x^3\left(\frac{1}{x^2}\right)(2x) + \ln x^2(3x^2) = 2x^2 + 6x^2 \ln x = 2x^2(1 + 3\ln x)$$

(c) $y = e^x \ln x$

By the product rule,

$$y' = e^x\left(\frac{1}{x}\right) + (\ln x)(e^x) = e^x\left(\frac{1}{x} + \ln x\right)$$

(d) $y = e^{-2x} \ln 2x$

$$y' = e^{-2x}\left(\frac{1}{2x}\right)(2) + \ln 2x(-2e^{-2x}) = e^{-2x}\left(\frac{1}{x} - 2\ln 2x\right)$$

(e) $y = \ln e^{3x+2}$

$$y' = \frac{1}{e^{3x+2}}(3e^{3x+2}) = 3$$

since $\ln e^{3x+2} = 3x + 2$, $d/dx(\ln e^{3x+2}) = d/dx(3x + 2) = 3$.

(f) $y = e^{\ln x}$

$$y' = e^{\ln x}\left(\frac{1}{x}\right) = x\left(\frac{1}{x}\right) = 1$$

since $e^{\ln x} = x$.

(g) $y = e^{\ln(2x+1)}$

$$y' = e^{\ln(2x+1)}\left(\frac{1}{2x+1}\right)(2) = 2$$

since $e^{\ln(2x+1)} = 2x + 1$.

(h) $y = e^{x \ln x}$

$$y' = e^{x \ln x}\frac{d}{dx}(x \ln x)$$

Then using the product rule for $d/dx(x \ln x)$,

$$y' = e^{x \ln x}\left[x\left(\frac{1}{x}\right) + (\ln x)(1)\right] = e^{x \ln x}(1 + \ln x)$$

(i) $y = e^{x^2 \ln 3x}$

$$y' = e^{x^2 \ln 3x}\left[x^2\left(\frac{1}{3x}\right)(3) + \ln 3x(2x)\right]$$
$$= e^{x^2 \ln 3x}(x + 2x \ln 3x) = xe^{x^2 \ln 3x}(1 + 2\ln 3x)$$

SLOPES OF EXPONENTIAL AND LOGARITHMIC FUNCTIONS

9.8. Evaluate the slope of each of the following functions at the point indicated:

(a) $y = 3e^{0.2x}$ at $x = 5$.

$$y' = 0.6e^{0.2x}$$

At $x = 5$, $\quad y' = 0.6e^{0.2(5)} = 0.6(2.71828) \approx 1.63097$.

(b) $y = 2e^{-1.5x}$ at $x = 4$.

$$y' = -3e^{-1.5x}$$

At $x = 4$, $y' = -3e^{-1.5(4)} = -3e^{-6} = -3(0.00248) \approx -0.00744$.

(c) $y = \ln(x^2 + 8x + 4)$ at $x = 2$.

$$y' = \frac{2x + 8}{x^2 + 8x + 4}$$

At $x = 2$, $y' = \frac{12}{24} = 0.5$.

(d) $y = \ln^2(x + 4)$ at $x = 6$.

At $x = 6$, $$y' = [2\ln(x + 4)]\left(\frac{1}{x + 4}\right)(1) = \frac{2\ln(x + 4)}{x + 4}$$

$$y' = \frac{2\ln 10}{10} = \frac{2(2.30259)}{10} \approx 0.46052$$

SECOND DERIVATIVES

9.9.   Find the first and second derivatives of the following functions:

(a) $y = e^{3x}$

$$y' = 3e^{3x}$$
$$y'' = 9e^{3x}$$

(b) $y = e^{-(1/2)x}$

$$y' = -\tfrac{1}{2}e^{-(1/2)x}$$
$$y'' = \tfrac{1}{4}e^{-(1/2)x}$$

(c) $y = 3e^{5x+1}$

$$y' = 15e^{5x+1}$$
$$y'' = 75e^{5x+1}$$

(d) $y = 2xe^x$

By the product rule,

$$y' = 2x(e^x) + e^x(2) = 2e^x(x + 1)$$
$$y'' = 2e^x(1) + (x + 1)(2e^x) = 2e^x(x + 2)$$

(e) $y = \ln 2x^5$

$$y' = \frac{1}{2x^5}(10x^4) = \frac{5}{x} = 5x^{-1}$$

$$y'' = -5x^{-2} = \frac{-5}{x^2}$$

(f) $y = 4\ln x$

$$y' = 4\left(\frac{1}{x}\right)(1) = \frac{4}{x} = 4x^{-1}$$

$$y'' = -4x^{-2}$$

9.10.   Take the first and second derivatives of each of the following functions:

(a) $y = a^{3x}$

$$y' = a^{3x}(3)\ln a = 3a^{3x}\ln a$$

where $\ln a = $ a constant. Thus,

$$y'' = (3a^{3x}\ln a)(3)\ln a = 9a^{3x}(\ln a)^2$$

(b) $y = a^{5x+1}$

$$y' = a^{5x+1}(5)\ln a = 5a^{5x+1}\ln a$$
$$y'' = (5a^{5x+1}\ln a)(5)\ln a = 25a^{5x+1}(\ln a)^2$$

(c) $y = \log_a 5x$

$$y' = \frac{1}{5x}(5)\frac{1}{\ln a} = \frac{1}{x\ln a} = (x\ln a)^{-1}$$

Using the generalized power function rule,

$$y'' = -1(x \ln a)^{-2} \ln a = \frac{-\ln a}{x^2 \ln^2 a} = -\frac{1}{x^2 \ln a}$$

(d) $y = \log_3 6x$

$$y' = \frac{1}{6x}(6)\left(\frac{1}{\ln 3}\right) = \frac{1}{x \ln 3} = (x \ln 3)^{-1}$$

$$y'' = -1(x \ln 3)^{-2}(\ln 3) = \frac{-\ln 3}{x^2 \ln^2 3} = -\frac{1}{x^2 \ln 3}$$

(e) $y = 3xe^x$

By the product rule,

$$y' = 3x(e^x) + e^x(3) = 3e^x(x + 1)$$
$$y'' = 3e^x(1) + (x + 1)(3e^x) = 3e^x(x + 2)$$

(f) $y = \dfrac{4x}{3 \ln x}$

By the quotient rule,

$$y' = \frac{(3 \ln x)(4) - 4x(3)(1/x)}{9 \ln^2 x} = \frac{12 \ln x - 12}{9 \ln^2 x} = \frac{12(\ln x - 1)}{9 \ln^2 x}$$

$$y'' = \frac{(9 \ln^2 x)[12(1/x)] - 12(\ln x - 1)\{[9(2) \ln x](1/x)\}}{81 \ln^4 x} = \frac{(108/x)(\ln^2 x) - (216/x)(\ln x - 1)(\ln x)}{81 \ln^4 x}$$

$$= \frac{4 \ln x - 8(\ln x - 1)}{3x \ln^3 x} = \frac{-4 \ln x + 8}{3x \ln^3 x} = \frac{4(2 - \ln x)}{3x \ln^3 x}$$

PARTIAL DERIVATIVES

9.11.   Find all the first and second partial derivatives for each of the following functions:

(a) $z = e^{x^2 + y^2}$

$$z_x = 2xe^{x^2+y^2} \qquad z_y = 2ye^{x^2+y^2}$$

By the product rule,

$$z_{xx} = 2x(2xe^{x^2+y^2}) + e^{x^2+y^2}(2) \qquad z_{yy} = 2y(2ye^{x^2+y^2}) + e^{x^2+y^2}(2)$$
$$= 2e^{x^2+y^2}(2x^2 + 1) \qquad\qquad = 2e^{x^2+y^2}(2y^2 + 1)$$
$$z_{xy} = 4xye^{x^2+y^2} = z_{yx}$$

(b) $z = e^{2x^2 + 3y}$

$$z_x = 4xe^{2x^2+3y} \qquad\qquad z_y = 3e^{2x^2+3y}$$
$$z_{xx} = 4x(4xe^{2x^2+3y}) + e^{2x^2+3y}(4) \qquad z_{yy} = 9e^{2x^2+3y}$$
$$= 4e^{2x^2+3y}(4x^2 + 1)$$
$$z_{xy} = 12xe^{2x^2+3y} = z_{yx}$$

(c) $z = a^{2x + 3y}$

$$z_x = a^{2x+3y}(2) \ln a \qquad\qquad z_y = a^{2x+3y}(3) \ln a$$
$$= 2a^{2x+3y} \ln a \qquad\qquad\quad = 3a^{2x+3y} \ln a$$
$$z_{xx} = 2a^{2x+3y}(\ln a)(2)(\ln a) \qquad z_{yy} = 3a^{2x+3y}(\ln a)(3)(\ln a)$$
$$= 4a^{2x+3y} \ln^2 a \qquad\qquad\quad = 9a^{2x+3y} \ln^2 a$$
$$z_{xy} = 6a^{2x+3y} \ln^2 a = z_{yx}$$

(d) $z = 4^{3x+5y}$

$$z_x = 4^{3x+5y}(3)\ln 4 \qquad\qquad z_y = 4^{3x+5y}(5)\ln 4$$
$$= 3(4)^{3x+5y}\ln 4 \qquad\qquad = 5(4)^{3x+5y}\ln 4$$
$$z_{xx} = 3(4)^{3x+5y}(\ln 4)(3)(\ln 4) \qquad z_{yy} = 5(4)^{3x+5y}(\ln 4)(5)(\ln 4)$$
$$= 9(4)^{3x+5y}\ln^2 4 \qquad\qquad = 25(4)^{3x+5y}\ln^2 4$$
$$z_{xy} = 15(4)^{3x+5y}\ln^2 4 = z_{yx}$$

(e) $z = \ln(7x + 2y)$

$$z_x = \frac{7}{7x+2y} \qquad z_y = \frac{2}{7x+2y}$$

By the quotient rule,

$$z_{xx} = \frac{(7x+2y)(0) - 7(7)}{(7x+2y)^2} = \frac{-49}{(7x+2y)^2} \qquad z_{yy} = \frac{(7x+2y)(0) - 2(2)}{(7x+2y)^2} = \frac{-4}{(7x+2y)^2}$$

$$z_{xy} = \frac{-14}{(7x+2y)^2} = z_{yx}$$

(f) $z = \ln(x^2 + 4y^2)$

$$z_x = \frac{2x}{x^2+4y^2} \qquad\qquad\qquad z_y = \frac{8y}{x^2+4y^2}$$

$$z_{xx} = \frac{(x^2+4y^2)(2) - 2x(2x)}{(x^2+4y^2)^2} = \frac{8y^2 - 2x^2}{(x^2+4y^2)^2} \qquad z_{yy} = \frac{(x^2+4y^2)(8) - 8y(8y)}{(x^2+4y^2)^2} = \frac{8x^2 - 32y^2}{(x^2+4y^2)^2}$$

$$z_{xy} = \frac{-16xy}{(x^2+4y^2)^2} = z_{yx}$$

(g) $z = \log_a(x - 2y)$

$$z_x = \frac{1}{(x-2y)\ln a} \qquad\qquad z_y = \frac{-2}{(x-2y)\ln a}$$

$$z_{xx} = \frac{-1\ln a}{(x-2y)^2\ln^2 a} = \frac{-1}{(x-2y)^2\ln a} \qquad z_{yy} = \frac{4\ln a}{(x-2y)^2\ln^2 a} = \frac{4}{(x-2y)^2\ln a}$$

$$z_{xy} = \frac{2}{(x-2y)^2\ln a} = z_{yx}$$

(h) $z = \log_a(3x^2 + y^2)$

$$z_x = \frac{6x}{(3x^2+y^2)\ln a} \qquad\qquad z_y = \frac{2y}{(3x^2+y^2)\ln a}$$

$$z_{xx} = \frac{(3x^2+y^2)(\ln a)(6) - 6x(6x\ln a)}{(3x^2+y^2)^2\ln^2 a} \qquad z_{yy} = \frac{(3x^2+y^2)(\ln a)(2) - 2y(2y\ln a)}{(3x^2+y^2)^2\ln^2 a}$$

$$= \frac{6y^2 - 18x^2}{(3x^2+y^2)^2\ln a} \qquad\qquad = \frac{6x^2 - 2y^2}{(3x^2+y^2)^2\ln a}$$

$$z_{xy} = \frac{-12xy}{(3x^2+y^2)^2\ln a} = z_{yx}$$

OPTIMIZATION OF EXPONENTIAL AND LOGARITHMIC FUNCTIONS

9.12. Given $y = 4xe^{3x}$, (a) find the critical values and (b) determine whether the function is maximized or minimized.

(a) By the product rule,

$$y' = 4x(3e^{3x}) + e^{3x}(4) = 0$$
$$4e^{3x}(3x + 1) = 0$$

Since there is no value of x for which $4e^{3x} = 0$, or for which $e^x = 0$,

$$3x + 1 = 0 \qquad \bar{x} = -\tfrac{1}{3}$$

(b) $$y'' = 4e^{3x}(3) + (3x + 1)(12e^{3x}) = 12e^{3x}(3x + 2)$$

At $\bar{x} = -\tfrac{1}{3}$, $y'' = 12e^{-1}(1)$. And $y'' = 12(0.36788) > 0$. The function is minimized.

9.13. Redo Problem 9.12, given $y = 5xe^{-0.2x}$.

(a) $$y' = 5x(-0.2e^{-0.2x}) + e^{-0.2x}(5) = 0$$
$$5e^{-0.2x}(1 - 0.2x) = 0$$

Since $5e^{-0.2x} \neq 0$, $(1 - 0.2x) = 0 \qquad \bar{x} = 5$

(b) $$y'' = 5e^{-0.2x}(-0.2) + (1 - 0.2x)(-1e^{-0.2x}) = e^{-0.2x}(0.2x - 2)$$

At $\bar{x} = 5$, $y'' = e^{-1}(1 - 2)$. And $y'' = (0.36788)(-1) < 0$. The function is at a maximum.

9.14. Redo Problem 9.12, given $y = \ln(x^2 - 8x + 20)$.

(a) $$y' = \frac{2x - 8}{x^2 - 8x + 20} = 0$$

Multiplying both sides by $x^2 - 8x + 20$ gives $2x - 8 = 0$ and $\bar{x} = 4$.

(b) $$y'' = \frac{(x^2 - 8x + 20)(2) - (2x - 8)(2x - 8)}{(x^2 - 8x + 20)^2}$$

At $\bar{x} = 4$, $y'' = \tfrac{8}{16} > 0$. The function is at a minimum.

9.15. Redo Problem 9.12, given $y = \ln(2x^2 - 20x + 5)$.

(a) $$y' = \frac{4x - 20}{2x^2 - 20x + 5} = 0$$

$$4x - 20 = 0 \qquad \bar{x} = 5$$

(b) $$y'' = \frac{(2x^2 - 20x + 5)(4) - (4x - 20)(4x - 20)}{(2x^2 - 20x + 5)^2}$$

At $\bar{x} = 5$, $y'' = -180/2025 < 0$. The function is at a maximum.

9.16. Given the function $z = \ln(2x^2 - 12x + y^2 - 10y)$, (a) find the critical values and (b) indicate whether the function is at a maximum or minimum.

(a) $$z_x = \frac{4x - 12}{2x^2 - 12x + y^2 - 10y} = 0 \qquad z_y = \frac{2y - 10}{2x^2 - 12x + y^2 - 10y} = 0$$

$$4x - 12 = 0 \qquad \bar{x} = 3 \qquad\qquad 2y - 10 = 0 \qquad \bar{y} = 5$$

(b) $$z_{xx} = \frac{(2x^2 - 12x + y^2 - 10y)(4) - (4x - 12)(4x - 12)}{(2x^2 - 12x + y^2 - 10y)^2}$$

$$z_{yy} = \frac{(2x^2 - 12x + y^2 - 10y)(2) - (2y - 10)(2y - 10)}{(2x^2 - 12x + y^2 - 10y)^2}$$

Evaluated at $\bar{x} = 3$, $\bar{y} = 5$,

$$z_{xx} = \frac{(-43)(4) - 0}{(-43)^2} = \frac{-172}{1849} < 0 \qquad z_{yy} = \frac{(-43)(2) - 0}{(-43)^2} = \frac{-86}{1849} < 0$$

$$z_{xy} = \frac{-(4x - 12)(2y - 10)}{(2x^2 - 12x + y^2 - 10y)^2} = z_{yx}$$

At $\bar{x} = 3$, $\bar{y} = 5$, $z_{xy} = 0 = z_{yx}$. With $z_{xx}, z_{yy} < 0$ and $z_{xx} z_{yy} > (z_{xy})^2$, the function is at a maximum.

9.17. Redo Problem 9.16, given $z = \ln(x^2 - 4x + 3y^2 - 6y)$.

(a)
$$z_x = \frac{2x - 4}{x^2 - 4x + 3y^2 - 6y} = 0 \qquad z_y = \frac{6y - 6}{x^2 - 4x + 3y^2 - 6y} = 0$$
$$2x - 4 = 0 \qquad \bar{x} = 2 \qquad 6y - 6 = 0 \qquad \bar{y} = 1$$

(b)
$$z_{xx} = \frac{(x^2 - 4x + 3y^2 - 6y)(2) - (2x - 4)(2x - 4)}{(x^2 - 4x + 3y^2 - 6y)^2}$$
$$z_{yy} = \frac{(x^2 - 4x + 3y^2 - 6y)(6) - (6y - 6)(6y - 6)}{(x^2 - 4x + 3y^2 - 6y)^2}$$

At $\bar{x} = 2$, $\bar{y} = 1$,

$$z_{xx} = \frac{(-7)(2) - 0}{(-7)^2} = -\frac{14}{49} < 0 \qquad z_{yy} = \frac{(-7)(6) - 0}{(-7)^2} = -\frac{42}{49} < 0$$

$$z_{xy} = \frac{-(2x - 4)(6y - 6)}{(x^2 - 4x + 3y^2 - 6y)^2} = z_{yx}$$

At $\bar{x} = 2$, $\bar{y} = 1$, $z_{xy} = 0 = z_{yx}$. With $z_{xx}, z_{yy} < 0$ and $z_{xx} z_{yy} > (z_{xy})^2$, the function is at a maximum.

9.18. Redo Problem 9.16, given $z = e^{(3x^2 - 6x + y^2 - 8y)}$.

(a)
$$z_x = (6x - 6)e^{(3x^2 - 6x + y^2 - 8y)} = 0 \qquad z_y = (2y - 8)e^{(3x^2 - 6x + y^2 - 8y)} = 0$$
$$6x - 6 = 0 \qquad \bar{x} = 1 \qquad 2y - 8 = 0 \qquad \bar{y} = 4$$

(b) Using the product rule,

$$z_{xx} = (6x - 6)(6x - 6)e^{(3x^2 - 6x + y^2 - 8y)} + e^{(3x^2 - 6x + y^2 - 8y)}(6)$$
$$z_{yy} = (2y - 8)(2y - 8)e^{(3x^2 - 6x + y^2 - 8y)} + e^{(3x^2 - 6x + y^2 - 8y)}(2)$$

Evaluated at $\bar{x} = 1$, $\bar{y} = 4$,

$$z_{xx} = 0 + 6e^{-19} > 0 \qquad z_{yy} = 0 + 2e^{-19} > 0$$

Then testing the cross partials,

$$z_{xy} = (6x - 6)(2y - 8)e^{(3x^2 - 6x + y^2 - 8y)} = z_{yx}$$

At $\bar{x} = 1$, $\bar{y} = 4$, $z_{xy} = 0 = z_{yx}$. The function is at a minimum since $z_{xx}, z_{yy} > 0$ and $z_{xx} z_{yy} > (z_{xy})^2$.

9.19. Given $z = e^{(2x^2 - 12x - 2xy + y^2 - 4y)}$, redo Problem 9.16.

(a)
$$z_x = (4x - 12 - 2y)e^{(2x^2 - 12x - 2xy + y^2 - 4y)} = 0$$
$$4x - 2y - 12 = 0 \qquad (9.10)$$
$$z_y = (-2x + 2y - 4)e^{(2x^2 - 12x - 2xy + y^2 - 4y)} = 0$$
$$-2x + 2y - 4 = 0 \qquad (9.11)$$

Solving (9.10) and (9.11) simultaneously, $\bar{x} = 8$, $\bar{y} = 10$.

(b)
$$z_{xx} = (4x - 12 - 2y)(4x - 12 - 2y)e^{(2x^2 - 12x - 2xy + y^2 - 4y)} + e^{(2x^2 - 12x - 2xy + y^2 - 4y)}(4)$$
$$z_{yy} = (-2x + 2y - 4)(-2x + 2y - 4)e^{(2x^2 - 12x - 2xy + y^2 - 4y)} + e^{(2x^2 - 12x - 2xy + y^2 - 4y)}(2)$$

Evaluated at $\bar{x} = 8$, $\bar{y} = 10$,

$$z_{xx} = 0 + 4e^{-68} > 0 \qquad z_{yy} = 0 + 2e^{-68} > 0$$

Testing the mixed partials, by the product rule,

$$z_{xy} = (4x - 12 - 2y)(-2x + 2y - 4)e^{(2x^2 - 12x - 2xy + y^2 - 4y)} + e^{(2x^2 - 12x - 2xy + y^2 - 4y)}(-2) = z_{yx}$$

Evaluated at $\bar{x} = 8$, $\bar{y} = 10$, $z_{xy} = 0 - 2e^{-68} = z_{yx}$. Since $z_{xx}, z_{yy} > 0$ and $z_{xx} z_{yy} > (z_{xy})^2$, the function is at a minimum.

9.20. Given the demand function

$$P = 8.25e^{-0.02Q} \tag{9.12}$$

(a) determine the quantity and price at which total revenue will be maximized and (b) test the second-order condition.

(a)
$$\text{TR} = PQ = (8.25e^{-0.02Q})Q$$

By the product rule,

$$\frac{d\text{TR}}{dQ} = (8.25e^{-0.02Q})(1) + Q(-0.02)(8.25e^{-0.02Q}) = 0$$

$$(8.25e^{-0.02Q})(1 - 0.02Q) = 0$$

Since $(8.25e^{-0.02Q}) \neq 0$ for any value of Q, $1 - 0.02Q = 0$; $\bar{Q} = 50$.
Substituting $\bar{Q} = 50$ in (9.12), $P = 8.25e^{-0.02(50)} = 8.25e^{-1}$. And $P = 8.25(0.36788) = 3.04$.

(b) By the product rule,

$$\frac{d^2\text{TR}}{dQ^2} = (8.25e^{-0.02Q})(-0.02) + (1 - 0.02Q)(-0.02)(8.25e^{-0.02Q}) = (-0.02)(8.25e^{-0.02Q})(2 - 0.02Q)$$

Evaluated at $\bar{Q} = 50$, $d^2\text{TR}/dQ^2 = (-0.02)(8.25e^{-1})(1) = -0.165(0.36788) < 0$. TR is at a maximum.

9.21. (a) Find the price and quantity that will maximize total revenue, given the demand function $P = 12.50e^{-0.005Q}$. (b) Check the second-order condition.

(a)
$$\text{TR} = (12.50e^{-0.005Q})Q$$

$$\frac{d\text{TR}}{dQ} = (12.50e^{-0.005Q})(1) + Q(-0.005)(12.50e^{-0.005Q})$$

$$= (12.50e^{-0.005Q})(1 - 0.005Q) = 0$$
$$1 - 0.005Q = 0 \qquad \bar{Q} = 200$$

Thus,
$$P = 12.50e^{-0.005(200)} = 12.50e^{-1} = 12.50(0.36788) = 4.60$$

(b)
$$\frac{d^2\text{TR}}{dQ^2} = (12.50e^{-0.005Q})(-0.005) + (1 - 0.005Q)(-0.005)(12.50e^{-0.005Q})$$

$$= (-0.005)(12.50e^{-0.005Q})(2 - 0.005Q)$$

Evaluated at $\bar{Q} = 200$, $d^2\text{TR}/dQ^2 = (-0.005)(12.50e^{-1})(1) = -0.0625(0.36788) < 0$. The function is maximized.

LOGARITHMIC DIFFERENTIATION

9.22. Use logarithmic differentiation to find the derivatives for the following functions:

(a)
$$g(x) = (x^3 - 2)(x^2 - 3)(8x - 5) \tag{9.13}$$

(1) Take the natural logarithm of both sides.

$$\ln g(x) = \ln(x^3 - 2) + \ln(x^2 - 3) + \ln(8x - 5)$$

(2) Take the derivative of $\ln g(x)$.

$$\frac{d}{dx}[\ln g(x)] = \frac{g'(x)}{g(x)} = \frac{3x^2}{x^3 - 2} + \frac{2x}{x^2 - 3} + \frac{8}{8x - 5} \tag{9.14}$$

(3) Solve algebraically for $g'(x)$ in (9.14).

$$g'(x) = \left(\frac{3x^2}{x^3 - 2} + \frac{2x}{x^2 - 3} + \frac{8}{8x - 5}\right) \cdot g(x) \tag{9.15}$$

(4) Then substitute (9.13) for $g(x)$ in (9.15).

$$g'(x) = \left(\frac{3x^2}{x^3 - 2} + \frac{2x}{x^2 - 3} + \frac{8}{8x - 5}\right)[(x^3 - 2)(x^2 - 3)(8x - 5)]$$

(b)
$$g(x) = (x^4 + 7)(x^5 + 6)(x^3 + 2) \tag{9.16}$$

(1)
$$\ln g(x) = \ln(x^4 + 7) + \ln(x^5 + 6) + \ln(x^3 + 2)$$

(2)
$$\frac{d}{dx}[\ln g(x)] = \frac{g'(x)}{g(x)} = \frac{4x^3}{x^4 + 7} + \frac{5x^4}{x^5 + 6} + \frac{3x^2}{x^3 + 2}$$

(3)
$$g'(x) = \left(\frac{4x^3}{x^4 + 7} + \frac{5x^4}{x^5 + 6} + \frac{3x^2}{x^3 + 2}\right) \cdot g(x) \tag{9.17}$$

(4) Finally, substituting (9.16) for $g(x)$ in (9.17),

$$g'(x) = \left(\frac{4x^3}{x^4 + 7} + \frac{5x^4}{x^5 + 6} + \frac{3x^2}{x^3 + 2}\right) \cdot (x^4 + 7)(x^5 + 6)(x^3 + 2)$$

(c)
$$g(x) = \frac{(3x^5 - 4)(2x^3 + 9)}{(7x^4 - 5)}$$

(1)
$$\ln g(x) = \ln(3x^5 - 4) + \ln(2x^3 + 9) - \ln(7x^4 - 5)$$

(2)
$$\frac{d}{dx}[\ln g(x)] = \frac{g'(x)}{g(x)} = \frac{15x^4}{3x^5 - 4} + \frac{6x^2}{2x^3 + 9} - \frac{28x^3}{7x^4 - 5}$$

(3)
$$g'(x) = \left(\frac{15x^4}{3x^5 - 4} + \frac{6x^2}{2x^3 + 9} - \frac{28x^3}{7x^4 - 5}\right) \cdot g(x)$$

(4)
$$g'(x) = \left(\frac{15x^4}{3x^5 - 4} + \frac{6x^2}{2x^3 + 9} - \frac{28x^3}{7x^4 - 5}\right) \cdot \frac{(3x^5 - 4)(2x^3 + 9)}{(7x^4 - 5)}$$

GROWTH

9.23. The price of agricultural goods is going up by 4 percent each year; the quantity by 2 percent. What is the annual rate of growth of revenue R derived from the agricultural sector?

Converting the revenue formula $R = PQ$ to natural logs,

$$\ln R = \ln P + \ln Q$$

The derivative of the natural log function equals the instantaneous rate of growth G of the function (see Section 9.6). Thus,

$$G = \frac{d}{dt}(\ln R) = \frac{d}{dt}(\ln P) + \frac{d}{dt}(\ln Q)$$

But
$$\frac{d}{dt}(\ln P) = \text{growth of } P = 4\% \qquad \frac{d}{dt}(\ln Q) = \text{growth of } Q = 2\%$$

Thus,
$$G = \frac{d}{dt}(\ln R) = 0.04 + 0.02 = 0.06$$

The rate of growth of a function involving a product is the sum of the rates of growth of the individual components.

9.24. A firm experiences a 10 percent increase in the use of inputs at a time when input costs are rising by 3 percent. What is the rate of increase in total input costs?

$$C = PQ$$
$$\ln C = \ln P + \ln Q$$
$$G = \frac{d}{dt}(\ln C) = \frac{d}{dt}(\ln P) + \frac{d}{dt}(\ln Q) = 0.03 + 0.10 = 0.13$$

9.25. Employment opportunities E are increasing by 4 percent a year and population P by 2.5 percent. What is the rate of growth of per capita employment PCE?

$$PCE = \frac{E}{P}$$
$$\ln PCE = \ln E - \ln P$$

Taking the derivative to find the growth rate,

$$G = \frac{d}{dt}(\ln PCE) = \frac{d}{dt}(\ln E) - \frac{d}{dt}(\ln P) = 0.04 - 0.025 = 0.015 = 1.5\%$$

The rate of growth of a function involving a quotient is the difference between the rate of growth of the numerator and denominator.

9.26. National income Y is increasing by 1.5 percent a year and population P by 2.5 percent a year. What is the rate of growth of per capita income PCY?

$$PCY = \frac{Y}{P}$$
$$\ln PCY = \ln Y - \ln P$$
$$G = \frac{d}{dt}(\ln PCY) = \frac{d}{dt}(\ln Y) - \frac{d}{dt}(\ln P) = 0.015 - 0.025 = -0.01 = -1\%$$

Per capita income is falling by 1 percent a year.

9.27. A country exports two goods, copper c and bananas b, where earnings in terms of million dollars are

$$c = c(t_0) = 4 \qquad b = b(t_0) = 1$$

If c grows by 10 percent and b by 20 percent, what is the rate of growth of export earnings E?

$$E = c + b$$
$$\ln E = \ln(c + b)$$
$$G = \frac{d}{dt}(\ln E) = \frac{d}{dt}\ln(c + b)$$

From the rules of derivatives in Section 9.1.3,

$$G_E = \frac{1}{c+b}\left[c'(t) + b'(t)\right] \qquad (9.18)$$

From Section 9.6,

$$G_c = \frac{c'(t)}{c(t)} \qquad G_b = \frac{b'(t)}{b(t)}$$

Thus, $\qquad\qquad c'(t) = G_c\,c(t) \qquad b'(t) = G_b\,b(t)$

Substituting in (9.18),

$$G_E = \frac{1}{c+b}\left[G_c\,c(t) + G_b\,b(t)\right]$$

Rearranging terms,

$$G_E = \frac{c(t)}{c+b}\,G_c + \frac{b(t)}{c+b}\,G_b$$

Then substituting the given values,

$$G_E = \frac{4}{4+1}\,(0.10) + \frac{1}{4+1}\,(0.20) = \frac{4}{5}\,(0.10) + \frac{1}{5}\,(0.20) = 0.12 \quad \text{or} \quad 12\%$$

The growth rate of a function involving the sum of other functions is the sum of the weighted average of the growth of the other functions.

9.28. A company derives 70 percent of its revenue from bathing suits, 20 percent from bathing caps, and 10 percent from bathing slippers. If revenues from bathing suits increase by 15 percent, from caps by 5 percent, and from slippers by 4 percent, what is the rate of growth of total revenue?

$$G_R = 0.70(0.15) + 0.20(0.05) + 0.10(0.04) = 0.105 + 0.01 + 0.004 = 0.119 \quad \text{or} \quad 11.9\%$$

9.29. Find the relative growth rate G of sales at $t = 4$, given $S(t) = 100\,000e^{0.5\sqrt{t}}$.

$$\ln S(t) = \ln 100\,000 + \ln e^{0.5\sqrt{t}} = \ln 100\,000 + 0.5\sqrt{t}$$

Take the derivative and recall that $0.5\sqrt{t} = 0.5t^{1/2}$,

$$G = \frac{d}{dt}\ln S(t) = \frac{S'(t)}{S(t)} = 0.5\left(\frac{1}{2}\right)t^{-1/2} = \frac{0.25}{\sqrt{t}}$$

At $t = 4$, $\qquad\qquad G = \frac{0.25}{\sqrt{4}} = 0.125 = 12.5\%$

9.30. Find the relative growth of profits at $t = 8$, given $\pi(t) = 250\,000e^{1.2t^{1/3}}$.

$$\ln \pi(t) = \ln 250\,000 + 1.2t^{1/3}$$

and $\qquad\qquad G = \frac{d}{dt}\ln \pi(t) = \frac{\pi'(t)}{\pi(t)} = 1.2\left(\frac{1}{3}\right)t^{-2/3} = \frac{0.4}{t^{2/3}}$

At $t = 8$, $\qquad\qquad G = \frac{0.4}{8^{2/3}} = \frac{0.4}{4} = 0.1 = 10\%$

OPTIMAL TIMING

9.31. Cut glass currently worth \$100 is appreciating in value according to the formula

$$V = 100e^{\sqrt{t}} = 100e^{t^{1/2}}$$

How long should the cut glass be kept to maximize its present value if under continuous compounding (a) $r = 0.08$ and (b) $r = 0.12$?

(a) The present value P is $P = Ve^{-rt}$. Substituting for V and r,

$$P = 100e^{\sqrt{t}}e^{-0.08t} = 100e^{\sqrt{t}-0.08t}$$

Converting to natural logs, $\ln P = \ln 100 + \ln e^{\sqrt{t}-0.08t} = \ln 100 + t^{1/2} - 0.08t$. Taking the derivative, setting it equal to zero, and recalling that $\ln 100$ is a constant,

$$\frac{d}{dt}(\ln P) = \frac{1}{P}\frac{dP}{dt} = \frac{1}{2}t^{-1/2} - 0.08$$

$$\frac{dP}{dt} = P\left(\frac{1}{2}t^{-1/2} - 0.08\right) = 0 \qquad\qquad (9.19)$$

Since $P \neq 0$,

$$\tfrac{1}{2}t^{-1/2} = 0.08$$
$$t^{-1/2} = 0.16$$

$$t = (0.16)^{-2} = \frac{1}{0.0256} = 39.06$$

Testing the second-order condition, and using the product rule since $P = f(t)$,

$$\frac{d^2P}{dt^2} = P\left(-\frac{1}{4}t^{-3/2}\right) + \left(\frac{1}{2}t^{-1/2} - 0.08\right)\frac{dP}{dt}$$

Since $dP/dt = 0$ at the critical value,

$$\frac{d^2P}{dt^2} = \frac{-P}{4\sqrt{t^3}}$$

which is negative, since P and t must both be positive. Thus, $t = 39.06$ maximizes the function.

(b) If $r = 0.12$, substituting 0.12 for 0.08 in (9.19) above,

$$\frac{dP}{dt} = P\left(\frac{1}{2}t^{-1/2} - 0.12\right) = 0$$

$$\tfrac{1}{2}t^{-1/2} = 0.12$$

$$t = (0.24)^{-2} = \frac{1}{0.0576} = 17.36$$

The second-order condition is unchanged. Note that the higher the rate of discount r, the shorter the period of storage.

9.32. Land bought for speculation is increasing in value according to the formula

$$V = 1000e^{3\sqrt{t}}$$

The discount rate under continuous compounding is 0.09. How long should the land be held to maximize the present value?

$$P = 1000e^{3\sqrt{t}}e^{-0.09t} = 1000e^{3\sqrt{t}-0.09t}$$

Convert to natural logs. $\ln P = \ln 1000 + t^{1/3} - 0.09t$

Take the derivative. $\dfrac{d}{dt}(\ln P) = \dfrac{1}{P}\dfrac{dP}{dt} = \dfrac{1}{3}t^{-2/3} - 0.09 = 0$

$$\frac{dP}{dt} = P\left(\frac{1}{3}t^{-2/3} - 0.09\right) = 0$$

$$\tfrac{1}{3}t^{-2/3} = 0.09 \qquad t = 0.27^{-3/2} \approx 7.13 \text{ years}$$

The second-order condition, recalling $dP/dt = 0$ at the critical value, is

$$\frac{d^2P}{dt^2} = P\left(-\frac{2}{9}t^{-5/3}\right) + \left(\frac{1}{3}t^{-2/3} - 0.09\right)\frac{dP}{dt} = -\frac{2P}{9\sqrt[3]{t^5}} < 0$$

9.33. The art collection of a recently deceased painter has an estimated value of

$$V = 200\,000(1.25)^{3\sqrt{t^2}}$$

How long should the executor of the estate hold on to the collection before putting it up for sale if the discount rate under continuous compounding is 6 percent?

Substituting the value of V in $P = Ve^{-rt}$,

$$P = 200\,000(1.25)^{t^{2/3}}e^{-0.06t}$$

$$\ln P = \ln 200\,000 + t^{2/3}\ln 1.25 - 0.06t$$

$$\frac{d}{dt}(\ln P) = \frac{1}{P}\frac{dP}{dt} = \frac{2}{3}(\ln 1.25)t^{-1/3} - 0.06 = 0$$

$$\frac{dP}{dt} = P\left[\frac{2}{3}(\ln 1.25)t^{-1/3} - 0.06\right] = 0$$

$$t^{-1/3} = \frac{3(0.06)}{2\ln 1.25} \qquad t = \left[\frac{0.18}{2(0.22314)}\right]^{-3} = (0.403)^{-3} \approx 15.3 \text{ years}$$

9.34. The estimated value of a diamond bought for investment purposes is

$$V = 250\,000(1.75)^{4\sqrt{t}}$$

If the discount rate under continuous compounding is 7 percent, how long should the diamond be held?

$$P = 250\,000(1.75)^{t^{1/4}}e^{-0.07t}$$

$$\ln P = \ln 250\,000 + t^{1/4}(\ln 1.75) - 0.07t$$

$$\frac{d}{dt}(\ln P) = \frac{1}{P}\frac{dP}{dt} = \frac{1}{4}(\ln 1.75)t^{-3/4} - 0.07 = 0$$

$$\frac{dP}{dt} = P\left[\frac{1}{4}(\ln 1.75)t^{-3/4} - 0.07\right] = 0$$

$$\frac{1}{4}(\ln 1.75)t^{-3/4} - 0.07 = 0 \qquad t = \left(\frac{0.28}{\ln 1.75}\right)^{-4/3} = (0.50)^{-4/3} \approx 2.52 \text{ years}$$

SELECTED PROOFS

9.35. Derive the derivative for $\ln x$.

From the definition of a derivative in Equation (3.2),

$$f'(x) = \lim_{\Delta x \to 0}\frac{f(x + \Delta x) - f(x)}{\Delta x}$$

Specifying $f(x) = \ln x$,

$$\frac{d}{dx}(\ln x) = \lim_{\Delta x \to 0}\frac{\ln(x + \Delta x) - \ln x}{\Delta x}$$

From the properties of logs, where $\ln a - \ln b = \ln(a/b)$,

$$\frac{d}{dx}(\ln x) = \lim_{\Delta x \to 0}\frac{\ln[(x + \Delta x)/x]}{\Delta x}$$

Rearranging first the denominator and then the numerator,

$$\frac{d}{dx}(\ln x) = \lim_{\Delta x \to 0}\left(\frac{1}{\Delta x}\ln\frac{x + \Delta x}{x}\right) = \lim_{\Delta x \to 0}\left[\frac{1}{\Delta x}\ln\left(1 + \frac{\Delta x}{x}\right)\right]$$

Chapter 10

The Fundamentals of Linear
(or Matrix) Algebra

10.1 THE ROLE OF LINEAR ALGEBRA

Linear algebra (1) permits expression of a complicated system of equations in a succinct, simplified way, (2) provides a shorthand method to determine whether a solution exists before it is attempted, and (3) furnishes the means of solving the equation system. Linear algebra, however, can be applied *only* to systems of linear equations. Since many economic relationships can be approximated by linear equations and others can be converted to linear relationships, this limitation generally presents no serious problem. See Example 2 and Section 7.6.

EXAMPLE 1. For a company with several different outlets selling several different products, a matrix provides a concise way of keeping track of stock.

Outlet	Skis	Poles	Bindings	Outfits
1	120	110	90	150
2	200	180	210	110
3	175	190	160	80
4	140	170	180	140

By reading across a row of the matrix, the firm can determine the level of stock in any of its outlets. By reading down a column of the matrix, the firm can determine the stock of any line of its products.

EXAMPLE 2. A nonlinear function, such as the rational function $z = x^{0.3}/y^{0.6}$, can be easily converted to a linear function by a simple rearrangement

$$z = \frac{x^{0.3}}{y^{0.6}} = x^{0.3} y^{-0.6}$$

followed by a logarithmic transformation

$$\ln z = 0.3 \ln x - 0.6 \ln y$$

which is log-linear. In similar fashion, many exponential and power functions are readily convertible to linear functions and then handled by linear algebra. See Section 7.6.

10.2 DEFINITIONS AND TERMS

A *matrix* is a rectangular array of numbers, parameters, or variables, each of which has a carefully ordered place within the matrix. The numbers (parameters, or variables) are referred to as *elements* of the matrix. The numbers in a horizontal line are called *rows*; the numbers in a vertical line are called *columns*. The number of rows r and columns c defines the *dimensions* of the matrix ($r \times c$), which is read "r by c." The row number always precedes the column number. In a *square matrix*, the number of rows equals the number of columns (that is, $r = c$). If the matrix is composed of a single column, such that its dimensions are $r \times 1$, it is a *column vector*; if a matrix is a single row, with dimensions $1 \times c$, it is a *row vector*. A matrix which converts the rows of A to columns and the columns of A to rows is called the *transpose* of A and is designated by A' (or A^T). See Example 3 and Problems 10.1 to 10.3.

EXAMPLE 3.   Given

$$A = \begin{bmatrix} a_{11} & a_{12} & a_{13} \\ a_{21} & a_{22} & a_{23} \\ a_{31} & a_{32} & a_{33} \end{bmatrix}_{3 \times 3} \qquad B = \begin{bmatrix} 3 & 9 & 8 \\ 4 & 2 & 7 \end{bmatrix}_{2 \times 3} \qquad C = \begin{bmatrix} 7 \\ 4 \\ 5 \end{bmatrix}_{3 \times 1} \qquad D = \begin{bmatrix} 3 & 0 & 1 \end{bmatrix}_{1 \times 3}$$

Here A is a general matrix composed of $3 \times 3 = 9$ elements, arranged in three rows and three columns. It is thus a square matrix. Note that no punctuation separates the elements of a matrix. The elements all have double subscripts which give the *address* or placement of the element in the matrix; the first subscript identifies the row in which the element appears, and the second identifies the column. Positioning is precise within a matrix. Thus, a_{23} is the element which appears in the second row, third column; a_{32} is the element which appears in the third row, second column. Since row always precedes column in matrix notation, it might be helpful to think of the subscripts in terms of RC cola or some other mnemonic device. To determine the number of rows, always count down; to find the number of columns, count across.

Here B is a 2×3 matrix. Its b_{12} element is 9, its b_{21} element is 4. And C is a column vector with dimensions 3×1; D is a row vector with dimensions 1×3.

The transpose of A is

$$A' = \begin{bmatrix} a_{11} & a_{21} & a_{31} \\ a_{12} & a_{22} & a_{32} \\ a_{13} & a_{23} & a_{33} \end{bmatrix}$$

and the transpose of C is

$$C' = \begin{bmatrix} 7 & 4 & 5 \end{bmatrix}$$

10.3   ADDITION AND SUBTRACTION OF MATRICES

Addition (and subtraction) of two matrices $A + B$ (or $A - B$) requires that the matrices be of equal dimensions. Each element of one matrix is then added to (subtracted from) the corresponding element of the other matrix. Thus, a_{11} in A will be added to (subtracted from) b_{11} in B; a_{12} to b_{12}; etc. See Examples 4 and 5 and Problems 10.4 to 10.8.

EXAMPLE 4.   The sum $A + B$ is calculated below, given matrices A and B:

$$A = \begin{bmatrix} 8 & 9 & 7 \\ 3 & 6 & 2 \\ 4 & 5 & 10 \end{bmatrix}_{3 \times 3} \qquad B = \begin{bmatrix} 1 & 3 & 6 \\ 5 & 2 & 4 \\ 7 & 9 & 2 \end{bmatrix}_{3 \times 3} \qquad A + B = \begin{bmatrix} 8+1 & 9+3 & 7+6 \\ 3+5 & 6+2 & 2+4 \\ 4+7 & 5+9 & 10+2 \end{bmatrix}_{3 \times 3} = \begin{bmatrix} 9 & 12 & 13 \\ 8 & 8 & 6 \\ 11 & 14 & 12 \end{bmatrix}_{3 \times 3}$$

The difference $C - D$, given matrices C and D, is found as follows:

$$C = \begin{bmatrix} 4 & 9 \\ 2 & 6 \end{bmatrix}_{2 \times 2} \qquad D = \begin{bmatrix} 1 & 7 \\ 5 & 4 \end{bmatrix}_{2 \times 2} \qquad C - D = \begin{bmatrix} 4-1 & 9-7 \\ 2-5 & 6-4 \end{bmatrix}_{2 \times 2} = \begin{bmatrix} 3 & 2 \\ -3 & 2 \end{bmatrix}_{2 \times 2}$$

EXAMPLE 5.   Suppose that deliveries D are made to the outlets of the firm in Example 1. What is the new level of stock?

$$D = \begin{bmatrix} 40 & 20 & 50 & 10 \\ 25 & 30 & 10 & 60 \\ 15 & 0 & 40 & 70 \\ 60 & 40 & 10 & 50 \end{bmatrix}$$

To find the new level of stock, label the initial matrix S, and solve for $S + D$. Adding the corresponding elements of each matrix,

$$S + D = \begin{bmatrix} 120 + 40 & 110 + 20 & 90 + 50 & 150 + 10 \\ 200 + 25 & 180 + 30 & 210 + 10 & 110 + 60 \\ 175 + 15 & 190 + 0 & 160 + 40 & 80 + 70 \\ 140 + 60 & 170 + 40 & 180 + 10 & 140 + 50 \end{bmatrix} = \begin{bmatrix} 160 & 130 & 140 & 160 \\ 225 & 210 & 220 & 170 \\ 190 & 190 & 200 & 150 \\ 200 & 210 & 190 & 190 \end{bmatrix}$$

10.4   SCALAR MULTIPLICATION

In matrix algebra, a simple number such as 12, -2, or 0.07 is called a *scalar*. Multiplication of a matrix by a number or scalar involves multiplication of every element of the matrix by the number. The process is called *scalar multiplication* because it scales the matrix up or down according to the size of the number. See Example 6 and Problems 10.10 to 10.12.

EXAMPLE 6.   The result of scalar multiplication kA, given $k = 8$ and

$$A = \begin{bmatrix} 6 & 9 \\ 2 & 7 \\ 8 & 4 \end{bmatrix}_{3 \times 2}$$

is shown below

$$kA = \begin{bmatrix} 8(6) & 8(9) \\ 8(2) & 8(7) \\ 8(8) & 8(4) \end{bmatrix}_{3 \times 2} = \begin{bmatrix} 48 & 72 \\ 16 & 56 \\ 64 & 32 \end{bmatrix}_{3 \times 2}$$

10.5   VECTOR MULTIPLICATION

Multiplication of a row vector A by a column vector B requires as a precondition that each vector have precisely the same number of elements. The product is then found by multiplying the individual elements of the row vector by their corresponding elements in the column vector and summing the products:

$$AB = (a_{11} \times b_{11}) + (a_{12} \times b_{21}) + (a_{13} \times b_{31}) \qquad \text{etc.}$$

The product of row-column multiplication will thus be a single number or scalar. Row-column vector multiplication is of paramount importance. It serves as the basis for all matrix multiplication. See Example 7 and Problems 10.13 to 10.18.

EXAMPLE 7.   The product AB of the row vector A and the column vector B, given

$$A = \begin{bmatrix} 4 & 7 & 2 & 9 \end{bmatrix}_{1 \times 4} \qquad B = \begin{bmatrix} 12 \\ 1 \\ 5 \\ 6 \end{bmatrix}_{4 \times 1}$$

is calculated as follows:

$$AB = 4(12) + 7(1) + 2(5) + 9(6) = 48 + 7 + 10 + 54 = 119$$

The product of vectors

$$C = \begin{bmatrix} 3 & 6 & 8 \end{bmatrix}_{1 \times 3} \qquad D = \begin{bmatrix} 2 \\ 4 \\ 5 \end{bmatrix}_{3 \times 1}$$

is

$$CD = (3 \times 2) + (6 \times 4) + (8 \times 5) = 6 + 24 + 40 = 70$$

Note that since each set of vectors above has the same number of elements, multiplication is possible.

Reversing the order of multiplication in either of the above and having column-row vector multiplication (BA or DC) will give a totally different answer. See Problem 10.36.

10.6   MULTIPLICATION OF MATRICES

Multiplication of two matrices with dimensions $(r \times c)_1$ and $(r \times c)_2$ requires that the matrices be *conformable*, i.e., that $c_1 = r_2$, or the number of columns in 1, the *lead matrix*, equal the number of rows in 2, the *lag matrix*. Each row vector in the lead matrix is then multiplied by each column vector of the lag matrix, according to the rules for multiplying row and column vectors discussed in Section 10.5. The row-column products, called *inner products*, are then used as elements in the formation of the product matrix, such that each element c_{ij} of the product matrix C is a scalar derived from the multiplication of the ith row of the lead matrix and the jth column of the lag matrix. See Examples 8 to 10 and Problems 10.19 to 10.33.

EXAMPLE 8.   Given

$$A = \begin{bmatrix} 3 & 6 & 7 \\ 12 & 9 & 11 \end{bmatrix}_{2 \times 3} \qquad B = \begin{bmatrix} 6 & 12 \\ 5 & 10 \\ 13 & 2 \end{bmatrix}_{3 \times 2} \qquad C = \begin{bmatrix} 1 & 7 & 8 \\ 2 & 4 & 3 \end{bmatrix}_{2 \times 3}$$

A shorthand test for conformability, which should be applied before undertaking any matrix multiplication, is to place the two sets of dimensions in the order in which the matrices are to be multiplied, then mentally circle the last number of the first set and the first number of the second set. If the two numbers are equal, the number of columns in the lead matrix will equal the number of rows in the lag matrix, and the two matrices will be conformable for multiplication in the given order. Moreover, the numbers outside the circle will provide, in proper order, the dimensions of the resulting product matrix. Thus, for AB

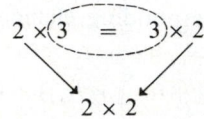

The number of columns in the lead matrix equals the number of rows in the lag matrix, $3 = 3$; the matrices are conformable for multiplication; and the dimensions of the product matrix AB will be 2×2. When two matrices such as A and B are conformable for multiplication, the product AB is said to be *defined*.

For BC,

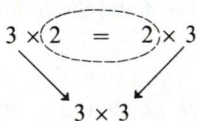

The number of columns in the lead matrix equals the number of rows in the lag matrix, $2 = 2$; hence B and C are conformable. The product BC is defined, and BC will be a 3×3 matrix.

For AC,

$$2 \times \boxed{3 \quad \neq \quad 2} \times 3$$

A and C are not conformable for multiplication. Thus, AC is not defined.

EXAMPLE 9.   Having determined that A and B in Example 8 are conformable, the product $AB = D$ can be found. Remembering to use only rows R from the lead matrix and only columns C from the lag matrix, multiply the first row R_1 of the lead matrix by the first column C_1 of the lag matrix to find the first element d_{11} $(= R_1 C_1)$ of the product matrix D. Then multiply the first row R_1 of the lead matrix by the second column C_2 of the lag matrix to get d_{12} ($= R_1 C_2$). Since there are no more columns left in the lag matrix to be multiplied by the first row of the lead matrix, move to the second row of the lead matrix. Multiply the second row R_2 of the lead matrix by the first column C_1 of the lag matrix to get d_{21} ($= R_2 C_1$). Finally, multiply the second row R_2 of the lead matrix by the second column C_2 of the lag matrix to get d_{22} ($= R_2 C_2$). Thus,

$$AB = D = \begin{bmatrix} R_1 C_1 & R_1 C_2 \\ R_2 C_1 & R_2 C_2 \end{bmatrix} = \begin{bmatrix} 3(6) + 6(5) + 7(13) & 3(12) + 6(10) + 7(2) \\ 12(6) + 9(5) + 11(13) & 12(12) + 9(10) + 11(2) \end{bmatrix}_{2 \times 2} = \begin{bmatrix} 139 & 110 \\ 260 & 256 \end{bmatrix}_{2 \times 2}$$

The product of BC is calculated below, using the same method:

$$BC = E = \begin{bmatrix} R_1 C_1 & R_1 C_2 & R_1 C_3 \\ R_2 C_1 & R_2 C_2 & R_2 C_3 \\ R_3 C_1 & R_3 C_2 & R_3 C_3 \end{bmatrix} = \begin{bmatrix} 6(1) + 12(2) & 6(7) + 12(4) & 6(8) + 12(3) \\ 5(1) + 10(2) & 5(7) + 10(4) & 5(8) + 10(3) \\ 13(1) + 2(2) & 13(7) + 2(4) & 13(8) + 2(3) \end{bmatrix}_{3 \times 3} = \begin{bmatrix} 30 & 90 & 84 \\ 25 & 75 & 70 \\ 17 & 99 & 110 \end{bmatrix}_{3 \times 3}$$

EXAMPLE 10.   Referring to Example 1, suppose that the price of skis is \$200, poles \$50, bindings \$100, and outfits \$150. To find the value V of the stock in the different outlets, express the prices as a column vector P, and multiply S by P:

$$V = SP = \begin{bmatrix} 120 & 110 & 90 & 150 \\ 200 & 180 & 210 & 110 \\ 175 & 190 & 160 & 80 \\ 140 & 170 & 180 & 140 \end{bmatrix}_{4 \times 4} \begin{bmatrix} 200 \\ 50 \\ 100 \\ 150 \end{bmatrix}_{4 \times 1}$$

The matrices are conformable, and the product matrix will be 4×1 since

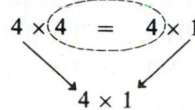

Thus,

$$V = \begin{bmatrix} R_1 C_1 \\ R_2 C_1 \\ R_3 C_1 \\ R_4 C_1 \end{bmatrix} = \begin{bmatrix} 120(200) + 110(50) + 90(100) + 150(150) \\ 200(200) + 180(50) + 210(100) + 110(150) \\ 175(200) + 190(50) + 160(100) + 80(150) \\ 140(200) + 170(50) + 180(100) + 140(150) \end{bmatrix}_{4 \times 1} = \begin{bmatrix} 61\,000 \\ 86\,500 \\ 72\,500 \\ 75\,500 \end{bmatrix}_{4 \times 1}$$

10.7 COMMUTATIVE, ASSOCIATIVE, AND DISTRIBUTIVE LAWS IN MATRIX ALGEBRA

Matrix addition is commutative (that is, $A + B = B + A$) since matrix addition merely involves the summing of corresponding elements of two matrices and the order in which the addition takes place is inconsequential. For the same reason, matrix addition is also associative, $(A + B) + C = A + (B + C)$. The same is true of matrix subtraction. Since matrix subtraction $A - B$ can be converted to matrix addition $A + (-B)$, matrix subtraction is also commutative and associative.

Matrix multiplication, with few exceptions, is not commutative (that is, $AB \neq BA$). Scalar multiplication, however, is commutative (that is, $kA = Ak$). If three or more matrices are conformable, that is, $X_{a \times b}$, $Y_{c \times d}$, $Z_{e \times f}$, where $b = c$ and $d = e$, the associative law will apply as long as the matrices are multiplied in the order of conformability. Thus $(XY)Z = X(YZ)$. Subject to these same conditions, matrix multiplication is also distributive: $A(B + C) = AB + AC$. See Examples 11 to 13 and Problems 10.34 to 10.48.

EXAMPLE 11.   Given

$$A = \begin{bmatrix} 4 & 11 \\ 17 & 6 \end{bmatrix} \qquad B = \begin{bmatrix} 3 & 7 \\ 6 & 2 \end{bmatrix}$$

To show that matrix addition and matrix subtraction are commutative, demonstrate that (1) $A + B = B + A$ and (2) $A - B = -B + A$. The calculations are shown below.

(1) $\qquad A + B = \begin{bmatrix} 4+3 & 11+7 \\ 17+6 & 6+2 \end{bmatrix} = \begin{bmatrix} 7 & 18 \\ 23 & 8 \end{bmatrix} = B + A = \begin{bmatrix} 3+4 & 7+11 \\ 6+17 & 2+6 \end{bmatrix} = \begin{bmatrix} 7 & 18 \\ 23 & 8 \end{bmatrix}$

(2) $\qquad A - B = \begin{bmatrix} 4-3 & 11-7 \\ 17-6 & 6-2 \end{bmatrix} = \begin{bmatrix} 1 & 4 \\ 11 & 4 \end{bmatrix} = -B + A = \begin{bmatrix} -3+4 & -7+11 \\ -6+17 & -2+6 \end{bmatrix} = \begin{bmatrix} 1 & 4 \\ 11 & 4 \end{bmatrix}$

EXAMPLE 12. Given

$$A = \begin{bmatrix} 3 & 6 & 7 \\ 12 & 9 & 11 \end{bmatrix}_{2 \times 3} \qquad B = \begin{bmatrix} 6 & 12 \\ 5 & 10 \\ 13 & 2 \end{bmatrix}_{3 \times 2}$$

It can be demonstrated that matrix multiplication is not commutative, by showing $AB \neq BA$, as follows:

Matrix AB is conformable. $\qquad 2 \times 3 \ = \ 3 \times 2 \qquad AB$ will be 2×2

$$AB = \begin{bmatrix} 3(6) + 6(5) + 7(13) & 3(12) + 6(10) + 7(2) \\ 12(6) + 9(5) + 11(13) & 12(12) + 9(10) + 11(2) \end{bmatrix}_{2 \times 2} = \begin{bmatrix} 139 & 110 \\ 260 & 256 \end{bmatrix}_{2 \times 2}$$

Matrix BA is conformable. $\qquad 3 \times 2 \ = \ 2 \times 3 \qquad BA$ will be 3×3

$$BA = \begin{bmatrix} 6(3) + 12(12) & 6(6) + 12(9) & 6(7) + 12(11) \\ 5(3) + 10(12) & 5(6) + 10(9) & 5(7) + 10(11) \\ 13(3) + 2(12) & 13(6) + 2(9) & 13(7) + 2(11) \end{bmatrix}_{3 \times 3} = \begin{bmatrix} 162 & 144 & 174 \\ 135 & 120 & 145 \\ 63 & 96 & 113 \end{bmatrix}_{3 \times 3}$$

Hence $AB \neq BA$. Frequently matrices will not even be conformable in two directions.

EXAMPLE 13. Given

$$A = \begin{bmatrix} 7 & 5 \\ 1 & 3 \\ 8 & 6 \end{bmatrix}_{3 \times 2} \qquad B = \begin{bmatrix} 4 & 9 & 10 \\ 2 & 6 & 5 \end{bmatrix}_{2 \times 3} \qquad C = \begin{bmatrix} 2 \\ 6 \\ 7 \end{bmatrix}_{3 \times 1}$$

To illustrate that matrix multiplication is associative, that is, $(AB)C = A(BC)$, the calculations are as follows:

$$AB = \begin{bmatrix} 7(4) + 5(2) & 7(9) + 5(6) & 7(10) + 5(5) \\ 1(4) + 3(2) & 1(9) + 3(6) & 1(10) + 3(5) \\ 8(4) + 6(2) & 8(9) + 6(6) & 8(10) + 6(5) \end{bmatrix}_{3 \times 3} = \begin{bmatrix} 38 & 93 & 95 \\ 10 & 27 & 25 \\ 44 & 108 & 110 \end{bmatrix}_{3 \times 3}$$

$$(AB)C = \begin{bmatrix} 38 & 93 & 95 \\ 10 & 27 & 25 \\ 44 & 108 & 110 \end{bmatrix}_{3 \times 3} \begin{bmatrix} 2 \\ 6 \\ 7 \end{bmatrix}_{3 \times 1} = \begin{bmatrix} 38(2) + 93(6) + 95(7) \\ 10(2) + 27(6) + 25(7) \\ 44(2) + 108(6) + 110(7) \end{bmatrix}_{3 \times 1} = \begin{bmatrix} 1299 \\ 357 \\ 1506 \end{bmatrix}_{3 \times 1}$$

$$BC = \begin{bmatrix} 4(2) + 9(6) + 10(7) \\ 2(2) + 6(6) + 5(7) \end{bmatrix}_{2 \times 1} = \begin{bmatrix} 132 \\ 75 \end{bmatrix}_{2 \times 1}$$

$$A(BC) = \begin{bmatrix} 7 & 5 \\ 1 & 3 \\ 8 & 6 \end{bmatrix}_{3 \times 2} \begin{bmatrix} 132 \\ 75 \end{bmatrix}_{2 \times 1} = \begin{bmatrix} 7(132) + 5(75) \\ 1(132) + 3(75) \\ 8(132) + 6(75) \end{bmatrix}_{3 \times 1} = \begin{bmatrix} 1299 \\ 357 \\ 1506 \end{bmatrix}_{3 \times 1} \qquad \text{Q.E.D.}$$

10.8 IDENTITY AND NULL MATRICES

An identity matrix I is a square matrix which has 1 for every element on the principal diagonal from left to right and 0 everywhere else. See Example 14. When a subscript is used, as in I_n, n denotes the dimensions of the matrix $(n \times n)$. The identity matrix is similar to the number 1 in algebra since multiplication of a matrix by an identity matrix leaves the original matrix unchanged (that is, $AI = IA = A$). Multiplication of an identity matrix by itself leaves the identity matrix unchanged: $I \times I = I^2 = I$. Any matrix for which $A = A'$ is a *symmetric matrix*. A symmetric matrix for which $A \times A = A$ is an *idempotent matrix*. The identity matrix is symmetric and idempotent.

A *null matrix* is composed of all 0s and can be of any dimension; it is not necessarily square. Addition or subtraction of the null matrix leaves the original matrix unchanged; multiplication by a null matrix produces a null matrix. See Example 14 and Problems 10.49 to 10.51.

EXAMPLE 14.   Given

$$A = \begin{bmatrix} 7 & 10 & 14 \\ 9 & 2 & 6 \\ 1 & 3 & 7 \end{bmatrix} \qquad B = \begin{bmatrix} 5 & 12 \\ 20 & 4 \end{bmatrix} \qquad N = \begin{bmatrix} 0 & 0 \\ 0 & 0 \end{bmatrix} \qquad I = \begin{bmatrix} 1 & 0 & 0 \\ 0 & 1 & 0 \\ 0 & 0 & 1 \end{bmatrix}$$

it is possible to show that (1) multiplication by an identity matrix leaves the original matrix unchanged, that is, $AI = A$, (2) multiplication by a null matrix produces a null matrix, that is, $BN = N$, and (3) addition or subtraction of a null matrix leaves the original matrix unchanged, that is, $B + N = B$. The calculations are shown below.

$$(1) \quad AI = \begin{bmatrix} 7 & 10 & 14 \\ 9 & 2 & 6 \\ 1 & 3 & 7 \end{bmatrix}\begin{bmatrix} 1 & 0 & 0 \\ 0 & 1 & 0 \\ 0 & 0 & 1 \end{bmatrix} = \begin{bmatrix} 7(1) + 10(0) + 14(0) & 7(0) + 10(1) + 14(0) & 7(0) + 10(0) + 14(1) \\ 9(1) + 2(0) + 6(0) & 9(0) + 2(1) + 6(0) & 9(0) + 2(0) + 6(1) \\ 1(1) + 3(0) + 7(0) & 1(0) + 3(1) + 7(0) & 1(0) + 3(0) + 7(1) \end{bmatrix}$$

$$= \begin{bmatrix} 7 & 10 & 14 \\ 9 & 2 & 6 \\ 1 & 3 & 7 \end{bmatrix} \qquad \text{Q.E.D.}$$

$$(2) \qquad BN = \begin{bmatrix} 5(0) + 12(0) & 5(0) + 12(0) \\ 20(0) + 4(0) & 20(0) + 4(0) \end{bmatrix} = \begin{bmatrix} 0 & 0 \\ 0 & 0 \end{bmatrix} \qquad \text{Q.E.D.}$$

$$(3) \qquad B + N = \begin{bmatrix} 5 + 0 & 12 + 0 \\ 20 + 0 & 4 + 0 \end{bmatrix} = \begin{bmatrix} 5 & 12 \\ 20 & 4 \end{bmatrix} \qquad \text{Q.E.D.}$$

10.9   MATRIX EXPRESSION OF A SYSTEM OF LINEAR EQUATIONS

Matrix algebra permits the concise expression of a system of linear equations. As a simple illustration, note that the system of linear equations

$$7x_1 + 3x_2 = 45$$
$$4x_1 + 5x_2 = 29$$

can be expressed in matrix form

$$AX = B$$

where
$$A = \begin{bmatrix} 7 & 3 \\ 4 & 5 \end{bmatrix} \qquad X = \begin{bmatrix} x_1 \\ x_2 \end{bmatrix} \qquad \text{and} \qquad B = \begin{bmatrix} 45 \\ 29 \end{bmatrix}$$

Here A is the *coefficient matrix*, X is the *solution vector*, and B is the *vector of constant terms*. And X and B will always be column vectors. See Examples 15 and 16.

EXAMPLE 15.   To show that $AX = B$ accurately represents the given system of equations above, find the product AX. Multiplication is possible since AX is conformable, and the product matrix will be 2×1.

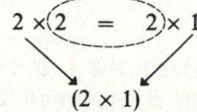

$$2 \times 2 \;=\; 2 \times 1$$
$$(2 \times 1)$$

Thus,
$$AX = \begin{bmatrix} 7 & 3 \\ 4 & 5 \end{bmatrix} \begin{bmatrix} x_1 \\ x_2 \end{bmatrix} = \begin{bmatrix} 7x_1 + 3x_2 \\ 4x_1 + 5x_2 \end{bmatrix}_{2 \times 1}$$

and
$$AX = B: \quad \begin{bmatrix} 7x_1 + 3x_2 \\ 4x_1 + 5x_2 \end{bmatrix} = \begin{bmatrix} 45 \\ 29 \end{bmatrix} \quad Q.E.D.$$

Here, despite appearances, AX is a 2×1 column vector since each row is composed of a single element which cannot be simplified further through addition.

EXAMPLE 16.   Given

$$8w + 12x - 7y + 2z = 139$$
$$3w - 13x + 4y + 9z = 242$$

To express this system of equations in matrix notation, mentally reverse the order of matrix multiplication:

$$\begin{bmatrix} 8 & 12 & -7 & 2 \\ 3 & -13 & 4 & 9 \end{bmatrix}_{2 \times 4} \begin{bmatrix} w \\ x \\ y \\ z \end{bmatrix}_{4 \times 1} = \begin{bmatrix} 139 \\ 242 \end{bmatrix}_{2 \times 1}$$

Then, letting $A =$ matrix of coefficients, $W =$ the column vector of variables, and $B =$ the column vector of constants, the given system of equations can be expressed in matrix form

$$A_{2 \times 4} W_{4 \times 1} = B_{2 \times 1}$$

10.10   ROW OPERATIONS

Row operations involve the application of simple algebraic operations to the rows of a matrix. With no change in the linear relationship, the three basic row operations allow (1) any two rows of a matrix to be interchanged, (2) any row or rows to be multiplied by a constant, provided the constant does not equal zero, and (3) any multiple of a row to be added to or subtracted from any other row. See Example 17.

EXAMPLE 17.   Row operations, which should be familiar from algebra, are illustrated below, given

$$5x + 2y = 16$$
$$8x + 4y = 28$$

Without any change in the linear relationship, one may

1.   Interchange the two rows:

$$8x + 4y = 28$$
$$5x + 2y = 16$$

2.   Multiply any row by a constant, here $8x + 4y = 28$ by $\frac{1}{4}$, leaving

$$2x + y = 7$$
$$5x + 2y = 16$$

3.   Subtract a multiple of one row from another, here $2(2x + y = 7)$ from $5x + 2y = 16$, leaving

$$5x + 2y = 16$$
$$\underline{-4x - 2y = -14}$$
$$x = 2$$

10.11   AUGMENTED MATRIX

Given a system of equations in matrix form $AX = B$, the augmented matrix $A | B$ is the coefficient matrix A with the column vector of constants B set alongside it, separated by a line or bar. Thus, for the system of equations in Section 10.9,

$$A\,|\,B = \begin{bmatrix} 7 & 3 & | & 45 \\ 4 & 5 & | & 29 \end{bmatrix}$$

Augmented matrices are used as a means of solving a system of linear equations.

EXAMPLE 18.   The augmented matrix $A\,|\,B$ for

$$4x_1 + 5x_2 + 7x_3 = 42$$
$$2x_1 + 3x_2 + 8x_3 = 40$$
$$6x_1 + 4x_2 + x_3 = 18$$

is

$$A\,|\,B = \begin{bmatrix} 4 & 5 & 7 & | & 42 \\ 2 & 3 & 8 & | & 40 \\ 6 & 4 & 1 & | & 18 \end{bmatrix}$$

10.12   GAUSSIAN METHOD OF SOLVING LINEAR EQUATIONS

To use the Gaussian elimination method of solving linear equations, simply express the system of equations as an augmented matrix and apply repeated row operations to the augmented matrix until the coefficient matrix A is reduced to an identity matrix. The solution to the system of equations can then be read from the remaining elements in the column vector B (see Example 19). To transform the coefficient matrix to an identity matrix, work along the principal axis. First obtain a 1 in the a_{11} position of the coefficient matrix; then use row operations to obtain 0s everywhere else in the first column. Next obtain a 1 in the a_{22} position, and use row operations to get 0s everywhere else in the column. Continue getting 1s along the principal diagonal and then clearing the column until the identity matrix is completed. See Example 19 and Problems 10.52 to 10.59.

EXAMPLE 19.   The Gaussian elimination method is used below to solve for x_1 and x_2 in the system of equations

$$2x_1 + 12x_2 = 40$$
$$8x_1 + 4x_2 = 28$$

First express the equations in an augmented matrix,

$$A\,|\,B = \begin{bmatrix} 2 & 12 & | & 40 \\ 8 & 4 & | & 28 \end{bmatrix}$$

Then

1a.   Multiply the first row by $\frac{1}{2}$ to obtain 1 in the a_{11} position.

$$\begin{bmatrix} 1 & 6 & | & 20 \\ 8 & 4 & | & 28 \end{bmatrix}$$

1b.   Subtract 8 times the first row from the second row to clear the first column.

$$\begin{bmatrix} 1 & 6 & | & 20 \\ 0 & -44 & | & -132 \end{bmatrix}$$

2a.   Multiply the second row by $-\frac{1}{44}$ to obtain 1 in a_{22}.

$$\begin{bmatrix} 1 & 6 & | & 20 \\ 0 & 1 & | & 3 \end{bmatrix}$$

2b.   Subtract 6 times the second row from the first row to clear the second column.

$$\begin{bmatrix} 1 & 0 & | & 2 \\ 0 & 1 & | & 3 \end{bmatrix}$$

The solution is $x_1 = 2$, $x_2 = 3$ since

$$\begin{bmatrix} 1 & 0 \\ 0 & 1 \end{bmatrix} \begin{bmatrix} x_1 \\ x_2 \end{bmatrix} = \begin{bmatrix} 2 \\ 3 \end{bmatrix}$$
$$x_1 + 0 = 2$$
$$0 + x_2 = 3$$

Solved Problems

MATRIX FORMAT

10.1. (a) Give the dimensions of each of the following matrices. (b) Give their transposes and indicate the new dimensions.

$$A = \begin{bmatrix} 6 & 7 & 9 \\ 2 & 8 & 4 \end{bmatrix} \qquad B = \begin{bmatrix} 12 & 9 & 2 & 6 \\ 7 & 5 & 8 & 3 \\ 9 & 1 & 0 & 4 \end{bmatrix} \qquad C = \begin{bmatrix} 12 \\ 19 \\ 25 \end{bmatrix}$$

$$D = \begin{bmatrix} 2 & 1 \\ 7 & 8 \\ 3 & 0 \\ 9 & 5 \end{bmatrix} \qquad E = \begin{bmatrix} 10 & 2 & 9 & 6 & 8 & 1 \end{bmatrix} \qquad F = \begin{bmatrix} 1 & 2 & 5 \\ 5 & 9 & 3 \\ 6 & 7 & 6 \\ 3 & 8 & 9 \end{bmatrix}$$

(a) Recalling that dimensions are always listed row by column or rc, $A = 2 \times 3$, $B = 3 \times 4$, $C = 3 \times 1$, $D = 4 \times 2$, $E = 1 \times 6$, and $F = 4 \times 3$. C is also called a column vector; E, a row vector.

(b) The transpose of A converts the rows of A to columns and the columns of A to rows.

$$A' = \begin{bmatrix} 6 & 2 \\ 7 & 8 \\ 9 & 4 \end{bmatrix}_{3 \times 2} \qquad B' = \begin{bmatrix} 12 & 7 & 9 \\ 9 & 5 & 1 \\ 2 & 8 & 0 \\ 6 & 3 & 4 \end{bmatrix}_{4 \times 3} \qquad C' = \begin{bmatrix} 12 & 19 & 25 \end{bmatrix}_{1 \times 3}$$

$$D' = \begin{bmatrix} 2 & 7 & 3 & 9 \\ 1 & 8 & 0 & 5 \end{bmatrix}_{2 \times 4} \qquad E' = \begin{bmatrix} 10 \\ 2 \\ 9 \\ 6 \\ 8 \\ 1 \end{bmatrix}_{6 \times 1} \qquad F' = \begin{bmatrix} 1 & 5 & 6 & 3 \\ 2 & 9 & 7 & 8 \\ 5 & 3 & 6 & 9 \end{bmatrix}_{3 \times 4}$$

10.2. Given $a_{21} = 4$, $a_{32} = 5$, $a_{13} = 3$, $a_{23} = 6$, $a_{12} = 10$, and $a_{31} = -5$, use your knowledge of subscripts to complete the following matrix:

$$A = \begin{bmatrix} 6 & \underline{\quad} & \underline{\quad} \\ \underline{\quad} & 7 & \underline{\quad} \\ \underline{\quad} & \underline{\quad} & 9 \end{bmatrix}$$

Since the subscripts are always given in row-column order, $a_{21} = 4$ means that 4 is located in the second row, first column; $a_{32} = 5$ means that 5 appears in the third row, second column; etc. Thus,

$$A = \begin{bmatrix} 6 & 10 & 3 \\ 4 & 7 & 6 \\ -5 & 5 & 9 \end{bmatrix}$$

10.3. A firm with five retail stores has 10 TVs t, 15 stereos s, 9 tape decks d, and 12 recorders r in store 1; $20t$, $14s$, $8d$, and $5r$ in store 2; $16t$, $8s$, $15d$, and $6r$ in store 3; $25t$, $15s$, $7d$, and $16r$ in store 4; and $5t$, $12s$, $20d$, and $18r$ in store 5. Express present inventory in matrix form.

$$
\begin{array}{c}
\text{Retail} \\
\text{store}
\end{array}
\begin{array}{cccc}
t & s & d & r
\end{array}
$$

$$
\begin{array}{c}
1 \\
2 \\
3 \\
4 \\
5
\end{array}
\begin{bmatrix}
10 & 15 & 9 & 12 \\
20 & 14 & 8 & 5 \\
16 & 8 & 15 & 6 \\
25 & 15 & 7 & 16 \\
5 & 12 & 20 & 18
\end{bmatrix}
$$

MATRIX ADDITION AND SUBTRACTION

10.4. Find the sums $A + B$ of the following matrices:

(a) $A = \begin{bmatrix} 8 & 9 \\ 12 & 7 \end{bmatrix}$ $B = \begin{bmatrix} 13 & 4 \\ 2 & 6 \end{bmatrix}$

$$
A + B = \begin{bmatrix} 8 + 13 & 9 + 4 \\ 12 + 2 & 7 + 6 \end{bmatrix} = \begin{bmatrix} 21 & 13 \\ 14 & 13 \end{bmatrix}
$$

(b) $A = \begin{bmatrix} 7 & -10 \\ -8 & 2 \end{bmatrix}$ $B = \begin{bmatrix} -8 & 4 \\ 12 & -6 \end{bmatrix}$

$$
A + B = \begin{bmatrix} 7 + (-8) & -10 + 4 \\ -8 + 12 & 2 + (-6) \end{bmatrix} = \begin{bmatrix} -1 & -6 \\ 4 & -4 \end{bmatrix}
$$

(c) $A = \begin{bmatrix} 12 & 16 & 2 & 7 & 8 \end{bmatrix}$ $B = \begin{bmatrix} 0 & 1 & 9 & 5 & 6 \end{bmatrix}$

$$
A + B = \begin{bmatrix} 12 & 17 & 11 & 12 & 14 \end{bmatrix}
$$

(d) $A = \begin{bmatrix} 9 & 4 \\ 2 & 7 \\ 3 & 5 \\ 8 & 6 \end{bmatrix}$ $B = \begin{bmatrix} 1 & 3 \\ 6 & 5 \\ 2 & 8 \\ 9 & 2 \end{bmatrix}$

$$
A + B = \begin{bmatrix} 10 & 7 \\ 8 & 12 \\ 5 & 13 \\ 17 & 8 \end{bmatrix}
$$

10.5. Redo Problem 10.4, given

$$
A = \begin{bmatrix} 0 & 1 & -6 & 2 \\ -3 & 5 & 8 & 7 \\ 2 & 9 & -1 & 6 \end{bmatrix}
\quad
B = \begin{bmatrix} 7 & 2 & 12 & 6 & 5 \\ 4 & 3 & 8 & 10 & 6 \\ 1 & 0 & 5 & 11 & 9 \end{bmatrix}
$$

Matrices A and B are not conformable for addition because they are not of equal dimensions; $A = 3 \times 4$, $B = 3 \times 5$.

10.6. The parent company in Problem 10.3 sends out deliveries D to its stores:

$$D = \begin{bmatrix} 4 & 3 & 5 & 2 \\ 0 & 9 & 6 & 1 \\ 5 & 7 & 2 & 6 \\ 12 & 2 & 4 & 8 \\ 9 & 6 & 3 & 5 \end{bmatrix}$$

What is the new level of stock?

$$I_2 = I_1 + D = \begin{bmatrix} 10 & 15 & 9 & 12 \\ 20 & 14 & 8 & 5 \\ 16 & 8 & 15 & 6 \\ 25 & 15 & 7 & 16 \\ 5 & 12 & 20 & 18 \end{bmatrix} + \begin{bmatrix} 4 & 3 & 5 & 2 \\ 0 & 9 & 6 & 1 \\ 5 & 7 & 2 & 6 \\ 12 & 2 & 4 & 8 \\ 9 & 6 & 3 & 5 \end{bmatrix} = \begin{bmatrix} 14 & 18 & 14 & 14 \\ 20 & 23 & 14 & 6 \\ 21 & 15 & 17 & 12 \\ 37 & 17 & 11 & 24 \\ 14 & 18 & 23 & 23 \end{bmatrix}$$

10.7. Find the difference $A - B$ for each of the following:

(a) $A = \begin{bmatrix} 3 & 7 & 11 \\ 12 & 9 & 2 \end{bmatrix}$ $B = \begin{bmatrix} 6 & 8 & 1 \\ 9 & 5 & 8 \end{bmatrix}$

$$A - B = \begin{bmatrix} 3-6 & 7-8 & 11-1 \\ 12-9 & 9-5 & 2-8 \end{bmatrix} = \begin{bmatrix} -3 & -1 & 10 \\ 3 & 4 & -6 \end{bmatrix}$$

(b) $A = \begin{bmatrix} 16 \\ 2 \\ 15 \\ 9 \end{bmatrix}$ $B = \begin{bmatrix} 7 \\ 11 \\ 3 \\ 8 \end{bmatrix}$

$$A - B = \begin{bmatrix} 16-7 \\ 2-11 \\ 15-3 \\ 9-8 \end{bmatrix} = \begin{bmatrix} 9 \\ -9 \\ 12 \\ 1 \end{bmatrix}$$

(c) $A = \begin{bmatrix} 13 & -5 & 8 \\ 4 & 9 & 1 \\ 10 & 6 & -2 \end{bmatrix}$ $B = \begin{bmatrix} 14 & 2 & -5 \\ 9 & 6 & 8 \\ -3 & 13 & 11 \end{bmatrix}$

$$A - B = \begin{bmatrix} -1 & -7 & 13 \\ -5 & 3 & -7 \\ 13 & -7 & -13 \end{bmatrix}$$

10.8. A monthly report R on sales for the company in Problem 10.6 indicates

$$R = \begin{bmatrix} 8 & 12 & 6 & 9 \\ 10 & 11 & 8 & 3 \\ 15 & 6 & 9 & 7 \\ 21 & 14 & 5 & 18 \\ 6 & 11 & 13 & 9 \end{bmatrix}$$

What is the inventory left at the end of the month?

$$I_2 - R = \begin{bmatrix} 14 & 18 & 14 & 14 \\ 20 & 23 & 14 & 6 \\ 21 & 15 & 17 & 12 \\ 37 & 17 & 11 & 24 \\ 14 & 18 & 23 & 23 \end{bmatrix} - \begin{bmatrix} 8 & 12 & 6 & 9 \\ 10 & 11 & 8 & 3 \\ 15 & 6 & 9 & 7 \\ 21 & 14 & 5 & 18 \\ 6 & 11 & 13 & 9 \end{bmatrix} = \begin{bmatrix} 6 & 6 & 8 & 5 \\ 10 & 12 & 6 & 3 \\ 6 & 9 & 8 & 5 \\ 16 & 3 & 6 & 6 \\ 8 & 7 & 10 & 14 \end{bmatrix}$$

CONFORMABILITY

10.9. Given

$$A = \begin{bmatrix} 7 & 2 & 6 \\ 5 & 4 & 8 \\ 3 & 1 & 9 \end{bmatrix} \qquad B = \begin{bmatrix} 6 & 2 \\ 5 & 0 \end{bmatrix} \qquad C = \begin{bmatrix} 11 \\ 4 \\ 13 \end{bmatrix}$$

$$D = \begin{bmatrix} 14 \\ 4 \end{bmatrix} \qquad E = [8 \quad 1 \quad 10] \qquad F = [13 \quad 3]$$

Determine for each of the following whether the products are defined, i.e., conformable for multiplication. If so, indicate the dimensions of the product matrix. (a) AC, (b) BD, (c) EC, (d) DF, (e) CA, (f) DE, (g) DB, (h) CF, (i) EF.

(a)   The dimensions of AC, in the order of multiplication, are 3 × 3 = 3 × 1. Matrix AC is defined since the numbers within the dashed circle indicate that the number of columns in A equals the number of rows in C. The numbers outside the circle indicate that the product matrix will be 3 × 1.

(b)   The dimensions of BD are 2 × 2 = 2 × 1. Matrix BD is defined; the product matrix will be 2 × 1.

(c)   The dimensions of EC are 1 × 3 = 3 × 1. Matrix EC is defined; the product matrix will be 1 × 1, or a scalar.

(d)   The dimensions of DF are 2 × 1 = 1 × 2. Matrix DF is defined; the product matrix will be 2 × 2.

(e)   The dimensions of CA are 3 × 1 ≠ 3 × 3. Matrix CA is undefined. The matrices are not conformable for multiplication in that order. [Note that AC in part (a) is defined. This illustrates that matrix multiplication is not commutative: $AC \neq CA$.]

(f)   The dimensions of DE are 2 × 1 = 1 × 3. Matrix DE is defined; the product matrix will be 2 × 3.

(g)   The dimensions of DB are 2 × 1 ≠ 2 × 2. The matrices are not conformable for multiplication. Matrix DB is not defined.

(h)   The dimensions of CF are 3 × 1 = 1 × 2. The matrices are conformable; the product matrix will be 3 × 2.

(i)   The dimensions of EF are 1 × 3 ≠ 1 × 2. The matrices are not conformable, and EF is not defined.

SCALAR AND VECTOR MULTIPLICATION

10.10. Determine Ak, given

$$A = \begin{bmatrix} 3 & 2 \\ 9 & 5 \\ 6 & 7 \end{bmatrix} \qquad k = 4$$

Here k is a scalar, and scalar multiplication is possible with a matrix of any dimension. Hence the product is defined.

$$Ak = \begin{bmatrix} 3(4) & 2(4) \\ 9(4) & 5(4) \\ 6(4) & 7(4) \end{bmatrix} = \begin{bmatrix} 12 & 8 \\ 36 & 20 \\ 24 & 28 \end{bmatrix}$$

10.11. Find kA, given

$$k = -2 \qquad A = \begin{bmatrix} 7 & -3 & 2 \\ -5 & 6 & 8 \\ 2 & -7 & -9 \end{bmatrix}$$

$$kA = \begin{bmatrix} -2(7) & -2(-3) & -2(2) \\ -2(-5) & -2(6) & -2(8) \\ -2(2) & -2(-7) & -2(-9) \end{bmatrix} = \begin{bmatrix} -14 & 6 & -4 \\ 10 & -12 & -16 \\ -4 & 14 & 18 \end{bmatrix}$$

10.12. A clothing store discounts all its slacks, jackets, and suits by 20 percent at the end of the year. If V_1 is the value of stock in its three branches prior to the discount, find the value V_2 after the discount, when

$$V_1 = \begin{bmatrix} 5\,000 & 4\,500 & 6\,000 \\ 10\,000 & 12\,000 & 7\,500 \\ 8\,000 & 9\,000 & 11\,000 \end{bmatrix}$$

A 20 percent reduction means that the clothing is selling for 80 percent of its original value. Hence $V_2 = 0.8V_1$, and

$$V_2 = 0.8 \begin{bmatrix} 5\,000 & 4\,500 & 6\,000 \\ 10\,000 & 12\,000 & 7\,500 \\ 8\,000 & 9\,000 & 11\,000 \end{bmatrix} = \begin{bmatrix} 4\,000 & 3\,600 & 4\,800 \\ 8\,000 & 9\,600 & 6\,000 \\ 6\,400 & 7\,200 & 8\,800 \end{bmatrix}$$

10.13. Find AB, given

$$A = [9 \quad 11 \quad 3] \qquad B = \begin{bmatrix} 2 \\ 6 \\ 7 \end{bmatrix}$$

Matrix AB is defined; $1 \times \overparen{3 = 3} \times 1$; the product will be a scalar, derived by multiplying each element of the row vector by its corresponding element in the column vector and then summing the products.

$$AB = 9(2) + 11(6) + 3(7) = 18 + 66 + 21 = 105$$

10.14. Find AB, given

$$A = [12 \quad -5 \quad 6 \quad 11] \qquad B = \begin{bmatrix} 3 \\ 2 \\ -8 \\ 6 \end{bmatrix}$$

Matrix AB is defined; $1 \times \overparen{4 = 4} \times 1$.

$$AB = 12(3) + (-5)(2) + 6(-8) + 11(6) = 44$$

10.15. Find AB, given

$$A = [9 \quad 6 \quad 2 \quad 0 \quad -5] \qquad B = \begin{bmatrix} 2 \\ 13 \\ 5 \\ 8 \\ 1 \end{bmatrix}$$

Matrix AB is defined; $1 \times \overparen{5 = 5} \times 1$.

$$AB = 9(2) + 6(13) + 2(5) + 0(8) + (-5)(1) = 101$$

10.16. Find AB, given

$$A = [12 \quad 9 \quad 2 \quad 4] \qquad B = \begin{bmatrix} 6 \\ 1 \\ 2 \end{bmatrix}$$

Matrix AB is undefined; $1 \times \boxed{4 \quad \neq \quad 3} \times 1$. Multiplication is not possible.

10.17. If the price of a TV is \$300, the price of a stereo is \$250, the price of a tape deck is \$175, and the price of a recorder is \$125, use vectors to determine the value of stock for outlet 2 in Problem 10.3.

The value of stock is $V = QP$. The physical volume of stock in outlet 2 in vector form is $Q = [20 \quad 14 \quad 8 \quad 5]$. The price vector P can be written

$$P = \begin{bmatrix} 300 \\ 250 \\ 175 \\ 125 \end{bmatrix}$$

Matrix QP is defined; $1 \times \boxed{4 \quad = \quad 4} \times 1$. Thus

$$V = QP$$
$$= 20(300) + 14(250) + 8(175) + 5(125) = 11\,525$$

10.18. Redo Problem 10.17 for outlet 5 in Problem 10.3.

Here $Q = [5 \quad 12 \quad 20 \quad 18]$, P remains the same. Matrix QP is defined. Thus,

$$V = 5(300) + 12(250) + 20(175) + 18(125) = 10\,250$$

MATRIX MULTIPLICATION

10.19. Determine whether AB is defined, indicate what the dimensions of the product matrix will be, and find the product matrix AB, given

$$A = \begin{bmatrix} 12 & 14 \\ 20 & 5 \end{bmatrix} \qquad B = \begin{bmatrix} 3 & 9 \\ 0 & 2 \end{bmatrix}$$

Matrix AB is defined; $2 \times \boxed{2 \quad = \quad 2} \times 2$; the product matrix will be 2×2. Matrix multiplication is nothing but a series of row-column vector multiplications in which the a_{11} element of the product matrix is determined by the product of the first row R_1 of the lead matrix and the first column C_1 of the lag matrix; the a_{12} element of the product matrix is determined by the product of the first row R_1 of the lead matrix and the second column C_2 of the lag matrix; the a_{ij} element of the product matrix is determined by the product of the ith row R_i of the lead matrix and the jth column C_j of the lag matrix, etc. Thus,

$$AB = \begin{bmatrix} R_1C_1 & R_1C_2 \\ R_2C_1 & R_2C_2 \end{bmatrix} = \begin{bmatrix} 12(3) + 14(0) & 12(9) + 14(2) \\ 20(3) + 5(0) & 20(9) + 5(2) \end{bmatrix} = \begin{bmatrix} 36 & 136 \\ 60 & 190 \end{bmatrix}$$

10.20. Redo Problem 10.19, given

$$A = \begin{bmatrix} 4 & 7 \\ 9 & 1 \end{bmatrix} \qquad B = \begin{bmatrix} 3 & 8 & 5 \\ 2 & 6 & 7 \end{bmatrix}$$

Matrix AB is defined; $2 \times \boxed{2 \quad = \quad 2} \times 3$; the product matrix will be 2×3.

$$AB = \begin{bmatrix} R_1C_1 & R_1C_2 & R_1C_3 \\ R_2C_1 & R_2C_2 & R_2C_3 \end{bmatrix} = \begin{bmatrix} 4(3) + 7(2) & 4(8) + 7(6) & 4(5) + 7(7) \\ 9(3) + 1(2) & 9(8) + 1(6) & 9(5) + 1(7) \end{bmatrix} = \begin{bmatrix} 26 & 74 & 69 \\ 29 & 78 & 52 \end{bmatrix}$$

10.21. Redo Problem 10.19, given

$$A = \begin{bmatrix} 3 & 1 \\ 8 & 2 \end{bmatrix} \qquad B = \begin{bmatrix} 2 & 9 \\ 4 & 6 \\ 7 & 5 \end{bmatrix}$$

Matrix AB is not defined; $2 \times 2 \neq 3 \times 2$. The matrices cannot be multiplied because they are not conformable in the given order. The number of columns (2) in A does not equal the number of rows (3) in B.

10.22. Redo Problem 10.19 for BA in Problem 10.21.

Matrix BA is defined; $3 \times 2 = 2 \times 2$; the product matrix will be 3×2.

$$BA = \begin{bmatrix} 2 & 9 \\ 4 & 6 \\ 7 & 5 \end{bmatrix} \begin{bmatrix} 3 & 1 \\ 8 & 2 \end{bmatrix} = \begin{bmatrix} R_1 C_1 & R_1 C_2 \\ R_2 C_1 & R_2 C_2 \\ R_3 C_1 & R_3 C_2 \end{bmatrix} = \begin{bmatrix} 2(3) + 9(8) & 2(1) + 9(2) \\ 4(3) + 6(8) & 4(1) + 6(2) \\ 7(3) + 5(8) & 7(1) + 5(2) \end{bmatrix} = \begin{bmatrix} 78 & 20 \\ 60 & 16 \\ 61 & 17 \end{bmatrix}$$

10.23. Redo Problem 10.19 for AB' in Problem 10.21, where B' is the transpose of B:

$$B' = \begin{bmatrix} 2 & 4 & 7 \\ 9 & 6 & 5 \end{bmatrix}$$

Matrix AB' is defined; $2 \times 2 = 2 \times 3$; the product will be a 2×3 matrix.

$$AB' = \begin{bmatrix} 3 & 1 \\ 8 & 2 \end{bmatrix} \begin{bmatrix} 2 & 4 & 7 \\ 9 & 6 & 5 \end{bmatrix} = \begin{bmatrix} 3(2) + 1(9) & 3(4) + 1(6) & 3(7) + 1(5) \\ 8(2) + 2(9) & 8(4) + 2(6) & 8(7) + 2(5) \end{bmatrix} = \begin{bmatrix} 15 & 18 & 26 \\ 34 & 44 & 66 \end{bmatrix}$$

(Note from Problems 10.21 to 10.23 that $AB \neq BA \neq AB'$. The noncommutative aspects of matrix multiplication are treated in Problems 10.36 to 10.41.)

10.24. Redo Problem 10.19, given

$$A = \begin{bmatrix} 7 & 11 \\ 2 & 9 \\ 10 & 6 \end{bmatrix} \qquad B = \begin{bmatrix} 12 & 4 & 5 \\ 3 & 6 & 1 \end{bmatrix}$$

Matrix AB is defined; $3 \times 2 = 2 \times 3$. The product matrix will be 3×3.

$$AB = \begin{bmatrix} R_1 C_1 & R_1 C_2 & R_1 C_3 \\ R_2 C_1 & R_2 C_2 & R_2 C_3 \\ R_3 C_1 & R_3 C_2 & R_3 C_3 \end{bmatrix} = \begin{bmatrix} 7(12) + 11(3) & 7(4) + 11(6) & 7(5) + 11(1) \\ 2(12) + 9(3) & 2(4) + 9(6) & 2(5) + 9(1) \\ 10(12) + 6(3) & 10(4) + 6(6) & 10(5) + 6(1) \end{bmatrix} = \begin{bmatrix} 117 & 94 & 46 \\ 51 & 62 & 19 \\ 138 & 76 & 56 \end{bmatrix}$$

10.25. Redo Problem 10.19, given

$$A = \begin{bmatrix} 6 & 2 & 5 \\ 7 & 9 & 4 \end{bmatrix} \qquad B = \begin{bmatrix} 10 & 1 \\ 11 & 3 \\ 2 & 9 \end{bmatrix}$$

Matrix AB is defined; $2 \times 3 = 3 \times 2$. The product matrix will be 2×2.

$$AB = \begin{bmatrix} R_1 C_1 & R_1 C_2 \\ R_2 C_1 & R_2 C_2 \end{bmatrix} = \begin{bmatrix} 6(10) + 2(11) + 5(2) & 6(1) + 2(3) + 5(9) \\ 7(10) + 9(11) + 4(2) & 7(1) + 9(3) + 4(9) \end{bmatrix} = \begin{bmatrix} 92 & 57 \\ 177 & 70 \end{bmatrix}$$

10.26. Redo Problem 10.19, given

$$A = [2 \quad 3 \quad 5] \qquad B = \begin{bmatrix} 7 & 1 & 6 \\ 5 & 2 & 4 \\ 9 & 2 & 7 \end{bmatrix}$$

Matrix AB is defined; $1 \times \boxed{3 \;=\; 3} \times 3$. The product matrix will be 1×3.

$$AB = [R_1C_1 \quad R_1C_2 \quad R_1C_3] = [2(7) + 3(5) + 5(9) \quad 2(1) + 3(2) + 5(2) \quad 2(6) + 3(4) + 5(7)] = [74 \quad 18 \quad 59]$$

10.27. Redo Problem 10.19, given

$$A = \begin{bmatrix} 5 \\ 1 \\ 10 \end{bmatrix} \qquad B = \begin{bmatrix} 3 & 9 & 4 \\ 2 & 1 & 8 \\ 5 & 6 & 1 \end{bmatrix}$$

Matrix AB is not defined; $3 \times \boxed{1 \;\neq\; 3} \times 3$. Multiplication is impossible in the given order.

10.28. Find BA from Problem 10.27.

Matrix BA is defined; $3 \times \boxed{3 \;=\; 3} \times 1$. The product matrix will be 3×1.

$$BA = \begin{bmatrix} 3 & 9 & 4 \\ 2 & 1 & 8 \\ 5 & 6 & 1 \end{bmatrix} \begin{bmatrix} 5 \\ 1 \\ 10 \end{bmatrix} = \begin{bmatrix} R_1C_1 \\ R_2C_1 \\ R_3C_1 \end{bmatrix} = \begin{bmatrix} 3(5) + 9(1) + 4(10) \\ 2(5) + 1(1) + 8(10) \\ 5(5) + 6(1) + 1(10) \end{bmatrix} = \begin{bmatrix} 64 \\ 91 \\ 41 \end{bmatrix}$$

10.29. Redo Problem 10.19, given

$$A = \begin{bmatrix} 2 & 1 & 5 \\ 3 & 2 & 6 \\ 1 & 4 & 3 \end{bmatrix} \qquad B = \begin{bmatrix} 10 & 1 & 2 \\ 5 & 3 & 6 \\ 2 & 1 & 2 \end{bmatrix}$$

Matrix AB is defined; $3 \times \boxed{3 \;=\; 3} \times 3$. The product matrix will be 3×3.

$$AB = \begin{bmatrix} R_1C_1 & R_1C_2 & R_1C_3 \\ R_2C_1 & R_2C_2 & R_2C_3 \\ R_3C_1 & R_3C_2 & R_3C_3 \end{bmatrix} = \begin{bmatrix} 2(10) + 1(5) + 5(2) & 2(1) + 1(3) + 5(1) & 2(2) + 1(6) + 5(2) \\ 3(10) + 2(5) + 6(2) & 3(1) + 2(3) + 6(1) & 3(2) + 2(6) + 6(2) \\ 1(10) + 4(5) + 3(2) & 1(1) + 4(3) + 3(1) & 1(2) + 4(6) + 3(2) \end{bmatrix}$$

$$= \begin{bmatrix} 35 & 10 & 20 \\ 52 & 15 & 30 \\ 36 & 16 & 32 \end{bmatrix}$$

10.30. Redo Problem 10.19, given

$$A = \begin{bmatrix} 3 \\ 1 \\ 4 \\ 5 \end{bmatrix} \qquad B = [2 \quad 6 \quad 5 \quad 3]$$

Matrix AB is defined; $4 \times \boxed{1 \;=\; 1} \times 4$. The product matrix will be 4×4.

$$AB = \begin{bmatrix} R_1C_1 & R_1C_2 & R_1C_3 & R_1C_4 \\ R_2C_1 & R_2C_2 & R_2C_3 & R_2C_4 \\ R_3C_1 & R_3C_2 & R_3C_3 & R_3C_4 \\ R_4C_1 & R_4C_2 & R_4C_3 & R_4C_4 \end{bmatrix} = \begin{bmatrix} 3(2) & 3(6) & 3(5) & 3(3) \\ 1(2) & 1(6) & 1(5) & 1(3) \\ 4(2) & 4(6) & 4(5) & 4(3) \\ 5(2) & 5(6) & 5(5) & 5(3) \end{bmatrix} = \begin{bmatrix} 6 & 18 & 15 & 9 \\ 2 & 6 & 5 & 3 \\ 8 & 24 & 20 & 12 \\ 10 & 30 & 25 & 15 \end{bmatrix}$$

10.31. Find AB when

$$A = \begin{bmatrix} 3 & 9 & 8 & 7 \end{bmatrix} \qquad B = \begin{bmatrix} 2 \\ 5 \\ 3 \end{bmatrix}$$

Matrix AB is undefined and cannot be multiplied as given; $1 \times 4 \neq 3 \times 1$.

10.32. Find BA from Problem 10.31.

Matrix BA is defined; $3 \times 1 = 1 \times 4$. The product matrix will be 3×4.

$$BA = \begin{bmatrix} R_1C_1 & R_1C_2 & R_1C_3 & R_1C_4 \\ R_2C_1 & R_2C_2 & R_2C_3 & R_2C_4 \\ R_3C_1 & R_3C_2 & R_3C_3 & R_3C_4 \end{bmatrix} = \begin{bmatrix} 2 \\ 5 \\ 3 \end{bmatrix} \begin{bmatrix} 3 & 9 & 8 & 7 \end{bmatrix}$$

$$= \begin{bmatrix} 2(3) & 2(9) & 2(8) & 2(7) \\ 5(3) & 5(9) & 5(8) & 5(7) \\ 3(3) & 3(9) & 3(8) & 3(7) \end{bmatrix} = \begin{bmatrix} 6 & 18 & 16 & 14 \\ 15 & 45 & 40 & 35 \\ 9 & 27 & 24 & 21 \end{bmatrix}$$

10.33. Use the inventory matrix for the company in Problem 10.3 and the price vector from Problem 10.17 to determine the value of inventory in all five of the company's outlets.

$V = QP.$ $\qquad QP$ is defined; $5 \times 4 = 4 \times 1$; V will be 5×1.

$$V = \begin{bmatrix} 10 & 15 & 9 & 12 \\ 20 & 14 & 8 & 5 \\ 16 & 8 & 15 & 6 \\ 25 & 15 & 7 & 16 \\ 5 & 12 & 20 & 18 \end{bmatrix} \begin{bmatrix} 300 \\ 250 \\ 175 \\ 125 \end{bmatrix} = \begin{bmatrix} R_1C_1 \\ R_2C_1 \\ R_3C_1 \\ R_4C_1 \\ R_5C_1 \end{bmatrix} = \begin{bmatrix} 10(300) + 15(250) + 9(175) + 12(125) \\ 20(300) + 14(250) + 8(175) + 5(125) \\ 16(300) + 8(250) + 15(175) + 6(125) \\ 25(300) + 15(250) + 7(175) + 16(125) \\ 5(300) + 12(250) + 20(175) + 18(125) \end{bmatrix} = \begin{bmatrix} 9\,825 \\ 11\,525 \\ 10\,175 \\ 14\,475 \\ 10\,250 \end{bmatrix}$$

THE COMMUTATIVE LAW AND MATRIX OPERATIONS

10.34. To illustrate the commutative or noncommutative aspects of matrix operations (that is, $A \pm B = B \pm A$, but in general, $AB \neq BA$), find (a) $A + B$ and (b) $B + A$, given

$$A = \begin{bmatrix} 7 & 3 & 2 \\ 1 & 4 & 6 \\ 2 & 5 & 4 \end{bmatrix} \qquad B = \begin{bmatrix} 2 & 0 & 5 \\ 3 & 4 & 1 \\ 7 & 9 & 6 \end{bmatrix}$$

(a) $\quad A + B = \begin{bmatrix} 7+2 & 3+0 & 2+5 \\ 1+3 & 4+4 & 6+1 \\ 2+7 & 5+9 & 4+6 \end{bmatrix} = \begin{bmatrix} 9 & 3 & 7 \\ 4 & 8 & 7 \\ 9 & 14 & 10 \end{bmatrix}$

(b) $\quad B + A = \begin{bmatrix} 2+7 & 0+3 & 5+2 \\ 3+1 & 4+4 & 1+6 \\ 7+2 & 9+5 & 6+4 \end{bmatrix} = \begin{bmatrix} 9 & 3 & 7 \\ 4 & 8 & 7 \\ 9 & 14 & 10 \end{bmatrix}$

$A + B = B + A$. This illustrates that the commutative law does apply to matrix addition.

Problems 10.35 to 10.42 illustrate the application of the commutative law to other matrix operations.

10.35. Find (a) $A - B$ and (b) $-B + A$, given

$$A = \begin{bmatrix} 5 & 3 \\ 4 & 9 \\ 10 & 8 \\ 6 & 12 \end{bmatrix} \qquad B = \begin{bmatrix} 3 & 13 \\ 7 & 9 \\ 2 & 1 \\ 8 & 6 \end{bmatrix}$$

(a) $A - B = \begin{bmatrix} 5-3 & 3-13 \\ 4-7 & 9-9 \\ 10-2 & 8-1 \\ 6-8 & 12-6 \end{bmatrix} = \begin{bmatrix} 2 & -10 \\ -3 & 0 \\ 8 & 7 \\ -2 & 6 \end{bmatrix}$

(b) $-B + A = \begin{bmatrix} -3+5 & -13+3 \\ -7+4 & -9+9 \\ -2+10 & -1+8 \\ -8+6 & -6+12 \end{bmatrix} = \begin{bmatrix} 2 & -10 \\ -3 & 0 \\ 8 & 7 \\ -2 & 6 \end{bmatrix}$

$A - B = -B + A$. This illustrates that matrix subtraction is commutative.

10.36. Find (a) AB and (b) BA, given

$$A = \begin{bmatrix} 4 & 12 & 9 & 6 \end{bmatrix} \qquad B = \begin{bmatrix} 13 \\ 5 \\ -2 \\ 7 \end{bmatrix}$$

Check for conformability first and indicate the dimensions of the product matrix.

(a) Matrix AB is defined; $1 \times \overparen{4 \quad = \quad 4} \times 1$. The product will be a 1×1 matrix or scalar.

$$AB = [4(13) + 12(5) + 9(-2) + 6(7)] = 136$$

(b) Matrix BA is also defined; $4 \times \overparen{1 \quad = \quad 1} \times 4$; the product will be a 4×4 matrix.

$$BA = \begin{bmatrix} 13(4) & 13(12) & 13(9) & 13(6) \\ 5(4) & 5(12) & 5(9) & 5(6) \\ -2(4) & -2(12) & -2(9) & -2(6) \\ 7(4) & 7(12) & 7(9) & 7(6) \end{bmatrix} = \begin{bmatrix} 52 & 156 & 117 & 78 \\ 20 & 60 & 45 & 30 \\ -8 & -24 & -18 & -12 \\ 28 & 84 & 63 & 42 \end{bmatrix}$$

$AB \neq BA$. This illustrates the noncommutative aspect of matrix multiplication. Products generally differ in dimensions and elements if the order of multiplication is reversed.

10.37. Find (a) AB and (b) BA, given

$$A = \begin{bmatrix} 7 & 4 \\ 6 & 2 \\ 1 & 8 \end{bmatrix} \qquad B = \begin{bmatrix} -3 & 9 & 1 \\ 2 & 12 & 7 \end{bmatrix}$$

(a) Matrix AB is defined; $3 \times 2 = 2 \times 3$; the product will be 3×3.

$$AB = \begin{bmatrix} 7(-3)+4(2) & 7(9)+4(12) & 7(1)+4(7) \\ 6(-3)+2(2) & 6(9)+2(12) & 6(1)+2(7) \\ 1(-3)+8(2) & 1(9)+8(12) & 1(1)+8(7) \end{bmatrix} = \begin{bmatrix} -13 & 111 & 35 \\ -14 & 78 & 20 \\ 13 & 105 & 57 \end{bmatrix}$$

(b) Matrix BA is also defined; $2 \times 3 = 3 \times 2$; the product will be 2×2.

$$BA = \begin{bmatrix} -3(7)+9(6)+1(1) & -3(4)+9(2)+1(8) \\ 2(7)+12(6)+7(1) & 2(4)+12(2)+7(8) \end{bmatrix} = \begin{bmatrix} 34 & 14 \\ 93 & 88 \end{bmatrix}$$

$AB \neq BA$. Matrix multiplication is not commutative. Here the products again differ in dimensions and elements.

10.38. Find (a) AB and (b) BA, given

$$A = \begin{bmatrix} 4 & 9 & 8 \\ 7 & 6 & 2 \\ 1 & 5 & 3 \end{bmatrix} \qquad B = \begin{bmatrix} 1 & 2 & 0 \\ 5 & 3 & 1 \\ 0 & 2 & 4 \end{bmatrix}$$

(a) Matrix AB is defined; $3 \times 3 = 3 \times 3$; the product will be 3×3.

$$AB = \begin{bmatrix} 4(1)+9(5)+8(0) & 4(2)+9(3)+8(2) & 4(0)+9(1)+8(4) \\ 7(1)+6(5)+2(0) & 7(2)+6(3)+2(2) & 7(0)+6(1)+2(4) \\ 1(1)+5(5)+3(0) & 1(2)+5(3)+3(2) & 1(0)+5(1)+3(4) \end{bmatrix} = \begin{bmatrix} 49 & 51 & 41 \\ 37 & 36 & 14 \\ 26 & 23 & 17 \end{bmatrix}$$

(b) Matrix BA is also defined and will result in a 3×3 matrix.

$$BA = \begin{bmatrix} 1(4)+2(7)+0(1) & 1(9)+2(6)+0(5) & 1(8)+2(2)+0(3) \\ 5(4)+3(7)+1(1) & 5(9)+3(6)+1(5) & 5(8)+3(2)+1(3) \\ 0(4)+2(7)+4(1) & 0(9)+2(6)+4(5) & 0(8)+2(2)+4(3) \end{bmatrix} = \begin{bmatrix} 18 & 21 & 12 \\ 42 & 68 & 49 \\ 18 & 32 & 16 \end{bmatrix}$$

$AB \neq BA$. The dimensions are the same but the elements differ.

10.39. Find (a) AB and (b) BA, given

$$A = \begin{bmatrix} 7 & 5 & 2 & 6 \\ 1 & 3 & 9 & 4 \end{bmatrix} \qquad B = \begin{bmatrix} 1 \\ 0 \\ -1 \\ 3 \end{bmatrix}$$

(a) Matrix AB is defined; $2 \times 4 = 4 \times 1$; the product will be 2×1.

$$AB = \begin{bmatrix} 7(1)+5(0)+2(-1)+6(3) \\ 1(1)+3(0)+9(-1)+4(3) \end{bmatrix} = \begin{bmatrix} 23 \\ 4 \end{bmatrix}$$

(b) Matrix BA is not defined; $4 \times 1 \neq 2 \times 4$. Multiplication is impossible. This is but another way in which matrix multiplication is noncommutative.

10.40. Find (a) AB and (b) BA, given

$$A = \begin{bmatrix} 11 & 14 \\ 2 & 6 \end{bmatrix} \qquad B = \begin{bmatrix} 7 & 6 \\ 4 & 5 \\ 1 & 3 \end{bmatrix}$$

(a) Matrix AB is not defined; $2 \times 2 \neq 3 \times 2$ and so cannot be multiplied.

(b) Matrix BA is defined; $3 \times 2 = 2 \times 2$ and will produce a 3×2 matrix.

$$BA = \begin{bmatrix} 7(11) + 6(2) & 7(14) + 6(6) \\ 4(11) + 5(2) & 4(14) + 5(6) \\ 1(11) + 3(2) & 1(14) + 3(6) \end{bmatrix} = \begin{bmatrix} 89 & 134 \\ 54 & 86 \\ 17 & 32 \end{bmatrix}$$

$BA \neq AB$, because AB does not exist.

10.41. Find (a) AB and (b) BA, given

$$A = \begin{bmatrix} -2 \\ 4 \\ 7 \end{bmatrix} \qquad B = \begin{bmatrix} 3 & 6 & -2 \end{bmatrix}$$

(a) Matrix AB is defined; $3 \times 1 = 1 \times 3$; the product will be a 3×3 matrix.

$$AB = \begin{bmatrix} -2(3) & -2(6) & -2(-2) \\ 4(3) & 4(6) & 4(-2) \\ 7(3) & 7(6) & 7(-2) \end{bmatrix} = \begin{bmatrix} -6 & -12 & 4 \\ 12 & 24 & -8 \\ 21 & 42 & -14 \end{bmatrix}$$

(b) Matrix BA is also defined; $1 \times 3 = 3 \times 1$, producing a 1×1 matrix or scalar.

$$BA = [3(-2) + 6(4) + (-2)(7)] = 4$$

Since matrix multiplication is not commutative, reversing the order of multiplication can lead to widely different answers. Matrix AB results in a 3×3 matrix, BA results in a scalar.

10.42. Find (a) AB and (b) BA, for a case where B is an identity matrix, given

$$A = \begin{bmatrix} 23 & 6 & 14 \\ 18 & 12 & 9 \\ 24 & 2 & 6 \end{bmatrix} \qquad B = \begin{bmatrix} 1 & 0 & 0 \\ 0 & 1 & 0 \\ 0 & 0 & 1 \end{bmatrix}$$

(a) Matrix AB is defined; $3 \times 3 = 3 \times 3$. The product matrix will also be 3×3.

$$AB = \begin{bmatrix} 23(1) + 6(0) + 14(0) & 23(0) + 6(1) + 14(0) & 23(0) + 6(0) + 14(1) \\ 18(1) + 12(0) + 9(0) & 18(0) + 12(1) + 9(0) & 18(0) + 12(0) + 9(1) \\ 24(1) + 2(0) + 6(0) & 24(0) + 2(1) + 6(0) & 24(0) + 2(0) + 6(1) \end{bmatrix} = \begin{bmatrix} 23 & 6 & 14 \\ 18 & 12 & 9 \\ 24 & 2 & 6 \end{bmatrix}$$

(b) Matrix BA is also defined; $3 \times 3 = 3 \times 3$. The product matrix will also be 3×3.

$$BA = \begin{bmatrix} 1(23) + 0(18) + 0(24) & 1(6) + 0(12) + 0(2) & 1(14) + 0(9) + 0(6) \\ 0(23) + 1(18) + 0(24) & 0(6) + 1(12) + 0(2) & 0(14) + 1(9) + 0(6) \\ 0(23) + 0(18) + 1(24) & 0(6) + 0(12) + 1(2) & 0(14) + 0(9) + 1(6) \end{bmatrix} = \begin{bmatrix} 23 & 6 & 14 \\ 18 & 12 & 9 \\ 24 & 2 & 6 \end{bmatrix}$$

Here $AB = BA$. Premultiplication or postmultiplication by an identity matrix gives the original matrix. Thus in the case of an identity matrix, matrix multiplication is commutative. This will also be true of a matrix and its inverse. See Section 11.7.

ASSOCIATIVE AND DISTRIBUTIVE LAWS

10.43. To illustrate whether the associative and distributive laws apply to matrix operations [that is, $(A + B) + C = A + (B + C)$, $(AB)C = A(BC)$, and $A(B + C) = AB + AC$, subject to the conditions in Section 10.7], find (a) $(A + B) + C$ and (b) $A + (B + C)$, given

$$A = \begin{bmatrix} 6 & 2 & 7 \\ 9 & 5 & 3 \end{bmatrix} \qquad B = \begin{bmatrix} 9 & 1 & 3 \\ 4 & 2 & 6 \end{bmatrix} \qquad C = \begin{bmatrix} 7 & 5 & 1 \\ 10 & 3 & 8 \end{bmatrix}$$

(a)
$$A + B = \begin{bmatrix} 6+9 & 2+1 & 7+3 \\ 9+4 & 5+2 & 3+6 \end{bmatrix} = \begin{bmatrix} 15 & 3 & 10 \\ 13 & 7 & 9 \end{bmatrix}$$

$$(A + B) + C = \begin{bmatrix} 15+7 & 3+5 & 10+1 \\ 13+10 & 7+3 & 9+8 \end{bmatrix} = \begin{bmatrix} 22 & 8 & 11 \\ 23 & 10 & 17 \end{bmatrix}$$

(b)
$$B + C = \begin{bmatrix} 9+7 & 1+5 & 3+1 \\ 4+10 & 2+3 & 6+8 \end{bmatrix} = \begin{bmatrix} 16 & 6 & 4 \\ 14 & 5 & 14 \end{bmatrix}$$

$$A + (B + C) = \begin{bmatrix} 6+16 & 2+6 & 7+4 \\ 9+14 & 5+5 & 3+14 \end{bmatrix} = \begin{bmatrix} 22 & 8 & 11 \\ 23 & 10 & 17 \end{bmatrix}$$

Thus, $(A + B) + C = A + (B + C)$. This illustrates that matrix addition is associative. Other aspects of these laws are demonstrated in Problems 10.44 to 10.47.

10.44. Find (a) $(A - B) + C$ and (b) $A + (-B + C)$, given

$$A = \begin{bmatrix} 7 \\ 6 \\ 12 \end{bmatrix} \qquad B = \begin{bmatrix} 3 \\ 8 \\ 5 \end{bmatrix} \qquad C = \begin{bmatrix} 13 \\ 2 \\ 6 \end{bmatrix}$$

(a) $A - B = \begin{bmatrix} 7-3 \\ 6-8 \\ 12-5 \end{bmatrix} = \begin{bmatrix} 4 \\ -2 \\ 7 \end{bmatrix}$ (b) $-B + C = \begin{bmatrix} -3+13 \\ -8+2 \\ -5+6 \end{bmatrix} = \begin{bmatrix} 10 \\ -6 \\ 1 \end{bmatrix}$

$(A - B) + C = \begin{bmatrix} 4+13 \\ -2+2 \\ 7+6 \end{bmatrix} = \begin{bmatrix} 17 \\ 0 \\ 13 \end{bmatrix}$ $A + (-B + C) = \begin{bmatrix} 7+10 \\ 6+(-6) \\ 12+1 \end{bmatrix} = \begin{bmatrix} 17 \\ 0 \\ 13 \end{bmatrix}$

Matrix subtraction is also associative.

10.45. Find (a) $(AB)C$ and (b) $A(BC)$, given

$$A = \begin{bmatrix} 7 & 1 & 5 \end{bmatrix} \qquad B = \begin{bmatrix} 6 & 5 \\ 2 & 4 \\ 3 & 8 \end{bmatrix} \qquad C = \begin{bmatrix} 9 & 4 \\ 3 & 10 \end{bmatrix}$$

(a)   Matrix AB is defined; $1 \times \overset{\frown}{3} = \overset{\frown}{3} \times 2$, producing a 1×2 matrix.

$$AB = [7(6) + 1(2) + 5(3) \quad 7(5) + 1(4) + 5(8)] = [59 \quad 79]$$

Matrix $(AB)C$ is defined; $1 \times \overset{\frown}{2} = \overset{\frown}{2} \times 2$, leaving a 1×2 matrix.

$$(AB)C = [59(9) + 79(3) \quad 59(4) + 79(10)] = [768 \quad 1026]$$

(b)   Matrix BC is defined; $3 \times \overset{\frown}{2} = \overset{\frown}{2} \times 2$, creating a 3×2 matrix.

$$BC = \begin{bmatrix} 6(9) + 5(3) & 6(4) + 5(10) \\ 2(9) + 4(3) & 2(4) + 4(10) \\ 3(9) + 8(3) & 3(4) + 8(10) \end{bmatrix} = \begin{bmatrix} 69 & 74 \\ 30 & 48 \\ 51 & 92 \end{bmatrix}$$

Matrix $A(BC)$ is also defined; $1 \times \overset{\frown}{3} = \overset{\frown}{3} \times 2$, producing a 1×2 matrix.

$$A(BC) = [7(69) + 1(30) + 5(51) \quad 7(74) + 1(48) + 5(92)] = [768 \quad 1026]$$

Matrix multiplication is associative, provided the proper order of multiplication is maintained.

10.46. Find (a) $A(B + C)$ and (b) $AB + AC$, given

$$A = [4 \quad 7 \quad 2] \qquad B = \begin{bmatrix} 6 \\ 5 \\ 1 \end{bmatrix} \qquad C = \begin{bmatrix} 9 \\ 5 \\ 8 \end{bmatrix}$$

(a)

$$B + C = \begin{bmatrix} 6 + 9 \\ 5 + 5 \\ 1 + 8 \end{bmatrix} = \begin{bmatrix} 15 \\ 10 \\ 9 \end{bmatrix}$$

Matrix $A(B + C)$ is defined; $1 \times 3 = 3 \times 1$. The product matrix will be 1×1.

$$A(B + C) = [4(15) + 7(10) + 2(9)] = 148$$

(b) Matrix AB is defined; $1 \times 3 = 3 \times 1$, producing a 1×1 matrix.

$$AB = [4(6) + 7(5) + 2(1)] = 61$$

Matrix AC is defined; $1 \times 3 = 3 \times 1$, also producing a 1×1 matrix.

$$AC = [4(9) + 7(5) + 2(8)] = 87$$

Thus, $AB + AC = 61 + 87 = 148$. This illustrates the distributive law of matrix multiplication.

10.47. A hamburger chain sells 1000 hamburgers, 600 cheeseburgers, and 1200 milk shakes in a week. The price of a hamburger is 45¢, a cheeseburger 60¢, and a milk shake 50¢. The cost to the chain of a hamburger is 38¢, a cheeseburger 42¢, and a milk shake 32¢. Find the firm's profit for the week, using (a) total concepts and (b) per-unit analysis to prove that matrix multiplication is distributive.

(a) The quantity of goods sold Q, the selling price of the goods P, and the cost of goods C can all be represented in matrix form:

$$Q = \begin{bmatrix} 1000 \\ 600 \\ 1200 \end{bmatrix} \qquad P = \begin{bmatrix} 0.45 \\ 0.60 \\ 0.50 \end{bmatrix} \qquad C = \begin{bmatrix} 0.38 \\ 0.42 \\ 0.32 \end{bmatrix}$$

Total revenue TR is

$$TR = PQ = \begin{bmatrix} 0.45 \\ 0.60 \\ 0.50 \end{bmatrix} \begin{bmatrix} 1000 \\ 600 \\ 1200 \end{bmatrix}$$

which is not defined as given. Taking the transpose of P or Q will render the vectors conformable for multiplication. Note that the order of multiplication is all-important. Row-vector multiplication ($P'Q$ or $Q'P$) will produce the scalar required; vector-row multiplication (PQ' or QP') will produce a 3×3 matrix that has no economic meaning. Thus, taking the transpose of P and premultiplying, we get

$$TR = P'Q = [0.45 \quad 0.60 \quad 0.50] \begin{bmatrix} 1000 \\ 600 \\ 1200 \end{bmatrix}$$

where $P'Q$ is defined; $1 \times 3 = 3 \times 1$, producing a 1×1 matrix or scalar.

$$TR = [0.45(1000) + 0.60(600) + 0.50(1200)] = 1410$$

Similarly, total cost TC is $TC = C'Q$:

$$TC = [0.38 \quad 0.42 \quad 0.32] \begin{bmatrix} 1000 \\ 600 \\ 1200 \end{bmatrix} = [0.38(1000) + 0.42(600) + 0.32(1200)] = 1016$$

Profits, therefore, are

$$\Pi = TR - TC = 1410 - 1016 = 394$$

(b) Using per-unit analysis, the per-unit profit U is

$$U = P - C = \begin{bmatrix} 0.45 \\ 0.60 \\ 0.50 \end{bmatrix} - \begin{bmatrix} 0.38 \\ 0.42 \\ 0.32 \end{bmatrix} = \begin{bmatrix} 0.07 \\ 0.18 \\ 0.18 \end{bmatrix}$$

Total profit Π is per-unit profit times the number of items sold

$$\Pi = UQ = \begin{bmatrix} 0.07 \\ 0.18 \\ 0.18 \end{bmatrix} \begin{bmatrix} 1000 \\ 600 \\ 1200 \end{bmatrix}$$

which is undefined. Taking the transpose of U,

$$\Pi = U'P = [0.07 \quad 0.18 \quad 0.18] \begin{bmatrix} 1000 \\ 600 \\ 1200 \end{bmatrix}$$

$$= [0.07(1000) + 0.18(600) + 0.18(1200)] = 394 \qquad \text{Q.E.D.}$$

10.48. Crazy Teddie's sells 700 CDs, 400 cassettes, and 200 CD players each week. The selling price of CDs is \$4, cassettes \$6, and CD players \$150. The cost to the shop is \$3.25 for a CD, \$4.75 for a cassette, and \$125 for a CD player. Find weekly profits by using (a) total and (b) per-unit concepts.

(a)
$$Q = \begin{bmatrix} 700 \\ 400 \\ 200 \end{bmatrix} \qquad P = \begin{bmatrix} 4 \\ 6 \\ 150 \end{bmatrix} \qquad C = \begin{bmatrix} 3.25 \\ 4.75 \\ 125.00 \end{bmatrix}$$

$$TR = P'Q = [4 \quad 6 \quad 150] \begin{bmatrix} 700 \\ 400 \\ 200 \end{bmatrix} = [4(700) + 6(400) + 150(200)] = 35\,200$$

$$TC = C'Q = [3.25 \quad 4.75 \quad 125] \begin{bmatrix} 700 \\ 400 \\ 200 \end{bmatrix} = [3.25(700) + 4.75(400) + 125(200)] = 29\,175$$

$$\Pi = TR - TC = 35\,200 - 29\,175 = 6025$$

(b) Per-unit profit U is

$$U = P - C = \begin{bmatrix} 4 \\ 6 \\ 150 \end{bmatrix} - \begin{bmatrix} 3.25 \\ 4.75 \\ 125.00 \end{bmatrix} = \begin{bmatrix} 0.75 \\ 1.25 \\ 25.00 \end{bmatrix}$$

Total profit Π is

$$\Pi = U'Q = [0.75 \quad 1.25 \quad 25] \begin{bmatrix} 700 \\ 400 \\ 200 \end{bmatrix} = [0.75(700) + 1.25(400) + 25(200)] = 6025$$

UNIQUE PROPERTIES OF MATRICES

10.49. Given

$$A = \begin{bmatrix} 6 & -12 \\ -3 & 6 \end{bmatrix} \qquad B = \begin{bmatrix} 12 & 6 \\ 6 & 3 \end{bmatrix}$$

(a) Find AB. (b) Why is the product unique?

(a)

$$AB = \begin{bmatrix} 6(12) - 12(6) & 6(6) - 12(3) \\ -3(12) + 6(6) & -3(6) + 6(3) \end{bmatrix} = \begin{bmatrix} 0 & 0 \\ 0 & 0 \end{bmatrix}$$

(b) The product AB is unique to matrix algebra in that, unlike ordinary algebra in which the product of two nonzero numbers can never equal zero, the product of two non-null matrices may produce a null matrix. The reason for this is that the two original matrices are singular. A *singular matrix* is one in which a row or column is a multiple of another row or column (see Section 11.1). In this problem, row 1 of A is -2 times row 2, and column 2 is -2 times column 1. In B, row 1 is 2 times row 2, and column 1 is 2 times column 2. Thus, in matrix algebra, multiplication involving singular matrices may, but need not, produce a null matrix as a solution. See Problem 10.50.

10.50. (a) Find AB and (b) comment on the solution, given

$$A = \begin{bmatrix} 6 & 12 \\ 3 & 6 \end{bmatrix} \qquad B = \begin{bmatrix} 12 & 6 \\ 6 & 3 \end{bmatrix}$$

(a)

$$AB = \begin{bmatrix} 6(12) + 12(6) & 6(6) + 12(3) \\ 3(12) + 6(6) & 3(6) + 6(3) \end{bmatrix} = \begin{bmatrix} 144 & 72 \\ 72 & 36 \end{bmatrix}$$

(b) While both A and B are singular, they do not produce a null matrix. The product AB, however, is also singular.

10.51. Given

$$A = \begin{bmatrix} 4 & 8 \\ 1 & 2 \end{bmatrix} \qquad B = \begin{bmatrix} 2 & 1 \\ 2 & 2 \end{bmatrix} \qquad C = \begin{bmatrix} -2 & 1 \\ 4 & 2 \end{bmatrix}$$

(a) Find AB and AC. (b) Comment on the unusual property of the solutions.

(a)

$$AB = \begin{bmatrix} 4(2) + 8(2) & 4(1) + 8(2) \\ 1(2) + 2(2) & 1(1) + 2(2) \end{bmatrix} = \begin{bmatrix} 24 & 20 \\ 6 & 5 \end{bmatrix}$$

$$AC = \begin{bmatrix} 4(-2) + 8(4) & 4(1) + 8(2) \\ 1(-2) + 2(4) & 1(1) + 2(2) \end{bmatrix} = \begin{bmatrix} 24 & 20 \\ 6 & 5 \end{bmatrix}$$

(b) Even though $B \neq C$, $AB = AC$. Unlike algebra where multiplication of one number by two different numbers cannot give the same product, in matrix algebra multiplication of one matrix by two different matrices may, but need not, produce identical matrices. In this case, A is a singular matrix.

GAUSSIAN METHOD OF SOLVING MATRIX EQUATIONS

10.52. Express the following system of linear equations in (a) matrix form and (b) an augmented matrix, letting $A =$ the coefficient matrix, $X =$ the column vector of variables, and $B =$ the column vector of parameters.

$$7x_1 + 8x_2 = 120$$
$$6x_1 + 9x_2 = 98$$

(a)

$$AX = B$$

$$\begin{bmatrix} 7 & 8 \\ 6 & 9 \end{bmatrix} \begin{bmatrix} x_1 \\ x_2 \end{bmatrix} = \begin{bmatrix} 120 \\ 98 \end{bmatrix}$$

(b)
$$A\,|\,B = \begin{bmatrix} 7 & 8 & 120 \\ 6 & 9 & 98 \end{bmatrix}$$

10.53. Redo Problem 10.52, given

$$4x_1 + 2x_2 + 9x_3 = 149$$
$$2x_1 + 8x_2 + 7x_3 = 204$$
$$5x_1 + 6x_2 + 3x_3 = 168$$

(a)
$$AX = B$$
$$\begin{bmatrix} 4 & 2 & 9 \\ 2 & 8 & 7 \\ 5 & 6 & 3 \end{bmatrix}\begin{bmatrix} x_1 \\ x_2 \\ x_3 \end{bmatrix} = \begin{bmatrix} 149 \\ 204 \\ 168 \end{bmatrix}$$

(b)
$$A\,|\,B = \begin{bmatrix} 4 & 2 & 9 & 149 \\ 2 & 8 & 7 & 204 \\ 5 & 6 & 3 & 168 \end{bmatrix}$$

10.54. Use the Gaussian elimination method to solve the following system of linear equations:

$$3x_1 + 6x_2 = 60$$
$$5x_1 + 4x_2 = 52$$

First, express the system of equations in augmented matrix form.

$$\begin{bmatrix} 3 & 6 & 60 \\ 5 & 4 & 52 \end{bmatrix}$$

Then apply row operations to convert the coefficient matrix on the left to an identity matrix. The simplest way to do this is to get 1 as the first element on the principal diagonal and clear column 1, then get 1 as the second element on the principal diagonal and clear column 2, etc., as follows:

1a.   Multiply row 1 by $\frac{1}{3}$:

$$\begin{bmatrix} 1 & 2 & 20 \\ 5 & 4 & 52 \end{bmatrix}$$

1b.   Subtract 5 times row 1 from row 2:

$$\begin{bmatrix} 1 & 2 & 20 \\ 0 & -6 & -48 \end{bmatrix}$$

2a.   Multiply row 2 by $-\frac{1}{6}$:

$$\begin{bmatrix} 1 & 2 & 20 \\ 0 & 1 & 8 \end{bmatrix}$$

2b.   Finally, subtract 2 times row 2 from row 1:

$$\begin{bmatrix} 1 & 0 & 4 \\ 0 & 1 & 8 \end{bmatrix}$$

Thus, $x_1 = 4$ and $x_2 = 8$, since

$$\begin{bmatrix} 1 & 0 \\ 0 & 1 \end{bmatrix}\begin{bmatrix} x_1 \\ x_2 \end{bmatrix} = \begin{bmatrix} 4 \\ 8 \end{bmatrix}$$

10.55. Redo Problem 10.54, given

$$2x_1 + 8x_2 = 34$$
$$4x_1 + 12x_2 = 56$$

The augmented matrix is

$$\begin{bmatrix} 2 & 8 & | & 34 \\ 4 & 12 & | & 56 \end{bmatrix}$$

1a. Multiply row 1 by $\frac{1}{2}$:

$$\begin{bmatrix} 1 & 4 & | & 17 \\ 4 & 12 & | & 56 \end{bmatrix}$$

1b. Subtract 4 times row 1 from row 2:

$$\begin{bmatrix} 1 & 4 & | & 17 \\ 0 & -4 & | & -12 \end{bmatrix}$$

2a. Multiply row 2 by $-\frac{1}{4}$:

$$\begin{bmatrix} 1 & 4 & | & 17 \\ 0 & 1 & | & 3 \end{bmatrix}$$

2b. Subtract 4 times row 2 from row 1:

$$\begin{bmatrix} 1 & 0 & | & 5 \\ 0 & 1 & | & 3 \end{bmatrix}$$

Thus, $x_1 = 5$ and $x_2 = 3$.

10.56. Redo Problem 10.54, given

$$4x_1 + 10x_2 = 30$$
$$6x_1 + 25x_2 = 67$$

The augmented matrix is

$$\begin{bmatrix} 4 & 10 & | & 30 \\ 6 & 25 & | & 67 \end{bmatrix}$$

1a. Multiply row 1 by $\frac{1}{4}$:

$$\begin{bmatrix} 1 & 2.5 & | & 7.5 \\ 6 & 25 & | & 67 \end{bmatrix}$$

1b. Subtract 6 times row 1 from row 2:

$$\begin{bmatrix} 1 & 2.5 & | & 7.5 \\ 0 & 10 & | & 22 \end{bmatrix}$$

2a. Multiply row 2 by $\frac{1}{10}$:

$$\begin{bmatrix} 1 & 2.5 & | & 7.5 \\ 0 & 1 & | & 2.2 \end{bmatrix}$$

2b. Subtract 2.5 times row 2 from row 1:

$$\begin{bmatrix} 1 & 0 & | & 2 \\ 0 & 1 & | & 2.2 \end{bmatrix}$$

Thus, $x_1 = 2$ and $x_2 = 2.2$.

10.57. Redo Problem 10.54, given

$$3x_1 + 7x_2 = 67$$
$$2x_1 + 9x_2 = 75$$

The augmented matrix is

$$\begin{bmatrix} 3 & 7 & | & 67 \\ 2 & 9 & | & 75 \end{bmatrix}$$

1a. Multiply row 1 by $\frac{1}{3}$:

$$\begin{bmatrix} 1 & \frac{7}{3} & | & \frac{67}{3} \\ 2 & 9 & | & 75 \end{bmatrix}$$

1b. Subtract 2 times row 1 from row 2:

$$\begin{bmatrix} 1 & \frac{7}{3} & | & \frac{67}{3} \\ 0 & \frac{13}{3} & | & \frac{91}{3} \end{bmatrix}$$

2a. Multiply row 2 by $\frac{3}{13}$:

$$\begin{bmatrix} 1 & \frac{7}{3} & | & \frac{67}{3} \\ 0 & 1 & | & 7 \end{bmatrix}$$

2b. Subtract $\frac{7}{3}$ times row 2 from row 1:

$$\begin{bmatrix} 1 & 0 & | & 6 \\ 0 & 1 & | & 7 \end{bmatrix}$$

Thus, $x_1 = 6$ and $x_2 = 7$.

10.58. Solve the following system of linear equations, using the Gaussian elimination method:

$$3x_1 + 2x_2 + 6x_3 = 24$$
$$2x_1 + 4x_2 + 3x_3 = 23$$
$$5x_1 + 3x_2 + 4x_3 = 33$$

The augmented matrix is

$$\begin{bmatrix} 3 & 2 & 6 & | & 24 \\ 2 & 4 & 3 & | & 23 \\ 5 & 3 & 4 & | & 33 \end{bmatrix}$$

1a. Multiply row 1 by $\frac{1}{3}$:

$$\begin{bmatrix} 1 & \frac{2}{3} & 2 & | & 8 \\ 2 & 4 & 3 & | & 23 \\ 5 & 3 & 4 & | & 33 \end{bmatrix}$$

1b. Subtract 2 times row 1 from row 2 and 5 times row 1 from row 3:

$$\begin{bmatrix} 1 & \frac{2}{3} & 2 & | & 8 \\ 0 & \frac{8}{3} & -1 & | & 7 \\ 0 & -\frac{1}{3} & -6 & | & -7 \end{bmatrix}$$

2a. Multiply row 2 by $\frac{3}{8}$:

$$\begin{bmatrix} 1 & \frac{2}{3} & 2 & | & 8 \\ 0 & 1 & -\frac{3}{8} & | & \frac{21}{8} \\ 0 & -\frac{1}{3} & -6 & | & -7 \end{bmatrix}$$

2b. Subtract $\frac{2}{3}$ times row 2 from row 1 and add $\frac{1}{3}$ times row 2 to row 3:

$$\begin{bmatrix} 1 & 0 & \frac{9}{4} & | & \frac{25}{4} \\ 0 & 1 & -\frac{3}{8} & | & \frac{21}{8} \\ 0 & 0 & -\frac{49}{8} & | & -\frac{49}{8} \end{bmatrix}$$

3a. Multiply row 3 by $-\frac{8}{49}$:

$$\begin{bmatrix} 1 & 0 & \frac{9}{4} & | & \frac{25}{4} \\ 0 & 1 & -\frac{3}{8} & | & \frac{21}{8} \\ 0 & 0 & 1 & | & 1 \end{bmatrix}$$

3b. Subtract $\frac{9}{4}$ times row 3 from row 1 and add $\frac{3}{8}$ times row 3 to row 2:

$$\begin{bmatrix} 1 & 0 & 0 & | & 4 \\ 0 & 1 & 0 & | & 3 \\ 0 & 0 & 1 & | & 1 \end{bmatrix}$$

Thus, $x_1 = 4$, $x_2 = 3$, and $x_3 = 1$.

10.59. Redo Problem 10.58, given

$$6x_1 + 2x_2 + 5x_3 = 73$$
$$7x_1 - 3x_2 + x_3 = -1$$
$$4x_1 + 8x_2 - 9x_3 = -9$$

The augmented matrix in this case is

$$\begin{bmatrix} 6 & 2 & 5 & | & 73 \\ 7 & -3 & 1 & | & -1 \\ 4 & 8 & -9 & | & -9 \end{bmatrix}$$

1a. Multiply row 1 by $\frac{1}{6}$:

$$\begin{bmatrix} 1 & \frac{1}{3} & \frac{5}{6} & \Big| & \frac{73}{6} \\ 7 & -3 & 1 & \Big| & -1 \\ 4 & 8 & -9 & \Big| & -9 \end{bmatrix}$$

1b. Subtract 7 times row 1 from row 2 and subtract 4 times row 1 from row 3:

$$\begin{bmatrix} 1 & \frac{1}{3} & \frac{5}{6} & \Big| & \frac{73}{6} \\ 0 & -\frac{16}{3} & -\frac{29}{6} & \Big| & -\frac{517}{6} \\ 0 & \frac{20}{3} & -\frac{74}{6} & \Big| & -\frac{173}{3} \end{bmatrix}$$

2a. Multiply row 2 by $-\frac{3}{16}$:

$$\begin{bmatrix} 1 & \frac{1}{3} & \frac{5}{6} & \Big| & \frac{73}{6} \\ 0 & 1 & \frac{29}{32} & \Big| & \frac{517}{32} \\ 0 & \frac{20}{3} & -\frac{74}{6} & \Big| & -\frac{173}{3} \end{bmatrix}$$

2b. Subtract $\frac{1}{3}$ times row 2 from row 1 and subtract $\frac{20}{3}$ times row 2 from row 3:

$$\begin{bmatrix} 1 & 0 & \frac{51}{96} & \Big| & \frac{651}{96} \\ 0 & 1 & \frac{29}{32} & \Big| & \frac{517}{32} \\ 0 & 0 & -\frac{441}{24} & \Big| & -\frac{3969}{24} \end{bmatrix}$$

3a. Multiply row 3 by $-\frac{24}{441}$:

$$\begin{bmatrix} 1 & 0 & \frac{51}{96} & \Big| & \frac{651}{96} \\ 0 & 1 & \frac{29}{32} & \Big| & \frac{517}{32} \\ 0 & 0 & 1 & \Big| & 9 \end{bmatrix}$$

3b. Subtract $\frac{51}{96}$ times row 3 from row 1 and subtract $\frac{29}{32}$ times row 3 from row 2:

$$\begin{bmatrix} 1 & 0 & 0 & \Big| & 2 \\ 0 & 1 & 0 & \Big| & 8 \\ 0 & 0 & 1 & \Big| & 9 \end{bmatrix}$$

Thus, $x_1 = 2$, $x_2 = 8$, and $x_3 = 9$.

Chapter 11

Matrix Inversion

11.1 DETERMINANTS AND NONSINGULARITY

The determinant $|A|$ of a 2×2 matrix, called a *second-order determinant*, is derived by taking the product of the two elements on the principal diagonal and subtracting from it the product of the two elements off the principal diagonal. Given a general 2×2 matrix

$$A = \begin{bmatrix} a_{11} & a_{12} \\ a_{21} & a_{22} \end{bmatrix}$$

the determinant is

$$|A| = \begin{vmatrix} a_{11} & a_{12} \\ a_{21} & a_{22} \end{vmatrix} \begin{matrix} (-) \\ (+) \end{matrix} = a_{11}a_{22} - a_{12}a_{21}$$

The determinant is a single number or scalar and is found only for square matrices. If the determinant of a matrix is equal to zero, the determinant is said to *vanish* and the matrix is termed *singular*. A *singular matrix* is one in which there exists linear dependence between at least two rows or columns. If $|A| \neq 0$, matrix A is *nonsingular* and all its rows and columns are linearly independent.

The *rank ρ* of a matrix is defined as the maximum number of linearly independent rows or columns in the matrix. See Example 1 and Problems 11.1, 11.3, and 11.22. For proof of nonsingularity and linear independence, see Problem 11.21.

EXAMPLE 1. Determinants are calculated as follows, given

$$A = \begin{bmatrix} 6 & 4 \\ 7 & 9 \end{bmatrix} \qquad B = \begin{bmatrix} 4 & 6 \\ 6 & 9 \end{bmatrix}$$

From the rules stated above,

$$|A| = 6(9) - 4(7) = 26$$

Since $|A| \neq 0$, the matrix is nonsingular, i.e., there is no linear dependence between any of its rows or columns. The rank of A is 2, written $\rho(A) = 2$. By way of contrast,

$$|B| = 4(9) - 6(6) = 0$$

With $|B| = 0$, B is singular and linear dependence exists between its rows and columns. Closer inspection reveals that row 2 and column 2 are equal to 1.5 times row 1 and column 1, respectively. Hence $\rho(B) = 1$.

11.2 THIRD-ORDER DETERMINANTS

The determinant of a 3×3 matrix

$$A = \begin{bmatrix} a_{11} & a_{12} & a_{13} \\ a_{21} & a_{22} & a_{23} \\ a_{31} & a_{32} & a_{33} \end{bmatrix}$$

is called a *third-order determinant* and is the summation of three products. To derive the three products:

1. Take the first element of the first row, a_{11}, and mentally delete the row and column in which it appears. See (a) below. Then multiply a_{11} by the determinant of the remaining elements.

2. Take the second element of the first row, a_{12}, and mentally delete the row and column in which it appears. See (b) below. Then multiply a_{12} by -1 times the determinant of the remaining elements.

3. Take the third element of the first row, a_{13}, and mentally delete the row and column in which it appears. See (c) below. Then multiply a_{13} by the determinant of the remaining elements.

$$
\begin{bmatrix} a_{11} & a_{12} & a_{13} \\ a_{21} & a_{22} & a_{23} \\ a_{31} & a_{32} & a_{33} \end{bmatrix}
\qquad
\begin{bmatrix} a_{11} & a_{12} & a_{13} \\ a_{21} & a_{22} & a_{23} \\ a_{31} & a_{32} & a_{33} \end{bmatrix}
\qquad
\begin{bmatrix} a_{11} & a_{12} & a_{13} \\ a_{21} & a_{22} & a_{23} \\ a_{31} & a_{32} & a_{33} \end{bmatrix}
$$

$$(a)\qquad\qquad\qquad\qquad (b)\qquad\qquad\qquad\qquad (c)$$

Thus, the calculations for the determinant are as follows:

$$
|A| = a_{11}\begin{vmatrix} a_{22} & a_{23} \\ a_{32} & a_{33} \end{vmatrix} + a_{12}(-1)\begin{vmatrix} a_{21} & a_{23} \\ a_{31} & a_{33} \end{vmatrix} + a_{13}\begin{vmatrix} a_{21} & a_{22} \\ a_{31} & a_{32} \end{vmatrix} \tag{11.1}
$$

$$
= a_{11}(a_{22}a_{33} - a_{23}a_{32}) - a_{12}(a_{21}a_{33} - a_{23}a_{31}) + a_{13}(a_{21}a_{32} - a_{22}a_{31})
$$

$$
= \text{a scalar}
$$

See Examples 2 and 3 and Problems 11.2, 11.3, and 11.22.

In like manner, the determinant of a 4×4 matrix is the sum of four products; the determinant of a 5×5 matrix is the sum of five products; etc. See Section 11.4 and Example 6.

EXAMPLE 2.   Given

$$
A = \begin{bmatrix} 8 & 3 & 2 \\ 6 & 4 & 7 \\ 5 & 1 & 3 \end{bmatrix}
$$

the determinant $|A|$ is calculated as follows:

$$
|A| = 8\begin{vmatrix} 4 & 7 \\ 1 & 3 \end{vmatrix} + 3(-1)\begin{vmatrix} 6 & 7 \\ 5 & 3 \end{vmatrix} + 2\begin{vmatrix} 6 & 4 \\ 5 & 1 \end{vmatrix}
$$

$$
= 8\,[4(3) - 7(1)] - 3\,[6(3) - 7(5)] + 2\,[6(1) - 4(5)]
$$

$$
= 8(5) - 3(-17) + 2(-14) = 63
$$

With $|A| \neq 0$, A is nonsingular and $\rho(A) = 3$.

EXAMPLE 3.   An alternative method for calculating a 3×3 determinant is illustrated in Fig. 11-1. To find the determinant of A, simply multiply each of the three elements in the first row by the two elements to which they are connected by a *solid* line and *add* their products. Then multiply each of the same three elements in the first row by the two elements to which they are connected by a *dashed* line and *subtract* the sum of their products from the previous total.

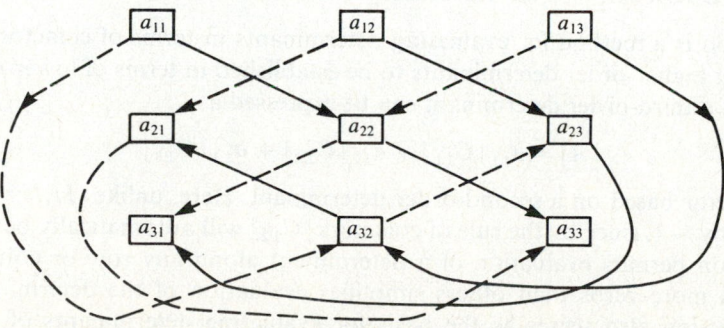

Fig. 11-1

Applying this method to matrix A from Example 2,

$$|A| = (8)(4)(3) + (3)(7)(5) + (2)(1)(6) - [(8)(1)(7) + (3)(6)(3) + (2)(4)(5)]$$
$$= 96 + 105 + 12 - (56 + 54 + 40) = 213 - 150 = 63$$

See Problem 11.2. While convenient, this method unfortunately is not applicable for determinants higher than third-order.

11.3 MINORS AND COFACTORS

The elements of a matrix remaining after the deletion process described in Section 11.2 form a subdeterminant of the matrix called a *minor*. Thus, a *minor* $|M_{ij}|$ is the determinant of the submatrix formed by deleting the ith row and jth column of the matrix. Using the matrix from Section 11.2,

$$|M_{11}| = \begin{vmatrix} a_{22} & a_{23} \\ a_{32} & a_{33} \end{vmatrix} \qquad |M_{12}| = \begin{vmatrix} a_{21} & a_{23} \\ a_{31} & a_{33} \end{vmatrix} \qquad |M_{13}| = \begin{vmatrix} a_{21} & a_{22} \\ a_{31} & a_{32} \end{vmatrix}$$

where $|M_{11}|$ is the minor of a_{11}, $|M_{12}|$ the minor of a_{12}, and $|M_{13}|$ the minor of a_{13}. Thus, the determinant in (11.1) can be written

$$|A| = a_{11}|M_{11}| + a_{12}(-1)|M_{12}| + a_{13}|M_{13}| \qquad (11.2)$$

A *cofactor* $|C_{ij}|$ is a minor with a prescribed sign. The rule for the sign of a cofactor is

$$|C_{ij}| = (-1)^{i+j}|M_{ij}|$$

Thus if the sum of the subscripts is an even number, $|C_{ij}| = |M_{ij}|$, since -1 raised to an even power is positive. If $i + j$ is equal to an odd number, $|C_{ij}| = -|M_{ij}|$, since -1 raised to an odd power is negative. See Example 4 and Problems 11.23 to 11.29.

EXAMPLE 4. The cofactors (1) $|C_{11}|$, (2) $|C_{12}|$, and (3) $|C_{13}|$ for the matrix in Section 11.2 are found as follows:

(1)
$$|C_{11}| = (-1)^{1+1}|M_{11}|$$

Since $(-1)^{1+1} = (-1)^2 = 1$,

$$|C_{11}| = |M_{11}| = \begin{vmatrix} a_{22} & a_{23} \\ a_{32} & a_{33} \end{vmatrix}$$

(2) $\qquad |C_{12}| = (-1)^{1+2}|M_{12}|$ (3) $\qquad |C_{13}| = (-1)^{1+3}|M_{13}|$

Since $(-1)^{1+2} = (-1)^3 = -1$, Since $(-1)^{1+3} = (-1)^4 = 1$,

$$|C_{12}| = -|M_{12}| = -\begin{vmatrix} a_{21} & a_{23} \\ a_{31} & a_{33} \end{vmatrix} \qquad\qquad |C_{13}| = |M_{13}| = \begin{vmatrix} a_{21} & a_{22} \\ a_{31} & a_{32} \end{vmatrix}$$

11.4 LAPLACE EXPANSION AND HIGHER-ORDER DETERMINANTS

Laplace expansion is a method for evaluating determinants in terms of cofactors. It thus simplifies matters by permitting higher-order determinants to be established in terms of lower-order determinants. Laplace expansion of a third-order determinant can be expressed as

$$|A| = a_{11}|C_{11}| + a_{12}|C_{12}| + a_{13}|C_{13}| \qquad (11.3)$$

where $|C_{ij}|$ is a cofactor based on a second-order determinant. Here, unlike (11.1) and (11.2), a_{12} is not explicitly multiplied by -1, since by the rule of cofactors $|C_{12}|$ will automatically be multiplied by -1.

Laplace expansion permits evaluation of a determinant along any row or column. Selection of a row or column with more zeros than others simplifies evaluation of the determinant by eliminating terms. Laplace expansion also serves as the basis for evaluating determinants of orders higher than three. See Examples 5 and 6 and Problem 11.30.

EXAMPLE 5.   Given

$$A = \begin{bmatrix} 12 & 7 & 0 \\ 5 & 8 & 3 \\ 6 & 7 & 0 \end{bmatrix}$$

the determinant is found by Laplace expansion along the third column, as demonstrated below:

$$|A| = a_{13}|C_{13}| + a_{23}|C_{23}| + a_{33}|C_{33}|$$

Since a_{13} and $a_{33} = 0$

$$|A| = a_{23}|C_{23}| \tag{11.4}$$

Deleting row 2 and column 3 to find $|C_{23}|$,

$$|C_{23}| = (-1)^{2+3} \begin{vmatrix} 12 & 7 \\ 6 & 7 \end{vmatrix}$$
$$= (-1)[12(7) - 7(6)] = -42$$

Then substituting in *(11.4)* where $a_{23} = 3$, $|A| = 3(-42) = -126$. So A is nonsingular and $\rho(A) = 3$.

The accuracy of this answer can be readily checked by expanding along the first row and solving for $|A|$.

EXAMPLE 6.   Laplace expansion for a fourth-order determinant is

$$|A| = a_{11}|C_{11}| + a_{12}|C_{12}| + a_{13}|C_{13}| + a_{14}|C_{14}|$$

where the cofactors are third-order subdeterminants which in turn can be reduced to second-order subdeterminants, as above. Fifth-order determinants and higher are treated in similar fashion. See Problem 11.30(*d*) to (*f*).

11.5   PROPERTIES OF A DETERMINANT

The following seven properties of determinants provide the ways in which a matrix can be manipulated to simplify its elements or reduce part of them to zero, before evaluating a determinant:

1. Adding or subtracting any nonzero multiple of one row (or column) from another row (or column) will have no effect on the determinant.
2. Interchanging any two rows or columns of a matrix will change the sign, but not the absolute value, of the determinant.
3. Multiplying the elements of any row or column by a constant will cause the determinant to be multiplied by the constant.
4. The determinant of a *triangular matrix*, i.e., a matrix with zero elements everywhere above *or* below the principal diagonal, is equal to the product of the elements on the principal diagonal.
5. The determinant of a matrix equals the determinant of its transpose: $|A| = |A'|$.
6. If all the elements of any row or column are zero, the determinant is zero.
7. If two rows or columns are identical or proportional, i.e., linearly dependent, the determinant is zero.

These properties and their use in matrix manipulation are treated in Problems 11.4 to 11.20.

11.6   COFACTOR AND ADJOINT MATRICES

A *cofactor matrix* is a matrix in which every element a_{ij} is replaced with its cofactor $|C_{ij}|$. An *adjoint matrix* is the transpose of a cofactor matrix. Thus,

$$C = \begin{bmatrix} |C_{11}| & |C_{12}| & |C_{13}| \\ |C_{21}| & |C_{22}| & |C_{23}| \\ |C_{31}| & |C_{32}| & |C_{33}| \end{bmatrix} \qquad \text{Adj } A = C' = \begin{bmatrix} |C_{11}| & |C_{21}| & |C_{31}| \\ |C_{12}| & |C_{22}| & |C_{32}| \\ |C_{13}| & |C_{23}| & |C_{33}| \end{bmatrix}$$

EXAMPLE 7.   The cofactor matrix C and the adjoint matrix Adj A are found below, given

$$A = \begin{bmatrix} 2 & 3 & 1 \\ 4 & 1 & 2 \\ 5 & 3 & 4 \end{bmatrix}$$

Replacing the elements a_{ij} with their cofactors $|C_{ij}|$ according to the laws of cofactors,

$$C = \begin{bmatrix} \begin{vmatrix} 1 & 2 \\ 3 & 4 \end{vmatrix} & -\begin{vmatrix} 4 & 2 \\ 5 & 4 \end{vmatrix} & \begin{vmatrix} 4 & 1 \\ 5 & 3 \end{vmatrix} \\ -\begin{vmatrix} 3 & 1 \\ 3 & 4 \end{vmatrix} & \begin{vmatrix} 2 & 1 \\ 5 & 4 \end{vmatrix} & -\begin{vmatrix} 2 & 3 \\ 5 & 3 \end{vmatrix} \\ \begin{vmatrix} 3 & 1 \\ 1 & 2 \end{vmatrix} & -\begin{vmatrix} 2 & 1 \\ 4 & 2 \end{vmatrix} & \begin{vmatrix} 2 & 3 \\ 4 & 1 \end{vmatrix} \end{bmatrix} = \begin{bmatrix} -2 & -6 & 7 \\ -9 & 3 & 9 \\ 5 & 0 & -10 \end{bmatrix}$$

The adjoint matrix Adj A is the transpose of C,

$$\text{Adj } A = C' = \begin{bmatrix} -2 & -9 & 5 \\ -6 & 3 & 0 \\ 7 & 9 & -10 \end{bmatrix}$$

11.7   INVERSE MATRICES

An *inverse matrix* A^{-1}, which can be found only for a square, nonsingular matrix A, is a unique matrix satisfying the relationship

$$AA^{-1} = I = A^{-1}A$$

Multiplying a matrix by its inverse reduces it to an identity matrix. Thus, the inverse matrix in linear algebra performs much the same function as the reciprocal in ordinary algebra. The formula for deriving the inverse is

$$A^{-1} = \frac{1}{|A|} \text{ Adj } A$$

See Example 8 and Problem 11.31.

EXAMPLE 8.   Find the inverse for

$$A = \begin{bmatrix} 4 & 1 & -5 \\ -2 & 3 & 1 \\ 3 & -1 & 4 \end{bmatrix}$$

1.   Check that it is a square matrix, here 3×3, since only square matrices can have inverses.
2.   Evaluate the determinant to be sure $|A| \neq 0$, since only nonsingular matrices can have inverses.

$$|A| = 4[3(4) - 1(-1)] - 1[(-2)(4) - 1(3)] + (-5)[(-2)(-1) - 3(3)]$$
$$= 52 + 11 + 35 = 98 \neq 0$$

Matrix A is nonsingular; $\rho(A) = 3$.

3.   Find the cofactor matrix of A,

$$C = \begin{bmatrix} \begin{vmatrix} 3 & 1 \\ -1 & 4 \end{vmatrix} & -\begin{vmatrix} -2 & 1 \\ 3 & 4 \end{vmatrix} & \begin{vmatrix} -2 & 3 \\ 3 & -1 \end{vmatrix} \\ -\begin{vmatrix} 1 & -5 \\ -1 & 4 \end{vmatrix} & \begin{vmatrix} 4 & -5 \\ 3 & 4 \end{vmatrix} & -\begin{vmatrix} 4 & 1 \\ 3 & -1 \end{vmatrix} \\ \begin{vmatrix} 1 & -5 \\ 3 & 1 \end{vmatrix} & -\begin{vmatrix} 4 & -5 \\ -2 & 1 \end{vmatrix} & \begin{vmatrix} 4 & 1 \\ -2 & 3 \end{vmatrix} \end{bmatrix} = \begin{bmatrix} 13 & 11 & -7 \\ 1 & 31 & 7 \\ 16 & 6 & 14 \end{bmatrix}$$

Then transpose the cofactor matrix to get the adjoint matrix.

$$\text{Adj } A = C' = \begin{bmatrix} 13 & 1 & 16 \\ 11 & 31 & 6 \\ -7 & 7 & 14 \end{bmatrix}$$

4. Multiply the adjoint matrix by $1/|A| = \frac{1}{98}$ to get A^{-1}.

$$A^{-1} = \frac{1}{98} \begin{bmatrix} 13 & 1 & 16 \\ 11 & 31 & 6 \\ -7 & 7 & 14 \end{bmatrix} = \begin{bmatrix} \frac{13}{98} & \frac{1}{98} & \frac{16}{98} \\ \frac{11}{98} & \frac{31}{98} & \frac{6}{98} \\ -\frac{1}{14} & \frac{1}{14} & \frac{1}{7} \end{bmatrix} = \begin{bmatrix} 0.1327 & 0.0102 & 0.1633 \\ 0.1122 & 0.3163 & 0.0612 \\ -0.0714 & 0.0714 & 0.1429 \end{bmatrix}$$

5. To check your answer, multiply AA^{-1} or $A^{-1}A$. Both products will equal I if the answer is correct. An inverse is checked in Problem 11.31(a).

11.8   SOLVING LINEAR EQUATIONS WITH THE INVERSE

An inverse matrix can be used to solve matrix equations. If

$$A_{n \times n} X_{n \times 1} = B_{n \times 1}$$

and the inverse A^{-1} exists, multiplication of both sides of the equation by A^{-1}, following the laws of conformability, gives

$$A^{-1}_{n \times n} A_{n \times n} X_{n \times 1} = A^{-1}_{n \times n} B_{n \times 1}$$

From Section 11.7, $A^{-1}A = I$. Thus,

$$I_{n \times n} X_{n \times 1} = A^{-1}_{n \times n} B_{n \times 1}$$

From Section 10.8, $IX = X$. Therefore,

$$X_{n \times 1} = (A^{-1}B)_{n \times 1}$$

The solution of the equation is given by the product of the inverse of the coefficient matrix A^{-1} and the column vector of constants B.   See Problems 11.32 to 11.39.

EXAMPLE 9.   Matrix equations and the inverse are used below to solve for x_1, x_2, and x_3, given

$$\begin{aligned} 4x_1 + x_2 - 5x_3 &= 8 \\ -2x_1 + 3x_2 + x_3 &= 12 \\ 3x_1 - x_2 + 4x_3 &= 5 \end{aligned}$$

First, express the system of equations in matrix form,

$$AX = B$$

$$\begin{bmatrix} 4 & 1 & -5 \\ -2 & 3 & 1 \\ 3 & -1 & 4 \end{bmatrix} \begin{bmatrix} x_1 \\ x_2 \\ x_3 \end{bmatrix} = \begin{bmatrix} 8 \\ 12 \\ 5 \end{bmatrix}$$

From Section 11.8,

$$X = A^{-1}B$$

Since A^{-1} has already been found in Example 8,

$$X = \begin{bmatrix} \frac{13}{98} & \frac{1}{98} & \frac{16}{98} \\ \frac{11}{98} & \frac{31}{98} & \frac{6}{98} \\ -\frac{1}{14} & \frac{1}{14} & \frac{1}{7} \end{bmatrix} \begin{bmatrix} 8 \\ 12 \\ 5 \end{bmatrix} = \begin{bmatrix} \frac{104}{98} + \frac{12}{98} + \frac{80}{98} \\ \frac{88}{98} + \frac{372}{98} + \frac{30}{98} \\ -\frac{8}{14} + \frac{12}{14} + \frac{5}{7} \end{bmatrix} = \begin{bmatrix} \frac{196}{98} \\ \frac{490}{98} \\ \frac{14}{14} \end{bmatrix} = \begin{bmatrix} 2 \\ 5 \\ 1 \end{bmatrix}$$

Thus, $\overline{x}_1 = 2$, $\overline{x}_2 = 5$, and $\overline{x}_3 = 1$.

11.9   CRAMER'S RULE FOR MATRIX SOLUTIONS

Cramer's rule provides a simplified method of solving a system of linear equations through the use of determinants. Cramer's rule states

$$\bar{x}_i = \frac{|A_i|}{|A|}$$

where x_i is the ith unknown variable in a series of equations, $|A|$ is the determinant of the coefficient matrix, and $|A_i|$ is the determinant of a special matrix formed from the original coefficient matrix by replacing the column of coefficients of x_i with the column vector of constants. See Example 10 and Problems 11.40 to 11.43. Proof for Cramer's rule is given in Problem 11.44.

EXAMPLE 10.   Cramer's rule is used below to solve the system of equations

$$6x_1 + 5x_2 = 49$$
$$3x_1 + 4x_2 = 32$$

1.   Express the equations in matrix form.

$$AX = B$$

$$\begin{bmatrix} 6 & 5 \\ 3 & 4 \end{bmatrix} \begin{bmatrix} x_1 \\ x_2 \end{bmatrix} = \begin{bmatrix} 49 \\ 32 \end{bmatrix}$$

2.   Find the determinant of A.

$$|A| = 6(4) - 5(3) = 9$$

3.   Then to solve for x_1, replace column 1, the coefficients of x_1, with the vector of constants B, forming a new matrix A_1.

$$A_1 = \begin{bmatrix} 49 & 5 \\ 32 & 4 \end{bmatrix}$$

Find the determinant of A_1,

$$|A_1| = 49(4) - 5(32) = 36$$

and use the formula for Cramer's rule,

$$\bar{x}_1 = \frac{|A_1|}{|A|} = \frac{36}{9} = 4$$

4.   To solve for x_2, replace column 2, the coefficients of x_2, from the *original* matrix, with the column vector of constants B, forming a new matrix A_2.

$$A_2 = \begin{bmatrix} 6 & 49 \\ 3 & 32 \end{bmatrix}$$

Take the determinant,

$$|A_2| = 6(32) - 49(3) = 45$$

and use the formula

$$\bar{x}_2 = \frac{|A_2|}{|A|} = \frac{45}{9} = 5$$

For a system of three linear equations, see Problem 11.41(b) to (e).

11.10 THE GAUSSIAN METHOD OF INVERTING A MATRIX

The Gaussian method can also be used to invert a matrix. Simply set up an augmented matrix with the identity matrix on the right. Then apply row operations until the coefficient matrix on the left is reduced to an identity matrix. At that point, the matrix on the right will be the inverse.

The rationale behind this method can be seen in a few mathematical steps. Start with the augmented matrix $A\,|\,I$ and multiply both sides by the inverse A^{-1}, $AA^{-1}\,|\,IA^{-1}$. From Sections 11.7 and 10.8, this reduces to $I\,|\,A^{-1}$, where the identity matrix is now on the left and the inverse is on the right. See Example 11 and Problems 11.45 and 11.46.

EXAMPLE 11.　To use the Gaussian elimination method to find the inverse for

$$A = \begin{bmatrix} 4 & 1 & -5 \\ -2 & 3 & 1 \\ 3 & -1 & 4 \end{bmatrix}$$

set up the augmented matrix with the identity matrix on the right, as follows:

$$\left[\begin{array}{ccc|ccc} 4 & 1 & -5 & 1 & 0 & 0 \\ -2 & 3 & 1 & 0 & 1 & 0 \\ 3 & -1 & 4 & 0 & 0 & 1 \end{array}\right]$$

Then reduce the coefficient matrix on the left to an identity matrix by applying the row operations outlined in Section 10.12.

1a.　Multiply row 1 by $\frac{1}{4}$,

$$\left[\begin{array}{ccc|ccc} 1 & \frac{1}{4} & -\frac{5}{4} & \frac{1}{4} & 0 & 0 \\ -2 & 3 & 1 & 0 & 1 & 0 \\ 3 & -1 & 4 & 0 & 0 & 1 \end{array}\right]$$

1b.　Add 2 times row 1 to row 2 and subtract 3 times row 1 from row 3,

$$\left[\begin{array}{ccc|ccc} 1 & \frac{1}{4} & -\frac{5}{4} & \frac{1}{4} & 0 & 0 \\ 0 & \frac{7}{2} & -\frac{3}{2} & \frac{1}{2} & 1 & 0 \\ 0 & -\frac{7}{4} & \frac{31}{4} & -\frac{3}{4} & 0 & 1 \end{array}\right]$$

2a.　Multiply row 2 by $\frac{2}{7}$,

$$\left[\begin{array}{ccc|ccc} 1 & \frac{1}{4} & -\frac{5}{4} & \frac{1}{4} & 0 & 0 \\ 0 & 1 & -\frac{3}{7} & \frac{1}{7} & \frac{2}{7} & 0 \\ 0 & -\frac{7}{4} & \frac{31}{4} & -\frac{3}{4} & 0 & 1 \end{array}\right]$$

2b.　Subtract $\frac{1}{4}$ row 2 from row 1 and add $\frac{7}{4}$ row 2 to row 3,

$$\left[\begin{array}{ccc|ccc} 1 & 0 & -\frac{8}{7} & \frac{3}{14} & -\frac{1}{14} & 0 \\ 0 & 1 & -\frac{3}{7} & \frac{1}{7} & \frac{2}{7} & 0 \\ 0 & 0 & 7 & -\frac{1}{2} & \frac{1}{2} & 1 \end{array}\right]$$

3a.　Multiply row 3 by $\frac{1}{7}$,

$$\left[\begin{array}{ccc|ccc} 1 & 0 & -\frac{8}{7} & \frac{3}{14} & -\frac{1}{14} & 0 \\ 0 & 1 & -\frac{3}{7} & \frac{1}{7} & \frac{2}{7} & 0 \\ 0 & 0 & 1 & -\frac{1}{14} & \frac{1}{14} & \frac{1}{7} \end{array}\right]$$

3b.   Add $\frac{8}{7}$ row 3 to row 1 and $\frac{3}{7}$ row 3 to row 2,

$$\left[\begin{array}{ccc|ccc} 1 & 0 & 0 & \frac{13}{98} & \frac{1}{98} & \frac{8}{49} \\ 0 & 1 & 0 & \frac{11}{98} & \frac{31}{98} & \frac{3}{49} \\ 0 & 0 & 1 & -\frac{1}{14} & \frac{1}{14} & \frac{1}{7} \end{array}\right]$$

Thus,

$$A^{-1} = \begin{bmatrix} \frac{13}{98} & \frac{1}{98} & \frac{8}{49} \\ \frac{11}{98} & \frac{31}{98} & \frac{3}{49} \\ -\frac{1}{14} & \frac{1}{14} & \frac{1}{7} \end{bmatrix}$$

as found in Example 8 using the adjoint matrix.

Solved Problems

DETERMINANTS

11.1.   Find the determinant $|A|$ for the following matrices:

(a) $A = \begin{bmatrix} 9 & 13 \\ 15 & 18 \end{bmatrix}$
                            (b) $A = \begin{bmatrix} 40 & -10 \\ 25 & -5 \end{bmatrix}$

         $|A| = 9(18) - 13(15) = -33$
                       $|A| = 40(-5) - (-10)(25) = 50$

(c) $A = \begin{bmatrix} 7 & 6 \\ 9 & 5 \\ 2 & 12 \end{bmatrix}$

       The determinant does not exist because A is a 3×2 matrix and only a square matrix can have a determinant.

11.2.   Find the determinant $|A|$ for the following matrices, using (1) the method presented in Section 11.2 and (2) the technique set forth in Fig. 11-1 of Example 3. Notice how the presence of zeros simplifies the task of evaluating a determinant.

(a) $A = \begin{bmatrix} 3 & 6 & 5 \\ 2 & 1 & 8 \\ 7 & 9 & 1 \end{bmatrix}$

(1) $|A| = 3\begin{vmatrix} 1 & 8 \\ 9 & 1 \end{vmatrix} - 6\begin{vmatrix} 2 & 8 \\ 7 & 1 \end{vmatrix} + 5\begin{vmatrix} 2 & 1 \\ 7 & 9 \end{vmatrix}$

                 $= 3\,[1(1) - 8(9)] - 6\,[2(1) - 8(7)] + 5\,[2(9) - 1(7)]$

                 $= 3(-71) - 6(-54) + 5(11) = 166$

(2) $|A| = (3)(1)(1) + (6)(8)(7) + (5)(9)(2) - [(3)(9)(8) + (6)(2)(1) + (5)(1)(7)]$

             $= 3 + 336 + 90 - (216 + 12 + 35) = 166$

(b) $A = \begin{bmatrix} 12 & 0 & 3 \\ 9 & 2 & 5 \\ 4 & 6 & 1 \end{bmatrix}$

(1) $|A| = 12\begin{vmatrix} 2 & 5 \\ 6 & 1 \end{vmatrix} - 0\begin{vmatrix} 9 & 5 \\ 4 & 1 \end{vmatrix} + 3\begin{vmatrix} 9 & 2 \\ 4 & 6 \end{vmatrix}$

                 $= 12(2 - 30) - 0 + 3(54 - 8) = -198$

(2) $$|A| = (12)(2)(1) + (0)(5)(4) + (3)(6)(9) - [(12)(6)(5) + (0)(9)(1) + (3)(2)(4)]$$
$$= 24 + 0 + 162 - (360 + 0 + 24) = -198$$

(c) $A = \begin{bmatrix} 0 & 6 & 0 \\ 3 & 5 & 2 \\ 7 & 6 & 9 \end{bmatrix}$

(1) $$|A| = 0\begin{vmatrix} 5 & 2 \\ 6 & 9 \end{vmatrix} - 6\begin{vmatrix} 3 & 2 \\ 7 & 9 \end{vmatrix} + 0\begin{vmatrix} 3 & 5 \\ 7 & 6 \end{vmatrix}$$
$$= 0 - 6(27 - 14) + 0 = -78$$

(2) $$|A| = (0)(5)(9) + (6)(2)(7) + (0)(6)(3) - [(0)(6)(2) + (6)(3)(9) + (0)(5)(7)]$$
$$= 0 + 84 + 0 - (0 + 162 + 0) = -78$$

Of more general application, the method used in step 1 will predominate in future discussions, but both methods are helpful.

RANK OF A MATRIX

11.3. Determine the rank ρ of the following matrices:

(a) $A = \begin{bmatrix} -3 & 6 & 2 \\ 1 & 5 & 4 \\ 4 & -8 & 2 \end{bmatrix}$

$$|A| = -3\begin{vmatrix} 5 & 4 \\ -8 & 2 \end{vmatrix} + 6(-1)\begin{vmatrix} 1 & 4 \\ 4 & 2 \end{vmatrix} + 2\begin{vmatrix} 1 & 5 \\ 4 & -8 \end{vmatrix}$$
$$= -3[10 - (-32)] - 6(2 - 16) + 2(-8 - 20) = -98$$

With $|A| \neq 0$, A is nonsingular and the three rows and columns are linearly independent. Hence, $\rho(A) = 3$.

(b) $B = \begin{bmatrix} 5 & -9 & 3 \\ 2 & 12 & -4 \\ -3 & -18 & 6 \end{bmatrix}$

$$|B| = 5\begin{vmatrix} 12 & -4 \\ -18 & 6 \end{vmatrix} - 9(-1)\begin{vmatrix} 2 & -4 \\ -3 & 6 \end{vmatrix} + 3\begin{vmatrix} 2 & 12 \\ -3 & -18 \end{vmatrix}$$
$$= 5[72 - (+72)] + 9[12 - (+12)] + 3[-36 - (-36)]$$
$$= 5(0) + 9(0) + 3(0) = 0$$

With $|B| = 0$, B is singular and the three rows and columns are not linearly independent. Hence, $\rho(A) \neq 3$. Now test to see if any two rows or columns are independent. Starting with the submatrix in the upper left corner, take the 2×2 determinant.

$$\begin{vmatrix} 5 & -9 \\ 2 & 12 \end{vmatrix} = 60 - (-18) = 78 \neq 0$$

Thus, $\rho(B) = 2$. There are only two linearly independent rows and columns in B. Row 3 is -1.5 times row 2, and column 3 is $-\frac{1}{3}$ times column 2.

(c) $C = \begin{bmatrix} -8 & 2 & -6 \\ 10 & -2.5 & 7.5 \\ 24 & -6 & 18 \end{bmatrix}$

$$|C| = -8\begin{vmatrix} -2.5 & 7.5 \\ -6 & 18 \end{vmatrix} + 2(-1)\begin{vmatrix} 10 & 7.5 \\ 24 & 18 \end{vmatrix} - 6\begin{vmatrix} 10 & -2.5 \\ 24 & -6 \end{vmatrix}$$
$$= -8[-45 - (-45)] - 2(180 - 180) - 6[-60 - (-60)] = 0$$

With $|C| = 0$, $\rho(C) \neq 3$. Trying various 2×2 submatrices,

$$\begin{vmatrix} -8 & 2 \\ 10 & -2.5 \end{vmatrix} = 20 - 20 = 0 \qquad \begin{vmatrix} 2 & -6 \\ -2.5 & 7.5 \end{vmatrix} = 15 - 15 = 0$$

$$\begin{vmatrix} 10 & -2.5 \\ 24 & -6 \end{vmatrix} = -60 - (-60) = 0 \qquad \begin{vmatrix} -2.5 & 7.5 \\ -6 & 18 \end{vmatrix} = -45 - (-45) = 0$$

With all the determinants of the different 2×2 submatrices equal to zero, no two rows or columns of C are linearly independent. So $\rho(C) \neq 2$ and $\rho(C) = 1$. Row 2 is -1.25 times row 1, row 3 is -3 times row 1, column 2 is $-\frac{1}{4}$ times column 1, and column 3 is $\frac{3}{4}$ times column 1.

(d) $D = \begin{bmatrix} 2 & 5 \\ 7 & 11 \\ 3 & 1 \end{bmatrix}$

Since the maximum number of linearly independent rows (columns) must equal the maximum number of linearly independent columns (rows), the rank of D cannot exceed 2. Testing a submatrix,

$$\begin{vmatrix} 2 & 5 \\ 7 & 11 \end{vmatrix} = 22 - 35 = -13 \neq 0 \qquad \rho(D) = 2$$

While it is clear that there are only two linearly independent columns, there are also only two linearly independent rows because row 2 = 2 times row 1 plus row 3.

PROPERTIES OF DETERMINANTS

11.4.   Given

$$A = \begin{bmatrix} 2 & 5 & 1 \\ 3 & 2 & 4 \\ 1 & 4 & 2 \end{bmatrix}$$

Compare (a) the determinant of A and (b) the determinant of the transpose of A. (c) Specify which property of determinants the comparison illustrates.

(a) $|A| = 2(4 - 16) - 5(6 - 4) + 1(12 - 2) = -24$

(b) $A' = \begin{bmatrix} 2 & 3 & 1 \\ 5 & 2 & 4 \\ 1 & 4 & 2 \end{bmatrix}$

$$|A'| = 2(4 - 16) - 3(10 - 4) + 1(20 - 2) = -24$$

(c)   This illustrates that the determinant of a matrix equals the determinant of its transpose. See Section 11.5.

11.5.   Compare (a) the determinant of A and (b) the determinant of A', given

$$A = \begin{bmatrix} a_{11} & a_{12} \\ a_{21} & a_{22} \end{bmatrix}$$

(a) $|A| = a_{11}a_{22} - a_{12}a_{21}$ (b) $A' = \begin{bmatrix} a_{11} & a_{21} \\ a_{12} & a_{22} \end{bmatrix}$ $|A'| = a_{11}a_{22} - a_{21}a_{12}$

11.6.   Given

$$A = \begin{bmatrix} 1 & 4 & 2 \\ 3 & 5 & 4 \\ 2 & 3 & 2 \end{bmatrix}$$

(a) Find the determinant of A. (b) Form a new matrix B by interchanging row 1 and row 2 of A, and find $|B|$. (c) Form another matrix C by interchanging column 1 and column 3 of A, and find $|C|$. (d) Compare determinants and specify which property of determinants is illustrated.

(a)
$$|A| = 1(10 - 12) - 4(6 - 8) + 2(9 - 10) = 4$$

(b)
$$B = \begin{bmatrix} 3 & 5 & 4 \\ 1 & 4 & 2 \\ 2 & 3 & 2 \end{bmatrix}$$
$$|B| = 3(8 - 6) - 5(2 - 4) + 4(3 - 8) = -4$$

(c)
$$C = \begin{bmatrix} 2 & 4 & 1 \\ 4 & 5 & 3 \\ 2 & 3 & 2 \end{bmatrix}$$
$$|C| = 2(10 - 9) - 4(8 - 6) + 1(12 - 10) = -4$$

(d) $|B| = -|A|$. Interchanging any two rows or columns will affect the sign of the determinant, but not the absolute value of the determinant.

11.7.   Given
$$W = \begin{bmatrix} w & x \\ y & z \end{bmatrix}$$

(a) Find the determinant of W. (b) Interchange row 1 and row 2 of W, forming a new matrix Y, and compare the determinant of Y with that of W.

(a)
$$|W| = wz - yx$$

(b)
$$Y = \begin{bmatrix} y & z \\ w & x \end{bmatrix} \qquad |Y| = yx - wz = -(wz - yx) = -|W|$$

11.8.   Given
$$A = \begin{bmatrix} 3 & 5 & 7 \\ 2 & 1 & 4 \\ 4 & 2 & 3 \end{bmatrix}$$

(a) Find the determinant of A. (b) Form a new matrix B by multiplying the first row of A by 2, and find the determinant of B. (c) Compare determinants and indicate which property of determinants this illustrates.

(a)
$$|A| = 3(3 - 8) - 5(6 - 16) + 7(4 - 4) = 35$$

(b)
$$B = \begin{bmatrix} 6 & 10 & 14 \\ 2 & 1 & 4 \\ 4 & 2 & 3 \end{bmatrix} \qquad |B| = 6(3 - 8) - 10(6 - 16) + 14(4 - 4) = 70$$

(c) $|B| = 2|A|$. Multiplying a single row or column of a matrix by a scalar will cause the value of the determinant to be multiplied by the scalar. Here doubling row 1 doubles the determinant.

11.9.   Given
$$A = \begin{bmatrix} 2 & 5 & 8 \\ 3 & 10 & 1 \\ 1 & 15 & 4 \end{bmatrix}$$

(a) Find $|A|$. (b) Form a new matrix B by multiplying column 2 by $\frac{1}{5}$ and find $|B|$. (c) Compare determinants.

(a)
$$|A| = 2(40 - 15) - 5(12 - 1) + 8(45 - 10) = 275$$

(b)   Recalling that multiplying by $\frac{1}{5}$ is the same thing as dividing by or factoring out 5,
$$B = \begin{bmatrix} 2 & 1 & 8 \\ 3 & 2 & 1 \\ 1 & 3 & 4 \end{bmatrix} \qquad |B| = 2(8 - 3) - 1(12 - 1) + 8(9 - 2) = 55$$

(c)
$$|B| = \tfrac{1}{5}|A|$$

11.10. Given
$$A = \begin{bmatrix} a_{11} & a_{12} \\ a_{21} & a_{22} \end{bmatrix} \qquad B = \begin{bmatrix} a_{11} & ka_{12} \\ a_{21} & ka_{22} \end{bmatrix}$$

Compare (a) the determinant of A and (b) the determinant of B.

(a) $|A| = a_{11}a_{22} - a_{12}a_{21}$

(b) $|B| = a_{11}ka_{22} - ka_{12}a_{21} = k(a_{11}a_{22}) - k(a_{12}a_{21})$
$$= k(a_{11}a_{22} - a_{12}a_{21}) = k|A|$$

11.11. Given
$$A = \begin{bmatrix} 5 & 1 & 4 \\ 3 & 2 & 5 \\ 4 & 1 & 6 \end{bmatrix}$$

(a) Find $|A|$. (b) Subtract 5 times column 2 from column 1, forming a new matrix B, and find $|B|$. (c) Compare determinants and indicate which property of determinants is illustrated.

(a)
$$|A| = 5(12 - 5) - 1(18 - 20) + 4(3 - 8) = 17$$

(b)
$$B = \begin{bmatrix} 0 & 1 & 4 \\ -7 & 2 & 5 \\ -1 & 1 & 6 \end{bmatrix} \qquad |B| = 0 - 1(-42 + 5) + 4(-7 + 2) = 17$$

(c) $|B| = |A|$. Addition or subtraction of a nonzero multiple of any row or column to or from another row or column does not change the value of the determinant.

11.12. (a) Subtract row 3 from row 1 in A of Problem 11.11, forming a new matrix C, and (b) find $|C|$.

(a)
$$C = \begin{bmatrix} 1 & 0 & -2 \\ 3 & 2 & 5 \\ 4 & 1 & 6 \end{bmatrix}$$

(b)
$$|C| = 1(12 - 5) - 0 + (-2)(3 - 8) = 17$$

11.13. Given the *upper-triangular matrix*
$$A = \begin{bmatrix} -3 & 0 & 0 \\ 2 & -5 & 0 \\ 6 & 1 & 4 \end{bmatrix}$$

which has zero elements everywhere above the principal diagonal, (a) find $|A|$. (b) Find the product of the elements along the principal diagonal and (c) specify which property of determinants this illustrates.

(a)
$$|A| = -3(-20 - 0) - 0 + 0 = 60$$

(b)   Multiplying the elements along the principal diagonal, $(-3)(-5)(4) = 60$.

(c)   The determinant of a triangular matrix is equal to the product of the elements along the principal diagonal.

11.14. Given the *lower-triangular matrix*
$$A = \begin{bmatrix} 2 & -5 & -1 \\ 0 & 3 & 6 \\ 0 & 0 & -7 \end{bmatrix}$$

which has zero elements everywhere below the principal diagonal, find (a) $|A|$ and (b) the product of the diagonal elements.

(a)
$$|A| = 2(-21 - 0) - (-5)(0 - 0) - 1(0 - 0) = -42$$

(b)
$$2(3)(-7) = -42$$

11.15. Given
$$A = \begin{bmatrix} 12 & 16 & 13 \\ 0 & 0 & 0 \\ -15 & 20 & -9 \end{bmatrix}$$

(a) Find $|A|$. (b) What property of determinants is illustrated?

(a)
$$|A| = 12(0 - 0) - 16(0 - 0) + 13(0 - 0) = 0$$

(b)   If all the elements of a row or column equal zero, the determinant will equal zero. With all the elements of row 2 in A equal to zero, the matrix is, in effect, a 2×3 matrix, not a 3×3 matrix. Only square matrices have determinants.

MATRIX SIMPLIFICATION PRIOR TO DETERMINANT EVALUATION

11.16. Using the information from Problems 11.4 to 11.15, simplify the following matrices, where possible, before finding the determinant. Start by factoring and remember to compensate for any factoring when finding a determinant. While the exercises are limited to 3×3 determinants for ease of computation, mastery of the techniques employed will prove particularly helpful in evaluating determinants of higher order.

(a) $A = \begin{bmatrix} -4 & 7 & 6 \\ 24 & -60 & 36 \\ 3 & -1 & 5 \end{bmatrix}$

Row 2 can be factored by 12. Thus,

$$|A| = 12 \begin{vmatrix} -4 & 7 & 6 \\ 2 & -5 & 3 \\ 3 & -1 & 5 \end{vmatrix}$$
$$= 12\,[-4(-25 + 3) - 7(10 - 9) + 6(-2 + 15)] = 12(159) = 1908$$

(b) $A = \begin{bmatrix} 10 & 52 & 7 \\ 12 & 78 & 5 \\ 4 & 65 & 11 \end{bmatrix}$

Factoring out 13 from column 2,

$$|A| = 13 \begin{vmatrix} 10 & 4 & 7 \\ 12 & 6 & 5 \\ 4 & 5 & 11 \end{vmatrix}$$

Then factoring out 2 from column 1,

$$|A| = 13(2) \begin{vmatrix} 5 & 4 & 7 \\ 6 & 6 & 5 \\ 2 & 5 & 11 \end{vmatrix}$$
$$= 26\,[5(66 - 25) - 4(66 - 10) + 7(30 - 12)] = 26(107) = 2782$$

(c) $A = \begin{bmatrix} 24 & 16 & 20 \\ 18 & 4 & 5 \\ 6 & 7 & 15 \end{bmatrix}$

Row 1 can be factored by 4.

$$|A| = 4 \begin{vmatrix} 6 & 4 & 5 \\ 18 & 4 & 5 \\ 6 & 7 & 15 \end{vmatrix}$$

Column 1 can be factored by 6, and column 3 can be factored by 5.

$$|A| = 4(6)(5) \begin{vmatrix} 1 & 4 & 1 \\ 3 & 4 & 1 \\ 1 & 7 & 3 \end{vmatrix}$$
$$= 120\,[1(12 - 7) - 4(9 - 1) + 1(21 - 4)] = 120(-10) = -1200$$

11.17. Simplify the following matrices by adding or subtracting nonzero multiples of rows or columns, and then find the determinant:

(a) $A = \begin{bmatrix} 3 & 3 & 6 \\ 4 & 2 & 4 \\ 9 & 5 & 1 \end{bmatrix}$

Subtracting column 2 from column 1 will leave 0 as the a_{11} element. Thus,

$$A = \begin{bmatrix} 0 & 3 & 6 \\ 2 & 2 & 4 \\ 4 & 5 & 1 \end{bmatrix}$$

Subtracting 2 times column 2 from column 3 will leave 0 in the a_{13} position.

$$A = \begin{bmatrix} 0 & 3 & 0 \\ 2 & 2 & 0 \\ 4 & 5 & -9 \end{bmatrix}$$

Thus, $|A| = 0 - 3(-18 - 0) + 0 = 54$

(b) $A = \begin{bmatrix} 28 & 34 & 2 \\ 23 & 45 & 3 \\ 19 & 41 & 1 \end{bmatrix}$

Subtracting 14 times column 3 from column 1 will leave 0 in the a_{11} position.

$$A = \begin{bmatrix} 0 & 34 & 2 \\ -19 & 45 & 3 \\ 5 & 41 & 1 \end{bmatrix}$$

Subtracting 17 times column 3 from column 2 will leave 0 in the a_{12} positiom.

$$A = \begin{bmatrix} 0 & 0 & 2 \\ -19 & -6 & 3 \\ 5 & 24 & 1 \end{bmatrix}$$

Thus, $|A| = 2(-456 + 30) = -852$

11.18. Check your answer to Problem 11.17(b), without simplifying the matrix.

$$|A| = 28(45 - 123) - 34(23 - 57) + 2(943 - 855) = -2184 + 1156 + 176 = -852$$

11.19. Given

$$A = \begin{bmatrix} 4 & 36 & 28 \\ 5 & 35 & 55 \\ 3 & 23 & 18 \end{bmatrix}$$

(a) Reduce A to an upper-triangular matrix and find $|A|$. (b) Check your answer.

(a) Subtract 9 times column 1 from column 2 and 7 times column 1 from column 3.

$$A = \begin{bmatrix} 4 & 0 & 0 \\ 5 & -10 & 20 \\ 3 & -4 & -3 \end{bmatrix}$$

Then add 2 times column 2 to column 3.

$$A = \begin{bmatrix} 4 & 0 & 0 \\ 5 & -10 & 0 \\ 3 & -4 & -11 \end{bmatrix}$$

Thus, $|A| = 4(-10)(-11) = 440$.

(b) $|A| = 4(630 - 1265) - 36(90 - 165) + 28(115 - 105) = -2540 + 2700 + 280 = 440$

11.20. Given

$$A = \begin{bmatrix} 71 & -26 & 5 \\ 58 & 32 & 6 \\ 63 & -45 & 3 \end{bmatrix} \qquad B = \begin{bmatrix} 126 & 42 & 63 \\ 108 & 56 & 49 \\ 96 & 60 & 74 \end{bmatrix}$$

(a) Reduce A to a lower-triangular matrix and find $|A|$. (b) Reduce B to an upper-triangular matrix and find $|B|$.

(a) Subtract 21 times column 3 from column 1, and add 15 times column 3 to column 2.

$$A = \begin{bmatrix} -34 & 49 & 5 \\ -68 & 122 & 6 \\ 0 & 0 & 3 \end{bmatrix}$$

Then, subtract 2 times row 1 from row 2.

$$A = \begin{bmatrix} -34 & 49 & 5 \\ 0 & 24 & -4 \\ 0 & 0 & 3 \end{bmatrix}$$
$$|A| = (-34)(24)(3) = -2448$$

(b) Subtract $\frac{1}{3}$ column 1 from column 2 and $\frac{1}{2}$ column 1 from column 3.

$$B = \begin{bmatrix} 126 & 0 & 0 \\ 108 & 20 & -5 \\ 96 & 28 & 26 \end{bmatrix}$$

Then add $\frac{1}{4}$ column 2 to column 3.

$$B = \begin{bmatrix} 126 & 0 & 0 \\ 108 & 20 & 0 \\ 96 & 28 & 33 \end{bmatrix}$$

$$|B| = 126(20)(33) = 83\,160$$

SINGULAR AND NONSINGULAR MATRICES

11.21. Using a 2×2 coefficient matrix A, prove that if $|A| \neq 0$, there is linear independence between the rows and columns of A and a unique solution exists for the system of equations.

Start with two linear equations in two unknowns

$$a_{11}x + a_{12}y = b_1 \tag{11.5}$$

$$a_{21}x + a_{22}y = b_2 \tag{11.6}$$

and solve for x by multiplying (11.5) by a_{22} and (11.6) by $-a_{12}$ and then adding to eliminate y.

$$\begin{aligned}
a_{11}a_{22}x + a_{12}a_{22}y &= a_{22}b_1 \\
-a_{12}a_{21}x - a_{12}a_{22}y &= -a_{12}b_2 \\
\hline
(a_{11}a_{22} - a_{12}a_{21})x &= a_{22}b_1 - a_{12}b_2 \\
x &= \frac{a_{22}b_1 - a_{12}b_2}{a_{11}a_{22} - a_{12}a_{21}}
\end{aligned} \tag{11.7}$$

where $a_{11}a_{22} - a_{12}a_{21} = |A|$. If, in (11.7), $|A| = a_{11}a_{22} - a_{12}a_{21} = 0$, x has no unique solution, indicating linear dependence between the equations; if $|A| = a_{11}a_{22} - a_{12}a_{21} \neq 0$, x has a unique solution and the equations must be linearly independent.

11.22. Use determinants to determine whether a unique solution exists for each of the following systems of equations:

(a) $12x_1 + 7x_2 = 147$
      $15x_1 + 19x_2 = 168$

To determine whether a unique solution exists, find the coefficient matrix A and take the determinant $|A|$. If $|A| \neq 0$, the matrix is nonsingular and a unique solution exists. If $|A| = 0$, the matrix is singular and there is no unique solution. Thus,

$$A = \begin{bmatrix} 12 & 7 \\ 15 & 19 \end{bmatrix}$$
$$|A| = 12(19) - (7)15 = 123$$

Since $|A| \neq 0$, A is nonsingular and a unique solution exists.

(b) $2x_1 + 3x_2 = 27$
      $6x_1 + 9x_2 = 81$

$$A = \begin{bmatrix} 2 & 3 \\ 6 & 9 \end{bmatrix} \qquad |A| = 2(9) - 6(3) = 0$$

There is no unique solution. The equations are linearly dependent. The second equation is 3 times the first equation.

(c) $72x_1 - 54x_2 = 216$
      $64x_1 - 48x_2 = 192$

$$A = \begin{bmatrix} 72 & -54 \\ 64 & -48 \end{bmatrix} \qquad |A| = 72(-48) - (-54)(64) = -3456 + 3456 = 0$$

A unique solution does not exist because the equations are linearly dependent. Closer inspection reveals the second equation is $\frac{8}{3}$ times the first equation.

(d) $4x_1 + 3x_2 + 5x_3 = 27$
     $x_1 + 6x_2 + 2x_3 = 19$
     $3x_1 + x_2 + 3x_3 = 15$

$$A = \begin{bmatrix} 4 & 3 & 5 \\ 1 & 6 & 2 \\ 3 & 1 & 3 \end{bmatrix} \qquad |A| = 4(18 - 2) - 3(3 - 6) + 5(1 - 18) = -12$$

A unique solution exists.

(e) $4x_1 + 2x_2 + 6x_3 = 28$
     $3x_1 + x_2 + 2x_3 = 20$
     $10x_1 + 5x_2 + 15x_3 = 70$

$$A = \begin{bmatrix} 4 & 2 & 6 \\ 3 & 1 & 2 \\ 10 & 5 & 15 \end{bmatrix} \qquad |A| = 4(15 - 10) - 2(45 - 20) + 6(15 - 10) = 0$$

There is no unique solution because the equations are linearly dependent. Closer examination reveals the third equation is 2.5 times the first equation.

(f) $56x_1 + 47x_2 + 8x_3 = 365$
     $84x_1 - 39x_2 + 12x_3 = 249$
     $28x_1 - 81x_2 + 4x_3 = 168$

$$A = \begin{bmatrix} 56 & 47 & 8 \\ 84 & -39 & 12 \\ 28 & -81 & 4 \end{bmatrix}$$

Factoring out 28 from column 1 and 4 from column 3 before taking the determinant,

$$|A| = 28(4) \begin{vmatrix} 2 & 47 & 2 \\ 3 & -39 & 3 \\ 1 & -81 & 1 \end{vmatrix}$$

The linear dependence between column 1 and column 3 is now evident. The determinant will therefore be zero, and no unique solution exists.

$$|A| = 112\,[2(-39 + 243) - 47(0) + 2(-243 + 39)] = 112(0) = 0$$

MINORS AND COFACTORS

11.23. Find (a) the minor $|M_{ij}|$ and (b) the cofactor $|C_{ij}|$ for each of the elements in the first row, given

$$A = \begin{bmatrix} a_{11} & a_{12} \\ a_{21} & a_{22} \end{bmatrix}$$

(a) To find the minor of a_{11}, mentally delete the row and column in which it appears. The remaining element is the minor. Thus, $|M_{11}| = a_{22}$. Similarly, $|M_{12}| = a_{21}$.

(b) From the rule of cofactors,

$$|C_{11}| = (-1)^{1+1}|M_{11}| = +1(a_{22}) = a_{22}$$
$$|C_{12}| = (-1)^{1+2}|M_{12}| = -1(a_{21}) = -a_{21}$$

11.24. Find (a) the minors and (b) the cofactors for the elements of the second row, given

$$A = \begin{bmatrix} 13 & 17 \\ 19 & 15 \end{bmatrix}$$

(a)
$$|M_{21}| = 17 \quad |M_{22}| = 13$$

(b)
$$|C_{21}| = (-1)^{2+1}|M_{21}| = -1(17) = -17$$
$$|C_{22}| = (-1)^{2+2}|M_{22}| = +1(13) = 13$$

11.25. Find (a) the minors and (b) the cofactors for the elements of the second column, given

$$A = \begin{bmatrix} 6 & 7 \\ 12 & 9 \end{bmatrix}$$

(a)
$$|M_{12}| = 12 \quad |M_{22}| = 6$$

(b)
$$|C_{12}| = (-1)^{1+2}|M_{12}| = -12$$
$$|C_{22}| = (-1)^{2+2}|M_{22}| = 6$$

11.26. Find (a) the minors and (b) the cofactors for the elements of the first row, given

$$A = \begin{bmatrix} 5 & 2 & -4 \\ 6 & -3 & 7 \\ 1 & 2 & 4 \end{bmatrix}$$

(a) Deleting row 1 and column 1,

$$|M_{11}| = \begin{vmatrix} -3 & 7 \\ 2 & 4 \end{vmatrix} = -26$$

Similarly,
$$|M_{12}| = \begin{vmatrix} 6 & 7 \\ 1 & 4 \end{vmatrix} = 17$$

$$|M_{13}| = \begin{vmatrix} 6 & -3 \\ 1 & 2 \end{vmatrix} = 15$$

(b)
$$|C_{11}| = (-1)^2|M_{11}| = -26$$
$$|C_{12}| = (-1)^3|M_{12}| = -17$$
$$|C_{13}| = (-1)^4|M_{13}| = 15$$

11.27. Find (a) the minors and (b) the cofactors for the elements of the third row, given

$$A = \begin{bmatrix} 9 & 11 & 4 \\ 3 & 2 & 7 \\ 6 & 10 & 4 \end{bmatrix}$$

(a) Deleting row 3 and column 1,

$$|M_{31}| = \begin{vmatrix} 11 & 4 \\ 2 & 7 \end{vmatrix} = 69$$

Similarly,
$$|M_{32}| = \begin{vmatrix} 9 & 4 \\ 3 & 7 \end{vmatrix} = 51$$

$$|M_{33}| = \begin{vmatrix} 9 & 11 \\ 3 & 2 \end{vmatrix} = -15$$

(b)
$$|C_{31}| = (-1)^4|M_{31}| = 69$$
$$|C_{32}| = (-1)^5|M_{32}| = -51$$
$$|C_{33}| = (-1)^6|M_{33}| = -15$$

11.28. Find (a) the minors and (b) the cofactors for the elements in the second column, given

$$A = \begin{bmatrix} 13 & 6 & 11 \\ 12 & 9 & 4 \\ 7 & 10 & 2 \end{bmatrix}$$

(a)
$$|M_{12}| = \begin{vmatrix} 12 & 4 \\ 7 & 2 \end{vmatrix} = -4$$
$$|M_{22}| = \begin{vmatrix} 13 & 11 \\ 7 & 2 \end{vmatrix} = -51$$
$$|M_{32}| = \begin{vmatrix} 13 & 11 \\ 12 & 4 \end{vmatrix} = -80$$

(b)
$$|C_{12}| = (-1)^3|M_{12}| = -1(-4) = 4$$
$$|C_{22}| = (-1)^4|M_{22}| = -51$$
$$|C_{32}| = (-1)^5|M_{32}| = -1(-80) = 80$$

11.29. Find (1) the cofactor matrix C and (2) the adjoint matrix Adj A for each of the following:

(a) $A = \begin{bmatrix} 7 & 12 \\ 4 & 3 \end{bmatrix}$

(1) $C = \begin{bmatrix} |C_{11}| & |C_{12}| \\ |C_{21}| & |C_{22}| \end{bmatrix} = \begin{bmatrix} |M_{11}| & -|M_{12}| \\ -|M_{21}| & |M_{22}| \end{bmatrix} = \begin{bmatrix} 3 & -4 \\ -12 & 7 \end{bmatrix}$

(2) Adj $A = C' = \begin{bmatrix} 3 & -12 \\ -4 & 7 \end{bmatrix}$

(b) $A = \begin{bmatrix} -2 & 5 \\ 13 & 6 \end{bmatrix}$

(1) $C = \begin{bmatrix} 6 & -13 \\ -5 & -2 \end{bmatrix}$ (2) Adj $A = \begin{bmatrix} 6 & -5 \\ -13 & -2 \end{bmatrix}$

(c) $A = \begin{bmatrix} 9 & -16 \\ -20 & 7 \end{bmatrix}$

(1) $C = \begin{bmatrix} 7 & 20 \\ 16 & 9 \end{bmatrix}$ (2) Adj $A = \begin{bmatrix} 7 & 16 \\ 20 & 9 \end{bmatrix}$

(d) $A = \begin{bmatrix} 6 & 2 & 7 \\ 5 & 4 & 9 \\ 3 & 3 & 1 \end{bmatrix}$

(1) $C = \begin{bmatrix} |C_{11}| & |C_{12}| & |C_{13}| \\ |C_{21}| & |C_{22}| & |C_{23}| \\ |C_{31}| & |C_{32}| & |C_{33}| \end{bmatrix} = \begin{bmatrix} \begin{vmatrix} 4 & 9 \\ 3 & 1 \end{vmatrix} & -\begin{vmatrix} 5 & 9 \\ 3 & 1 \end{vmatrix} & \begin{vmatrix} 5 & 4 \\ 3 & 3 \end{vmatrix} \\ -\begin{vmatrix} 2 & 7 \\ 3 & 1 \end{vmatrix} & \begin{vmatrix} 6 & 7 \\ 3 & 1 \end{vmatrix} & -\begin{vmatrix} 6 & 2 \\ 3 & 3 \end{vmatrix} \\ \begin{vmatrix} 2 & 7 \\ 4 & 9 \end{vmatrix} & -\begin{vmatrix} 6 & 7 \\ 5 & 9 \end{vmatrix} & \begin{vmatrix} 6 & 2 \\ 5 & 4 \end{vmatrix} \end{bmatrix} = \begin{bmatrix} -23 & 22 & 3 \\ 19 & -15 & -12 \\ -10 & -19 & 14 \end{bmatrix}$

(2)   Adj $A = C' = \begin{bmatrix} -23 & 19 & -10 \\ 22 & -15 & -19 \\ 3 & -12 & 14 \end{bmatrix}$

(e) $A = \begin{bmatrix} 13 & -2 & 8 \\ -9 & 6 & -4 \\ -3 & 2 & -1 \end{bmatrix}$

(1) $C = \begin{bmatrix} \begin{vmatrix} 6 & -4 \\ 2 & -1 \end{vmatrix} & -\begin{vmatrix} -9 & -4 \\ -3 & -1 \end{vmatrix} & \begin{vmatrix} -9 & 6 \\ -3 & 2 \end{vmatrix} \\ -\begin{vmatrix} -2 & 8 \\ 2 & -1 \end{vmatrix} & \begin{vmatrix} 13 & 8 \\ -3 & -1 \end{vmatrix} & -\begin{vmatrix} 13 & -2 \\ -3 & 2 \end{vmatrix} \\ \begin{vmatrix} -2 & 8 \\ 6 & -4 \end{vmatrix} & -\begin{vmatrix} 13 & 8 \\ -9 & -4 \end{vmatrix} & \begin{vmatrix} 13 & -2 \\ -9 & 6 \end{vmatrix} \end{bmatrix} = \begin{bmatrix} 2 & 3 & 0 \\ 14 & 11 & -20 \\ -40 & -20 & 60 \end{bmatrix}$

(2)   Adj $A = C' = \begin{bmatrix} 2 & 14 & -40 \\ 3 & 11 & -20 \\ 0 & -20 & 60 \end{bmatrix}$

LAPLACE EXPANSION

11.30. Use Laplace expansion to find the determinants for each of the following, using whatever row or column is easiest:

(a) $A = \begin{bmatrix} 15 & 7 & 9 \\ 2 & 5 & 6 \\ 9 & 0 & 12 \end{bmatrix}$

Expanding along the second column,

$$|A| = a_{12}|C_{12}| + a_{22}|C_{22}| + a_{32}|C_{32}| = 7(-1)\begin{vmatrix} 2 & 6 \\ 9 & 12 \end{vmatrix} + 5\begin{vmatrix} 15 & 9 \\ 9 & 12 \end{vmatrix} + 0$$
$$= -7(-30) + 5(99) = 705$$

(b) $A = \begin{bmatrix} 23 & 35 & 0 \\ 72 & 46 & 10 \\ 15 & 29 & 0 \end{bmatrix}$

Expanding along the third column,

$$|A| = a_{13}|C_{13}| + a_{23}|C_{23}| + a_{33}|C_{33}|$$
$$= 0 + 10(-1)\begin{vmatrix} 23 & 35 \\ 15 & 29 \end{vmatrix} + 0 = -10(142) = -1420$$

(c) $A = \begin{bmatrix} 12 & 98 & 15 \\ 0 & 25 & 0 \\ 21 & 84 & 19 \end{bmatrix}$

Expanding along the second row,

$$|A| = a_{21}|C_{21}| + a_{22}|C_{22}| + a_{23}|C_{23}| = 0 + 25\begin{vmatrix} 12 & 15 \\ 21 & 19 \end{vmatrix} + 0 = 25(-87) = -2175$$

(d) $A = \begin{bmatrix} 2 & 4 & 1 & 5 \\ 3 & 2 & 5 & 1 \\ 1 & 2 & 1 & 4 \\ 3 & 4 & 3 & 2 \end{bmatrix}$

Expanding along the first row,

$$|A| = a_{11}|C_{11}| + a_{12}|C_{12}| + a_{13}|C_{13}| + a_{14}|C_{14}|$$

$$= 2(-1)^{1+1}\begin{vmatrix} 2 & 5 & 1 \\ 2 & 1 & 4 \\ 4 & 3 & 2 \end{vmatrix} + 4(-1)^{1+2}\begin{vmatrix} 3 & 5 & 1 \\ 1 & 1 & 4 \\ 3 & 3 & 2 \end{vmatrix} + 1(-1)^{1+3}\begin{vmatrix} 3 & 2 & 1 \\ 1 & 2 & 4 \\ 3 & 4 & 2 \end{vmatrix} + 5(-1)^{1+4}\begin{vmatrix} 3 & 2 & 5 \\ 1 & 2 & 1 \\ 3 & 4 & 3 \end{vmatrix}$$

Then expanding each of the 3×3 subdeterminants along the first row,

$$|A| = 2\left[2\begin{vmatrix} 1 & 4 \\ 3 & 2 \end{vmatrix} - 5\begin{vmatrix} 2 & 4 \\ 4 & 2 \end{vmatrix} + 1\begin{vmatrix} 2 & 1 \\ 4 & 3 \end{vmatrix} \right] - 4\left[3\begin{vmatrix} 1 & 4 \\ 3 & 2 \end{vmatrix} - 5\begin{vmatrix} 1 & 4 \\ 3 & 2 \end{vmatrix} + 1\begin{vmatrix} 1 & 1 \\ 3 & 3 \end{vmatrix} \right]$$

$$+ 1\left[3\begin{vmatrix} 2 & 4 \\ 4 & 2 \end{vmatrix} - 2\begin{vmatrix} 1 & 4 \\ 3 & 2 \end{vmatrix} + 1\begin{vmatrix} 1 & 2 \\ 3 & 4 \end{vmatrix} \right] - 5\left[3\begin{vmatrix} 2 & 1 \\ 4 & 3 \end{vmatrix} - 2\begin{vmatrix} 1 & 1 \\ 3 & 3 \end{vmatrix} + 5\begin{vmatrix} 1 & 2 \\ 3 & 4 \end{vmatrix} \right]$$

$$= 2[2(-10) - 5(-12) + 1(2)] - 4[3(-10) - 5(-10) + 1(0)]$$
$$+ 1[3(-12) - 2(-10) + 1(-2)] - 5[3(2) - 2(0) + 5(-2)]$$

$$= 2(42) - 4(20) + 1(-18) - 5(-4) = 6$$

(e) $A = \begin{bmatrix} 5 & 0 & 1 & 3 \\ 4 & 2 & 6 & 0 \\ 3 & 0 & 1 & 5 \\ 0 & 1 & 4 & 2 \end{bmatrix}$

Expanding along the second column,

$$|A| = a_{12}|C_{12}| + a_{22}|C_{22}| + a_{32}|C_{32}| + a_{42}|C_{42}|$$

$$= 0 + 2(-1)^{2+2}\begin{vmatrix} 5 & 1 & 3 \\ 3 & 1 & 5 \\ 0 & 4 & 2 \end{vmatrix} + 0 + 1(-1)^{4+2}\begin{vmatrix} 5 & 1 & 3 \\ 4 & 6 & 0 \\ 3 & 1 & 5 \end{vmatrix}$$

Then substituting the values for the 3×3 subdeterminants,

$$|A| = 2(-60) + 1(88) = -32$$

(f) $A = \begin{bmatrix} 7 & 3 & 5 & 1 \\ 2 & 4 & 3 & 6 \\ 1 & 0 & 9 & 5 \\ 2 & 5 & 4 & 3 \end{bmatrix}$

Simplifying the matrix first by subtracting 7 times column 4 from column 1, 3 times column 4 from column 2, and 5 times column 4 from column 3,

$$A = \begin{bmatrix} 0 & 0 & 0 & 1 \\ -40 & -14 & -27 & 6 \\ -34 & -15 & -16 & 5 \\ -19 & -4 & -11 & 3 \end{bmatrix}$$

Then expanding along row 1,

$$|A| = a_{11}|C_{11}| + a_{12}|C_{12}| + a_{13}|C_{13}| + a_{14}|C_{14}| = 0 + 0 + 0 + 1(-1)^{1+4}\begin{vmatrix} -40 & -14 & -27 \\ -34 & -15 & -16 \\ -19 & -4 & -11 \end{vmatrix}$$

Substituting the value of the 3×3 determinant in parentheses,

$$|A| = -1(963) = -963$$

INVERTING A MATRIX

11.31. Find the inverse A^{-1} for the following matrices. Check your answer to part (*a*).

(*a*) $A = \begin{bmatrix} 24 & 15 \\ 8 & 7 \end{bmatrix}$

$$A^{-1} = \frac{1}{|A|} \text{Adj } A$$

Evaluating the determinant, $|A| = 24(7) - 15(8) = 48$

Then finding the cofactor matrix to get the adjoint,

$$C = \begin{bmatrix} 7 & -8 \\ -15 & 24 \end{bmatrix}$$

and $\text{Adj } A = C' = \begin{bmatrix} 7 & -15 \\ -8 & 24 \end{bmatrix}$

Thus, $A^{-1} = \frac{1}{48} \begin{bmatrix} 7 & -15 \\ -8 & 24 \end{bmatrix} = \begin{bmatrix} \frac{7}{48} & -\frac{5}{16} \\ -\frac{1}{6} & \frac{1}{2} \end{bmatrix}$ (*11.8*)

Checking to make sure $A^{-1}A = I$, and using the unreduced form of A^{-1} from (*11.8*) for easier computation,

$$A^{-1}A = \frac{1}{48} \begin{bmatrix} 7 & -15 \\ -8 & 24 \end{bmatrix} \begin{bmatrix} 24 & 15 \\ 8 & 7 \end{bmatrix} = \frac{1}{48} \begin{bmatrix} 7(24) - 15(8) & 7(15) - 15(7) \\ -8(24) + 24(8) & -8(15) + 24(7) \end{bmatrix}$$

$$= \frac{1}{48} \begin{bmatrix} 48 & 0 \\ 0 & 48 \end{bmatrix} = \begin{bmatrix} 1 & 0 \\ 0 & 1 \end{bmatrix}$$

(*b*) $A = \begin{bmatrix} 7 & 9 \\ 6 & 12 \end{bmatrix}$

$$|A| = 7(12) - 9(6) = 30$$

The cofactor matrix is

$$C = \begin{bmatrix} 12 & -6 \\ -9 & 7 \end{bmatrix}$$

and $\text{Adj } A = C' = \begin{bmatrix} 12 & -9 \\ -6 & 7 \end{bmatrix}$

Thus, $A^{-1} = \frac{1}{30} \begin{bmatrix} 12 & -9 \\ -6 & 7 \end{bmatrix} = \begin{bmatrix} \frac{2}{5} & -\frac{3}{10} \\ -\frac{1}{5} & \frac{7}{30} \end{bmatrix}$

(*c*) $A = \begin{bmatrix} -7 & 16 \\ -9 & 13 \end{bmatrix}$

$$|A| = -7(13) - 16(-9) = 53$$

$$C = \begin{bmatrix} 13 & 9 \\ -16 & -7 \end{bmatrix}$$

$$\text{Adj } A = C' = \begin{bmatrix} 13 & -16 \\ 9 & -7 \end{bmatrix}$$

$$A^{-1} = \frac{1}{53} \begin{bmatrix} 13 & -16 \\ 9 & -7 \end{bmatrix} = \begin{bmatrix} \frac{13}{53} & -\frac{16}{53} \\ \frac{9}{53} & -\frac{7}{53} \end{bmatrix}$$

(d) $A = \begin{bmatrix} 4 & 2 & 5 \\ 3 & 1 & 8 \\ 9 & 6 & 7 \end{bmatrix}$

$$|A| = 4(7 - 48) - 2(21 - 72) + 5(18 - 9) = -17$$

The cofactor matrix is

$$C = \begin{bmatrix} \begin{vmatrix} 1 & 8 \\ 6 & 7 \end{vmatrix} & -\begin{vmatrix} 3 & 8 \\ 9 & 7 \end{vmatrix} & \begin{vmatrix} 3 & 1 \\ 9 & 6 \end{vmatrix} \\ -\begin{vmatrix} 2 & 5 \\ 6 & 7 \end{vmatrix} & \begin{vmatrix} 4 & 5 \\ 9 & 7 \end{vmatrix} & -\begin{vmatrix} 4 & 2 \\ 9 & 6 \end{vmatrix} \\ \begin{vmatrix} 2 & 5 \\ 1 & 8 \end{vmatrix} & -\begin{vmatrix} 4 & 5 \\ 3 & 8 \end{vmatrix} & \begin{vmatrix} 4 & 2 \\ 3 & 1 \end{vmatrix} \end{bmatrix} = \begin{bmatrix} -41 & 51 & 9 \\ 16 & -17 & -6 \\ 11 & -17 & -2 \end{bmatrix}$$

and $\text{Adj } A = C' = \begin{bmatrix} -41 & 16 & 11 \\ 51 & -17 & -17 \\ 9 & -6 & -2 \end{bmatrix}$

Thus,

$$A^{-1} = -\frac{1}{17} \begin{bmatrix} -41 & 16 & 11 \\ 51 & -17 & -17 \\ 9 & -6 & -2 \end{bmatrix} = \begin{bmatrix} \frac{41}{17} & -\frac{16}{17} & -\frac{11}{17} \\ -3 & 1 & 1 \\ -\frac{9}{17} & \frac{6}{17} & \frac{2}{17} \end{bmatrix}$$

(e) $A = \begin{bmatrix} 14 & 0 & 6 \\ 9 & 5 & 0 \\ 0 & 11 & 8 \end{bmatrix}$

$$|A| = 14(40) - 0 + 6(99) = 1154$$

The cofactor matrix is

$$C = \begin{bmatrix} 40 & -72 & 99 \\ 66 & 112 & -154 \\ -30 & 54 & 70 \end{bmatrix}$$

The adjoint is

$$\text{Adj } A = \begin{bmatrix} 40 & 66 & -30 \\ -72 & 112 & 54 \\ 99 & -154 & 70 \end{bmatrix}$$

Then $A^{-1} = \frac{1}{1154} \begin{bmatrix} 40 & 66 & -30 \\ -72 & 112 & 54 \\ 99 & -154 & 70 \end{bmatrix} = \begin{bmatrix} \frac{20}{577} & \frac{33}{577} & -\frac{15}{577} \\ -\frac{36}{577} & \frac{56}{577} & \frac{27}{577} \\ \frac{99}{1154} & -\frac{77}{577} & \frac{35}{577} \end{bmatrix}$

MATRIX INVERSION IN EQUATION SOLUTIONS

11.32. Use matrix inversion to solve the following systems of linear equations. Check your answers on your own by substituting into the original equations.

(a) $4x_1 + 3x_2 = 28$
      $2x_1 + 5x_2 = 42$

$$\begin{bmatrix} 4 & 3 \\ 2 & 5 \end{bmatrix} \begin{bmatrix} x_1 \\ x_2 \end{bmatrix} = \begin{bmatrix} 28 \\ 42 \end{bmatrix}$$

where from Section 11.8, $X = A^{-1}B$. Find first the inverse of A, where $|A| = 4(5) - 3(2) = 14$. The cofactor matrix of A is

$$C = \begin{bmatrix} 5 & -2 \\ -3 & 4 \end{bmatrix}$$

and
$$\text{Adj } A = C' = \begin{bmatrix} 5 & -3 \\ -2 & 4 \end{bmatrix}$$

Thus,
$$A^{-1} = \frac{1}{14} \begin{bmatrix} 5 & -3 \\ -2 & 4 \end{bmatrix} = \begin{bmatrix} \frac{5}{14} & -\frac{3}{14} \\ -\frac{1}{7} & \frac{2}{7} \end{bmatrix}$$

Then substituting in $X = A^{-1}B$ and simply multiplying matrices,
$$X = \begin{bmatrix} \frac{5}{14} & -\frac{3}{14} \\ -\frac{1}{7} & \frac{2}{7} \end{bmatrix}_{2 \times 2} \begin{bmatrix} 28 \\ 42 \end{bmatrix}_{2 \times 1} = \begin{bmatrix} 10 - 9 \\ -4 + 12 \end{bmatrix}_{2 \times 1} = \begin{bmatrix} 1 \\ 8 \end{bmatrix}_{2 \times 1}$$

Thus, $\bar{x} = 1$ and $\bar{x}_2 = 8$.

(b) $6x_1 + 7x_2 = 56$
$2x_1 + 3x_2 = 44$

$$\begin{bmatrix} 6 & 7 \\ 2 & 3 \end{bmatrix}\begin{bmatrix} x_1 \\ x_2 \end{bmatrix} = \begin{bmatrix} 56 \\ 44 \end{bmatrix}$$

where $|A| = 6(3) - 7(2) = 4$.

$$C = \begin{bmatrix} 3 & -2 \\ -7 & 6 \end{bmatrix} \qquad \text{Adj } A = C' = \begin{bmatrix} 3 & -7 \\ -2 & 6 \end{bmatrix}$$

and
$$A^{-1} = \frac{1}{4} \begin{bmatrix} 3 & -7 \\ -2 & 6 \end{bmatrix} = \begin{bmatrix} \frac{3}{4} & -\frac{7}{4} \\ -\frac{1}{2} & \frac{3}{2} \end{bmatrix}$$

Thus,
$$X = \begin{bmatrix} \frac{3}{4} & -\frac{7}{4} \\ -\frac{1}{2} & \frac{3}{2} \end{bmatrix}_{2 \times 2} \begin{bmatrix} 56 \\ 44 \end{bmatrix}_{2 \times 1} = \begin{bmatrix} 42 - 77 \\ -28 + 66 \end{bmatrix}_{2 \times 1} = \begin{bmatrix} -35 \\ 38 \end{bmatrix}_{2 \times 1}$$

and $\bar{x}_1 = -35$ and $\bar{x}_2 = 38$.

11.33. The equilibrium conditions for two related markets (pork and beef) are given by
$$18P_b - \quad P_p = 87$$
$$-2P_b + 36P_p = 98$$

Find the equilibrium price for each market.
$$\begin{bmatrix} 18 & -1 \\ -2 & 36 \end{bmatrix}\begin{bmatrix} P_b \\ P_p \end{bmatrix} = \begin{bmatrix} 87 \\ 98 \end{bmatrix}$$

where $|A| = 18(36) - (-1)(-2) = 646$.

$$C = \begin{bmatrix} 36 & 2 \\ 1 & 18 \end{bmatrix} \qquad \text{Adj } A = \begin{bmatrix} 36 & 1 \\ 2 & 18 \end{bmatrix}$$

and
$$A^{-1} = \frac{1}{646} \begin{bmatrix} 36 & 1 \\ 2 & 18 \end{bmatrix} = \begin{bmatrix} \frac{18}{323} & \frac{1}{646} \\ \frac{1}{323} & \frac{9}{323} \end{bmatrix}$$

Thus,
$$X = \begin{bmatrix} \frac{18}{323} & \frac{1}{646} \\ \frac{1}{323} & \frac{9}{323} \end{bmatrix}\begin{bmatrix} 87 \\ 98 \end{bmatrix} = \begin{bmatrix} \frac{1615}{323} \\ \frac{969}{323} \end{bmatrix} = \begin{bmatrix} 5 \\ 3 \end{bmatrix}$$

and $\bar{P}_b = 5$ and $\bar{P}_p = 3$.

This is the same solution as that obtained by simultaneous equations in Problem 2.12. For practice try the inverse matrix solution for Problem 2.13.

11.34. The equilibrium condition for two substitute goods is given by
$$5P_1 - 2P_2 = 15$$
$$-P_1 + 8P_2 = 16$$

Find the equilibrium prices.

$$\begin{bmatrix} 5 & -2 \\ -1 & 8 \end{bmatrix}\begin{bmatrix} P_1 \\ P_2 \end{bmatrix} = \begin{bmatrix} 15 \\ 16 \end{bmatrix}$$

where $|A| = 5(8) - (-1)(-2) = 38$.

$$C = \begin{bmatrix} 8 & 1 \\ 2 & 5 \end{bmatrix} \qquad \text{Adj } A = \begin{bmatrix} 8 & 2 \\ 1 & 5 \end{bmatrix}$$

and

$$A^{-1} = \frac{1}{38}\begin{bmatrix} 8 & 2 \\ 1 & 5 \end{bmatrix} = \begin{bmatrix} \frac{4}{19} & \frac{1}{19} \\ \frac{1}{38} & \frac{5}{38} \end{bmatrix}$$

Thus,

$$X = \begin{bmatrix} \frac{4}{19} & \frac{1}{19} \\ \frac{1}{38} & \frac{5}{38} \end{bmatrix}\begin{bmatrix} 15 \\ 16 \end{bmatrix} = \begin{bmatrix} \dfrac{60 + 16}{19} \\ \dfrac{15 + 80}{38} \end{bmatrix} = \begin{bmatrix} 4 \\ 2.5 \end{bmatrix}$$

and $\bar{P}_1 = 4$ and $\bar{P}_2 = 2.5$.

11.35. Given: the IS equation $0.3Y + 100i - 252 = 0$ and the LM equation $0.25Y - 200i - 176 = 0$. Find the equilibrium level of income and rate of interest.

The IS and LM equations can be reduced to the form

$$0.3Y + 100i = 252$$
$$0.25Y - 200i = 176$$

and then expressed in matrix form where

$$A = \begin{bmatrix} 0.3 & 100 \\ 0.25 & -200 \end{bmatrix} \qquad X = \begin{bmatrix} Y \\ i \end{bmatrix} \qquad B = \begin{bmatrix} 252 \\ 176 \end{bmatrix}$$

Thus,

$$|A| = 0.3(-200) - 100(0.25) = -85$$

$$C = \begin{bmatrix} -200 & -0.25 \\ -100 & 0.3 \end{bmatrix}$$

$$\text{Adj } A = \begin{bmatrix} -200 & -100 \\ -0.25 & 0.3 \end{bmatrix}$$

and

$$A^{-1} = -\frac{1}{85}\begin{bmatrix} -200 & -100 \\ -0.25 & 0.3 \end{bmatrix} = \begin{bmatrix} \dfrac{40}{17} & \dfrac{20}{17} \\ \dfrac{0.05}{17} & -\dfrac{0.06}{17} \end{bmatrix}$$

Thus,

$$X = \begin{bmatrix} \dfrac{40}{17} & \dfrac{20}{17} \\ \dfrac{0.05}{17} & -\dfrac{0.06}{17} \end{bmatrix}\begin{bmatrix} 252 \\ 176 \end{bmatrix} = \begin{bmatrix} \dfrac{10\,080 + 3520}{17} \\ \dfrac{12.6 - 10.56}{17} \end{bmatrix} = \begin{bmatrix} 800 \\ 0.12 \end{bmatrix}$$

In equilibrium $\bar{Y} = 800$ and $\bar{i} = 0.12$ as found in Problem 2.23 where simultaneous equations were used. On your own, practice with Problem 2.24.

11.36. Use matrix inversion to solve for the unknowns in the system of linear equations given below.

$$3x_1 + 5x_2 + x_3 = 36$$
$$x_1 + 2x_2 + 4x_3 = 42$$
$$4x_1 + 3x_2 + 2x_3 = 28$$

$$\begin{bmatrix} 3 & 5 & 1 \\ 1 & 2 & 4 \\ 4 & 3 & 2 \end{bmatrix}\begin{bmatrix} x_1 \\ x_2 \\ x_3 \end{bmatrix} = \begin{bmatrix} 36 \\ 42 \\ 28 \end{bmatrix}$$

where $|A| = 3(4 - 12) - 5(2 - 16) + 1(3 - 8) = 41$.

$$C = \begin{bmatrix} \begin{vmatrix} 2 & 4 \\ 3 & 2 \end{vmatrix} & -\begin{vmatrix} 1 & 4 \\ 4 & 2 \end{vmatrix} & \begin{vmatrix} 1 & 2 \\ 4 & 3 \end{vmatrix} \\ -\begin{vmatrix} 5 & 1 \\ 3 & 2 \end{vmatrix} & \begin{vmatrix} 3 & 1 \\ 4 & 2 \end{vmatrix} & -\begin{vmatrix} 3 & 5 \\ 4 & 3 \end{vmatrix} \\ \begin{vmatrix} 5 & 1 \\ 2 & 4 \end{vmatrix} & -\begin{vmatrix} 3 & 1 \\ 1 & 4 \end{vmatrix} & \begin{vmatrix} 3 & 5 \\ 1 & 2 \end{vmatrix} \end{bmatrix} = \begin{bmatrix} -8 & 14 & -5 \\ -7 & 2 & 11 \\ 18 & -11 & 1 \end{bmatrix}$$

$$\text{Adj } A = \begin{bmatrix} -8 & -7 & 18 \\ 14 & 2 & -11 \\ -5 & 11 & 1 \end{bmatrix}$$

and

$$A^{-1} = \frac{1}{41}\begin{bmatrix} -8 & -7 & 18 \\ 14 & 2 & -11 \\ -5 & 11 & 1 \end{bmatrix} = \begin{bmatrix} -\frac{8}{41} & -\frac{7}{41} & \frac{18}{41} \\ \frac{14}{41} & \frac{2}{41} & -\frac{11}{41} \\ -\frac{5}{41} & \frac{11}{41} & \frac{1}{41} \end{bmatrix}$$

Thus,

$$X = \begin{bmatrix} -\frac{8}{41} & -\frac{7}{41} & \frac{18}{41} \\ \frac{14}{41} & \frac{2}{41} & -\frac{11}{41} \\ -\frac{5}{41} & \frac{11}{41} & \frac{1}{41} \end{bmatrix}\begin{bmatrix} 36 \\ 42 \\ 28 \end{bmatrix} = \begin{bmatrix} \dfrac{-288 - 294 + 504}{41} \\ \dfrac{504 + 84 - 308}{41} \\ \dfrac{-180 + 462 + 28}{41} \end{bmatrix} = \begin{bmatrix} -1.902 \\ 6.829 \\ 7.561 \end{bmatrix} = \begin{bmatrix} \bar{x}_1 \\ \bar{x}_2 \\ \bar{x}_3 \end{bmatrix}$$

11.37. Redo Problem 11.36, given

$$2x_1 + 4x_2 - 3x_3 = 12$$
$$3x_1 - 5x_2 + 2x_3 = 13$$
$$-x_1 + 3x_2 + 2x_3 = 17$$

$$\begin{bmatrix} 2 & 4 & -3 \\ 3 & -5 & 2 \\ -1 & 3 & 2 \end{bmatrix}\begin{bmatrix} x_1 \\ x_2 \\ x_3 \end{bmatrix} = \begin{bmatrix} 12 \\ 13 \\ 17 \end{bmatrix}$$

where $|A| = 2(-16) - 4(8) - 3(4) = -76$.

$$C = \begin{bmatrix} \begin{vmatrix} -5 & 2 \\ 3 & 2 \end{vmatrix} & -\begin{vmatrix} 3 & 2 \\ -1 & 2 \end{vmatrix} & \begin{vmatrix} 3 & -5 \\ -1 & 3 \end{vmatrix} \\ -\begin{vmatrix} 4 & -3 \\ 3 & 2 \end{vmatrix} & \begin{vmatrix} 2 & -3 \\ -1 & 2 \end{vmatrix} & -\begin{vmatrix} 2 & 4 \\ -1 & 3 \end{vmatrix} \\ \begin{vmatrix} 4 & -3 \\ -5 & 2 \end{vmatrix} & -\begin{vmatrix} 2 & -3 \\ 3 & 2 \end{vmatrix} & \begin{vmatrix} 2 & 4 \\ 3 & -5 \end{vmatrix} \end{bmatrix} = \begin{bmatrix} -16 & -8 & 4 \\ -17 & 1 & -10 \\ -7 & -13 & -22 \end{bmatrix}$$

$$\text{Adj } A = \begin{bmatrix} -16 & -17 & -7 \\ -8 & 1 & -13 \\ 4 & -10 & -22 \end{bmatrix}$$

$$A^{-1} = -\frac{1}{76} \begin{bmatrix} -16 & -17 & -7 \\ -8 & 1 & -13 \\ 4 & -10 & -22 \end{bmatrix} = \begin{bmatrix} \frac{16}{76} & \frac{17}{76} & \frac{7}{76} \\ \frac{8}{76} & -\frac{1}{76} & \frac{13}{76} \\ -\frac{4}{76} & \frac{10}{76} & \frac{22}{76} \end{bmatrix}$$

where the common denominator 76 is deliberately kept to simplify later calculations.

Thus,

$$X = \begin{bmatrix} \frac{16}{76} & \frac{17}{76} & \frac{7}{76} \\ \frac{8}{76} & -\frac{1}{76} & \frac{13}{76} \\ -\frac{4}{76} & \frac{10}{76} & \frac{22}{76} \end{bmatrix} \begin{bmatrix} 12 \\ 13 \\ 17 \end{bmatrix} = \begin{bmatrix} \dfrac{192 + 221 + 119}{76} \\ \dfrac{96 - 13 + 221}{76} \\ \dfrac{-48 + 130 + 374}{76} \end{bmatrix} = \begin{bmatrix} 7 \\ 4 \\ 6 \end{bmatrix} = \begin{bmatrix} \overline{x}_1 \\ \overline{x}_2 \\ \overline{x}_3 \end{bmatrix}$$

11.38. The equilibrium condition for three related markets is given by

$$\begin{aligned} 11P_1 - P_2 - P_3 &= 31 \\ -P_1 + 6P_2 - 2P_3 &= 26 \\ -P_1 - 2P_2 + 7P_3 &= 24 \end{aligned}$$

Find the equilibrium price for each market.

$$\begin{bmatrix} 11 & -1 & -1 \\ -1 & 6 & -2 \\ -1 & -2 & 7 \end{bmatrix} \begin{bmatrix} P_1 \\ P_2 \\ P_3 \end{bmatrix} = \begin{bmatrix} 31 \\ 26 \\ 24 \end{bmatrix}$$

where $|A| = 11(38) + 1(-9) - 1(8) = 401$.

$$C = \begin{bmatrix} \begin{vmatrix} 6 & -2 \\ -2 & 7 \end{vmatrix} & -\begin{vmatrix} -1 & -2 \\ -1 & 7 \end{vmatrix} & \begin{vmatrix} -1 & 6 \\ -1 & -2 \end{vmatrix} \\ -\begin{vmatrix} -1 & -1 \\ -2 & 7 \end{vmatrix} & \begin{vmatrix} 11 & -1 \\ -1 & 7 \end{vmatrix} & -\begin{vmatrix} 11 & -1 \\ -1 & -2 \end{vmatrix} \\ \begin{vmatrix} -1 & -1 \\ 6 & -2 \end{vmatrix} & -\begin{vmatrix} 11 & -1 \\ -1 & -2 \end{vmatrix} & \begin{vmatrix} 11 & -1 \\ -1 & 6 \end{vmatrix} \end{bmatrix} = \begin{bmatrix} 38 & 9 & 8 \\ 9 & 76 & 23 \\ 8 & 23 & 65 \end{bmatrix}$$

$$\text{Adj } A = \begin{bmatrix} 38 & 9 & 8 \\ 9 & 76 & 23 \\ 8 & 23 & 65 \end{bmatrix}$$

$$A^{-1} = \frac{1}{401} \begin{bmatrix} 38 & 9 & 8 \\ 9 & 76 & 23 \\ 8 & 23 & 65 \end{bmatrix} = \begin{bmatrix} \frac{38}{401} & \frac{9}{401} & \frac{8}{401} \\ \frac{9}{401} & \frac{76}{401} & \frac{23}{401} \\ \frac{8}{401} & \frac{23}{401} & \frac{65}{401} \end{bmatrix}$$

$$X = \begin{bmatrix} \frac{38}{401} & \frac{9}{401} & \frac{8}{401} \\ \frac{9}{401} & \frac{76}{401} & \frac{23}{401} \\ \frac{8}{401} & \frac{23}{401} & \frac{65}{401} \end{bmatrix} \begin{bmatrix} 31 \\ 26 \\ 24 \end{bmatrix} = \begin{bmatrix} \dfrac{1178 + 234 + 192}{401} \\ \dfrac{279 + 1976 + 552}{401} \\ \dfrac{248 + 598 + 1560}{401} \end{bmatrix} = \begin{bmatrix} 4 \\ 7 \\ 6 \end{bmatrix} = \begin{bmatrix} \overline{P}_1 \\ \overline{P}_2 \\ \overline{P}_3 \end{bmatrix}$$

See Problem 2.16 for the same solution with simultaneous equations.

11.39. Given $Y = C + I_0$, where $C = C_0 + bY$. Use matrix inversion to find the equilibrium level of Y and C.

The given equations can first be rearranged so that the endogenous variables C and Y, together with their coefficients $-b$, are on the left-hand side of the equation and the exogenous variables C_0 and I_0 are on the right.

$$Y - C = I_0$$
$$-bY + C = C_0$$

Thus,

$$\begin{bmatrix} 1 & -1 \\ -b & 1 \end{bmatrix} \begin{bmatrix} Y \\ C \end{bmatrix} = \begin{bmatrix} I_0 \\ C_0 \end{bmatrix}$$

The determinant of the coefficient matrix is $|A| = 1(1) + 1(-b) = 1 - b$. The cofactor matrix is

$$C = \begin{bmatrix} 1 & b \\ 1 & 1 \end{bmatrix}$$

$$\text{Adj } A = \begin{bmatrix} 1 & 1 \\ b & 1 \end{bmatrix}$$

and

$$A^{-1} = \frac{1}{1-b} \begin{bmatrix} 1 & 1 \\ b & 1 \end{bmatrix}$$

Letting $X = \begin{bmatrix} Y \\ C \end{bmatrix}$,

$$X = \frac{1}{1-b} \begin{bmatrix} 1 & 1 \\ b & 1 \end{bmatrix} \begin{bmatrix} I_0 \\ C_0 \end{bmatrix} = \frac{1}{1-b} \begin{bmatrix} I_0 + C_0 \\ bI_0 + C_0 \end{bmatrix}$$

Thus,

$$\bar{Y} = \frac{1}{1-b}(I_0 + C_0) \qquad \bar{C} = \frac{1}{1-b}(C_0 + bI_0)$$

Example 3 in Chapter 2 was solved for the equilibrium level of income without matrices.

CRAMER'S RULE

11.40. Use Cramer's rule to solve for the unknowns in each of the following:

(a) $2x_1 + 6x_2 = 22$
        $-x_1 + 5x_2 = 53$

From Cramer's rule,

$$\bar{x}_i = \frac{|A_i|}{|A|}$$

where A_i is a special matrix formed by replacing the column of coefficients of x_i with the column of constants. Thus, from the original data,

$$\begin{bmatrix} 2 & 6 \\ -1 & 5 \end{bmatrix} \begin{bmatrix} x_1 \\ x_2 \end{bmatrix} = \begin{bmatrix} 22 \\ 53 \end{bmatrix}$$

where $|A| = 2(5) - 6(-1) = 16$.
Replacing the first column of the coefficient matrix with the column of constants,

$$A_1 = \begin{bmatrix} 22 & 6 \\ 53 & 5 \end{bmatrix}$$

where $|A_1| = 22(5) - 6(53) = -208$. Thus,

$$\bar{x}_1 = \frac{|A_1|}{|A|} = -\frac{208}{16} = -13$$

Replacing the second column of the original coefficient matrix with the column of constants,

$$A_2 = \begin{bmatrix} 2 & 22 \\ -1 & 53 \end{bmatrix}$$

where $|A_2| = 2(53) - 22(-1) = 128$. Thus,

$$\bar{x}_2 = \frac{|A_2|}{|A|} = \frac{128}{16} = 8$$

(b) $5x_1 - 3x_2 = 28$
       $-2x_1 + 4x_2 = 14$

$$A = \begin{bmatrix} 5 & -3 \\ -2 & 4 \end{bmatrix}$$

where $|A| = 5(4) - (-3)(-2) = 14$.

$$A_1 = \begin{bmatrix} 28 & -3 \\ 14 & 4 \end{bmatrix}$$

where $|A_1| = 28(4) - (-3)(14) = 154$.

$$A_2 = \begin{bmatrix} 5 & 28 \\ -2 & 14 \end{bmatrix}$$

where $|A_2| = 5(14) - 28(-2) = 126$. Thus,

$$\bar{x}_1 = \frac{|A_1|}{|A|} = \frac{154}{14} = 11 \quad \text{and} \quad \bar{x}_2 = \frac{|A_2|}{|A|} = \frac{126}{14} = 9$$

(c) $7p_1 + 2p_2 = 60$
       $p_1 + 8p_2 = 78$

$$A = \begin{bmatrix} 7 & 2 \\ 1 & 8 \end{bmatrix}$$

where $|A| = 7(8) - 2(1) = 54$.

$$A_1 = \begin{bmatrix} 60 & 2 \\ 78 & 8 \end{bmatrix}$$

where $|A_1| = 60(8) - 2(78) = 324$.

$$A_2 = \begin{bmatrix} 7 & 60 \\ 1 & 78 \end{bmatrix}$$

where $|A_2| = 7(78) - 60(1) = 486$.

$$\bar{p}_1 = \frac{|A_1|}{|A|} = \frac{324}{54} = 6 \quad \text{and} \quad \bar{p}_2 = \frac{|A_2|}{|A|} = \frac{486}{54} = 9$$

(d) $18P_b - P_p = 87$
       $-2P_b + 36P_p = 98$

$$A = \begin{bmatrix} 18 & -1 \\ -2 & 36 \end{bmatrix}$$

where $|A| = 18(36) - (-1)(-2) = 646$.

$$A_1 = \begin{bmatrix} 87 & -1 \\ 98 & 36 \end{bmatrix}$$

where $|A_1| = 87(36) + 1(98) = 3230$.

$$A_2 = \begin{bmatrix} 18 & 87 \\ -2 & 98 \end{bmatrix}$$

where $|A_2| = 18(98) - 87(-2) = 1938$.

$$\bar{P}_b = \frac{|A_1|}{|A|} = \frac{3230}{646} = 5 \quad \text{and} \quad \bar{P}_p = \frac{|A_2|}{|A|} = \frac{1938}{646} = 3$$

Compare the work involved in this method of solution with the work involved in Problems 2.12 and 11.33 where the same problem is treated first with simultaneous equations and then with matrix inversion.

11.41. Redo Problem 11.40 for each of the following:

(a) $0.4Y + 150i = 209$
$0.1Y - 250i = 35$

$$A = \begin{bmatrix} 0.4 & 150 \\ 0.1 & -250 \end{bmatrix}$$

where $|A| = 0.4(-250) - 150(0.1) = -115$.

$$A_1 = \begin{bmatrix} 209 & 150 \\ 35 & -250 \end{bmatrix}$$

where $|A_1| = 209(-250) - 150(35) = -57\,500$.

$$A_2 = \begin{bmatrix} 0.4 & 209 \\ 0.1 & 35 \end{bmatrix}$$

where $|A_2| = 0.4(35) - 209(0.1) = -6.9$.

$$\bar{Y} = \frac{|A_1|}{|A|} = \frac{-57\,500}{-115} = 500 \quad \text{and} \quad \bar{i} = \frac{|A_2|}{|A|} = \frac{-6.9}{-115} = 0.06$$

Compare this method of solution with Problem 2.24.

(b) $5x_1 - 2x_2 + 3x_3 = 16$
$2x_1 + 3x_2 - 5x_3 = 2$
$4x_1 - 5x_2 + 6x_3 = 7$

$$|A| = \begin{vmatrix} 5 & -2 & 3 \\ 2 & 3 & -5 \\ 4 & -5 & 6 \end{vmatrix} = 5(18 - 25) + 2(12 + 20) + 3(-10 - 12) = -37$$

$$|A_1| = \begin{vmatrix} 16 & -2 & 3 \\ 2 & 3 & -5 \\ 7 & -5 & 6 \end{vmatrix} = 16(18 - 25) + 2(12 + 35) + 3(-10 - 21) = -111$$

$$|A_2| = \begin{vmatrix} 5 & 16 & 3 \\ 2 & 2 & -5 \\ 4 & 7 & 6 \end{vmatrix} = 5(12 + 35) - 16(12 + 20) + 3(14 - 8) = -259$$

$$|A_3| = \begin{vmatrix} 5 & -2 & 16 \\ 2 & 3 & 2 \\ 4 & -5 & 7 \end{vmatrix} = 5(21 + 10) + 2(14 - 8) + 16(-10 - 12) = -185$$

$$\bar{x}_1 = \frac{|A_1|}{|A|} = \frac{-111}{-37} = 3 \quad \bar{x}_2 = \frac{|A_2|}{|A|} = \frac{-259}{-37} = 7 \quad \bar{x}_3 = \frac{|A_3|}{|A|} = \frac{-185}{-37} = 5$$

(c) $5x_1 - 4x_2 \qquad = 10$

$\qquad 4x_2 - 5x_3 = -5$

$\quad 3x_1 \qquad - 2x_3 = 20$

$$|A| = \begin{vmatrix} 5 & -4 & 0 \\ 0 & 4 & -5 \\ 3 & 0 & -2 \end{vmatrix} = 5(-8) + 4(15) = 20$$

$$|A_1| = \begin{vmatrix} 10 & -4 & 0 \\ -5 & 4 & -5 \\ 20 & 0 & -2 \end{vmatrix} = 10(-8) + 4(110) = 360$$

$$|A_2| = \begin{vmatrix} 5 & 10 & 0 \\ 0 & -5 & -5 \\ 3 & 20 & -2 \end{vmatrix} = 5(110) - 10(15) = 400$$

$$|A_3| = \begin{vmatrix} 5 & -4 & 10 \\ 0 & 4 & -5 \\ 3 & 0 & 20 \end{vmatrix} = 5(80) + 3(-20) = 340$$

$$\bar{x}_1 = \frac{|A_1|}{|A|} = \frac{360}{20} = 18 \qquad \bar{x}_2 = \frac{|A_2|}{|A|} = \frac{400}{20} = 20 \qquad \bar{x}_3 = \frac{|A_3|}{|A|} = \frac{340}{20} = 17$$

(d) $2x_1 + 4x_2 - x_3 = 52$

$\quad -x_1 + 5x_2 + 3x_3 = 72$

$\quad 3x_1 - 7x_2 + 2x_3 = 10$

$$|A| = \begin{vmatrix} 2 & 4 & -1 \\ -1 & 5 & 3 \\ 3 & -7 & 2 \end{vmatrix} = 2(31) - 4(-11) - 1(-8) = 114$$

$$|A_1| = \begin{vmatrix} 52 & 4 & -1 \\ 72 & 5 & 3 \\ 10 & -7 & 2 \end{vmatrix} = 52(31) - 4(114) - 1(-554) = 1710$$

$$|A_2| = \begin{vmatrix} 2 & 52 & -1 \\ -1 & 72 & 3 \\ 3 & 10 & 2 \end{vmatrix} = 2(114) - 52(-11) - 1(-226) = 1026$$

$$|A_3| = \begin{vmatrix} 2 & 4 & 52 \\ -1 & 5 & 72 \\ 3 & -7 & 10 \end{vmatrix} = 2(554) - 4(-226) + 52(-8) = 1596$$

$$\bar{x}_1 = \frac{|A_1|}{|A|} = \frac{1710}{114} = 15 \qquad \bar{x}_2 = \frac{|A_2|}{|A|} = \frac{1026}{114} = 9 \qquad \bar{x}_3 = \frac{|A_3|}{|A|} = \frac{1596}{114} = 14$$

(e) $11p_1 - p_2 - p_3 = 31$

$\quad -p_1 + 6p_2 - 2p_3 = 26$

$\quad -p_1 - 2p_2 + 7p_3 = 24$

$$|A| = \begin{vmatrix} 11 & -1 & -1 \\ -1 & 6 & -2 \\ -1 & -2 & 7 \end{vmatrix} = 11(38) + 1(-9) - 1(8) = 401$$

$$|A_1| = \begin{vmatrix} 31 & -1 & -1 \\ 26 & 6 & -2 \\ 24 & -2 & 7 \end{vmatrix} = 31(38) + 1(230) - 1(-196) = 1604$$

$$|A_2| = \begin{vmatrix} 11 & 31 & -1 \\ -1 & 26 & -2 \\ -1 & 24 & 7 \end{vmatrix} = 11(230) - 31(-9) - 1(2) = 2807$$

$$|A_3| = \begin{vmatrix} 11 & -1 & 31 \\ -1 & 6 & 26 \\ -1 & -2 & 24 \end{vmatrix} = 11(196) + 1(2) + 31(8) = 2406$$

Thus, $\quad \bar{p}_1 = \dfrac{|A_1|}{|A|} = \dfrac{1604}{401} = 4 \quad \bar{p}_2 = \dfrac{|A_2|}{|A|} = \dfrac{2807}{401} = 7 \quad \bar{p}_3 = \dfrac{|A_3|}{|A|} = \dfrac{2406}{401} = 6$

Compare the work involved in this type of solution with the work involved in Problems 2.16 and 11.38.

11.42. Use Cramer's rule to solve for x and y, given the first-order conditions for constrained optimization from Example 7 of Chapter 6:

$$\frac{\partial TC}{\partial x} = 16x - y - \lambda = 0$$

$$\frac{\partial TC}{\partial y} = 24y - x - \lambda = 0$$

$$\frac{\partial TC}{\partial \lambda} = 42 - x - y = 0$$

Rearrange the equations,

$$\begin{aligned} 16x - \quad y - \lambda &= \quad 0 \\ -x + 24y - \lambda &= \quad 0 \\ -x - \quad y \quad\quad &= -42 \end{aligned}$$

and set them in matrix form.

$$\begin{bmatrix} 16 & -1 & -1 \\ -1 & 24 & -1 \\ -1 & -1 & 0 \end{bmatrix} \begin{bmatrix} x \\ y \\ \lambda \end{bmatrix} = \begin{bmatrix} 0 \\ 0 \\ -42 \end{bmatrix}$$

Expanding along the third column,

$$|A| = (-1)(1 + 24) - (-1)(-16 - 1) + 0 = -42$$

$$A_1 = \begin{bmatrix} 0 & -1 & -1 \\ 0 & 24 & -1 \\ -42 & -1 & 0 \end{bmatrix}$$

Expanding along the first column, $|A_1| = -42(1 + 24) = -1050$.

$$A_2 = \begin{bmatrix} 16 & 0 & -1 \\ -1 & 0 & -1 \\ -1 & -42 & 0 \end{bmatrix}$$

Expanding along the second column, $|A_2| = -(-42)(-16 - 1) = -714$.

$$A_3 = \begin{bmatrix} 16 & -1 & 0 \\ -1 & 24 & 0 \\ -1 & -1 & -42 \end{bmatrix}$$

Expanding along the third column, $|A_3| = -42(384 - 1) = -16086$.

Thus,
$$\bar{x} = \frac{|A_1|}{|A|} = \frac{-1050}{-42} = 25 \qquad \bar{y} = \frac{|A_2|}{|A|} = \frac{-714}{-42} = 17$$

and
$$\bar{\lambda} = \frac{|A_3|}{|A|} = \frac{-16\,086}{-42} = 383$$

11.43. Use Cramer's rule to find the critical values of Q_1 and Q_2, given the first-order conditions for constrained utility maximization in Problem 6.37: $Q_2 - 10\lambda = 0$, $Q_1 - 2\lambda = 0$, and $240 - 10Q_1 - 2Q_2 = 0$.

$$\begin{bmatrix} 0 & 1 & -10 \\ 1 & 0 & -2 \\ -10 & -2 & 0 \end{bmatrix} \begin{bmatrix} Q_1 \\ Q_2 \\ \lambda \end{bmatrix} = \begin{bmatrix} 0 \\ 0 \\ -240 \end{bmatrix}$$

Thus,
$$|A| = -(1)(-20) + (-10)(-2) = 40.$$

$$A_1 = \begin{bmatrix} 0 & 1 & -10 \\ 0 & 0 & -2 \\ -240 & -2 & 0 \end{bmatrix} = -240(-2) = 480$$

$$A_2 = \begin{bmatrix} 0 & 0 & -10 \\ 1 & 0 & -2 \\ -10 & -240 & 0 \end{bmatrix} = -(-240)(10) = 2400$$

$$A_3 = \begin{bmatrix} 0 & 1 & 0 \\ 1 & 0 & 0 \\ -10 & -2 & -240 \end{bmatrix} = -240(-1) = 240$$

Thus,
$$\bar{Q}_1 = \frac{|A_1|}{|A|} = \frac{480}{40} = 12 \qquad \bar{Q}_2 = \frac{|A_2|}{|A|} = \frac{2400}{40} = 60$$

and
$$\bar{\lambda} = \frac{|A_3|}{|A|} = \frac{240}{40} = 6$$

11.44. Given
$$ax_1 + bx_2 = g \qquad (11.9)$$
$$cx_1 + dx_2 = h \qquad (11.10)$$

Prove Cramer's rule by showing

$$\bar{x}_1 = \frac{\begin{vmatrix} g & b \\ h & d \end{vmatrix}}{\begin{vmatrix} a & b \\ c & d \end{vmatrix}} = \frac{|A_1|}{|A|} \qquad \bar{x}_2 = \frac{\begin{vmatrix} a & g \\ c & h \end{vmatrix}}{\begin{vmatrix} a & b \\ c & d \end{vmatrix}} = \frac{|A_2|}{|A|}$$

Dividing (11.9) by b,
$$\frac{a}{b} x_1 + x_2 = \frac{g}{b} \qquad (11.11)$$

Multiplying (11.11) by d and subtracting (11.10),

$$\frac{ad}{b} x_1 + dx_2 = \frac{dg}{b}$$
$$-cx_1 - dx_2 = -h$$
$$\overline{\left(\frac{ad - cb}{b}\right) x_1 \qquad\qquad = \frac{dg - hb}{b}}$$

$$\bar{x}_1 = \frac{dg - hb}{ad - cb} = \frac{\begin{vmatrix} g & b \\ h & d \end{vmatrix}}{\begin{vmatrix} a & b \\ c & d \end{vmatrix}} = \frac{|A_1|}{|A|}$$

Similarly, dividing (11.9) by a,

$$x_1 + \frac{b}{a} x_2 = \frac{g}{a} \tag{11.12}$$

Multiplying (11.12) by $-c$ and adding to (11.10),

$$-cx_1 - \frac{bc}{a} x_2 = -\frac{cg}{a}$$

$$\underline{cx_1 + \quad dx_2 = h}$$

$$\left(\frac{ad - bc}{a}\right)x_2 = \frac{ah - cg}{a}$$

$$\bar{x}_2 = \frac{ah - cg}{ad - bc} = \frac{\begin{vmatrix} a & g \\ c & h \end{vmatrix}}{\begin{vmatrix} a & b \\ c & d \end{vmatrix}} = \frac{|A_2|}{|A|} \qquad \text{Q.E.D.}$$

GAUSSIAN METHOD FOR FINDING THE INVERSE

11.45. Use the Gaussian elimination method to find the inverse of the following matrix:

$$A = \begin{bmatrix} 7 & 9 \\ 6 & 12 \end{bmatrix}$$

Set up an augmented matrix with the identity matrix to the right. Then apply row operations until the original matrix is reduced to an identity matrix. The matrix on the right will then be the inverse A^{-1}. Thus,

$$A \,|\, B = \begin{bmatrix} 7 & 9 & 1 & 0 \\ 6 & 12 & 0 & 1 \end{bmatrix}$$

1a.   Multiply row 1 by $\frac{1}{7}$,

$$\begin{bmatrix} 1 & \frac{9}{7} & \frac{1}{7} & 0 \\ 6 & 12 & 0 & 1 \end{bmatrix}$$

1b.   Subtract 6 times row 1 from row 2,

$$\begin{bmatrix} 1 & \frac{9}{7} & \frac{1}{7} & 0 \\ 0 & \frac{30}{7} & -\frac{6}{7} & 1 \end{bmatrix}$$

2a.   Multiply row 2 by $\frac{7}{30}$,

$$\begin{bmatrix} 1 & \frac{9}{7} & \frac{1}{7} & 0 \\ 0 & 1 & -\frac{1}{5} & \frac{7}{30} \end{bmatrix}$$

2b.   Subtract $\frac{9}{7}$ times row 2 from row 1,

$$\begin{bmatrix} 1 & 0 & \frac{2}{5} & -\frac{3}{10} \\ 0 & 1 & -\frac{1}{5} & \frac{7}{30} \end{bmatrix}$$

Thus,

$$A^{-1} = \begin{bmatrix} \frac{2}{5} & -\frac{3}{10} \\ -\frac{1}{5} & \frac{7}{30} \end{bmatrix}$$

as was found by the adjoint method in Problem 11.31(b).

11.46. Redo Problem 11.45, given

$$A = \begin{bmatrix} 4 & 2 & 5 \\ 3 & 1 & 8 \\ 9 & 6 & 7 \end{bmatrix}$$

$$A\,|\,B = \begin{bmatrix} 4 & 2 & 5 & 1 & 0 & 0 \\ 3 & 1 & 8 & 0 & 1 & 0 \\ 9 & 6 & 7 & 0 & 0 & 1 \end{bmatrix}$$

1. Multiply row 1 by $\frac{1}{4}$,

$$\begin{bmatrix} 1 & \frac{1}{2} & \frac{5}{4} & \frac{1}{4} & 0 & 0 \\ 3 & 1 & 8 & 0 & 1 & 0 \\ 9 & 6 & 7 & 0 & 0 & 1 \end{bmatrix}$$

2. Subtract 3 times row 1 from row 2 and 9 times row 1 from row 3,

$$\begin{bmatrix} 1 & \frac{1}{2} & \frac{5}{4} & \frac{1}{4} & 0 & 0 \\ 0 & -\frac{1}{2} & \frac{17}{4} & -\frac{3}{4} & 1 & 0 \\ 0 & \frac{3}{2} & -\frac{17}{4} & -\frac{9}{4} & 0 & 1 \end{bmatrix}$$

3. Multiply row 2 by -2,

$$\begin{bmatrix} 1 & \frac{1}{2} & \frac{5}{4} & \frac{1}{4} & 0 & 0 \\ 0 & 1 & -\frac{17}{2} & \frac{3}{2} & -2 & 0 \\ 0 & \frac{3}{2} & -\frac{17}{4} & -\frac{9}{4} & 0 & 1 \end{bmatrix}$$

4. Subtract $\frac{1}{2}$ row 2 from row 1 and $\frac{3}{2}$ row 2 from row 3,

$$\begin{bmatrix} 1 & 0 & \frac{11}{2} & -\frac{1}{2} & 1 & 0 \\ 0 & 1 & -\frac{17}{2} & \frac{3}{2} & -2 & 0 \\ 0 & 0 & \frac{17}{2} & -\frac{9}{2} & 3 & 1 \end{bmatrix}$$

5. Multiply row 3 by $\frac{2}{17}$,

$$\begin{bmatrix} 1 & 0 & \frac{11}{2} & -\frac{1}{2} & 1 & 0 \\ 0 & 1 & -\frac{17}{2} & \frac{3}{2} & -2 & 0 \\ 0 & 0 & 1 & -\frac{9}{17} & \frac{6}{17} & \frac{2}{17} \end{bmatrix}$$

6. Subtract $\frac{11}{2}$ times row 3 from row 1 and add $\frac{17}{2}$ times row 3 to row 2,

$$\begin{bmatrix} 1 & 0 & 0 & \frac{41}{17} & -\frac{16}{17} & -\frac{11}{17} \\ 0 & 1 & 0 & -3 & 1 & 1 \\ 0 & 0 & 1 & -\frac{9}{17} & \frac{6}{17} & \frac{2}{17} \end{bmatrix}$$

Thus,

$$A^{-1} = \begin{bmatrix} \frac{41}{17} & -\frac{16}{17} & -\frac{11}{17} \\ -3 & 1 & 1 \\ -\frac{9}{17} & \frac{6}{17} & \frac{2}{17} \end{bmatrix}$$

as was found by the adjoint method in Problem 11.31(d).

Chapter 12

Special Determinants and Matrices
and Their Use in Economics

12.1 THE JACOBIAN

Section 11.1 showed how to test for linear dependence through the use of a simple determinant. In contrast, a *Jacobian determinant* permits testing for functional dependence, both linear *and* nonlinear. A Jacobian determinant $|J|$ is composed of all the first-order partial derivatives of a system of equations, arranged in ordered sequence. Given

$$y_1 = f_1(x_1, x_2, x_3)$$
$$y_2 = f_2(x_1, x_2, x_3)$$
$$y_3 = f_3(x_1, x_2, x_3)$$

$$|J| = \begin{vmatrix} \partial y_1, \partial y_2, \partial y_3 \\ \partial x_1, \partial x_2, \partial x_3 \end{vmatrix} = \begin{vmatrix} \dfrac{\partial y_1}{\partial x_1} & \dfrac{\partial y_1}{\partial x_2} & \dfrac{\partial y_1}{\partial x_3} \\ \dfrac{\partial y_2}{\partial x_1} & \dfrac{\partial y_2}{\partial x_2} & \dfrac{\partial y_2}{\partial x_3} \\ \dfrac{\partial y_3}{\partial x_1} & \dfrac{\partial y_3}{\partial x_2} & \dfrac{\partial y_3}{\partial x_3} \end{vmatrix}$$

Notice that the elements of each row are the partial derivatives of one function y_i with respect to each of the independent variables x_1, x_2, x_3, and the elements of each column are the partial derivatives of each of the functions y_1, y_2, y_3 with respect to one of the independent variables x_j. If $|J| = 0$, the equations are functionally dependent; if $|J| \neq 0$, the equations are functionally independent. See Example 1 and Problems 12.1 to 12.4.

EXAMPLE 1. Use of the Jacobian to test for functional dependence is demonstrated below, given

$$y_1 = 5x_1 + 3x_2$$
$$y_2 = 25x_1^2 + 30x_1x_2 + 9x_2^2$$

First, take the first-order partials,

$$\frac{\partial y_1}{\partial x_1} = 5 \qquad \frac{\partial y_1}{\partial x_2} = 3 \qquad \frac{\partial y_2}{\partial x_1} = 50x_1 + 30x_2 \qquad \frac{\partial y_2}{\partial x_2} = 30x_1 + 18x_2$$

Then set up the Jacobian,

$$|J| = \begin{vmatrix} 5 & 3 \\ 50x_1 + 30x_2 & 30x_1 + 18x_2 \end{vmatrix}$$

and evaluate,

$$|J| = 5(30x_1 + 18x_2) - 3(50x_1 + 30x_2) = 0$$

Since $|J| = 0$, there is functional dependence between the equations. In this, the simplest of cases, $(5x_1 + 3x_2)^2 = 25x_1^2 + 30x_1x_2 + 9x_2^2$.

12.2 THE HESSIAN

Given that the first-order conditions $z_x = z_y = 0$ are met, a sufficient condition for a multivariable function $x = f(x, y)$ to be at an optimum is

(1)
$$z_{xx}, z_{yy} > 0 \qquad \text{for a minimum}$$
$$z_{xx}, z_{yy} < 0 \qquad \text{for a maximum}$$
(2)
$$z_{xx} z_{yy} > (z_{xy})^2$$

See Section 5.4. A convenient test for this second-order condition is the Hessian. A *Hessian* $|H|$ is a determinant composed of all the second-order partial derivatives, with the second-order direct partials on the principal diagonal and the second-order cross partials off the principal diagonal. Thus,

$$|H| = \begin{vmatrix} z_{xx} & z_{xy} \\ z_{yx} & z_{yy} \end{vmatrix}$$

where $z_{xy} = z_{yx}$. If the first element on the principal diagonal, the *first principal minor*, $|H_1| = z_{xx}$ is positive and the *second principal minor*

$$|H_2| = \begin{vmatrix} z_{xx} & z_{xy} \\ z_{xy} & z_{yy} \end{vmatrix} = z_{xx} z_{yy} - (z_{xy})^2 > 0$$

the second-order conditions for a minimum are met. When $|H_1| > 0$ and $|H_2| > 0$, the Hessian $|H|$ is called *positive definite*. A positive definite Hessian fulfills the second-order conditions for a minimum.

If the first principal minor $|H_1| = z_{xx} < 0$ and the second principal minor

$$|H_2| = \begin{vmatrix} z_{xx} & z_{xy} \\ z_{xy} & z_{yy} \end{vmatrix} > 0$$

the second-order conditions for a maximum are met. When $|H_1| < 0$, $|H_2| > 0$, the Hessian $|H|$ is *negative definite*. A negative definite Hessian fulfills the second-order conditions for a maximum. See Example 2 and Problems 12.10 to 12.13.

EXAMPLE 2. In Problem 5.10(a) it was found that

$$z = 3x^2 - xy + 2y^2 - 4x - 7y + 12$$

is optimized at $x_0 = 1$ and $y_0 = 2$. The second partials were $z_{xx} = 6$, $z_{yy} = 4$, and $z_{xy} = -1$. Using the Hessian to test the second-order conditions,

$$|H| = \begin{vmatrix} z_{xx} & z_{xy} \\ z_{yx} & z_{yy} \end{vmatrix} = \begin{vmatrix} 6 & -1 \\ -1 & 4 \end{vmatrix}$$

Taking the principal minors, $|H_1| = 6 > 0$ and

$$|H_2| = \begin{vmatrix} 6 & -1 \\ -1 & 4 \end{vmatrix} = 6(4) - (-1)(-1) = 23 > 0$$

With $|H_1| > 0$ and $|H_2| > 0$, the Hessian $|H|$ is positive definite, and z is minimized at the critical values.

12.3 THE DISCRIMINANT

Determinants may be used to test for positive or negative definiteness of any quadratic form. The determinant of a quadratic form is called a *discriminant* $|D|$. Given the quadratic form

$$z = ax^2 + bxy + cy^2$$

the discriminant is formed by placing the coefficients of the squared terms on the principal diagonal and dividing the coefficients of the nonsquared term equally between the off-diagonal positions. Thus,

$$|D| = \begin{vmatrix} a & \dfrac{b}{2} \\ \dfrac{b}{2} & c \end{vmatrix}$$

Then evaluate the principal minors as in the Hessian test, where

$$|D_1| = a \quad \text{and} \quad |D_2| = \begin{vmatrix} a & \dfrac{b}{2} \\ \dfrac{b}{2} & c \end{vmatrix} = ac - \dfrac{b^2}{4}$$

If $|D_1|, |D_2| > 0, |D|$ is positive definite and z is positive for all nonzero values of x and y. If $|D_1| < 0$ and $|D_2| > 0$, z is negative definite and z is negative for all nonzero values of x and y. If $|D_2| > 0$, z is not sign definite and z may assume both positive and negative values. See Example 3 and Problems 12.5 to 12.7.

EXAMPLE 3.   To test for sign definiteness, given the quadratic form

$$z = 2x^2 + 5xy + 8y^2$$

form the discriminant as explained in Section 12.3.

$$|D| = \begin{vmatrix} 2 & 2.5 \\ 2.5 & 8 \end{vmatrix}$$

Then evaluate the principal minors as in the Hessian test.

$$|D_1| = 2 > 0 \qquad |D_2| = \begin{vmatrix} 2 & 2.5 \\ 2.5 & 8 \end{vmatrix} = 16 - 6.25 = 9.75 > 0$$

Thus, z is positive definite, meaning that it will be greater than zero for all nonzero values of x and y.

12.4   HIGHER-ORDER HESSIANS

Given $y = f(x_1, x_2, x_3)$, the third-order Hessian is

$$|H| = \begin{vmatrix} y_{11} & y_{12} & y_{13} \\ y_{21} & y_{22} & y_{23} \\ y_{31} & y_{32} & y_{33} \end{vmatrix}$$

where the elements are the various second-order partial derivatives of y:

$$y_{11} = \frac{\partial^2 y}{\partial x_1^2} \qquad y_{12} = \frac{\partial^2 y}{\partial x_2 \, \partial x_1} \qquad y_{23} = \frac{\partial^2 y}{\partial x_3 \, \partial x_2} \qquad \text{etc.}$$

Conditions for a relative minimum or maximum depend on the signs of the first, second, and third principal minors, respectively. If $|H_1| = y_{11} > 0$,

$$|H_2| = \begin{vmatrix} y_{11} & y_{12} \\ y_{21} & y_{22} \end{vmatrix} > 0 \qquad \text{and} \qquad |H_3| = |H| > 0$$

where $|H_3|$ is the *third principal minor*, $|H|$ is positive definite and fulfills the second-order conditions for a minimum. If $|H_1| = y_{11} < 0$,

$$|H_2| = \begin{vmatrix} y_{11} & y_{12} \\ y_{21} & y_{22} \end{vmatrix} > 0 \qquad \text{and} \qquad |H_3| = |H| < 0$$

$|H|$ is negative definite and will fulfill the second-order conditions for a maximum. Higher-order Hessians follow in analogous fashion. If all the principal minors of $|H|$ are positive, $|H|$ is positive definite and the second-order conditions for a relative minimum are met. If all the principal minors of $|H|$ alternate in sign between negative and positive, $|H|$ is negative definite and the second-order conditions for a relative maximum are met. See Example 4 and Problems 12.8, 12.9, and 12.14 to 12.22.

EXAMPLE 4.   The function

$$y = -5x_1^2 + 10x_1 + x_1x_3 - 2x_2^2 + 4x_2 + 2x_2x_3 - 4x_3^2$$

is optimized as follows, using the Hessian to test the second-order conditions.

   The first-order conditions are

$$\frac{\partial y}{\partial x_1} = y_1 = -10x_1 + 10 + x_3 = 0$$

$$\frac{\partial y}{\partial x_2} = y_2 = -4x_2 + 2x_3 + 4 = 0$$

$$\frac{\partial y}{\partial x_3} = y_3 = x_1 + 2x_2 - 8x_3 = 0$$

which can be expressed in matrix form as

$$\begin{bmatrix} -10 & 0 & 1 \\ 0 & -4 & 2 \\ 1 & 2 & -8 \end{bmatrix} \begin{bmatrix} x_1 \\ x_2 \\ x_3 \end{bmatrix} = \begin{bmatrix} -10 \\ -4 \\ 0 \end{bmatrix} \qquad (12.1)$$

Using Cramer's rule (see Section 11.9) and taking the different determinants, $|A| = -10(28) + 1(4) = -276 \neq 0$. Since $|A|$ in this case is the Jacobian and does not equal zero, the three equations are functionally independent.

$$|A_1| = -10(28) + 1(-8) = -288 \qquad |A_2| = -10(32) - (-10)(-2) + 1(4) = -336$$

$$|A_3| = -10(8) - 10(4) = -120$$

Thus, $\bar{x}_1 = \dfrac{|A_1|}{|A|} = \dfrac{-288}{-276} \cong 1.04 \qquad \bar{x}_2 = \dfrac{|A_2|}{|A|} = \dfrac{-336}{-276} \cong 1.22 \qquad \bar{x}_3 = \dfrac{|A_3|}{|A|} = \dfrac{-120}{-276} \cong 0.43$

Taking the second partial derivatives from the first-order conditions to prepare the Hessian,

$$y_{11} = -10 \qquad y_{12} = 0 \qquad y_{13} = 1$$
$$y_{21} = 0 \qquad y_{22} = -4 \qquad y_{23} = 2$$
$$y_{31} = 1 \qquad y_{32} = 2 \qquad y_{33} = -8$$

Thus, $$|H| = \begin{vmatrix} -10 & 0 & 1 \\ 0 & -4 & 2 \\ 1 & 2 & -8 \end{vmatrix}$$

which has the same elements as the coefficient matrix in (12.1) since the first-order partials are all linear. Finally, applying the Hessian test, by checking the signs of the first, second, and third principal minors, respectively,

$$|H_1| = -10 < 0 \qquad |H_2| = \begin{vmatrix} -10 & 0 \\ 0 & -4 \end{vmatrix} = 40 > 0 \qquad |H_3| = |H| = |A| = -276 < 0$$

Since the principal minors alternate correctly in sign, the Hessian is negative definite and the function is maximized at $\bar{x}_1 = 1.04$, $\bar{x}_2 = 1.22$, and $\bar{x}_3 = 0.43$.

12.5   THE BORDERED HESSIAN FOR CONSTRAINED OPTIMIZATION

   To optimize a function $f(x, y)$ subject to a constraint $g(x, y)$, Section 5.5 showed that a new function could be formed $F(x, y, \lambda) = f(x, y) + \lambda[k - g(x, y)]$, where the first-order conditions are $F_x = F_y = F_\lambda = 0$.

The second-order conditions can now be expressed in terms of a *bordered Hessian* $|\bar{H}|$ in either of two ways:

$$|\bar{H}| = \begin{vmatrix} F_{xx} & F_{xy} & g_x \\ F_{yx} & F_{yy} & g_y \\ g_x & g_y & 0 \end{vmatrix} \quad \text{or} \quad \begin{vmatrix} 0 & g_x & g_y \\ g_x & F_{xx} & F_{xy} \\ g_y & F_{yx} & F_{yy} \end{vmatrix}$$

which is simply the plain Hessian

$$\begin{vmatrix} F_{xx} & F_{xy} \\ F_{yx} & F_{yy} \end{vmatrix}$$

bordered by the first derivatives of the constraint with zero on the principal diagonal. The order of a *bordered principal minor* is determined by the order of the principal minor being bordered. Hence $|\bar{H}|$ above represents a second bordered principal minor $|\bar{H}_2|$, because the principal minor being bordered is 2×2.

For a function in n variables $f(x_1, x_2, \ldots, x_n)$, subject to $g(x_1, x_2, \ldots, x_n)$,

$$|\bar{H}| = \begin{vmatrix} F_{11} & F_{12} & \cdots & F_{1n} & g_1 \\ F_{21} & F_{22} & \cdots & F_{2n} & g_2 \\ \hline \\ F_{n1} & F_{n2} & \cdots & F_{nn} & g_n \\ g_1 & g_2 & \cdots & g_n & 0 \end{vmatrix} \quad \text{or} \quad \begin{vmatrix} 0 & g_1 & g_2 & \cdots & g_n \\ g_1 & F_{11} & F_{12} & \cdots & F_{1n} \\ g_2 & F_{21} & F_{22} & \cdots & F_{2n} \\ \hline \\ g_n & F_{n1} & F_{n2} & \cdots & F_{nn} \end{vmatrix}$$

where $|\bar{H}| = |\bar{H}_n|$, because of the $n \times n$ principal minor being bordered.

If $|\bar{H}_2|, |\bar{H}_3|, \ldots, |\bar{H}_n| < 0$, the bordered Hessian is positive definite, which is a sufficient condition for a minimum. Note that the test starts with $|\bar{H}_2|$, and *not* $|\bar{H}_1|$.

If $|\bar{H}_2| > 0$, $|\bar{H}_3| < 0$, $|\bar{H}_4| > 0$, etc., the bordered Hessian is negative definite, which is a sufficient condition for a maximum. If a given $|\bar{H}|$ meets the criteria, one is assured of a minimum or a maximum. Further tests beyond the scope of the present book are needed if the criteria are not met, since the given criteria represent sufficient conditions, and not necessary conditions. See Examples 5 and 6 and Problems 12.23 to 12.31. For a 4×4 bordered Hessian, see Problem 12.32.

EXAMPLE 5.   Refer to Example 9 in Chapter 5. The bordered Hessian can be used to check the second-order conditions of the optimized function and to determine if Z is maximized or minimized, as demonstrated below.

From Equations (5.8) and (5.9), $Z_{xx} = 8$, $Z_{yy} = 12$, $Z_{xy} = Z_{yx} = 3$. From the constraint, $x + y = 56$, $g_x = 1$, and $g_y = 1$. Thus,

$$|\bar{H}| = \begin{vmatrix} 8 & 3 & 1 \\ 3 & 12 & 1 \\ 1 & 1 & 0 \end{vmatrix}$$

Starting with the second principal minor $|\bar{H}_2|$,

$$|\bar{H}_2| = |\bar{H}| = 8(-1) - 3(-1) + 1(3 - 12) = -14$$

With $|\bar{H}_2| < 0$, $|\bar{H}|$ is positive definite, which means that Z is at a minimum. See Problems 12.23 — 12.26.

EXAMPLE 6.   The bordered Hessian is applied below to test the second-order condition of the generalized Cobb-Douglas production function maximized in Example 12 of Chapter 6.

From Equations (6.15) and (6.16), $Q_{KK} = -0.24K^{-1.6}L^{0.5}$, $Q_{LL} = -0.25K^{0.4}L^{-1.5}$, $Q_{KL} = Q_{LK} = 0.2K^{-0.6}L^{-0.5}$; and from the constraint, $3K + 4L = 108$, $g_K = 3$, $g_L = 4$,

$$|\bar{H}| = \begin{vmatrix} -0.24K^{-1.6}L^{0.5} & 0.2K^{-0.6}L^{-0.5} & 3 \\ 0.2K^{-0.6}L^{-0.5} & -0.25K^{0.4}L^{-1.5} & 4 \\ 3 & 4 & 0 \end{vmatrix}$$

Starting with $|\bar{H}_2|$ and expanding along the third row,

$$|\bar{H}_2| = 3(0.8K^{-0.6}L^{-0.5} + 0.75K^{0.4}L^{-1.5}) - 4(-0.96K^{-1.6}L^{0.5} - 0.6K^{-0.6}L^{-0.5})$$

$$= 2.25K^{0.4}L^{-1.5} + 4.8K^{-0.6}L^{-0.5} + 3.84K^{-1.6}L^{0.5} = \frac{2.25K^{0.4}}{L^{1.5}} + \frac{4.8}{K^{0.6}L^{0.5}} + \frac{3.84L^{0.5}}{K^{1.6}} > 0$$

With $|\bar{H}_2| > 0$, $|\bar{H}|$ is negative definite and Q is maximized. See Problems 12.27 — 12.32.

12.6 DERIVATION OF A MARSHALLIAN DEMAND FUNCTION

A Marshallian demand function expresses the amount of a good a consumer will buy as a function of commodity prices and available income. The Marshallian demand function is derived by means of utility maximization subjected to a budgetary constraint. Given $u = Q_1Q_2$ subject to $P_1Q_1 + P_2Q_2 = B$, where $B = $ the budget or amount of income available, the Lagrangian function is

$$U = Q_1Q_2 + \lambda(B - P_1Q_1 - P_2Q_2)$$

Thus,

$$U_1 = Q_2 - \lambda P_1 = 0 \tag{12.2}$$

$$U_2 = Q_1 - \lambda P_2 = 0 \tag{12.3}$$

$$U_\lambda = B - P_1Q_1 - P_2Q_2 = 0 \tag{12.4}$$

Solving simultaneously, from (12.2) and (12.3),

$$\frac{Q_2}{P_1} = \lambda = \frac{Q_1}{P_2}$$

Thus,

$$Q_2 = \frac{Q_1P_1}{P_2} \qquad Q_1 = \frac{Q_2P_2}{P_1}$$

Substituting $Q_2 = Q_1P_1/P_2$ in (12.4),

$$B = P_1Q_1 + \frac{P_2(Q_1P_1)}{P_2} \qquad \bar{Q}_1 = \frac{B}{2P_1}$$

Similarly, substituting $Q_1 = Q_2P_2/P_1$ in (12.4),

$$\bar{Q}_2 = \frac{B}{2P_2}$$

These are the Marshallian demand functions for Q_1 and Q_2, maximizing the consumer's satisfaction subject to income and commodity prices.

Then testing the second-order conditions, where from (12.2) and (12.3) $U_{11} = 0$, $U_{22} = 0$, $U_{12} = U_{21} = 1$, $g_1 = P_1$, and $g_2 = P_2$,

$$|\bar{H}| = \begin{vmatrix} 0 & 1 & P_1 \\ 1 & 0 & P_2 \\ P_1 & P_2 & 0 \end{vmatrix}$$

$$|\bar{H}_2| = -1(-P_1P_2) + P_1(P_2) = 2P_1P_2 > 0$$

With $|\bar{H}_2| > 0$, $|\bar{H}|$ is negative definite and U is maximized. See Example 7 and Problems 12.33 and 12.34.

EXAMPLE 7.   Given $B = 250$, the demand function for Q_1 at $P_1 = 5$, 10, and 25 is derived as follows on the basis of the preceding discussion:

At $P_1 = 5$, $$\bar{Q}_1 = \frac{250}{2(5)} = 25$$

At $P_1 = 10$, $$\bar{Q}_1 = \frac{250}{2(10)} = 12.5$$

At $P_1 = 25$, $$\bar{Q}_1 = \frac{250}{2(25)} = 5$$

(Since in this simple model demand for each good depends in the same way on income and its own price, both demand functions will be identical. For more realistic functions see Problems 12.33 and 12.34.)

12.7   INPUT-OUTPUT ANALYSIS

In a modern economy where the production of one good requires the input of many other goods as *intermediate goods* in the production process (steel requires coal, iron ore, electricity, etc.), total demand x for product i will be the summation of all intermediate demand for the product plus the *final demand* b for the product arising from consumers, investors, the government, and exporters, as ultimate users. If a_{ij} is a *technical coefficient* expressing the value of input i required to produce one dollar's worth of product j, the total demand for product i can be expressed as

$$x_i = a_{i1}x_1 + a_{i2}x_2 + \cdots + a_{in}x_n + b_i$$

for $i = 1, 2, \ldots, n$. In matrix form this can be expressed as

$$X = AX + B \qquad\qquad (12.5)$$

where
$$X = \begin{bmatrix} x_1 \\ x_2 \\ \vdots \\ x_n \end{bmatrix} \qquad A = \begin{bmatrix} a_{11} & a_{12} & \cdots & a_{1n} \\ a_{21} & a_{22} & \cdots & a_{2n} \\ \hdashline a_{n1} & a_{n2} & \cdots & a_{nn} \end{bmatrix} \qquad B = \begin{bmatrix} b_1 \\ b_2 \\ \vdots \\ b_n \end{bmatrix}$$

and A is called the *matrix of technical coefficients*. To find the level of total output (intermediate and final) needed to satisfy final demand, we can solve for X in terms of the matrix of technical coefficients and the column vector of final demand, both of which are given. From (12.5),

$$X - AX = B$$
$$(I - A)X = B$$
$$X = (I - A)^{-1}B \qquad\qquad (12.6)$$

Thus, for a three-sector economy

$$\begin{bmatrix} x_1 \\ x_2 \\ x_3 \end{bmatrix} = \begin{bmatrix} 1 - a_{11} & -a_{12} & -a_{13} \\ -a_{21} & 1 - a_{22} & -a_{23} \\ -a_{31} & -a_{32} & 1 - a_{33} \end{bmatrix}^{-1} \begin{bmatrix} b_1 \\ b_2 \\ b_3 \end{bmatrix}$$

where the $I - A$ matrix is called the *Leontief matrix*. In a complete input-output table, labor and capital would also be included as inputs, constituting value added by the firm. The vertical summation of elements along column j in such a model would equal 1: the input cost of producing one unit or one dollar's worth of the commodity, as seen in Problem 12.45. See Example 8 and Problems 12.35 to 12.45.

EXAMPLE 8. Determine the total demand x for industries 1, 2, and 3, given the matrix of technical coefficients A and the final demand vector B.

$$A = \begin{bmatrix} 0.3 & 0.4 & 0.1 \\ 0.5 & 0.2 & 0.6 \\ 0.1 & 0.3 & 0.1 \end{bmatrix} \qquad B = \begin{bmatrix} 20 \\ 10 \\ 30 \end{bmatrix}$$

From (12.6), $X = (I - A)^{-1}B$, where

$$I - A = \begin{bmatrix} 1 & 0 & 0 \\ 0 & 1 & 0 \\ 0 & 0 & 1 \end{bmatrix} - \begin{bmatrix} 0.3 & 0.4 & 0.1 \\ 0.5 & 0.2 & 0.6 \\ 0.1 & 0.3 & 0.1 \end{bmatrix} = \begin{bmatrix} 0.7 & -0.4 & -0.1 \\ -0.5 & 0.8 & -0.6 \\ -0.1 & -0.3 & 0.9 \end{bmatrix}$$

Taking the inverse,

$$(I - A)^{-1} = \frac{1}{0.151} \begin{bmatrix} 0.54 & 0.39 & 0.32 \\ 0.51 & 0.62 & 0.47 \\ 0.23 & 0.25 & 0.36 \end{bmatrix}$$

and substituting in (12.6),

$$X = \frac{1}{0.151} \begin{bmatrix} 0.54 & 0.39 & 0.32 \\ 0.51 & 0.62 & 0.47 \\ 0.23 & 0.25 & 0.36 \end{bmatrix} \begin{bmatrix} 20 \\ 10 \\ 30 \end{bmatrix} = \frac{1}{0.151} \begin{bmatrix} 24.3 \\ 30.5 \\ 17.9 \end{bmatrix} = \begin{bmatrix} 160.93 \\ 201.99 \\ 118.54 \end{bmatrix} = \begin{bmatrix} x_1 \\ x_2 \\ x_3 \end{bmatrix}$$

12.8   CHARACTERISTIC ROOTS AND VECTORS (EIGENVALUES, EIGENVECTORS)

To this point, the sign definiteness of a Hessian and a quadratic form has been tested by using the principal minors. Sign definiteness can also be tested by using the characteristic roots of a matrix. Given a square matrix A, if it is possible to find a vector $V \neq 0$ and a scalar c such that

$$AV = cV \tag{12.7}$$

the scalar c is called the *characteristic root*, *latent root*, or *eigenvalue*; and the vector is called the *characteristic vector*, *latent vector*, or *eigenvector*. Equation (12.7) can also be expressed

$$AV = cIV$$

which can be rearranged so that

$$AV - cIV = 0$$
$$(A - cI)V = 0 \tag{12.8}$$

where $A - cI$ is called the *characteristic matrix* of A. Since by assumption $V \neq 0$, the characteristic matrix $A - cI$ must be singular (see Problem 10.49) and thus its determinant must vanish. If $A = 3 \times 3$ matrix, then

$$|A - cI| = \begin{vmatrix} a_{11} - c & a_{12} & a_{13} \\ a_{21} & a_{22} - c & a_{23} \\ a_{31} & a_{32} & a_{33} - c \end{vmatrix} = 0$$

With $|A - cI| = 0$ in (12.8), there will be an infinite number of solutions for V. To force a unique solution, the solution is *normalized* by requiring of the elements v_i of V that $\Sigma v_i^2 = 1$, as shown in Example 10.

If
(1)   All characteristic roots (c) are positive, A is positive definite.
(2)   All c's are negative, A is negative definite.
(3)   All c's are nonnegative and at least one $c = 0$, A is positive semidefinite.

(4) All c's are nonpositive and at least one $c = 0$, A is negative semidefinite.

(5) Some c's are positive and others negative, A is indefinite.

See Examples 9 and 10 and Problems 12.46 to 12.51.

EXAMPLE 9.   Given

$$A = \begin{bmatrix} -6 & 3 \\ 3 & -6 \end{bmatrix}$$

To find the characteristic roots of A, the determinant of the characteristic matrix $A - cI$ must equal zero. Thus,

$$|A - cI| = \begin{vmatrix} -6 - c & 3 \\ 3 & -6 - c \end{vmatrix} = 0 \qquad (12.9)$$

$$(-6 - c)(-6 - c) - (3)(3) = 0$$

$$c^2 + 12c + 27 = 0 \qquad (c + 9)(c + 3) = 0$$

$$c_1 = -9 \qquad c_2 = -3$$

Testing for sign definiteness, since both characteristic roots are negative, A is negative definite.

EXAMPLE 10.   Continuing with Example 9, the first root $c_1 = -9$ is now used to find the characteristic vector. Substituting $c = -9$ in (12.9),

$$\begin{bmatrix} -6 - (-9) & 3 \\ 3 & -6 - (-9) \end{bmatrix} \begin{bmatrix} v_1 \\ v_2 \end{bmatrix} = 0$$

$$\begin{bmatrix} 3 & 3 \\ 3 & 3 \end{bmatrix} \begin{bmatrix} v_1 \\ v_2 \end{bmatrix} = 0 \qquad (12.10)$$

Since the coefficient matrix is linearly dependent, (12.10) is capable of an infinite number of solutions. The product of the matrices gives two equations which are identical:

$$3v_1 + 3v_2 = 0$$

Solving for v_2 in terms of v_1,

$$v_2 = -v_1 \qquad (12.11)$$

Then, normalizing the solution in (12.11) so that

$$v_1^2 + v_2^2 = 1 \qquad (12.12)$$

$v_2 = -v_1$ is substituted in (12.12), getting

$$v_1^2 + (-v_1)^2 = 1$$

Thus, $2v_1^2 = 1$, $v_1^2 = \frac{1}{2}$. Then taking the positive square root, $v_1 = \sqrt{\frac{1}{2}} = \sqrt{0.5}$. From (12.11), $v_2 = -v_1$. Thus, $v_2 = -\sqrt{0.5}$, and the first characteristic vector is

$$V_1 = \begin{bmatrix} \sqrt{0.5} \\ -\sqrt{0.5} \end{bmatrix}$$

When the second characteristic root $c_2 = -3$ is used,

$$\begin{bmatrix} -6 - (-3) & 3 \\ 3 & -6 - (-3) \end{bmatrix} \begin{bmatrix} v_1 \\ v_2 \end{bmatrix} = \begin{bmatrix} -3 & 3 \\ 3 & -3 \end{bmatrix} \begin{bmatrix} v_1 \\ v_2 \end{bmatrix} = 0$$

Multiplying the 2×2 matrix by the column vector,

$$-3v_1 + 3v_2 = 0$$

$$3v_1 - 3v_2 = 0$$

Thus, $v_1 = v_2$. Normalizing,

$$v_1^2 + v_2^2 = 1$$
$$(v_2)^2 + v_2^2 = 1$$
$$2v_2^2 = 1$$
$$v_2 = \sqrt{0.5} \qquad v_1 = \sqrt{0.5}$$

Thus,
$$V_2 = \begin{bmatrix} \sqrt{0.5} \\ \sqrt{0.5} \end{bmatrix}$$

12.9 TRANSFORMATION MATRIX

Having found the characteristic vectors V_1 and V_2, a *transformation matrix* $T = [V_1 \quad V_2]$ can be found such that the product $T'AT$ will be a diagonal matrix with the characteristic roots as the diagonal elements. Thus for a 3×3 matrix,

$$T'AT = \begin{bmatrix} c_1 & 0 & 0 \\ 0 & c_2 & 0 \\ 0 & 0 & c_3 \end{bmatrix}$$

See Example 11 and Problems 12.52 to 12.55.

EXAMPLE 11. Using the data from Examples 9 and 10, the transformation matrix T is

$$T = [V_1 \quad V_2] = \begin{bmatrix} \sqrt{0.5} & \sqrt{0.5} \\ -\sqrt{0.5} & \sqrt{0.5} \end{bmatrix} \quad \text{and} \quad T' = \begin{bmatrix} \sqrt{0.5} & -\sqrt{0.5} \\ \sqrt{0.5} & \sqrt{0.5} \end{bmatrix}$$

Thus,
$$T'AT = \begin{bmatrix} \sqrt{0.5} & -\sqrt{0.5} \\ \sqrt{0.5} & \sqrt{0.5} \end{bmatrix}\begin{bmatrix} -6 & 3 \\ 3 & -6 \end{bmatrix}\begin{bmatrix} \sqrt{0.5} & \sqrt{0.5} \\ -\sqrt{0.5} & \sqrt{0.5} \end{bmatrix}$$

where
$$T'A = \begin{bmatrix} -9\sqrt{0.5} & 9\sqrt{0.5} \\ -3\sqrt{0.5} & -3\sqrt{0.5} \end{bmatrix}$$

and
$$T'AT = \begin{bmatrix} -18(0.5) & 0 \\ 0 & -6(0.5) \end{bmatrix} = \begin{bmatrix} -9 & 0 \\ 0 & -3 \end{bmatrix} = \begin{bmatrix} c_1 & 0 \\ 0 & c_2 \end{bmatrix}$$

Solved Problems

THE JACOBIAN

12.1. Use the Jacobian to test for functional dependence in the following system of equations:

$$y_1 = 6x_1 + 4x_2$$
$$y_2 = 7x_1 + 9x_2$$

Taking the first-order partials to set up the Jacobian $|J|$,

$$\frac{\partial y_1}{\partial x_1} = 6 \qquad \frac{\partial y_1}{\partial x_2} = 4 \qquad \frac{\partial y_2}{\partial x_1} = 7 \qquad \frac{\partial y_2}{\partial x_2} = 9$$

Thus,
$$|J| = \begin{vmatrix} 6 & 4 \\ 7 & 9 \end{vmatrix} = 6(9) - 7(4) = 26$$

Since $|J| \neq 0$, there is no functional dependence. Notice that in a system of linear equations the Jacobian $|J|$ equals the determinant $|A|$ of the coefficient matrix, and all their elements are identical. See Section 11.1, where the determinant test for nonsingularity of a matrix is nothing more than an application of the Jacobian to a system of linear equations.

12.2. Redo Problem 12.1, given

$$y_1 = 3x_1 - 4x_2$$
$$y_2 = 9x_1^2 - 24x_1x_2 + 16x_2^2$$

The first-order partials are

$$\frac{\partial y_1}{\partial x_1} = 3 \qquad \frac{\partial y_1}{\partial x_2} = -4 \qquad \frac{\partial y_2}{\partial x_1} = 18x_1 - 24x_2 \qquad \frac{\partial y_2}{\partial x_2} = -24x_1 + 32x_2$$

Thus,
$$|J| = \begin{vmatrix} 3 & -4 \\ 18x_1 - 24x_2 & -24x_1 + 32x_2 \end{vmatrix} = 3(-24x_1 + 32x_2) + 4(18x_1 - 24x_2) = 0$$

There is functional dependence: $(3x_1 - 4x_2)^2 = 9x_1^2 - 24x_1x_2 + 16x_2^2$.

12.3. Redo Problem 12.1, given

$$y_1 = x_1^2 - 3x_2 + 5$$
$$y_2 = x_1^4 - 6x_1^2x_2 + 9x_2^2$$

$$\frac{\partial y_1}{\partial x_1} = 2x_1 \qquad \frac{\partial y_1}{\partial x_2} = -3 \qquad \frac{\partial y_2}{\partial x_1} = 4x_1^3 - 12x_1x_2 \qquad \frac{\partial y_2}{\partial x_2} = -6x_1^2 + 18x_2$$

$$|J| = \begin{vmatrix} 2x_1 & -3 \\ 4x_1^3 - 12x_1x_2 & -6x_1^2 + 18x_2 \end{vmatrix} = 2x_1(-6x_1^2 + 18x_2) + 3(4x_1^3 - 12x_1x_2) = 0$$

There is functional dependence: $y_2 = (y_1 - 5)^2$, where

$$y_1 - 5 = x_1^2 - 3x_2 + 5 - 5 = x_1^2 - 3x_2$$

and
$$(x_1^2 - 3x_2)^2 = x_1^4 - 6x_1^2x_2 + 9x_2^2$$

12.4. Test for functional dependence in each of the following by means of the Jacobian:

(a) $y_1 = 4x_1 - x_2$
$y_2 = 16x_1^2 + 8x_1x_2 + x_2^2$

$$|J| = \begin{vmatrix} 4 & -1 \\ 32x_1 + 8x_2 & 8x_1 + 2x_2 \end{vmatrix} = 4(8x_1 + 2x_2) + 1(32x_1 + 8x_2) = 64x_1 + 16x_2 \neq 0$$

The equations are functionally independent.

(b) $y_1 = 1.5x_1^2 + 12x_1x_2 + 24x_2^2$
$y_2 = 2x_1 + 8x_2$

$$|J| = \begin{vmatrix} 3x_1 + 12x_2 & 12x_1 + 48x_2 \\ 2 & 8 \end{vmatrix} = 8(3x_1 + 12x_2) - 2(12x_1 + 48x_2) = 0$$

There is functional dependence between the equations.

(c) $y_1 = 4x_1^2 + 3x_2 + 9$
$y_2 = 16x_1^4 + 24x_1^2x_2 + 9x_2^2 + 12$

$$|J| = \begin{vmatrix} 8x_1 & 3 \\ 64x_1^3 + 48x_1x_2 & 24x_1^2 + 18x_2 \end{vmatrix} = 8x_1(24x_1^2 + 18x_2) - 3(64x_1^3 + 48x_1x_2) = 0$$

The equations are functionally dependent.

DISCRIMINANTS AND SIGN DEFINITENESS OF QUADRATIC FUNCTIONS

12.5. Use discriminants to determine whether each of the following quadratic functions is positive or negative definite:

(a) $y = -3x_1^2 + 4x_1x_2 - 4x_2^2$

Since the coefficients of the squared terms are placed on the principal diagonal and the coefficient of the nonsquared term x_1x_2 is divided evenly between the a_{12} and a_{21} positions, in this case,

$$|D| = \begin{vmatrix} -3 & 2 \\ 2 & -4 \end{vmatrix}$$

where $|D_1| = -3 < 0$ $|D_2| = \begin{vmatrix} -3 & 2 \\ 2 & -4 \end{vmatrix} = (-3)(-4) - (2)(2) = 8 > 0$

With $|D_1| < 0$ and $|D_2| > 0$, y is negative definite and y will be negative for all nonzero values of x_1 and x_2.

(b) $y = 5x_1^2 - 2x_1x_2 + 7x_2^2$

The discriminant is $|D| = \begin{vmatrix} 5 & -1 \\ -1 & 7 \end{vmatrix}$

where $|D_1| = 5 > 0$ and $|D_2| = |D| = 5(7) - (-1)(-1) = 34 > 0$. With $|D_1| > 0$ and $|D_2| > 0$, y is positive definite and y will be positive for all nonzero values of x_1 and x_2.

12.6.   Redo Problem 12.5 for $y = 5x_1^2 - 6x_1x_2 + 3x_2^2 - 2x_2x_3 + 8x_3^2 - 3x_1x_3$.

For a quadratic form in three variables, the coefficients of the squared terms continue to go on the principal diagonal, while the coefficient of x_1x_3 is divided evenly between the a_{13} and a_{31} positions, the coefficient of x_2x_3 is divided between the a_{23} and a_{32} positions, etc. Thus,

$$|D| = \begin{vmatrix} 5 & -3 & -1.5 \\ -3 & 3 & -1 \\ -1.5 & -1 & 8 \end{vmatrix}$$

where $|D_1| = 5 > 0$ $|D_2| = \begin{vmatrix} 5 & -3 \\ -3 & 3 \end{vmatrix} = 6 > 0$

and $|D_3| = |D| = 5(23) + 3(-25.5) - 1.5(7.5) = 27.25 > 0$. Therefore, y is positive definite.

12.7.   Use discriminants to determine the sign definiteness of the following functions:

(a) $y = -2x_1^2 + 4x_1x_2 - 5x_2^2 + 2x_2x_3 - 3x_3^2 + 2x_1x_3$

$$|D| = \begin{vmatrix} -2 & 2 & 1 \\ 2 & -5 & 1 \\ 1 & 1 & -3 \end{vmatrix}$$

where $|D_1| = -2 < 0$ $|D_2| = \begin{vmatrix} -2 & 2 \\ 2 & -5 \end{vmatrix} = 6 > 0$

and $|D_3| = |D| = -2(14) - 2(-7) + 1(7) = -7 < 0$. So y is negative definite.

(b) $y = -7x_1^2 - 2x_2^2 + 2x_2x_3 - 4x_3^2 - 6x_1x_3$

$$|D| = \begin{vmatrix} -7 & 0 & -3 \\ 0 & -2 & 1 \\ -3 & 1 & -4 \end{vmatrix}$$

where $|D_1| = -7$ $|D_2| = \begin{vmatrix} -7 & 0 \\ 0 & -2 \end{vmatrix} = 14$

and $|D_3| = |D| = -7(7) - 3(-6) = -31$. And y is negative definite.

THE HESSIAN IN OPTIMIZATION PROBLEMS

12.8. Optimize the following function, using (a) Cramer's rule for the first-order condition and (b) the Hessian for the second-order condition:

$$y = 3x_1^2 - 5x_1 - x_1x_2 + 6x_2^2 - 4x_2 + 2x_2x_3 + 4x_3^2 + 2x_3 - 3x_1x_3$$

(a) The first-order conditions are

$$
\begin{aligned}
y_1 &= 6x_1 - 5 - x_2 - 3x_3 = 0 \\
y_2 &= -x_1 + 12x_2 - 4 + 2x_3 = 0 \\
y_3 &= 2x_2 + 8x_3 + 2 - 3x_1 = 0
\end{aligned}
\tag{12.13}
$$

which in matrix form is

$$
\begin{bmatrix} 6 & -1 & -3 \\ -1 & 12 & 2 \\ -3 & 2 & 8 \end{bmatrix}
\begin{bmatrix} x_1 \\ x_2 \\ x_3 \end{bmatrix} =
\begin{bmatrix} 5 \\ 4 \\ -2 \end{bmatrix}
$$

Using Cramer's rule, $|A| = 6(92) + 1(-2) - 3(34) = 448$. Since $|A|$ also equals $|J|$, the equations are functionally independent.

$$
\begin{aligned}
|A_1| &= 5(92) + 1(36) - 3(32) = 400 \\
|A_2| &= 6(36) - 5(-2) - 3(14) = 184 \\
|A_3| &= 6(-32) + 1(14) + 5(34) = -8
\end{aligned}
$$

Thus, $\bar{x}_1 = \dfrac{400}{448} \approx 0.89 \qquad \bar{x}_2 = \dfrac{184}{448} \approx 0.41 \qquad \bar{x}_3 = \dfrac{-8}{448} \approx -0.02$

(b) Testing the second-order condition by taking the second-order partials of (12.13) to form the Hessian,

$$
\begin{aligned}
y_{11} &= 6 & y_{12} &= -1 & y_{13} &= -3 \\
y_{21} &= -1 & y_{22} &= 12 & y_{23} &= 2 \\
y_{31} &= -3 & y_{32} &= 2 & y_{33} &= 8
\end{aligned}
$$

Thus, $|H| = \begin{vmatrix} 6 & -1 & -3 \\ -1 & 12 & 2 \\ -3 & 2 & 8 \end{vmatrix}$

where $|H_1| = 6 > 0 \qquad |H_2| = \begin{vmatrix} 6 & -1 \\ -1 & 12 \end{vmatrix} = 71 > 0$

and $|H_3| = |H| = |A| = 448 > 0$. With $|H|$ positive definite, y is minimized at the critical values.

12.9. Redo Problem 12.8, given $y = -5x_1^2 + 10x_1 + x_1x_3 - 2x_2^2 + 4x_2 + 2x_2x_3 - 4x_3^2$.

(a) $\begin{aligned}
y_1 &= -10x_1 + 10 + x_3 = 0 \\
y_2 &= -4x_2 + 4 + 2x_3 = 0 \\
y_3 &= x_1 + 2x_2 - 8x_3 = 0
\end{aligned} \tag{12.14}$

In matrix form, $\begin{bmatrix} -10 & 0 & 1 \\ 0 & -4 & 2 \\ 1 & 2 & -8 \end{bmatrix} \begin{bmatrix} x_1 \\ x_2 \\ x_3 \end{bmatrix} = \begin{bmatrix} -10 \\ -4 \\ 0 \end{bmatrix}$

Using Cramer's rule, $\begin{aligned}
|A| &= -10(28) + 1(4) = -276 \\
|A_1| &= -10(28) + 1(-8) = -288 \\
|A_2| &= -10(32) + 10(-2) + 1(4) = -336 \\
|A_3| &= -10(8) - 10(4) = -120
\end{aligned}$

Thus, $\bar{x}_1 = \dfrac{-288}{-276} \approx 1.04 \qquad \bar{x}_2 = \dfrac{-336}{-276} \approx 1.22 \qquad \bar{x}_3 = \dfrac{-120}{-276} \approx 0.43$

(b) Taking the second partials of (12.14) and forming the Hessian,

$$|H| = \begin{vmatrix} -10 & 0 & 1 \\ 0 & -4 & 2 \\ 1 & 2 & -8 \end{vmatrix}$$

where $|H_1| = -10 < 0$, $|H_2| = 40 > 0$, and $|H_3| = |A| = -276 < 0$. Thus, $|H|$ is negative definite, and y is maximized.

12.10. A firm produces two goods in pure competition and has the following total revenue and total cost functions:

$$\text{TR} = 15Q_1 + 18Q_2 \qquad \text{TC} = 2Q_1^2 + 2Q_1Q_2 + 3Q_2^2$$

The two goods are *technically related in production*, since the marginal cost of one is dependent on the level of output of the other (for example, $\partial \text{TC}/\partial Q_1 = 4Q_1 + 2Q_2$). Maximize profits for the firm, using (a) Cramer's rule for the first-order condition and (b) the Hessian for the second-order condition.

(a)
$$\Pi = \text{TR} - \text{TC} = 15Q_1 + 18Q_2 - 2Q_1^2 - 2Q_1Q_2 - 3Q_2^2$$

The first-order conditions are

$$\Pi_1 = 15 - 4Q_1 - 2Q_2 = 0$$
$$\Pi_2 = 18 - 2Q_1 - 6Q_2 = 0$$

In matrix form,

$$\begin{bmatrix} -4 & -2 \\ -2 & -6 \end{bmatrix} \begin{bmatrix} Q_1 \\ Q_2 \end{bmatrix} = \begin{bmatrix} -15 \\ -18 \end{bmatrix}$$

Solving by Cramer's rule,

$$|A| = 24 - 4 = 20 \qquad |A_1| = 90 - 36 = 54 \qquad |A_2| = 72 - 30 = 42$$

Thus,
$$\bar{Q}_1 = \frac{54}{20} = 2.7 \qquad \bar{Q}_2 = \frac{42}{20} = 2.1$$

(b) Using the Hessian to test for the second-order condition,

$$|H| = \begin{vmatrix} -4 & -2 \\ -2 & -6 \end{vmatrix}$$

where $|H_1| = -4$ and $|H_2| = 20$. With $|H|$ negative definite, Π is maximized.

12.11 Using the techniques of Problem 12.10, maximize profits for the competitive firm whose goods are not technically related in production. The firm's total revenue and total cost functions are

$$\text{TR} = 7Q_1 + 9Q_2 \qquad \text{TC} = Q_1^2 + 2Q_1 + 5Q_2 + 2Q_2^2$$

(a)
$$\Pi = 7Q_1 + 9Q_2 - Q_1^2 - 2Q_1 - 5Q_2 - 2Q_2^2$$

$$\Pi_1 = 7 - 2Q_1 - 2 = 0 \qquad \bar{Q}_1 = 2.5$$
$$\Pi_2 = 9 - 5 - 4Q_2 = 0 \qquad \bar{Q}_2 = 1$$

(b)
$$|H| = \begin{vmatrix} -2 & 0 \\ 0 & -4 \end{vmatrix}$$

where $|H_1| = -2$ and $|H_2| = 8$. So $|H|$ is negative definite, and Π is maximized.

12.12. Maximize profits for a monopolistic firm producing two related goods, i.e.,

$$P_1 = f(Q_1, Q_2)$$

when the goods are substitutes and the demand and total cost functions are

$$P_1 = 80 - 5Q_1 - 2Q_2 \qquad P_2 = 50 - Q_1 - 3Q_2 \qquad TC = 3Q_1^2 + Q_1Q_2 + 2Q_2^2$$

Use (a) Cramer's rule and (b) the Hessian, as in Problem 12.10.

(a) $\Pi = TR - TC$, where $TR = P_1Q_1 + P_2Q_2$.

$$\Pi = (80 - 5Q_1 - 2Q_2)Q_1 + (50 - Q_1 - 3Q_2)Q_2 - (3Q_1^2 + Q_1Q_2 + 2Q_2^2)$$
$$= 80Q_1 + 50Q_2 - 4Q_1Q_2 - 8Q_1^2 - 5Q_2^2$$
$$\Pi_1 = 80 - 4Q_2 - 16Q_1 = 0 \qquad \Pi_2 = 50 - 4Q_1 - 10Q_2 = 0$$

In matrix form,
$$\begin{bmatrix} -16 & -4 \\ -4 & -10 \end{bmatrix} \begin{bmatrix} Q_1 \\ Q_2 \end{bmatrix} = \begin{bmatrix} -80 \\ -50 \end{bmatrix}$$

$$|A| = 160 - 16 = 144 \qquad |A_1| = 800 - 200 = 600 \qquad |A_2| = 800 - 320 = 480$$

and
$$\bar{Q}_1 = \frac{600}{144} \approx 4.17 \qquad \bar{Q}_2 = \frac{480}{144} \approx 3.33$$

(b)
$$|H| = \begin{vmatrix} -16 & -4 \\ -4 & -10 \end{vmatrix}$$

where $|H_1| = -16$ and $|H_2| = 144$. So Π is maximized.

12.13. Maximize profits for a producer of two substitute goods, given

$$P_1 = 130 - 4Q_1 - Q_2 \qquad P_2 = 160 - 2Q_1 - 5Q_2 \qquad TC = 2Q_1^2 + 2Q_1Q_2 + 4Q_2^2$$

Use (a) Cramer's rule for the first-order condition and (b) the Hessian for the second-order condition.

(a)
$$\Pi = (130 - 4Q_1 - Q_2)Q_1 + (160 - 2Q_1 - 5Q_2)Q_2 - (2Q_1^2 + 2Q_1Q_2 + 4Q_2^2)$$
$$= 130Q_1 + 160Q_2 - 5Q_1Q_2 - 6Q_1^2 - 9Q_2^2$$
$$\Pi_1 = 130 - 5Q_2 - 12Q_1 = 0 \qquad \Pi_2 = 160 - 5Q_1 - 18Q_2 = 0$$

Thus,
$$\begin{bmatrix} -12 & -5 \\ -5 & -18 \end{bmatrix} \begin{bmatrix} Q_1 \\ Q_2 \end{bmatrix} = \begin{bmatrix} -130 \\ -160 \end{bmatrix}$$

$$|A| = 191$$

$$|A_1| = 1540 \qquad \bar{Q}_1 = \frac{1540}{191} \approx 8.06$$

$$|A_2| = 1270 \qquad \bar{Q}_2 = \frac{1270}{191} \approx 6.65$$

(b)
$$|H| = \begin{vmatrix} -12 & -5 \\ -5 & -18 \end{vmatrix}$$

$|H_1| = -12$ and $|H_2| = 191$. So Π is maximized.

12.14. Redo Problem 12.13 for a monopolistic firm producing three related goods, when the demand functions and the cost function are

$$P_1 = 180 - 3Q_1 - Q_2 - 2Q_3 \qquad P_2 = 200 - Q_1 - 4Q_2 \qquad P_3 = 150 - Q_2 - 3Q_3$$
$$TC = Q_1^2 + Q_1Q_2 + Q_2^2 + Q_2Q_3 + Q_3^2$$

(a)
$$\Pi = (180 - 3Q_1 - Q_2 - 2Q_3)Q_1 + (200 - Q_1 - 4Q_2)Q_2 + (150 - Q_2 - 3Q_3)Q_3$$
$$- (Q_1^2 + Q_1Q_2 + Q_2^2 + Q_2Q_3 + Q_3^2)$$
$$= 180Q_1 + 200Q_2 + 150Q_3 - 3Q_1Q_2 - 2Q_2Q_3 - 2Q_1Q_3 - 4Q_1^2 - 5Q_2^2 - 4Q_3^2$$
$$\Pi_1 = 180 - 3Q_2 - 2Q_3 - 8Q_1 = 0 \qquad \Pi_2 = 200 - 3Q_1 - 2Q_3 - 10Q_2 = 0$$
$$\Pi_3 = 150 - 2Q_2 - 2Q_1 - 8Q_3 = 0$$

In matrix form,

$$\begin{bmatrix} -8 & -3 & -2 \\ -3 & -10 & -2 \\ -2 & -2 & -8 \end{bmatrix}\begin{bmatrix} Q_1 \\ Q_2 \\ Q_3 \end{bmatrix} = \begin{bmatrix} -180 \\ -200 \\ -150 \end{bmatrix}$$

$$|A| = -8(76) + 3(20) - 2(-14) = -520$$
$$|A_1| = -180(76) + 3(1300) - 2(-1100) = -7580$$
$$|A_2| = -8(1300) + 180(20) - 2(50) = -6900$$
$$|A_3| = -8(1100) + 3(50) - 180(-14) = -6130$$

Thus, $$\bar{Q}_1 = \frac{-7580}{-520} \approx 14.58 \qquad \bar{Q}_2 = \frac{-6900}{-520} \approx 13.27 \qquad \bar{Q}_3 = \frac{-6130}{-520} \approx 11.79$$

(b)
$$|H| = \begin{vmatrix} -8 & -3 & -2 \\ -3 & -10 & -2 \\ -2 & -2 & -8 \end{vmatrix}$$

where $|H_1| = -8$, $|H_2| = 71$, and $|H_3| = |H| = |A| = -520$. And Π is maximized.

12.15. Maximize profits as in Problem 12.14, given

$$P_1 = 70 - 2Q_1 - Q_2 - Q_3 \qquad P_2 = 120 - Q_1 - 4Q_2 - 2Q_3 \qquad P_3 = 90 - Q_1 - Q_2 - 3Q_3$$
$$\text{TC} = Q_1^2 + Q_1Q_2 + 2Q_2^2 + 2Q_2Q_3 + Q_3^2 + Q_1Q_3$$

(a)
$$\Pi = 70Q_1 + 120Q_2 + 90Q_3 - 3Q_1Q_2 - 5Q_2Q_3 - 3Q_1Q_3 - 3Q_1^2 - 6Q_2^2 - 4Q_3^2$$
$$\Pi_1 = 70 - 3Q_2 - 3Q_3 - 6Q_1 = 0 \qquad \Pi_2 = 120 - 3Q_1 - 5Q_3 - 12Q_2 = 0$$
$$\Pi_3 = 90 - 3Q_1 - 5Q_2 - 8Q_3 = 0$$

Thus,

$$\begin{bmatrix} -6 & -3 & -3 \\ -3 & -12 & -5 \\ -3 & -5 & -8 \end{bmatrix}\begin{bmatrix} Q_1 \\ Q_2 \\ Q_3 \end{bmatrix} = \begin{bmatrix} -70 \\ -120 \\ -90 \end{bmatrix}$$

$$|A| = -336$$

$$|A_1| = -2000 \qquad \bar{Q}_1 = \frac{-2000}{-336} \approx 5.95$$

$$|A_2| = -2160 \qquad \bar{Q}_2 = \frac{-2160}{-336} \approx 6.43$$

$$|A_3| = -1680 \qquad \bar{Q}_3 = \frac{-1680}{-336} = 5$$

(b)
$$|H| = \begin{vmatrix} -6 & -3 & -3 \\ -3 & -12 & -5 \\ -3 & -5 & -8 \end{vmatrix}$$

where $|H_1| = -6$, $|H_2| = 63$, and $|H_3| = |H| = |A| = -336$. Π is maximized.

12.16. Given that $Q = F(P)$, maximize profits by (a) finding the inverse function $P = f(Q)$, (b) using Cramer's rule for the first-order condition, and (c) using the Hessian for the second-order condition. The demand functions and total cost function are

$$Q_1 = 100 - 3P_1 + 2P_2 \qquad Q_2 = 75 + 0.5P_1 - P_2 \qquad \text{TC} = Q_1^2 + 2Q_1Q_2 + Q_2^2$$

where Q_1 and Q_2 are substitute goods, as indicated by the opposite signs for P_1 and P_2 in each equation (i.e., an increase in P_2 will increase demand for Q_1 and an increase in P_1 will increase demand for Q_2).

(a) Since the markets are interrelated, the inverse functions must be found simultaneously. Rearranging the demand functions to get $P = f(Q)$, in order ultimately to maximize Π as a function of Q alone,

$$-3P_1 + 2P_2 = Q_1 - 100$$
$$0.5P_1 - P_2 = Q_2 - 75$$

In matrix form,

$$\begin{bmatrix} -3 & 2 \\ 0.5 & -1 \end{bmatrix}\begin{bmatrix} P_1 \\ P_2 \end{bmatrix} = \begin{bmatrix} Q_1 - 100 \\ Q_2 - 75 \end{bmatrix}$$

Using Cramer's rule,

$$|A| = 2$$

$$|A_1| = \begin{vmatrix} Q_1 - 100 & 2 \\ Q_2 - 75 & -1 \end{vmatrix} = -Q_1 + 100 - 2Q_2 + 150 = 250 - Q_1 - 2Q_2$$

$$P_1 = \frac{|A_1|}{|A|} = \frac{250 - Q_1 - 2Q_2}{2} = 125 - 0.5Q_1 - Q_2$$

$$|A_2| = \begin{vmatrix} -3 & Q_1 - 100 \\ 0.5 & Q_2 - 75 \end{vmatrix} = -3Q_2 + 225 - 0.5Q_1 + 50 = 275 - 0.5Q_1 - 3Q_2$$

$$P_2 = \frac{|A_2|}{|A|} = \frac{275 - 0.5Q_1 - 3Q_2}{2} = 137.5 - 0.25Q_1 - 1.5Q_2$$

(b)
$$\Pi = (125 - 0.5Q_1 - Q_2)Q_1 + (137.5 - 0.25Q_1 - 1.5Q_2)Q_2 - (Q_1^2 + 2Q_1Q_2 + Q_2^2)$$
$$= 125Q_1 + 137.5Q_2 - 3.25Q_1Q_2 - 1.5Q_1^2 - 2.5Q_2^2$$
$$\Pi_1 = 125 - 3.25Q_2 - 3Q_1 = 0 \qquad \Pi_2 = 137.5 - 3.25Q_1 - 5Q_2 = 0$$

Thus,

$$\begin{bmatrix} -3 & -3.25 \\ -3.25 & -5 \end{bmatrix}\begin{bmatrix} Q_1 \\ Q_2 \end{bmatrix} = \begin{bmatrix} -125 \\ -137.5 \end{bmatrix}$$

$$|A| = 4.4375$$

$$|A_1| = 178.125 \qquad \bar{Q}_1 = \frac{178.125}{4.4375} \approx 40.14$$

$$|A_2| = 6.25 \qquad \bar{Q}_2 = \frac{6.25}{4.4375} \approx 1.4$$

(c)
$$|H| = \begin{vmatrix} -3 & -3.25 \\ -3.25 & -5 \end{vmatrix}$$

$|H_1| = -3, |H_2| = |H| = |A| = 4.4375$, and Π is maximized.

12.17. Redo Problem 12.16 by maximizing profits for

$$Q_1 = 90 - 6P_1 - 2P_2 \qquad Q_2 = 80 - 2P_1 - 4P_2 \qquad TC = 2Q_1^2 + 3Q_1Q_2 + 2Q_2^2$$

where Q_1 and Q_2 are complements, as indicated by the same sign for P_1 and P_2 in each equation.

(a)　Converting the demand functions to functions of Q,

$$\begin{bmatrix} -6 & -2 \\ -2 & -4 \end{bmatrix}\begin{bmatrix} P_1 \\ P_2 \end{bmatrix} = \begin{bmatrix} Q_1 - 90 \\ Q_2 - 80 \end{bmatrix}$$

$$|A| = 20$$

$$|A_1| = \begin{vmatrix} Q_1 - 90 & -2 \\ Q_2 - 80 & -4 \end{vmatrix} = -4Q_1 + 360 + 2Q_2 - 160 = 200 - 4Q_1 + 2Q_2$$

$$P_1 = \frac{200 - 4Q_1 + 2Q_2}{20} = 10 - 0.2Q_1 + 0.1Q_2$$

$$|A_2| = \begin{vmatrix} -6 & Q_1 - 90 \\ -2 & Q_2 - 80 \end{vmatrix} = -6Q_2 + 480 + 2Q_1 - 180 = 300 - 6Q_2 + 2Q_1$$

$$P_2 = \frac{300 - 6Q_2 + 2Q_1}{20} = 15 - 0.3Q_2 + 0.1Q_1$$

(b)　　$$\Pi = (10 - 0.2Q_1 + 0.1Q_2)Q_1 + (15 - 0.3Q_2 + 0.1Q_1)Q_2 - (2Q_1^2 + 3Q_1Q_2 + 2Q_2^2)$$
$$= 10Q_1 + 15Q_2 - 2.8Q_1Q_2 - 2.2Q_1^2 - 2.3Q_2^2$$
$$\Pi_1 = 10 - 2.8Q_2 - 4.4Q_1 = 0 \qquad \Pi_2 = 15 - 2.8Q_1 - 4.6Q_2 = 0$$

Thus,
$$\begin{bmatrix} -4.4 & -2.8 \\ -2.8 & -4.6 \end{bmatrix}\begin{bmatrix} Q_1 \\ Q_2 \end{bmatrix} = \begin{bmatrix} -10 \\ -15 \end{bmatrix}$$

$$|A| = 12.4$$

$$|A_1| = 4 \qquad \bar{Q}_1 = \frac{4}{12.4} \approx 0.32$$

$$|A_2| = 38 \qquad \bar{Q}_2 = \frac{38}{12.4} \approx 3.06$$

(c)　　$$|H| = \begin{vmatrix} -4.4 & -2.8 \\ -2.8 & -4.6 \end{vmatrix}$$

$|H_1| = -4.4, |H_2| = |A| = 12.4$, and Π is maximized.

12.18. Redo Problem 12.16, given

$$Q_1 = 150 - 3P_1 + P_2 + P_3 \qquad Q_2 = 180 + P_1 - 4P_2 + 2P_3 \qquad Q_3 = 200 + 2P_1 + P_2 - 5P_3$$
$$TC = Q_1^2 + Q_1Q_2 + 2Q_2^2 + Q_2Q_3 + Q_3^2 + Q_1Q_3$$

(a)　Finding the inverses of the demand functions

$$\begin{bmatrix} -3 & 1 & 1 \\ 1 & -4 & 2 \\ 2 & 1 & -5 \end{bmatrix}\begin{bmatrix} P_1 \\ P_2 \\ P_3 \end{bmatrix} = \begin{bmatrix} Q_1 - 150 \\ Q_2 - 180 \\ Q_3 - 200 \end{bmatrix}$$

$$|A| = -36$$
$$|A_1| = (Q_1 - 150)(20 - 2) - 1(-5Q_2 + 900 - 2Q_3 + 400) + 1(Q_2 - 180 + 4Q_3 - 800)$$
$$= -4980 + 18Q_1 + 6Q_2 + 6Q_3$$
$$P_1 = \frac{-4980 + 18Q_1 + 6Q_2 + 6Q_3}{-36} = 138.33 - 0.5Q_1 - 0.17Q_2 - 0.17Q_3$$
$$|A_2| = -3(-5Q_2 + 900 - 2Q_3 + 400) - (Q_1 - 150)(-5 - 4) + 1(Q_3 - 200 - 2Q_2 + 360)$$
$$= -5090 + 9Q_1 + 13Q_2 + 7Q_3$$
$$P_2 = \frac{-5090 + 9Q_1 + 13Q_2 + 7Q_3}{-36} = 141.39 - 0.25Q_1 - 0.36Q_2 - 0.19Q_3$$
$$|A_3| = -3(-4Q_3 + 800 - Q_2 + 180) - 1(Q_3 - 200 - 2Q_2 + 360) + (Q_1 - 150)(1 + 8)$$
$$= -4450 + 9Q_1 + 5Q_2 + 11Q_3$$
$$P_3 = \frac{-4450 + 9Q_1 + 5Q_2 + 11Q_3}{-36} = 123.61 - 0.25Q_1 - 0.14Q_2 - 0.31Q_3$$

(b)
$$\Pi = P_1 Q_1 + P_2 Q_2 + P_3 Q_3 - TC$$
$$= 138.33 Q_1 + 141.39 Q_2 + 123.61 Q_3 - 1.42 Q_1 Q_2$$
$$- 1.33 Q_2 Q_3 - 1.42 Q_1 Q_3 - 1.5 Q_1^2 - 2.36 Q_2^2 - 1.31 Q_3^2$$

$$\Pi_1 = 138.33 - 1.42 Q_2 - 1.42 Q_3 - 3 Q_1 = 0$$
$$\Pi_2 = 141.39 - 1.42 Q_1 - 1.33 Q_3 - 4.72 Q_2 = 0$$
$$\Pi_3 = 123.61 - 1.33 Q_2 - 1.42 Q_1 - 2.62 Q_3 = 0$$

Thus,

$$\begin{bmatrix} -3 & -1.42 & -1.42 \\ -1.42 & -4.72 & -1.33 \\ -1.42 & -1.33 & -2.62 \end{bmatrix} \begin{bmatrix} Q_1 \\ Q_2 \\ Q_3 \end{bmatrix} = \begin{bmatrix} -138.33 \\ -141.39 \\ -123.61 \end{bmatrix}$$

$$|A| = -22.37$$

$$|A_1| = -612.27 \qquad \bar{Q}_1 = \frac{-612.27}{-22.37} \approx 27.37$$

$$|A_2| = -329.14 \qquad \bar{Q}_2 = \frac{-329.14}{-22.37} \approx 14.71$$

$$|A_3| = -556.64 \qquad \bar{Q}_3 = \frac{-556.64}{-22.37} \approx 24.88$$

(c)
$$|H_1| = \begin{vmatrix} -3 & -1.42 & -1.42 \\ -1.42 & -4.72 & -1.33 \\ -1.42 & -1.33 & -2.62 \end{vmatrix}$$

$|H_1| = -3$, $|H_2| = 12.14$, and $|H_3| = |A| = -22.37$. And Π is maximized.

PRICE DISCRIMINATION AND ELASTICITY OF DEMAND

Note: While the parameters of the problems in this section are kept unrealistically low for easier computation, the economic significance is not affected.

12.19. A telephone company has isolated three distinct demands for its service:

Weekdays: $\qquad\qquad\qquad\qquad Q_1 = 90 - 0.5 P_1$

Holidays: $\qquad\qquad\qquad\qquad Q_2 = 35 - 0.25 P_2$ $\qquad\qquad$ (12.15)

Nights: $\qquad\qquad\qquad\qquad Q_3 = 30 - 0.2 P_3$

$TC = 25 + 20Q$ where $Q = Q_1 + Q_2 + Q_3$.

Show that as a discriminating monopolist this company will maximize profits by charging the highest price in the market where the price elasticity $|\epsilon|$ of demand is lowest, by finding (a) the profit-maximizing level of output, (b) the profit-maximizing price, and (c) the price elasticity of demand in each market. Use Cramer's rule for solving simultaneous equations and the Hessian for second-order conditions.

(a) From (12.15),

$$P_1 = 180 - 2Q_1 \qquad P_2 = 140 - 4Q_2 \qquad P_3 = 150 - 5Q_3 \qquad (12.16)$$

Thus,

$$\Pi = (180 - 2Q_1)Q_1 + (140 - 4Q_2)Q_2 + (150 - 5Q_3)Q_3 - (25 + 20Q_1 + 20Q_2 + 20Q_3)$$
$$= 160Q_1 - 2Q_1^2 + 120Q_2 - 4Q_2^2 + 130Q_3 - 5Q_3^2 - 25$$

$$\Pi_1 = 160 - 4Q_1 = 0 \qquad \bar{Q}_1 = 40 \qquad \Pi_2 = 120 - 8Q_2 = 0 \qquad \bar{Q}_2 = 15$$
$$\Pi_3 = 130 - 10Q_3 = 0 \qquad \bar{Q}_3 = 13 \qquad\qquad (12.17)$$

Taking the second partials of (12.17) and forming the Hessian to test for the second-order condition,

$$|H| = \begin{vmatrix} -4 & 0 & 0 \\ 0 & -8 & 0 \\ 0 & 0 & -10 \end{vmatrix}$$

$|H_1| = -4$, $|H_2| = 32$, $|H_3| = -320$, and Π is maximized.

(b) Substituting the critical values in (12.16),

$$\bar{P}_1 = 180 - 2(40) = 100 \qquad \bar{P}_2 = 140 - 4(15) = 80 \qquad \bar{P}_3 = 150 - 5(13) = 85$$

(c)
$$\epsilon_i = \frac{dQ_i}{dP_i}\frac{P_i}{Q_i}$$

Taking the derivatives of (12.15) and using the equilibrium prices and quantities,

$$\epsilon_1 = -0.5(\tfrac{100}{40}) = -1.25 \qquad \epsilon_2 = -0.25(\tfrac{80}{15}) = -1.33 \qquad \epsilon_3 = -0.2(\tfrac{85}{13}) = -1.31$$

For profit maximization, market 1 is charged the highest price ($P_1 = 100$) because elasticity $|\epsilon|$ is lowest ($|\epsilon_1| = |-1.25|$); market 2 is charged the lowest price ($P_2 = 80$) because elasticity $|\epsilon|$ is highest ($|\epsilon_2| = |-1.33|$).

12.20. Redo Problem 12.19 for an airline which has isolated three distinct demands for air flight services, as follows:

Day service: $\qquad\qquad Q_1 = 12 - \tfrac{1}{12}P_1$

Night coach: $\qquad\qquad Q_2 = 11 - \tfrac{1}{10}P_2 \qquad\qquad$ (12.18)

Standby: $\qquad\qquad Q_3 = 13 - \tfrac{1}{8}P_3$

$$TC = 40 + 10Q + 0.5Q^2 \qquad\qquad (12.19)$$

where $Q = Q_1 + Q_2 + Q_3$.

(a) From (12.18), $\qquad P_1 = 144 - 12Q_1 \qquad P_2 = 110 - 10Q_2 \qquad P_3 = 104 - 8Q_3 \qquad$ (12.20)

$$\Pi = (144 - 12Q_1)Q_1 + (110 - 10Q_2)Q_2 + (104 - 8Q_3)Q_3 - TC$$

Substituting $Q = Q_1 + Q_2 + Q_3$ in (12.19),

$$TC = 0.5Q_1^2 + Q_1Q_2 + 10Q_1 + 0.5Q_2^2 + Q_2Q_3 + 10Q_2 + 0.5Q_3^2 + Q_1Q_3 + 10Q_3 + 40$$

Thus,

$$\Pi = -12.5Q_1^2 + 134Q_1 - Q_1Q_2 - 10.5Q_2^2 + 100Q_2 - Q_2Q_3 - 8.5Q_3^2 + 94Q_3 - Q_1Q_3 - 40$$

$$\Pi_1 = -25Q_1 + 134 - Q_2 - Q_3 = 0 \qquad \Pi_2 = -Q_1 - 21Q_2 + 100 - Q_3 = 0$$
$$\Pi_3 = -17Q_3 + 94 - Q_2 - Q_1 = 0 \qquad\qquad (12.21)$$

Thus,

$$\begin{bmatrix} -25 & -1 & -1 \\ -1 & -21 & -1 \\ -1 & -1 & -17 \end{bmatrix}\begin{bmatrix} Q_1 \\ Q_2 \\ Q_3 \end{bmatrix} = \begin{bmatrix} -134 \\ -100 \\ -94 \end{bmatrix}$$

$$|A| = -8864$$

$$|A_1| = -44\,224 \qquad \bar{Q}_1 = \frac{-44\,224}{-8864} \approx 4.99$$

$$|A_2| = -38\,000 \qquad \bar{Q}_2 = \frac{-38\,000}{-8864} \approx 4.29$$

$$|A_3| = -44\,176 \qquad \bar{Q}_3 = \frac{-44\,176}{-8864} \approx 4.98$$

Taking the second partials of (12.21) to form the Hessian,

$$|H| = \begin{vmatrix} -25 & -1 & -1 \\ -1 & -21 & -1 \\ -1 & -1 & -17 \end{vmatrix}$$

$|H_1| = -25, |H_2| = 524,$ and $|H_3| = |A| = -8864$; and Π is maximized.

(b) Substituting the critical values in (12.20), $\bar{P}_1 = 84.12, \bar{P}_2 = 67.10,$ and $\bar{P}_3 = 64.16$.

(c)
$$\epsilon_i = \frac{dQ_i}{dP_i} \frac{P_i}{Q_i}$$

Thus,

$$\epsilon_1 = \frac{-1}{12}\left(\frac{84.12}{4.99}\right) \approx -1.40 \qquad \epsilon_2 = \frac{-1}{10}\left(\frac{67.10}{4.29}\right) \approx -1.56 \qquad \epsilon_3 = -\frac{1}{8}\left(\frac{64.16}{4.98}\right) \approx -1.61$$

The airline maximizes profit by charging the highest price in the market where $|\epsilon|$ is lowest.

12.21. A university club can distinguish three separate demands for membership:

Student membership: $\qquad\qquad\qquad Q_1 = 46.67 - \frac{1}{6}P_1$

Junior membership: $\qquad\qquad\qquad Q_2 = 72.86 - \frac{1}{7}P_2 \qquad\qquad\qquad$ (12.22)

Senior membership: $\qquad\qquad\qquad Q_3 = 80 - \frac{1}{8}P_3$

$$TC = Q^2 + 30Q + 75 \qquad\qquad\qquad (12.23)$$

where $Q = Q_1 + Q_2 + Q_3$.

Redo Problem 12.19 for this club, using the MR $=$ MC approach.

(a) From (12.22),

$$P_1 = 280 - 6Q_1 \qquad P_2 = 510 - 7Q_2 \qquad P_3 = 640 - 8Q_3 \qquad (12.24)$$

With TR $=$ PQ,

$$TR_1 = 280Q_1 - 6Q_1^2 \qquad TR_2 = 510Q_2 - 7Q_2^2 \qquad TR_3 = 640Q_3 - 8Q_3^2 \qquad (12.25)$$

Taking the derivatives of (12.25) and (12.23) to get marginal revenue and marginal cost (see Problem 4.22),

$$MR_1 = 280 - 12Q_1 \qquad MR_2 = 510 - 14Q_2 \qquad MR_3 = 640 - 16Q_3 \qquad (12.26)$$

$$MC = 30 + 2Q \qquad\qquad\qquad (12.27)$$

Substituting $Q = Q_1 + Q_2 + Q_3$ in (12.27),

$$MC = 30 + 2Q_1 + 2Q_2 + 2Q_3 \qquad\qquad\qquad (12.27a)$$

Equating MR and MC in each market in order to maximize profits,

$$280 - 12Q_1 = 30 + 2Q_1 + 2Q_2 + 2Q_3$$
$$510 - 14Q_2 = 30 + 2Q_1 + 2Q_2 + 2Q_3$$
$$640 - 16Q_3 = 30 + 2Q_1 + 2Q_2 + 2Q_3$$

Simplifying by subtracting MC from MR,

$$250 - 14Q_1 - 2Q_2 - 2Q_3 = 0$$
$$480 - 2Q_1 - 16Q_2 - 2Q_3 = 0 \qquad\qquad\qquad (12.28)$$
$$610 - 2Q_1 - 2Q_2 - 18Q_3 = 0$$

In matrix form,

$$\begin{bmatrix} -14 & -2 & -2 \\ -2 & -16 & -2 \\ -2 & -2 & -18 \end{bmatrix}\begin{bmatrix} Q_1 \\ Q_2 \\ Q_3 \end{bmatrix} = \begin{bmatrix} -250 \\ -480 \\ -610 \end{bmatrix}$$

$$|A| = -3856$$

$$|A_1| = -38\,560 \qquad \bar{Q}_1 = \frac{-38\,560}{-3856} = 10$$

$$|A_2| = -96\,400 \qquad \bar{Q}_2 = \frac{-96\,400}{-3856} = 25$$

$$|A_3| = -115\,680 \qquad \bar{Q}_3 = \frac{-115\,680}{-3856} = 30$$

To test for the second-order condition, we can take the second partials of (12.28) because (12.28) was derived by subtracting MC from MR. This is equivalent to the first partials of the profit function since

$$\frac{d\Pi}{dQ} = \frac{d\text{TR}}{dQ} - \frac{d\text{TC}}{dQ} = \text{MR} - \text{MC}$$

Thus,

$$|H| = \begin{vmatrix} -14 & -2 & -2 \\ -2 & -16 & -2 \\ -2 & -2 & -18 \end{vmatrix}$$

$|H_1| = -14$, $|H_2| = 220$, and $|H_3| = |A| = -3856$; so Π is maximized.

(b)   Substituting the critical values in (12.24), $\bar{P}_1 = 220$, $\bar{P}_2 = 335$, and $\bar{P}_3 = 400$.

(c) $\epsilon_1 = -\frac{1}{6}\left(\frac{220}{10}\right) \approx -3.67 \qquad \epsilon_2 = -\frac{1}{7}\left(\frac{335}{25}\right) \approx -1.91 \qquad \epsilon_3 = -\frac{1}{8}\left(\frac{400}{30}\right) \approx -1.67$

12.22. It can be demonstrated that

$$\text{MR} = P\left(1 - \frac{1}{|\epsilon|}\right)$$

Check the answer for market 1 in Problem 12.21.

$$\text{MR}_1 = 220\left(1 - \frac{1}{3.67}\right) \approx 160$$

In comparison, by substituting $\bar{Q}_1 = 10$ in (12.26), $\text{MR}_1 = 280 - 12(10) = 160$.
On your own, check your answers for MR_2 and MR_3.

THE BORDERED HESSIAN IN CONSTRAINED OPTIMIZATION

12.23. Maximize utility $u = 2xy$ subject to a budget constraint equal to $3x + 4y = 90$ by (a) finding the critical values $\bar{x}$, $\bar{y}$, and $\bar{\lambda}$ and (b) using the bordered Hessian $|\bar{H}|$ to test the second-order condition.

(a)   The Lagrangian function is $U = 2xy + \lambda(90 - 3x - 4y)$

The first-order conditions are

$$U_x = 2y - 3\lambda = 0 \qquad U_y = 2x - 4\lambda = 0 \qquad U_\lambda = 90 - 3x - 4y = 0$$

In matrix form,

$$\begin{bmatrix} 0 & 2 & -3 \\ 2 & 0 & -4 \\ -3 & -4 & 0 \end{bmatrix}\begin{bmatrix} x \\ y \\ \lambda \end{bmatrix} = \begin{bmatrix} 0 \\ 0 \\ -90 \end{bmatrix} \qquad (12.29)$$

Solving by Cramer's rule, $|A| = 48$, $|A_1| = 720$, $|A_2| = 540$, and $|A_3| = 360$. Thus, $\bar{x} = 15$, $\bar{y} = 11.25$, and $\bar{\lambda} = 7.5$.

(b) Taking the second partials of U with respect to x and y and the first partials of the constraint with respect to x and y to form the bordered Hessian,

$$U_{xx} = 0 \qquad U_{yy} = 0 \qquad U_{xy} = 2 = U_{yx} \qquad c_x = 3 \qquad c_y = 4$$

From Section 12.5,

$$|\bar{H}| = \begin{vmatrix} 0 & 2 & 3 \\ 2 & 0 & 4 \\ 3 & 4 & 0 \end{vmatrix} \qquad \text{or} \qquad |\bar{H}| = \begin{vmatrix} 0 & 3 & 4 \\ 3 & 0 & 2 \\ 4 & 2 & 0 \end{vmatrix}$$

$$|\bar{H}_2| = |\bar{H}| = -2(-12) + 3(8) = 48 > 0 \qquad |\bar{H}_2| = |\bar{H}| = -3(-8) + 4(6) = 48 > 0$$

The bordered Hessian can be set up in either of the above forms without affecting the value of the principal minor. With $|\bar{H}| = |A| > 0$, from the rules of Section 12.5 $|\bar{H}|$ is negative definite, and U is maximized.

12.24. Maximize utility $u = xy + x$ subject to the budget constraint $6x + 2y = 110$, by using the techniques of Problem 12.23.

(a)
$$U = xy + x + \lambda(110 - 6x - 2y)$$

$$U_x = y + 1 - 6\lambda = 0 \qquad U_y = x - 2\lambda = 0 \qquad U_\lambda = 110 - 6x - 2y = 0$$

In matrix form,

$$\begin{bmatrix} 0 & 1 & -6 \\ 1 & 0 & -2 \\ -6 & -2 & 0 \end{bmatrix} \begin{bmatrix} x \\ y \\ \lambda \end{bmatrix} = \begin{bmatrix} -1 \\ 0 \\ -110 \end{bmatrix}$$

Solving by Cramer's rule, $\bar{x} = 9\frac{1}{3}$, $\bar{y} = 27$, and $\bar{\lambda} = 4\frac{2}{3}$.

(b) Since $U_{xx} = 0$, $U_{yy} = 0$, $U_{xy} = 1 = U_{yx}$, $c_x = 6$, and $c_y = 2$,

$$|\bar{H}| = \begin{vmatrix} 0 & 1 & 6 \\ 1 & 0 & 2 \\ 6 & 2 & 0 \end{vmatrix} \qquad |\bar{H}_2| = |\bar{H}| = 24$$

With $|\bar{H}_2| > 0$, $|\bar{H}|$ is negative definite, and U is maximized.

12.25. Minimize a firm's total costs $c = 45x^2 + 90xy + 90y^2$ when the firm has to meet a production quota g equal to $2x + 3y = 60$ by (a) finding the critical values and (b) using the bordered Hessian to test the second-order conditions.

(a)
$$C = 45x^2 + 90xy + 90y^2 + \lambda(60 - 2x - 3y)$$

$$C_x = 90x + 90y - 2\lambda = 0 \qquad C_y = 90x + 180y - 3\lambda = 0$$
$$C_\lambda = 60 - 2x - 3y = 0$$

In matrix form,

$$\begin{bmatrix} 90 & 90 & -2 \\ 90 & 180 & -3 \\ -2 & -3 & 0 \end{bmatrix} \begin{bmatrix} x \\ y \\ \lambda \end{bmatrix} = \begin{bmatrix} 0 \\ 0 \\ -60 \end{bmatrix}$$

Solving by Cramer's rule, $\bar{x} = 12$, $\bar{y} = 12$, and $\bar{\lambda} = 1080$.

(b) Since $C_{xx} = 90$, $C_{yy} = 180$, $C_{xy} = 90 = C_{yx}$, $g_x = 2$, and $g_y = 3$,

$$|\bar{H}| = \begin{vmatrix} 90 & 90 & 2 \\ 90 & 180 & 3 \\ 2 & 3 & 0 \end{vmatrix}$$

$|\bar{H}_2| = -450$. With $|\bar{H}_2| < 0$, $|\bar{H}|$ is positive definite and C is minimized.

12.26. Minimize a firm's costs $c = 3x^2 + 5xy + 6y^2$ when the firm must meet a production quota of $5x + 7y = 732$, using the techniques of Problem 12.25.

(a)
$$C = 3x^2 + 5xy + 6y^2 + \lambda(732 - 5x - 7y)$$

$$C_x = 6x + 5y - 5\lambda = 0 \qquad C_y = 5x + 12y - 7\lambda = 0$$
$$C_\lambda = 732 - 5x - 7y = 0$$

Solving simultaneously, $\qquad \bar{x} = 75 \qquad \bar{y} = 51 \qquad \bar{\lambda} = 141$

(b) With $C_{xx} = 6, C_{yy} = 12, C_{xy} = 5 = C_{yx}, g_x = 5$, and $g_y = 7$,

$$|\bar{H}| = \begin{vmatrix} 6 & 5 & 5 \\ 5 & 12 & 7 \\ 5 & 7 & 0 \end{vmatrix}$$

$|\bar{H}_2| = 5(35 - 60) - 7(42 - 25) = -244$. Thus, $|\bar{H}|$ is positive definite, and C is minimized.

12.27. Redo Problem 12.25 by maximizing utility $u = x^{0.5}y^{0.3}$ subject to the budget constraint $10x + 3y = 140$.

(a)
$$U = x^{0.5}y^{0.3} + \lambda(140 - 10x - 3y)$$

$$U_x = 0.5x^{-0.5}y^{0.3} - 10\lambda = 0 \qquad U_y = 0.3x^{0.5}y^{-0.7} - 3\lambda = 0$$
$$U_\lambda = 140 - 10x - 3y = 0$$

Solving simultaneously, as shown in Example 12 of Chapter 6,

$$\bar{x} = 8.75 \qquad \bar{y} = 17.5 \qquad \text{and} \qquad \bar{\lambda} = 0.04$$

(b) With $U_{xx} = -0.25x^{-1.5}y^{0.3}, U_{yy} = -0.21x^{0.5}y^{-1.7}, U_{xy} = U_{yx} = 0.15x^{-0.5}y^{-0.7}, g_x = 10$, and $g_y = 3$,

$$|\bar{H}| = \begin{vmatrix} -0.25x^{-1.5}y^{0.3} & 0.15x^{-0.5}y^{-0.7} & 10 \\ 0.15x^{-0.5}y^{-0.7} & -0.21x^{0.5}y^{-1.7} & 3 \\ 10 & 3 & 0 \end{vmatrix}$$

Expanding along the third column,

$$|\bar{H}_2| = 10(0.45x^{-0.5}y^{-0.7} + 2.1x^{0.5}y^{-1.7}) - 3(-0.75x^{-1.5}y^{0.3} - 1.5x^{-0.5}y^{-0.7})$$
$$= 21x^{0.5}y^{-1.7} + 9x^{-0.5}y^{-0.7} + 2.25x^{-1.5}y^{0.3} > 0$$

since x and $y > 0$, and a positive number x raised to a negative power $-n$ equals $1/x^n$, which is also positive. With $|\bar{H}_2| > 0, |\bar{H}|$ is negative definite, and U is maximized.

12.28. Maximize utility $u = x^{0.25}y^{0.4}$ subject to the budget constraint $2x + 8y = 104$, as in Problem 12.27.

(a)
$$U = x^{0.25}y^{0.4} + \lambda(104 - 2x - 8y)$$

$$U_x = 0.25x^{-0.75}y^{0.4} - 2\lambda = 0 \qquad U_y = 0.4x^{0.25}y^{-0.6} - 8\lambda = 0$$
$$U_\lambda = 104 - 2x - 8y = 0$$

Solving simultaneously, $\bar{x} = 20, \bar{y} = 8$, and $\bar{\lambda} = 0.03$.

(b)
$$|\bar{H}| = \begin{vmatrix} -0.1875x^{-1.75}y^{0.4} & 0.1x^{-0.75}y^{-0.6} & 2 \\ 0.1x^{-0.75}y^{-0.6} & -0.24x^{0.25}y^{-1.6} & 8 \\ 2 & 8 & 0 \end{vmatrix}$$

Expanding along the third row,

$$|\bar{H}_2| = 2(0.8x^{-0.75}y^{-0.6} + 0.48x^{0.25}y^{-1.6}) - 8(-1.5x^{-1.75}y^{0.4} - 0.2x^{-0.75}y^{-0.6})$$
$$= 0.96x^{0.25}y^{-1.6} + 3.2x^{-0.75}y^{-0.6} + 12x^{-1.75}y^{0.4} > 0$$

Thus, $|\bar{H}|$ is negative definite, and U is maximized.

12.29. Minimize costs $c = 3x + 4y$ subject to the constraint $2xy = 337.5$, using the techniques of Problem 12.25(a) and (b). (c) Discuss the relationship between this solution and that for Problem 12.23.

(a)
$$C = 3x + 4y + \lambda(337.5 - 2xy)$$

$$C_x = 3 - 2\lambda y = 0 \qquad \lambda = \frac{1.5}{y} \qquad\qquad (12.30)$$

$$C_y = 4 - 2\lambda x = 0 \qquad \lambda = \frac{2}{x} \qquad\qquad (12.31)$$

$$C_\lambda = 337.5 - 2xy = 0 \qquad\qquad (12.32)$$

Equate λ's in (12.30) and (12.31).

$$\frac{1.5}{y} = \frac{2}{x} \qquad y = 0.75x$$

Substitute in (12.32).

$$337.5 = 2x(0.75x) = 1.5x^2$$
$$x^2 = 225 \qquad \bar{x} = 15$$

Thus, $\bar{y} = 11.25$ and $\bar{\lambda} = 0.133$.

(b) With $C_{xx} = 0$, $C_{yy} = 0$, and $C_{xy} = C_{yx} = -2\lambda$ and from the constraint $2xy = 337.5$, $g_x = 2y$, and $g_y = 2x$,

$$|\bar{H}| = \begin{vmatrix} 0 & -2\lambda & 2y \\ -2\lambda & 0 & 2x \\ 2y & 2x & 0 \end{vmatrix}$$

$|\bar{H}_2| = -(-2\lambda)(-4xy) + 2y(-4x\lambda) = -16\lambda xy$. With $\bar{\lambda}, \bar{x}, \bar{y} > 0$, $|\bar{H}_2| < 0$. Hence $|\bar{H}|$ is positive definite, and C is minimized.

(c) This problem and Problem 12.23 are the same, except that the objective functions and constraints are reversed. In Problem 12.23, the objective function $u = 2xy$ was maximized subject to the constraint $3x + 4y = 90$; in this problem the objective function $c = 3x + 4y$ was minimized subject to the constraint $2xy = 337.5$. Therefore, one may maximize utility subject to a budget constraint *or* minimize the cost of achieving a given level of utility.

12.30. Minimize the cost of 434 units of production for a firm when $Q = 10K^{0.7}L^{0.1}$ and $P_K = 28$, $P_L = 10$ by (a) finding the critical values and (b) using the bordered Hessian. (c) Check the answer with that of Problem 6.45(b).

(a) The objective function is $c = 28K + 10L$, and the constraint is $10K^{0.7}L^{0.1} = 434$. Thus,

$$C = 28K + 10L + \lambda(434 - 10K^{0.7}L^{0.1})$$

$$C_K = 28 - 7\lambda K^{-0.3}L^{0.1} = 0 \qquad \lambda = 4K^{0.3}L^{-0.1} \qquad (12.33)$$

$$C_L = 10 - \lambda K^{0.7}L^{-0.9} = 0 \qquad \lambda = 10K^{-0.7}L^{0.9} \qquad (12.34)$$

$$C_\lambda = 434 - 10K^{0.7}L^{0.1} = 0 \qquad\qquad (12.35)$$

Equate λ's in (12.33) and (12.34).

$$4K^{0.3}L^{-0.1} = 10K^{-0.7}L^{0.9} \qquad K = 2.5L$$

Substitute in (12.35) and use a calculator.

$$434 = 10(2.5)^{0.7}L^{0.7}L^{0.1} \qquad 434 = 19L^{0.8}$$
$$\bar{L} = (22.8)^{1/0.8} = (22.8)^{1.25} \approx 50$$

Thus, $\bar{K} = 125$ and $\bar{\lambda} = 11.5$.

(b) With $C_{KK} = 2.1\lambda K^{-1.3}L^{0.1}$, $C_{LL} = 0.9\lambda K^{0.7}L^{-1.9}$, and $C_{KL} = -0.7\lambda K^{-0.3}L^{-0.9} = C_{LK}$ and from the constraint $g_K = 7K^{-0.3}L^{0.1}$ and $g_L = K^{0.7}L^{-0.9}$,

$$|\bar{H}| = \begin{vmatrix} 2.1\lambda K^{-1.3}L^{0.1} & -0.7\lambda K^{-0.3}L^{-0.9} & 7K^{-0.3}L^{0.1} \\ -0.7\lambda K^{-0.3}L^{-0.9} & 0.9\lambda K^{0.7}L^{-1.9} & K^{0.7}L^{-0.9} \\ 7K^{-0.3}L^{0.1} & K^{0.7}L^{-0.9} & 0 \end{vmatrix}$$

Expanding along the third row,

$$|\bar{H}_2| = 7K^{-0.3}L^{0.1}(-0.7\lambda K^{0.4}L^{-1.8} - 6.3\lambda K^{0.4}L^{-1.8}) - K^{0.7}L^{-0.9}(2.1\lambda K^{-0.6}L^{-0.8} + 4.9\lambda K^{-0.6}L^{-0.8})$$
$$= -49\lambda K^{0.1}L^{-1.7} - 7\lambda K^{0.1}L^{-1.7} = -56\lambda K^{0.1}L^{-1.7}$$

With $K, L, \lambda > 0$, $|\bar{H}_2| < 0$; $|\bar{H}|$ is positive definite, and C is minimized.

(c) The answers are identical with those in Problem 6.45(b), but note the difference in the work involved when the linear function is selected as the objective function and not the constraint. See also the bordered Hessian for Problem 6.45(b), which is calculated in Problem 12.31(c).

12.31. Use the bordered Hessian to check the second-order conditions for (a) Example 7 of Chapter 6, (b) Problem 6.45(a), and (c) Problem 6.45(b).

(a)
$$|\bar{H}| = \begin{vmatrix} 16 & -1 & 1 \\ -1 & 24 & 1 \\ 1 & 1 & 0 \end{vmatrix}$$

$|\bar{H}_2| = 1(-1 - 24) - 1(16 + 1) = -42$. With $|\bar{H}_2| < 0$, $|\bar{H}|$ is positive definite and C is minimized.

(b)
$$|\bar{H}| = \begin{vmatrix} -0.21K^{-1.7}L^{0.5} & 0.15K^{-0.7}L^{-0.5} & 6 \\ 0.15K^{-0.7}L^{-0.5} & -0.25K^{0.3}L^{-1.5} & 2 \\ 6 & 2 & 0 \end{vmatrix}$$

$$|\bar{H}_2| = 6(0.30K^{-0.7}L^{-0.5} + 1.5K^{0.3}L^{-1.5}) - 2(-0.42K^{-1.7}L^{0.5} - 0.9K^{-0.7}L^{-0.5})$$
$$= 9K^{0.3}L^{-1.5} + 3.6K^{-0.7}L^{-0.5} + 0.84K^{-1.7}L^{0.5} > 0$$

With $|\bar{H}_2| > 0$, $|\bar{H}|$ is negative definite, and Q is maximized.

(c)
$$|\bar{H}| = \begin{vmatrix} -2.1K^{-1.3}L^{0.1} & 0.7K^{-0.3}L^{-0.9} & 28 \\ 0.7K^{-0.3}L^{-0.9} & -0.9K^{0.7}L^{-1.9} & 10 \\ 28 & 10 & 0 \end{vmatrix}$$

$$|\bar{H}_2| = 28(7K^{-0.3}L^{-0.9} + 25.2K^{0.7}L^{-1.9}) - 10(-21K^{-1.3}L^{0.1} - 19.6K^{-0.3}L^{-0.9})$$
$$= 705.6K^{0.7}L^{-1.9} + 392K^{-0.3}L^{-0.9} + 210K^{-1.3}L^{0.1} > 0$$

With $|\bar{H}_2| > 0$, $|\bar{H}|$ is negative definite, and Q is maximized.

12.32. Use the bordered Hessian to check the second-order conditions in Problem 5.12(c), where $4xyz^2$ was optimized subject to the constraint $x + y + z = 56$; the first-order conditions were $F_x = 4yz^2 - \lambda = 0$, $F_y = 4xz^2 - \lambda = 0$, and $F_z = 8xyz - \lambda = 0$; and the critical values were $\bar{x} = 14$, $\bar{y} = 14$, and $\bar{z} = 28$.

Take the second partial derivatives of F and the first partials of the constraint, and set up the bordered Hessian, as follows:

$$|\bar{H}| = \begin{vmatrix} F_{xx} & F_{xy} & F_{xz} & g_x \\ F_{yx} & F_{yy} & F_{yz} & g_y \\ F_{zx} & F_{zy} & F_{zz} & g_z \\ g_x & g_y & g_z & 0 \end{vmatrix} = \begin{vmatrix} 0 & 4z^2 & 8yz & 1 \\ 4z^2 & 0 & 8xz & 1 \\ 8yz & 8xz & 8xy & 1 \\ 1 & 1 & 1 & 0 \end{vmatrix}$$

Start with $|H_2|$, the 3×3 submatrix in the upper left-hand corner.

$$|\bar{H}_2| = 0 - 4z^2[(4z^2 \cdot 8xy) - (8yz \cdot 8xz)] + 8yz(4z^2 \cdot 8xz - 0)$$
$$= -128xyz^4 + 256xyz^4 + 256xyz^4 = 384xyz^4 > 0$$

Next evaluate $|\bar{H}_3|$, which here equals $|\bar{H}|$.

$$|\bar{H}_3| = 0 - 4z^2 \begin{vmatrix} 4z^2 & 8xz & 1 \\ 8yz & 8xy & 1 \\ 1 & 1 & 0 \end{vmatrix} + 8yz \begin{vmatrix} 4z^2 & 0 & 1 \\ 8yz & 8xz & 1 \\ 1 & 1 & 0 \end{vmatrix} - (1) \begin{vmatrix} 4z^2 & 0 & 8xz \\ 8yz & 8xz & 8xy \\ 1 & 1 & 1 \end{vmatrix}$$

$$= -4z^2[4z^2(0 - 1) - 8xz(0 - 1) + 1(8yz - 8xy)] + 8yz[4z^2(0 - 1) - 0 + 1(8yz - 8xz)]$$
$$- 1[4z^2(8xz - 8xy) - 0 + 8xz(8yz - 8xz)]$$

$$= -4z^2(-4z^2 + 8xz + 8yz - 8xy) + 8yz(-4z^2 + 8yz - 8xz) - (32xz^3 - 32xyz^2 + 64xyz^2 - 64x^2z^2)$$

$$= 16z^4 - 64xz^3 - 64yz^3 - 64xyz^2 + 64x^2z^2 + 64y^2z^2$$

Evaluated at $\bar{x} = 14, \bar{y} = 14, \bar{z} = 28$,

$$|\bar{H}_3| = -19\,668\,992 < 0$$

With $|\bar{H}_2| > 0$ and $|\bar{H}_3| < 0$, $|\bar{H}|$ is negative definite, and the function is maximized.

CONSTRUCTION OF MARSHALLIAN DEMAND FUNCTIONS

12.33. Given the utility function and budget constraint

$$u = 3x + xy + 2y \qquad P_x x + P_y y = B$$

(a) Construct the Marshallian demand function.

(b) Estimate the demand for x at $P_x = 2, 4$, when $B = 60, P_y = 4$.

(c) Estimate the demand for y at $P_y = 2, 4$, when $B = 60, P_x = 4$.

(a) Forming the Lagrangian expression and taking the first partials,

$$U = xy + 3x + 2y + \lambda(P_x x + P_y y - B)$$
$$U_x = y + 3 + \lambda P_x = 0 \qquad U_y = x + 2 + \lambda P_y = 0 \qquad U_\lambda = P_x x + P_y y - B = 0$$

In matrix form,

$$\begin{bmatrix} 0 & 1 & P_x \\ 1 & 0 & P_y \\ P_x & P_y & 0 \end{bmatrix} \begin{bmatrix} x \\ y \\ \lambda \end{bmatrix} = \begin{bmatrix} -3 \\ -2 \\ B \end{bmatrix}$$

Using Cramer's rule, $|A| = -1(-P_x P_y) + P_x(P_y) = 2P_x P_y$. Expanding along the third column here and below,

$$|A_1| = \begin{vmatrix} -3 & 1 & P_x \\ -2 & 0 & P_y \\ B & P_y & 0 \end{vmatrix} = P_x(-2P_y) - P_y(-3P_y - B)$$

$$\bar{x} = \frac{|A_1|}{|A|} = \frac{-2P_x P_y + 3P_y^2 + P_y B}{2P_x P_y} = \frac{B - 2P_x + 3P_y}{2P_x}$$

$$|A_2| = \begin{vmatrix} 0 & -3 & P_x \\ 1 & -2 & P_y \\ P_x & B & 0 \end{vmatrix} = P_x(B + 2P_x) - P_y(3P_x)$$

$$\bar{y} = \frac{|A_2|}{|A|} = \frac{BP_x + 2P_x^2 - 3P_x P_y}{2P_x P_y} = \frac{B + 2P_x - 3P_y}{2P_y}$$

Testing the second-order condition,

$$|\bar{H}| = \begin{vmatrix} 0 & 1 & P_x \\ 1 & 0 & P_y \\ P_x & P_y & 0 \end{vmatrix} = |A| = 2P_x P_y > 0$$

Thus $|\bar{H}|$ is negative definite, and U is maximized.

(b)   Given $B = 60$, $P_y = 4$ and having found

$$x = \frac{B - 2P_x + 3P_y}{2P_x}$$

At $P_x = 2$, $x = \dfrac{60 - 2(2) + 3(4)}{2(2)} = \dfrac{68}{4} = 17$

At $P_x = 4$, $x = \dfrac{60 - 2(4) + 3(4)}{2(4)} = \dfrac{64}{8} = 8$

(c)   At $B = 60$, $P_x = 4$,

$$y = \frac{B + 2P_x - 3P_y}{2P_y}$$

At $P_y = 2$, $y = \dfrac{60 + 2(4) - 3(2)}{2(2)} = \dfrac{62}{4} = 15.5$

At $P_y = 4$, $y = \dfrac{60 + 2(4) - 3(4)}{2(4)} = \dfrac{56}{8} = 7$

12.34. (a)   Derive the Marshallian demand function, given

$$u = 2x + 2xy + 5y \qquad P_x x + P_y y = B$$

(b)   Estimate the demand for x and y when $B = 100$, $P_x = 2$, and $P_y = 10$.

(a)

$$U = 2xy + 2x + 5y + \lambda(P_x x + P_y y - B)$$
$$U_x = 2y + 2 + \lambda P_x = 0 \qquad U_y = 2x + 5 + \lambda P_y = 0 \qquad U_\lambda = P_x x + P_y y - B = 0$$

In matrix form,

$$\begin{bmatrix} 0 & 2 & P_x \\ 2 & 0 & P_y \\ P_x & P_y & 0 \end{bmatrix} \begin{bmatrix} x \\ y \\ \lambda \end{bmatrix} = \begin{bmatrix} -2 \\ -5 \\ B \end{bmatrix}$$

Solving by Cramer's rule, $|A| = -2(-P_x P_y) + P_x(2P_y) = 4P_x P_y$. Expanding along the third column,

$$|A_1| = P_x(-5P_y) - P_y(-2P_y - 2B)$$
$$\bar{x} = \frac{|A_1|}{|A|} = \frac{-5P_x P_y + 2P_y^2 + 2P_y B}{4P_x P_y} = \frac{2B - 5P_x + 2P_y}{4P_x}$$
$$|A_2| = P_x(2B + 5P_x) - P_y(2P_x)$$
$$\bar{y} = \frac{|A_2|}{|A|} = \frac{2P_x B + 5P_x^2 - 2P_x P_y}{4P_x P_y} = \frac{2B + 5P_x - 2P_y}{4P_y}$$

Testing the second-order condition,

$$|\bar{H}| = \begin{vmatrix} 0 & 2 & P_x \\ 2 & 0 & P_y \\ P_x & P_y & 0 \end{vmatrix} = |A| = 4P_x P_y > 0$$

$|\bar{H}|$ is negative definite, and U is maximized.

(b) At $B = 100$, $P_x = 2$, and $P_y = 10$,

$$\bar{x} = \frac{2(100) - 5(2) + 2(10)}{4(2)} = 26.25 \qquad \bar{y} = \frac{2(100) + 5(2) - 2(10)}{4(10)} = 4.75$$

INPUT-OUTPUT ANALYSIS

12.35. Determine the total demand for industries 1, 2, and 3, given the matrix of technical coefficients A and the final demand vector B below.

$$
\begin{array}{c}
\text{Output industry}\\
\begin{array}{ccc} 1 & 2 & 3 \end{array}
\end{array}
$$

$$
A = \begin{bmatrix} 0.2 & 0.3 & 0.2 \\ 0.4 & 0.1 & 0.3 \\ 0.3 & 0.5 & 0.2 \end{bmatrix} \begin{array}{l} 1 \\ 2 \\ 3 \end{array} \begin{array}{l} \text{Input} \\ \text{industry} \end{array} \qquad B = \begin{bmatrix} 150 \\ 200 \\ 210 \end{bmatrix}
$$

From *(12.6)*, the total demand vector is $X = (I - A)^{-1}B$, where

$$
I - A = \begin{bmatrix} 0.8 & -0.3 & -0.2 \\ -0.4 & 0.9 & -0.3 \\ -0.3 & -0.5 & 0.8 \end{bmatrix}
$$

Taking the inverse of $I - A$,

$$
(I - A)^{-1} = \frac{1}{0.239} \begin{bmatrix} 0.57 & 0.34 & 0.27 \\ 0.41 & 0.58 & 0.32 \\ 0.47 & 0.49 & 0.60 \end{bmatrix}
$$

Substituting in $X = (I - A)^{-1}B$,

$$
X = \frac{1}{0.239} \begin{bmatrix} 0.57 & 0.34 & 0.27 \\ 0.41 & 0.58 & 0.32 \\ 0.47 & 0.49 & 0.60 \end{bmatrix} \begin{bmatrix} 150 \\ 200 \\ 210 \end{bmatrix} = \frac{1}{0.239} \begin{bmatrix} 210.2 \\ 244.7 \\ 294.5 \end{bmatrix} = \begin{bmatrix} 879.50 \\ 1023.85 \\ 1232.22 \end{bmatrix} = \begin{bmatrix} x_1 \\ x_2 \\ x_3 \end{bmatrix}
$$

12.36. Determine the new level of total demand X_2 for Problem 12.35 if final demand increases by 40 in industry 1, 20 in industry 2, and 25 in industry 3.

$$\Delta X = (I - A)^{-1}\Delta B$$

$$
\Delta X = \frac{1}{0.239} \begin{bmatrix} 0.57 & 0.34 & 0.27 \\ 0.41 & 0.58 & 0.32 \\ 0.47 & 0.49 & 0.60 \end{bmatrix} \begin{bmatrix} 40 \\ 20 \\ 25 \end{bmatrix} = \frac{1}{0.239} \begin{bmatrix} 36.35 \\ 36.00 \\ 43.60 \end{bmatrix} = \begin{bmatrix} 152.09 \\ 150.63 \\ 182.43 \end{bmatrix}
$$

$$
X_2 = X_1 + \Delta X = \begin{bmatrix} 879.50 \\ 1023.85 \\ 1232.22 \end{bmatrix} + \begin{bmatrix} 152.09 \\ 150.63 \\ 182.43 \end{bmatrix} = \begin{bmatrix} 1031.59 \\ 1174.48 \\ 1414.65 \end{bmatrix}
$$

12.37. Determine the total demand for industries 1, 2, and 3, given the matrix of technical coefficients A and the final demand vector B below.

$$
\begin{array}{c}
\text{Output industry}\\
\begin{array}{ccc} 1 & 2 & 3 \end{array}
\end{array}
$$

$$
A = \begin{bmatrix} 0.4 & 0.3 & 0.1 \\ 0.2 & 0.2 & 0.3 \\ 0.2 & 0.4 & 0.2 \end{bmatrix} \begin{array}{l} 1 \\ 2 \\ 3 \end{array} \begin{array}{l} \text{Input} \\ \text{industry} \end{array} \qquad B = \begin{bmatrix} 140 \\ 220 \\ 180 \end{bmatrix}
$$

$$X = (I - A)^{-1}B$$

where

$$I - A = \begin{bmatrix} 0.6 & -0.3 & -0.1 \\ -0.2 & 0.8 & -0.3 \\ -0.2 & -0.4 & 0.8 \end{bmatrix}$$

and the inverse

$$(I - A)^{-1} = \frac{1}{0.222} \begin{bmatrix} 0.52 & 0.28 & 0.17 \\ 0.22 & 0.46 & 0.20 \\ 0.24 & 0.30 & 0.42 \end{bmatrix}$$

Thus,

$$X = \frac{1}{0.222} \begin{bmatrix} 0.52 & 0.28 & 0.17 \\ 0.22 & 0.46 & 0.20 \\ 0.24 & 0.30 & 0.42 \end{bmatrix} \begin{bmatrix} 140 \\ 220 \\ 180 \end{bmatrix} = \begin{bmatrix} 743.24 \\ 756.76 \\ 789.19 \end{bmatrix} = \begin{bmatrix} x_1 \\ x_2 \\ x_3 \end{bmatrix}$$

12.38. Determine the new total demand X_2 if final demand increases by 30 for industry 1 and decreases by 15 and 35 for industries 2 and 3, respectively, in Problem 12.37.

$$\Delta X = (I - A)^{-1} \Delta B$$

$$\Delta X = \frac{1}{0.222} \begin{bmatrix} 0.52 & 0.28 & 0.17 \\ 0.22 & 0.46 & 0.20 \\ 0.24 & 0.30 & 0.42 \end{bmatrix} \begin{bmatrix} 30 \\ -15 \\ -35 \end{bmatrix} = \frac{1}{0.222} \begin{bmatrix} 5.45 \\ -7.30 \\ -12.00 \end{bmatrix} = \begin{bmatrix} 24.55 \\ -32.88 \\ -54.05 \end{bmatrix}$$

$$X_2 = X_1 + \Delta X = \begin{bmatrix} 743.24 \\ 756.76 \\ 789.19 \end{bmatrix} + \begin{bmatrix} 24.55 \\ -32.88 \\ -54.05 \end{bmatrix} = \begin{bmatrix} 767.79 \\ 723.88 \\ 735.14 \end{bmatrix}$$

12.39. Given the interindustry transaction demand table in millions of dollars below, find the matrix of technical coefficients.

Sector of Origin	Sector of Destination				Final Demand	Total Demand
	Steel	Coal	Iron	Auto		
Steel	80	20	110	230	160	600
Coal	200	50	90	120	140	600
Iron	220	110	30	40	0	400
Auto	60	140	160	240	400	1000
Value added	40	280	10	370		
Gross production	600	600	400	1000		

The technical coefficient a_{ij} expresses the number of units or dollars of input i required to produce one unit or one dollar of product j. Thus a_{11} = the percentage of steel in one dollar of steel, a_{21} = the percentage of coal in one dollar of steel, a_{31} = the percentage of iron in one dollar of steel, and a_{41} = the percentage of autos in one dollar of steel. To find the technical coefficients, simply divide every element in each column by the value of gross production at the bottom of the column, omitting value added. Thus,

$$A = \begin{bmatrix} \frac{80}{600} & \frac{20}{600} & \frac{110}{400} & \frac{230}{1000} \\ \frac{200}{600} & \frac{50}{600} & \frac{90}{400} & \frac{120}{1000} \\ \frac{220}{600} & \frac{110}{600} & \frac{30}{400} & \frac{40}{1000} \\ \frac{60}{600} & \frac{140}{600} & \frac{160}{400} & \frac{240}{1000} \end{bmatrix} = \begin{bmatrix} 0.133 & 0.033 & 0.275 & 0.23 \\ 0.333 & 0.083 & 0.225 & 0.12 \\ 0.367 & 0.183 & 0.075 & 0.04 \\ 0.10 & 0.233 & 0.40 & 0.24 \end{bmatrix}$$

12.40. Check the matrix of technical coefficients A in Problem 12.39.

To check matrix A, multiply it by the column vector of total demand X. The product should equal the intermediate demand which is total demand X − final demand B. Allow for slight errors due to rounding.

$$AX = \begin{bmatrix} 0.133 & 0.033 & 0.275 & 0.23 \\ 0.333 & 0.083 & 0.225 & 0.12 \\ 0.367 & 0.183 & 0.075 & 0.04 \\ 0.10 & 0.233 & 0.40 & 0.24 \end{bmatrix} \begin{bmatrix} 600 \\ 600 \\ 400 \\ 1000 \end{bmatrix} = \begin{bmatrix} 439.6 \\ 459.6 \\ 400 \\ 599.8 \end{bmatrix}$$

$$X - B = \begin{bmatrix} 600 \\ 600 \\ 400 \\ 1000 \end{bmatrix} - \begin{bmatrix} 160 \\ 140 \\ 0 \\ 400 \end{bmatrix} = \begin{bmatrix} 440 \\ 460 \\ 400 \\ 600 \end{bmatrix}$$

12.41. Given the interindustry transaction demand table below, (a) find the matrix of technical coefficients and (b) check your answer.

	Sector of Destination				
Sector of Origin	1	2	3	Final Demand	Total Demand
1	20	60	10	50	140
2	50	10	80	10	150
3	40	30	20	40	130
Value added	30	50	20		
Gross production	140	150	130		

(a)
$$A = \begin{bmatrix} \frac{20}{140} & \frac{60}{150} & \frac{10}{130} \\ \frac{50}{140} & \frac{10}{150} & \frac{80}{130} \\ \frac{40}{140} & \frac{30}{150} & \frac{20}{130} \end{bmatrix} = \begin{bmatrix} 0.143 & 0.4 & 0.077 \\ 0.357 & 0.067 & 0.615 \\ 0.286 & 0.2 & 0.154 \end{bmatrix}$$

(b)
$$AX = \begin{bmatrix} 0.143 & 0.4 & 0.077 \\ 0.357 & 0.067 & 0.615 \\ 0.286 & 0.2 & 0.154 \end{bmatrix} \begin{bmatrix} 140 \\ 150 \\ 130 \end{bmatrix} = \begin{bmatrix} 90 \\ 140 \\ 90 \end{bmatrix}$$

$$X - B = \begin{bmatrix} 140 \\ 150 \\ 130 \end{bmatrix} - \begin{bmatrix} 50 \\ 10 \\ 40 \end{bmatrix} = \begin{bmatrix} 90 \\ 140 \\ 90 \end{bmatrix}$$

12.42. Find the new level of total demand in Problem 12.41 if in year 2 final demand is 70 in industry 1, 25 in industry 2, and 50 in industry 3.

$$X = (I - A)^{-1}B$$

where $I - A = \begin{bmatrix} 0.857 & -0.4 & -0.077 \\ -0.357 & 0.933 & -0.615 \\ -0.286 & -0.2 & 0.846 \end{bmatrix}$ and $(I - A)^{-1} = \frac{1}{0.354} \begin{bmatrix} 0.666 & 0.354 & 0.318 \\ 0.478 & 0.703 & 0.555 \\ 0.338 & 0.286 & 0.657 \end{bmatrix}$

Thus,

$$X = \frac{1}{0.354} \begin{bmatrix} 0.666 & 0.354 & 0.318 \\ 0.478 & 0.703 & 0.555 \\ 0.338 & 0.286 & 0.657 \end{bmatrix} \begin{bmatrix} 70 \\ 25 \\ 50 \end{bmatrix} = \frac{1}{0.354} \begin{bmatrix} 71.37 \\ 78.79 \\ 63.66 \end{bmatrix} = \begin{bmatrix} 201.61 \\ 222.57 \\ 179.83 \end{bmatrix}$$

12.43. Having found the inverse of $I - A$, use it to check the accuracy of the matrix of coefficients derived in Problem 12.41; i.e., check to see if $(I - A)^{-1}B = X$.

$$(I - A)^{-1}B = \frac{1}{0.354}\begin{bmatrix} 0.666 & 0.354 & 0.318 \\ 0.478 & 0.703 & 0.555 \\ 0.338 & 0.286 & 0.657 \end{bmatrix}\begin{bmatrix} 50 \\ 10 \\ 40 \end{bmatrix} = \frac{1}{0.354}\begin{bmatrix} 49.56 \\ 53.13 \\ 46.04 \end{bmatrix} = \begin{bmatrix} 140 \\ 150 \\ 130 \end{bmatrix}$$

12.44. Assume in Problem 12.41 that value added is composed entirely of the primary input labor. How much labor would be necessary to obtain the final demand (a) in Problem 12.41 and (b) in Problem 12.42? (c) If the amount of labor available in the economy is 100, is the output mix feasible?

(a) To get the technical coefficient of labor a_{Lj} in Problem 12.41, simply divide the value added in each column by the gross production. Thus, $a_{L1} = \frac{30}{140} = 0.214$, $a_{L2} = \frac{50}{150} = 0.333$, and $a_{L3} = \frac{20}{130} = 0.154$. The amount of labor needed to meet the final demand will then equal the row of technical coefficients for labor times the column vector of total demand, since labor must also be used to produce the intermediate products. Thus,

$$L_1 = \begin{bmatrix} 0.214 & 0.333 & 0.154 \end{bmatrix}\begin{bmatrix} 140 \\ 150 \\ 130 \end{bmatrix} = 99.93$$

(b)
$$L_2 = \begin{bmatrix} 0.214 & 0.333 & 0.154 \end{bmatrix}\begin{bmatrix} 201.61 \\ 222.57 \\ 179.83 \end{bmatrix} = 144.95$$

(c) Final demand in Problem 12.41 is feasible since $99.93 < 100$. Final demand in Problem 12.42 is not feasible since society does not have sufficient labor resources to produce it.

12.45. Check the accuracy of the technical coefficients found in Problem 12.44.

Having found the technical coefficients of labor for Problem 12.41, where value added was due totally to labor inputs, the accuracy of the technical coefficients can be easily checked. Since each dollar of output must be completely accounted for in terms of inputs, simply add each column of technical coefficients to be sure it equals 1.

	1	2	3
1	0.143	0.4	0.077
2	0.357	0.067	0.615
3	0.286	0.2	0.154
Value added (labor)	0.214	0.333	0.154
	1.000	1.000	1.000

EIGENVALUES, EIGENVECTORS

12.46. Use eigenvalues (characteristic roots, latent roots) to determine sign definiteness for

$$A = \begin{bmatrix} 10 & 3 \\ 3 & 4 \end{bmatrix}$$

To find the characteristic roots of A, the determinant of the characteristic matrix $A - cI$ must equal zero. Thus,

$$|A - cI| = \begin{vmatrix} 10 - c & 3 \\ 3 & 4 - c \end{vmatrix} = 0$$

$$40 + c^2 - 14c - 9 = 0 \qquad c^2 - 14c + 31 = 0$$

Using the quadratic formula,

$$c = \frac{14 \pm \sqrt{196 - 4(31)}}{2} = \frac{14 \pm 8.485}{2}$$

$$c_1 = 11.2425 \qquad c_2 = 2.7575$$

With both characteristic roots positive, A is positive definite.

12.47. Redo Problem 12.46, given

$$A = \begin{bmatrix} -4 & -2 \\ -2 & -6 \end{bmatrix}$$

$$|A - cI| = \begin{vmatrix} -4 - c & -2 \\ -2 & -6 - c \end{vmatrix} = 0$$

$$24 + c^2 + 10c - 4 = 0 \qquad c^2 + 10c + 20 = 0$$

$$c = \frac{-10 \pm \sqrt{100 - 4(20)}}{2} = \frac{-10 \pm 4.4721}{2}$$

$$c_1 = \frac{-5.5279}{2} = -2.764 \qquad c_2 = \frac{-14.4721}{2} = -7.236$$

With both characteristic roots negative, A is negative definite.

12.48. Redo Problem 12.46, given

$$A = \begin{bmatrix} 6 & 2 \\ 2 & 2 \end{bmatrix}$$

$$|A - cI| = \begin{vmatrix} 6 - c & 2 \\ 2 & 2 - c \end{vmatrix} = 0$$

$$12 + c^2 - 8c - 4 = 0 \qquad c^2 - 8c + 8 = 0$$

$$c = \frac{8 \pm \sqrt{64 - 4(8)}}{2} = \frac{8 \pm 5.66}{2}$$

$$c_1 = 1.17 \quad c_2 = 6.83$$

A is positive definite.

12.49. Redo Problem 12.46, given

$$A = \begin{bmatrix} 4 & 6 & 3 \\ 0 & 2 & 5 \\ 0 & 1 & 3 \end{bmatrix}$$

$$|A - cI| = \begin{vmatrix} 4 - c & 6 & 3 \\ 0 & 2 - c & 5 \\ 0 & 1 & 3 - c \end{vmatrix} = 0$$

Expanding along the first column,

$$|A - cI| = (4 - c)[(2 - c)(3 - c) - 5] = 0 \qquad (12.36)$$

$$-c^3 + 9c^2 - 21c + 4 = 0 \qquad (12.37)$$

To solve (12.37), we may use a standard formula for finding cube roots or note that (12.37) will equal zero if in (12.36)

$$4 - c = 0 \qquad \text{or} \qquad (2 - c)(3 - c) - 5 = 0$$

Thus, the characteristic roots are

$$4 - c = 0 \qquad (2 - c)(3 - c) - 5 = 0$$
$$c_1 = 4 \qquad\qquad c^2 - 5c + 1 = 0$$
$$c = \frac{5 \pm \sqrt{25 - 4}}{2} = \frac{5 \pm 4.58}{2}$$
$$c_2 = 4.79 \qquad c_3 = 0.21$$

With all three characteristic roots positive, A is positive definite.

12.50. Redo Problem 12.46, given

$$A = \begin{bmatrix} 6 & 1 & 0 \\ 13 & 4 & 0 \\ 5 & 1 & 9 \end{bmatrix}$$

$$|A - cI| = \begin{vmatrix} 6 - c & 1 & 0 \\ 13 & 4 - c & 0 \\ 5 & 1 & 9 - c \end{vmatrix} = 0$$

Expanding along the third column,

$$|A - cI| = (9 - c)[(6 - c)(4 - c) - 13] = 0 \qquad (12.38)$$
$$-c^3 + 19c^2 - 101c + 99 = 0 \qquad (12.39)$$

which will equal zero if in (12.38)

$$9 - c = 0 \qquad \text{or} \qquad (6 - c)(4 - c) - 13 = 0$$

Thus,
$$c_1 = 9 \qquad\qquad c^2 - 10c + 11 = 0$$
$$c = \frac{10 \pm \sqrt{100 - 4(11)}}{2} = \frac{10 \pm 7.48}{2}$$
$$c_2 = 8.74 \qquad c_3 = 1.26$$

With all latent roots positive, A is positive definite.

12.51. Redo Problem 12.46, given

$$A = \begin{bmatrix} -5 & 1 & 2 \\ 0 & -2 & 0 \\ 4 & 2 & -3 \end{bmatrix}$$

$$|A - cI| = \begin{vmatrix} -5 - c & 1 & 2 \\ 0 & -2 - c & 0 \\ 4 & 2 & -3 - c \end{vmatrix} = 0$$

Expanding along the second row,

$$|A - cI| = (-2 - c)[(-5 - c)(-3 - c) - 8] = 0$$

Thus,
$$-2 - c = 0 \qquad \text{or} \qquad (-5 - c)(-3 - c) - 8 = 0$$
$$c_1 = -2 \qquad\qquad c^2 + 8c + 7 = 0$$
$$(c + 7)(c + 1) = 0$$
$$c_2 = -7 \qquad c_3 = -1$$

With all latent roots negative, A is negative definite.

12.52. Given

$$A = \begin{bmatrix} 6 & 6 \\ 6 & -3 \end{bmatrix}$$

Find (*a*) the characteristic roots and (*b*) the characteristic vectors. (*c*) Check the characteristic vectors with the transformation matrix, showing

$$T'AT = \begin{bmatrix} c_1 & 0 \\ 0 & c_2 \end{bmatrix}$$

(*a*)

$$|A - cI| = \begin{vmatrix} 6 - c & 6 \\ 6 & -3 - c \end{vmatrix} = 0$$

$$-18 + c^2 - 3c - 36 = 0$$
$$c^2 - 3c - 54 = 0$$
$$(c - 9)(c + 6) = 0$$
$$c_1 = 9 \qquad c_2 = -6$$

With one root positive and the other negative, A is indefinite.

(*b*)   Using $c_1 = 9$ for the first characteristic vector V_1,

$$\begin{bmatrix} 6 - 9 & 6 \\ 6 & -3 - 9 \end{bmatrix}\begin{bmatrix} v_1 \\ v_2 \end{bmatrix} = \begin{bmatrix} -3 & 6 \\ 6 & -12 \end{bmatrix}\begin{bmatrix} v_1 \\ v_2 \end{bmatrix} = 0$$

$$v_1 = 2v_2$$

Normalizing, as in Example 10,

$$(2v_2)^2 + v_2^2 = 1$$
$$5v_2^2 = 1$$
$$v_2 = \sqrt{0.2} \qquad v_1 = 2v_2 = 2\sqrt{0.2}$$

Thus,

$$V_1 = \begin{bmatrix} 2\sqrt{0.2} \\ \sqrt{0.2} \end{bmatrix}$$

Using $c_2 = -6$ for the second characteristic vector,

$$\begin{bmatrix} 6 - (-6) & 6 \\ 6 & -3 - (-6) \end{bmatrix}\begin{bmatrix} v_1 \\ v_2 \end{bmatrix} = \begin{bmatrix} 12 & 6 \\ 6 & 3 \end{bmatrix}\begin{bmatrix} v_1 \\ v_2 \end{bmatrix} = 0$$

$$v_2 = -2v_1$$

Normalizing,

$$v_1^2 + (-2v_1)^2 = 1$$
$$5v_1^2 = 1$$
$$v_1 = \sqrt{0.2} \qquad v_2 = -2v_1 = -2\sqrt{0.2}$$

Thus,

$$V_2 = \begin{bmatrix} \sqrt{0.2} \\ -2\sqrt{0.2} \end{bmatrix}$$

(*c*)

$$T = [V_1 \quad V_2] = \begin{bmatrix} 2\sqrt{0.2} & \sqrt{0.2} \\ \sqrt{0.2} & -2\sqrt{0.2} \end{bmatrix}$$

Thus,

$$T'AT = \begin{bmatrix} 2\sqrt{0.2} & \sqrt{0.2} \\ \sqrt{0.2} & -2\sqrt{0.2} \end{bmatrix}\begin{bmatrix} 6 & 6 \\ 6 & -3 \end{bmatrix}\begin{bmatrix} 2\sqrt{0.2} & \sqrt{0.2} \\ \sqrt{0.2} & -2\sqrt{0.2} \end{bmatrix}$$

where

$$T'A = \begin{bmatrix} 2\sqrt{0.2} & \sqrt{0.2} \\ \sqrt{0.2} & -2\sqrt{0.2} \end{bmatrix}\begin{bmatrix} 6 & 6 \\ 6 & -3 \end{bmatrix} = \begin{bmatrix} 18\sqrt{0.2} & 9\sqrt{0.2} \\ -6\sqrt{0.2} & 12\sqrt{0.2} \end{bmatrix}$$

and

$$T'AT = \begin{bmatrix} 18\sqrt{0.2} & 9\sqrt{0.2} \\ -6\sqrt{0.2} & 12\sqrt{0.2} \end{bmatrix} \begin{bmatrix} 2\sqrt{0.2} & \sqrt{0.2} \\ \sqrt{0.2} & -2\sqrt{0.2} \end{bmatrix} = \begin{bmatrix} 45(0.2) & 0 \\ 0 & -30(0.2) \end{bmatrix}$$

$$= \begin{bmatrix} 9 & 0 \\ 0 & -6 \end{bmatrix} = \begin{bmatrix} c_1 & 0 \\ 0 & c_2 \end{bmatrix}$$

12.53. Redo Problem 12.52, given $\qquad A = \begin{bmatrix} 6 & 3 \\ 3 & -2 \end{bmatrix}$

(a)
$$|A - cI| = \begin{vmatrix} 6 - c & 3 \\ 3 & -2 - c \end{vmatrix} = 0$$

$$c^2 - 4c - 21 = 0$$

$$c_1 = 7 \qquad c_2 = -3$$

With $c_1 > 0$ and $c_2 < 0$, A is indefinite.

(b) Using $c_1 = 7$ to form the first characteristic vector,

$$\begin{bmatrix} 6 - 7 & 3 \\ 3 & -2 - 7 \end{bmatrix} \begin{bmatrix} v_1 \\ v_2 \end{bmatrix} = \begin{bmatrix} -1 & 3 \\ 3 & -9 \end{bmatrix} \begin{bmatrix} v_1 \\ v_2 \end{bmatrix} = 0$$

$$v_1 = 3v_2$$

Normalizing,
$$(3v_2)^2 + v_2^2 = 1$$
$$9v_2^2 + v_2^2 = 1$$
$$10v_2^2 = 1$$
$$v_2 = \sqrt{0.1} \quad \text{and} \quad v_1 = 3v_2 = 3\sqrt{0.1}$$

Thus,
$$V_1 = \begin{bmatrix} 3\sqrt{0.1} \\ \sqrt{0.1} \end{bmatrix}$$

Using $c_2 = -3$,

$$\begin{bmatrix} 6 - (-3) & 3 \\ 3 & -2 - (-3) \end{bmatrix} \begin{bmatrix} v_1 \\ v_2 \end{bmatrix} = \begin{bmatrix} 9 & 3 \\ 3 & 1 \end{bmatrix} \begin{bmatrix} v_1 \\ v_2 \end{bmatrix} = 0$$

$$v_2 = -3v_1$$

Normalizing,
$$v_1^2 + (-3v_1)^2 = 1$$
$$10v_1^2 = 1$$
$$v_1 = \sqrt{0.1} \quad \text{and} \quad v_2 = -3v_1 = -3\sqrt{0.1}$$

Thus,
$$V_2 = \begin{bmatrix} \sqrt{0.1} \\ -3\sqrt{0.1} \end{bmatrix}$$

(c) Checking,
$$T'AT = \begin{bmatrix} 3\sqrt{0.1} & \sqrt{0.1} \\ \sqrt{0.1} & -3\sqrt{0.1} \end{bmatrix} \begin{bmatrix} 6 & 3 \\ 3 & -2 \end{bmatrix} \begin{bmatrix} 3\sqrt{0.1} & \sqrt{0.1} \\ \sqrt{0.1} & -3\sqrt{0.1} \end{bmatrix}$$

where
$$T'A = \begin{bmatrix} 21\sqrt{0.1} & 7\sqrt{0.1} \\ -3\sqrt{0.1} & 9\sqrt{0.1} \end{bmatrix}$$

and
$$T'AT = \begin{bmatrix} 21\sqrt{0.1} & 7\sqrt{0.1} \\ -3\sqrt{0.1} & 9\sqrt{0.1} \end{bmatrix} \begin{bmatrix} 3\sqrt{0.1} & \sqrt{0.1} \\ \sqrt{0.1} & -3\sqrt{0.1} \end{bmatrix} = \begin{bmatrix} 7 & 0 \\ 0 & -3 \end{bmatrix} = \begin{bmatrix} c_1 & 0 \\ 0 & c_2 \end{bmatrix}$$

12.54. Using the data from (a) Problem 12.52 and (b) Problem 12.53, prove that characteristic vectors are *orthonormal*, i.e., $V_i' V_i = 1$.

(a)
$$V_1' V_1 = [2\sqrt{0.2} \quad \sqrt{0.2}]\begin{bmatrix} 2\sqrt{0.2} \\ \sqrt{0.2} \end{bmatrix} = 4(0.2) + 0.2 = 1$$

$$V_2' V_2 = [\sqrt{0.2} \quad -2\sqrt{0.2}]\begin{bmatrix} \sqrt{0.2} \\ -2\sqrt{0.2} \end{bmatrix} = 0.2 + 4(0.2) = 1$$

(b)
$$V_1' V_1 = [3\sqrt{0.1} \quad \sqrt{0.1}]\begin{bmatrix} 3\sqrt{0.1} \\ \sqrt{0.1} \end{bmatrix} = 9(0.1) + 0.1 = 1$$

$$V_2' V_2 = [\sqrt{0.1} \quad -3\sqrt{0.1}]\begin{bmatrix} \sqrt{0.1} \\ -3\sqrt{0.1} \end{bmatrix} = 0.1 + 9(0.1) = 1$$

12.55. From Problem 12.54, prove that characteristic vectors are *orthogonal*, that is, $V_i' V_j = 0$.

(a)
$$V_1' V_2 = [2\sqrt{0.2} \quad \sqrt{0.2}]\begin{bmatrix} \sqrt{0.2} \\ -2\sqrt{0.2} \end{bmatrix} = 2(0.2) - 2(0.2) = 0$$

(b)
$$V_1' V_2 = [3\sqrt{0.1} \quad \sqrt{0.1}]\begin{bmatrix} \sqrt{0.1} \\ -3\sqrt{0.1} \end{bmatrix} = 3(0.1) - 3(0.1) = 0$$

Chapter 13

Linear Programming: A Graphic Approach

13.1 GRAPHIC SOLUTIONS

The objective of linear programming is to determine the optimal allocation of scarce resources among competing products or activities. Economic situations frequently call for optimizing a function subject to several inequality constraints. For optimization subject to a single inequality constraint, the Lagrangian method (see Section 6.7) is relatively simple. When more than one inequality constraint is involved, linear programming is easier. If the constraints, however numerous, are limited to two variables, the easiest solution is the graphic approach. The graphic approach for maximization and minimization is demonstrated in Examples 1 and 2, respectively.

EXAMPLE 1. A manufacturer produces tables x_1 and desks x_2. Each table requires 2.5 hours for assembling A, 3 hours for buffing B, and 1 hour for crating C. Each desk requires 1 hour for assembling, 3 hours for buffing, and 2 hours for crating. The firm can use no more than 20 hours for assembling, 30 hours for buffing, and 16 hours for crating each week. Its profit margin is \$3 per table and \$4 per desk.

The graphic approach is used below to find the output mix that will maximize the firm's weekly profits. It is demonstrated in four easy steps.

1. Express the data as equations or inequalities. The function to be optimized, the *objective function*, becomes

$$\Pi = 3x_1 + 4x_2 \tag{13.1}$$

subject to the constraints

Constraint from A:	$2.5x_1 + x_2 \le 20$
Constraint from B:	$3x_1 + 3x_2 \le 30$
Constraint from C:	$x_1 + 2x_2 \le 16$
Nonnegativity constraint:	$x_1, x_2 \ge 0$

The first three inequalities are *technical constraints* determined by the state of technology and the availability of inputs; the fourth is a *nonnegativity constraint* imposed on every problem to preclude negative (hence unacceptable) values from the solution.

2. Treat the three inequality constraints as equations, solve each one for x_2 in terms of x_1, and graph. Thus,

From A,	$x_2 = 20 - 2.5x_1$
From B,	$x_2 = 10 - x_1$
From C,	$x_2 = 8 - 0.5x_1$

The graph of the original "less than or equal to" inequality will include all the points *on the line and to the left of it*. See Fig. 13-1(a). The nonnegativity constraints $x_1, x_2 \ge 0$ are represented by the vertical and horizontal axes, respectively. The shaded area is called the *feasible region*. It contains all the points that satisfy all three constraints plus the nonnegativity constraints. The variables x_1 and x_2 are called *decision* or *structural variables*.

317

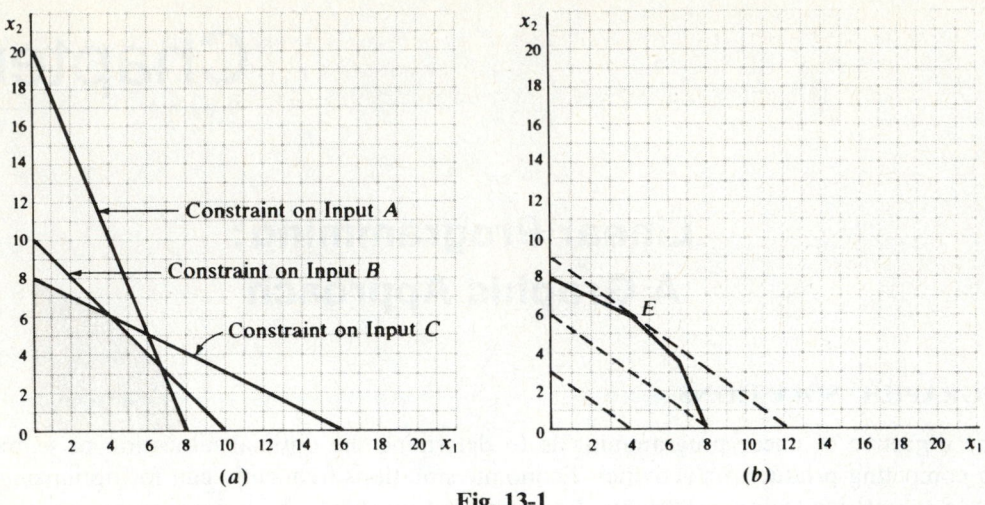

Fig. 13-1

3. To find the optimal solution within the feasible region, if it exists, graph the objective function as a series of isoprofit lines. From (*13.1*),

$$x_2 = \frac{\Pi}{4} - \frac{3}{4} x_1$$

Thus, the isoprofit line has a slope of $-\frac{3}{4}$. Drawing a series of (dashed) isoprofit lines allowing for larger and larger profits, we find the isoprofit line representing the largest possible profit touches the feasible region at E, where $\bar{x}_1 = 4$ and $\bar{x}_2 = 6$. See Fig. 13-1(*b*). Substituting in (*13.1*), $\bar{\Pi} = 3(4) + 4(6) = 36$.

4. Profit is maximized at the intersection of two constraints, called an *extreme point*.

13.2 THE EXTREME POINT THEOREM

The *extreme point theorem* states that if an optimal feasible value of the objective function exists, it will be found at one of the extreme (or corner) points of the boundary. Notice that there are 10 extreme points: $(0, 20)$, $(0, 10)$, $(6, 5)$, $(10, 0)$, $(16, 0)$, $(0, 8)$, $(4, 6)$, $(6\frac{2}{3}, 3\frac{1}{3})$, $(8, 0)$, and $(0, 0)$ in Fig. 13-1(*a*), the last being the intersection of the nonnegativity constraints. All are called *basic solutions*, but only the last five are basic *feasible* solutions since they violate none of the constraints. Ordinarily only one of the basic feasible solutions will be optimal. At $(6\frac{2}{3}, 3\frac{1}{3})$, for instance, $\Pi = 3(6\frac{2}{3}) + 4(3\frac{1}{3}) = 33\frac{1}{3}$, which is lower than $\Pi = 36$ above.

EXAMPLE 2.   A farmer wants to see that her herd gets the minimum daily requirement of three basic nutrients A, B, and C. Daily requirements are 14 for A, 12 for B, and 18 for C. Product y_1 has 2 units of A and 1 unit each of B and C; product y_2 has 1 unit each of A and B and 3 units of C. The cost of y_1 is \$2, and the cost of y_2 is \$4. The graphic method is used below to determine the least-cost combination of y_1 and y_2 that will fulfill all minimum requirements. Following the procedure used in Example 1,

1. The objective function to be minimized is

$$c = 2y_1 + 4y_2 \tag{13.2}$$

subject to the constraints

Constraint from A:	$2y_1 + y_2 \geq 14$
Constraint from B:	$y_1 + y_2 \geq 12$
Constraint from C:	$y_1 + 3y_2 \geq 18$
Nonnegativity constraint:	$y_1, y_2 \geq 0$

where the technical constraints read $\geq$ since minimum requirements must be fulfilled but may be exceeded.

2. Treat the inequalities as equations, solve each one for y_2 in terms of y_1, and graph. The graph of the original "greater than or equal to" inequality will include all the points *on the line and to the right of it*. See Fig. 13-2(a). The shaded area is the feasible region containing all the points that satisfy all three requirements plus the nonnegativity constraint.

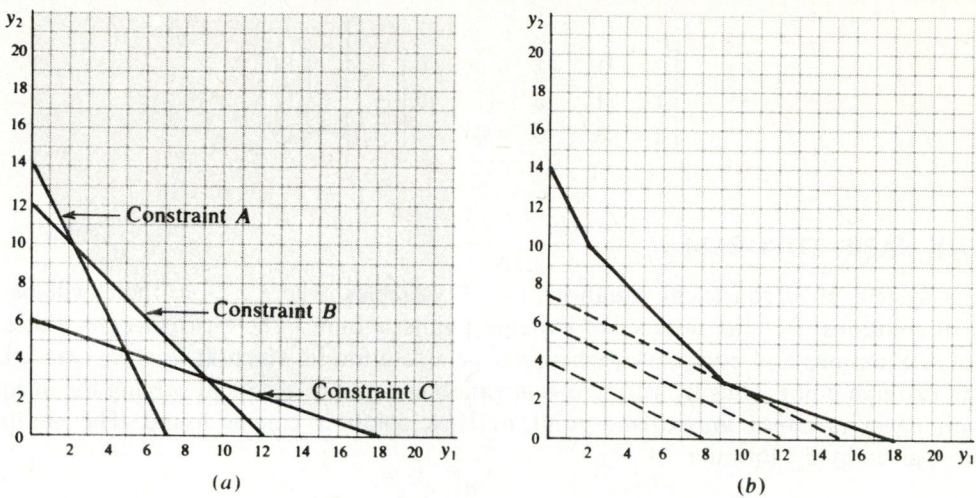

Fig. 13-2

3. To find the optimal solution, graph the objective function as a series of (dashed) isocost lines. From (13.2),

$$y_2 = \frac{c}{4} - \frac{1}{2} y_1$$

The lowest isocost line that will touch the feasible region is tangent at $\bar{y}_1 = 9$ and $\bar{y}_2 = 3$ in Fig. 13-2(b). Thus, $\bar{c} = 2(9) + 4(3) = 30$, which represents a cost lower than at any other feasible extreme point. For example, at $(2, 10)$, $c = 2(2) + 4(10) = 44$. [For minimization problems, $(0, 0)$ is not in the feasible region.]

13.3 SLACK AND SURPLUS VARIABLES

Problems involving more than two variables are beyond the scope of the two-dimensional graphic approach presented in the preceding sections. Because equations are needed, the system of linear inequalities must be converted to a system of linear equations. This is done by incorporating a separate slack or surplus variable s_i into each inequality (the ith constraint) in the system. See Example 3.

A "less than or equal to" inequality such as $5x_1 + 3x_2 \le 30$ can be converted to an equation by *adding a slack variable $s \ge 0$*, such that $5x_1 + 3x_2 + s = 30$. If $5x_1 + 3x_2 = 30$, the slack variable $s = 0$. If $5x_1 + 3x_2 < 30$, s is a positive value equal to the difference between $5x_1 + 3x_2$ and 30.

A "greater than or equal to" inequality such as $4x_1 + 7x_2 \ge 60$ is converted to an equation by *subtracting a surplus variable $s \ge 0$*, such that $4x_1 + 7x_2 - s = 60$. If $4x_1 + 7x_2 = 60$, the surplus variable $s = 0$. If $4x_1 + 7x_2 > 60$, s is a positive value equal to the difference between $4x_1 + 7x_2$ and 60.

EXAMPLE 3. Since the technical constraints in Example 1 all involve "less than or equal to" inequalities, slack variables are added, as follows:

$$2.5x_1 + x_2 + s_1 = 20 \qquad 3x_1 + 3x_2 + s_2 = 30 \qquad x_1 + 2x_2 + s_3 = 16$$

Expressed in matrix form,

$$\begin{bmatrix} 2.5 & 1 & 1 & 0 & 0 \\ 3 & 3 & 0 & 1 & 0 \\ 1 & 2 & 0 & 0 & 1 \end{bmatrix} \begin{bmatrix} x_1 \\ x_2 \\ s_1 \\ s_2 \\ s_3 \end{bmatrix} = \begin{bmatrix} 20 \\ 30 \\ 16 \end{bmatrix}$$

In contrast, the constraints in Example 2 are all "greater than or equal to." Hence surplus variables are subtracted.

$$2y_1 + y_2 - s_1 = 14 \qquad y_1 + y_2 - s_2 = 12 \qquad y_1 + 3y_2 - s_3 = 18$$

In matrix form,

$$\begin{bmatrix} 2 & 1 & -1 & 0 & 0 \\ 1 & 1 & 0 & -1 & 0 \\ 1 & 3 & 0 & 0 & -1 \end{bmatrix} \begin{bmatrix} y_1 \\ y_2 \\ s_1 \\ s_2 \\ s_3 \end{bmatrix} = \begin{bmatrix} 14 \\ 12 \\ 18 \end{bmatrix}$$

13.4 THE BASIS THEOREM

For a system of m consistent equations and n variables, where $n > m$, there will be an infinite number of solutions. But the number of extreme points is finite. The *basis theorem* states that for a system of m equations and n variables, where $n > m$, a solution in which at least $n - m$ variables equal zero is an extreme point. Thus by setting $n - m$ variables equal to zero and solving the m equations for the remaining m variables, an extreme point, or basic solution, can be found. The number of basic solutions is given by the formula

$$\frac{n!}{m!(n - m)!}$$

where $n!$ reads n *factorial*. See Example 4.

EXAMPLE 4.   Reducing the inequalities to equations in Example 3 left three equations and five variables. The calculations to determine (1) the number of variables that must be set equal to zero to find a basic solution and (2) the number of basic solutions that exist are demonstrated below.

1. Since there are 3 equations and 5 variables, and $n - m$ variables must equal zero for a basic solution, $5 - 3$ or 2 variables must equal zero for a basic solution or extreme point.
2. Using the formula for the number of basic solutions, $n!/[m!(n - m)!]$ and substituting the given parameters,

$$\frac{5!}{3!(2)!}$$

where $5! = 5(4)(3)(2)(1)$. Thus,

$$\frac{5(4)(3)(2)(1)}{3(2)(1)(2)(1)} = 10$$

EXAMPLE 5.   Some basic solutions can be read directly from matrices without any algebraic manipulation. Refer to Example 3.

In the first matrix, setting $x_1 = 0$ and $x_2 = 0$ leaves an identity matrix for s_1, s_2, s_3. Thus, $s_1 = 20$, $s_2 = 30$, and $s_3 = 16$ is a basic solution which can be read directly from the matrix.

In the second matrix, setting $y_1 = 0$ and $y_2 = 0$ leaves a negative identity matrix for s_1, s_2, s_3. Thus, $s_1 = -14$, $s_2 = -12$, and $s_3 = -18$ is a basic solution. Note, however, that it is not a basic *feasible* solution since it violates the nonnegativity constraint.

Solved Problems

MATHEMATICAL EXPRESSION OF ECONOMIC PROBLEMS

13.1.   A specialty steel manufacturer produces two types of steel g_1 and g_2. Type 1 requires 2 hours of melting, 4 hours of rolling, and 10 hours of cutting. Type 2 requires 5 hours of melting, 1 hour of rolling, and 5 hours of cutting. Forty hours are available for melting, 20 for rolling, and 60 for cutting. The profit margin for type 1 is 24; for type 2 it is 8. Reduce the data to the equations and inequalities necessary to determine the output mix that will maximize profits.

Maximize
$$\Pi = 24g_1 + 8g_2$$

subject to
$$2g_1 + 5g_2 \leq 40 \quad \text{melting constraint}$$
$$4g_1 + g_2 \leq 20 \quad \text{rolling constraint}$$
$$10g_1 + 5g_2 \leq 60 \quad \text{cutting constraint}$$
$$g_1, g_2 \geq 0$$

For a graphic solution, see Problem 13.9.

13.2. A manufacturer of pebbles for patios produces two different kinds: coarse x_1 and fine x_2. The coarse pebbles require 2 hours of crushing, 5 hours of sifting, and 8 hours of drying. The fine pebbles require 6 hours of crushing, 3 hours of sifting, and 2 hours of drying. The profit margin for coarse pebbles is 40; for fine pebbles it is 50. The manufacturer has available 36 hours for crushing, 30 hours for sifting, and 40 hours for drying.

Determine the profit-maximizing output mix by reducing these data to equations and inequalities.

Maximize
$$\Pi = 40x_1 + 50x_2$$

subject to
$$2x_1 + 6x_2 \leq 36 \quad \text{crushing constraint}$$
$$5x_1 + 3x_2 \leq 30 \quad \text{sifting constraint}$$
$$8x_1 + 2x_2 \leq 40 \quad \text{drying constraint}$$
$$x_1, x_2 \geq 0$$

For a graphic solution, see Problem 13.10.

13.3. A toy manufacturer makes two games: Bong g_1 and Zong g_2. The profit margin on Bong is 30; the profit margin on Zong is 20. Bong takes 6 hours of processing, 4 hours of assembly, and 5 hours of packaging. Zong takes 3 hours of processing, 6 hours of assembly, and 5 hours of packaging. If 54 hours are available for processing, 48 hours for assembling, and 50 hours for packaging, what is the profit-maximizing output mix in terms of equations and inequalities?

Maximize
$$\Pi = 30g_1 + 20g_2$$

subject to
$$6g_1 + 3g_2 \leq 54 \quad \text{processing constraint}$$
$$4g_1 + 6g_2 \leq 48 \quad \text{assembling constraint}$$
$$5g_1 + 5g_2 \leq 50 \quad \text{packaging constraint}$$
$$g_1, g_2 \geq 0$$

13.4. A stereo manufacturer makes three types of stereos: standard y_1, quality y_2, and deluxe y_3. His profit margin from each is 15, 20, and 24, respectively. The standard model requires 3 hours for wiring and 1 hour for encasing. The quality model requires 1 hour for wiring and 5 hours for encasing. The deluxe model requires 3 hours for wiring and 2 hours for encasing. If 120 hours are available for wiring and 60 hours for encasing, express the output mix that will maximize profits as equations and inequalities.

Maximize
$$\Pi = 15y_1 + 20y_2 + 24y_3$$

subject to
$$3y_1 + y_2 + 3y_3 \leq 120 \quad \text{wiring constraint}$$
$$y_1 + 5y_2 + 2y_3 \leq 60 \quad \text{encasing constraint}$$
$$y_1, y_2, y_3 \geq 0$$

13.5. A furniture manufacturer makes three types of end tables: provincial x_1, contemporary x_2, and modern x_3. The provincial model requires 2 hours for sanding and 3 hours for staining. Its profit margin is 36. The contemporary model requires 2 hours for sanding and 2 hours for staining. Its profit margin is 28. The modern model requires 4 hours for sanding and 1 hour for staining, while contributing a profit margin of 32. How should production be allocated to maximize profits if 60 hours are available for sanding and 80 hours for staining?

Maximize
$$\Pi = 36x_1 + 28x_2 + 32x_3$$

subject to
$$2x_1 + 2x_2 + 4x_3 \le 60 \qquad \text{sanding constraint}$$
$$3x_1 + 2x_2 + \ x_3 \le 80 \qquad \text{staining constraint}$$
$$x_1, x_2, x_3 \ge 0$$

13.6. A horticulturist wishes to mix fertilizer that will provide a minimum of 15 units of potash, 20 units of nitrates, and 24 units of phosphates. Brand 1 provides 3 units of potash, 1 unit of nitrates, and 3 units of phosphates; it costs \$120. Brand 2 provides 1 unit of potash, 5 units of nitrates, and 2 units of phosphates; it costs \$60. Express the least-cost combination of fertilizers that will meet the desired specifications as equations and inequalities.

Minimize
$$c = 120x_1 + 60x_2$$

subject to
$$3x_1 + \ x_2 \ge 15 \qquad \text{potash requirement}$$
$$x_1 + 5x_2 \ge 20 \qquad \text{nitrate requirement}$$
$$3x_1 + 2x_2 \ge 24 \qquad \text{phosphate requirement}$$
$$x_1, x_2 \ge 0$$

For a graphic solution, see Problem 13.14.

13.7. A health enthusiast wishes to have a minimum of 36 units of vitamin A each day, 28 units of vitamin C, and 32 units of vitamin D. Brand 1 costs \$3 and supplies 2 units of vitamin A, 2 units of vitamin C, and 8 units of vitamin D. Brand 2 costs \$4 and supplies 3 units of vitamin A, 2 units of vitamin C, and 2 units of vitamin D. In terms of equations and inequalities, what is the least-cost combination guaranteeing daily requirements?

Minimize
$$c = 3y_1 + 4y_2$$

Subject to
$$2y_1 + 3y_2 \ge 36 \qquad \text{vitamin A requirement}$$
$$2y_1 + 2y_2 \ge 28 \qquad \text{vitamin C requirement}$$
$$8y_1 + 2y_2 \ge 32 \qquad \text{vitamin D requirement}$$
$$y_1, y_2 \ge 0$$

For a graphic solution, see Problem 13.15.

13.8. Hank Burdue makes sure his chickens get at least 24 units of iron and 8 units of vitamins each day. Corn x_1 provides 2 units of iron and 5 units of vitamins. Bone meal x_2 provides 4 units of iron and 1 unit of vitamins. Millet x_3 provides 2 units of iron and 1 unit of vitamins. How should the feeds be mixed to provide least-cost satisfaction of daily requirements if feed costs are \$40, \$20, and \$60, respectively?

Minimize
$$c = 40x_1 + 20x_2 + 60x_3$$

subject to
$$2x_1 + 4x_2 + 2x_3 \ge 24 \qquad \text{iron requirement}$$
$$5x_1 + \ x_2 + \ x_3 \ge 8 \qquad \text{vitamin requirement}$$
$$x_1, x_2, x_3 \ge 0$$

GRAPHING THE SOLUTION

13.9. Using the data below,

(1) Graph the inequality constraints after solving each for g_2 in terms of g_1.

(2) Regraph and darken in the feasible region.

(3) Compute the slope of the feasible region. Set a ruler with this slope, move it to the point of contact with the feasible region, and construct a dashed line.

(4) Read the critical values for g_1 and g_2 at the point of contact, and evaluate the objective function at these values.

From Problem 13.1,

Maximize
$$\Pi = 24g_1 + 8g_2$$

subject to
$$2g_1 + 5g_2 \le 40 \qquad \text{constraint 1}$$
$$4g_1 + g_2 \le 20 \qquad \text{constraint 2}$$
$$10g_1 + 5g_2 \le 60 \qquad \text{constraint 3}$$
$$g_1 \ g_2 \ge 0$$

The inequality constraints should be graphed as shown in Fig. 13-3(a). For constraint 1, from $g_2 = 8 - \frac{2}{5}g_1$, when $g_1 = 0$, $g_2 = 8$; when $g_2 = 0$, $g_1 = 20$. Note that the nonnegativity constraints merely limit analysis to the first quadrant.

The feasible region is graphed in Fig. 13-3(b). From the objective function, $g_2 = \Pi/8 - 3g_1$; slope $= -3$. At the point of contact, $\bar{g}_1 = 4$ and $\bar{g}_2 = 4$. Thus, $\bar{\Pi} = 24(4) + 8(4) = 128$.

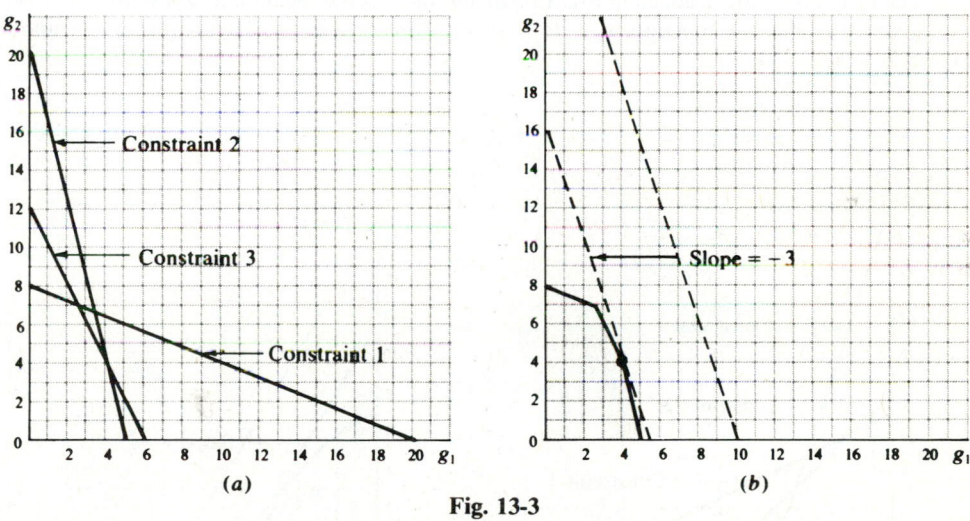

(a)   (b)

Fig. 13-3

13.10. Redo Problem 13.9, using the following data derived in Problem 13.2:

Maximize
$$\Pi = 40x_1 + 50x_2$$

subject to
$$2x_1 + 6x_2 \le 36 \qquad \text{constraint 1}$$
$$5x_1 + 3x_2 \le 30 \qquad \text{constraint 2}$$
$$8x_1 + 2x_2 \le 40 \qquad \text{constraint 3}$$
$$x_1, x_2 \ge 0$$

See Fig. 13-4(a) for the graphed constraints and Fig. 13-4(b) for the feasible region.

From the objective function, $x_2 = \Pi/50 - \frac{4}{5}x_1$; slope $= -\frac{4}{5}$. In Fig. 13-4(b), $\bar{x}_1 = 3$ and $\bar{x}_2 = 5$. Thus, $\bar{\Pi} = 40(3) + 50(5) = 370$.

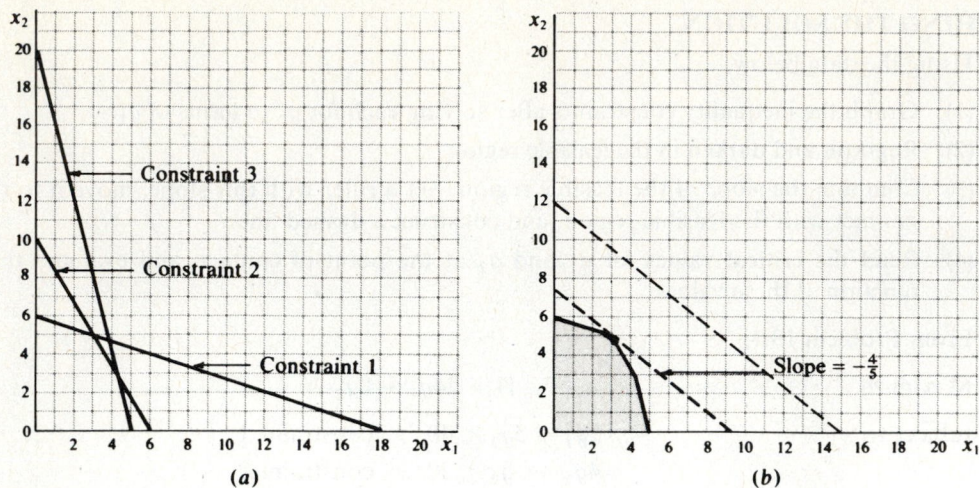

Fig. 13-4

13.11. Redo Problem 13.9 for the following data:

Maximize $\qquad\qquad\qquad\qquad \Pi = 5x_1 + 3x_2$

subject to $\qquad 6x_1 + 2x_2 \le 36 \qquad$ constraint 1 $\qquad 2x_1 + 4x_2 \le 28 \qquad$ constraint 3

$\qquad\qquad 5x_1 + 5x_2 \le 40 \qquad$ constraint 2 $\qquad\qquad x_1, x_2 \ge 0$

     The inequalities are graphed in Fig. 13-5(a) and the feasible region in Fig. 13-5(b).

     From the objective function, $x_2 = \Pi/3 - \frac{5}{3}x_1$; slope $= -\frac{5}{3}$. In Fig. 13-5(b), $\bar{x}_1 = 5$ and $\bar{x}_2 = 3$. Thus, $\bar{\Pi} = 5(5) + 3(3) = 34$.

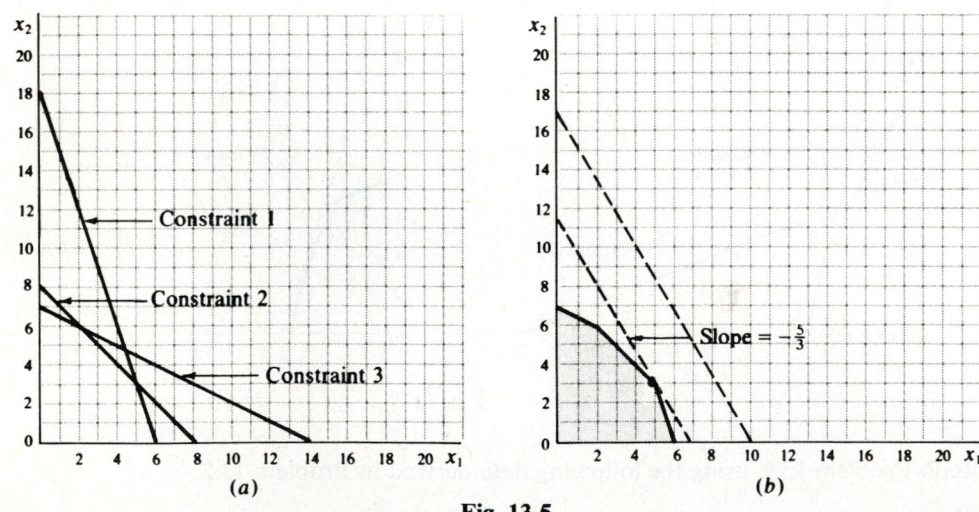

Fig. 13-5

13.12. Redo Problem 13.9, given the data below:

Maximize $\qquad\qquad\qquad\qquad \Pi = 40y_1 + 30y_2$

subject to $\qquad 5y_1 + 2y_2 \le 30 \qquad$ constraint 1 $\qquad y_2 \le 6 \qquad$ constraint 3

$\qquad\qquad 2y_1 + 4y_2 \le 28 \qquad$ constraint 2 $\qquad y_1, y_2 \ge 0$

     See Fig. 13-6(a) for the graphed constraints and Fig. 13-6(b) for the feasible region.

     From the critical values, $\bar{y}_1 = 4$, $\bar{y}_2 = 5$, and $\bar{\Pi} = 40(4) + 30(5) = 310$.

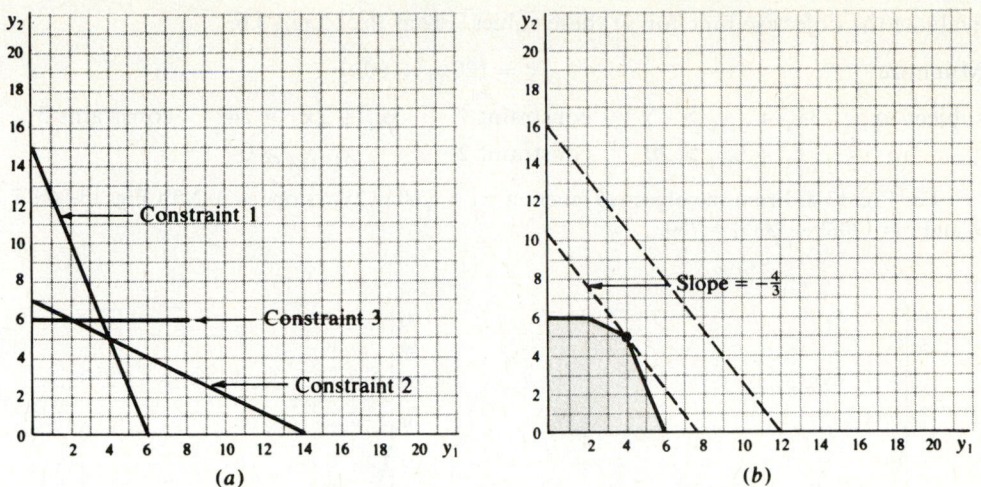

Fig. 13-6

13.13. Redo Problem 13.9, given the following data:

Maximize $$\Pi = 20x_1 + 10x_2$$

subject to $4x_1 + 3x_2 \le 48$ constraint 1 $x_1 \le 9$ constraint 3
             $3x_1 + 5x_2 \le 60$ constraint 2 $x_1, x_2 \ge 0$

See Fig. 13-7.

From the critical values, $\bar{x}_1 = 9$, $\bar{x}_2 = 4$, and $\bar{\Pi} = 20(9) + 10(4) = 220$.

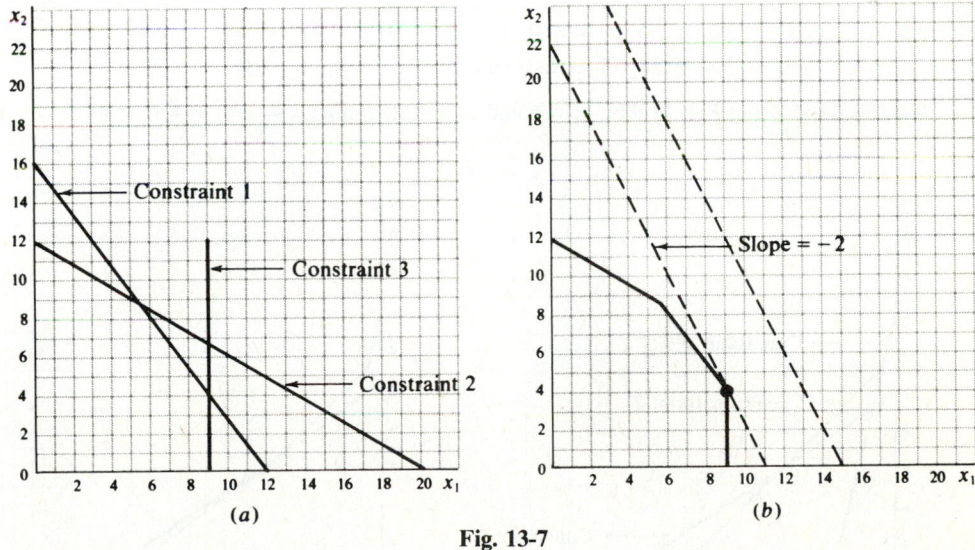

Fig. 13-7

13.14. Using the data provided, graph the inequality constraints after solving each for x_2 in terms of x_1. Regraph and darken in the feasible region. Compute the slope of the objective function, and construct a dashed line as in Problem 13.9. Read the critical values at the point of contact, and evaluate the objective function at these values. From Problem 13.6,

Minimize $$c = 120x_1 + 60x_2$$

subject to $3x_1 + x_2 \geq 15$ constraint 1 $3x_1 + 2x_2 \geq 24$ constraint 3

           $x_1 + 5x_2 \geq 20$ constraint 2 $x_1, x_2 \geq 0$

See Fig. 13-8. From the objective function, $x_2 = c/60 - 2x_1$; slope $= -2$. In Fig. 13-8(b), $\bar{x}_1 = 2$, $\bar{x}_2 = 9$, and $\bar{c} = 120(2) + 60(9) = 780$.

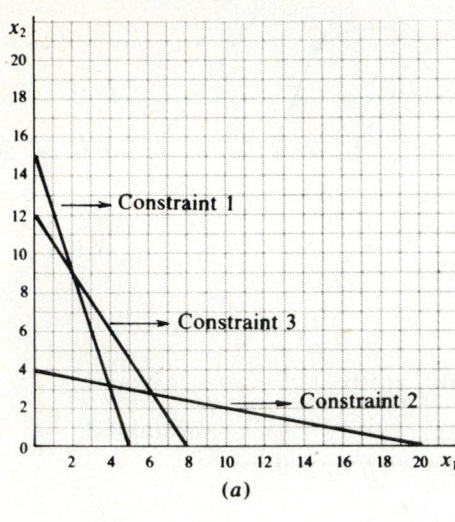 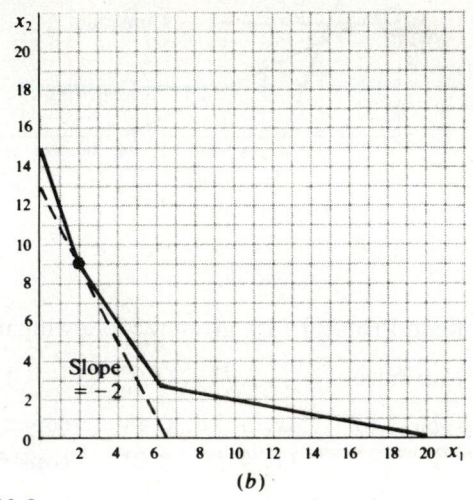

(a) (b)

Fig. 13-8

13.15. Redo Problem 13.14, using the data derived in Problem 13.7.

Minimize $$c = 3y_1 + 4y_2$$

subject to $2y_1 + 3y_2 \geq 36$ constraint 1 $8y_1 + 2y_2 \geq 32$ constraint 3

           $2y_1 + 2y_2 \geq 28$ constraint 2 $y_1, y_2 \geq 0$

See Fig. 13-9. From Fig. 13-9(b), $\bar{y}_1 = 6$ and $\bar{y}_2 = 8$; therefore, $\bar{c} = 3(6) + 4(8) = 50$.

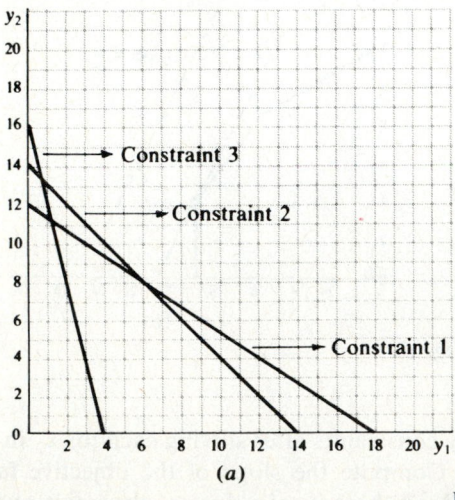 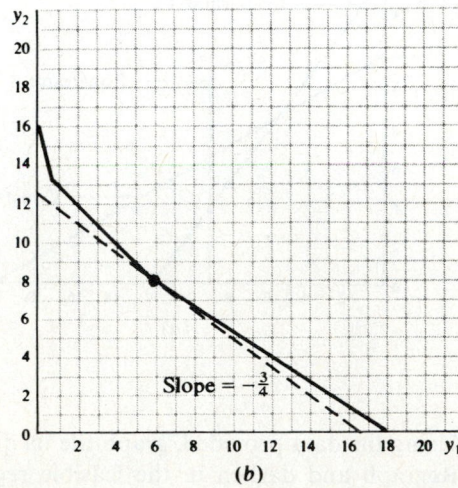

(a) (b)

Fig. 13-9

13.16. Redo Problem 13.14, using the following data:

Minimize $$c = 30x_1 + 50x_2$$

subject to $\quad 6x_1 + 2x_2 \geq 30 \quad$ constraint 1 $\quad 5x_1 + 10x_2 \geq 60 \quad$ constraint 3

$\qquad\qquad 3x_1 + 2x_2 \geq 24 \quad$ constraint 2 $\qquad x_1, x_2 \geq 0$

The constraints are graphed in Fig. 13-10(a) and the feasible region in Fig. 13-10(b). In Fig. 13-10(b), the slope $= -\frac{3}{5}$; $\bar{x}_1 = 6$ and $\bar{x}_2 = 3$. Thus, $\bar{c} = 30(6) + 50(3) = 330$.

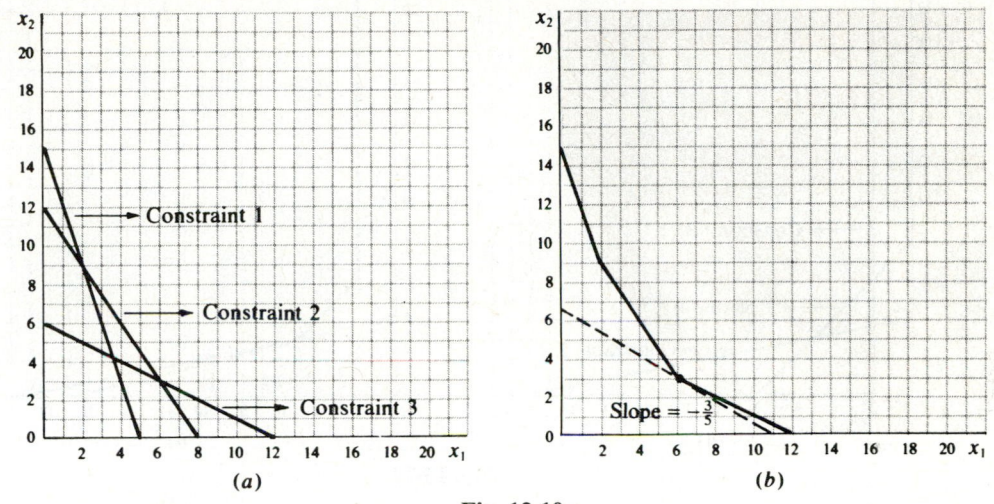

(a) (b)

Fig. 13-10

13.17. Redo Problem 13.14, given the data below:

Minimize $$c = 4g_1 + 5g_2$$

subject to $\quad 4g_1 + 2g_2 \geq 28 \quad$ constraint 1 $\qquad g_2 \geq 4 \quad$ constraint 3

$\qquad\qquad 2g_1 + 3g_2 \geq 30 \quad$ constraint 2 $\quad g_1, g_2 \geq 0$

See Fig. 13-11. In Fig. 13-11(b), the slope $= -\frac{4}{5}$, $\bar{g}_1 = 3$, and $\bar{g}_2 = 8$; $\bar{c} = 4(3) + 5(8) = 52$.

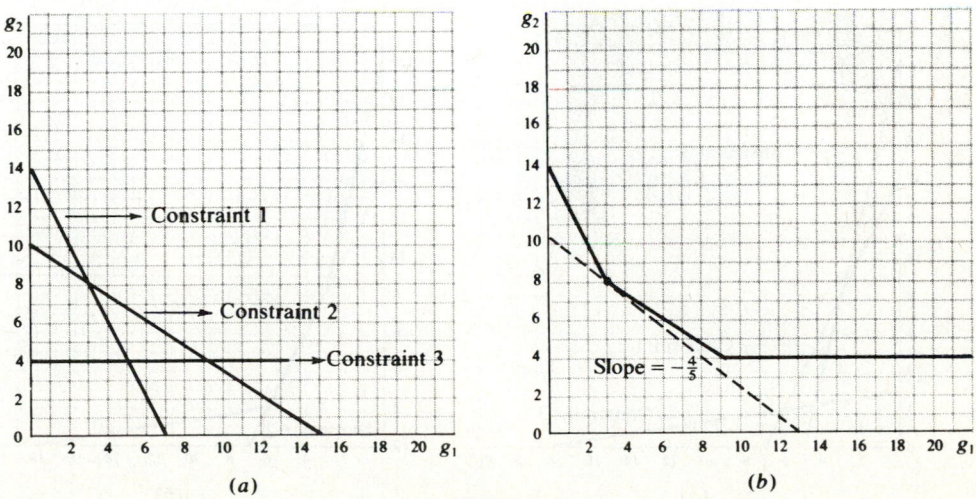

(a) (b)

Fig. 13-11

13.18. Redo Problem 13.14, using the following data:

Minimize $\qquad\qquad\qquad c = 2x_1 + 8x_2$

subject to $\quad 4x_1 + 4x_2 \geq 32 \quad$ constraint 1 $\qquad x_1 \geq 2 \qquad$ constraint 3

$\qquad\qquad\quad x_1 + 5x_2 \geq 20 \quad$ constraint 2 $\qquad x_1, x_2 \geq 0$

See Fig. 13-12.

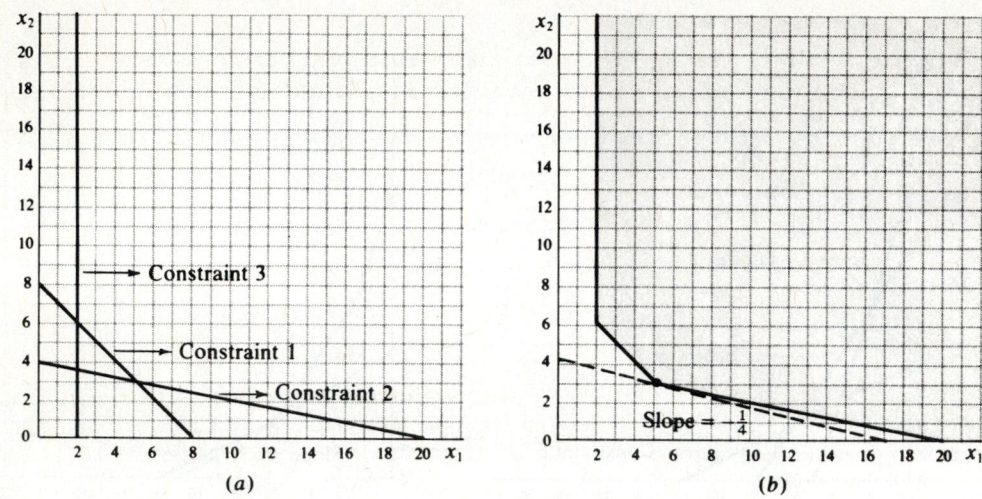

Fig. 13-12

From Fig. 13-12(b), the slope $= -\frac{1}{4}$, $\bar{x}_1 = 5$, and $\bar{x}_2 = 3$. Thus, $\bar{c} = 2(5) + 8(3) = 34$.

MULTIPLE OPTIMAL SOLUTIONS

13.19. Redo Problem 13.14, given the following data:

Minimize $\qquad\qquad\qquad c = 4x_1 + 2x_2$

subject to $\quad 4x_1 + x_2 \geq 20 \quad$ constraint 1 $\qquad x_1 + 6x_2 \geq 18 \qquad$ constraint 3

$\qquad\qquad\quad 2x_1 + x_2 \geq 14 \quad$ constraint 2 $\qquad\quad x_1, x_2 \geq 0$

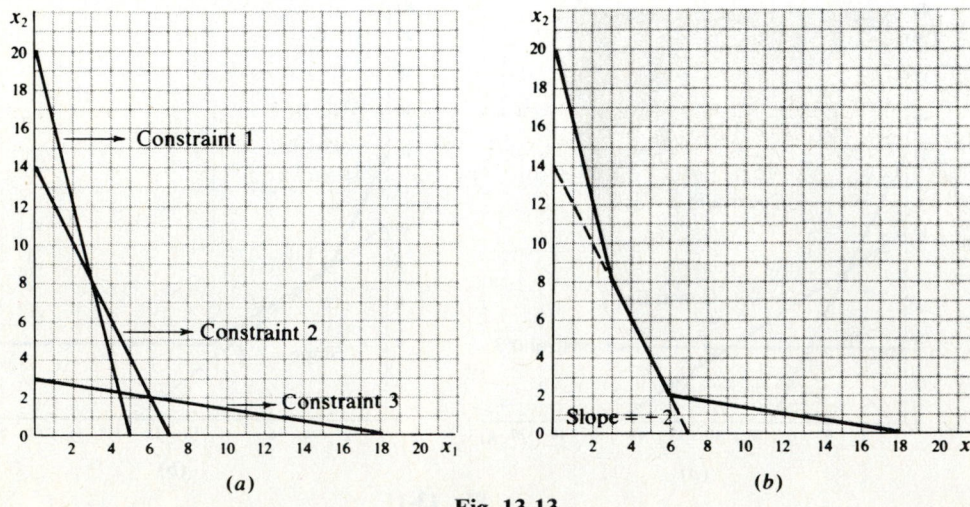

Fig. 13-13

In Fig. 13-13, with the isocost line tangent to the second constraint, there is no *unique* optimal feasible solution. Any point on the line between (3, 8) and (6, 2) will minimize the objective function subject to the constraints. Multiple optimal solutions occur whenever there is linear dependence between the objective function and one of the constraints. In this case, the objective function and constraint 2 are linearly dependent because one can be expressed as a multiple of the other. Notice that multiple optimal solutions do not contradict the extreme point theorem since the extreme points (3, 8) and (6, 2) are also included in the optimal solutions, to wit, $c = 4(3) + 2(8) = 28$ or $c = 4(6) + 2(2) = 28$.

SLACK AND SURPLUS VARIABLES

13.20. (*a*) Convert the inequality constraints in the following data to equations by adding slack variables or subtracting surplus variables, and (*b*) express the equations in matrix form.

Maximize $$\Pi = 24y_1 + 8y_2$$

subject to $$2y_1 + 5y_2 \le 40 \qquad 10y_1 + 5y_2 \le 60$$
$$4y_1 + y_2 \le 20 \qquad y_1, y_2 \ge 0$$

(*a*) For "less than or equal to" inequalities, add slack variables. Thus,

$$2y_1 + 5y_2 + s_1 = 40 \qquad 4y_1 + y_2 + s_2 = 20 \qquad 10y_1 + 5y_2 + s_3 = 60$$

(*b*)
$$\begin{bmatrix} 2 & 5 & 1 & 0 & 0 \\ 4 & 1 & 0 & 1 & 0 \\ 10 & 5 & 0 & 0 & 1 \end{bmatrix} \begin{bmatrix} y_1 \\ y_2 \\ s_1 \\ s_2 \\ s_3 \end{bmatrix} = \begin{bmatrix} 40 \\ 20 \\ 60 \end{bmatrix}$$

13.21. Redo Problem 13.20 for the following:

Minimize $$c = 60x_1 + 80x_2$$

subject to $$2x_1 + 3x_2 \ge 36 \qquad 8x_1 + 2x_2 \ge 32$$
$$2x_1 + 2x_2 \ge 28 \qquad x_1, x_2 \ge 0$$

(*a*) For "greater than or equal to" inequalities, subtract surplus variables.

$$2x_1 + 3x_2 - s_1 = 36 \qquad 2x_1 + 2x_2 - s_2 = 28 \qquad 8x_1 + 2x_2 - s_3 = 32$$

(*b*)
$$\begin{bmatrix} 2 & 3 & -1 & 0 & 0 \\ 2 & 2 & 0 & -1 & 0 \\ 8 & 2 & 0 & 0 & -1 \end{bmatrix} \begin{bmatrix} x_1 \\ x_2 \\ s_1 \\ s_2 \\ s_3 \end{bmatrix} = \begin{bmatrix} 36 \\ 28 \\ 32 \end{bmatrix}$$

13.22. (*a*) Reduce the inequality constraints of the following data to equations and express in matrix form. Determine (*b*) the number of variables that must be set equal to zero to find a basic solution and (*c*) the number of basic solutions that exist. (*d*) Read the first basic solution from the matrix.

Minimize $$c = 54g_1 + 48g_2 + 50g_3$$

subject to $$6g_1 + 4g_2 + 5g_3 \ge 30 \qquad 3g_1 + 6g_2 + 5g_3 \ge 20 \qquad g_1, g_2, g_3 \ge 0$$

(*a*)
$$6g_1 + 4g_2 + 5g_3 - s_1 = 30$$
$$3g_1 + 6g_2 + 5g_3 - s_2 = 20$$
$$\begin{bmatrix} 6 & 4 & 5 & -1 & 0 \\ 3 & 6 & 5 & 0 & -1 \end{bmatrix} \begin{bmatrix} g_1 \\ g_2 \\ g_3 \\ s_1 \\ s_2 \end{bmatrix} = \begin{bmatrix} 30 \\ 20 \end{bmatrix}$$

(b) Since there are two equations and five variables, $n - m = 5 - 2 = 3$ variables must be set equal to zero for a basic solution.

(c) The number of basic solutions is

$$\frac{n!}{m!(n-m)!} = \frac{5!}{2!(3)!} = \frac{5(4)(3)(2)(1)}{2(1)(3)(2)(1)} = 10$$

(d) Setting $g_1 = g_2 = g_3 = 0$, the first basic solution is $\bar{s}_1 = -30$ and $\bar{s}_2 = -20$. Since both are negative, they would fail to constitute a basic *feasible* solution.

Chapter 14

Linear Programming: The Simplex Algorithm

14.1 SIMPLEX ALGORITHM: MAXIMIZATION

An *algorithm* is a set of rules or a systematic procedure for finding the solution to a problem. The *simplex algorithm* is a method (or computational procedure) for determining basic feasible solutions to a system of equations and testing the solutions for optimality. Since at least $n - m$ variables must equal zero for a basic solution, $n - m$ variables are set equal to zero in each step of the procedure, and a basic solution is found by solving the m equations for the remaining m variables. The algorithm moves from one basic feasible solution to another, always improving upon the previous solution, until the optimal solution is reached. Those variables set equal to zero at a particular step are called *not in the basis*, or *not in the solution*. Those not set equal to zero are called *in the basis, in the solution*, or, more simply, *basic variables*. The simplex method is demonstrated in Example 1 for maximization and in Example 3 for minimization.

EXAMPLE 1. The simplex algorithm is used as follows to maximize profits, given

$$\Pi = 5x_1 + 3x_2$$

subject to the constraints

$$6x_1 + 2x_2 \le 36 \qquad 2x_1 + 4x_2 \le 28$$
$$5x_1 + 5x_2 \le 40 \qquad x_1, x_2 \ge 0$$

1. *The Initial Simplex Tableau (or Table)*

    i. Convert the inequalities to equations by adding slack variables.

    $$6x_1 + 2x_2 + s_1 = 36$$
    $$5x_1 + 5x_2 + s_2 = 40 \qquad\qquad (14.1)$$
    $$2x_1 + 4x_2 + s_3 = 28$$

    ii. Express the constraint equations in matrix form.

    $$\begin{bmatrix} 6 & 2 & 1 & 0 & 0 \\ 5 & 5 & 0 & 1 & 0 \\ 2 & 4 & 0 & 0 & 1 \end{bmatrix} \begin{bmatrix} x_1 \\ x_2 \\ s_1 \\ s_2 \\ s_3 \end{bmatrix} = \begin{bmatrix} 36 \\ 40 \\ 28 \end{bmatrix}$$

    iii. Set up an initial simplex tableau composed of the coefficient matrix of the constraint equations and the column vector of constants set above a row of *indicators* which are the negatives of the coefficients of the objective function and a zero coefficient for each slack variable. The constant column

331

entry of the last row is also zero, corresponding to the value of the objective function at the origin (when $x_1 = x_2 = 0$).

Initial simplex tableau:

x_1	x_2	s_1	s_2	s_3	Constant
⑥	2	1	0	0	36
5	5	0	1	0	40
2	4	0	0	1	28
−5	−3	0	0	0	0

↑   Indicators

iv.   The first basic feasible solution can be read from the initial simplex tableau. Setting $x_1 = 0$ and $x_2 = 0$, as in Chapter 13, Example 5, $s_1 = 36$, $s_2 = 40$, and $s_3 = 28$. At the first basic feasible solution, the objective function has a value of zero.

2. *The Pivot Element and a Change of Basis*

To increase the value of the objective function, a new basic solution is examined. To move to a new basic feasible solution, a new variable must be introduced into the basis, and one of the variables formerly in the basis must be excluded. The process of selecting the variable to be included and the variable to be excluded is called *change of basis*.

i.   The negative indicator with the largest absolute value determines the variable to enter the basis. Since -5 in the first (or x_1) column is the negative indicator with the largest absolute value, x_1 is brought into the basis. The x_1 column becomes the *pivot column* and is denoted by an arrow.

ii.   The variable to be eliminated is determined by the smallest *displacement ratio*. Displacement ratios are found by dividing the elements of the constant column by the elements of the pivot column. The row with the smallest displacement ratio (i.e., the *pivot row*), ignoring ratios less than or equal to 0, determines the variable to leave the basis. Since $\frac{36}{6}$ provides the smallest ratio ($\frac{36}{6} < \frac{40}{5} < \frac{28}{2}$), row 1 is the pivot row. Since the unit vector with 1 in the first row appears under the column for s_1, s_1 leaves the basis. The *pivot element* is ⑥, the element at the intersection of the column of the variable entering the basis and the row associated with the variable leaving the basis (i.e., the element at the intersection of the pivot row and the pivot column).

3. *Pivoting*

Pivoting is the process of solving the m equations in terms of the m variables presently in the basis. Since only one new variable enters the basis at each step of the process, and the previous step always involves an identity matrix, pivoting simply involves converting the pivot element to 1 and all the other elements in the pivot column to zero, as in the Gaussian elimination method (see Section 10.12), as follows:

i.   Multiply the pivot row by the reciprocal of the pivot element. In this case, multiply row 1 by $\frac{1}{6}$.

x_1	x_2	s_1	s_2	s_3	Constant
1	$\frac{1}{3}$	$\frac{1}{6}$	0	0	6
5	5	0	1	0	40
2	4	0	0	1	28
−5	−3	0	0	0	0

ii.   Having reduced the pivot element to 1, clear the pivot column. Here subtract 5 times row 1 from row 2, 2 times row 1 from row 3, and add 5 times row 1 to row 4. This gives the second tableau.

Second tableau:

x_1	x_2	s_1	s_2	s_3	Constant
1	$\frac{1}{3}$	$\frac{1}{6}$	0	0	6
0	$\left(\frac{10}{3}\right)$	$-\frac{5}{6}$	1	0	10
0	$\frac{10}{3}$	$-\frac{1}{3}$	0	1	16
0	$-\frac{4}{3}$	$\frac{5}{6}$	0	0	30

The second basic feasible solution can be read directly from the second tableau. Setting $x_2 = 0$ and $s_1 = 0$, we are left with an identity matrix which gives $x_1 = 6$, $s_2 = 10$, and $s_3 = 16$. The last element in the last row (in this case, 30) is the value of the objective function at the second basic feasible solution.

4.   *Optimization*

The objective function is maximized when there are no negative indicators in the last row. Changing the basis and pivoting continue according to the rules above until this is achieved. Since $-\frac{4}{3}$ in the second column is the only negative indicator, x_2 is introduced into the basis; column 2 becomes the pivot column. Dividing the constant column by the pivot column shows that the smallest ratio is in the second row. Thus, $\left(\frac{10}{3}\right)$ becomes the new pivot element. Since the unit vector with 1 in the second row is under s_2, s_2 will leave the basis. To pivot,

i.   Multiply row 2 by $\frac{3}{10}$.

x_1	x_2	s_1	s_2	s_3	Constant
1	$\frac{1}{3}$	$\frac{1}{6}$	0	0	6
0	1	$-\frac{1}{4}$	$\frac{3}{10}$	0	3
0	$\frac{10}{3}$	$-\frac{1}{3}$	0	1	16
0	$-\frac{4}{3}$	$\frac{5}{6}$	0	0	30

ii.   Then subtract $\frac{1}{3}$ times row 2 from row 1, $\frac{10}{3}$ times row 2 from row 3, and add $\frac{4}{3}$ times row 2 to row 4, deriving the third tableau.

Third tableau:

x_1	x_2	s_1	s_2	s_3	Constant
1	0	$\frac{1}{4}$	$-\frac{1}{10}$	0	5
0	1	$-\frac{1}{4}$	$\frac{3}{10}$	0	3
0	0	$\frac{1}{2}$	-1	1	6
0	0	$\frac{1}{2}$	$\frac{2}{5}$	0	34

The third basic feasible solution can be read directly from the tableau. With $s_1 = 0$ and $s_2 = 0$, $x_1 = 5$, $x_2 = 3$, and $s_3 = 6$. Since there are no negative indicators left in the last row, this is the optimal solution. The last element in the last row indicates that at $\bar{x}_1 = 5$, $\bar{x}_2 = 3$, $\bar{s}_1 = 0$, $\bar{s}_2 = 0$, and $\bar{s}_3 = 6$, the objective function reaches a maximum at $\bar{\Pi} = 34$. With $\bar{s}_1 = 0$ and $\bar{s}_2 = 0$, from (*14.1*) there is no slack in the first two constraints, and the first two inputs are all used up. With $\bar{s}_3 = 6$, however, 6 units of the third input remain unused. For a graphic representation, see Problem 13.11.

14.2   MARGINAL VALUE OR SHADOW PRICING

The value of the indicator under each slack variable in the final tableau expresses the marginal value or *shadow price* of the input associated with the variable, i.e., how much the value of the objective function would change as a result of a 1-unit increase in the input. Thus, in Example 1, profits would increase by $\frac{1}{2}$ unit or 50¢ for a 1-unit change in the constant value of constraint 1; by $\frac{2}{5}$ or 40¢ for a 1-unit increase in the constant value of constraint 2; and by 0 for a 1-unit increase in the constant value of constraint 3. Since constraint 3 has a positive slack variable, it is not fully utilized in the optimal solution, and its marginal value is zero (i.e., the addition of still another unit would add nothing to the profit function). The optimal value of the objective function will always equal the sum of the marginal value of each input times the amount available of each input.

EXAMPLE 2. The answer to Example 1 can be checked by (1) substituting the critical values in both the objective function and the constraint equations in (14.1) and (2) evaluating the sum of the marginal values of the resources. All conditions must be satisfied for an optimum. Let A, B, C symbolize the constants in constraints 1, 2, 3.

$$
\begin{aligned}
1. \qquad \Pi &= 5x_1 + 3x_2 & 5x_1 + 5x_2 + s_2 &= 40 \\
&= 5(5) + 3(3) = 34 & 5(5) + 5(3) + 0 &= 40 \\[2mm]
6x_1 + 2x_2 + s_1 &= 36 & 2x_1 + 4x_2 + s_3 &= 28 \\
6(5) + 2(3) + 0 &= 36 & 2(5) + 4(3) + 6 &= 28
\end{aligned}
$$

$$
2. \qquad \Pi = MV_A(A) + MV_B(B) + MV_C(C) = \tfrac{1}{2}(36) + \tfrac{2}{5}(40) + 0(28) = 34
$$

14.3 SIMPLEX ALGORITHM: MINIMIZATION

When the simplex algorithm is used to find a minimal value, the negative values generated by the surplus variables present a special problem. See Example 3. It is frequently easier to solve minimization problems by using the dual, which is treated in Chapter 15. The reader, therefore, may prefer to read Chapter 15 first.

EXAMPLE 3. The simplex algorithm is used below to minimize costs. The data are from Example 2 in Chapter 13, with x now used for y, where $c = 2x_1 + 4x_2$, subject to the nutritional constraints

$$
\begin{aligned}
2x_1 + x_2 &\geq 14 & x_1 + 3x_2 &\geq 18 \\
x_1 + x_2 &\geq 12 & x_1, x_2 &\geq 0
\end{aligned}
$$

1. *The Initial Simplex Tableau (slightly modified)*

    i. Convert the inequalities to equations by subtracting surplus variables.

$$
\begin{aligned}
2x_1 + x_2 - s_1 &= 14 \\
x_1 + x_2 - s_2 &= 12 \\
x_1 + 3x_2 - s_3 &= 18
\end{aligned}
$$

    ii. Express the constraint equations in matrix form.

$$
\begin{bmatrix} 2 & 1 & -1 & 0 & 0 \\ 1 & 1 & 0 & -1 & 0 \\ 1 & 3 & 0 & 0 & -1 \end{bmatrix}
\begin{bmatrix} x_1 \\ x_2 \\ s_1 \\ s_2 \\ s_3 \end{bmatrix}
=
\begin{bmatrix} 14 \\ 12 \\ 18 \end{bmatrix}
$$

From the matrix it is clear that if $x_1 = 0$ and $x_2 = 0$, as in the initial simplex tableau for maximization, the basic solution will not be feasible since $s_1 = -14$, $s_2 = -12$, $s_3 = -18$ and negative values are nonfeasible. To overcome the problem, artificial variables must be introduced.

iii. Add artificial variables. An *artificial variable* $A_i \geq 0$ is a dummy variable added for the specific purpose of generating an initial basic feasible solution. It has no economic meaning. A separate artificial variable is added for each original "greater than or equal to" inequality. Thus,

$$\begin{bmatrix} 2 & 1 & -1 & 0 & 0 & 1 & 0 & 0 \\ 1 & 1 & 0 & -1 & 0 & 0 & 1 & 0 \\ 1 & 3 & 0 & 0 & -1 & 0 & 0 & 1 \end{bmatrix} \begin{bmatrix} x_1 \\ x_2 \\ s_1 \\ s_2 \\ s_3 \\ A_1 \\ A_2 \\ A_3 \end{bmatrix} = \begin{bmatrix} 14 \\ 12 \\ 18 \end{bmatrix} \qquad (14.2)$$

2. The Initial Simplex Tableau Adapted for Minimization

i. Prepare the initial simplex tableau by setting the matrix of coefficients and the column vector of constants in (*14.2*) above a row of indicators which are the negatives of the coefficients of the objective function. The objective function has zero coefficients for the surplus variables and M coefficients for the artificial variables, where M is an impossibly large number to ensure that A will be excluded from the optimal solution.

x_1	x_2	s_1	s_2	s_3	A_1	A_2	A_3	Constant
2	1	-1	0	0	1	0	0	14
1	1	0	-1	0	0	1	0	12
1	3	0	0	-1	0	0	1	18
-2	-4	0	0	0	$-M$	$-M$	$-M$	

$$\underbrace{\qquad\qquad\qquad\qquad\qquad\qquad}_{\text{Indicators}}$$

ii. Then remove the M's from the columns of artificial variables by adding M times (row 1 + row 2 + row 3) to row 4. This gives the initial tableau.

Initial tableau:

x_1	x_2	s_1	s_2	s_3	A_1	A_2	A_3	Constant
2	1	-1	0	0	1	0	0	14
1	1	0	-1	0	0	1	0	12
1	③	0	0	-1	0	0	1	18
$4M - 2$	$5M - 4$	$-M$	$-M$	$-M$	0	0	0	$44M$

The first basic feasible solution can be read directly from the initial tableau. Letting $x_1 = x_2 = s_1 = s_2 = s_3 = 0$, the first basic feasible solution is $A_1 = 14$, $A_2 = 12$, $A_3 = 18$, and the objective function is $44M$, an impossibly large number. To reduce costs, seek a change of basis.

3. The Pivot Element

i. For minimization, the largest positive indicator determines the pivot column and the variable to enter the basis. Since the last entry of the bottom row, $44M$, is not an indicator, $5M - 4$ is the largest positive indicator. Thus, x_2 enters the basis, and the x_2 column becomes the pivot column, as indicated by the arrow.

ii. The pivot row and the variable to leave the basis are determined by the smallest ratio resulting from division of the elements of the constant column by the elements of the pivot column, exactly as for maximization problems. Since $\frac{18}{3} = 6$ is the smallest resulting ratio, row 3 becomes the pivot row. And A_3 leaves the basis since the unit vector with 1 in the third row is associated with A_3. The pivot element at the intersection of the pivot column and pivot row is (3).

4. Pivoting

i. Reduce the pivot element to 1 by multiplying row 3 by $\frac{1}{3}$.

2	1	-1	0	0	1	0	0	14
1	1	0	-1	0	0	1	0	12
$\frac{1}{3}$	1	0	0	$-\frac{1}{3}$	0	0	$\frac{1}{3}$	6
$4M - 2$	$5M - 4$	$-M$	$-M$	$-M$	0	0	0	$44M$

ii. Clear the pivot column by subtracting row 3 from row 1 and from row 2, and $(5M - 4)$ times row 3 from row 4.

Second tableau:

x_1	x_2	s_1	s_2	s_3	A_1	A_2	A_3	Constant
$\frac{5}{3}$	0	-1	0	$\frac{1}{3}$	1	0	$-\frac{1}{3}$	8
$\frac{2}{3}$	0	0	-1	$\frac{1}{3}$	0	1	$-\frac{1}{3}$	6
$\frac{1}{3}$	1	0	0	$-\frac{1}{3}$	0	0	$\frac{1}{3}$	6
$\dfrac{7M - 2}{3}$	0	$-M$	$-M$	$\dfrac{2M - 4}{3}$	0	0	$\dfrac{-5M + 4}{3}$	$14M + 24$

$\uparrow$

5. Reiteration

As long as a positive indicator remains, the process continues. The new pivot column becomes column 1; the new pivot row is row 1. Thus, x_1 enters the basis, and A_1 leaves the basis. The pivot element is $\frac{5}{3}$.

i. Multiply row 1 by $\frac{3}{5}$.

1	0	$-\frac{3}{5}$	0	$\frac{1}{5}$	$\frac{3}{5}$	0	$-\frac{1}{5}$	$\frac{24}{5}$
$\frac{2}{3}$	0	0	-1	$\frac{1}{3}$	0	1	$-\frac{1}{3}$	6
$\frac{1}{3}$	1	0	0	$-\frac{1}{3}$	0	0	$\frac{1}{3}$	6
$\dfrac{7M - 2}{3}$	0	$-M$	$-M$	$\dfrac{2M - 4}{3}$	0	0	$\dfrac{-5M + 4}{3}$	$14M + 24$

ii. Clear column 1 by subtracting $\frac{2}{3}$ row 1 from row 2, $\frac{1}{3}$ row 1 from row 3, and $[(7M - 2)/3]$ row 1 from row 4, deriving the third tableau.

Third tableau:

x_1	x_2	s_1	s_2	s_3	A_1	A_2	A_3	Constant
1	0	$-\frac{3}{5}$	0	$\frac{1}{5}$	$\frac{3}{5}$	0	$-\frac{1}{5}$	$\frac{24}{5}$
0	0	$\frac{2}{5}$	-1	$\frac{1}{5}$	$-\frac{2}{5}$	1	$-\frac{1}{5}$	$\frac{14}{5}$
0	1	$\frac{1}{5}$	0	$-\frac{2}{5}$	$-\frac{1}{5}$	0	$\frac{2}{5}$	$\frac{22}{5}$
0	0	$\dfrac{2M - 2}{5}$	$-M$	$\dfrac{M - 6}{5}$	$\dfrac{-7M + 2}{5}$	0	$\dfrac{-6M + 6}{5}$	$\dfrac{14M + 136}{5}$

$\uparrow$

6. *Fourth Pivot*

    i. Multiply row 2 by $\frac{5}{2}$.

1	0	$-\frac{3}{5}$	0	$\frac{1}{5}$	$\frac{3}{5}$	0	$-\frac{1}{5}$	$\frac{24}{5}$
0	0	1	$-\frac{5}{2}$	$\frac{1}{2}$	-1	$\frac{5}{2}$	$-\frac{1}{2}$	7
0	1	$\frac{1}{5}$	0	$-\frac{2}{5}$	$-\frac{1}{5}$	0	$\frac{2}{5}$	$\frac{22}{5}$
0	0	$\frac{2M-2}{5}$	$-M$	$\frac{M-6}{5}$	$\frac{-7M+2}{5}$	0	$\frac{-6M+6}{5}$	$\frac{14M+136}{5}$

    ii. Add $\frac{3}{5}$ row 2 to row 1, and subtract $\frac{1}{5}$ row 2 from row 3 and $[(2M-2)/5]$ row 2 from row 4.

Fourth tableau:

x_1	x_2	s_1	s_2	s_3	A_1	A_2	A_3	Constant
1	0	0	$-\frac{3}{2}$	$\frac{1}{2}$	0	$\frac{3}{2}$	$-\frac{1}{2}$	9
0	0	1	$-\frac{5}{2}$	$\frac{1}{2}$	-1	$\frac{5}{2}$	$-\frac{1}{2}$	7
0	1	0	$\frac{1}{2}$	$-\frac{1}{2}$	0	$-\frac{1}{2}$	$\frac{1}{2}$	3
0	0	0	-1	-1	$-M$	$-M+1$	$-M+1$	30

    With all indicators negative, an optimal feasible solution has been reached. Isolating the identity matrix, and noting that the unit vectors for x_2 and s_1 are reversed, the optimal feasible solution is read directly from the fourth tableau: $\bar{x}_1 = 9$, $\bar{x}_2 = 3$, $\bar{s}_1 = 7$, $\bar{s}_2 = 0$, and $\bar{s}_3 = 0$. The value of the objective function is indicated by the last element of the last row, where $\bar{c} = 30$.

Several points are worth noting:

1. With $\bar{s}_2 = \bar{s}_3 = 0$, the second and third requirements are exactly fulfilled. There is no surplus. With $\bar{s}_1 = 7$, the first requirement is overfulfilled by 7 units.
2. The absolute value of the indicators for the surplus variables gives the marginal value or shadow price of the constraint. With the indicator for s_1 equal to zero, a unit reduction in the first nutritional requirement would not reduce costs. However, a unit reduction in the second or third nutritional requirement would reduce costs by \$1, since the absolute value of the indicators for s_2 and s_3 is 1. As in the case of marginal value, total costs will equal the sum of the different requirements times their respective shadow prices.
3. The indicators of the artificial variables are all negative in the final tableau. This must always be true for an optimal solution.
4. The coefficient elements of the surplus variables (s_1, s_2, s_3) always equal the negative of the coefficient elements of their corresponding artificial variables (A_1, A_2, A_3). This must be true in each successive tableau and can be helpful in picking up mathematical errors.
5. An artificial variable will never appear in the basis of the final tableau if an optimal *feasible* solution has been reached.

For a dual solution to the same problem, see Examples 4 and 5 in Chapter 15.

EXAMPLE 4. The answer to Example 3 can be checked by (1) substituting the critical values in both the objective function and constraint equations and (2) evaluating the sum of the marginal cost of resources. Let A, B, C symbolize the constants in constraints 1, 2, 3.

1.
$$c = 2x_1 + 4x_2 \qquad\qquad x_1 + x_2 - s_2 = 12$$
$$= 2(9) + 4(3) = 30 \qquad 9 + 3 - 0 = 12$$
$$2x_1 + x_2 - s_1 = 14 \qquad x_1 + 3x_2 - s_3 = 18$$
$$2(9) + 3 - 7 = 14 \qquad 9 + 3(3) - 0 = 18$$

2.
$$c = \mathrm{MC}_A(A) + \mathrm{MC}_B(B) + \mathrm{MC}_C(C) = 0(14) + 1(12) + 1(18) = 30$$

Solved Problems

MAXIMIZATION

14.1. Use the simplex algorithm to solve the following system of equations and inequalities. Determine the shadow prices of the inputs (or requirements) of the constraints.

Maximize
$$\Pi = 3y_1 + 4y_2$$

subject to
$$2.5y_1 + y_2 \le 20 \qquad y_1 + 2y_2 \le 16$$
$$3y_1 + 3y_2 \le 30 \qquad y_1, y_2 \ge 0$$

1. Construct the initial simplex tableau.
    i. Add slack variables to the constraints to make them equations.

$$2.5y_1 + y_2 + s_1 = 20 \qquad 3y_1 + 3y_2 + s_2 = 30 \qquad y_1 + 2y_2 + s_3 = 16$$

   ii. Express the equations in matrix form.

$$\begin{bmatrix} 2.5 & 1 & 1 & 0 & 0 \\ 3 & 3 & 0 & 1 & 0 \\ 1 & 2 & 0 & 0 & 1 \end{bmatrix} \begin{bmatrix} y_1 \\ y_2 \\ s_1 \\ s_2 \\ s_3 \end{bmatrix} = \begin{bmatrix} 20 \\ 30 \\ 16 \end{bmatrix}$$

   iii. Form the initial simplex tableau composed of the coefficient matrix of the constraint equations and the column vector of constants set above a row of indicators which are the negatives of the coefficients of the objective function with zero coefficients for the slack variables.

Initial tableau:

y_1	y_2	s_1	s_2	s_3	Constant
$\frac{5}{2}$	1	1	0	0	20
3	3	0	1	0	30
1	②	0	0	1	16
-3	-4	0	0	0	0

Setting $y_1 = y_2 = 0$, the first basic feasible solution is $s_1 = 20$, $s_2 = 30$, and $s_3 = 16$. At the first basic feasible solution, $\Pi = 0$.

2. Change the basis. The negative indicator with the largest absolute value (arrow) determines the pivot column. The smallest displacement ratio arising from the division of the elements of the constant column by the elements of the pivot column determines the pivot row. Thus, ② becomes the pivot element, the element at the intersection of the pivot row and pivot column.

3. Pivot.
    i. Convert the pivot element to 1 by multiplying row 3 by $\frac{1}{2}$.

$\frac{5}{2}$	1	1	0	0	20
3	3	0	1	0	30
$\frac{1}{2}$	1	0	0	$\frac{1}{2}$	8
-3	-4	0	0	0	0

   ii. Clear the pivot column by subtracting row 3 from row 1, 3 times row 3 from row 2, and adding 4 times row 3 to row 4.

Second tableau:

y_1	y_2	s_1	s_2	s_3	Constant
2	0	1	0	$-\frac{1}{2}$	12
$\frac{3}{2}$	0	0	1	$-\frac{3}{2}$	6
$\frac{1}{2}$	1	0	0	$\frac{1}{2}$	8
-1	0	0	0	2	32

   ↑

4. Change the basis and pivot again. Column 1 is the pivot column, row 2 the pivot row, and $\frac{3}{2}$ the pivot element.

i. Multiply row 2 by $\frac{2}{3}$.

2	0	1	0	$-\frac{1}{2}$	12
1	0	0	$\frac{2}{3}$	-1	4
$\frac{1}{2}$	1	0	0	$\frac{1}{2}$	8
-1	0	0	0	2	32

ii. Clear the pivot column by subtracting 2 times row 2 from row 1, $\frac{1}{2}$ times row 2 from row 3, and adding row 2 to row 4.

Final tableau:

y_1	y_2	s_1	s_2	s_3	Constant
0	0	1	$-\frac{4}{3}$	$\frac{3}{2}$	4
1	0	0	$\frac{2}{3}$	-1	4
0	1	0	$-\frac{1}{3}$	1	6
0	0	0	$\frac{2}{3}$	1	36

Since there are no negative indicators left, the final tableau has been reached. Correcting for the fact that the unit vectors of the identity matrix are out of order, $\bar{y}_1 = 4$, $\bar{y}_2 = 6$, $\bar{s}_1 = 4$, $\bar{s}_2 = 0$, $\bar{s}_3 = 0$, and $\bar{\Pi} = 36$. See Example 1 in Chapter 13 where x was used in place of y. The shadow prices of the inputs are 0, $\frac{2}{3}$, and 1, respectively.

14.2. Redo Problem 14.1 for the equation and inequalities specified below:

Maximize
$$\Pi = 30x_1 + 24x_2 + 60x_3$$

subject to $6x_1 + 3x_2 + 5x_3 \le 30$ $2x_1 + 2x_2 + 10x_3 \le 50$ $x_1, x_2, x_3 \ge 0$

First, add the slack variables and express the constraint equations in matrix form.

$$6x_1 + 3x_2 + 5x_3 + s_1 = 30 \qquad 2x_1 + 2x_2 + 10x_3 + s_2 = 50$$

$$\begin{bmatrix} 6 & 3 & 5 & 1 & 0 \\ 2 & 2 & 10 & 0 & 1 \end{bmatrix} \begin{bmatrix} x_1 \\ x_2 \\ x_3 \\ s_1 \\ s_2 \end{bmatrix} = \begin{bmatrix} 30 \\ 50 \end{bmatrix}$$

Then set up the initial tableau.

Initial tableau:

x_1	x_2	x_3	s_1	s_2	Constant
6	3	5	1	0	30
2	2	⑩	0	1	50
-30	-24	-60	0	0	0

          ↑

Then, change the basis and pivot, as follows: (1) Multiply row 2 by $\frac{1}{10}$.

6	3	5	1	0	30
$\frac{1}{5}$	$\frac{1}{5}$	1	0	$\frac{1}{10}$	5
-30	-24	-60	0	0	0

(2) Clear the pivot column by subtracting 5 times row 2 from row 1 and adding 60 times row 2 to row 3.

Second tableau:

	x_1	x_2	x_3	s_1	s_2	Constant
	⑤	2	0	1	$-\frac{1}{2}$	5
	$\frac{1}{5}$	$\frac{1}{5}$	1	0	$\frac{1}{10}$	5
	-18	-12	0	0	6	300
	↑					

Change the basis and pivot again, as follows: (1) Multiply row 1 by $\frac{1}{5}$.

1	$\frac{2}{5}$	0	$\frac{1}{5}$	$-\frac{1}{10}$	1
$\frac{1}{5}$	$\frac{1}{5}$	1	0	$\frac{1}{10}$	5
-18	-12	0	0	6	300

(2) Clear the pivot column by subtracting $\frac{1}{5}$ row 1 from row 2 and adding 18 times row 1 to row 3.

Third tableau:

	x_1	x_2	x_3	s_1	s_2	Constant
	1	②/③	0	$\frac{1}{5}$	$-\frac{1}{10}$	1
	0	$\frac{3}{25}$	1	$-\frac{1}{25}$	$\frac{3}{25}$	$\frac{24}{5}$
	0	$-\frac{24}{5}$	0	$\frac{18}{5}$	$\frac{21}{5}$	318
		↑				

Pivot a third time. Note that x_1, which was brought into the basis by the second pivot, leaves the basis on the third pivot. It is possible for a variable to enter and leave; but note that the optimal value of the objective function continues to increase. (1) Multiply row 1 by $\frac{5}{2}$.

$\frac{5}{2}$	1	0	$\frac{1}{2}$	$-\frac{1}{4}$	$\frac{5}{2}$
0	$\frac{3}{25}$	1	$-\frac{1}{25}$	$\frac{3}{25}$	$\frac{24}{5}$
0	$-\frac{24}{5}$	0	$\frac{18}{5}$	$\frac{21}{5}$	318

(2) Subtract $\frac{3}{25}$ row 1 from row 2 and add $\frac{24}{5}$ row 1 to row 3.

Final tableau:

	x_1	x_2	x_3	s_1	s_2	Constant
	$\frac{5}{2}$	1	0	$\frac{1}{2}$	$-\frac{1}{4}$	$\frac{5}{2}$
	$-\frac{3}{10}$	0	1	$-\frac{1}{10}$	$\frac{3}{20}$	$\frac{9}{2}$
	12	0	0	6	3	330

In this case, $\bar{x}_1 = 0$, $\bar{x}_2 = 2.5$, $\bar{x}_3 = 4.5$, $\bar{s}_1 = 0$, $\bar{s}_2 = 0$, and $\bar{\Pi} = 330$. The shadow price of the first input is 6; of the second, 3.

14.3.   Redo Problem 14.1 for the data given below:

Maximize $$\Pi = 60g_1 + 100g_2$$

subject to $$4g_1 + 5g_2 \le 40 \qquad 2g_1 + 6g_2 \le 42$$
$$6g_1 + 3g_2 \le 42 \qquad\qquad g_1, g_2 \ge 0$$

1. Set up the initial tableau.

   Initial tableau:

	g_1	g_2	s_1	s_2	s_3	Constant
	4	5	1	0	0	40
	6	3	0	1	0	42
	2	⑥	0	0	1	42
	-60	-100	0	0	0	0
		↑				

2. Change the basis and pivot.
   i. Multiply row 3 by $\frac{1}{6}$.

g_1	g_2	s_1	s_2	s_3	Constant
4	5	1	0	0	40
6	3	0	1	0	42
$\frac{1}{3}$	1	0	0	$\frac{1}{6}$	7
-60	-100	0	0	0	0

   ii. Clear the pivot column by subtracting 5 times row 3 from row 1, 3 times row 3 from row 2, and adding 100 times row 3 to row 4.

   Second tableau:

	g_1	g_2	s_1	s_2	s_3	Constant
	$\left(\frac{7}{3}\right)$	0	1	0	$-\frac{5}{6}$	5
	5	0	0	1	$-\frac{1}{2}$	21
	$\frac{1}{3}$	1	0	0	$\frac{1}{6}$	7
	$-\frac{80}{3}$	0	0	0	$\frac{50}{3}$	700
	↑					

3. Change the basis and pivot again.
   i. Multiply row 1 by $\frac{3}{7}$.

g_1	g_2	s_1	s_2	s_3	Constant
1	0	$\frac{3}{7}$	0	$-\frac{5}{14}$	$\frac{15}{7}$
5	0	0	1	$-\frac{1}{2}$	21
$\frac{1}{3}$	1	0	0	$\frac{1}{6}$	7
$-\frac{80}{3}$	0	0	0	$\frac{50}{3}$	700

   ii. Clear the pivot column by subtracting 5 times row 1 from row 2, $\frac{1}{3}$ times row 1 from row 3, and adding $\frac{80}{3}$ row 1 to row 4.

   Final tableau:

	g_1	g_2	s_1	s_2	s_3	Constant
	1	0	$\frac{3}{7}$	0	$-\frac{5}{14}$	$\frac{15}{7}$
	0	0	$-\frac{15}{7}$	1	$\frac{9}{7}$	$\frac{72}{7}$
	0	1	$-\frac{1}{7}$	0	$\frac{4}{14}$	$\frac{44}{7}$
	0	0	$\frac{80}{7}$	0	$\frac{50}{7}$	$\frac{5300}{7}$

Noting the position of the unit vectors in the identity matrix portion of the tableau,

$$\bar{g}_1 = \tfrac{15}{7} = 2.14 \qquad \bar{s}_1 = 0 \qquad \bar{s}_3 = 0$$
$$\bar{g}_2 = \tfrac{44}{7} = 6.29 \qquad \bar{s}_2 = \tfrac{72}{7} = 10.29 \qquad \bar{\Pi} = \tfrac{5300}{7} = 757.14$$

The shadow prices of the inputs are 11.43, 0, and 7.14, respectively.

MINIMIZATION

14.4. Use the simplex algorithm to solve the equation and inequalities given below. Determine the shadow price of each constraint requirement.

Minimize
$$c = 60x_1 + 80x_2$$

subject to
$$2x_1 + 3x_2 \geq 36 \qquad 8x_1 + 2x_2 \geq 32$$
$$2x_1 + 2x_2 \geq 28 \qquad x_1, x_2 \geq 0$$

1. Convert the inequalities to equations by subtracting surplus variables, and express in matrix form.

$$2x_1 + 3x_2 - s_1 = 36 \qquad 2x_1 + 2x_2 - s_2 = 28 \qquad 8x_1 + 2x_2 - s_3 = 32$$

$$\begin{bmatrix} 2 & 3 & -1 & 0 & 0 \\ 2 & 2 & 0 & -1 & 0 \\ 8 & 2 & 0 & 0 & -1 \end{bmatrix} \begin{bmatrix} x_1 \\ x_2 \\ s_1 \\ s_2 \\ s_3 \end{bmatrix} = \begin{bmatrix} 36 \\ 28 \\ 32 \end{bmatrix}$$

Since the first basic solution will be nonfeasible, add artificial variables.

$$\begin{bmatrix} 2 & 3 & -1 & 0 & 0 & 1 & 0 & 0 \\ 2 & 2 & 0 & -1 & 0 & 0 & 1 & 0 \\ 8 & 2 & 0 & 0 & -1 & 0 & 0 & 1 \end{bmatrix} \begin{bmatrix} x_1 \\ x_2 \\ s_1 \\ s_2 \\ s_3 \\ A_1 \\ A_2 \\ A_3 \end{bmatrix} = \begin{bmatrix} 36 \\ 28 \\ 32 \end{bmatrix}$$

2. Prepare for the initial tableau by setting the coefficient matrix and the column vector of constants over the negatives of the coefficients of the objective function which has zero coefficients for the surplus variables and artificially large coefficients (M) for the artificial variables.

x_1	x_2	s_1	s_2	s_3	A_1	A_2	A_3	Constant
2	3	−1	0	0	1	0	0	36
2	2	0	−1	0	0	1	0	28
8	2	0	0	−1	0	0	1	32
−60	−80	0	0	0	−M	−M	−M	

Clear the artificial variable columns of M by adding M times (row 1 + row 2 + row 3) to row 4 to obtain the initial tableau.

Initial tableau:

x_1	x_2	s_1	s_2	s_3	A_1	A_2	A_3	Constant
2	3	−1	0	0	1	0	0	36
2	2	0	−1	0	0	1	0	28
⑧	2	0	0	−1	0	0	1	32
$12M − 60$	$7M − 80$	−M	−M	−M	0	0	0	$96M$
↑								

3. Choose the pivot element and pivot. Since $12M − 60$ is the largest positive indicator and $\frac{32}{8}$ is the smallest displacement ratio, 8 is the pivot element.

    i.   Multiply row 3 by $\frac{1}{8}$.

2	3	−1	0	0	1	0	0	36
2	2	0	−1	0	0	1	0	28
1	$\frac{1}{4}$	0	0	$-\frac{1}{8}$	0	0	$\frac{1}{8}$	4
$12M − 60$	$7M − 80$	−M	−M	−M	0	0	0	$96M$

ii. Subtract 2 times row 3 from row 1, 2 times row 3 from row 2, and $(12M - 60)$ times row 3 from row 4.

Second tableau:

x_1	x_2	s_1	s_2	s_3	A_1	A_2	A_3	Constant
0	$\frac{5}{2}$	-1	0	$\frac{1}{4}$	1	0	$-\frac{1}{4}$	28
0	$\frac{3}{2}$	0	-1	$\frac{1}{4}$	0	1	$-\frac{1}{4}$	20
1	$\frac{1}{4}$	0	0	$-\frac{1}{8}$	0	0	$\frac{1}{8}$	4
0	$4M - 65$	$-M$	$-M$	$\dfrac{M - 15}{2}$	0	0	$\dfrac{-3M + 15}{2}$	$48M + 240$

$\uparrow$

4. Pivot again.

i. Multiply row 1 by $\frac{2}{5}$.

0	1	$-\frac{2}{5}$	0	$\frac{1}{10}$	$\frac{2}{5}$	0	$-\frac{1}{10}$	$\frac{56}{5}$
0	$\frac{3}{2}$	0	-1	$\frac{1}{4}$	0	1	$-\frac{1}{4}$	20
1	$\frac{1}{4}$	0	0	$-\frac{1}{8}$	0	0	$\frac{1}{8}$	4
0	$4M - 65$	$-M$	$-M$	$\dfrac{M - 15}{2}$	0	0	$\dfrac{-3M + 15}{2}$	$48M + 240$

ii. Subtract $\frac{3}{2}$ row 1 from row 2, $\frac{1}{4}$ row 1 from row 3, and $(4M - 65)$ row 1 from row 4.

Third tableau:

x_1	x_2	s_1	s_2	s_3	A_1	A_2	A_3	Constant
0	1	$-\frac{2}{5}$	0	$\frac{1}{10}$	$\frac{2}{5}$	0	$-\frac{1}{10}$	$\frac{56}{5}$
0	0	$\left(\frac{3}{5}\right)$	-1	$\frac{1}{10}$	$-\frac{3}{5}$	1	$-\frac{1}{10}$	$\frac{16}{5}$
1	0	$\frac{1}{10}$	0	$-\frac{3}{20}$	$-\frac{1}{10}$	0	$\frac{3}{20}$	$\frac{6}{5}$
0	0	$\dfrac{3M}{5} - 26$	$-M$	$\dfrac{M}{10} - 1$	$\dfrac{-8M}{5} + 26$	0	$\dfrac{-11M}{10} + 1$	$\dfrac{16M}{5} + 968$

$\uparrow$

5. Pivot a third time. Recalling that negative elements cannot be used in the denominator of the displacement ratio, $\frac{3}{5}$ is the new pivot element.

i. Multiply row 2 by $\frac{5}{3}$.

0	1	$-\frac{2}{5}$	0	$\frac{1}{10}$	$\frac{2}{5}$	0	$-\frac{1}{10}$	$\frac{56}{5}$
0	0	1	$-\frac{5}{3}$	$\frac{1}{6}$	-1	$\frac{5}{3}$	$-\frac{1}{6}$	$\frac{16}{3}$
1	0	$\frac{1}{10}$	0	$-\frac{3}{20}$	$-\frac{1}{10}$	0	$\frac{3}{20}$	$\frac{6}{5}$
0	0	$\dfrac{3M}{5} - 26$	$-M$	$\dfrac{M}{10} - 1$	$\dfrac{-8M}{5} + 26$	0	$\dfrac{-11M}{10} + 1$	$\dfrac{16M}{5} + 968$

ii. Add $\frac{2}{5}$ times row 2 to row 1 and subtract $\frac{1}{10}$ times row 2 from row 3 and $[(3M/5) - 26]$ times row 2 from row 4.

Fourth tableau:

x_1	x_2	s_1	s_2	s_3	A_1	A_2	A_3	Constant
0	1	0	$-\frac{2}{3}$	$\frac{1}{6}$	0	$\frac{2}{3}$	$-\frac{1}{6}$	$\frac{40}{3}$
0	0	1	$-\frac{5}{3}$	$\left(\frac{1}{6}\right)$	-1	$\frac{5}{3}$	$-\frac{1}{6}$	$\frac{16}{3}$
1	0	0	$\frac{1}{6}$	$-\frac{1}{6}$	0	$-\frac{1}{6}$	$\frac{1}{6}$	$\frac{2}{3}$
0	0	0	$-\frac{130}{3}$	$\frac{10}{3}$	$-M$	$-M + \frac{130}{3}$	$-M - \frac{10}{3}$	$\frac{3320}{3}$

$\uparrow$

6. Pivot a fourth time.

    i. Multiply row 2 by 6.

$$\begin{array}{cccccccc|c}
0 & 1 & 0 & -\frac{2}{3} & \frac{1}{6} & 0 & \frac{2}{3} & -\frac{1}{6} & \frac{40}{3} \\
0 & 0 & 6 & -10 & 1 & -6 & 10 & -1 & 32 \\
1 & 0 & 0 & \frac{1}{6} & -\frac{1}{6} & 0 & -\frac{1}{6} & \frac{1}{6} & \frac{2}{3} \\
\hline
0 & 0 & 0 & -\frac{130}{3} & \frac{10}{3} & -M & -M+\frac{130}{3} & -M-\frac{10}{3} & \frac{3320}{3}
\end{array}$$

    ii. Subtract $\frac{1}{6}$ times row 2 from row 1, add $\frac{1}{6}$ times row 2 to row 3, and subtract $\frac{10}{3}$ times row 2 from row 4.

    Final tableau:

x_1	x_2	s_1	s_2	s_3	A_1	A_2	A_3	Constant
0	1	-1	1	0	1	-1	0	8
0	0	6	-10	1	-6	10	-1	32
1	0	1	$-\frac{3}{2}$	0	-1	$\frac{3}{2}$	0	6
0	0	-20	-10	0	$-M+20$	$-M+10$	$-M$	1000

Noting the order of the unit vectors, $\bar{x}_1 = 6$, $\bar{x}_2 = 8$, $\bar{s}_1 = \bar{s}_2 = 0$, $\bar{s}_3 = 32$, and $\bar{c} = 1000$. The shadow prices of the constraint requirements are 20, 10, and 0, respectively.

14.5. Redo Problem 14.4 for the data specified below:

Minimize $c = 36x_1 + 40x_2 + 28x_3$

subject to $6x_1 + 5x_2 + 2x_3 \geq 5$ $2x_1 + 5x_2 + 4x_3 \geq 3$ $x_1, x_2, x_3 \geq 0$

1. Convert the constraint inequalities to equations by subtracting surplus variables and add the necessary artificial variables.

$$6x_1 + 5x_2 + 2x_3 - s_1 + A_1 = 5 \qquad 2x_1 + 5x_2 + 4x_3 - s_2 + A_2 = 3$$

2. Prepare for the initial tableau.

x_1	x_2	x_3	s_1	s_2	A_1	A_2	Constant
6	5	2	-1	0	1	0	5
2	5	4	0	-1	0	1	3
-36	-40	-28	0	0	$-M$	$-M$	

Clear the artificial variable columns to obtain the initial tableau.

Initial tableau:

x_1	x_2	x_3	s_1	s_2	A_1	A_2	Constant
6	5	2	-1	0	1	0	5
2	⑤	4	0	-1	0	1	3
$8M - 36$	$10M - 40$	$6M - 28$	$-M$	$-M$	0	0	$8M$

                                               ↑

3. Pivot by multiplying row 2 by $\frac{1}{5}$. Having reduced the pivot element to 1, subtract 5 times row 2 from row 1, and $(10M - 40)$ times row 2 from row 3.

Second tableau:

x_1	x_2	x_3	s_1	s_2	A_1	A_2	Constant
④	0	-2	-1	1	1	-1	2
$\frac{2}{5}$	1	$\frac{4}{5}$	0	$-\frac{1}{5}$	0	$\frac{1}{5}$	$\frac{3}{5}$
$4M - 20$	0	$-2M + 4$	$-M$	$M - 8$	0	$-2M + 8$	$2M + 24$

 ↑

4. Pivot again. Multiply row 1 by $\frac{1}{4}$. Then having reduced the pivot element to 1, subtract $\frac{2}{5}$ times row 1 from row 2 and $(4M - 20)$ times row 1 from row 3.

Final tableau:

x_1	x_2	x_3	s_1	s_2	A_1	A_2	Constant
1	0	$-\frac{1}{2}$	$-\frac{1}{4}$	$\frac{1}{4}$	$\frac{1}{4}$	$-\frac{1}{4}$	$\frac{1}{2}$
0	1	1	$\frac{1}{10}$	$-\frac{3}{10}$	$-\frac{1}{10}$	$\frac{3}{10}$	$\frac{2}{5}$
0	0	-6	-5	-3	$-M + 5$	$-M + 3$	34

Thus, $\bar{x}_1 = \frac{1}{2}$, $\bar{x}_2 = \frac{2}{5}$, $\bar{x}_3 = 0$, $\bar{s}_1 = 0$, $\bar{s}_2 = 0$, and $\bar{c} = 34$. With $\bar{s}_1 = \bar{s}_2 = 0$, the constraints are exactly fulfilled, and there is no surplus. The shadow prices of the constraint requirements are 5 and 3, respectively.

14.6. Redo Problem 14.4 for the following data:

Minimize
$$c = 20y_1 + 30y_2 + 16y_3$$

subject to $2.5y_1 + 3y_2 + y_3 \geq 3$ $y_1 + 3y_2 + 2y_3 \geq 4$ $y_1, y_2, y_3 \geq 0$

1. Set up the initial tableau.

Initial tableau:

y_1	y_2	y_3	s_1	s_2	A_1	A_2	Constant
$\frac{5}{2}$	③	1	-1	0	1	0	3
1	3	2	0	-1	0	1	4
$\frac{7M}{2} - 20$	$6M - 30$	$3M - 16$	$-M$	$-M$	0	0	$7M$

    ↑

2. Pivot.

y_1	y_2	y_3	s_1	s_2	A_1	A_2	Constant
$\frac{5}{6}$	1	$\frac{1}{3}$	$-\frac{1}{3}$	0	$\frac{1}{3}$	0	1
$-\frac{3}{2}$	0	①	1	-1	-1	1	1
$\frac{-3M}{2} + 5$	0	$M - 6$	$M - 10$	$-M$	$-2M + 10$	0	$M + 30$

    ↑

3. Pivot again.

y_1	y_2	y_3	s_1	s_2	A_1	A_2	Constant
$\frac{4}{3}$	1	0	$-\frac{2}{3}$	$\frac{1}{3}$	$\frac{2}{3}$	$-\frac{1}{3}$	$\frac{2}{3}$
$-\frac{3}{2}$	0	1	1	-1	-1	1	1
-4	0	0	-4	-6	$-M + 4$	$-M + 6$	36

Thus, $\bar{y}_1 = 0$, $\bar{y}_2 = \frac{2}{3}$, $\bar{y}_3 = 1$, $\bar{s}_1 = 0$, $\bar{s}_2 = 0$, and $\bar{c} = 36$. The shadow prices of the constraint requirements are 4 and 6, respectively.

MULTIPLE OPTIMAL SOLUTIONS

14.7. Use the simplex algorithm to solve the following equation and inequalities:

Minimize
$$c = 4x_1 + 2x_2$$

subject to
$$4x_1 + x_2 \geq 20 \qquad x_1 + 6x_2 \geq 18$$
$$2x_1 + x_2 \geq 14 \qquad x_1, x_2 \geq 0$$

1. Set up the initial tableau.

Initial tableau:

x_1	x_2	s_1	s_2	s_3	A_1	A_2	A_3	Constant
4	1	-1	0	0	1	0	0	20
2	1	0	-1	0	0	1	0	14
1	⑥	0	0	-1	0	0	1	18
$7M-4$	$8M-2$	$-M$	$-M$	$-M$	0	0	0	$52M$

2. Pivot. Multiply row 3 by $\frac{1}{6}$. Having reduced the pivot element to 1, subtract row 3 from row 1 and from row 2, and $(8M-2)$ times row 3 from row 4, deriving the second tableau.

Second tableau:

x_1	x_2	s_1	s_2	s_3	A_1	A_2	A_3	Constant
$\boxed{\frac{23}{6}}$	0	-1	0	$\frac{1}{6}$	1	0	$-\frac{1}{6}$	17
$\frac{11}{6}$	0	0	-1	$\frac{1}{6}$	0	1	$-\frac{1}{6}$	11
$\frac{1}{6}$	1	0	0	$-\frac{1}{6}$	0	0	$\frac{1}{6}$	3
$\frac{17M-11}{3}$	0	$-M$	$-M$	$\frac{M-1}{3}$	0	0	$\frac{-4M+1}{3}$	$28M+6$

3. Pivot again. Multiply row 1 by $\frac{6}{23}$. Then subtract $\frac{11}{6}$ times row 1 from row 2, $\frac{1}{6}$ times row 1 from row 3, and $[(17M-11)/3]$ times row 1 from row 4.

Third tableau:

x_1	x_2	s_1	s_2	s_3	A_1	A_2	A_3	Constant
1	0	$-\frac{6}{23}$	0	$\frac{1}{23}$	$\frac{6}{23}$	0	$-\frac{1}{23}$	$\frac{102}{23}$
0	0	$\boxed{\frac{11}{23}}$	-1	$\frac{2}{23}$	$-\frac{11}{23}$	1	$-\frac{2}{23}$	$\frac{66}{23}$
0	1	$\frac{1}{23}$	0	$-\frac{4}{23}$	$-\frac{1}{23}$	0	$\frac{4}{23}$	$\frac{52}{23}$
0	0	$\frac{11M-22}{23}$	$-M$	$\frac{2M-4}{23}$	$\frac{-34M+22}{23}$	0	$\frac{-25M+4}{23}$	$\frac{66M+512}{23}$

4. Pivot a third time. Multiply row 2 by $\frac{23}{11}$. Then add $\frac{6}{23}$ times row 2 to row 1, subtract $\frac{1}{23}$ times row 2 from row 3, and $[(11M-22)/23]$ times row 2 from row 4.

Final tableau:

x_1	x_2	s_1	s_2	s_3	A_1	A_2	A_3	Constant
1	0	0	$-\frac{6}{11}$	$\frac{1}{11}$	0	$\frac{6}{11}$	$-\frac{1}{11}$	6
0	0	1	$-\frac{23}{11}$	$\frac{2}{11}$	-1	$\frac{23}{11}$	$-\frac{2}{11}$	6
0	1	0	$\frac{1}{11}$	$-\frac{2}{11}$	0	$-\frac{1}{11}$	$\frac{2}{11}$	2
0	0	0	-2	0	$-M$	$-M+2$	$-M$	28

From the final tableau, $\bar{x}_1 = 6$, $\bar{x}_2 = 2$, $\bar{s}_1 = 6$, $\bar{s}_2 = 0$, $\bar{s}_3 = 0$, and $\bar{c} = 28$. But s_3, which is not in the final basis, has a zero indicator. This means that the variable s_3 can be included in the basis without affecting the value of the objective function. Since the objective function is already at an optimum, it follows that there must be more than one optimal solution. Whenever a variable not in the basis has a zero indicator, the objective function must have multiple optimal solutions. For a graphic solution to this problem, see Problem 13.19.

Chapter 15

Linear Programming: The Dual

15.1 THE DUAL

Every maximization (minimization) problem in linear programming has a corresponding minimization (maximization) problem. The original problem is called the *primal*; the corresponding problem is called the *dual*. The relationship between the two can best be expressed through the use of the parameters they share in common. [For similar properties in Lagrangian functions, see Problems 12.29(c) and 12.30(c).]

EXAMPLE 1. Given an original or primal problem,

Maximize
$$\Pi = g_1 x_1 + g_2 x_2 + g_3 x_3$$

subject to
$$a_{11} x_1 + a_{12} x_2 + a_{13} x_3 \leq b_1$$
$$a_{21} x_1 + a_{22} x_2 + a_{23} x_3 \leq b_2$$
$$a_{31} x_1 + a_{32} x_2 + a_{33} x_3 \leq b_3$$
$$x_1, x_2, x_3 \geq 0$$

the related dual problem is

Minimize
$$c = b_1 z_1 + b_2 z_2 + b_3 z_3$$

subject to
$$a_{11} z_1 + a_{21} z_2 + a_{31} z_3 \geq g_1$$
$$a_{12} z_1 + a_{22} z_2 + a_{32} z_3 \geq g_2$$
$$a_{13} z_1 + a_{23} z_2 + a_{33} z_3 \geq g_3$$
$$z_1, z_2, z_3 \geq 0$$

15.2 RULES OF TRANSFORMATION TO OBTAIN THE DUAL

In the formulation of a dual from a primal problem,

1. The direction of optimization is reversed. Maximization in the primal becomes minimization in the dual and vice versa.
2. The inequality signs of the technical constraints are reversed, but the nonnegativity constraint on decision variables is always maintained.
3. The rows of the coefficient matrix of the constraints in the primal are transposed to columns for the coefficient matrix of constraints in the dual.
4. The row vector of coefficients in the objective function in the primal is transposed to a column vector of constants for the dual constraints.
5. The column vector of constants from the primal constraints is transposed to a row vector of coefficients for the objective function in the dual.
6. Primal decision variables x_j are replaced by dual decision variables z_i.

EXAMPLE 2. The dual of the linear programming problem

Maximize
$$\Pi = 5x_1 + 3x_2$$

subject to
$$6x_1 + 2x_2 \leq 36$$
$$5x_1 + 5x_2 \leq 40$$
$$2x_1 + 4x_2 \leq 28 \qquad x_1, x_2 \geq 0$$

is

Minimize
$$c = 36z_1 + 40z_2 + 28z_3$$

subject to
$$6z_1 + 5z_2 + 2z_3 \geq 5 \qquad 2z_1 + 5z_2 + 4z_3 \geq 3 \qquad z_1, z_2, z_3 \geq 0$$

EXAMPLE 3. The dual of the linear programming problem

Minimize
$$c = 20z_1 + 30z_2 + 16z_3$$

subject to
$$2.5z_1 + 3z_2 + z_3 \geq 3$$
$$z_1 + 3z_2 + 2z_3 \geq 4 \qquad z_1, z_2, z_3 \geq 0$$

is

Maximize
$$\Pi = 3x_1 + 4x_2$$

subject to
$$2.5x_1 + x_2 \leq 20 \qquad x_1 + 2x_2 \leq 16$$
$$3x_1 + 3x_2 \leq 30 \qquad x_1, x_2 \geq 0$$

Note that if the dual of the dual were taken here or in the examples above, the corresponding primal would be obtained.

15.3   THE DUAL THEOREMS

Two dual theorems are of extreme importance for linear programming. They state:

1. The optimal value of the primal objective function always equals the optimal value of the dual objective function, provided an optimal feasible solution exists.
2. If in the optimal feasible solution
    i.   A decision variable in the primal program has a nonzero value, the corresponding slack (or surplus) variable in the dual program must have an optimal value of zero.
    ii. A slack (or surplus) variable in the primal has a nonzero value, the corresponding decision variable in the dual program must have an optimal value of zero.

EXAMPLE 4. Given the following linear programming problem

Maximize:
$$\Pi = 14x_1 + 12x_2 + 18x_3$$

subject to
$$2x_1 + x_2 + x_3 \leq 2$$
$$x_1 + x_2 + 3x_3 \leq 4 \qquad x_1, x_2, x_3 \geq 0$$

The dual theorems are used as follows to find the optimal value of (1) the primal objective function and (2) the primal decision variables. The dual program is

Minimize
$$c = 2z_1 + 4z_2$$

subject to
$$2z_1 + z_2 \geq 14$$
$$z_1 + z_2 \geq 12$$
$$z_1 + 3z_2 \geq 18 \qquad z_1, z_2 \geq 0$$

1. The optimal values of the dual program were found graphically in Chapter 13, Example 2: $\bar{z}_1 = 9$, $\bar{z}_2 = 3$, and $\bar{c} = 30$. With the optimal value of the dual equal to 30, it is clear from the first dual theorem that $\bar{\Pi}$ must also equal 30.

2. To find the optimal values of the primal decision variables, convert the inequality constraints to equations by adding slack variables to the primal (I) and subtracting surplus variables from the dual (II). To distinguish the slack variables of the primal from the surplus variables of the dual, s_i is used for the primal and t_i for the dual.

$$\text{I.} \quad \begin{aligned} 2x_1 + x_2 + x_3 + s_1 &= 2 \\ x_1 + x_2 + 3x_3 + s_2 &= 4 \end{aligned} \tag{15.1}$$

$$\text{II.} \quad \begin{aligned} 2z_1 + z_2 - t_1 &= 14 \\ z_1 + z_2 - t_2 &= 12 \\ z_1 + 3z_2 - t_3 &= 18 \end{aligned} \tag{15.2}$$

Substitute $\bar{z}_1 = 9$, $\bar{z}_2 = 3$ in (15.2) to find $\bar{t}_1, \bar{t}_2, \bar{t}_3$ as follows:

$$\begin{aligned} 2(9) + 3 - t_1 &= 14 & \bar{t}_1 &= 7 \\ 9 + 3 - t_2 &= 12 & \bar{t}_2 &= 0 \\ 9 + 3(3) - t_3 &= 18 & \bar{t}_3 &= 0 \end{aligned}$$

With the surplus variables $\bar{t}_2, \bar{t}_3$ for the second and third dual constraints equal to zero, according to the second dual theorem, the corresponding primal decision variables $\bar{x}_2, \bar{x}_3$ must be nonzero. With $\bar{t}_1 \neq 0$, the corresponding decision variable $\bar{x}_1$ must equal zero. Therefore $\bar{x}_1 = 0$.

The second dual theorem also states that if the optimal dual decision variables $\bar{z}_1, \bar{z}_2$ do not equal zero in the dual, the corresponding primal slack variables $\bar{s}_1, \bar{s}_2$ in the primary must equal zero. Substituting $\bar{s}_1 = \bar{s}_2 = 0$ in (15.1), and recalling that $\bar{x}_1 = 0$, (15.1) reduces to

$$x_2 + x_3 = 2 \qquad x_2 + 3x_3 = 4$$

Solving simultaneously by Cramer's rule, $\bar{x}_2 = 1$ and $\bar{x}_3 = 1$. Thus the optimal decision variables are $\bar{x}_1 = 0$, $\bar{x}_2 = 1$, and $\bar{x}_3 = 1$, which can be easily checked by substitution into the objective function: $\Pi = 14(0) + 12(1) + 18(1) = 30$.

EXAMPLE 5. The dual in Example 4 was solved as a primal in Chapter 14, Example 3. Converting x_i to z_i and s_i to t_i for the dual form, the final tableau reads

Final tableau:

	z_1	z_2	t_1	t_2	t_3	A_1	A_2	A_3	Constant
	1	0	0	$-\frac{3}{2}$	$\frac{1}{2}$	0	$\frac{3}{2}$	$-\frac{1}{2}$	9
	0	0	1	$-\frac{5}{2}$	$\frac{1}{2}$	-1	$\frac{5}{2}$	$-\frac{1}{2}$	7
	0	1	0	$\frac{1}{2}$	$-\frac{1}{2}$	0	$-\frac{1}{2}$	$\frac{1}{2}$	3
	0	0	$\boxed{0 \quad -1 \quad -1}$			$-M$	$-M+1$	$-M+1$	30

The final tableau of the dual can be used to determine the optimal values of (1) the primal objective function and (2) the primal decision variables.

1. The optimal value of the primal objective function, just as the optimal value for the dual objective function, is indicated by the last element of the last row: 30.
2. The optimal values for the primal decision variables can also be read directly from the dual tableau. They are given by the absolute values of the indicators in the columns under the corresponding dual surplus variables. Since t_1 is the surplus variable for the first dual constraint and it corresponds to x_1 in the primal, $\bar{x}_1 = 0$. Since t_2 is the dual surplus variable for the second constraint and it corresponds to x_2 in the primal, $\bar{x}_2 = 1$. Similarly, $\bar{x}_3 = 1$. The dual indicators whose absolute values give the optimal values of the primal decision variables are boxed. The indicators in the artificial variable columns have no economic meaning.

15.4 ADVANTAGES OF THE DUAL

From the relationship between the primal and dual, as outlined above, it is clear that the optimal value of the objective function can be found through either the primal or dual. Because of the complementary relationship between decision variables in one program and slack (or surplus) variables in the other, solution of one program provides full solution of the other. This is beneficial because

1. It enables minimization problems to be solved in terms of maximization, which is frequently easier.

2. For primal problems with three decision variables, the dual reduces the program to two decision variables (see Example 3), which can then be graphed.

EXAMPLE 6.   The dual is used below to find the optimal values of the minimization problem in Example 3.

The dual of the minimization problem in Example 3 is graphed in Chapter 13, Example 1, where $\bar{x}_1 = 4$, $\bar{x}_2 = 6$, and $\bar{\Pi} = 36$. Costs for the primal problem in Example 3 are minimized at $\bar{c} = 36$. Using the techniques in Example 4, $\bar{z}_1 = 0$, $\bar{z}_2 = \frac{2}{3}$, and $\bar{z}_3 = 1$. For similar solutions, see Problems 15.1 to 15.4. For solution by the simplex algorithm, see Problem 15.8.

15.5 SHADOW PRICES IN THE DUAL

When using the dual to solve the primal, the marginal value or shadow price of the ith resource in the primal is given directly by the corresponding decision variable in the objective function of the dual. Thus, z_i in the dual gives the shadow price of the ith resource in the primal. The optimal value of the objective function will always equal the sum of resources times their respective shadow prices. In terms of the parameters of Example 1,

$$\Pi = \sum_{i=1}^{3} b_i z_i = b_1 z_1 + b_2 z_2 + b_3 z_3 \tag{15.3}$$

EXAMPLE 7.   The final tableau for the dual in Example 5 is used to determine the shadow prices of the primal resources in Example 4, as follows: Correcting for the order of unit vectors in the identity-matrix portion of the final dual tableau, $\bar{z}_1 = 9$ and $\bar{z}_2 = 3$. Since z_1 and z_2 are the dual decision variables corresponding to the two resources in the primal constraints, the shadow price of the first resource is 9; the shadow price of the second resource is 3.

These shadow prices can be used to determine the optimal value of the primal objective function. From the primal constraints in Example 4, there are 2 units of the first resource and 4 units of the second. Multiplying the available resources by their shadow prices and adding the products, $\Pi = 2(9) + 4(3) = 30$.

15.6 SHADOW PRICES AND THE LAGRANGIAN MULTIPLIER

Shadow prices serve the same function as Lagrangian multipliers (see Section 5.6). They estimate the change in the objective function arising from a small change in the constraint. This is easily demonstrated by taking the partial derivatives of (15.3) with respect to the constraints b_1, b_2, and b_3:

$$\frac{\partial \Pi}{\partial b_1} = z_1 \qquad \frac{\partial \Pi}{\partial b_2} = z_2 \qquad \frac{\partial \Pi}{\partial b_3} = z_3 \tag{15.4}$$

From (15.4) it is clear that for a 1-unit change in the constraints b_1, b_2, or b_3, the objective function will change by z_1, z_2, or z_3, respectively.

Solved Problems

SOLVING THE PRIMAL THROUGH THE DUAL

15.1.   For the following primal problem, (a) formulate the dual. (b) Solve the dual graphically. Then use the dual solution to find the optimal values of (c) the primal objective function and (d) the primal decision variables.

Minimize $c = 40x_1 + 20x_2 + 60x_3$

subject to $2x_1 + 4x_2 + 10x_3 \geq 24$
$$5x_1 + x_2 + 5x_3 \geq 8 \qquad x_1, x_2, x_3 \geq 0$$

(a) The dual is

Maximize $\qquad\qquad\qquad\qquad \Pi = 24z_1 + 8z_2$

subject to $\qquad\qquad\qquad\qquad 2z_1 + 5z_2 \leq 40$

$$4z_1 + z_2 \leq 20$$
$$10z_1 + 5z_2 \leq 60 \qquad z_1, z_2 \geq 0$$

(b) The dual was solved graphically as a primal in Problem 13.9. Converting x_i to z_i, $\bar{z}_1 = 4$, $\bar{z}_2 = 4$, and $\bar{\Pi} = 128$.

(c) With $\bar{\Pi} = 128$, $\bar{c} = 128$.

(d) To find the primal decision variables x_1, x_2, x_3 from the dual decision variables z_1, z_2, first convert the primal (I) and dual (II) inequalities to equations.

$$\text{I.} \quad 2x_1 + 4x_2 + 10x_3 - s_1 = 24 \qquad \text{II.} \quad 2z_1 + 5z_2 + t_1 = 40$$
$$5x_1 + x_2 + 5x_3 - s_2 = 8 \qquad\qquad\quad 4z_1 + z_2 + t_2 = 20$$
$$10z_1 + 5z_2 + t_3 = 60$$

Then substitute $\bar{z}_1 = \bar{z}_2 = 4$ into the dual constraint equations to solve for the slack variables.

$$2(4) + 5(4) + t_1 = 40 \qquad \bar{t}_1 = 12$$
$$4(4) + 4 + t_2 = 20 \qquad \bar{t}_2 = 0$$
$$10(4) + 5(4) + t_3 = 60 \qquad \bar{t}_3 = 0$$

With $\bar{t}_1 \neq 0$, the corresponding primal decision variable $\bar{x}_1$ must equal zero. With $\bar{t}_2 = \bar{t}_3 = 0$, $\bar{x}_2, \bar{x}_3 \neq 0$.

Since the optimal values of the dual decision variables z_1, z_2 do not equal zero, the corresponding primal surplus variables s_1, s_2 must equal zero. Incorporating the knowledge that $\bar{x}_1 = \bar{s}_1 = \bar{s}_2 = 0$ into the primal constraint equations,

$$2(0) + 4x_2 + 10x_3 - 0 = 24 \qquad 5(0) + x_2 + 5x_3 - 0 = 8$$

Solved simultaneously, $\bar{x}_2 = 4$ and $\bar{x}_3 = 0.8$. Thus the primal decision variables are $\bar{x}_1 = 0$, $\bar{x}_2 = 4$, and $\bar{x}_3 = 0.8$.

15.2. Redo Problem 15.1 for the following primal problem:

Minimize $\qquad\qquad\qquad\qquad c = 36x_1 + 30x_2 + 40x_3$

subject to $\qquad\qquad\qquad\qquad 2x_1 + 5x_2 + 8x_3 \geq 40$

$$6x_1 + 3x_2 + 2x_3 \geq 50 \qquad x_1, x_2, x_3 \geq 0$$

(a) Maximize $\qquad\qquad\qquad\qquad \Pi = 40z_1 + 50z_2$

subject to $\qquad\qquad\qquad\qquad 2z_1 + 6z_2 \leq 36$

$$5z_1 + 3z_2 \leq 30$$
$$8z_1 + 2z_2 \leq 40 \qquad z_1, z_2 \geq 0$$

(b) The equivalent of the dual was solved graphically in Problem 13.10: $\bar{z}_1 = 3$, $\bar{z}_2 = 5$, and $\bar{\Pi} = 370$.

(c) With $\bar{\Pi} = 370$, $\bar{c} = 370$.

(d)

$$\text{I.} \quad 2x_1 + 5x_2 + 8x_3 - s_1 = 40 \qquad \text{II.} \quad 2z_1 + 6z_2 + t_1 = 36$$
$$6x_1 + 3x_2 + 2x_3 - s_2 = 50 \qquad\qquad\quad 5z_1 + 3z_2 + t_2 = 30$$
$$8z_1 + 2z_2 + t_3 = 40$$

Substituting $\bar{z}_1 = 3$ and $\bar{z}_2 = 5$ in Π,

$$2(3) + 6(5) + t_1 = 36 \qquad \bar{t}_1 = 0$$
$$5(3) + 3(5) + t_2 = 30 \qquad \bar{t}_2 = 0$$
$$8(3) + 2(5) + t_3 = 40 \qquad \bar{t}_3 = 6$$

With $\bar{t}_1 = \bar{t}_2 = 0$, $\bar{x}_1, \bar{x}_2 \neq 0$. Since $\bar{t}_3 \neq 0$, $\bar{x}_3 = 0$. With $\bar{z}_1, \bar{z}_2 \neq 0$, $\bar{s}_1 = \bar{s}_2 = 0$. Substituting in I,

$$2x_1 + 5x_2 + 8(0) - 0 = 40 \qquad 6x_1 + 3x_2 + 2(0) - 0 = 50$$

Thus, $\bar{x}_1 = 5.42$, $\bar{x}_2 = 5.83$, and $\bar{x}_3 = 0$.

15.3. Redo Problem 15.1, given the following linear programming problem:

Maximize
$$\Pi = 15x_1 + 20x_2 + 24x_3$$

subject to
$$3x_1 + x_2 + 3x_3 \leq 120$$
$$x_1 + 5x_2 + 2x_3 \leq 60 \qquad x_1, x_2, x_3 \geq 0$$

(a) Minimize
$$c = 120z_1 + 60z_2$$

subject to
$$3z_1 + z_2 \geq 15$$
$$z_1 + 5z_2 \geq 20$$
$$3z_1 + 2z_2 \geq 24 \qquad z_1, z_2 \geq 0$$

(b) The equivalent of the dual was solved in Problem 13.14: $\bar{z}_1 = 2$, $\bar{z}_2 = 9$, and $\bar{c} = 780$.

(c) With $\bar{c} = 780$, $\bar{\Pi} = 780$.

(d)
$$\text{I.} \quad 3x_1 + x_2 + 3x_3 + s_1 = 120 \qquad \text{II.} \quad 3z_1 + z_2 - t_1 = 15$$
$$x_1 + 5x_2 + 2x_3 + s_2 = 60 \qquad \qquad z_1 + 5z_2 - t_2 = 20$$
$$3z_1 + 2z_2 - t_3 = 24$$

Substituting $\bar{z}_1 = 2$ and $\bar{z}_2 = 9$ in Π,

$$3(2) + 9 - t_1 = 15 \qquad \bar{t}_1 = 0$$
$$2 + 5(9) - t_2 = 20 \qquad \bar{t}_2 = 27$$
$$3(2) + 2(9) - t_3 = 24 \qquad \bar{t}_3 = 0$$

With $\bar{t}_1 = \bar{t}_3 = 0$, $\bar{x}_1, \bar{x}_3 \neq 0$. Since $\bar{t}_2 \neq 0$, $\bar{x}_2 = 0$. With $\bar{z}_1, \bar{z}_2 \neq 0$, $\bar{s}_1 = \bar{s}_2 = 0$. Substituting in I,

$$3x_1 + 0 + 3x_3 + 0 = 120 \qquad x_1 + 5(0) + 2x_3 + 0 = 60$$

Thus, $\bar{x}_1 = 20$, $\bar{x}_2 = 0$, and $\bar{x}_3 = 20$.

15.4. Redo Problem 15.1, given the linear programming problem below:

Maximize
$$\Pi = 36x_1 + 28x_2 + 32x_3$$

subject to
$$2x_1 + 2x_2 + 8x_3 \leq 3$$
$$3x_1 + 2x_2 + 2x_3 \leq 4 \qquad x_1, x_2, x_3 \geq 0$$

(a) Minimize
$$c = 3z_1 + 4z_2$$

subject to
$$2z_1 + 3z_2 \geq 36$$
$$2z_1 + 2z_2 \geq 28$$
$$8z_1 + 2z_2 \geq 32 \qquad z_1, z_2 \geq 0$$

(b) The equivalent of the dual was solved in Problem 13.15: $\bar{z}_1 = 6$, $\bar{z}_2 = 8$, and $\bar{c} = 50$.

(c) With $\bar{c} = 50$, $\bar{\Pi} = 50$.

(d)
$$\text{I.} \quad 2x_1 + 2x_2 + 8x_3 + s_1 = 3 \qquad \text{II.} \quad 2z_1 + 3z_2 - t_1 = 36$$
$$3x_1 + 2x_2 + 2x_3 + s_2 = 4 \qquad \qquad 2z_1 + 2z_2 - t_2 = 28$$
$$8z_1 + 2z_2 - t_3 = 32$$

Substituting $\bar{z}_1 = 6$ and $\bar{z}_2 = 8$ in Π,

$$2(6) + 3(8) - t_1 = 36 \qquad \bar{t}_1 = 0$$
$$2(6) + 2(8) - t_2 = 28 \qquad \bar{t}_2 = 0$$
$$8(6) + 2(8) - t_3 = 32 \qquad \bar{t}_3 = 32$$

With $\bar{t}_1 = \bar{t}_2 = 0$, $\bar{x}_1, \bar{x}_2 \neq 0$; $\bar{x}_3 = 0$ since $\bar{t}_3 \neq 0$. With $\bar{z}_1, \bar{z}_2 \neq 0$, $\bar{s}_1 = \bar{s}_2 = 0$. Substituting in I,

$$2x_1 + 2x_2 + 8(0) + 0 = 3 \qquad 3x_1 + 2x_2 + 2(0) + 0 = 4$$

Thus, $\bar{x}_1 = 1$, $\bar{x}_2 = \frac{1}{2}$, and $\bar{x}_3 = 0$.

15.5. Use the duals in Problems 15.1 to 15.4 to determine the shadow prices or marginal values (MVs) of the resources in the primal constraints. Use A and B for the resources in constraints 1 and 2, respectively.

The shadow prices of resources A and B in the primal constraints are given by the optimal values of the dual decision variables z_1 and z_2. Thus,

For Problem 15.1, $MV_A = \bar{z}_1 = 4$ and $MV_B = \bar{z}_2 = 4$.
For Problem 15.2, $MV_A = \bar{z}_1 = 3$ and $MV_B = \bar{z}_2 = 5$.
For Problem 15.3, $MV_A = \bar{z}_1 = 2$ and $MV_B = \bar{z}_2 = 9$.
For Problem 15.4, $MV_A = \bar{z}_1 = 6$ and $MV_B = \bar{z}_2 = 8$.

SIMPLEX ALGORITHM AND THE DUAL

15.6. For the following problem, (a) formulate the dual and (b) solve it, using the simplex method. (c) Use the final dual tableau to determine the optimal values of the primal objective function and decision variables.

Maximize
$$\Pi = 5x_1 + 3x_2$$

subject to
$$6x_1 + 2x_2 \leq 36$$
$$5x_1 + 5x_2 \leq 40$$
$$2x_1 + 4x_2 \leq 28 \qquad x_1, x_2 \geq 0$$

(a) Minimize
$$c = 36z_1 + 40z_2 + 28z_3$$

subject to
$$6z_1 + 5z_2 + 2z_3 \geq 5$$
$$2z_1 + 5z_2 + 4z_3 \geq 3 \qquad z_1, z_2, z_3 \geq 0$$

(b) The dual was solved as a primal in Problem 14.5. Converting x_i to z_i and s_i to t_i, the final tableau reads

Final tableau:	z_1	z_2	z_3	t_1	t_2	A_1	A_2	Constant
	1	0	$-\frac{1}{2}$	$-\frac{1}{4}$	$\frac{1}{4}$	$\frac{1}{4}$	$-\frac{1}{4}$	$\frac{1}{2}$
	0	1	1	$\frac{1}{10}$	$-\frac{3}{10}$	$-\frac{1}{10}$	$\frac{3}{10}$	$\frac{2}{5}$
	0	0	-6	$\boxed{-5}$	-3	$-M+5$	$-M+3$	34

(c) The absolute value of the indicators under the dual surplus variables t_1 and t_2 in the final tableau gives the optimal values of the primal decision variables x_1 and x_2. Thus, $\bar{x}_1 = 5$, $\bar{x}_2 = 3$, and $\bar{\Pi} = 34$. Check this answer with Example 1 in Chapter 14, where the primal was solved directly.

15.7. Redo Problem 15.6 for the following problem:

Minimize
$$c = 30x_1 + 50x_2$$

subject to
$$6x_1 + 2x_2 \geq 30$$
$$3x_1 + 2x_2 \geq 24$$
$$5x_1 + 10x_2 \geq 60 \qquad x_1, x_2 \geq 0$$

(a) Maximize
$$\Pi = 30z_1 + 24z_2 + 60z_3$$

subject to
$$6z_1 + 3z_2 + 5z_3 \leq 30$$
$$2z_1 + 2z_2 + 10z_3 \leq 50 \qquad z_1, z_2, z_3 \geq 0$$

(b) The dual was solved as a primal in Problem 14.2. Making the necessary adjustments for variable notation, the final tableau is

Final tableau:

	z_1	z_2	z_3	t_1	t_2	Constant
	$\frac{5}{2}$	1	0	$\frac{1}{2}$	$-\frac{1}{4}$	$\frac{5}{2}$
	$-\frac{3}{10}$	0	1	$-\frac{1}{10}$	$\frac{3}{20}$	$\frac{9}{2}$
	12	0	0	$\boxed{6}$	$\boxed{3}$	330

(c) Thus, $\bar{x}_1 = 6$, $\bar{x}_2 = 3$, and $\bar{c} = 330$. See Problem 13.16, where the primal was solved graphically.

15.8. Redo Problem 15.6 for the following linear programming problem:

Minimize $$c = 20x_1 + 30x_2 + 16x_3$$

subject to
$$2.5x_1 + 3x_2 + x_3 \geq 3$$
$$x_1 + 3x_2 + 2x_3 \geq 4 \qquad x_1, x_2, x_3 \geq 0$$

(a) Maximize $$\Pi = 3z_1 + 4z_2$$

subject to
$$2.5z_1 + z_2 \leq 20$$
$$3z_1 + 3z_2 \leq 30$$
$$z_1 + 2z_2 \leq 16 \qquad z_1, z_2 \geq 0$$

(b) The dual was solved as a primal in Problem 14.1. Making the necessary adjustments to accommodate dual notation, the final tableau reads

Final tableau:

	z_1	z_2	t_1	t_2	t_3	Constant
	0	0	1	$-\frac{4}{3}$	$\frac{3}{2}$	4
	1	0	0	$\frac{2}{3}$	-1	4
	0	1	0	$-\frac{1}{3}$	1	6
	0	0	$\boxed{0}$	$\boxed{\frac{2}{3}}$	$\boxed{1}$	36

(c) Thus, $\bar{x}_1 = 0$, $\bar{x}_2 = \frac{2}{3}$, $\bar{x}_3 = 1$, and $\bar{c} = 36$. See Example 6 for an earlier approach to this problem.

15.9. Redo Problem 15.6 for the following problem:

Maximize $$\Pi = 36x_1 + 28x_2 + 32x_3$$

subject to
$$2x_1 + 2x_2 + 8x_3 \leq 60$$
$$3x_1 + 2x_2 + 2x_3 \leq 80 \qquad x_1, x_2, x_3 \geq 0$$

(a) Minimize $$c = 60z_1 + 80z_2$$

subject to
$$2z_1 + 3z_2 \geq 36$$
$$2z_1 + 2z_2 \geq 28$$
$$8z_1 + 2z_2 \geq 32 \qquad z_1, z_2 \geq 0$$

(b) The dual was solved as a primal in Problem 14.4. The adjusted final tableau reads

Final tableau:	z_1	z_2	t_1	t_2	t_3	A_1	A_2	A_3	Constant
	0	1	-1	1	0	1	-1	0	8
	0	0	6	-10	1	-6	10	-1	32
	1	0	1	$-\frac{3}{2}$	0	-1	$\frac{3}{2}$	0	6
	0	0	$\boxed{-20}$	$\boxed{-10}$	$\boxed{0}$	$-M + 20$	$-M + 10$	$-M$	1000

(c) Thus, $\bar{x}_1 = 20$, $\bar{x}_2 = 10$, $\bar{x}_3 = 0$, and $\bar{\Pi} = 1000$.

DEGENERACY

15.10. A linear program is said to *degenerate* if any of the variables *in the basis* assumes a value of zero. In effect, it means that there is linear dependence between column vectors, precluding a unique optimal solution. For the following problem, (*a*) formulate the dual, (*b*) solve it by the simplex method, and (*c*) determine the optimal primal values.

Minimize $$c = 4x_1 + 2x_2 \qquad\qquad (15.5)$$

subject to
$$4x_1 + x_2 \geq 20$$
$$2x_1 + x_2 \geq 14$$
$$x_1 + 6x_2 \geq 18 \qquad x_1, x_2 \geq 0$$

(*a*)   Maximize $$\Pi = 20z_1 + 14z_2 + 18z_3 \qquad\qquad (15.6)$$

subject to
$$4z_1 + 2z_2 + z_3 \leq 4$$
$$z_1 + z_2 + 6z_3 \leq 2 \qquad z_1, z_2, z_3 \geq 0$$

(*b*)   Express the constraints as equations in matrix form.

$$\begin{bmatrix} 4 & 2 & 1 & 1 & 0 \\ 1 & 1 & 6 & 0 & 1 \end{bmatrix} \begin{bmatrix} z_1 \\ z_2 \\ z_3 \\ t_1 \\ t_2 \end{bmatrix} = \begin{bmatrix} 4 \\ 2 \end{bmatrix} \qquad\qquad (15.7)$$

Set up the initial tableau.

Initial tableau:

z_1	z_2	z_3	t_1	t_2	Constant
④	2	1	1	0	4
1	1	6	0	1	2
-20	-14	-18	0	0	0
↑					

Pivot by first multiplying row 1 by $\frac{1}{4}$, then subtracting row 1 from row 2, and adding 20 times row 1 to row 3.

Second tableau:

z_1	z_2	z_3	t_1	t_2	Constant
1	$\frac{1}{2}$	$\frac{1}{4}$	$\frac{1}{4}$	0	1
0	$\frac{1}{2}$	$\left(\frac{23}{4}\right)$	$-\frac{1}{4}$	1	1
0	-4	-13	5	0	20
		↑			

Pivot again. Multiply row 2 by $\frac{4}{23}$; then subtract $\frac{1}{4}$ times row 2 from row 1, and add 13 times row 2 to row 3.

Third tableau:

z_1	z_2	z_3	t_1	t_2	Constant
1	$\left(\frac{11}{23}\right)$	0	$\frac{6}{23}$	$-\frac{1}{23}$	$\frac{22}{23}$
0	$\left(\frac{2}{23}\right)$	1	$-\frac{1}{23}$	$\frac{4}{23}$	$\frac{4}{23}$
0	$-\frac{66}{23}$	0	$\frac{102}{23}$	$\frac{52}{23}$	$\frac{512}{23}$
	↑				

Pivot a third time. Here the displacement ratios are equal:

$$\frac{22}{23}\left(\frac{23}{11}\right) = 2 = \frac{4}{23}\left(\frac{23}{2}\right)$$

When two or more displacement ratios are equal, the linear program will degenerate; i.e., not all the variables in the basis will assume nonzero values. In the event of equal displacement ratios, either row in which they occur may be selected as the pivot row, but the one which will help form an identity matrix to the left of the tableau is often most useful. Here, selecting $\left(\frac{2}{23}\right)$ as the pivot element will generate an identity matrix in the first two columns. Then, multiply row 2 by $\frac{23}{2}$; subtract $\frac{11}{23}$ times row 2 from row 1, and add $\frac{66}{23}$ times row 2 to row 3.

Final tableau:

z_1	z_2	z_3	t_1	t_2	Constant
1	0	$-\frac{11}{2}$	$\frac{1}{2}$	-1	0
0	1	$\frac{23}{2}$	$-\frac{1}{2}$	2	2
0	0	33	3	8	28

The final tableau indicates that $\bar{z}_1 = 0$, $\bar{z}_2 = 2$, $\bar{z}_3 = 0$, $\bar{t}_1 = 0$, $\bar{t}_2 = 0$, and $\bar{\Pi} = 28$, which checks with the initial dual program in (15.6):

$$\Pi = 20(0) + 14(2) + 18(0) = 28$$

Converting to the primal, it indicates that $\bar{x}_1 = 3$, $\bar{x}_2 = 8$, and $\bar{c} = 28$, which also checks with (15.5): $c = 4(3) + 2(8) = 28$.

But since one of the variables *in the basis* of the final tableau has a zero value, there is linear dependence and multiple optimal solutions exist. Note the linear dependence between column 2 of the coefficient matrix and the column vector of constants in (15.7). See Problem 14.7 where the primal was solved directly, where $\bar{x}_1 = 6$, $\bar{x}_2 = 2$, and $\bar{c} = 28$; this also checks with (15.5). For a graphic solution, see Problem 13.19.

Chapter 16

Integral Calculus:
The Indefinite Integral

16.1 INTEGRATION

Chapters 3 to 6 were devoted to differential calculus, which measures the rate of change of functions. Differentiation, we learned, is the process of finding the derivative $F'(x)$ of a function $F(x)$. Frequently in economics, however, we know the rate of change of a function $F'(x)$ and want to find the original function. Reversing the process of differentiation and finding the original function from the derivative is called *integration*, or *antidifferentiation*. The original function $F(x)$ is called the *integral*, or *antiderivative*, of $F'(x)$.

EXAMPLE 1. Letting $f(x) = F'(x)$ for simplicity, the antiderivative of $f(x)$ is expressed mathematically as

$$\int f(x)\,dx = F(x) + c$$

Here the left-hand side of the equation is read, "the *indefinite integral* of f of x with respect to x." The symbol $\int$ is an *integral sign*, $f(x)$ is the *integrand*, and c is the *constant of integration*, which is explained in Example 3.

16.2 RULES OF INTEGRATION

The following rules of integration are obtained by reversing the corresponding rules of differentiation. Their accuracy is easily checked, since the derivative of the integral must equal the integrand. Each rule is illustrated in Example 2 and Problems 16.1 to 16.6.

Rule 1. The integral of a constant k is

$$\int k\,dx = kx + c$$

Rule 2. The integral of 1, written simply as dx, not 1 dx, is

$$\int dx = x + c$$

Rule 3. The integral of a power function x^n, where $n \neq -1$, is given by the *power rule*:

$$\int x^n\,dx = \frac{1}{n+1}\,x^{n+1} + c \qquad n \neq -1$$

Rule 4. The integral of x^{-1} (or $1/x$) is

$$\int x^{-1}\,dx = \ln x + c \qquad x > 0$$

The condition $x > 0$ is added because only positive numbers have logarithms. For negative numbers,

$$\int x^{-1}\,dx = \ln|x| + c \qquad x \neq 0$$

Rule 5. The integral of an exponential function is

$$\int a^{kx}\, dx = \frac{a^{kx}}{k \ln a} + c$$

Rule 6. The integral of a natural exponential function is

$$\int e^{kx}\, dx = \frac{e^{kx}}{k} + c \qquad \text{since} \qquad \ln e = 1$$

Rule 7. The integral of a constant times a function equals the constant times the integral of the function.

$$\int k f(x)\, dx = k \int f(x)\, dx$$

Rule 8. The integral of the sum or difference of two or more functions equals the sum or difference of their integrals.

$$\int [f(x) + g(x)]\, dx = \int f(x)\, dx + \int g(x)\, dx$$

Rule 9. The integral of the negative of a function equals the negative of the integral of that function.

$$\int -f(x)\, dx = -\int f(x)\, dx$$

EXAMPLE 2. The rules of integration are illustrated below. Check each answer on your own by making sure that the derivative of the integral equals the integrand.

$$(i) \quad \int 3\, dx = 3x + c \qquad\qquad \text{(Rule 1)}$$

$$(ii) \quad \int x^2\, dx = \frac{1}{2+1} x^{2+1} + c = \frac{1}{3} x^3 + c \qquad \text{(Rule 3)}$$

$$(iii) \quad \int 5x^4\, dx = 5 \int x^4\, dx \qquad\qquad \text{(Rule 7)}$$

$$= 5\left(\frac{1}{5} x^5 + c_1\right) \qquad\qquad \text{(Rule 3)}$$

$$= x^5 + c$$

where c_1 and c are arbitrary constants and $5c_1 = c$. Since c is an arbitrary constant, it can be ignored in the preliminary calculation and included only in the final solution.

$$(iv) \quad \int (3x^3 - x + 1)\, dx = 3 \int x^3\, dx - \int x\, dx + \int dx \qquad \text{(Rules 7, 8, and 9)}$$

$$= 3(\tfrac{1}{4} x^4) - \tfrac{1}{2} x^2 + x + c \qquad \text{(Rules 2 and 3)}$$

$$= \tfrac{3}{4} x^4 - \tfrac{1}{2} x^2 + x + c$$

$$(v) \quad \int 3x^{-1}\, dx = 3 \int x^{-1}\, dx \qquad\qquad \text{(Rule 7)}$$

$$= 3 \ln |x| + c \qquad\qquad \text{(Rule 4)}$$

$$(vi) \quad \int 2^{3x}\, dx = \frac{2^{3x}}{3 \ln 2} + c \qquad\qquad \text{(Rule 5)}$$

$$(vii) \quad \int 9e^{-3x}\, dx = \frac{9e^{-3x}}{-3} + c \qquad\qquad \text{(Rule 6)}$$

$$= -3e^{-3x} + c$$

EXAMPLE 3. Functions which differ by only a constant have the same derivative. The function $F(x) = 2x + k$ has the same derivative, $F'(x) = f(x) = 2$, for any infinite number of possible values for k. If the process is reversed, it is clear that $\int 2\, dx$ must be the antiderivative or indefinite integral for an infinite number of functions differing from each other by only a constant. The constant of integration c thus represents the value of any constant which was part of the primitive function but precluded from the derivative by the rules of differentiation.

The graph of an indefinite integral $\int f(x)\, dx = F(x) + c$, where c is unspecified, is a family of curves parallel in the sense that the slope of the tangent to any of them at x is $f(x)$. Specifying c specifies the curve; changing c shifts the curve. This is illustrated in Fig. 16-1 for the indefinite integral $\int 2\, dx = 2x + c$ where $c = -7, -3, 1,$ and 5, respectively. If $c = 0$, the curve begins at the origin.

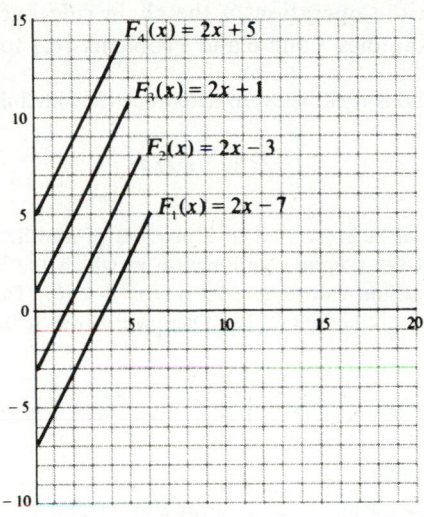

Fig. 16-1

16.3   INITIAL CONDITIONS AND BOUNDARY CONDITIONS

In many problems an *initial condition* ($y = y_0$ when $x = 0$) or a *boundary condition* ($y = y_0$ when $x = x_0$) is given which uniquely determines the constant of integration. By permitting a unique determination of c, the initial or boundary condition singles out a specific curve from the family of curves illustrated in Example 3 and Problems 16.3 to 16.5.

EXAMPLE 4. Given the boundary condition $y = 11$ when $x = 3$, the integral $y = \int 2\, dx$ is evaluated as follows:

$$y = \int 2\, dx = 2x + c$$

Substituting $y = 11$ when $x = 3$,

$$11 = 2(3) + c \qquad c = 5$$

Therefore, $y = 2x + 5$. Note that even though c is specified, $\int 2\, dx$ remains an *indefinite* integral because x is unspecified. Thus, the integral $2x + 5$ can assume an infinite number of possible values.

16.4   INTEGRATION BY SUBSTITUTION

Integration of a product or quotient of two differentiable functions of x, such as

$$\int 12x^2(x^3 + 2)\, dx$$

cannot be done directly by using the simple rules above. However, if the integrand can be expressed as a *constant* multiple of another function u and its derivative du/dx, integration by substitution is possible. By expressing the integrand $f(x)$ as a function of u and its derivative du/dx and integrating with respect to x,

$$\int f(x) \, dx = \int \left(u \frac{du}{dx} \right) dx$$

$$\int f(x) \, dx = \int u \, du = F(u) + c$$

The substitution method reverses the operation of the chain rule and the generalized power function rule in differential calculus. See Examples 5 and 6 and Problems 16.7 to 16.18.

EXAMPLE 5.   The substitution method is used below to determine the indefinite integral

$$\int 12x^2(x^3 + 2) \, dx$$

1. Be sure that the integrand can be converted to a product of another function u and its derivative du/dx times a *constant* multiple. (*a*) Let u equal the function in which the independent variable is raised to the higher power in terms of absolute value; here let $u = x^3 + 2$. (*b*) Take the derivative of u; $du/dx = 3x^2$. (*c*) Solve algebraically for dx; $dx = du/3x^2$. (*d*) Then substitute u for $x^3 + 2$ and $du/3x^2$ for dx in the original integrand:

$$\int 12x^2(x^3 + 2) \, dx = \int 12x^2 \cdot u \cdot \frac{du}{3x^2} = \int 4u \, du = 4 \int u \, du$$

   where 4 is a *constant* multiple of u.

2. Integrate with respect to u, using Rule 3 and ignoring c in the first step of the calculation.

$$4 \int u \, du = 4(\tfrac{1}{2}u^2) = 2u^2 + c$$

3. Convert back to the terms of the original problem by substituting $x^3 + 2$ for u.

$$\int 12x^2(x^3 + 2) \, dx = 2u^2 + c = 2(x^3 + 2)^2 + c$$

4. Check the answer by differentiating with the generalized power function rule or chain rule.

$$\frac{d}{dx} [2(x^3 + 2)^2 + c] = 4(x^3 + 2)(3x^2) = 12x^2(x^3 + 2)$$

   See also Problems 16.7 to 16.18.

EXAMPLE 6.   Determine the integral $\int 4x(x + 1)^3 \, dx$.
    Let $u = x + 1$. Then $du/dx = 1$ and $dx = du/1 = du$. Substitute $u = x + 1$ and $dx = du$ in the original integrand.

$$\int 4x(x + 1)^3 \, dx = \int 4xu^3 \, du = 4 \int xu^3 \, du$$

Since x is a *variable* multiple which cannot be factored out, the original integrand cannot be transformed to a *constant* multiple of $u \, du/dx$. Hence the substitution method is ineffectual. Integration by parts (Section 16.5) may be helpful.

16.5   INTEGRATION BY PARTS

If an integrand is a product or quotient of differentiable functions of x and cannot be expressed as a constant multiple of $u \, du/dx$, integration by parts is frequently useful. The method is derived by reversing the process of differentiating a product. From the product rule in Section 3.7.5,

$$\frac{d}{dx}\,[f(x)\,g(x)] = f(x)\,g'(x) + g(x)f'(x)$$

Taking the integral of the derivative gives

$$f(x)\,g(x) = \int f(x)\,g'(x)\,dx + \int g(x)f'(x)\,dx$$

Then solving algebraically for the first integral on the right-hand side,

$$\int f(x)\,g'(x)\,dx = f(x)\,g(x) - \int g(x)f'(x)\,dx \qquad (16.1)$$

See Examples 7 and 8 and Problems 16.19 to 16.24.

For more complicated functions, *integration tables* are generally used. Integration tables provide formulas for the integrals of as many as 500 different functions, and they can be found in mathematical handbooks.

EXAMPLE 7.   Integration by parts is used below to determine

$$\int 4x(x + 1)^3\,dx$$

1. Separate the integrand into two parts amenable to the formula in (16.1). As a general rule, consider first the simpler function for $f(x)$ and the more complicated function for $g'(x)$. By letting $f(x) = 4x$ and $g'(x) = (x + 1)^3$, then $f'(x) = 4$ and $g(x) = \int (x + 1)^3\,dx$, which can be integrated by using the simple power rule (Rule 3):

$$g(x) = \int (x + 1)^3\,dx = \tfrac{1}{4}(x + 1)^4 + c_1$$

2. Substitute the values for $f(x), f'(x)$, and $g(x)$ in (16.1); and note that $g'(x)$ is not used in the formula.

$$\int 4x(x + 1)^3\,dx = f(x) \cdot g(x) - \int [g(x) \cdot f'(x)]\,dx$$

$$= 4x\,[\tfrac{1}{4}(x + 1)^4 + c_1] - \int [\tfrac{1}{4}(x + 1)^4 + c_1](4)\,dx$$

$$= x\,(x + 1)^4 + 4c_1 x - \int [(x + 1)^4 + 4c_1]\,dx$$

3. Use Rule 3 to compute the final integral and substitute.

$$\int 4x(x + 1)^3\,dx = x(x + 1)^4 + 4c_1 x - \tfrac{1}{5}(x + 1)^5 - 4c_1 x + c$$

$$= x(x + 1)^4 - \tfrac{1}{5}(x + 1)^5 + c$$

   Note that the c_1 term does not appear in the final solution. Since this is common to integration by parts, c_1 will henceforth be assumed equal to 0 and not formally included in future problem solving.

4. Check the answer by letting $y(x) = x(x + 1)^4 - \tfrac{1}{5}(x + 1)^5 + c$ and using the product and generalized power function rules.

$$y'(x) = [x \cdot 4(x + 1)^3 + (x + 1)^4 \cdot 1] - (x + 1)^4 = 4x(x + 1)^3$$

EXAMPLE 8.   The integral $\int 2xe^x\,dx$ is determined as follows:

Let $f(x) = 2x$ and $g'(x) = e^x$; then $f'(x) = 2$, and by Rule 6, $g(x) = \int e^x\,dx = e^x$. Substitute in (16.1).

$$\int 2xe^x\,dx = f(x) \cdot g(x) - \int g(x) \cdot f'(x)\,dx$$

$$= 2x \cdot e^x - \int e^x \cdot 2\,dx = 2xe^x - 2\int e^x\,dx$$

Apply Rule 6 again and remember the constant of integration.

$$\int 2xe^x \, dx = 2xe^x - 2e^x + c$$

Then let $y(x) = 2xe^x - 2e^x + c$ and check the answer.

$$y'(x) = 2x \cdot e^x + e^x \cdot 2 - 2e^x = 2xe^x$$

16.6 ECONOMIC APPLICATIONS

Net investment I is defined as the rate of change in capital stock formation K over time t. If the process of capital formation is continuous over time, $I(t) = dK(t)/dt = K'(t)$. From the rate of investment, the level of capital stock can be estimated. Capital stock is the integral with respect to time of net investment:

$$K_t = \int I(t) \, dt = K(t) + c = K(t) + K_0$$

where $c = $ the initial capital stock K_0.

Similarly, the integral can be used to estimate total cost from marginal cost. Since marginal cost is the change in total cost from an incremental change in output, $\text{MC} = d\text{TC}/dQ$, and only variable costs change with the level of output

$$\text{TC} = \int \text{MC} \, dQ = \text{VC} + c = \text{VC} + \text{FC}$$

since $c = $ the fixed or initial cost FC. Economic analysis which traces the time path of variables or attempts to determine whether variables will converge toward equilibrium over time is called *dynamics*. For similar applications, see Example 9 and Problems 16.25 to 16.35.

EXAMPLE 9. The rate of net investment is given by $I(t) = 140t^{3/4}$, and the initial stock of capital at $t = 0$ is 150. Determining the function for capital K, the time path $K(t)$,

$$K = \int 140t^{3/4} \, dt = 140 \int t^{3/4} \, dt$$

By the power rule,

$$K = 140(\tfrac{4}{7}t^{7/4}) + c = 80t^{7/4} + c$$

But $c = K_0 = 150$. Therefore, $K = 80t^{7/4} + 150$.

Solved Problems

INDEFINITE INTEGRALS

16.1. Determine the following integrals. Check the answers on your own by making sure that the derivative of the integral equals the integrand.

(a) $\displaystyle\int 3.5\,dx$

$$\int 3.5\,dx = 3.5x + c \qquad\qquad\text{(Rule 1)}$$

(b) $\displaystyle\int -\tfrac{1}{2}\,dx$

$$\int -\tfrac{1}{2}\,dx = -\int \tfrac{1}{2}\,dx = -\tfrac{1}{2}x + c \qquad\qquad\text{(Rules 1 and 9)}$$

(c) $\displaystyle\int dx$

$$\int dx = x + c \qquad\qquad\text{(Rule 2)}$$

(d) $\displaystyle\int x^5\,dx$

$$\int x^5\,dx = \tfrac{1}{6}x^6 + c \qquad\qquad\text{(Rule 3)}$$

(e) $\displaystyle\int 4x^3\,dx$

$$\int 4x^3\,dx = 4\int x^3\,dx \qquad\qquad\text{(Rule 7)}$$
$$= 4(\tfrac{1}{4}x^4) + c = x^4 + c \qquad\qquad\text{(Rule 3)}$$

(f) $\displaystyle\int x^{2/3}\,dx$

$$\int x^{2/3}\,dx = \tfrac{3}{5}x^{5/3} + c \qquad\qquad\text{(Rule 3)}$$

(g) $\displaystyle\int x^{-1/5}\,dx$

$$\int x^{-1/5}\,dx = \tfrac{5}{4}x^{4/5} + c \qquad\qquad\text{(Rule 3)}$$

(h) $\displaystyle\int 4x^{-2}\,dx$

$$\int 4x^{-2}\,dx = -4x^{-1} + c = -\frac{4}{x} + c \qquad\qquad\text{(Rule 3)}$$

(i) $\displaystyle\int x^{-5/2}\,dx$

$$\int x^{-5/2}\,dx = -\frac{2}{3}x^{-3/2} + c = \frac{-2}{3\sqrt{x^3}} + c \qquad\qquad\text{(Rule 3)}$$

16.2. Redo Problem 16.1 for each of the following:

(a) $\displaystyle\int \frac{dx}{x}$

$$\int \frac{dx}{x} = \int \frac{1}{x}\,dx = \ln|x| + c \qquad\qquad\text{(Rule 4)}$$

(b) $\displaystyle\int 5x^{-1}\,dx$

$$\int 5x^{-1}\,dx = 5\ln|x| + c \qquad\qquad \text{(Rules 7 and 4)}$$

(c) $\displaystyle\int \frac{1}{3x}\,dx$

$$\int \frac{1}{3x}\,dx = \frac{1}{3}\int \frac{1}{x}\,dx = \frac{1}{3}\ln|x| + c \qquad\qquad \text{(Rules 7 and 4)}$$

(d) $\displaystyle\int \sqrt{x}\,dx$

$$\int \sqrt{x}\,dx = \int x^{1/2}\,dx = \tfrac{2}{3}x^{3/2} + c \qquad\qquad \text{(Rule 3)}$$

(e) $\displaystyle\int \frac{dx}{x^4}$

$$\int \frac{dx}{x^4} = \int x^{-4}\,dx = -\frac{1}{3}x^{-3} + c \qquad\qquad \text{(Rule 3)}$$

(f) $\displaystyle\int \frac{dx}{\sqrt[3]{x}}$

$$\int \frac{dx}{\sqrt[3]{x}} = \int x^{-1/3}\,dx = \frac{3}{2}x^{2/3} + c \qquad\qquad \text{(Rule 3)}$$

(g) $\displaystyle\int (5x^3 + 2x^2 + 3x)\,dx$

$$\int (5x^3 + 2x^2 + 3x)\,dx = 5\int x^3\,dx + 2\int x^2\,dx + 3\int x\,dx \qquad \text{(Rules 7 and 8)}$$
$$= 5(\tfrac{1}{4}x^4) + 2(\tfrac{1}{3}x^3) + 3(\tfrac{1}{2}x^2) + c \qquad \text{(Rule 3)}$$
$$= \tfrac{5}{4}x^4 + \tfrac{2}{3}x^3 + \tfrac{3}{2}x^2 + c$$

(h) $\displaystyle\int (2x^6 - 3x^4)\,dx$

$$\int (2x^6 - 3x^4)\,dx = \tfrac{2}{7}x^7 - \tfrac{3}{5}x^5 + c \qquad\qquad \text{(Rules 3, 7, 8, and 9)}$$

16.3. Find the integral for $y = \int (x^{1/2} + 3x^{-1/2})\,dx$, given the initial condition $y = 0$ when $x = 0$.

$$y = \int (x^{1/2} + 3x^{-1/2})\,dx = \tfrac{2}{3}x^{3/2} + 6x^{1/2} + c$$

Substituting the initial condition $y = 0$ when $x = 0$ above, $c = 0$. Hence, $y = \tfrac{2}{3}x^{3/2} + 6x^{1/2}$.

16.4. Find the integral for $y = \int (2x^5 - 3x^{-1/4})\,dx$, given the initial condition $y = 6$ when $x = 0$.

$$y = \int (2x^5 - 3x^{-1/4})\,dx = \tfrac{1}{3}x^6 - 4x^{3/4} + c$$

Substituting $y = 6$ and $x = 0$, $c = 6$. Thus, $y = \tfrac{1}{3}x^6 - 4x^{3/4} + 6$.

16.5. Find the integral for $y = \int (10x^4 - 3)\, dx$, given the boundary condition $y = 21$ when $x = 1$.

$$y = \int (10x^4 - 3)\, dx = 2x^5 - 3x + c$$

Substituting $y = 21$ and $x = 1$, $21 = 2(1)^5 - 3(1) + c$ $c = 22$

$$y = 2x^5 - 3x + 22$$

16.6. Redo Problem 16.1 for each of the following:

(a) $\displaystyle\int 2^{4x}\, dx$

$$\int 2^{4x}\, dx = \frac{2^{4x}}{4\ln 2} + c \quad \text{(Rule 5)}$$

(b) $\displaystyle\int 8^x\, dx$

$$\int 8^x\, dx = \frac{8^x}{\ln 8} + c$$

(c) $\displaystyle\int e^{5x}\, dx$

$$\int e^{5x}\, dx = \frac{e^{5x}}{5} + c \quad \text{(Rule 6)}$$

$$= \tfrac{1}{5}e^{5x} + c$$

(d) $\displaystyle\int 16e^{-4x}\, dx$

$$\int 16e^{-4x}\, dx = \frac{16e^{-4x}}{-4} + c = -4e^{-4x} + c$$

(e) $\displaystyle\int (6e^{3x} - 8e^{-2x})\, dx$

$$\int (6e^{3x} - 8e^{-2x})\, dx = \frac{6e^{3x}}{3} - \frac{8e^{-2x}}{-2} + c = 2e^{3x} + 4e^{-2x} + c$$

INTEGRATION BY SUBSTITUTION

16.7. Determine the following integral, using the substitution method. Check the answer on your own. Given $\int 10x(x^2 + 3)^4\, dx$.

Let $u = x^2 + 3$. Then $du/dx = 2x$ and $dx = du/2x$. Substituting in the original integrand to reduce it to a function of $u\, du/dx$,

$$\int 10x(x^2 + 3)^4\, dx = \int 10xu^4\, \frac{du}{2x} = 5\int u^4\, du$$

Integrating by the power rule, $5\displaystyle\int u^4\, du = 5(\tfrac{1}{5}u^5) = u^5 + c$

Substituting $u = x^2 + 3$, $\int 10x(x^2 + 3)^4\, dx = u^5 + c = (x^2 + 3)^5 + c$

16.8. Redo Problem 16.7, given $\int x^4(2x^5 - 5)^4\, dx$.

Let $u = 2x^5 - 5$, $du/dx = 10x^4$, and $dx = du/10x^4$. Substituting in the original integrand,

$$\int x^4(2x^5 - 5)^4\, dx = \int x^4 u^4\, \frac{du}{10x^4} = \frac{1}{10}\int u^4\, du$$

Integrating,
$$\tfrac{1}{10}\int u^4\,du = \tfrac{1}{10}\left(\tfrac{1}{5}u^5\right) = \tfrac{1}{50}u^5 + c$$

Substituting,
$$\int x^4(2x^5 - 5)^4\,dx = \tfrac{1}{50}u^5 + c = \tfrac{1}{50}(2x^5 - 5)^5 + c$$

16.9. Redo Problem 16.7, given $\int (x - 9)^{7/4}\,dx$.

Let $u = x - 9$. Then $du/dx = 1$ and $dx = du$. Substituting,
$$\int (x - 9)^{7/4}\,dx = \int u^{7/4}\,du$$

Integrating,
$$\int u^{7/4}\,du = \tfrac{4}{11}u^{11/4} + c$$

Substituting,
$$\int (x - 9)^{7/4}\,dx = \tfrac{4}{11}(x - 9)^{11/4} + c$$

Whenever $du/dx = 1$, the power rule can be used immediately for integration by substitution.

16.10. Redo Problem 16.7, given $\int (6x - 11)^{-5}\,dx$.

Let $u = 6x - 11$. Then $du/dx = 6$ and $dx = du/6$. Substituting,
$$\int (6x - 11)^{-5}\,dx = \int u^{-5}\frac{du}{6} = \frac{1}{6}\int u^{-5}\,du$$

Integrating,
$$\frac{1}{6}\int u^{-5}\,du = \frac{1}{6}\left(\frac{1}{-4}u^{-4}\right) = -\frac{1}{24}u^{-4} + c$$

Substituting,
$$\int (6x - 11)^{-5}\,dx = -\tfrac{1}{24}(6x - 11)^{-4} + c$$

Notice that here $du/dx = 6 \neq 1$, and the power rule cannot be used directly.

16.11. Redo Problem 16.7, given
$$\int \frac{x^2}{(4x^3 + 7)^2}\,dx$$

$$\int \frac{x^2}{(4x^3 + 7)^2}\,dx = \int x^2(4x^3 + 7)^{-2}\,dx$$

Let $u = 4x^3 + 7$, $du/dx = 12x^2$, and $dx = du/12x^2$. Substituting,
$$\int x^2 u^{-2}\frac{du}{12x^2} = \frac{1}{12}\int u^{-2}\,du$$

Integrating,
$$\tfrac{1}{12}\int u^{-2}\,du = -\tfrac{1}{12}u^{-1} + c$$

Substituting,
$$\int \frac{x^2}{(4x^3 + 7)^2}\,dx = -\frac{1}{12(4x^3 + 7)} + c$$

16.12. Redo Problem 16.7, given
$$\int \frac{6x^2 + 4x + 10}{(x^3 + x^2 + 5x)^3}\,dx$$

Let $u = x^3 + x^2 + 5x$. Then $du/dx = 3x^2 + 2x + 5$ and $dx = du/(3x^2 + 2x + 5)$. Substituting,

$$\int (6x^2 + 4x + 10)u^{-3} \frac{du}{3x^2 + 2x + 5} = 2 \int u^{-3}\, du$$

Integrating,

$$2 \int u^{-3}\, du = -u^{-2} + c$$

Substituting,

$$\int \frac{6x^2 + 4x + 10}{(x^3 + x^2 + 5x)^3}\, dx = -\frac{1}{(x^3 + x^2 + 5x)^2} + c$$

16.13. Redo Problem 16.7, given

$$\int \frac{dx}{9x - 5}$$

$$\int \frac{dx}{9x - 5} = \int (9x - 5)^{-1}\, dx$$

Let $u = 9x - 5$, $du/dx = 9$, and $dx = du/9$. Substituting,

$$\int u^{-1} \frac{du}{9} = \frac{1}{9} \int u^{-1}\, du$$

Integrating with Rule 4, $\frac{1}{9} \int u^{-1}\, du = \frac{1}{9} \ln|u| + c$. Since u may be $\gtrless 0$, and only positive numbers have logs, always use the absolute value of u. See Rule 4. Substituting,

$$\int \frac{dx}{9x - 5} = \frac{1}{9} \ln|9x - 5| + c$$

16.14. Redo Problem 16.7, given

$$\int \frac{3x^2 + 2}{4x^3 + 8x}\, dx$$

Let $u = 4x^3 + 8x$, $du/dx = 12x^2 + 8$, and $dx = du/(12x^2 + 8)$. Substituting,

$$\int (3x^2 + 2)u^{-1} \frac{du}{12x^2 + 8} = \frac{1}{4} \int u^{-1}\, du$$

Integrating,

$$\frac{1}{4} \int u^{-1}\, du = \frac{1}{4} \ln|u| + c$$

Substituting,

$$\int \frac{3x^2 + 2}{4x^3 + 8x}\, dx = \frac{1}{4} \ln|4x^3 + 8x| + c$$

16.15. Use the substitution method to find the integral for $\int x^3 e^{x^4}\, dx$. Check your answer.

Let $u = x^4$. Then $du/dx = 4x^3$ and $dx = du/4x^3$. Substituting, and noting that u is now an exponent,

$$\int x^3 e^u \frac{du}{4x^3} = \frac{1}{4} \int e^u\, du$$

Integrating with Rule 6,

$$\frac{1}{4} \int e^u\, du = \frac{1}{4} e^u + c$$

Substituting,

$$\int x^3 e^{x^4}\, dx = \frac{1}{4} e^{x^4} + c$$

16.16. Redo Problem 16.15, given $\int 24xe^{3x^2}\, dx$.

Let $u = 3x^2$, $du/dx = 6x$, and $dx = du/6x$. Substituting,

$$\int 24xe^u\, \frac{du}{6x} = 4 \int e^u\, du$$

Integrating,

$$4 \int e^u\, du = 4e^u + c$$

Substituting,

$$\int 24xe^{3x^2}\, dx = 4e^{3x^2} + c$$

16.17. Redo Problem 16.15, given $\int 14e^{2x+7}\, dx$.

Let $u = 2x + 7$; then $du/dx = 2$ and $dx = du/2$. Substituting,

$$\int 14e^u\, \frac{du}{2} = 7 \int e^u\, du = 7e^u + c$$

Substituting,

$$\int 14e^{2x+7}\, dx = 7e^{2x+7} + c$$

16.18. Redo Problem 16.15, given $\int 5xe^{5x^2+3}\, dx$.

Let $u = 5x^2 + 3$, $du/dx = 10x$, and $dx = du/10x$. Substituting,

$$\int 5xe^u\, \frac{du}{10x} = \frac{1}{2} \int e^u\, du$$

Integrating,

$$\tfrac{1}{2} \int e^u\, du = \tfrac{1}{2}e^u + c$$

Substituting,

$$\int 5xe^{5x^2+3}\, dx = \tfrac{1}{2}e^{5x^2+3} + c$$

INTEGRATION BY PARTS

16.19. Use integration by parts to evaluate the following integral. Keep in the habit of checking your answers. Given $\int 15x(x + 4)^{3/2}\, dx$.

Let $f(x) = 15x$, then $f'(x) = 15$. Let $g'(x) = (x + 4)^{3/2}$, then $g(x) = \int (x + 4)^{3/2}\, dx = \tfrac{2}{5}(x + 4)^{5/2}$. Substituting in (16.1),

$$\int 15x(x + 4)^{3/2}\, dx = f(x)\, g(x) - \int g(x) f'(x)\, dx$$

$$= 15x\, [\tfrac{2}{5}(x + 4)^{5/2}] - \int \tfrac{2}{5}(x + 4)^{5/2} 15\, dx = 6x(x + 4)^{5/2} - 6 \int (x + 4)^{5/2}\, dx$$

Evaluating the remaining integral,

$$\int 15x(x + 4)^{3/2}\, dx = 6x(x + 4)^{5/2} - \tfrac{12}{7}(x + 4)^{7/2} + c$$

16.20. Redo Problem 16.19, given

$$\int \frac{2x}{(x - 8)^3}\, dx$$

Let $f(x) = 2x$, $f'(x) = 2$, and $g'(x) = (x - 8)^{-3}$; then $g(x) = \int (x - 8)^{-3}\, dx = -\frac{1}{2}(x - 8)^{-2}$. Substituting in (16.1),

$$\int \frac{2x}{(x - 8)^3}\, dx = 2x\left[-\frac{1}{2}(x - 8)^{-2}\right] - \int -\frac{1}{2}(x - 8)^{-2}\, 2\, dx = -x(x - 8)^{-2} + \int (x - 8)^{-2}\, dx$$

Integrating for the last time,

$$\int \frac{2x}{(x - 8)^3}\, dx = -x(x - 8)^{-2} - (x - 8)^{-1} + c = \frac{-x}{(x - 8)^2} - \frac{1}{x - 8} + c$$

16.21. Redo Problem 16.19, given

$$\int \frac{5x}{(x - 1)^2}\, dx$$

Let $f(x) = 5x$, $f'(x) = 5$, and $g'(x) = (x - 1)^{-2}$; then $g(x) = \int (x - 1)^{-2}\, dx = -(x - 1)^{-1}$. Substituting in (16.1),

$$\int \frac{5x}{(x - 1)^2}\, dx = 5x[-(x - 1)^{-1}] - \int -(x - 1)^{-1}5\, dx = -5x(x - 1)^{-1} + 5 \int (x - 1)^{-1}\, dx$$

Integrating again,

$$\int \frac{5x}{(x - 1)^2}\, dx = -5x(x - 1)^{-1} + 5\ln|x - 1| + c = \frac{-5x}{x - 1} + 5\ln|x - 1| + c$$

16.22. Redo Problem 16.19, given $\int 6xe^{x+7}\, dx$.

Let $f(x) = 6x$, $f'(x) = 6$, $g'(x) = e^{x+7}$, and $g(x) = \int e^{x+7}\, dx = e^{x+7}$. Using (16.1),

$$\int 6xe^{x+7}\, dx = 6xe^{x+7} - \int e^{x+7}6\, dx = 6xe^{x+7} - 6 \int e^{x+7}\, dx$$

Integrating again,

$$\int 6xe^{x+7}\, dx = 6xe^{x+7} - 6e^{x+7} + c$$

16.23. Use integration by parts to evaluate $\int 16xe^{-(x+9)}\, dx$.

Let $f(x) = 16x$, $f'(x) = 16$, $g'(x) = e^{-(x+9)}$, and $g(x) = \int e^{-(x+9)}\, dx = -e^{-(x+9)}$. Using (16.1),

$$\int 16xe^{-(x+9)}\, dx = -16xe^{-(x+9)} - \int -e^{-(x+9)}16\, dx = -16xe^{-(x+9)} + 16 \int e^{-(x+9)}\, dx$$

Integrating once more,

$$\int 16xe^{-(x+9)}\, dx = -16xe^{-(x+9)} - 16e^{-(x+9)} + c$$

16.24. Redo Problem 16.23, given $\int x^2 e^{2x}\, dx$.

Let $f(x) = x^2$, $f'(x) = 2x$, $g'(x) = e^{2x}$, and $g(x) = \int e^{2x}\, dx = \frac{1}{2}e^{2x}$. Substituting in (16.1),

$$\int x^2 e^{2x}\, dx = x^2(\tfrac{1}{2}e^{2x}) - \int \tfrac{1}{2}e^{2x}(2x)\, dx = \tfrac{1}{2}x^2 e^{2x} - \int xe^{2x}\, dx \qquad (16.2)$$

Using parts again for the remaining integral, $f(x) = x$, $f'(x) = 1$, $g'(x) = e^{2x}$, and $g(x) = \int e^{2x}\, dx = \frac{1}{2}e^{2x}$. Using (16.1),

$$\int xe^{2x}\, dx = x(\tfrac{1}{2}e^{2x}) - \int \tfrac{1}{2}e^{2x}\, dx = \tfrac{1}{2}xe^{2x} - \tfrac{1}{2}(\tfrac{1}{2}e^{2x})$$

Finally, substituting in (16.2),

$$\int x^2 e^{2x}\, dx = \tfrac{1}{2}x^2 e^{2x} - \tfrac{1}{2}xe^{2x} + \tfrac{1}{4}e^{2x} + c$$

ECONOMIC APPLICATIONS

16.25. The rate of net investment is $I = 40t^{3/5}$, and capital stock at $t = 0$ is 75. Find the capital function K.

$$K = \int I\, dt = \int 40t^{3/5}\, dt = 40(\tfrac{5}{8}t^{8/5}) + c = 25t^{8/5} + c$$

Substituting $t = 0$ and $K = 75$,

$$75 = 0 + c \qquad c = 75$$

Thus, $K = 25t^{8/5} + 75$.

16.26. The rate of net investment is $I = 60t^{1/3}$, and capital stock at $t = 1$ is 85. Find K.

$$K = \int 60t^{1/3}\, dt = 45t^{4/3} + c$$

At $t = 1$ and $K = 85$,

$$85 = 45(1) + c \qquad c = 40$$

Thus, $K = 45t^{4/3} + 40$.

16.27. Marginal cost is given by $MC = dTC/dQ = 25 + 30Q - 9Q^2$. Fixed cost is 55. Find the (a) total cost, (b) average cost, and (c) variable cost functions.

(a)
$$TC = \int MC\, dQ = \int (25 + 30Q - 9Q^2)\, dQ = 25Q + 15Q^2 - 3Q^3 + c$$

With $FC = 55$, at $Q = 0$, $TC = FC = 55$. Thus, $c = FC = 55$ and $TC = 25Q + 15Q^2 - 3Q^3 + 55$.

(b)
$$AC = \frac{TC}{Q} = 25 + 15Q - 3Q^2 + \frac{55}{Q}$$

(c)
$$VC = TC - FC = 25Q + 15Q^2 - 3Q^3$$

16.28. Given $MC = dTC/dQ = 32 + 18Q - 12Q^2$, $FC = 43$. Find the (a) TC, (b) AC, and (c) VC functions.

(a)
$$TC = \int MC\, dQ = \int (32 + 18Q - 12Q^2)\, dQ = 32Q + 9Q^2 - 4Q^3 + c$$

At $Q = 0$, $TC = FC = 43$, $TC = 32Q + 9Q^2 - 4Q^3 + 43$.

(b)
$$AC = \frac{TC}{Q} = 32 + 9Q - 4Q^2 + \frac{43}{Q}$$

(c)
$$VC = TC - FC = 32Q + 9Q^2 - 4Q^3$$

16.29. Marginal revenue is given by $\text{MR} = d\text{TR}/dQ = 60 - 2Q - 2Q^2$. Find (a) the TR function and (b) the demand function $P = f(Q)$.

(a)
$$\text{TR} = \int \text{MR} \, dQ = \int (60 - 2Q - 2Q^2) \, dQ = 60Q - Q^2 - \tfrac{2}{3}Q^3 + c$$

At $Q = 0$, $\text{TR} = 0$. Therefore $c = 0$. Thus, $\text{TR} = 60Q - Q^2 - \tfrac{2}{3}Q^3$.

(b) $\text{TR} = PQ$. Therefore, $P = \text{TR}/Q$, which is the same as saying that the demand function and the average revenue function are identical. Thus, $P = \text{AR} = \text{TR}/Q = 60 - Q - \tfrac{2}{3}Q^2$.

16.30. Find (a) the total revenue function and (b) the demand function, given

$$\text{MR} = 84 - 4Q - Q^2$$

(a)
$$\text{TR} = \int \text{MR} \, dQ = \int (84 - 4Q - Q^2) \, dQ = 84Q - 2Q^2 - \tfrac{1}{3}Q^3 + c$$

At $Q = 0$, $\text{TR} = 0$. Therefore $c = 0$. Thus, $\text{TR} = 84Q - 2Q^2 - \tfrac{1}{3}Q^3$.

(b)
$$P = \text{AR} = \frac{\text{TR}}{Q} = 84 - 2Q - \frac{1}{3} Q^2$$

16.31. With $C = f(Y)$, the marginal propensity to consume is given by $\text{MPC} = dC/dY = f'(Y)$. If the $\text{MPC} = 0.8$ and consumption is 40 when income is zero, find the consumption function.

$$C = \int f'(Y) \, dY = \int 0.8 \, dY = 0.8Y + c$$

At $Y = 0$, $C = 40$. Thus, $c = 40$ and $C = 0.8Y + 40$.

16.32. Given $dC/dY = 0.6 + 0.1/\sqrt[3]{Y} = \text{MPC}$ and $C = 45$ when $Y = 0$. Find the consumption function.

$$C = \int \left(0.6 + \frac{0.1}{\sqrt[3]{Y}} \right) dY = \int (0.6 + 0.1Y^{-1/3}) \, dY = 0.6Y + 0.15Y^{2/3} + c$$

At $Y = 0$, $C = 45$. Thus, $C = 0.6Y + 0.15Y^{2/3} + 45$.

16.33. The marginal propensity to save is given by $dS/dY = 0.5 - 0.2Y^{-1/2}$. There is dissaving of 3.5 when income is 25, that is, $S = -3.5$ when $Y = 25$. Find the savings function.

$$S = \int (0.5 - 0.2Y^{-1/2}) \, dY = 0.5Y - 0.4Y^{1/2} + c$$

At $Y = 25$, $S = -3.5$.

$$-3.5 = 0.5(25) - 0.4(\sqrt{25}) + c \qquad c = -14$$

Thus, $S = 0.5Y - 0.4Y^{1/2} - 14$.

16.34. Given $\text{MC} = d\text{TC}/dQ = 12e^{0.5Q}$ and $\text{FC} = 36$. Find the total cost.

$$\text{TC} = \int 12e^{0.5Q} \, dQ = 12 \frac{1}{0.5} e^{0.5Q} + c = 24e^{0.5Q} + c$$

With $\text{FC} = 36$, $\text{TC} = 36$ when $Q = 0$. Substituting, $36 = 24e^{0.5(0)} + c$. Since $e^0 = 1$, $36 = 24 + c$, and $c = 12$. Thus, $\text{TC} = 24e^{0.5Q} + 12$. Notice that c does not always equal FC.

16.35. Given $MC = 16e^{0.4Q}$ and $FC = 100$. Find TC.

$$TC = \int 16e^{0.4Q}\, dQ = 16\left(\frac{1}{0.4}\right)e^{0.4Q} + c = 40e^{0.4Q} + c$$

At $Q = 0$, $TC = 100$.

$$100 = 40e^0 + c \qquad c = 60$$

Thus, $TC = 40e^{0.4Q} + 60$.

Chapter 17

Integral Calculus: The Definite Integral

17.1 AREA UNDER A CURVE

There is no geometric formula for the area under an irregularly shaped curve, such as $y = f(x)$ between $x = a$ and $x = b$ in Fig. 17-1(a). If the interval $[a, b]$ is divided into n subintervals $[x_1, x_2]$, $[x_2, x_3]$, etc., and rectangles are constructed such that the height of each is equal to the smallest value of the function in the subinterval, as in Fig. 17-1(b), then the sum of the areas of the rectangles $\sum_{i=1}^{n} f(x_i) \, \Delta x_i$, called a *Riemann sum*, will approximate, but underestimate, the actual area under the

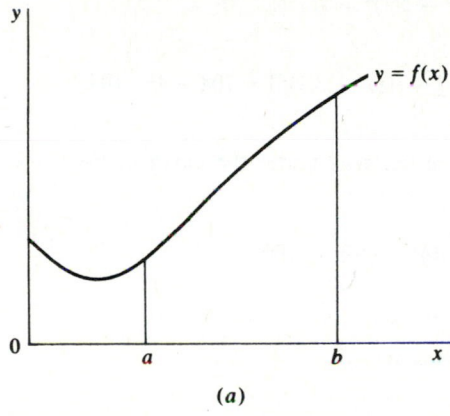

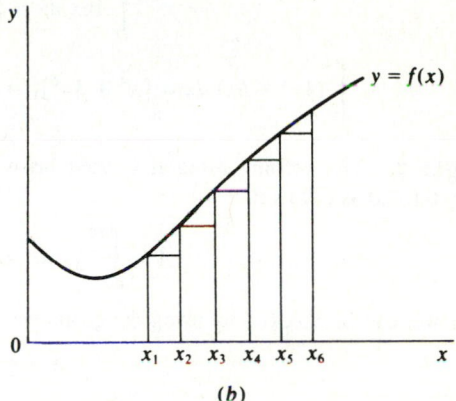

$$(a) \qquad\qquad (b)$$

Fig. 17-1

curve. The smaller the subintervals (the smaller the Δx_i), the more rectangles are created and the closer the combined area of the rectangles $\sum_{i=1}^{n} f(x_i) \, \Delta x_i$ approaches the actual area under the curve. If the number of subintervals is increased so that $n \to \infty$, each subinterval becomes infinitesimal ($\Delta x_i = dx_i = dx$) and the area A under the curve can be expressed mathematically as

$$A = \lim_{n \to \infty} \sum_{i=1}^{n} f(x_i) \, \Delta x_i$$

17.2 THE DEFINITE INTEGRAL

The area under a graph of a continuous function such as that in Fig. 17-1 from a to b ($a < b$) can be expressed more succinctly as the *definite integral* of $f(x)$ over the interval a to b. Put mathematically,

$$\int_a^b f(x) \, dx = \lim_{n \to \infty} \sum_{i=1}^{n} f(x_i) \, \Delta x_i$$

Here the left-hand side is read, "the integral from a to b of f of x dx." Here a is called the *lower limit* of integration and b the *upper limit* of integration. Unlike the indefinite integral which is a set of functions containing all the antiderivatives of $f(x)$, as explained in Example 3 of Chapter 16, the definite integral is a real number which can be evaluated by using the fundamental theorem of calculus (Section 17.3).

17.3 THE FUNDAMENTAL THEOREM OF CALCULUS

The *fundamental theorem of calculus* states that the numerical value of the definite integral of a continuous function $f(x)$ over the interval from a to b is given by the indefinite integral $F(x) + c$ evaluated at the upper limit of integration b, minus the same indefinite integral $F(x) + c$ evaluated at the lower limit of integration a. Since c is common to both, the constant of integration is eliminated in subtraction. Expressed mathematically,

$$\int_a^b f(x)\, dx = F(x)\Big|_a^b = F(b) - F(a)$$

where the symbol $|_a^b$, $]_a^b$, or $[\cdots]_a^b$ indicates that b and a are to be substituted successively for x. See Examples 1 and 2 and Problems 17.1 to 17.10.

EXAMPLE 1. The definite integrals given below

$$(1)\quad \int_1^4 10x\, dx \qquad (2)\quad \int_1^3 (4x^3 + 6x)\, dx$$

are evaluated as follows:

$$(1)\qquad \int_1^4 10x\, dx = 5x^2\Big|_1^4 = 5(4)^2 - 5(1)^2 = 75$$

$$(2)\qquad \int_1^3 (4x^3 + 6x)\, dx = [x^4 + 3x^2]_1^3 = [(3)^4 + 3(3)^2] - [(1)^4 + 3(1)^2] = 108 - 4 = 104$$

EXAMPLE 2. The definite integral is used below to determine the area under the curve in Fig. 17-2 over the interval 0 to 20 as follows:

$$A = \int_0^{20} \tfrac{1}{2}x\, dx = \tfrac{1}{4}x^2\Big|_0^{20} = \tfrac{1}{4}(20)^2 - \tfrac{1}{4}(0)^2 = 100$$

The answer can be checked by using the geometric formula $A = \tfrac{1}{2}xy$:

$$A = \tfrac{1}{2}xy = \tfrac{1}{2}(20)(10) = 100$$

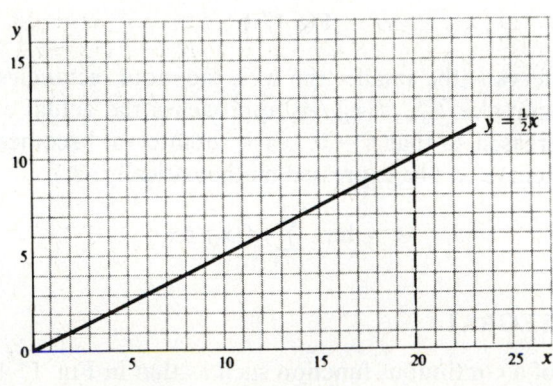

Fig. 17-2

17.4 PROPERTIES OF DEFINITE INTEGRALS

1. Reversing the order of the limits changes the sign of the definite integral.

$$\int_a^b f(x)\, dx = -\int_b^a f(x)\, dx \qquad (17.1)$$

2. If the upper limit of integration equals the lower limit of integration, the value of the definite
    integral is zero.

$$\int_a^a f(x)\, dx = F(a) - F(a) = 0 \tag{17.2}$$

3. The definite integral can be expressed as the sum of component subintegrals.

$$\int_a^c f(x)\, dx = \int_a^b f(x)\, dx + \int_b^c f(x)\, dx \qquad a \leq b \leq c \tag{17.3}$$

4. The sum or difference of two definite integrals with identical limits of integration is equal to the
    definite integral of the sum or difference of the two functions.

$$\int_a^b f(x)\, dx \pm \int_a^b g(x)\, dx = \int_a^b [f(x) \pm g(x)]\, dx \tag{17.4}$$

5. The definite integral of a constant times a function is equal to the constant times the definite
    integral of the function.

$$\int_a^b kf(x)\, dx = k \int_a^b f(x)\, dx \tag{17.5}$$

See Example 3 and Problems 17.11 to 17.14.

EXAMPLE 3.   To illustrate a sampling of the properties presented above, the following definite integrals are evaluated:

1. $\displaystyle\int_1^3 2x^3\, dx = -\int_3^1 2x^3\, dx$

$$\int_1^3 2x^3\, dx = \tfrac{1}{2}x^4 \Big|_1^3 = \tfrac{1}{2}(3)^4 - \tfrac{1}{2}(1)^4 = 40$$

Checking this answer,

$$\int_3^1 2x^3\, dx = \tfrac{1}{2}x^4 \Big|_3^1 = \tfrac{1}{2}(1)^4 - \tfrac{1}{2}(3)^4 = -40$$

2. $\displaystyle\int_5^5 (2x + 3)\, dx = 0$

Checking this answer,

$$\int_5^5 (2x + 3)\, dx = [x^2 + 3x]_5^5 = [(5)^2 + 3(5)] - [(5)^2 + 3(5)] = 0$$

3. $\displaystyle\int_0^4 6x\, dx = \int_0^3 6x\, dx + \int_3^4 6x\, dx$

$$\int_0^4 6x\, dx = 3x^2 \Big|_0^4 = 3(4)^2 - 3(0)^2 = 48$$

$$\int_0^3 6x\, dx = 3x^2 \Big|_0^3 = 3(3)^2 - 3(0)^2 = 27$$

$$\int_3^4 6x\, dx = 3x^2 \Big|_3^4 = 3(4)^2 - 3(3)^2 = 21$$

Checking this answer, $48 = 27 + 21$

17.5   AREA BETWEEN CURVES

The area of a region between two or more curves can be evaluated by applying the properties of definite integrals outlined above. The procedure is demonstrated in Example 4 and treated in Problems 17.15 to 17.18.

EXAMPLE 4.   Using the properties of integrals, the area of the region between two functions such as $y_1 = 3x^2 - 6x + 8$ and $y_2 = -2x^2 + 4x + 1$ from $x = 0$ to $x = 2$ is found in the following way:

(a)   Draw a rough sketch of the graph of the functions and shade in the desired area as in Fig. 17-3.

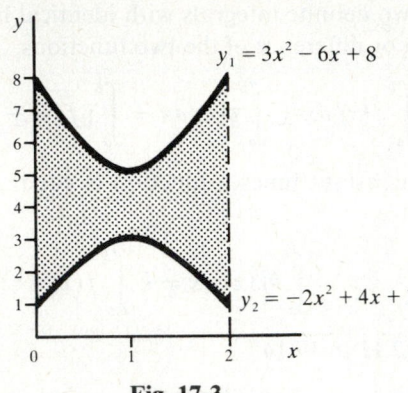

Fig. 17-3

(b)   Note the relationship between the curves. Since y_1 lies above y_2, the desired region is simply the area under y_1 minus the area under y_2 between $x = 0$ and $x = 2$. Hence,

$$A = \int_0^2 (3x^2 - 6x + 8)\, dx - \int_0^2 (-2x^2 + 4x + 1)\, dx$$

From (17.4),
$$A = \int_0^2 [(3x^2 - 6x + 8) - (-2x^2 + 4x + 1)]\, dx$$

$$= \int_0^2 (5x^2 - 10x + 7)\, dx$$

$$= (\tfrac{5}{3}x^3 - 5x^2 + 7x)\big|_0^2 = 7\tfrac{1}{3} - 0 = 7\tfrac{1}{3}$$

17.6   IMPROPER INTEGRALS

The area under some curves that extend infinitely far along the x axis, as in Fig. 17-4(a), may be estimated with the help of improper integrals. A definite integral with infinity for either an upper or lower limit of integration is called an *improper integral*.

$$\int_a^\infty f(x)\, dx \qquad \text{and} \qquad \int_{-\infty}^b f(x)\, dx$$

are improper integrals because ∞ is not a number and cannot be substituted for x in $F(x)$. They can, however, be defined as the limits of other integrals, as shown below.

$$\int_a^\infty f(x)\, dx = \lim_{b \to \infty} \int_a^b f(x)\, dx \qquad \text{and} \qquad \int_{-\infty}^b f(x)\, dx = \lim_{a \to -\infty} \int_a^b f(x)\, dx$$

If the limit in either case exists, the improper integral is said to *converge*. The integral has a definite value, and the area under the curve can be evaluated. If the limit does not exist, the improper integral *diverges* and is meaningless. See Example 5 and Problems 17.19 to 17.25.

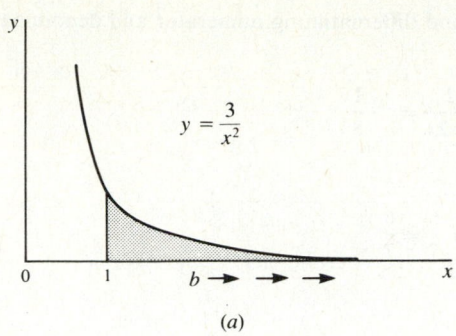
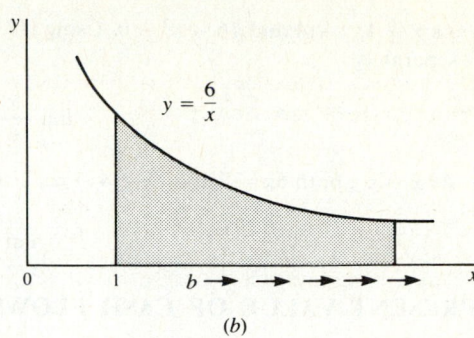

(a) (b)

Fig. 17-4

EXAMPLE 5.   The improper integrals given below

$$(a)\quad \int_1^\infty \frac{3}{x^2}\, dx \qquad (b)\quad \int_1^\infty \frac{6}{x}\, dx$$

are sketched in Fig. 17-4(a) and (b) and evaluated as follows:

(a)
$$\int_1^\infty \frac{3}{x^2}\, dx = \lim_{b\to\infty} \int_1^b \frac{3}{x^2}\, dx = \lim_{b\to\infty}\left[\frac{-3}{x}\right]_1^b$$
$$= \lim_{b\to\infty}\left[\frac{-3}{b} - \frac{(-3)}{1}\right] = \lim_{b\to\infty}\left(\frac{-3}{b} + 3\right) = 3$$

because as $b\to\infty$, $-3/b \to 0$. Hence the improper integral is convergent and the area under the curve in Fig. 17-4(a) equals 3.

(b)
$$\int_1^\infty \frac{6}{x}\, dx = \lim_{b\to\infty} \int_1^b \frac{6}{x}\, dx$$
$$= \lim_{b\to\infty} \left[6\ln|x|\right]_1^b = \lim_{b\to\infty}\left[6\ln|b| - 6\ln|1|\right]$$
$$= \lim_{b\to\infty}\left[6\ln|b|\right] \qquad \text{since}\quad \ln|1| = 0$$

As $b\to\infty$, $6\ln|b| \to \infty$. The improper integral diverges and has no definite value. The area under the curve in Fig. 17-4(b) cannot be computed even though the graph is deceptively similar to the one in (a).

17.7   L'HÔPITAL'S RULE

If the limit of a function $f(x) = g(x)/h(x)$ as $x\to a$ cannot be evaluated, such as (1) when both numerator and denominator approach zero, giving rise to the indeterminate form 0/0, or (2) when both numerator and denominator approach infinity, giving rise to the indeterminate form ∞/∞, *L'Hôpital's rule* can often be helpful. L'Hôpital's rule states:

$$\lim_{x\to a} \frac{g(x)}{h(x)} = \lim_{x\to a} \frac{g'(x)}{h'(x)} \tag{17.6}$$

It is illustrated in Example 6 and Problem 17.26.

EXAMPLE 6.   The limits of the functions given below are found as follows, using L'Hôpital's rule. Note that numerator and denominator are differentiated separately, not as a quotient.

$$(a)\quad \lim_{x\to 4}\frac{x-4}{16-x^2} \qquad (b)\quad \lim_{x\to\infty}\frac{6x-2}{7x+4}$$

(a) As $x \to 4$, $x - 4$ and $16 - x^2 \to 0$. Using (17.6), therefore, and differentiating numerator and denominator separately,

$$\lim_{x \to 4} \frac{x - 4}{16 - x^2} = \lim_{x \to 4} \frac{1}{-2x} = -\frac{1}{8}$$

(b) As $x \to \infty$, both $6x - 2$ and $7x + 4 \to \infty$. Using (17.6),

$$\lim_{x \to \infty} \frac{6x - 2}{7x + 4} = \lim_{x \to \infty} \frac{6}{7} = \frac{6}{7}$$

17.8 PRESENT VALUE OF CASH FLOWS

In Section 8.3, the present value of a sum of money to be received in the future, when interest is compounded continuously, was given by $P = Se^{-rt}$. The present value of a *stream of future income* (money to be received *each year* for n years), therefore, is given by the integral

$$P_n = \int_0^n Se^{-rt}\, dt = S \int_0^n e^{-rt}\, dt = S\left[-\frac{1}{r} e^{-rt} \right]_0^n = -\frac{S}{r} [e^{-rt}]_0^n$$

$$= -\frac{S}{r} (e^{-rn} - e^{-r(0)}) = -\frac{S}{r} (e^{-rn} - 1)$$

$$= \frac{S}{r} (1 - e^{-rn}) \tag{17.7}$$

Notice the similarity to the formula in Section 8.4 for the present value of a future stream of income under conditions of annual compounding.

EXAMPLE 7. The present value of \$1000 to be paid each year for 3 years when the interest rate is 5 percent compounded continuously is calculated below, using (17.7).

$$P_n = \frac{1000}{0.05} (1 - e^{-(0.05)(3)}) = 20\,000(1 - e^{-0.15}) = 20\,000(1 - 0.8607) = \$2786$$

17.9 CONSUMERS' AND PRODUCERS' SURPLUS

A demand function $P_1 = f_1(Q)$, as in Fig. 17-5(a), represents the different prices consumers are willing to pay for different quantities of a good. If equilibrium in the market is at (Q_0, P_0), then the consumers who would be willing to pay more than P_0 benefit. Total benefit to consumers is represented by the shaded area and is called *consumers' surplus*. Mathematically,

$$\text{Consumers' surplus} = \int_0^{Q_0} f_1(Q)\, dQ - Q_0 P_0 \tag{17.8}$$

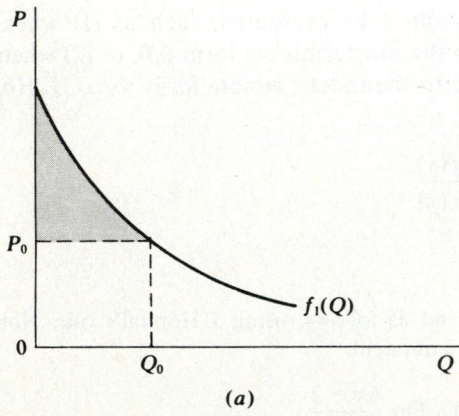
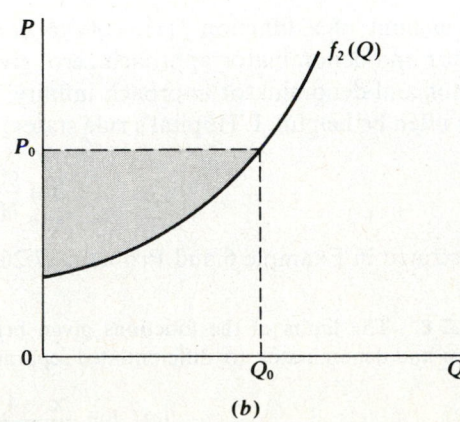

(a)   (b)

Fig. 17-5

A supply function $P_2 = f_2(Q)$, as in Fig. 17-5(b), represents the prices at which different quantities of a good will be supplied. If market equilibrium occurs at (Q_0, P_0), the producers who would supply at a lower price than P_0 benefit. Total gain to producers is called *producers' surplus* and is designated by the shaded area. Mathematically,

$$\text{Producers' surplus} = Q_0 P_0 - \int_0^{Q_0} f_2(Q)\, dQ \qquad (17.9)$$

See Example 8 and Problems 17.27 to 17.31.

EXAMPLE 8. Given the demand function $P = 42 - 5Q - Q^2$. Assuming that the equilibrium price is 6, the consumers' surplus is evaluated as follows:

At $P_0 = 6$,
$$42 - 5Q - Q^2 = 6$$
$$36 - 5Q - Q^2 = 0$$
$$(Q + 9)(-Q + 4) = 0$$

So $Q_0 = 4$, because $Q = -9$ is not feasible. Substituting in (17.8),

$$\text{Consumers' surplus} = \int_0^4 (42 - 5Q - Q^2)\, dQ - (4)(6)$$
$$= [42Q - 2.5Q^2 - \tfrac{1}{3}Q^3]_0^4 - 24$$
$$= (168 - 40 - 21\tfrac{1}{3}) - 0 - 24 = 82\tfrac{2}{3}$$

17.10   THE DEFINITE INTEGRAL AND PROBABILITY

The probability P that an event will occur can be measured by the corresponding area under a probability density function. A *probability density* or *frequency function* is a continuous function $f(x)$ such that:

1. $f(x) \geq 0$. Probability cannot be negative.
2. $\int_{-\infty}^{\infty} f(x)\, dx = 1$. The probability of the event occurring over the entire range of x is 1.
3. $P(a < x < b) = \int_a^b f(x)\, dx$. The probability of the value of x falling within the interval $[a, b]$ is the value of the definite integral from a to b.

See Example 9 and Problems 17.32 and 17.33.

EXAMPLE 9. The time in minutes between cars passing on a highway is given by the frequency function $f(t) = 2e^{-2t}$ for $t \geq 0$. The probability of a car passing in 0.25 minute is calculated as follows:

$$P = \int_0^{0.25} 2e^{-2t}\, dt = -e^{-2t}\Big|_0^{0.25} = -e^{-0.5} - (-e^0) = -0.606531 + 1 = 0.393469$$

Solved Problems

DEFINITE INTEGRALS

17.1.   Evaluate the following definite integrals:

(a) $\displaystyle \int_0^6 5x\, dx$

$$\int_0^6 5x\, dx = 2.5x^2\Big|_0^6 = 2.5(6)^2 - 2.5(0)^2 = 90$$

(b) $\displaystyle\int_{1}^{10} 3x^2 \, dx$

$$\int_{1}^{10} 3x^2 \, dx = x^3 \Big|_{1}^{10} = (10)^3 - (1)^3 = 999$$

(c) $\displaystyle\int_{1}^{64} x^{-2/3} \, dx$

$$\int_{1}^{64} x^{-2/3} \, dx = 3x^{1/3} \Big|_{1}^{64} = 3\sqrt[3]{64} - 3\sqrt[3]{1} = 9$$

(d) $\displaystyle\int_{1}^{3} (x^3 + x + 6) \, dx$

$$\int_{1}^{3} (x^3 + x + 6) \, dx = (\tfrac{1}{4}x^4 + \tfrac{1}{2}x^2 + 6x) \Big|_{1}^{3} = \tfrac{1}{4}(3)^4 + \tfrac{1}{2}(3)^2 + 6(3) - [\tfrac{1}{4}(1)^4 + \tfrac{1}{2}(1)^2 + 6(1)] = 36$$

(e) $\displaystyle\int_{1}^{4} (x^{-1/2} + 3x^{1/2}) \, dx$

$$\int_{1}^{4} (x^{-1/2} + 3x^{1/2}) \, dx = (2x^{1/2} + 2x^{3/2}) \Big|_{1}^{4} = 2\sqrt{4} + 2\sqrt{4^3} - (2\sqrt{1} + 2\sqrt{1^3}) = 16$$

(f) $\displaystyle\int_{0}^{3} 4e^{2x} \, dx$

$$\int_{0}^{3} 4e^{2x} \, dx = 2e^{2x} \Big|_{0}^{3} = 2(e^{2(3)} - e^{2(0)})$$
$$= 2(403.4 - 1) = 804.8$$

(g) $\displaystyle\int_{0}^{10} 2e^{-2x} \, dx$

$$\int_{0}^{10} 2e^{-2x} \, dx = -e^{-2x} \Big|_{0}^{10} = -e^{-2(10)} - (-e^{-2(0)}) = -e^{-20} + e^0 = 1$$

SUBSTITUTION METHOD

17.2. Use the substitution method to integrate the following definite integral:

$$\int_{0}^{3} 8x(2x^2 + 3) \, dx$$

Let $u = 2x^2 + 3$. Then $du/dx = 4x$ and $dx = du/4x$. Ignore the limits of integration for the moment, and treat the integral as an indefinite integral. Substituting in the original integrand,

$$\int 8x(2x^2 + 3) \, dx = \int 8xu \, \frac{du}{4x} = 2 \int u \, du$$

Integrating with respect to u,

$$2 \int u \, du = 2\left(\frac{u^2}{2}\right) + c = u^2 + c \qquad (17.10)$$

Finally, by substituting $u = 2x^2 + 3$ in (17.10) and recalling that c will drop out in the integration, the definite integral can be written in terms of x, incorporating the original limits:

$$\int_{0}^{3} 8x(2x^2 + 3) \, dx = (2x^2 + 3)^2 \Big|_{0}^{3} = [2(3)^2 + 3]^2 - [2(0)^2 + 3]^2 = 441 - 9 = 432$$

Because in the original substitution $u \neq x$ but $2x^2 + 3$, the limits of integration in terms of x will differ from the limits of integration in terms of u. The limits can be expressed in terms of u, if so desired. Since we have set $u = 2x^2 + 3$ and x ranges from 0 to 3, the limits in terms of u are $u = 2(3)^2 + 3 = 21$ and $u = 2(0)^2 + 3 = 3$. Using these limits with the integral expressed in terms of u, as in (17.10),

$$2 \int_3^{21} u \, du = u^2 \Big|_3^{21} = 441 - 9 = 432$$

17.3. Redo Problem 17.2, given $\int_1^2 x^2(x^3 - 5)^2 \, dx$.

Let $u = x^3 - 5$, $du/dx = 3x^2$, and $dx = du/3x^2$. Substituting independently of the limits,

$$\int x^2(x^3 - 5)^2 \, dx = \int x^2 u^2 \frac{du}{3x^2} = \frac{1}{3} \int u^2 \, du$$

Integrating with respect to u and ignoring the constant,

$$\frac{1}{3} \int u^2 \, du = \frac{1}{3}(\frac{1}{3}u^3) = \frac{1}{9}u^3$$

Substituting $u = x^3 - 5$ and incorporating the limits for x,

$$\int_1^2 x^2(x^3 - 5)^2 \, dx = [\frac{1}{9}(x^3 - 5)^3]_1^2$$

$$= \frac{1}{9}[(2)^3 - 5]^3 - \frac{1}{9}[(1)^3 - 5]^3 = \frac{1}{9}(27) - \frac{1}{9}(-64) = 10.11$$

Since $u = x^3 - 5$ and the limits for x are $x = 1$ and $x = 2$, by substitution the limits for u are $u = (1)^3 - 5 = -4$ and $u = (2)^3 - 5 = 3$. Incorporating these limits for the integral with respect to u,

$$\frac{1}{3} \int_{-4}^3 u^2 \, du = [\frac{1}{9}u^3]_{-4}^3 = \frac{1}{9}(3)^3 - \frac{1}{9}(-4)^3 = 10.11$$

17.4. Redo Problem 17.2, given

$$\int_0^2 \frac{3x^2}{(x^3 + 1)^2} \, dx$$

Let $u = x^3 + 1$. Then $du/dx = 3x^2$ and $dx = du/3x^2$. Substituting,

$$\int \frac{3x^2}{(x^3 + 1)^2} \, dx = \int 3x^2 u^{-2} \frac{du}{3x^2} = \int u^{-2} \, du$$

Integrating with respect to u and ignoring the constant,

$$\int u^{-2} \, du = -u^{-1}$$

Substituting $u = x^3 + 1$ with the original limits,

$$\int_0^2 \frac{3x^2}{(x^3 + 1)^2} \, dx = -(x^3 + 1)^{-1} \Big|_0^2 = \frac{-1}{2^3 + 1} - \frac{-1}{0^3 + 1} = -\frac{1}{9} + 1 = \frac{8}{9}$$

With $u = x^3 + 1$, and the limits of x ranging from 0 to 2, the limits of u are $u = (0)^3 + 1 = 1$ and $u = (2)^3 + 1 = 9$. Thus,

$$\int_1^9 u^{-2} \, du = -u^{-1} \Big|_1^9 = (-\frac{1}{9}) - (-\frac{1}{1}) = \frac{8}{9}$$

17.5. Integrate the following definite integral by means of the substitution method:

$$\int_0^3 \frac{6x}{x^2 + 1} \, dx$$

Let $u = x^2 + 1$, $du/dx = 2x$, and $dx = du/2x$. Substituting,

$$\int \frac{6x}{x^2 + 1}\, dx = \int 6xu^{-1}\frac{du}{2x} = 3\int u^{-1}\, du$$

Integrating with respect to u,

$$3\int u^{-1}\, du = 3\ln|u|$$

Substituting $u = x^2 + 1$,

$$\int_0^3 \frac{6x}{x^2 + 1}\, dx = 3\ln|x^2 + 1|\,\Big|_0^3$$

$$= 3\ln|3^2 + 1| - 3\ln|0^2 + 1| = 3\ln 10 - 3\ln 1$$

Since $\ln 1 = 0$, $\qquad\qquad\qquad = 3\ln 10 = 6.9078$

The limits of u are $u = (0)^2 + 1 = 1$ and $u = (3)^2 + 1 = 10$. Integrating with respect to u,

$$3\int_1^{10} u^{-1}\, du = 3\ln|u|\,\Big|_1^{10} = 3\ln 10 - 3\ln 1 = 3\ln 10 = 6.9078$$

17.6. Redo Problem 17.5, given $\int_1^2 4xe^{x^2+2}\, dx$.

Let $u = x^2 + 2$. Then $du/dx = 2x$ and $dx = du/2x$. Substituting,

$$\int 4xe^{x^2+2}\, dx = \int 4xe^u \frac{du}{2x} = 2\int e^u\, du$$

Integrating with respect to u and ignoring the constant,

$$2\int e^u\, du = 2e^u$$

Substituting $u = x^2 + 2$,

$$\int_1^2 4xe^{x^2+2}\, dx = 2e^{x^2+2}\,\Big|_1^2 = 2(e^{(2)^2+2} - e^{(1)^2+2}) = 2(e^6 - e^3)$$

$$= 2(403.43 - 20.09) = 766.68$$

With $u = x^2 + 2$, the limits of u are $u = (1)^2 + 2 = 3$ and $u = (2)^2 + 2 = 6$.

$$2\int_3^6 e^u\, du = 2e^u\,\Big|_3^6 = 2(e^6 - e^3) = 766.68$$

17.7. Redo Problem 17.5, given $\int_0^1 3x^2 e^{2x^3+1}\, dx$.

Let $u = 2x^3 + 1$, $du/dx = 6x^2$, and $dx = du/6x^2$. Substituting,

$$\int 3x^2 e^{2x^3+1}\, dx = \int 3x^2 e^u \frac{du}{6x^2} = \frac{1}{2}\int e^u\, du$$

Integrating with respect to u,

$$\frac{1}{2}\int e^u\, du = \frac{1}{2}e^u$$

Substituting $u = 2x^3 + 1$,

$$\int_0^1 3x^2 e^{2x^3+1}\, dx = \frac{1}{2}e^{2x^3+1}\,\Big|_0^1 = \frac{1}{2}(e^3 - e^1) = \frac{1}{2}(20.086 - 2.718) = 8.684$$

With $u = 2x^3 + 1$, the limits of u are $u = 2(0)^3 + 1 = 1$ and $u = 2(1)^3 + 1 = 3$. Thus

$$\frac{1}{2} \int_1^3 e^u \, du = \frac{1}{2} e^u \Big|_1^3 = \frac{1}{2}(e^3 - e^1) = 8.68$$

INTEGRATION BY PARTS

17.8. Integrate the following definite integral, using the method of integration by parts:

$$\int_2^5 \frac{3x}{(x + 1)^2} \, dx$$

Let $f(x) = 3x$; then $f'(x) = 3$. Let $g'(x) = (x + 1)^{-2}$; then $g(x) = \int (x + 1)^{-2} \, dx = -(x + 1)^{-1}$. Substituting in (16.1),

$$\int \frac{3x}{(x + 1)^2} \, dx = 3x[-(x + 1)^{-1}] - \int -(x + 1)^{-1} 3 \, dx$$

$$= -3x(x + 1)^{-1} + 3 \int (x + 1)^{-1} \, dx$$

Integrating and ignoring the constant,

$$\int \frac{3x}{(x + 1)^2} \, dx = -3x(x + 1)^{-1} + 3 \ln |x + 1|$$

Applying the limits,

$$\int_2^5 \frac{3x}{(x + 1)^2} \, dx = [-3x(x + 1)^{-1} + 3 \ln |x + 1|]_2^5$$

$$= \left[-\frac{3(5)}{5 + 1} + 3 \ln |5 + 1| \right] - \left[-\frac{3(2)}{2 + 1} + 3 \ln |2 + 1| \right]$$

$$= -\frac{5}{2} + 3 \ln 6 + 2 - 3 \ln 3$$

$$= 3(\ln 6 - \ln 3) - \frac{1}{2} = 3(1.7918 - 1.0986) - 0.5 = 1.5796$$

17.9. Redo Problem 17.8, given

$$\int_1^3 \frac{4x}{(x + 2)^3} \, dx$$

Let $f(x) = 4x$, $f'(x) = 4$, $g'(x) = (x + 2)^{-3}$, and $g(x) = \int (x + 2)^{-3} \, dx = -\frac{1}{2}(x + 2)^{-2}$. Substituting in (16.1),

$$\int \frac{4x}{(x + 2)^3} \, dx = 4x \left[-\frac{1}{2}(x + 2)^{-2} \right] - \int -\frac{1}{2}(x + 2)^{-2} 4 \, dx$$

$$= -2x(x + 2)^{-2} + 2 \int (x + 2)^{-2} \, dx$$

Integrating,

$$\int \frac{4x}{(x + 2)^3} \, dx = -2x(x + 2)^{-2} - 2(x + 2)^{-1}$$

Applying the limits,

$$\int_1^3 \frac{4x}{(x + 2)^3} \, dx = [-2x(x + 2)^{-2} - 2(x + 2)^{-1}]_1^3$$

$$= [-2(3)(3 + 2)^{-2} - 2(3 + 2)^{-1}] - [-2(1)(1 + 2)^{-2} - 2(1 + 2)^{-1}]$$

$$= -\frac{6}{25} - \frac{2}{5} + \frac{2}{9} + \frac{2}{3} = \frac{56}{225}$$

17.10. Redo Problem 17.8, given $\int_1^3 5xe^{x+2}\,dx$.

Let $f(x) = 5x$, $f'(x) = 5$, $g'(x) = e^{x+2}$, and $g(x) = \int e^{x+2}\,dx = e^{x+2}$. Applying (16.1),

$$\int 5xe^{x+2}\,dx = 5xe^{x+2} - \int e^{x+2}5\,dx = 5xe^{x+2} - 5\int e^{x+2}\,dx$$

Integrating,

$$\int 5xe^{x+2}\,dx = 5xe^{x+2} - 5e^{x+2}$$

Applying the limits,

$$\int_1^3 5xe^{x+2}\,dx = [5xe^{x+2} - 5e^{x+2}]_1^3 = (15e^5 - 5e^5) - (5e^3 - 5e^3) = 10e^5 = 10(148.4) = 1484$$

PROPERTIES OF DEFINITE INTEGRALS

17.11. Show $\int_{-4}^4 (8x^3 + 9x^2)\,dx = \int_{-4}^0 (8x^3 + 9x^2)\,dx + \int_0^4 (8x^3 + 9x^2)\,dx$.

$$\int_{-4}^4 (8x^3 + 9x^2)\,dx = 2x^4 + 3x^3 \Big|_{-4}^4 = 704 - 320 = 384$$

$$\int_{-4}^0 (8x^3 + 9x^2)\,dx = 2x^4 + 3x^3 \Big|_{-4}^0 = 0 - 320 = -320$$

$$\int_0^4 (8x^3 + 9x^2)\,dx = 2x^4 + 3x^3 \Big|_0^4 = 704 - 0 = 704$$

Checking this answer, $-320 + 704 = 384$

17.12. Show $\int_0^{16} (x^{-1/2} + 3x)\,dx = \int_0^4 (x^{-1/2} + 3x)\,dx + \int_4^9 (x^{-1/2} + 3x)\,dx + \int_9^{16} (x^{-1/2} + 3x)\,dx$.

$$\int_0^{16} (x^{-1/2} + 3x)\,dx = 2x^{1/2} + 1.5x^2 \Big|_0^{16} = 392 - 0 = 392$$

$$\int_0^4 (x^{-1/2} + 3x)\,dx = 2x^{1/2} + 1.5x^2 \Big|_0^4 = 28 - 0 = 28$$

$$\int_4^9 (x^{-1/2} + 3x)\,dx = 2x^{1/2} + 1.5x^2 \Big|_4^9 = 127.5 - 28 = 99.5$$

$$\int_9^{16} (x^{-1/2} + 3x)\,dx = 2x^{1/2} + 1.5x^2 \Big|_9^{16} = 392 - 127.5 = 264.5$$

Checking this answer, $28 + 99.5 + 264.5 = 392$

17.13. Show

$$\int_0^3 \frac{6x}{x^2 + 1}\,dx = \int_0^1 \frac{6x}{x^2 + 1}\,dx + \int_1^2 \frac{6x}{x^2 + 1}\,dx + \int_2^3 \frac{6x}{x^2 + 1}\,dx$$

From Problem 17.5,

$$\int_0^3 \frac{6x}{x^2 + 1}\,dx = 3\ln|x^2 + 1| \Big|_0^3 = 3\ln 10$$

$$\int_0^1 \frac{6x}{x^2 + 1}\,dx = 3\ln|x^2 + 1| \Big|_0^1 = 3\ln 2 - 0 = 3\ln 2$$

$$\int_1^2 \frac{6x}{x^2 + 1}\,dx = 3\ln|x^2 + 1| \Big|_1^2 = 3\ln 5 - 3\ln 2$$

$$\int_2^3 \frac{6x}{x^2 + 1}\,dx = 3\ln|x^2 + 1| \Big|_2^3 = 3\ln 10 - 3\ln 5$$

Checking this answer, $3\ln 2 + 3\ln 5 - 3\ln 2 + 3\ln 10 - 3\ln 5 = 3\ln 10$

17.14. Show $\int_1^3 5xe^{x+2}\, dx = \int_1^2 5xe^{x+2}\, dx + \int_2^3 5xe^{x+2}\, dx$.

From Problem 17.10,

$$\int_1^3 5xe^{x+2}\, dx = [5xe^{x+2} - 5e^{x+2}]_1^3 = 10e^5$$

$$\int_1^2 5xe^{x+2}\, dx = [5xe^{x+2} - 5e^{x+2}]_1^2 = (10e^4 - 5e^4) - (5e^3 - 5e^3) = 5e^4$$

$$\int_2^3 5xe^{x+2}\, dx = [5xe^{x+2} - 5e^{x+2}]_2^3 = (15e^5 - 5e^5) - (10e^4 - 5e^4) = 10e^5 - 5e^4$$

Checking this answer, $\qquad\qquad\qquad 5e^4 + 10e^5 - 5e^4 = 10e^5$

AREA BETWEEN CURVES

17.15. (*a*) Draw the graphs of the following functions, and (*b*) evaluate the area between the curves over the stated interval:

$$y_1 = 7 - x \qquad \text{and} \qquad y_2 = 4x - x^2 \qquad \text{from } x = 1 \text{ to } x = 4$$

(*a*) See Fig. 17-6.

(*b*) From Fig. 17-6, the desired region is the area under the curve specified by $y_1 = 7 - x$ from $x = 1$ to $x = 4$ minus the area under the curve specified by $y_2 = 4x - x^2$ from $x = 1$ to $x = 4$. Using the properties of definite integrals,

$$A = \int_1^4 (7 - x)\, dx - \int_1^4 (4x - x^2)\, dx = \int_1^4 (x^2 - 5x + 7)\, dx$$
$$= [\tfrac{1}{3}x^3 - 2.5x^2 + 7x]_1^4$$
$$= [\tfrac{1}{3}(4)^3 - 2.5(4)^2 + 7(4)] - [\tfrac{1}{3}(1)^3 - 2.5(1)^2 + 7(1)] = 4.5$$

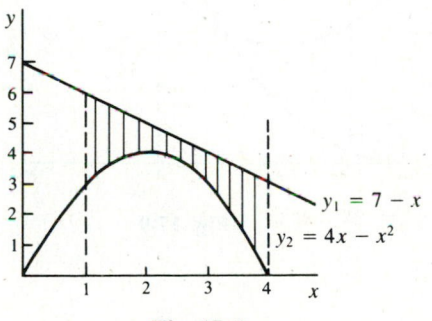

Fig. 17-6

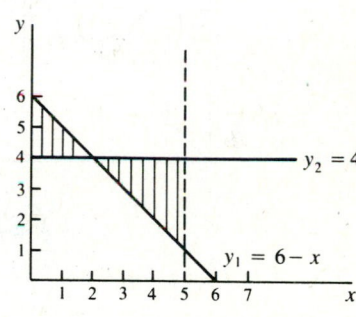

Fig. 17-7

17.16. Redo Problem 17.15, given

$$y_1 = 6 - x \qquad \text{and} \qquad y_2 = 4 \qquad \text{from } x = 0 \text{ to } x = 5$$

Notice the shift in the relative positions of the curves at the point of intersection.

(*a*) See Fig. 17-7.

(*b*) From Fig. 17-7, the desired area is the area between $y_1 = 6 - x$ and $y_2 = 4$ from $x = 0$ to $x = 2$ plus the area between $y_2 = 4$ and $y_1 = 6 - x$ from $x = 2$ to $x = 5$. Mathematically,

$$A = \int_0^2 [(6 - x) - 4]\, dx + \int_2^5 [4 - (6 - x)]\, dx$$
$$= \int_0^2 (2 - x)\, dx + \int_2^5 (x - 2)\, dx$$
$$= [2x - \tfrac{1}{2}x^2]_0^2 + [\tfrac{1}{2}x^2 - 2x]_2^5 = 2 - 0 + 2.5 - (-2) = 6.5$$

17.17. Redo Problem 17.15, given

$$y_1 = x^2 - 4x + 8 \quad \text{and} \quad y_2 = 2x \quad \text{from } x = 0 \text{ to } x = 3$$

(a)   See Fig. 17-8.

(b)
$$A = \int_0^2 [(x^2 - 4x + 8) - 2x] \, dx + \int_2^3 [2x - (x^2 - 4x + 8)] \, dx$$

$$= \int_0^2 (x^2 - 6x + 8) \, dx + \int_2^3 (-x^2 + 6x - 8) \, dx$$

$$= [\tfrac{1}{3}x^3 - 3x^2 + 8x]_0^2 + [-\tfrac{1}{3}x^3 + 3x^2 - 8x]_2^3 = 7\tfrac{1}{3}$$

17.18. Redo Problem 17.15, given

$$y_1 = x^2 - 4x + 12 \quad \text{and} \quad y_2 = x^2 \quad \text{from } x = 0 \text{ to } x = 4$$

(a)   See Fig. 17-9.

(b)
$$A = \int_0^3 [(x^2 - 4x + 12) - x^2] \, dx + \int_3^4 [x^2 - (x^2 - 4x + 12)] \, dx$$

$$= \int_0^3 (12 - 4x) \, dx + \int_3^4 (4x - 12) \, dx$$

$$= [12x - 2x^2]_0^3 + [2x^2 - 12x]_3^4 = 20$$

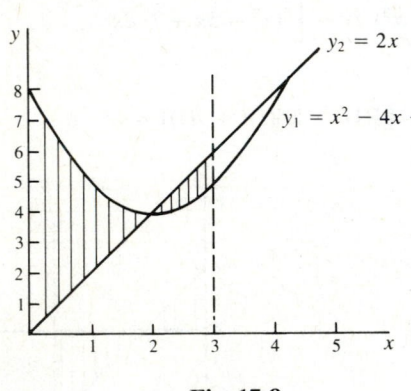

Fig. 17-8

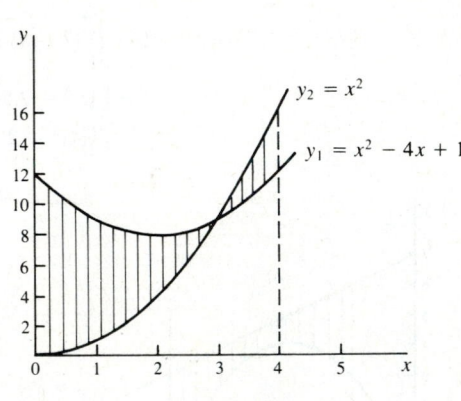

Fig. 17-9

IMPROPER INTEGRALS AND L'HÔPITAL'S RULE

17.19. (a) Specify why the integral given below is improper and (b) test for convergence. Evaluate where possible.

$$\int_1^\infty \frac{2x}{(x^2 + 1)^2} \, dx$$

(a)   This is an example of an improper integral because the upper limit of integration is infinite.

(b)
$$\int_1^\infty \frac{2x}{(x^2 + 1)^2} \, dx = \lim_{b \to \infty} \int_1^b \frac{2x}{(x^2 + 1)^2} \, dx$$

Let $u = x^2 + 1$, $du/dx = 2x$, and $dx = du/2x$. Substituting,

$$\int \frac{2x}{(x^2 + 1)^2} \, dx = \int 2xu^{-2} \frac{du}{2x} = \int u^{-2} \, du$$

Integrating with respect to u and ignoring the constant,

$$\int u^{-2} \, du = -u^{-1}$$

Substituting $u = x^2 + 1$ and incorporating the limits of x,

$$\int_1^\infty \frac{2x}{(x^2+1)^2} \, dx = \lim_{b \to \infty} \int_1^b \frac{2x}{(x^2+1)^2} \, dx = -(x^2+1)^{-1} \Big|_1^b$$

$$= \frac{-1}{b^2+1} + \frac{1}{(1)^2+1} = \frac{1}{2} - \frac{1}{b^2+1}$$

As $b \to \infty$, $1/(b^2+1) \to 0$. The integral converges and has a value of $\frac{1}{2}$.

17.20. Redo Problem 17.19, given

$$\int_1^\infty \frac{dx}{x+7}$$

(a) This is an improper integral because one of its limits of integration is infinite.

(b)
$$\int_1^\infty \frac{dx}{x+7} = \lim_{b \to \infty} \int_1^b \frac{dx}{x+7} = \ln|x+7| \Big|_1^b$$
$$= \ln|b+7| - \ln|1+7|$$

As $b \to \infty$, $\ln|b+7| \to \infty$. The integral diverges and is meaningless.

17.21. Redo Problem 17.19, given $\int_{-\infty}^0 e^{3x} \, dx$.

(a) The lower limit is infinite.

(b)
$$\int_{-\infty}^0 e^{3x} \, dx = \lim_{a \to -\infty} \int_a^0 e^{3x} \, dx = \tfrac{1}{3} e^{3x} \Big|_a^0$$
$$= \tfrac{1}{3} e^{3(0)} - \tfrac{1}{3} e^{3a} = \tfrac{1}{3} - \tfrac{1}{3} e^{3a}$$

As $a \to -\infty$, $\tfrac{1}{3} e^{3a} \to 0$. The integral converges and has a value of $\frac{1}{3}$.

17.22. (a) Specify why the integral given below is improper and (b) test for convergence. Evaluate where possible.

$$\int_{-\infty}^0 (5-x)^{-2} \, dx$$

(a) The lower limit is infinite.

(b)
$$\int_{-\infty}^0 (5-x)^{-2} \, dx = \lim_{a \to -\infty} \int_a^0 (5-x)^{-2} \, dx$$

Let $u = 5 - x$, $du/dx = -1$, and $dx = -du$. Substituting,

$$\int (5-x)^{-2} \, dx = \int u^{-2}(-du) = -\int u^{-2} \, du$$

Integrating with respect to u,

$$-\int u^{-2} \, du = u^{-1}$$

Substituting $u = 5 - x$ and incorporating the limits of x,

$$\int_{-\infty}^{0} (5 - x)^{-2}\, dx = \lim_{a \to -\infty} \int_{a}^{0} (5 - x)^{-2}\, dx = (5 - x)^{-1} \Big|_{a}^{0}$$

$$= \frac{1}{5 - 0} - \frac{1}{5 - a} = \frac{1}{5} - \frac{1}{5 - a}$$

As $a \to -\infty$, $1/(5 - a) \to 0$. The integral converges and equals $\frac{1}{5}$.

17.23. Redo Problem 17.22, given $\int_{-\infty}^{0} 2xe^x\, dx$.

(a) The lower limit is infinite.

(b)
$$\int_{-\infty}^{0} 2xe^x\, dx = \lim_{a \to -\infty} \int_{a}^{0} 2xe^x\, dx$$

Using integration by parts, let $f(x) = 2x$, $f'(x) = 2$, $g'(x) = e^x$, and $g(x) = \int e^x\, dx = e^x$. Substituting in (16.1),

$$\int 2xe^x\, dx = 2xe^x - \int e^x 2\, dx$$

Integrating once again,

$$\int 2xe^x\, dx = 2xe^x - 2e^x$$

Incorporating the limits,

$$\int_{-\infty}^{0} 2xe^x\, dx = \lim_{a \to -\infty} \int_{a}^{0} 2xe^x\, dx = (2xe^x - 2e^x) \Big|_{a}^{0}$$

$$= [2(0)e^0 - 2e^0] - (2ae^a - 2e^a)$$

$$= -2 - 2ae^a + 2e^a \qquad \text{since} \quad e^0 = 1$$

As $a \to -\infty$, $e^a \to 0$. Therefore the integral converges and has a value of -2.

17.24. Redo Problem 17.22, given

$$\int_{0}^{6} \frac{dx}{x - 6}$$

(a) This is also an improper integral because, as x approaches 6 from the left $(x \to 6^-)$, the integrand $\to -\infty$.

(b)
$$\int_{0}^{6} \frac{dx}{x - 6} = \lim_{b \to 6} \int_{0}^{b} \frac{dx}{x - 6} = \ln|x - 6| \Big|_{0}^{b}$$

$$= \ln|b - 6| - \ln|0 - 6|$$

As $b \to 6^-$, $|b - 6| \to 0$ and $\ln 0$ is undefined. Therefore, the integral diverges and is meaningless.

17.25. Redo Problem 17.22, given $\int_{0}^{8} (8 - x)^{-1/2}\, dx$.

(a) As $x \to 8^-$, the integrand approaches infinity.

(b)
$$\int_{0}^{8} (8 - x)^{-1/2}\, dx = \lim_{b \to 8} \int_{0}^{b} (8 - x)^{-1/2}\, dx = -2(8 - x)^{1/2} \Big|_{0}^{b}$$

$$= (-2\sqrt{8 - b}) - (-2\sqrt{8 - 0}) = 2\sqrt{8} - 2\sqrt{8 - b}$$

As $b \to 8^-$, $-2\sqrt{8 - b} \to 0$. The integral converges and has a value of $2\sqrt{8} = 4\sqrt{2}$.

17.26. Use L'Hôpital's rule to evaluate the following limits:

(a) $\lim\limits_{x \to \infty} \dfrac{5x - 9}{e^x}$

As $x \to \infty$, both $5x - 9$ and e^x tend to ∞, giving rise to the indeterminate form ∞/∞. Using (17.6), therefore, and differentiating numerator and denominator separately,

$$\lim_{x \to \infty} \frac{5x - 9}{e^x} = \lim_{x \to \infty} \frac{5}{e^x} = \frac{5}{\infty} = 0$$

(b) $\lim\limits_{x \to \infty} \dfrac{1 - e^{1/x}}{1/x}$

As $x \to \infty$, $1 - e^{1/x}$ and $1/x \to 0$. Using (17.6), therefore, and recalling that $1/x = x^{-1}$,

$$\lim_{x \to \infty} \frac{1 - e^{1/x}}{1/x} = \lim_{x \to \infty} \frac{-(-1/x^2)e^{1/x}}{-1/x^2}$$

Simplifying algebraically,

$$\lim_{x \to \infty} \frac{1 - e^{1/x}}{1/x} = \lim_{x \to \infty} (-e^{1/x}) = -e^0 = -1$$

(c) $\lim\limits_{x \to \infty} \dfrac{\ln 2x}{e^{5x}}$

As $x \to \infty$, $\ln 2x$ and $e^{5x} \to \infty$. Again using (17.6),

$$\lim_{x \to \infty} \frac{\ln 2x}{e^{5x}} = \lim_{x \to \infty} \frac{1/x}{5e^{5x}} = \frac{0}{\infty} = 0 \qquad \text{since } \frac{0}{\infty} \text{ is not an indeterminate form}$$

(d) $\lim\limits_{x \to \infty} \dfrac{6x^3 - 7}{3x^2 + 9}$

$$\lim_{x \to \infty} \frac{6x^3 - 7}{3x^2 + 9} = \lim_{x \to \infty} \frac{18x^2}{6x} = \lim_{x \to \infty} 3x = \infty$$

(e) $\lim\limits_{x \to \infty} \dfrac{3x^2 - 7x}{4x^2 - 21}$

$$\lim_{x \to \infty} \frac{3x^2 - 7x}{4x^2 - 21} = \lim_{x \to \infty} \frac{6x - 7}{8x}$$

Whenever application of L'Hôpital's rule gives rise to a new quotient whose limit is also an indeterminate form, L'Hôpital's rule must be applied again. Thus,

$$\lim_{x \to \infty} \frac{6x - 7}{8x} = \lim_{x \to \infty} \frac{6}{8} = \frac{3}{4} \qquad \text{See Problem 3.4(c)}.$$

(f) $\lim\limits_{x \to \infty} \dfrac{8x^3 - 5x^2 + 13x}{2x^3 + 7x^2 - 18x}$

Using L'Hôpital's rule repeatedly,

$$\lim_{x \to \infty} \frac{8x^3 - 5x^2 + 13x}{2x^3 + 7x^2 - 18x} = \lim_{x \to \infty} \frac{24x^2 - 10x + 13}{6x^2 + 14x - 18} = \lim_{x \to \infty} \frac{48x - 10}{12x + 14}$$

$$= \lim_{x \to \infty} \tfrac{48}{12} = 4$$

CONSUMERS' AND PRODUCERS' SURPLUS

17.27. Given the demand function $P = 45 - 0.5Q$, find the consumers' surplus CS when $P_0 = 32.5$ and $Q_0 = 25$.

Using (17.8),

$$CS = \int_0^{25} (45 - 0.5Q)\, dQ - (32.5)(25) = [45Q - 0.25Q^2]_0^{25} - 812.5$$

$$= [45(25) - 0.25(25)^2] - 0 - 812.5 = 156.25$$

17.28. Given the supply function $P = (Q + 3)^2$, find the producers' surplus PS at $P_0 = 81$ and $Q_0 = 6$.

From (17.9),

$$PS = (81)(6) - \int_0^6 (Q + 3)^2\, dQ = 486 - [\tfrac{1}{3}(Q + 3)^3]_0^6$$

$$= 486 - [\tfrac{1}{3}(6 + 3)^3 - \tfrac{1}{3}(0 + 3)^3] = 252$$

17.29. Given the demand function $P_d = 25 - Q^2$ and the supply function $P_s = 2Q + 1$. Assuming pure competition, find (a) the consumers' surplus and (b) the producers' surplus.

For market equilibrium, $s = d$. Thus,

$$2Q + 1 = 25 - Q^2 \qquad Q^2 + 2Q - 24 = 0$$
$$(Q + 6)(Q - 4) = 0 \qquad Q_0 = 4 \qquad P_0 = 9$$

since Q_0 cannot equal -6.

(a)
$$CS = \int_0^4 (25 - Q^2)\, dQ - (9)(4) = [25Q - \tfrac{1}{3}Q^3]_0^4 - 36$$

$$= [25(4) - \tfrac{1}{3}(4)^3] - 0 - 36 = 42.67$$

(b)
$$PS = (9)(4) - \int_0^4 (2Q + 1)\, dQ$$

$$= 36 - [Q^2 + Q]_0^4 = 16$$

17.30. Given the demand function $P_d = 113 - Q^2$ and the supply function $P_s = (Q + 1)^2$ under pure competition, find (a) CS and (b) PS.

Multiplying the supply function out and equating supply and demand,

$$Q^2 + 2Q + 1 = 113 - Q^2 \qquad 2(Q^2 + Q - 56) = 0$$
$$(Q + 8)(Q - 7) = 0 \qquad Q_0 = 7 \qquad P_0 = 64$$

(a)
$$CS = \int_0^7 (113 - Q^2)\, dQ - (64)(7) = [113Q - \tfrac{1}{3}Q^3]_0^7 - 448 = 228.67$$

(b)
$$PS = (64)(7) - \int_0^7 (Q + 1)^2\, dQ = 448 - [\tfrac{1}{3}(Q + 1)^3]_0^7 = 448 - (170.67 - 0.33) = 277.67$$

17.31. Under a monopoly, the quantity sold and market price are determined by the demand function. If the demand function for a profit-maximizing monopolist is $P = 274 - Q^2$ and MC $= 4 + 3Q$, find the consumers' surplus.

Given $P = 274 - Q^2$,

$$TR = PQ = (274 - Q^2)Q = 274Q - Q^3$$

and
$$MR = \frac{dTR}{dQ} = 274 - 3Q^2$$

The monopolist maximizes profit at $MR = MC$. Thus,

$$274 - 3Q^2 = 4 + 3Q \qquad 3(Q^2 + Q - 90) = 0$$
$$(Q + 10)(Q - 9) = 0 \qquad Q_0 = 9 \qquad P_0 = 193$$

and

$$CS = \int_0^9 (274 - Q^2)\, dQ - (193)(9) = [274Q - \tfrac{1}{3}Q^3]_0^9 - 1737 = 486$$

FREQUENCY FUNCTIONS AND PROBABILITY

17.32. The probability in minutes of being waited on in a large chain restaurant is given by the frequency function $f(t) = \frac{4}{81}t^3$ for $0 \le t \le 3$. What is the probability of being waited on between 1 and 2 minutes?

$$P = \int_1^2 \tfrac{4}{81}t^3\, dt = \tfrac{1}{81}t^4 \Big|_1^2 = \tfrac{1}{81}(16) - \tfrac{1}{81}(1) = 0.1852$$

17.33. The proportion of assignments completed within a given day is described by the probability density function $f(x) = 12(x^2 - x^3)$ for $0 \le x \le 1$. What is the probability that (a) 50 percent or less of the assignments will be completed within the day and (b) 50 percent or more will be completed?

(a)
$$P_a = \int_0^{0.5} 12(x^2 - x^3)\, dx = 12\left[\frac{x^3}{3} - \frac{x^4}{4}\right]_0^{0.5}$$
$$= 12\left[\left(\frac{0.125}{3} - \frac{0.0625}{4}\right) - 0\right] = 0.3125$$

(b)
$$P_b = \int_{0.5}^1 12(x^2 - x^3)\, dx = 12\left[\frac{x^3}{3} - \frac{x^4}{4}\right]_{0.5}^1$$
$$= 12\left[\left(\frac{1}{3} - \frac{1}{4}\right) - \left(\frac{0.125}{3} - \frac{0.0625}{4}\right)\right] = 0.6875$$

As expected, $P_a + P_b = 0.3125 + 0.6875 = 1$.

OTHER ECONOMIC APPLICATIONS

17.34. Given $I(t) = 9t^{1/2}$, find the level of capital formation in (a) 8 years and (b) for the fifth through the eighth years (interval $[4, 8]$).

(a)
$$K = \int_0^8 9t^{1/2}\, dt = 6t^{3/2} \Big|_0^8 = 6(8)^{3/2} - 0 = 96\sqrt{2} = 135.76$$

(b)
$$K = \int_4^8 9t^{1/2}\, dt = 6t^{3/2} \Big|_4^8 = 6(8)^{3/2} - 6(4)^{3/2} = 135.76 - 48 = 87.76$$

Chapter 18

Differential Equations

18.1 DEFINITIONS AND CONCEPTS

A *differential equation* is an equation which expresses an explicit or implicit relationship between a function $y = f(t)$ and one or more of its derivatives or differentials. Examples of differential equations include

$$\frac{dy}{dt} = 5t + 9 \qquad y' = 12y \qquad \text{and} \qquad y'' - 2y' + 19 = 0$$

Equations involving a single independent variable, such as those above, are called *ordinary differential equations*. The *solution* or *integral* of a differential equation is any equation, without derivative or differential, that is defined over an interval and satisfies the differential equation for all the values of the independent variable(s) in the interval. See Example 1.

The *order* of a differential equation is the order of the highest derivative in the equation. The *degree* of a differential equation is the highest power to which the derivative of highest order is raised. See Example 2 and Problem 18.1.

EXAMPLE 1. To solve the differential equation $y''(t) = 7$ for all the functions $y(t)$ which satisfy the equation, simply integrate both sides of the equation to find the integrals.

$$y'(t) = \int 7 \, dt = 7t + c_1$$

$$y(t) = \int (7t + c_1) \, dt = 3.5t^2 + c_1 t + c$$

This is called a *general solution* which indicates that when c is unspecified, a differential equation has an infinite number of possible solutions. If c can be specified, the differential equation has a *particular* or *definite solution* which alone of all possible solutions is relevant.

EXAMPLE 2. The order and degree of differential equations are shown below.

1. $\dfrac{dy}{dt} = 2x + 6$ first-order, first-degree

2. $\left(\dfrac{dy}{dt}\right)^4 - 5t^5 = 0$ first-order, fourth-degree

3. $\dfrac{d^2 y}{dt^2} + \left(\dfrac{dy}{dt}\right)^3 + x^2 = 0$ second-order, first-degree

4. $\left(\dfrac{d^2 y}{dt^2}\right)^7 + \left(\dfrac{d^3 y}{dt^3}\right)^5 = 75y$ third-order, fifth-degree

18.2 GENERAL FORMULA FOR FIRST-ORDER LINEAR DIFFERENTIAL EQUATIONS

For a first-order *linear* differential equation, dy/dt and y must be of the first degree, and no product $y(dy/dt)$ may occur. For such an equation

$$\frac{dy}{dt} + vy = z$$

392

where v and z may be constants or functions of time, the formula for a *general solution* is

$$y(t) = e^{-\int v\, dt}\left(A + \int ze^{\int v\, dt}\, dt\right) \tag{18.1}$$

where A is an arbitrary constant. A solution is composed of two parts: $e^{-\int v\, dt}A$ is called the *complementary function*, and $e^{-\int v\, dt}\int ze^{\int v\, dt}\, dt$ is called the *particular integral*. The particular integral y_p equals the *intertemporal equilibrium level* of $y(t)$; the complementary function y_c represents the *deviation from the equilibrium*. For $y(t)$ to be *dynamically stable*, y_c must approach zero as t approaches infinity (that is, k in e^{kt} must be negative). The solution of a differential equation can always be checked by differentiation. See Examples 3 to 5, Problems 18.2 to 18.12, and Problem 21.30.

EXAMPLE 3. The general solution for the differential equation $dy/dt + 4y = 12$ is calculated as follows. Since $v = 4$ and $z = 12$, substituting in (18.1) gives

$$y(t) = e^{-\int 4\, dt}\left(A + \int 12e^{\int 4\, dt}\, dt\right)$$

From Section 16.2, $\int 4\, dt = 4t + c$. When (18.1) is used, c is always ignored and subsumed under A. Thus,

$$y(t) = e^{-4t}\left(A + \int 12e^{4t}\, dt\right) \tag{18.2}$$

Integrating the remaining integral gives $\int 12e^{4t}\, dt = 3e^{4t} + c$. Ignoring the constant again and substituting in (18.2),

$$y(t) = e^{-4t}(A + 3e^{4t}) = Ae^{-4t} + 3 \tag{18.3}$$

since $e^{-4t}e^{4t} = e^0 = 1$. As $t \to \infty$, $y_c = Ae^{-4t} \to 0$ and $y(t)$ approaches $y_p = 3$, the intertemporal equilibrium level. $y(t)$ is dynamically stable.

    To check this answer, which is a general solution because A has not been specified, start by taking the derivative of (18.3).

$$\frac{dy}{dt} = -4Ae^{-4t}$$

From the original problem,

$$\frac{dy}{dt} + 4y = 12 \qquad \frac{dy}{dt} = 12 - 4y$$

Substituting $y = Ae^{-4t} + 3$ from (18.3),

$$\frac{dy}{dt} = 12 - 4(Ae^{-4t} + 3) = -4Ae^{-4t}$$

EXAMPLE 4. Given $dy/dt + 3t^2y = t^2$ where $v = 3t^2$ and $z = t^2$. To find the general solution, first substitute in (18.1),

$$y(t) = e^{-\int 3t^2\, dt}\left(A + \int t^2 e^{\int 3t^2\, dt}\, dt\right) \tag{18.4}$$

Integrating the exponents, $\int 3t^2\, dt = t^3$. Substituting in (18.4),

$$y(t) = e^{-t^3}\left(A + \int t^2 e^{t^3}\, dt\right) \tag{18.5}$$

Integrating the remaining integral in (18.5) calls for the substitution method. Letting $u = t^3$, $du/dt = 3t^2$, and $dt = du/3t^2$,

$$\int t^2 e^{t^3}\, dt = \int t^2 e^u \frac{du}{3t^2} = \frac{1}{3}\int e^u\, du = \frac{1}{3}e^u = \frac{1}{3}e^{t^3}$$

Finally, substituting in (*18.5*),

$$y(t) = e^{-t^3}(A + \tfrac{1}{3}e^{t^3}) = Ae^{-t^3} + \tfrac{1}{3} \tag{18.6}$$

As $t \to \infty$, $y_c = Ae^{-t^3} \to 0$ and $y(t)$ approaches $\tfrac{1}{3}$. The equilibrium is dynamically stable.

Differentiating (*18.6*) to check the general solution, $dy/dt = -3t^2 Ae^{-t^3}$. From the original problem,

$$\frac{dy}{dt} + 3t^2 y = t^2 \qquad \frac{dy}{dt} = t^2 - 3t^2 y$$

Substituting y from (*18.6*),

$$\frac{dy}{dt} = t^2 - 3t^2 \left(Ae^{-t^3} + \frac{1}{3} \right) = -3t^2 Ae^{-t^3}$$

EXAMPLE 5. Suppose that $y(0) = 1$ in Example 4. The definite solution is calculated as follows: From (*18.6*), $y = Ae^{-t^3} + \tfrac{1}{3}$. At $t = 0$, $y(0) = 1$. Hence, $1 = A + \tfrac{1}{3}$ since $e^0 = 1$, and $A = \tfrac{2}{3}$. Substituting $A = \tfrac{2}{3}$ in (*18.6*), the definite solution is $y = \tfrac{2}{3}e^{-t^3} + \tfrac{1}{3}$.

18.3 EXACT DIFFERENTIAL EQUATIONS AND PARTIAL INTEGRATION

Given a function of more than one independent variable, such as $F(y, t)$ where $M = \partial F/\partial y$ and $N = \partial F/\partial t$, the total differential is written

$$dF(y, t) = M \, dy + N \, dt \tag{18.7}$$

Since F is a function of more than one independent variable, M and N are partial derivatives and Equation (*18.7*) is called a *partial differential equation*. If the differential is set equal to zero, so that $M \, dy + N \, dt = 0$, it is called an *exact differential equation* because the left side exactly equals the differential of the primitive function $F(y, t)$. For an exact differential equation, $\partial M/\partial t$ must equal $\partial N/\partial y$, that is, $\partial^2 F/(\partial t \, \partial y) = \partial^2 F/(\partial y \, \partial t)$. For proof of this proposition, see Problem 18.50.

Solution of an exact differential equation calls for successive integration with respect to one independent variable at a time while holding constant the other independent variable(s). The procedure, called *partial integration*, reverses the process of partial differentiation. See Example 6 and Problems 18.13 to 18.17.

EXAMPLE 6. Solve the exact nonlinear differential equation

$$(6yt + 9y^2) \, dy + (3y^2 + 8t) \, dt = 0 \tag{18.8}$$

1. Test to see if it is an exact differential equation. Here $M = 6yt + 9y^2$ and $N = 3y^2 + 8t$. Thus, $\partial M/\partial t = 6y$ and $\partial N/\partial y = 6y$. If $\partial M/\partial t \neq \partial N/\partial y$, it is not an exact differential equation.

2. Since $M = \partial F/\partial y$ is a partial derivative, integrate M partially with respect to y by treating t as a constant, and add a new function $Z(t)$ for any additive terms of t which would have been eliminated by the original differentiation with respect to y. Note that ∂y replaces dy in partial integration.

$$F(y, t) = \int (6yt + 9y^2) \, \partial y + Z(t) = 3y^2 t + 3y^3 + Z(t) \tag{18.9}$$

This gives the original function except for the unknown additive terms of t, $Z(t)$.

3. Differentiate (*18.9*) with respect to t to find $\partial F/\partial t$ (earlier called N). Thus,

$$\frac{\partial F}{\partial t} = 3y^2 + Z'(t) \tag{18.10}$$

Since $\partial F/\partial t = N$ and $N = 3y^2 + 8t$ from (*18.8*), substitute $\partial F/\partial t = 3y^2 + 8t$ in (*18.10*).

$$3y^2 + 8t = 3y^2 + Z'(t) \qquad Z'(t) = 8t$$

4. Next integrate $Z'(t)$ with respect to t to find the missing t terms.

$$Z(t) = \int Z'(t) \, dt = \int 8t \, dt = 4t^2 \qquad (18.11)$$

5. Substitute (18.11) in (18.9), and add a constant of integration.

$$F(y, t) = 3y^2 t + 3y^3 + 4t^2 + c$$

This is easily checked by differentiation.

18.4 INTEGRATING FACTORS

Not all differential equations are exact. However, some can be made exact by means of an *integrating factor*. This is a multiplier which permits the equation to be integrated. See Example 7 and Problems 18.18 to 18.22.

EXAMPLE 7. Testing the nonlinear differential equation $5yt \, dy + (5y^2 + 8t) \, dt = 0$ reveals that it is not exact. With $M = 5yt$ and $N = 5y^2 + 8t$, $\partial M/\partial t = 5y \neq \partial N/\partial y = 10y$. Multiplying by an integrating factor of t, however, makes it exact: $5yt^2 \, dy + (5y^2 t + 8t^2) \, dt = 0$. Now $\partial M/\partial t = 10yt = \partial N/\partial y$, and the equation can be solved by the procedure outlined above. See Problem 18.22.

To check the answer to a problem in which an integrating factor was used, take the total differential of the answer and then divide by the integrating factor.

18.5 RULES FOR THE INTEGRATING FACTOR

Two rules will help to find the integrating factor for a nonlinear first-order differential equation, if such a factor exists. Assuming $\partial M/\partial t \neq \partial N/\partial y$,

Rule 1. If $\dfrac{1}{N}\left(\dfrac{\partial M}{\partial t} - \dfrac{\partial N}{\partial y}\right) = f(y)$ alone, then $e^{\int f(y) \, dy}$ is an integrating factor.

Rule 2. If $\dfrac{1}{M}\left(\dfrac{\partial N}{\partial y} - \dfrac{\partial M}{\partial t}\right) = g(t)$ alone, then $e^{\int g(t) \, dt}$ is an integrating factor.

See Example 8 and Problems 18.23 to 18.28.

EXAMPLE 8. To illustrate the rules above, find the integrating factor given in Example 7, where

$$5yt \, dy + (5y^2 + 8t) \, dt = 0 \qquad M = 5yt \qquad N = 5y^2 + 8t \qquad \frac{\partial M}{\partial t} = 5y \neq \frac{\partial N}{\partial y} = 10y$$

Applying Rule 1,

$$\frac{1}{5y^2 + 8t}(5y - 10y) = \frac{-5y}{5y^2 + 8t}$$

which is not a function of y alone and will not supply an integrating factor for the equation. Applying Rule 2,

$$\frac{1}{5yt}(10y - 5y) = \frac{5y}{5yt} = \frac{1}{t}$$

which is a function of t alone. The integrating factor, therefore, is $e^{\int (1/t) \, dt} = e^{\ln t} = t$.

18.6 SEPARATION OF VARIABLES

Solution of nonlinear first-order first-degree differential equations is complex. (A first-order first-degree differential equation is one in which the highest derivative is the first derivative dy/dt and that derivative is raised to a power of 1. It is *nonlinear* if it contains a product of y and dy/dt, or y raised to a power other than 1.) If the equation is exact or can be rendered exact by an integrating factor, the procedure outlined in Example 6 can be used. If, however, the equation can be written in the form of *separated variables* such that $M(y)\,dy + N(t)\,dt = 0$, where M and N, respectively, are functions of y and t alone, the equation can be solved by ordinary integration. See Examples 9 and 10 and Problems 18.29 to 18.35.

EXAMPLE 9. The following calculations illustrate the separation of variables to solve the nonlinear differential equation

$$\frac{dy}{dt} = y^2 t \qquad (18.12)$$

First, rearranging terms, $dy/y^2 = t\,dt$. Thus, $M = 1/y^2$ and $N = t$. Integrating both sides,

$$\int y^{-2}\,dy = \int t\,dt$$

$$-y^{-1} + c_1 = \frac{t^2}{2} + c_2$$

$$-\frac{1}{y} = \frac{t^2 + 2c_2 - 2c_1}{2}$$

Letting $c = 2c_2 - 2c_1$,

$$y = \frac{-2}{t^2 + c} \qquad (18.13)$$

Since the constant of integration is arbitrary until it is evaluated to obtain a particular solution, it will be treated generally and not specifically in the initial steps of the solution. e^c and $\ln c$ can also be used to express the constant.

This solution can be checked as follows: Taking the derivative of $y = -2(t^2 + c)^{-1}$ by the generalized power function rule,

$$\frac{dy}{dt} = (-1)(-2)(t^2 + c)^{-2}(2t) = \frac{4t}{(t^2 + c)^2}$$

From (18.12), $dy/dt = y^2 t$. Substituting into (18.12) from (18.13),

$$\frac{dy}{dt} = \left(\frac{-2}{t^2 + c}\right)^2 t = \frac{4t}{(t^2 + c)^2}$$

EXAMPLE 10. Given the nonlinear differential equation

$$t^2\,dy + y^3\,dt = 0 \qquad (18.14)$$

where $M \neq f(y)$ and $N \neq f(t)$. But multiplying (18.14) by $1/(t^2 y^3)$ to separate the variables gives

$$\frac{1}{y^3}\,dy + \frac{1}{t^2}\,dt = 0 \qquad (18.14a)$$

Integrating the separated variables,

$$\int y^{-3}\,dy + \int t^{-2}\,dt = -\tfrac{1}{2}y^{-2} - t^{-1} + c$$

and

$$F(y, t) = -\tfrac{1}{2}y^{-2} - t^{-1} + c$$
$$= -\tfrac{1}{2y^2} - \tfrac{1}{t} + c$$

For complicated functions, the answer is frequently left in this form. It can be checked by differentiating and comparing with (18.14a), which can be reduced to (18.14) through multiplication by $y^3 t^2$. For other forms in which an answer can be expressed, see Problems 18.20 to 18.22 and 18.29 to 18.35.

18.7 BERNOULLI EQUATIONS

A *Bernoulli equation* is a nonlinear differential equation in the specific form

$$\frac{dy}{dt} + ay = by^n \tag{18.15}$$

where a and b are constants or functions of t, $n \neq 0$, and $n \neq 1$. By letting $w = y^{1-n}$, Equation (18.15) can be transformed to a linear equation of the form

$$\frac{dw}{dt} + (1 - n)aw = (1 - n)b \tag{18.15a}$$

which can be solved by (18.1) with $v = (1 - n)a$ and $z = (1 - n)b$. See Example 11 and Problems 18.36 to 18.38. For verification of (18.15a), see Problem 18.51.

EXAMPLE 11.   The Bernoulli equation, $dy/dt - y = ty^2$ is solved below.

Here $n = 2$, so $w = y^{1-2} = y^{-1}$; $a = -1$, $b = t$; and $1 - n = -1$. Substituting in (18.15a),

$$\frac{dw}{dt} + w = -t$$

Using (18.1) with $v = 1$ and $z = -t$,

$$w(t) = e^{-\int 1\, dt}\left(A + \int -te^{\int 1\, dt}\, dt\right) = e^{-t}\left(A + \int -te^t\, dt\right)$$

By parts, $$w(t) = e^{-t}(A - te^t + e^t) = Ae^{-t} - t + 1$$

Since $w(t) = y(t)^{-1}$, $$y(t) = (Ae^{-t} - t + 1)^{-1}$$

18.8 ECONOMIC APPLICATIONS

Differential equations serve many functions in economics. They are used to determine the conditions for dynamic stability in microeconomic models of market equilibria and to trace the time path of growth under various conditions in macroeconomics. Given the growth rate of a function, differential equations enable the economist to find the function whose growth is described; from point elasticity, they enable the economist to estimate the demand function (see Example 12 and Problems 18.39 to 18.49). In Section 16.6 they were used to estimate capital functions from investment functions and total cost and total revenue functions from marginal cost and marginal revenue functions.

EXAMPLE 12.   Given the demand function $Q_d = c + bP$ and the supply function $Q_s = g + hP$, the equilibrium price is

$$\bar{P} = \frac{c - g}{h - b} \tag{18.16}$$

Assume that the rate of change of price in the market dP/dt is a positive linear function of *excess demand* $Q_d - Q_s$ such that

$$\frac{dP}{dt} = m(Q_d - Q_s) \qquad m = \text{a constant} > 0 \tag{18.17}$$

The conditions for dynamic price stability in the market [i.e., under what conditions $P(t)$ will converge to $\bar{P}$ as $t \to \infty$] can be calculated as shown below.

Substituting the given parameters for Q_d and Q_s in (18.17),

$$\frac{dP}{dt} = m[(c + bP) - (g + hP)] = m(c + bP - g - hP)$$

Rearranging to fit the general format of Section 18.2, $dP/dt + m(h - b)P = m(c - g)$. Letting $v = m(h - b)$ and $z = m(c - g)$, and using (18.1),

$$P(t) = e^{-\int v \, dt}\left(A + \int z e^{\int v \, dt} \, dt\right) = e^{-vt}\left(A + \int z e^{vt} \, dt\right)$$

$$= e^{-vt}\left(A + \frac{z e^{vt}}{v}\right) = Ae^{-vt} + \frac{z}{v} \qquad (18.18)$$

At $t = 0$, $P(0) = A + z/v$ and $A = P(0) - z/v$.

Substituting in (18.18),

$$P(t) = \left[P(0) - \frac{z}{v}\right]e^{-vt} + \frac{z}{v}$$

Finally, replacing $v = m(h - b)$ and $z = m(c - g)$,

$$P(t) = \left[P(0) - \frac{c - g}{h - b}\right]e^{-m(h-b)t} + \frac{c - g}{h - b}$$

and making use of (18.16), the time path is

$$P(t) = [P(0) - \bar{P}]e^{-m(h-b)t} + \bar{P} \qquad (18.19)$$

Since $P(0)$, $\bar{P}$, $m > 0$, the first term on the right-hand side will converge toward zero as $t \to \infty$, and thus $P(t)$ will converge toward $\bar{P}$ only if $h - b > 0$. For normal cases where demand is negatively sloped ($b < 0$) and supply is positively sloped ($h > 0$), the dynamic stability condition is assured. Markets with positively sloped demand functions or negatively sloped supply functions will also be dynamically stable as long as $h > b$.

Solved Problems

ORDER AND DEGREE

18.1. Specify the order and degree of the following differential equations:

(a) $\dfrac{d^2y}{dx^2} + \left(\dfrac{dy}{dx}\right)^3 = 12x$

(b) $\dfrac{dy}{dx} = 3x^2$

(c) $\left(\dfrac{d^3y}{dx^3}\right)^4 + \left(\dfrac{d^2y}{dx^2}\right)^6 = 4 - y$

(d) $\left(\dfrac{d^2y}{dx^2}\right)^3 + \dfrac{d^4y}{dx^4} - 75y = 0$

(e) $\dfrac{d^3y}{dx^3} + x^2y\left(\dfrac{d^2y}{dx^2}\right) - 4y^4 = 0$

(a) Second order, first degree; (b) first order, first degree; (c) third order, fourth degree; (d) fourth order, first degree; (e) third order, first degree.

FIRST-ORDER FIRST-DEGREE LINEAR DIFFERENTIAL EQUATIONS

18.2. (a) Use the formula for a general solution to solve the following equation. (b) Check your answer.

$$\frac{dy}{dt} + 5y = 0 \qquad (18.20)$$

(a) Here $v = 5$ and $z = 0$. Substituting in (18.1),

$$y(t) = e^{-\int 5 \, dt}\left(A + \int 0 \, e^{\int 5 \, dt} \, dt\right)$$

Integrating the exponents, $\int 5\,dt = 5t + c$, where c can be ignored because it is subsumed under A. Thus, $y(t) = e^{-5t}(A + \int 0\,dt)$. And $\int 0\,dt = k$, a constant, which can also be subsumed under A. Hence,

$$y(t) = e^{-5t}A = Ae^{-5t} \tag{18.21}$$

(b) Taking the derivative of (18.21), $dy/dt = -5Ae^{-5t}$. From (18.20), $dy/dt = -5y$. Substituting y from (18.21),

$$\frac{dy}{dt} = -5(Ae^{-5t}) = -5Ae^{-5t}$$

18.3. Redo Problem 18.2, given

$$\frac{dy}{dt} = 3y \qquad y(0) = 2 \tag{18.22}$$

(a) Rearranging to obtain the general format,

$$\frac{dy}{dt} - 3y = 0$$

Here $v = -3$ and $z = 0$. Substituting in (18.1),

$$y(t) = e^{-\int -3\,dt}\left(A + \int 0\,e^{\int -3\,dt}\,dt\right)$$

Substituting $\int -3\,dt = -3t$, $y(t) = e^{3t}(A + \int 0\,dt) = Ae^{3t}$. At $t = 0$, $y = 2$. Thus, $2 = Ae^{3(0)}$, $A = 2$. Substituting,

$$y(t) = 2e^{3t} \tag{18.23}$$

(b) Taking the derivative of (18.23), $dy/dt = 6e^{3t}$. From (18.22), $dy/dt = 3y$. Substituting y from (18.23), $dy/dt = 3(2e^{3t}) = 6e^{3t}$.

18.4. Redo Problem 18.2, given

$$\frac{dy}{dt} = 15 \tag{18.24}$$

(a) Here $v = 0$ and $z = 15$. Thus,

$$y(t) = e^{-\int 0\,dt}\left(A + \int 15\,e^{\int 0\,dt}\,dt\right)$$

where $\int 0\,dt = k$, a constant. Substituting and recalling that e^k is also a constant,

$$y(t) = e^{-k}\left(A + \int 15e^k\,dt\right)$$

$$= e^{-k}(A + 15te^k) = Ae^{-k} + 15t = 15t + A \tag{18.25}$$

where A is an arbitrary constant equal to Ae^{-k} or simply c. Whenever the derivative is equal to a constant, simply integrate as in Example 1.

(b) Taking the derivative of (18.25), $dy/dt = 15$. From (18.24), $dy/dt = 15$.

18.5. Redo Problem 18.2, given

$$\frac{dy}{dt} - 6y = 18 \tag{18.26}$$

(a) Here $v = -6$, $z = 18$, and $\int -6\,dt = -6t$. Substituting in (18.1),

$$y(t) = e^{6t}\left(A + \int 18e^{-6t}\,dt\right)$$

where $\int 18e^{-6t}\,dt = -3e^{-6t}$. Thus,

$$y(t) = e^{6t}(A - 3e^{-6t}) = Ae^{6t} - 3 \qquad (18.27)$$

(b) Taking the derivative of (18.27), $dy/dt = 6Ae^{6t}$. From (18.26), $dy/dt = 18 + 6y$. Substituting y from (18.27), $dy/dt = 18 + 6(Ae^{6t} - 3) = 6Ae^{6t}$.

18.6. Redo Problem 18.2, given

$$\frac{dy}{dt} + 4y = -20 \qquad y(0) = 10 \qquad (18.28)$$

(a) Here $v = 4$, $z = -20$, and $\int 4\,dt = 4t$. Thus,

$$y(t) = e^{-4t}\left(A + \int -20e^{4t}\,dt\right)$$

where $\int -20e^{4t}\,dt = -5e^{4t}$. Substituting, $y(t) = e^{-4t}(A - 5e^{4t}) = Ae^{-4t} - 5$. At $t = 0$, $y = 10$. Thus, $10 = Ae^{-4(0)} - 5$, and $A = 15$. Substituting,

$$y(t) = 15e^{-4t} - 5 = 5(3e^{-4t} - 1) \qquad (18.29)$$

(b) The derivative of (18.29) is $dy/dt = -60e^{-4t}$. From (18.28), $dy/dt = -20 - 4y$. Substituting from (18.29) for y, $dy/dt = -20 - 4(15e^{-4t} - 5) = -60e^{-4t}$.

18.7. Redo Problem 18.2, given

$$\frac{dy}{dt} + 4ty = 6t \qquad (18.30)$$

(a) $v = 4t$, $z = 6t$, and $\int 4t\,dt = 2t^2$. Thus,

$$y(t) = e^{-2t^2}\left(A + \int 6te^{2t^2}\,dt\right) \qquad (18.31)$$

Using the substitution method for the remaining integral, let $u = 2t^2$, $du/dt = 4t$ and $dt = du/4t$. Thus,

$$\int 6te^{2t^2}\,dt = \int 6te^u\,\frac{du}{4t} = 1.5\int e^u\,du = 1.5e^{2t^2}$$

Substituting back in (18.31),

$$y(t) = e^{-2t^2}(A + 1.5e^{2t^2}) = Ae^{-2t^2} + 1.5 \qquad (18.32)$$

(b) The derivative of (18.32) is $dy/dt = -4tAe^{-2t^2}$. From (18.30), $dy/dt = 6t - 4ty$. Substituting from (18.32), $dy/dt = 6t - 4t(Ae^{-2t^2} + 1.5) = -4tAe^{-2t^2}$.

18.8. (a) Solve the equation below using the formula for a general solution. (b) Check your answer.

$$2\frac{dy}{dt} - 2t^2y = 9t^2 \qquad y(0) = -2.5 \qquad (18.33)$$

(a) Dividing through by 2, $dy/dt - t^2y = 4.5t^2$. Thus, $v = -t^2$, $z = 4.5t^2$, and $\int -t^2\,dt = -\frac{1}{3}t^3$. Substituting,

$$y(t) = e^{(1/3)t^3}\left(A + \int 4.5t^2e^{-(1/3)t^3}\,dt\right) \qquad (18.34)$$

Let $u = -\frac{1}{3}t^3$, $du/dt = -t^2$, and $dt = -du/t^2$. Thus,

$$\int 4.5t^2 e^{-(1/3)t^3}\, dt = \int 4.5t^2 e^u \frac{du}{-t^2} = -4.5 \int e^u\, du = -4.5 e^{-(1/3)t^3}$$

Substituting in (18.34),

$$y(t) = e^{(1/3)t^3}(A - 4.5e^{-(1/3)t^3}) = Ae^{(1/3)t^3} - 4.5$$

At $t = 0$, $-2.5 = A - 4.5$; $A = 2$. Thus,

$$y(t) = 2e^{(1/3)t^3} - 4.5 \tag{18.35}$$

(b) Taking the derivative of (18.35), $dy/dt = 2t^2 e^{(1/3)t^3}$. From (18.33), $dy/dt = 4.5t^2 + t^2 y$. Substituting from (18.35), $dy/dt = 4.5t^2 + t^2(2e^{(1/3)t^3} - 4.5) = 2t^2 e^{(1/3)t^3}$.

18.9. Redo Problem 18.8, given

$$\frac{dy}{dt} - 2ty = e^{t^2} \tag{18.36}$$

(a) $v = -2t$, $z = e^{t^2}$, and $\int -2t\, dt = -t^2$. Thus,

$$y(t) = e^{t^2}\left(A + \int e^{t^2} e^{-t^2}\, dt\right) = e^{t^2}\left(A + \int e^0\, dt\right)$$

where $e^0 = 1$ and $\int 1\, dt = t$. Substituting back,

$$y(t) = e^{t^2}(A + t) \tag{18.37}$$

(b) The derivative of (18.37), by the product rule, is $dy/dt = 2te^{t^2}(A + t) + e^{t^2}(1) = 2tAe^{t^2} + 2t^2 e^{t^2} + e^{t^2}$. From (18.36), $dy/dt = e^{t^2} + 2ty$. Substituting from (18.37),

$$\frac{dy}{dt} = e^{t^2} + 2t\left[e^{t^2}(A + t)\right] = e^{t^2} + 2tAe^{t^2} + 2t^2 e^{t^2}$$

18.10. Redo Problem 18.8, given

$$\frac{dy}{dt} + 3y = 6t \qquad y(0) = \frac{1}{3} \tag{18.38}$$

(a) $v = 3$, $z = 6t$, and $\int 3\, dt = 3t$. Then,

$$y(t) = e^{-3t}\left(A + \int 6te^{3t}\, dt\right) \tag{18.39}$$

Using integration by parts for the remaining integral, let $f(t) = 6t$, then $f'(t) = 6$; let $g'(t) = e^{3t}$, then $g(t) = \int e^{3t}\, dt = \frac{1}{3}e^{3t}$. Substituting in (16.1),

$$\int 6te^{3t}\, dt = 6t(\tfrac{1}{3}e^{3t}) - \int \tfrac{1}{3}e^{3t} 6\, dt$$

$$= 2te^{3t} - 2 \int e^{3t}\, dt = 2te^{3t} - \tfrac{2}{3}e^{3t}$$

Substituting back in (18.39),

$$y(t) = e^{-3t}(A + 2te^{3t} - \tfrac{2}{3}e^{3t}) = Ae^{-3t} + 2t - \tfrac{2}{3}$$

At $t = 0$, $\frac{1}{3} = Ae^{-3(0)} + 2(0) - \frac{2}{3}$; $A = 1$. Thus,

$$y(t) = e^{-3t} + 2t - \tfrac{2}{3} \tag{18.40}$$

(b) Taking the derivative of (18.40), $dy/dt = -3e^{-3t} + 2$. From (18.38), $dy/dt = 6t - 3y$. Substituting (18.40) directly above, $dy/dt = 6t - 3(e^{-3t} + 2t - \frac{2}{3}) = -3e^{-3t} + 2$.

18.11. Redo Problem 18.8, given

$$\frac{dy}{dt} - \frac{y}{t} = 0 \qquad y(3) = 12 \tag{18.41}$$

(a) $v = -1/t, z = 0$, and $\int -(1/t)\, dt = -\ln t$. Thus,

$$y(t) = e^{\ln t}\left(A + \int 0\, dt\right) = At$$

since $e^{\ln t} = t$. At $t = 3$, $12 = A(3)$; $A = 4$. Thus,

$$y(t) = 4t \tag{18.42}$$

(b) The derivative of (18.42) is $dy/dt = 4$. From (18.41), $dy/dt = y/t$. Substituting from (18.42), $dy/dt = 4t/t = 4$.

18.12. Redo Problem 18.8, given

$$\frac{dy}{dt} = -y \qquad y(3) = 20 \tag{18.43}$$

(a) With rearranging, $dy/dt + y = 0$. Therefore, $v = 1, z = 0$, and $\int 1\, dt = t$. Thus,

$$y(t) = e^{-t}\left(A + \int 0\, dt\right) = Ae^{-t}$$

At $t = 3$, $20 = Ae^{-3}$; $20 = A(0.05)$, so $A = 400$. Thus,

$$y(t) = 400e^{-t} \tag{18.44}$$

(b) Taking the derivative of (18.44), $dy/dt = -400e^{-t}$. From (18.43), $dy/dt = -y$. Substituting from (18.44), $dy/dt = -(400e^{-t}) = -400e^{-t}$.

EXACT DIFFERENTIAL EQUATIONS AND PARTIAL INTEGRATION

18.13. Solve the following exact differential equation. Check the answer on your own.

$$(4y + 8t^2)\, dy + (16yt - 3)\, dt = 0$$

As outlined in Example 6,

1. Check to see if it is an exact differential equation. Letting $M = 4y + 8t^2$ and $N = 16yt - 3$, $\partial M/\partial t = 16t = \partial N/\partial y$.

2. Integrate M partially with respect to y and add $Z(t)$ to get $F(y, t)$.

$$F(y, t) = \int (4y + 8t^2)\, \partial y + Z(t) = 2y^2 + 8t^2 y + Z(t) \tag{18.45}$$

3. Differentiate $F(y, t)$ partially with respect to t and equate with N above.

$$\frac{\partial F}{\partial t} = 16ty + Z'(t)$$

But $\partial F/\partial t = N = 16yt - 3$, so

$$16ty + Z'(t) = 16yt - 3 \qquad Z'(t) = -3$$

4. Integrate $Z'(t)$ with respect to t to get $Z(t)$.

$$Z(t) = \int Z'(t)\, dt = \int -3\, dt = -3t \tag{18.46}$$

5. Substitute (18.46) in (18.45) and add a constant of integration.

$$F(y, t) = 2y^2 + 8t^2 y - 3t + c$$

18.14. Redo Problem 18.13, given $(12y + 7t + 6)\,dy + (7y + 4t - 9)\,dt = 0$.

1. $\partial M/\partial t = 7 = \partial N/\partial y$.

2. $$F(y, t) = \int (12y + 7t + 6)\,\partial y + Z(t) = 6y^2 + 7yt + 6y + Z(t)$$

3. $\partial F/\partial t = 7y + Z'(t)$. But $\partial F/\partial t = N = 7y + 4t - 9$, so
$$7y + Z'(t) = 7y + 4t - 9 \qquad Z'(t) = 4t - 9$$

4. $$Z(t) = \int (4t - 9)\,dt = 2t^2 - 9t$$

5. $$F(y, t) = 6y^2 + 7yt + 6y + 2t^2 - 9t + c$$

18.15. Redo Problem 18.13, given $(12y^2 t^2 + 10y)\,dy + (8y^3 t)\,dt = 0$.

1. $\partial M/\partial t = 24y^2 t = \partial N/\partial y$.

2. $$F(y, t) = \int (12y^2 t^2 + 10y)\,\partial y + Z(t) = 4y^3 t^2 + 5y^2 + Z(t)$$

3. $\partial F/\partial t = 8y^3 t + Z'(t)$. But $N = 8y^3 t$, so
$$8y^3 t = 8y^3 t + Z'(t) \qquad Z'(t) = 0$$

4. $Z(t) = \int 0\,dt = k$, which will be subsumed under c.

5. $$F(y, t) = 4y^3 t^2 + 5y^2 + c$$

18.16. Redo Problem 18.13, given $8tyy' = -(3t^2 + 4y^2)$.

By rearranging,
$$8ty\,dy = -(3t^2 + 4y^2)\,dt \qquad 8ty\,dy + (3t^2 + 4y^2)\,dt = 0$$

1. $\partial M/\partial t = 8y = \partial N/\partial y$.

2. $$F(y, t) = \int 8ty\,\partial y + Z(t) = 4ty^2 + Z(t)$$

3. $\partial F/\partial t = 4y^2 + Z'(t)$. But $\partial F/\partial t = N = 3t^2 + 4y^2$, so
$$4y^2 + Z'(t) = 3t^2 + 4y^2 \qquad Z'(t) = 3t^2$$

4. $$Z(t) = \int 3t^2\,dt = t^3$$

5. $$F(y, t) = t^3 + 4ty^2 + c$$

18.17. Redo Problem 18.13, given $60ty^2 y' = -(12t^3 + 20y^3)$.

By rearranging, $\qquad 60ty^2\,dy + (12t^3 + 20y^3)\,dt = 0$

1. $\partial M/\partial t = 60y^2 = \partial N/\partial y$.

2. $$F(y, t) = \int 60ty^2\,\partial y + Z(t) = 20ty^3 + Z(t)$$

3. $\partial F/\partial t = 20y^3 + Z'(t)$. But $\partial F/\partial t = N = 12t^3 + 20y^3$, so
$$20y^3 + Z'(t) = 12t^3 + 20y^3 \qquad Z'(t) = 12t^3$$

4.
$$Z(t) = \int 12t^3 \, dt = 3t^4$$

5.
$$F(y, t) = 3t^4 + 20ty^3 + c$$

INTEGRATING FACTORS

18.18. Use the integrating factors provided in parentheses to solve the following differential equation. Check the answer on your own (remember to divide by the integrating factor after taking the total differential of the answer).

$$6t \, dy + 12y \, dt = 0 \qquad (t)$$

1. $\partial M/\partial t = 6 \neq \partial N/\partial y = 12$. But multiplying by the integrating factor t,

$$6t^2 \, dy + 12yt \, dt = 0$$

where $\partial M/\partial t = 12t = \partial N/\partial y$. Continuing with the new function,

2.
$$F(y, t) = \int 6t^2 \, dy + Z(t) = 6t^2 y + Z(t)$$

3. $\partial F/\partial t = 12ty + Z'(t)$. But $\partial F/\partial t = N = 12ty$, so $Z'(t) = 0$.

4. $Z(t) = \int 0 \, dt = k$, which will be subsumed under the c below.

5.
$$F(y, t) = 6t^2 y + c$$

18.19. Redo Problem 18.18, given

$$t^2 \, dy + 3yt \, dt = 0 \qquad (t)$$

1. $\partial M/\partial t = 2t \neq \partial N/\partial y = 3t$. But multiplying by t,

$$t^3 \, dy + 3yt^2 \, dt = 0$$

where $\partial M/\partial t = 3t^2 = \partial N/\partial y$.

2.
$$F(y, t) = \int t^3 \, dy + Z(t) = t^3 y + Z(t)$$

3. $\partial F/\partial t = 3t^2 y + Z'(t)$. But $\partial F/\partial t = N = 3t^2 y$, so $Z'(t) = 0$ and $F(y, t) = t^3 y + c$.

18.20. Redo Problem 18.18, given

$$\frac{dy}{dt} = \frac{y}{t} \qquad \left(\frac{1}{ty}\right)$$

Rearranging, $t \, dy = y \, dt \qquad t \, dy - y \, dt = 0$

1. $\partial M/\partial t = 1 \neq \partial N/\partial y = -1$. Multiplying by $1/(ty)$,

$$\frac{dy}{y} - \frac{dt}{t} = 0$$

where $\partial M/\partial t = 0 = \partial N/\partial y$, since neither function contains the variable with respect to which it is being partially differentiated.

2.
$$F(y, t) = \int \frac{1}{y} \, dy + Z(t) = \ln y + Z(t)$$

3. $\partial F/\partial t = Z'(t)$. But $\partial F/\partial t = N = -1/t$, so $Z'(t) = -1/t$.

4.
$$Z(t) = \int -\frac{1}{t}\, dt = -\ln t$$

5. $F(y, t) = \ln y - \ln t + c$ which can be expressed in different ways. Since c is an arbitrary constant, we can write $\ln y - \ln t = c$. Making use of the laws of logs (Section 7.3), $\ln y - \ln t = \ln (y/t)$. Thus, $\ln (y/t) = c$. Finally, expressing each side of the equation as exponents of e, and recalling that $e^{\ln x} = x$,

$$e^{\ln (y/t)} = e^c$$

$$\frac{y}{t} = e^c \qquad \text{or} \qquad y = te^c$$

For other treatments of c, see Problems 18.29 to 18.35.

18.21. Redo Problem 18.18, given

$$4t\, dy + (16y - t^2)\, dt = 0 \qquad (t^3)$$

1. $\partial M/\partial t = 4 \neq \partial N/\partial y = 16$. Multiplying by t^3, $4t^4\, dy + (16t^3y - t^5)\, dt = 0$ where $\partial M/\partial t = 16t^3 = \partial N/\partial y$.

2.
$$F(y, t) = \int 4t^4\, \partial y + Z(t) = 4t^4 y + Z(t)$$

3. $\partial F/\partial t = 16t^3 y + Z'(t)$. But $\partial F/\partial t = N = 16t^3 y - t^5$, so

$$16t^3 y + Z'(t) = 16t^3 y - t^5 \qquad Z'(t) = -t^5$$

4.
$$Z(t) = \int -t^5\, dt = -\tfrac{1}{6}t^6$$

5.
$$F(y, t) = 4t^4 y - \tfrac{1}{6}t^6 + c = 24t^4 y - t^6 + c$$

or
$$24t^4 y - t^6 = c$$

18.22. Redo Problem 18.18, given

$$5yt\, dy + (5y^2 + 8t)\, dt = 0 \qquad (t)$$

1. $\partial M/\partial t = 5y \neq \partial N/\partial y = 10y$. Multiplying by t, as in Example 7, $5yt^2\, dy + (5y^2 t + 8t^2)\, dt = 0$ where $\partial M/\partial t = 10yt = \partial N/\partial y$.

2.
$$F(y, t) = \int 5yt^2\, \partial y + Z(t) = 2.5y^2 t^2 + Z(t)$$

3. $\partial F/\partial t = 5y^2 t + Z'(t)$. But $\partial F/\partial t = N = 5y^2 t + 8t^2$, so

$$5y^2 t + Z'(t) = 5y^2 t + 8t^2 \qquad Z'(t) = 8t^2$$

4.
$$Z(t) = \int 8t^2\, dt = \tfrac{8}{3}t^3$$

5.
$$F(y, t) = 2.5y^2 t^2 + \tfrac{8}{3}t^3 + c = 7.5y^2 t^2 + 8t^3 + c$$

FINDING THE INTEGRATING FACTOR

18.23. (a) Find the integrating factor for the differential equation given below, and (b) solve the equation, using the five steps from Example 6.

$$(7y + 4t^2)\, dy + 4ty\, dt = 0 \qquad\qquad (18.47)$$

(a) $\partial M/\partial t = 8t \neq \partial N/\partial y = 4t$. Applying Rule 1 from Section 18.5, since $M = 7y + 4t^2$ and $N = 4ty$,

$$\frac{1}{4ty}(8t - 4t) = \frac{4t}{4ty} = \frac{1}{y} = f(y) \quad \text{alone}$$

Thus the integrating factor is

$$e^{\int (1/y)\,dy} = e^{\ln y} = y$$

(b)   Multiplying (18.47) by the integrating factor y, $(7y^2 + 4yt^2)\,dy + 4ty^2\,dt = 0$.

1. $\partial M/\partial t = 8yt = \partial N/\partial y$. Thus,

2. $F(y,\,t) = \displaystyle\int (7y^2 + 4yt^2)\,\partial y + Z(t) = \tfrac{7}{3}y^3 + 2y^2t^2 + Z(t)$

3. $\dfrac{\partial F}{\partial t} = 4y^2 t + Z'(t)$

4. $\partial F/\partial t = N = 4y^2 t$, so $Z'(t) = 0$ and $Z(t)$ is a constant. Thus,

5. $F(y,\,t) = \tfrac{7}{3}y^3 + 2y^2t^2 + c = 7y^3 + 6y^2t^2 + c$

18.24.   Redo Problem 18.23, given

$$y^3 t\,dy + \tfrac{1}{2}y^4\,dt = 0 \qquad\qquad (18.48)$$

(a) $\partial M/\partial t = y^3 \neq \partial N/\partial y = 2y^3$. Applying Rule 1,

$$\frac{1}{\frac{1}{2}y^4}(y^3 - 2y^3) = \frac{2}{y^4}(-y^3) = -\frac{2}{y} = f(y) \quad \text{alone}$$

Thus, $e^{\int -2y^{-1}\,dy} = e^{-2\ln y} = e^{\ln y^{-2}} = y^{-2}$

(b)   Multiplying (18.48) by y^{-2}, $yt\,dy + \tfrac{1}{2}y^2\,dt = 0$.

1. $\partial M/\partial t = y = \partial N/\partial y$. Thus,

2. $F(y,\,t) = \displaystyle\int yt\,\partial y + Z(t) = \tfrac{1}{2}y^2 t + Z(t)$

3. $\dfrac{\partial F}{\partial t} = \dfrac{1}{2}y^2 + Z'(t)$

4. $\partial F/\partial t = N = \tfrac{1}{2}y^2$, so $Z'(t) = 0$, and $Z(t)$ is a constant. Thus,

5. $F(y,\,t) = \tfrac{1}{2}y^2 t + c$

18.25.   Redo Problem 18.23, given

$$4t\,dy + (16y - t^2)\,dt = 0 \qquad\qquad (18.49)$$

(a) $M = 4t$, $N = 16y - t^2$, and $\partial M/\partial t = 4 \neq \partial N/\partial y = 16$. Applying Rule 1,

$$\frac{1}{16y - t^2}(4 - 16) = \frac{-12}{16y - t^2} \neq f(y) \quad \text{alone}$$

Applying Rule 2,

$$\frac{1}{4t}(16 - 4) = \frac{3}{t} = g(t) \quad \text{alone}$$

Thus, $e^{\int 3t^{-1}\,dt} = e^{3\ln t} = e^{\ln t^3} = t^3$

(b)   Multiplying (18.49) by t^3, $4t^4\,dy + (16yt^3 - t^5)\,dt = 0$ which was solved in Problem 18.21.

18.26. Redo Problem 18.23, given

$$t^2 \, dy + 3yt \, dt = 0 \tag{18.50}$$

(a) Here $M = t^2$, $N = 3yt$, and $\partial M/\partial t = 2t \neq \partial N/\partial y = 3t$. Applying Rule 1,

$$\frac{1}{3yt}(2t - 3t) = \frac{-t}{3yt} = \frac{-1}{3y} = f(y) \qquad \text{alone}$$

Thus,

$$e^{\int (-1/3y) \, dy} = e^{-(1/3)\ln y} = e^{\ln y^{-1/3}} = y^{-1/3}$$

Consequently, $y^{-1/3}$ is an integrating factor for the equation, although in Problem 18.19 t was given as an integrating factor. Let us check $y^{-1/3}$ first.

(b) Multiplying (18.50) by $y^{-1/3}$, $t^2 y^{-1/3} \, dy + 3ty^{2/3} \, dt = 0$.

    1. $\partial M/\partial t = 2ty^{-1/3} = \partial N/\partial y$. Thus,

    2.
$$F(y, t) = \int t^2 y^{-1/3} \, \partial y + Z(t) = 1.5t^2 y^{2/3} + Z(t)$$

    3.
$$\frac{\partial F}{\partial t} = 3ty^{2/3} + Z'(t)$$

    4. $\partial F/\partial t = N = 3ty^{2/3}$, so $Z'(t) = 0$ and $Z(t)$ is a constant. Hence,

    5.
$$F_1(y, t) = 1.5t^2 y^{2/3} + c \tag{18.51}$$

    Here F_1 is used to distinguish this function from the function F_2 below.

18.27. Test to see if t is a possible integrating factor in Problem 18.26.

    Applying Rule 2 to the original equation,

$$\frac{1}{t^2}(3t - 2t) = \frac{t}{t^2} = \frac{1}{t}$$

Thus,

$$e^{\int (1/t) \, dt} = e^{\ln t} = t$$

Hence t is also a possible integrating factor, as demonstrated in Problem 18.19, where the solution was $F_2(y, t) = t^3 y + c$. This differs from (18.51) but is equally correct, as you can check on your own.

18.28. Redo Problem 18.23, given

$$(y - t) \, dy - dt = 0 \tag{18.52}$$

(a) $M = y - t$, $N = -1$, and $\partial M/\partial t = -1 \neq \partial N/\partial y = 0$. Applying Rule 1,

$$\frac{1}{-1}(-1 - 0) = 1 = f(y) \qquad \text{alone}$$

Thus,

$$e^{\int 1 \, dy} = e^y$$

(b) Multiplying (18.52) by e^y,

$$(y - t)e^y \, dy - e^y \, dt = 0 \tag{18.53}$$

    1. $\partial M/\partial t = -e^y = \partial N/\partial y$. Thus,

    2.
$$F(y, t) = \int (y - t)e^y \, \partial y + Z(t) \tag{18.54}$$

which requires integration by parts. Let

$$f(y) = y - t \qquad f'(y) = 1 \qquad g'(y) = e^y \qquad g(y) = \int e^y \, dy = e^y$$

Substituting in (16.1),

$$\int (y - t)e^y \, \partial y = (y - t)e^y - \int e^y 1 \, dy = (y - t)e^y - e^y$$

Substituting in (18.54), $F(y, t) = (y - t)e^y - e^y + Z(t)$.

3.
$$\frac{\partial F}{\partial t} = -e^y + Z'(t)$$

4. $\partial F / \partial t = N = -e^y$ in (18.53), so $Z'(t) = 0$ and $Z(t)$ is a constant. Thus,

5.
$$F(y, t) = (y - t)e^y - e^y + c \quad \text{or} \quad (y - 1)e^y - te^y + c$$

SEPARATION OF VARIABLES

18.29. Solve the following differential equation, using the procedure for separating variables described in Section 18.6.

$$\frac{dy}{dt} = \frac{-5t}{y}$$

Separating the variables,

$$y \, dy = -5t \, dt \qquad y \, dy + 5t \, dt = 0$$

Integrating each term separately,

$$\frac{y^2}{2} + \frac{5t^2}{2} = c_1$$
$$y^2 + 5t^2 = 2c_1$$
$$y^2 + 5t^2 = c$$

Letting $c = 2c_1$,

18.30. Redo Problem 18.29, given

(a) $\dfrac{dy}{dt} = \dfrac{t^5}{y^4}$ (b) $t^2 \, dy - y^2 \, dt = 0$

$$y^4 \, dy - t^5 \, dt = 0 \qquad\qquad\qquad \frac{dy}{y^2} - \frac{dt}{t^2} = 0$$

Integrating, $\dfrac{y^5}{5} - \dfrac{t^6}{6} = c_1$ Integrating, $-\dfrac{1}{y} + \dfrac{1}{t} = c$

$$6y^5 - 5t^6 = 30c_1 \qquad\qquad\qquad y - t = cty$$

Letting $c = 30c_1$, $6y^5 - 5t^6 = c$

18.31. Redo Problem 18.29, given $t \, dy + y \, dt = 0$.

$$\frac{dy}{y} + \frac{dt}{t} = 0$$

Integrating, $\ln y + \ln t = \ln c$ (an arbitrary constant)

By the rule of logs, $\ln yt = \ln c \qquad yt = c$

18.32. Redo Problem 18.29, given $(t + 5)\, dy - (y + 9)\, dt = 0$.

$$\frac{dy}{y + 9} - \frac{dt}{t + 5} = 0$$

Integrating, $\qquad\qquad\qquad \ln(y + 9) - \ln(t + 5) = \ln c$

By the rule of logs, $\qquad\qquad \ln\frac{y + 9}{t + 5} = \ln c$

$$\frac{y + 9}{t + 5} = c \qquad \text{or} \qquad y + 9 = c(t + 5)$$

18.33. Using the procedure for separating variables, solve the differential equation $dy = 3t^2 y\, dt$.

$$\frac{dy}{y} - 3t^2\, dt = 0$$

Integrating, $\qquad\qquad\qquad \ln y - t^3 = \ln c$

Expressing each side of the equation as an exponent of e,

$$e^{\ln y - t^3} = e^{\ln c}$$
$$e^{\ln y} e^{-t^3} = e^{\ln c}$$
$$y e^{-t^3} = c$$
$$y = c e^{t^3}$$

18.34. Redo Problem 18.33, given $y^2(t^3 + 1)\, dy + t^2(y^3 - 5)\, dt = 0$.

$$\frac{y^2}{y^3 - 5}\, dy + \frac{t^2}{t^3 + 1}\, dt = 0$$

Integrating by substitution,

$$\tfrac{1}{3}\ln(y^3 - 5) + \tfrac{1}{3}\ln(t^3 + 1) = \ln c$$
$$\ln[(y^3 - 5)(t^3 + 1)] = \ln c \qquad (y^3 - 5)(t^3 + 1) = c$$

18.35. Redo Problem 18.33, given

$$3\, dy + \frac{t}{t^2 - 1}\, dt = 0$$

Integrating, $\qquad\qquad 3y + \tfrac{1}{2}\ln(t^2 - 1) = c$

Setting the left-hand side as an exponent of e and ignoring c, because, as an arbitrary constant, it can be expressed equally well as c or e^c,

$$e^{3y + (1/2)\ln(t^2 - 1)} = c$$
$$e^{3y} e^{\ln(t^2 - 1)^{1/2}} = c \qquad e^{3y}(t^2 - 1)^{1/2} = c$$

BERNOULLI EQUATIONS

18.36. Solve the following Bernoulli equation:

$$\frac{dy}{dt} + y = ty^3$$

Using the method outlined in Section 18.7, here $n = 3$, $w = y^{1-3} = y^{-2}$, $a = 1$, $b = t$, and $1 - n = -2$. Substituting in (18.15a),

$$\frac{dw}{dt} - 2w = -2t$$

Using (18.1) with $v = -2$ and $z = -2t$,

$$w(t) = e^{-\int -2\,dt}\left(A + \int -2te^{\int -2\,dt}\,dt\right) = e^{2t}\left(A + \int -2te^{-2t}\,dt\right)$$

By parts, $w(t) = e^{2t}(A + te^{-2t} + \tfrac{1}{2}e^{-2t}) = Ae^{2t} + t + \tfrac{1}{2}$

Since $w = y^{-2}$, $y = w^{-1/2}$. Thus, $y = (Ae^{2t} + t + \tfrac{1}{2})^{-1/2}$

18.37. Redo Problem 18.36, given

$$\frac{dy}{dt} + \frac{y}{t} = y^4$$

Here $n = 4$, $w = y^{1-4} = y^{-3}$, $a = 1/t$, $b = 1$, and $1 - n = -3$. Substituting in ($18.15a$),

$$\frac{dw}{dt} - \frac{3w}{t} = -3$$

Using (18.1) with $v = -3/t$ and $z = -3$,

$$w(t) = e^{-\int -(3/t)\,dt}\left(A + \int -3e^{\int -(3/t)\,dt}\,dt\right)$$

$$= e^{3\ln t}\left(A + \int -3e^{-3\ln t}\,dt\right) = t^3\left(A + \int -3t^{-3}\,dt\right)$$

$$= t^3(A + 1.5t^{-2}) = At^3 + 1.5t$$

Since $w(t) = y(t)^{-3}$, $y(t) = w(t)^{-1/3} = (At^3 + 1.5t)^{-1/3}$

18.38. Redo Problem 18.36, given

$$\frac{dy}{dt} + \frac{1}{2}y = \frac{1}{2}(t + 1)y^3$$

Here $n = 3$, $w = y^{1-3} = y^{-2}$, $a = \tfrac{1}{2}$, $b = \tfrac{1}{2}(t + 1)$, and $1 - n = -2$. Substituting in ($18.15a$),

$$\frac{dw}{dt} - w = -(t + 1)$$

Using (18.1) with $v = -1$ and $z = -(t + 1)$,

$$w(t) = e^{-\int -1\,dt}\left[A + \int -(t + 1)e^{\int -1\,dt}\,dt\right] = e^{t}\left[A - \int (t + 1)e^{-t}\,dt\right]$$

$$= e^{t}[A + (t + 1)e^{-t} + e^{-t}] = Ae^{t} + t + 1 + 1 = Ae^{t} + t + 2$$

Since $w = y^{-2}$, $y = w^{-1/2} = (Ae^{t} + t + 2)^{-1/2}$

USE OF DIFFERENTIAL EQUATIONS IN ECONOMICS

18.39. Find the demand function $Q = f(P)$ if point elasticity ϵ is -1 for all $P > 0$.

$$\epsilon = \frac{dQ}{dP}\frac{P}{Q} = -1 \qquad \frac{dQ}{dP} = -\frac{Q}{P}$$

Separating the variables,

$$\frac{dQ}{Q} + \frac{dP}{P} = 0$$

Integrating, $\ln Q + \ln P = \ln c$

$$QP = c \qquad Q = \frac{c}{P}$$

18.40. Find the demand function $Q = f(P)$ if $\epsilon = -k$, a constant.

$$\epsilon = \frac{dQ}{dP}\frac{P}{Q} = -k \qquad \frac{dQ}{dP} = -\frac{kQ}{P}$$

Separating the variables,

$$\frac{dQ}{Q} + \frac{k}{P}\,dP = 0$$
$$\ln Q + k \ln P = c$$
$$QP^k = c \qquad Q = cP^{-k}$$

18.41. Find the demand function $Q = f(P)$ if $\epsilon = -(5P + 2P^2)/Q$ and $Q = 500$ when $P = 10$.

$$\epsilon = \frac{dQ}{dP}\frac{P}{Q} = \frac{-(5P + 2P^2)}{Q}$$
$$\frac{dQ}{dP} = \frac{-(5P + 2P^2)}{Q}\frac{Q}{P} = -(5 + 2P)$$

Separating the variables,

$$dQ + (5 + 2P)\,dP = 0$$

Integrating, $Q + 5P + P^2 = c \qquad Q = -P^2 - 5P + c$

At $P = 10$ and $Q = 500$,

$$500 = -100 - 50 + c \qquad c = 650$$

Thus, $Q = 650 - 5P - P^2$.

18.42. Derive the formula $P = P(0)e^{it}$ for the total value of an initial sum of money $P(0)$ set out for t years at interest rate i, when i is compounded continuously.

If i is compounded continuously,

$$\frac{dP}{dt} = iP$$

Separating the variables,

$$\frac{dP}{P} - i\,dt = 0$$

Integrating, $\ln P - it = c$

Setting the left-hand side as an exponent of e,

$$e^{\ln P - it} = c$$
$$Pe^{-it} = c \qquad P = ce^{it}$$

At $t = 0$, $P = P(0)$. Thus $P(0) = ce^0$, $c = P(0)$, and $P = P(0)e^{it}$.

18.43. Determine the stability conditions for a two-sector income determination model in which $\hat{C}, \hat{I}, \hat{Y}$ are deviations of consumption, investment, and income, respectively, from their equilibrium values C_e, I_e, Y_e. That is, $\hat{C} = C(t) - C_e$, etc., where $\hat{C}$ is read "C hat." Income changes at a rate proportional to excess demand $C + I - Y$, and

$$\hat{C}(t) = g\hat{Y}(t) \qquad \hat{I}(t) = b\hat{Y}(t) \qquad \frac{d\hat{Y}(t)}{dt} = a(\hat{C} + \hat{I} - \hat{Y}) \qquad 0 < a, b, g < 1$$

Substituting the first two equations in the third,

$$\frac{d\hat{Y}}{dt} = a(g + b - 1)\hat{Y}$$

Separating the variables and then integrating,

$$\frac{d\hat{Y}}{\hat{Y}} = a(g + b - 1)\, dt$$

$$\ln \hat{Y} = a(g + b - 1)t + c$$
$$e^{\ln \hat{Y}} = e^{a(g+b-1)t+c}$$

Letting the constant $e^c = c$,

$$\hat{Y} = ce^{a(g+b-1)t}$$

At $t = 0$, $\hat{Y} = Y(0) - Y_e = c$. Substituting above, $\hat{Y} = [Y(0) - Y_e]e^{a(g+b-1)t}$. Since $\hat{Y} = Y(t) - Y_e$, $Y(t) = Y_e + \hat{Y}$. Thus,

$$Y(t) = Y_e + [Y(0) - Y_e]e^{a(g+b-1)t}$$

As $t \to \infty$, $Y(t) \to Y_e$ only if $g + b < 1$. The sum of the marginal propensity to consume g and the marginal propensity to invest b must be less than 1.

18.44. In Example 12 we found $P(t) = [P(0) - \bar{P}]e^{-m(h-b)t} + \bar{P}$. (a) Explain the time path if (1) the initial price $P(0) = \bar{P}$, (2) $P(0) > \bar{P}$, and (3) $P(0) < \bar{P}$. (b) Graph your findings.

(a) (1) If the initial price equals the equilibrium price, $P(0) = \bar{P}$, the first term on the right disappears and $P(t) = \bar{P}$. The time path is a horizontal line, and adjustment is immediate. See Fig. 18-1.

   (2) If $P(0) > \bar{P}$, the first term on the right is positive. Thus $P(t) > \bar{P}$ and $P(t)$ approaches $\bar{P}$ from above as $t \to \infty$ and the first term on the right $\to 0$.

   (3) If $P(0) < \bar{P}$, the first term on the right is negative. And $P(t) < \bar{P}$ and approaches it from below as $t \to \infty$ and the first term $\to 0$.

(b) See Fig. 18-1.

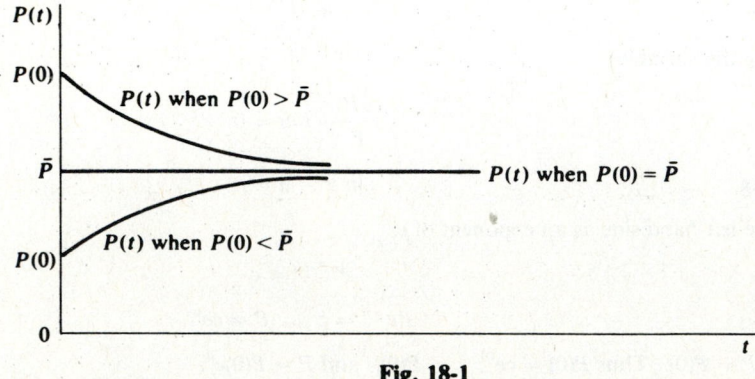

Fig. 18-1

18.45. A change in the rate of investment will affect both aggregate demand and the productive capability of an economy. The Domar model seeks to find the time path along which an economy can grow while maintaining full utilization of its productive capacity. If the marginal propensity to save s and the marginal capital-output ratio k are constant, find the investment function needed for the desired growth.

The change in aggregate demand is equal to the change in investment times the multiplier $1/s$,

$$\frac{dY}{dt} = \frac{1}{s}\frac{dI}{dt} \tag{18.55}$$

The change in productive capacity is equal to the change in the capital stock times the reciprocal of the marginal capital-output ratio,

$$\frac{dQ}{dt} = \frac{1}{k}\frac{dK}{dt} = \frac{1}{k}I \quad \text{since} \quad \frac{dK}{dt} = I \tag{18.56}$$

Equating (18.55) and (18.56) for fully utilized capacity,

$$\frac{1}{s}\frac{dI}{dt} = \frac{1}{k}I \qquad \frac{1}{s}dI = \frac{1}{k}I\,dt$$

Separating the variables,

$$\frac{dI}{I} - \frac{s}{k}dt = 0$$

Integrating,

$$\ln I - \frac{s}{k}t = c$$

$$Ie^{-(s/k)t} = c \qquad I = ce^{(s/k)t}$$

At $t = 0$, $I(0) = c$, and $I = I(0)e^{(s/k)t}$.

Investment must grow at a constant rate determined by s/k: the savings rate divided by the capital-output ratio.

18.46. The Solow model examines equilibrium growth paths with full employment of both capital and labor. Based on the assumptions that

1. Output is a linearly homogeneous function of capital and labor exhibiting constant returns to scale,

$$Y = f(K, L) \tag{18.57}$$

2. A constant proportion s of output is saved and invested,

$$\frac{dK}{dt} \equiv \dot{K} = sY \tag{18.58}$$

3. The supply of labor is growing at a constant rate r,

$$L = L_0\,e^{rt} \tag{18.59}$$

derive the differential equation in terms of the single variable K/L, which serves as the basis of the model.

Substituting Y from (18.57) in (18.58),

$$\frac{dK}{dt} = sf(K, L) \tag{18.60}$$

Substituting L from (18.59) in (18.60),

$$\frac{dK}{dt} = sf(K, L_0\,e^{rt}) \tag{18.61}$$

This is the time path capital formation (dK/dt) must follow for full employment of a growing labor force. Preparing to convert to a function of K/L, let $z = K/L$, then $K = zL$. Making use of (18.59),

$$K = zL_0 e^{rt} \tag{18.62}$$

Taking the derivative of (18.62) and using the product rule since z is a function of t,

$$\frac{dK}{dt} = z(rL_0 e^{rt}) + L_0 e^{rt}\frac{dz}{dt} = \left(zr + \frac{dz}{dt}\right)L_0 e^{rt} \tag{18.63}$$

Equating (18.61) and (18.63),

$$sf(K, L_0 e^{rt}) = \left(zr + \frac{dz}{dt}\right)L_0 e^{rt} \tag{18.64}$$

Since the left-hand side of (18.64) is a linearly homogeneous production function, we may divide both inputs by $L_0 e^{rt}$ and multiply the function itself by $L_0 e^{rt}$ without changing its value. Thus,

$$sf(K, L_0 e^{rt}) = sL_0 e^{rt}f\left(\frac{K}{L_0 e^{rt}}, 1\right) \tag{18.65}$$

Substituting (18.65) in (18.64) and dividing both sides by $L_0 e^{rt}$,

$$sf\left(\frac{K}{L_0 e^{rt}}, 1\right) = zr + \frac{dz}{dt} \tag{18.66}$$

Finally, substituting z for $K/L_0 e^{rt}$ and subtracting zr from both sides,

$$\frac{dz}{dt} = sf(z, 1) - zr \tag{18.67}$$

which is a differential equation in terms of the single variable z and two parameters r and s, where $z = K/L$, r = the rate of growth of the labor force, and s = the savings rate.

18.47. Suppose that the production function in (18.57) is further specified to be a strict Cobb-Douglas production function. Find the growth path of the capital-labor ratio that will provide full employment of all resources; i.e., solve the differential equation in (18.67), given the new conditions.

A strict Cobb-Douglas function has the form $Y = K^\alpha L^{1-\alpha} = L(K/L)^\alpha$ since $L^{1-\alpha} = L/L^\alpha$. Substituting $z = K/L$,

$$Y = Lz^\alpha \tag{18.68}$$

In the previously unspecified linearly homogeneous production function (18.57), $Y = f(K, L)$. Dividing the inputs by L and multiplying the function by L, as in (18.65), will leave the value of the function unaltered. Thus,

$$Y = f(K, L) = Lf\left(\frac{K}{L}, 1\right) = Lf(z, 1) \tag{18.69}$$

Equating Y in (18.68) and (18.69), since we now assume a strict Cobb-Douglas function,

$$Lz^\alpha = Lf(z, 1)$$
$$z^\alpha = f(z, 1) \tag{18.70}$$

Substituting (18.70) in (18.67) gives

$$\frac{dz}{dt} = sz^\alpha - zr \qquad \frac{dz}{dt} + rz = sz^\alpha \tag{18.71}$$

which is a Bernoulli equation, where $n = \alpha$, so $w = z^{1-\alpha}$, $a = r$, and $b = s$. Substituting in (18.15a),

$$\frac{dw}{dt} + (1-\alpha)rw = (1-\alpha)s$$

Using (18.1) where $v = (1 - \alpha)r$ and $z = (1 - \alpha)s$,

$$w(t) = e^{-\int (1-\alpha)r \, dt} \left[A + \int (1 - \alpha)se^{\int (1-\alpha)r \, dt} \, dt \right]$$

$$= e^{-(1-\alpha)rt} \left[A + \int (1 - \alpha)se^{(1-\alpha)rt} \, dt \right]$$

$$= e^{-(1-\alpha)rt} \left[A + \frac{(1-\alpha)s}{(1-\alpha)r} e^{(1-\alpha)rt} \right] = Ae^{-(1-\alpha)rt} + \frac{s}{r}$$

At $t = 0$, $w(0) = A + s/r$ and $A = w(0) - s/r$. Thus,

$$w(t) = \left[w(0) - \frac{s}{r} \right] e^{-(1-\alpha)rt} + \frac{s}{r}$$

Since $w(t) = z^{1-\alpha}$,

$$z^{1-\alpha} = \left[z(0)^{1-\alpha} - \frac{s}{r} \right] e^{-(1-\alpha)rt} + \frac{s}{r}$$

With $0 < \alpha < 1$ and $1 - \alpha$ and $r > 0$, as $t \to \infty$, $z^{1-\alpha} \to s/r$; and $z \to (s/r)^{1/(1-\alpha)}$. The capital-labor ratio z approaches $(s/r)^{1/(1-\alpha)}$ as its equilibrium value. In the Solow model the equilibrium level of the capital-labor ratio varies directly with the rate of savings s and inversely with the rate of growth of the supply of labor r.

18.48. Assume that the demand for money is for transaction purposes only. Thus,

$$M_d = kP(t)Q \tag{18.72}$$

where k is constant, P is the price level, and Q is real output. Assume $M_s = M_d$ and is exogenously determined by monetary authorities. If inflation or the rate of change of prices is proportional to excess demand for goods in society and, from Walras' law, an excess demand for goods is the same thing as an excess supply of money, so that

$$\frac{dP(t)}{dt} = b(M_s - M_d) \tag{18.73}$$

find the stability conditions, when real output Q is constant.

Substituting (18.72) in (18.73),

$$\frac{dP(t)}{dt} = bM_s - bkP(t)Q \tag{18.74}$$

If we let

$$\hat{P} = P(t) - P_e \tag{18.75}$$

where $\hat{P}$ is the deviation of prices from the equilibrium price level P_e, then taking the derivative of (18.75),

$$\frac{d\hat{P}}{dt} = \frac{dP(t)}{dt} - \frac{dP_e}{dt}$$

But in equilibrium $dP_e/dt = 0$. Hence,

$$\frac{d\hat{P}}{dt} = \frac{dP(t)}{dt} \tag{18.76}$$

Substituting in (18.74),

$$\frac{d\hat{P}}{dt} = bM_s - bkP(t)Q \tag{18.77}$$

In equilibrium, $M_s = M_d = kP_eQ$. Hence $M_s - kP_eQ = 0$ and $b(M_s - kP_eQ) = 0$. Subtracting this from (18.77),

$$\frac{d\hat{P}}{dt} = bM_s - bkP(t)Q - bM_s + bkP_eQ = -bkQ[P(t) - P_e] = -bkQ\hat{P} \tag{18.78}$$

which is a differential equation. Separating the variables,

$$\frac{d\hat{P}}{\hat{P}} = -bkQ \; dt$$

Integrating, $\ln \hat{P} = -bkQt + c$, $\hat{P} = Ae^{-bkQt}$, where $e^c = A$.

Since $b, k, Q > 0$, $\hat{P} \to 0$ as $t \to \infty$, and the system is stable. To find the time path $P(t)$ from $\hat{P}$, see the conclusion of Problem 18.43, where $Y(t)$ was derived from $\hat{Y}$.

18.49. If the expectation of inflation is a positive function of the present rate of inflation

$$\left[\frac{dP(t)}{dt}\right]_E = h \frac{dP(t)}{dt} \qquad (18.79)$$

and the expectation of inflation reduces people's desire to hold money, so that

$$M_d = kP(t)Q - g\left[\frac{dP(t)}{dt}\right]_E \qquad (18.80)$$

check the stability conditions, assuming that the rate of inflation is proportional to the excess supply of money as in (18.73).

Substituting (18.79) in (18.80),

$$M_d = kP(t)Q - gh \frac{dP(t)}{dt} \qquad (18.81)$$

Substituting (18.81) in (18.73),

$$\frac{dP(t)}{dt} = bM_s - b\left[kP(t)Q - gh \frac{dP(t)}{dt}\right]$$

By a process similar to the steps involving (18.75) to (18.78),

$$\frac{d\hat{P}}{dt} = bM_s - bkP(t)Q + bgh \frac{dP(t)}{dt} - bM_s + bkP_eQ = -bkQ\hat{P} + bgh \frac{dP(t)}{dt} \qquad (18.82)$$

Substituting (18.76) for $dP(t)/dt$ in (18.82),

$$\frac{d\hat{P}}{dt} = -bkQ\hat{P} + bgh \frac{d\hat{P}}{dt} = \frac{-bkQ\hat{P}}{1 - bgh}$$

Separating the variables,

$$\frac{d\hat{P}}{\hat{P}} = \frac{-bkQ}{1 - bgh} \; dt$$

Integrating, $\ln \hat{P} = -bkQt/(1 - bgh)$

$$\hat{P} = Ae^{-bkQt/(1 - bgh)}$$

Since $b, k, Q > 0$, $\hat{P} \to 0$ as $t \to \infty$, if $bgh < 1$. Hence even if h is greater than 1, meaning people expect inflation to accelerate, the economy need not be unstable, as long as b and g are sufficiently small.

PROOFS

18.50. If $dz = M(x, y) \; dx + N(x, y) \; dy$ and M and N are assumed to have continuous partial derivatives, prove that

$$\frac{\partial M}{\partial y} = \frac{\partial N}{\partial x}$$

Given
$$dz = M\,dx + N\,dy$$

But from (5.11),
$$dz = \frac{\partial z}{\partial x}\,dx + \frac{\partial z}{\partial y}\,dy$$

So
$$M = \frac{\partial z}{\partial x} \quad\text{and}\quad N = \frac{dz}{\partial y} \tag{18.83}$$

By Young's theorem,
$$\frac{\partial^2 z}{\partial y\,\partial x} = \frac{\partial^2 z}{\partial x\,\partial y}$$

and from (18.83),
$$\frac{\partial M}{\partial y} = \frac{\partial^2 z}{\partial y\,\partial x} \quad\text{and}\quad \frac{\partial N}{\partial x} = \frac{\partial^2 z}{\partial x\,\partial y}$$

Therefore,
$$\frac{\partial M}{\partial y} = \frac{\partial N}{\partial x}$$

18.51. Show that by letting $w = y^{1-n}$, a Bernoulli equation in the form

$$\frac{dy}{dt} + ay = by^n \tag{18.84}$$

can be transformed to the linear differential equation

$$\frac{dw}{dt} + (1-n)aw = (1-n)b \tag{18.85}$$

Dividing (18.84) by y^n,

$$y^{-n}\frac{dy}{dt} + ay^{1-n} = b \tag{18.86}$$

Letting $w = y^{1-n}$ and taking the derivative to facilitate substitution in (18.86),

$$\frac{dw}{dt} = \frac{dw}{dy}\frac{dy}{dt}$$

$$= (1-n)y^{-n}\frac{dy}{dt} \qquad y^{-n}\frac{dy}{dt} = \frac{1}{1-n}\frac{dw}{dt} \tag{18.87}$$

Substituting (18.87) and $w = y^{1-n}$ in (18.86), and multiplying by $1-n$,

$$\frac{dw}{dt} + (1-n)aw = (1-n)b \qquad \text{Q.E.D.} \tag{18.88}$$

Chapter 19

Difference Equations

19.1 DEFINITIONS AND CONCEPTS

A *difference equation* expresses a relationship between a dependent variable and a lagged independent variable (or variables) which changes at discrete intervals of time, for example, $I_t = f(Y_{t-1})$, where I and Y are measured at the end of each year. The *order* of a difference equation is determined by the greatest number of periods lagged. A *first-order* difference equation expresses a time lag of one period; a *second-order*, two periods; etc. The change in y as t changes from t to $t + 1$ is called the *first difference of y*. It is written

$$\frac{\Delta y}{\Delta t} = \Delta y_t = y_{t+1} - y_t \tag{19.1}$$

where Δ is an operator replacing d/dt that is used to measure continuous change in differential equations. The *solution* of a difference equation defines y for every value of t and does not contain a difference expression. See Examples 1 and 2.

EXAMPLE 1. Each of the following is a difference equation of the order indicated.

$$
\begin{aligned}
I_t &= a(Y_{t-1} - Y_{t-2}) & &\text{order 2}\\
Q_s &= a + bP_{t-1} & &\text{order 1}\\
y_{t+3} - 9y_{t+2} + 2y_{t+1} + 6y_t &= 8 & &\text{order 3}\\
\Delta y_t &= 5y_t & &\text{order 1}
\end{aligned}
$$

Substituting from (*19.1*) for Δy_t above,

$$y_{t+1} - y_t = 5y_t \qquad y_{t+1} = 6y_t \qquad \text{order 1}$$

EXAMPLE 2. Given that the initial value of y is y_0, in the difference equation

$$y_{t+1} = by_t \tag{19.2}$$

a solution is found as follows. By successive substitutions of $t = 0, 1, 2, 3$, etc. in (*19.2*),

$$
\begin{aligned}
y_1 &= by_0 & y_3 &= by_2 = b(b^2 y_0) = b^3 y_0\\
y_2 &= by_1 = b(by_0) = b^2 y_0 & y_4 &= by_3 = b(b^3 y_0) = b^4 y_0
\end{aligned}
$$

Thus, for any period t,

$$y_t = b^t y_0$$

This method is called the *iterative method*. Since y_0 is a constant, notice the crucial role b plays in determining values for y as t changes.

19.2 GENERAL FORMULA FOR FIRST-ORDER LINEAR DIFFERENCE EQUATIONS

Given a first-order difference equation which is *linear* (i.e., all the variables are raised to the first power and there are no cross products),

$$y_t = by_{t-1} + a \tag{19.3}$$

where b and a are constants, the general formula for a *definite solution* is

$$y_t = \left(y_0 - \frac{a}{1-b}\right)b^t + \frac{a}{1-b} \qquad \text{when} \quad b \neq 1 \qquad (19.4)$$

$$y_t = y_0 + at \qquad \text{when} \quad b = 1 \qquad (19.4a)$$

If no initial condition is given, an arbitrary constant A is used for $y_0 - a/(1-b)$ in (*19.4*) and for y_0 in (*19.4a*). This is called a *general solution*. See Example 3 and Problems 19.1 to 19.13.

EXAMPLE 3.   Given the difference equation $y_t = -7y_{t-1} + 16$ and $y_0 = 5$. In the equation, $b = -7$ and $a = 16$. Since $b \neq 1$, it is solved by using (*19.4*), as follows:

$$y_t = \left(5 - \frac{16}{1+7}\right)(-7)^t + \frac{16}{1+7} = 3(-7)^t + 2 \qquad (19.5)$$

To check the answer, substitute $t = 0$ and $t = 1$ in (*19.5*).

$$y_0 = 3(-7)^0 + 2 = 5 \qquad \text{since} \quad (-7)^0 = 1$$
$$y_1 = 3(-7)^1 + 2 = -19$$

Substituting $y_1 = -19$ for y_t and $y_0 = 5$ for y_{t-1} in the original equation,

$$-19 = -7(5) + 16 = -35 + 16$$

19.3   STABILITY CONDITIONS

Equation (*19.4*) can be expressed in the general form

$$y_t = Ab^t + c \qquad (19.6)$$

where $A = y_0 - a/(1-b)$ and $c = a/(1-b)$. Here Ab^t is called the *complementary function*, and c is the *particular solution*. The particular solution expresses the *intertemporal equilibrium level of y*; the complementary function represents the *deviations from that equilibrium*. Equation (*19.6*) will be dynamically stable, therefore, only if the complementary function $Ab^t \to 0$, as $t \to \infty$. All depends on the base b. Assuming $A = 1$ and $c = 0$ for the moment, the exponential expression b^t will generate seven different time paths depending on the value of b, as illustrated in Example 4. As seen there, if $|b| > 1$, the time path will explode and move farther and farther away from equilibrium; if $|b| < 1$, the time path will be damped and move toward equilibrium. If $b < 0$, the time path will oscillate between positive and negative values; if $b > 0$, the time path will be nonoscillating. If $A \neq 1$, the value of the multiplicative constant will scale up or down the magnitude of b^t, but will not change the basic pattern of movement. If $A = -1$, a mirror image of the time path of b^t with respect to the horizontal axis will be produced. If $c \neq 0$, the vertical intercept of the graph is affected, and the graph shifts up or down accordingly. See Examples 4 and 5 and Problems 19.1 to 19.13.

EXAMPLE 4.   In the equation $y_t = b^t$, b can range from $-\infty$ to ∞. Seven different time paths can be generated, each of which is explained below and graphed in Fig. 19-1.

1. If $b > 1$, b^t increases at an increasing rate as t increases, thus moving farther and farther away from the horizontal axis. This is illustrated in Fig. 19-1(*a*), which is a step function representing changes at discrete intervals of time, not a continuous function. Assume $b = 3$. Then as t goes from 0 to 4, $b^t = 1, 3, 9, 27, 81$.

2. If $b = 1$, $b^t = 1$ for all values of t. This is represented by a horizontal line in Fig. 19-1(*b*).

3. If $0 < b < 1$, then b is a positive fraction and b^t decreases as t increases, drawing closer and closer to the horizontal axis, but always remaining positive, as illustrated in Fig. 19-1(*c*). Assume $b = \frac{1}{3}$. Then as t goes from 0 to 4, $b^t = 1, \frac{1}{3}, \frac{1}{9}, \frac{1}{27}, \frac{1}{81}$.

4. If $b = 0$, then $b^t = 0$ for all values of t. See Fig. 19-1(*d*).

5. If $-1 < b < 0$, then b is a negative fraction; b^t will alternate in sign and draw closer and closer to the horizontal axis as t increases. See Fig. 19-1(*e*). Assume $b = -\frac{1}{3}$. Then as t goes from 0 to 4, $b^t = 1, -\frac{1}{3}, \frac{1}{9}, -\frac{1}{27}, \frac{1}{81}$.

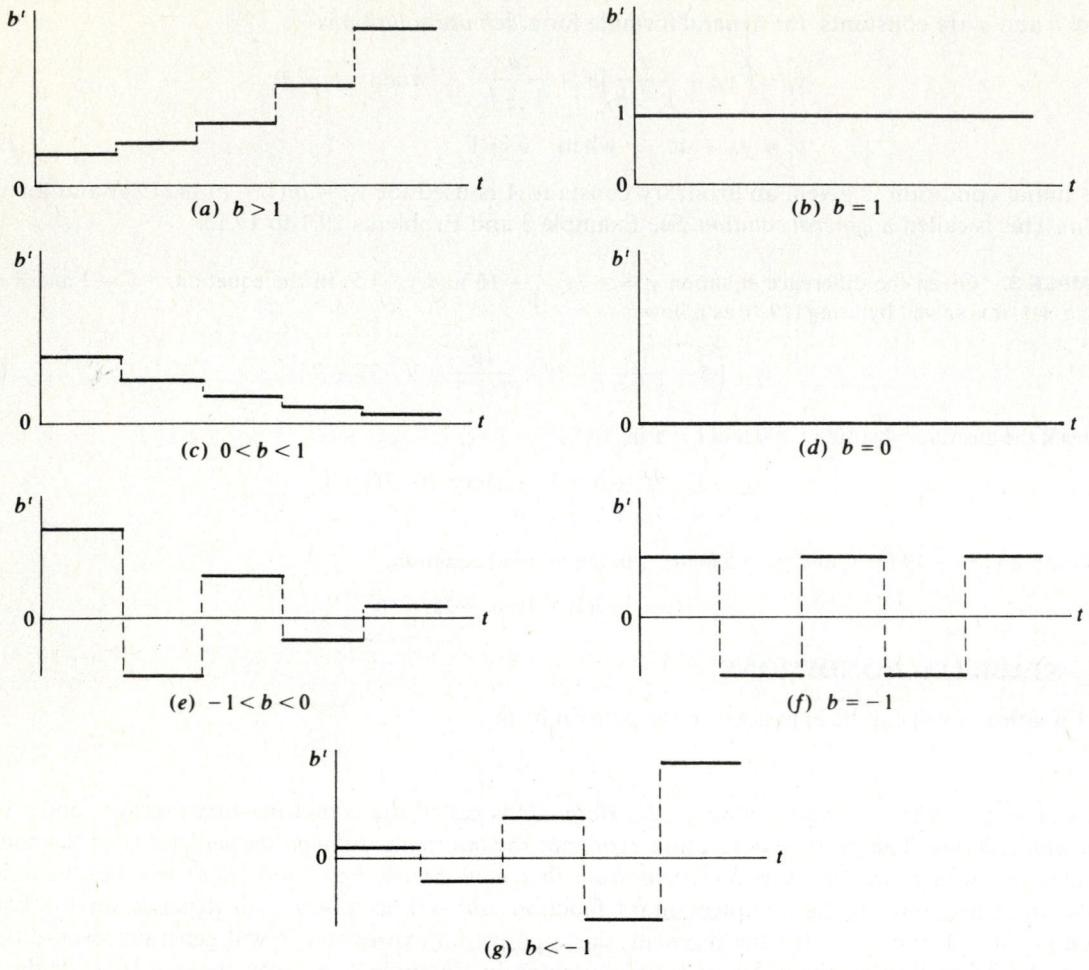

Fig. 19-1   Time path of b^t.

6. If $b = -1$, then b^t oscillates between $+1$ and -1. See Fig. 19-1(f).

7. If $b < -1$, then b^t will oscillate and move farther and farther away from the horizontal axis, as illustrated in Fig. 19-1(g). Assume $b = -3$. Then $b^t = 1, -3, 9, -27, 81$, as t goes from 0 to 4.

In short, if $|b| > 1$ the time path explodes

                      $|b| < 1$ the time path converges

                      $b > 0$ the time path is nonoscillating

                      $b < 0$ the time path oscillates

EXAMPLE 5.   In the equation $y_t = 6(-\frac{1}{4})^t + 6$, since $b = -\frac{1}{4} < 0$, the time path oscillates. Since $|b| < 1$, the time path converges.

When $y_t = 5(6)^t + 9$ and $b = 6 > 0$, there is no oscillation. With $|b| > 1$, the time path explodes.

19.4   LAGGED INCOME DETERMINATION MODEL

In the simple income determination model of Section 2.3 there were no lags. Now assume that consumption is a function of the previous period's income, so that

$$C_t = C_0 + cY_{t-1} \qquad Y_t = C_t + I_t$$

where $I_t = I_0$. Thus, $Y_t = C_0 + cY_{t-1} + I_0$. Rearranging terms to conform with (19.3),

$$Y_t = cY_{t-1} + C_0 + I_0 \qquad (19.7)$$

where $b = c$ and $a = C_0 + I_0$. Substituting these values in (19.4), since the marginal propensity to consume c cannot equal 1, and assuming $Y_t = Y_0$ at $t = 0$,

$$Y_t = \left(Y_0 - \frac{C_0 + I_0}{1 - c} \right)(c)^t + \frac{C_0 + I_0}{1 - c} \qquad (19.8)$$

The stability of the time path thus depends on c. Since $0 < \text{MPC} < 1$, $|c| < 1$ and the time path will converge. Since $c > 0$, there will be no oscillations. The equilibrium is stable, and as $t \to \infty$, $Y_t \to (C_0 + I_0)/(1 - c)$, which is the intertemporal equilibrium level of income. See Example 6 and Problems 19.14 to 19.20.

EXAMPLE 6. Given $Y_t = C_t + I_t$, $C_t = 200 + 0.9Y_{t-1}$, $I_t = 100$, and $Y_0 = 4500$. Solving for Y_t,

$$Y_t = 200 + 0.9Y_{t-1} + 100 = 0.9Y_{t-1} + 300 \qquad (19.9)$$

Using (19.4),

$$Y_t = \left(4500 - \frac{300}{1 - 0.9} \right)(0.9)^t + \frac{300}{1 - 0.9} = 1500(0.9)^t + 3000 \qquad (19.10)$$

With $|0.9| < 1$, the time path converges; with $0.9 > 0$, there is no oscillation. Thus, Y_t is dynamically stable. As $t \to \infty$, the first term on the right-hand side goes to zero, and Y_t approaches the intertemporal equilibrium level of income: $300/(1 - 0.9) = 3000$.

To check this answer, let $t = 0$ and $t = 1$ in (19.10). Thus,

$$Y_0 = 1500(0.9)^0 + 3000 = 4500$$
$$Y_1 = 1500(0.9)^1 + 3000 = 4350$$

Substituting $Y_1 = 4350$ for Y_t and $Y_0 = 4500$ for Y_{t-1} in (19.9),

$$4350 - 0.9(4500) = 300$$
$$4350 - 4050 = 300$$

19.5 THE COBWEB MODEL

For many products, such as agricultural commodities, which are planted a year before marketing, current supply depends on last year's price. This poses interesting stability questions. If

$$Q_{dt} = c + bP_t \qquad \text{and} \qquad Q_{st} = g + hP_{t-1}$$

in equilibrium,

$$c + bP_t = g + hP_{t-1} \qquad (19.11)$$

$$bP_t = hP_{t-1} + g - c \qquad (19.12)$$

Dividing (19.12) by b to conform to (19.3),

$$P_t = \frac{h}{b} P_{t-1} + \frac{g - c}{b}$$

Since $b < 0$ and $h > 0$ under normal demand and supply conditions, $h/b \neq 1$. Using (19.4),

$$P_t = \left[P_0 - \frac{(g - c)/b}{1 - h/b} \right] \left(\frac{h}{b} \right)^t + \frac{(g - c)/b}{1 - h/b}$$

$$= \left(P_0 - \frac{g - c}{b - h} \right) \left(\frac{h}{b} \right)^t + \frac{g - c}{b - h} \qquad (19.13)$$

When the model is in equilibrium, $P_t = P_{t-1}$. Substituting P_e for P_t and P_{t-1} in (19.11)

$$P_e = \frac{g - c}{b - h} \qquad (19.13a)$$

Substituting in (19.13),

$$P_t = (P_0 - P_e)\left(\frac{h}{b}\right)^t + P_e$$

With an ordinary negative demand function and positive supply function, $b < 0$ and $h > 0$. Therefore, $h/b < 0$ and the time path will oscillate.

If $|h| > |b|$, $|h/b| > 1$, and the time path P_t explodes.
If $|h| = |b|$, $h/b = -1$, and the time path oscillates uniformly.
If $|h| < |b|$, $|h/b| < 1$, and the time path converges, and P_t approaches P_e.

In short, for stability the supply curve must be flatter than the demand curve. See Example 7 and Problems 19.21 to 19.25.

EXAMPLE 7. Given $Q_{dt} = 86 - 0.8P_t$ and $Q_{st} = -10 + 0.2P_{t-1}$, the market price P_t for any time period and the equilibrium price P_e can be found as follows. Equating demand and supply,

$$86 - 0.8P_t = -10 + 0.2P_{t-1} \qquad -0.8P_t = 0.2P_{t-1} - 96$$

Dividing through by -0.8 to conform to (19.3), $P_t = -0.25P_{t-1} + 120$. Using (19.4),

$$P_t = \left(P_0 - \frac{120}{1 + 0.25}\right)(-0.25)^t + \frac{120}{1 + 0.25} = (P_0 - 96)(-0.25)^t + 96$$

which can be checked by substituting the appropriate values in (19.13). From (19.13a), $P_e = (-10 - 86)/(-0.8 - 0.2) = (-96)/(-1) = 96$.

With the base $b = -0.25$, which is negative and less than 1, the time path oscillates and converges. The equilibrium is stable, and P_t will converge to $P_e = 96$ as $t \to \infty$.

19.6 THE HARROD MODEL

The Harrod model attempts to explain the dynamics of growth in the economy. It assumes

$$S_t = sY_t$$

where s is a constant equal to both the MPS and APS. It also assumes the *acceleration principle*, i.e., investment is proportional to the rate of change of national income over time.

$$I_t = a(Y_t - Y_{t-1})$$

where a is a constant equal to both the marginal and average capital-output ratios. In equilibrium, $I_t = S_t$. Therefore,

$$a(Y_t - Y_{t-1}) = sY_t \qquad (a - s)Y_t = aY_{t-1}$$

Dividing through by $a - s$ to conform to (19.3), $Y_t = [a/(a - s)]Y_{t-1}$. Using (19.4) since $a/(a - s) \neq 1$,

$$Y_t = (Y_0 - 0)\left(\frac{a}{a - s}\right)^t + 0 = \left(\frac{a}{a - s}\right)^t Y_0 \qquad (19.14)$$

The stability of the time path thus depends on $a/(a - s)$. Since $a =$ the capital-output ratio, which is normally larger than 1, and since $s =$ MPS which is larger than 0 and less than 1, the base $a/(a - s)$ will be larger than 0 and usually larger than 1. Therefore, Y_t is explosive but nonoscillating. Income will expand indefinitely, which means it has no bounds. See Examples 8 and 9 and Problems 19.26 and 19.27. For other economic applications, see Problems 19.28 to 19.30.

EXAMPLE 8. The *warranted rate of growth* (i.e., the path the economy must follow to have equilibrium between saving and investment each year) can be found as follows in the Harrod model.

From (*19.14*) Y_t increases indefinitely. Income in one period is $a/(a-s)$ times the income of the previous period.

$$Y_1 = \left(\frac{a}{a-s}\right)Y_0 \tag{19.15}$$

The rate of growth G between the periods is defined as

$$G = \frac{Y_1 - Y_0}{Y_0}$$

Substituting from (*19.15*),

$$G = \frac{[a/(a-s)]Y_0 - Y_0}{Y_0} = \frac{[a/(a-s) - 1]Y_0}{Y_0}$$

$$= \frac{a}{a-s} - 1 = \frac{a}{a-s} - \frac{a-s}{a-s} = \frac{s}{a-s}$$

The warranted rate of growth, therefore, is

$$G_w = \frac{s}{a-s} \tag{19.16}$$

EXAMPLE 9. Assume that the marginal propensity to save in the Harrod model above is 0.12 and the capital-output ratio is 2.12. To find Y_t from (*19.14*),

$$Y_t = \left(\frac{2.12}{2.12 - 0.12}\right)^t Y_0 = (1.06)^t Y_0$$

The warranted rate of growth, from (*19.16*), is

$$G_w = \frac{0.12}{2.12 - 0.12} = \frac{0.12}{2} = 0.06$$

Solved Problems

USE OF GENERAL FORMULA FOR FIRST-ORDER LINEAR DIFFERENCE EQUATIONS

19.1. (*a*) Solve the difference equation given below; (*b*) check your answer, using $t = 0$ and $t = 1$; and (*c*) comment on the nature of the time path.

$$y_t = 6y_{t-1}$$

(*a*) Here $b = 6$ and $a = 0$. Using (*19.4*) for all cases in which $b \neq 1$,

$$y_t = (y_0 - 0)(6)^t + 0 = y_0(6)^t = A(6)^t \tag{19.17}$$

where A, as a more generally used unspecified constant, replaces y_0.

(*b*) Estimating (*19.17*) at $t = 0$ and $t = 1$,

$$y_0 = A(6)^0 = A \qquad y_1 = A(6) = 6A$$

Substituting $y_0 = A$ for y_{t-1} and $y_1 = 6A$ for y_t in the original problem, $6A = 6(A)$.

(*c*) With the base $b = 6$ in (*19.17*) positive and greater than 1, that is, $b > 0$ and $|b| > 1$, the time path is nonoscillating and explosive.

19.2. Redo Problem 19.1 for $y_t = \frac{1}{8}y_{t-1}$.

(a) Using (*19.4*),

$$y_t = (y_0 - 0)(\tfrac{1}{8})^t + 0 = y_0(\tfrac{1}{8})^t = A(\tfrac{1}{8})^t$$

(b) At $t = 0$, $y_0 = A(\tfrac{1}{8})^0 = A$. At $t = 1$, $y_1 = A(\tfrac{1}{8}) = \tfrac{1}{8}A$. Substituting $y_0 = A$ for y_{t-1} and $y_1 = \tfrac{1}{8}A$ for y_t in the original equation, $\tfrac{1}{8}A = \tfrac{1}{8}(A)$.

(c) With $b = \tfrac{1}{8}$, $b > 0$ and $|b| < 1$. The time path is nonoscillating and converging.

19.3. Redo Problem 19.1, given $y_t = -\frac{1}{4}y_{t-1} + 60$ and $y_0 = 8$.

(a)

$$y_t = \left(8 - \frac{60}{1 + \frac{1}{4}}\right)\left(-\frac{1}{4}\right)^t + \frac{60}{1 + \frac{1}{4}} = -40\left(-\frac{1}{4}\right)^t + 48$$

(b) At $t = 0$, $y_0 = -40(-\tfrac{1}{4})^0 + 48 = 8$. At $t = 1$, $y_1 = -40(-\tfrac{1}{4}) + 48 = 58$. Substituting in the original equation, $58 = -\tfrac{1}{4}(8) + 60 = 58$.

(c) With $b = -\tfrac{1}{4}$, $b < 0$ and $|b| < 1$. The time path oscillates and converges.

19.4. Redo Problem 19.1, given $x_t + 3x_{t-1} + 8 = 0$ and $x_0 = 16$.

(a) Rearranging to conform with (*19.3*),

$$x_t = -3x_{t-1} - 8$$

Thus, $b = -3$ and $a = -8$. Substituting in (*19.4*),

$$x_t = \left(16 + \frac{8}{1 + 3}\right)(-3)^t - \frac{8}{1 + 3} = 18(-3)^t - 2$$

(b) At $t = 0$, $x_0 = 18(-3)^0 - 2 = 16$. At $t = 1$, $x_1 = 18(-3) - 2 = -56$. Substituting in the original, $-56 + 3(16) + 8 = 0$.

(c) With $b = -3$, $b < 0$ and $|b| > 1$. The time path oscillates and explodes.

19.5. Redo Problem 19.1, given $y_t - y_{t-1} = 17$.

(a) Rearranging, $y_t = y_{t-1} + 17$. Here $b = 1$. Using (*19.4a*), therefore, $y_t = y_0 + 17t = A + 17t$.

(b) At $t = 0$, $y_0 = A$. At $t = 1$, $y_1 = A + 17$. Substituting in the original, $A + 17 - A = 17$.

(c) Here $b = 1$. Thus $b > 0$ and y_t will not oscillate. But with $|b| = 1$, $1 \not< |b| \not< 1$. This presents a special case. With $a \neq 0$, unless $y_0 = A = 0$, the time path is *divergent* because the complementary function A does not approach 0 as $t \to \infty$. Thus, y_t approaches $A + at$, and not the particular solution, at, itself. For $b = 1$ and $a = 0$, see Problem 19.17.

19.6. Redo Problem 19.1, given $g_t = g_{t-1} - 25$ and $g_0 = 40$.

(a) Using (*19.4a*), $g_t = 40 - 25t$.

(b) At $t = 0$, $g_0 = 40$. At $t = 1$, $g_t = 15$. Substituting in the original, $15 = 40 - 25$.

(c) With $b = 1$, $a \neq 0$ and $A = g_0 \neq 0$. The time path is nonoscillatory and divergent.

19.7. Redo Problem 19.1, given $2y_t = y_{t-1} - 18$.

(a) Dividing through by 2 to conform to (*19.3*) and then using (*19.4*),

$$y_t = \frac{1}{2}y_{t-1} - 9 = \left(y_0 + \frac{9}{1 - \frac{1}{2}}\right)\left(\frac{1}{2}\right)^t - \frac{9}{1 - \frac{1}{2}} = A\left(\frac{1}{2}\right)^t - 18$$

where A is an arbitrary constant for $y_0 + 18$.

(b)   At $t = 0$, $y_0 = A - 18$. At $t = 1$, $y_1 = \frac{1}{2}A - 18$. Substituting in the original, $2(\frac{1}{2}A - 18) = A - 18 - 18$;
$A - 36 = A - 36$.

(c)   With $b = \frac{1}{2}$, $b > 0$ and $|b| < 1$. So y_t is nonoscillating and convergent.

19.8.   (a) Solve the following difference equation; (b) check the answer, using $t = 0$ and $t = 1$; and (c) comment on the nature of the time path.

$$5y_t + 2y_{t-1} - 140 = 0 \qquad y_0 = 30$$

(a)   Dividing by 5, rearranging terms, and using (19.4),

$$y_t = -0.4y_{t-1} + 28 = \left(30 - \frac{28}{1 + 0.4}\right)(-0.4)^t + \frac{28}{1 + 0.4} = 10(-0.4)^t + 20$$

(b)   At $t = 0$, $y_0 = 30$. At $t = 1$, $y_1 = 16$. Substituting in the original, $5(16) + 2(30) - 140 = 0$.

(c)   With $b = -0.4$, $b < 0$ and $|b| < 1$. So y_t oscillates and converges.

19.9.   Redo Problem 19.8, given $x_{t+1} = 4x_t - 36$.

(a)   Shifting the time periods back one period to conform with (19.3), $x_t = 4x_{t-1} - 36$. Using (19.4) and allowing A to replace $x_0 - a/(1 - b)$ as in Problem 19.7,

$$x_t = A(4)^t - \frac{36}{1 - 4} = A(4)^t + 12$$

(b)   At $t = 0$, $x_0 = A + 12$. At $t = 1$, $x_1 = 4A + 12$. Substituting $x_1 = 4A + 12$ for x_{t+1} and $x_0 = A + 12$ for x_t in the original equation, $4A + 12 = 4(A + 12) - 36$; $4A + 12 = 4A + 12$.

(c)   With $b = 4$, $b > 0$ and $|b| > 1$. So x_t does not oscillate but it explodes.

19.10.   Redo Problem 19.8, given $y_{t+5} + 2y_{t+4} + 57 = 0$ and $y_0 = 11$.

(a)   Moving the time periods back 5 periods, rearranging terms, and using (19.4),

$$y_t = -2y_{t-1} - 57 = \left(11 + \frac{57}{1 + 2}\right)(-2)^t - \frac{57}{1 + 2} = 30(-2)^t - 19$$

(b)   At $t = 0$, $y_0 = 11$. At $t = 1$, $y_1 = -79$. Substituting y_1 for y_{t+5} and y_0 for y_{t+4} in the original equation, $-79 + 2(11) + 57 = 0$.

(c)   With $b = -2$, $b < 0$ and $|b| > 1$. y_t oscillates and explodes.

19.11.   Redo Problem 19.8, given $8y_{t-2} - 2y_{t-3} = 120$ and $y_0 = 28$.

(a)   Divide through by 8, shift the time periods ahead by 2, and rearrange terms.

$$y_t = \frac{1}{4}y_{t-1} + 15 = \left(28 - \frac{15}{1 - \frac{1}{4}}\right)\left(\frac{1}{4}\right)^t + \frac{15}{1 - \frac{1}{4}} = 8\left(\frac{1}{4}\right)^t + 20$$

(b)   At $t = 0$, $y_0 = 28$. At $t = 1$, $y_1 = 22$. Substitute y_1 for y_{t-2} and y_0 for y_{t-3}.

$$8(22) - 2(28) = 120 \qquad 120 = 120$$

(c)   With $b = \frac{1}{4}$, $b > 0$ and $|b| < 1$. So y_t is nonoscillating and convergent.

19.12.   Redo Problem 19.8, given $\Delta g_t = 14$.

(a)   Substituting (19.1) for Δg_t,

$$g_{t+1} - g_t = 14 \qquad\qquad\qquad\qquad\qquad (19.18)$$

Set the time periods back 1 and rearrange terms.

$$g_t = g_{t-1} + 14$$

Using $(19.4a)$, $g_t = g_0 + 14t = A + 14t$.

(b) At $t = 0$, $g_0 = A$. At $t = 1$, $g_1 = A + 14$. Substituting g_1 for g_{t+1} and g_0 for g_t in (19.18), $A + 14 - A = 14$.

(c) With $b = 1$, g_t is nonoscillatory. If $A \neq 0$, g_t is divergent.

19.13. Redo Problem 19.8, given $\Delta y_t = y_t + 13$ and $y_0 = 45$.

(a) Substituting from (19.1), moving the time periods back 1, and rearranging terms,

$$y_t = 2y_{t-1} + 13 \qquad (19.19)$$

Using (19.4), $\qquad y_t = \left(45 - \dfrac{13}{1-2}\right)(2)^t + \dfrac{13}{1-2} = 58(2)^t - 13$

(b) At $t = 0$, $y_0 = 45$. At $t = 1$, $y_1 = 103$. Substituting in (19.19), $103 = 2(45) + 13$; $103 = 103$.

(c) With $b = 2$, $b > 0$ and $|b| > 1$. Thus y_t is nonoscillatory and explosive.

LAGGED INCOME DETERMINATION MODELS

19.14. Given the data below, (a) find the time path of national income Y_t; (b) check your answer, using $t = 0$ and $t = 1$; and (c) comment on the stability of the time path.

$$C_t = 90 + 0.8Y_{t-1} \qquad I_t = 50 \qquad Y_0 = 1200$$

(a) In equilibrium, $Y_t = C_t + I_t$. Thus,

$$Y_t = 90 + 0.8Y_{t-1} + 50 = 0.8Y_{t-1} + 140 \qquad (19.20)$$

Using (19.4), $\qquad Y_t = \left(1200 - \dfrac{140}{1-0.8}\right)(0.8)^t + \dfrac{140}{1-0.8} = 500(0.8)^t + 700$

(b) $Y_0 = 1200$; $Y_1 = 1100$. Substituting in (19.20),

$$1100 = 0.8(1200) + 140 \qquad 1100 = 1100$$

(c) With $b = 0.8$, $b > 0$ and $|b| < 1$. The time path Y_t is nonoscillating and convergent. Y_t converges to the equilibrium level of income 700.

19.15. Redo Problem 19.14, given $C_t = 200 + 0.75Y_{t-1}$, $I_t = 50 + 0.15Y_{t-1}$, and $Y_0 = 3000$.

(a) $\qquad Y_t = 200 + 0.75Y_{t-1} + 50 + 0.15Y_{t-1} = 0.9Y_{t-1} + 250$

Using (19.4), $\qquad Y_t = \left(3000 - \dfrac{250}{1-0.9}\right)(0.9)^t + \dfrac{250}{1-0.9} = 500(0.9)^t + 2500$

(b) $Y_0 = 3000$; $Y_1 = 2950$. Substituting above, $2950 = 0.9(3000) + 250$; $2950 = 2950$.

(c) With $b = 0.9$, the time path Y_t is nonoscillatory and converges toward 2500.

19.16. Redo Problem 19.14, given $C_t = 300 + 0.87Y_{t-1}$, $I_t = 150 + 0.13Y_{t-1}$, and $Y_0 = 6000$.

(a) $\qquad Y_t = 300 + 0.87Y_{t-1} + 150 + 0.13Y_{t-1} = Y_{t-1} + 450 \qquad (19.21)$

Using $(19.4a)$, $Y_t = 6000 + 450t$.

(b) $Y_0 = 6000$; $Y_1 = 6450$. Substituting in (19.21) above, $6450 = 6000 + 450$.

(c) With $b = 1$ and $A \neq 0$, the time path Y_t is nonoscillatory but divergent. See Problem 19.5.

19.17. Redo Problem 19.14, given $C_t = 0.92Y_{t-1}$, $I_t = 0.08Y_{t-1}$, and $Y_0 = 4000$.

(a) $$Y_t = 0.92Y_{t-1} + 0.08Y_{t-1} = Y_{t-1}$$

Using (*19.4a*), $Y_t = 4000 + 0 = 4000$.

(b) $Y_0 = 4000 = Y_1$

(c) When $b = 1$ and $a = 0$, Y_t is a stationary path.

19.18. Redo Problem 19.14, given $C_t = 400 + 0.6Y_t + 0.35Y_{t-1}$, $I_t = 240 + 0.15Y_{t-1}$, and $Y_0 = 7000$.

(a) $$Y_t = 400 + 0.6Y_t + 0.35Y_{t-1} + 240 + 0.15Y_{t-1} \qquad 0.4Y_t = 0.5Y_{t-1} + 640$$

Divide through by 0.4 and then use (*19.4*).

$$Y_t = 1.25Y_{t-1} + 1600 = \left(7000 - \frac{1600}{1 - 1.25}\right)(1.25)^t + \frac{1600}{1 - 1.25} = 13\,400(1.25)^t - 6400$$

(b) $Y_0 = 7000$; $Y_1 = 10\,350$. Substituting in the initial equation,

$$10\,350 = 400 + 0.6(10\,350) + 0.35(7000) + 240 + 0.15(7000) = 10\,350$$

(c) With $b = 1.25$, the time path Y_t is nonoscillatory and explosive.

19.19. Redo Problem 19.14, given $C_t = 300 + 0.5Y_t + 0.4Y_{t-1}$, $I_t = 200 + 0.2Y_{t-1}$, and $Y_0 = 6500$.

(a) $$Y_t = 300 + 0.5Y_t + 0.4Y_{t-1} + 200 + 0.2Y_{t-1} \qquad 0.5Y_t = 0.6Y_{t-1} + 500$$

Dividing through by 0.5 and then using (*19.4*),

$$Y_t = 1.2Y_{t-1} + 1000 = \left(6500 - \frac{1000}{1 - 1.2}\right)(1.2)^t + \frac{1000}{1 - 1.2} = 11\,500(1.2)^t - 5000$$

(b) $Y_0 = 6500$; $Y_1 = 8800$. Substituting in the initial equation,

$$8800 = 300 + 0.5(8800) + 0.4(6500) + 200 + 0.2(6500) = 8800$$

(c) With $b = 1.2$, Y_t is nonoscillatory and explosive.

19.20. Redo Problem 19.14, given $C_t = 200 + 0.5Y_t$, $I_t = 3(Y_t - Y_{t-1})$, and $Y_0 = 10\,000$.

(a) $$Y_t = 200 + 0.5Y_t + 3(Y_t - Y_{t-1}) \qquad -2.5Y_t = -3Y_{t-1} + 200$$

Dividing through by -2.5 and then using (*19.4*),

$$Y_t = 1.2Y_{t-1} - 80 = \left(10\,000 + \frac{80}{1 - 1.2}\right)(1.2)^t - \frac{80}{1 - 1.2} = 9600(1.2)^t + 400$$

(b) $Y_0 = 10\,000$; $Y_1 = 11\,920$. Substituting in the initial equation,

$$11\,920 = 200 + 0.5(11\,920) + 3(11\,920 - 10\,000) = 11\,920$$

(c) With $b = 1.2$, the time path Y_t explodes but does not oscillate.

THE COBWEB MODEL

19.21. For the data given below, determine (a) the market price P_t in any time period, (b) the equilibrium price P_e, and (c) the stability of the time path.

$$Q_{dt} = 180 - 0.75P_t \qquad Q_{st} = -30 + 0.3P_{t-1} \qquad P_0 = 220$$

(a) Equating demand and supply,

$$180 - 0.75P_t = -30 + 0.3P_{t-1} \tag{19.22}$$
$$-0.75P_t = 0.3P_{t-1} - 210$$

Dividing through by -0.75 and using (19.4),

$$P_t = -0.4P_{t-1} + 280 = \left(220 - \frac{280}{1+0.4}\right)(-0.4)^t + \frac{280}{1+0.4} = 20(-0.4)^t + 200 \tag{19.23}$$

(b) If the market is in equilibrium, $P_t = P_{t-1}$. Substituting P_e for P_t and P_{t-1} in (19.22),

$$180 - 0.75P_e = -30 + 0.3P_e \qquad P_e = 200$$

which is the second term on the right-hand side of (19.23).

(c) With $b = -0.4$, the time path P_t will oscillate and converge.

19.22. Check the answer to Problem 19.21(a), using $t = 0$ and $t = 1$.

From (19.23), $P_0 = 20(-0.4)^0 + 200 = 220$ and $P_1 = 20(-0.4) + 200 = 192$. Substituting P_1 for P_t and P_0 for P_{t-1} in (19.22),

$$180 - 0.75(192) = -30 + 0.3(220)$$
$$36 = 36$$

19.23. Redo Problem 19.21, given $Q_{dt} = 160 - 0.8P_t$, $Q_{st} = -20 + 0.4P_{t-1}$, and $P_0 = 153$.

(a) $$160 - 0.8P_t = -20 + 0.4P_{t-1} \tag{19.24}$$
$$-0.8P_t = 0.4P_{t-1} - 180$$

Dividing through by -0.8 and using (19.4),

$$P_t = -0.5P_{t-1} + 225 = \left(153 - \frac{225}{1+0.5}\right)(-0.5)^t + \frac{225}{1+0.5} = 3(-0.5)^t + 150 \tag{19.25}$$

(b) As shown in Problem 19.21(b), $P_e = 150$. See also Section 19.5.

(c) With $b = -0.5$, P_t oscillates and converges toward 150.

19.24. Check the answer to Problem 19.23(a), using $t = 0$ and $t = 1$.

From (19.25), $P_0 = 3(-0.5)^0 + 150 = 153$ and $P_1 = 3(-0.5) + 150 = 148.5$. Substituting in (19.24),

$$160 - 0.8(148.5) = -20 + 0.4(153)$$
$$41.2 = 41.2$$

19.25. Redo Problem 19.21, given $Q_{dt} = 220 - 0.4P_t$, $Q_{st} = -30 + 0.6P_{t-1}$, and $P_0 = 254$.

(a) $$220 - 0.4P_t = -30 + 0.6P_{t-1}$$
$$-0.4P_t = 0.6P_{t-1} - 250$$

Dividing through by -0.4 and then using (19.4),

$$P_t = -1.5P_{t-1} + 625 = \left(254 - \frac{625}{1+1.5}\right)(-1.5)^t + \frac{625}{1+1.5} = 4(-1.5)^t + 250$$

(b) $$P_e = 250$$

(c) With $b = -1.5$, P_t oscillates and explodes.

THE HARROD GROWTH MODEL

19.26. For the following data, find (a) the level of income Y_t for any period and (b) the warranted rate of growth.

$$I_t = 2.66(Y_t - Y_{t-1}) \qquad S_t = 0.16Y_t \qquad Y_0 = 9000$$

(a) In equilibrium,

$$2.66(Y_t - Y_{t-1}) = 0.16Y_t \qquad 2.5Y_t = 2.66Y_{t-1}$$

Dividing through by 2.5 and then using (19.4),

$$Y_t = 1.064Y_{t-1} = (9000 - 0)(1.064)^t + 0 = 9000(1.064)^t$$

(b) From (19.16), $G_w = 0.16/(2.66 - 0.16) = 0.064$.

19.27. Redo Problem 19.26, given $I_t = 4.2(Y_t - Y_{t-1})$, $S_t = 0.2Y_t$, and $Y_0 = 5600$.

(a)
$$4.2(Y_t - Y_{t-1}) = 0.2Y_t$$
$$4Y_t = 4.2Y_{t-1}$$
$$Y_t = 1.05Y_{t-1}$$

Using (19.4), $Y_t = 5600(1.05)^t$.

(b)
$$G_w = \frac{0.2}{4.2 - 0.2} = 0.05$$

OTHER ECONOMIC APPLICATIONS

19.28. Derive the formula for the value P_t of an initial amount of money P_0 deposited at i interest for t years when compounded annually.

When interest is compounded annually,

$$P_{t+1} = P_t + iP_t = (1 + i)P_t$$

Moving the time periods back one to conform with (19.3),

$$P_t = (1 + i)P_{t-1}$$

Using (19.4) since $i \neq 0$, $\qquad P_t = (P_0 + 0)(1 + i)^t + 0 = P_0(1 + i)^t$

19.29. Assume that $Q_{dt} = c + zP_t$, $Q_{st} = g + hP_t$, and

$$P_{t+1} = P_t - a(Q_{st} - Q_{dt}) \qquad\qquad (19.26)$$

i.e., price is no longer determined by a market-clearing mechanism but by the level of inventory $Q_{st} - Q_{dt}$. Assume, too, that $a > 0$ since a buildup in inventory ($Q_{st} > Q_{dt}$) will tend to reduce price and a depletion of inventory ($Q_{st} < Q_{dt}$) will cause prices to rise. (a) Find the price P_t for any period and (b) comment on the stability conditions of the time path.

(a) Substituting Q_{st} and Q_{dt} in (19.26),

$$P_{t+1} = P_t - a(g + hP_t - c - zP_t)$$
$$= [1 - a(h - z)]P_t - a(g - c) = [1 + a(z - h)]P_t - a(g - c)$$

Shifting the time periods back 1 to conform to (19.3) and using (19.4),

$$P_t = \left\{ P_0 + \frac{a(g - c)}{1 - [1 + a(z - h)]} \right\} [1 + a(z - h)]^t - \frac{a(g - c)}{1 - [1 + a(z - h)]}$$

$$= \left(P_0 - \frac{g - c}{z - h} \right)[1 + a(z - h)]^t + \frac{g - c}{z - h} \qquad\qquad (19.27)$$

Substituting as in (19.13a),

$$P_t = (P_0 - P_e)[1 + a(z - h)]^t + P_e \qquad (19.28)$$

(b) The stability of the time path depends on $b = 1 + a(z - h)$. Since $a > 0$ and under normal conditions $z < 0$ and $h > 0$, $a(z - h) < 0$. Thus,

If $0 < |a(z - h)| < 1$,	$0 < b < 1$;	P_t converges and is nonoscillatory.
If $a(z - h) = -1$,	$b = 0$;	P_t remains in equilibrium ($P_t = P_0$).
If $-2 < a(z - h) < -1$,	$-1 < b < 0$;	P_t converges with oscillation.
If $a(z - h) = -2$,	$b = -1$;	uniform oscillation takes place.
If $a(z - h) < -2$,	$b < -1$;	P_t oscillates and explodes.

19.30. Given the following data, (a) find the price P_t for any time period; (b) check the answer, using $t = 0$ and $t = 1$; and (c) comment on the stability conditions.

$$Q_{dt} = 120 - 0.5P_t \qquad Q_{st} = -30 + 0.3P_t \qquad P_{t+1} = P_t - 0.2(Q_{st} - Q_{dt}) \qquad P_0 = 200$$

(a) Substituting, $\qquad P_{t+1} = P_t - 0.2(-30 + 0.3P_t - 120 + 0.5P_t) = 0.84P_t + 30$

Shifting time periods back 1 and using (19.4),

$$P_t = 0.84P_{t-1} + 30 = \left(200 - \frac{30}{1 - 0.84}\right)(0.84)^t + \frac{30}{1 - 0.84} = 12.5(0.84)^t + 187.5$$

(b) $P_0 = 200$; $P_1 = 198$. Substituting in the first equation of the solution, $198 = 200 - 0.2[-30 + 0.3(200) - 120 + 0.5(200)] = 198$.

(c) With $b = 0.84$, P_t converges without oscillation toward 187.5.

Chapter 20

Second-Order Differential Equations and Difference Equations

20.1 SECOND-ORDER DIFFERENTIAL EQUATIONS

Second-order differential equations require separate solution for the complementary function y_c and the particular integral y_p. The general solution is the sum of the two: $y(t) = y_c + y_p$. Given the second-order linear differential equation

$$y''(t) + b_1 y'(t) + b_2 y(t) = a \qquad (20.1)$$

where b_1, b_2, and a are constants, the particular integral will be

$$y_p = \frac{a}{b_2} \qquad b_2 \neq 0 \qquad (20.2)$$

$$y_p = \frac{a}{b_1} t \qquad b_2 = 0 \qquad b_1 \neq 0 \qquad (20.2a)$$

$$y_p = \frac{a}{2} t^2 \qquad b_1 = b_2 = 0 \qquad (20.2b)$$

The complementary function is

$$y_c = y_1 + y_2 \qquad (20.3)$$

where
$$y_1 = A_1 e^{r_1 t} \qquad (20.3a)$$
$$y_2 = A_2 e^{r_2 t} \qquad (20.3b)$$

and
$$r_1, r_2 = \frac{-b_1 \pm \sqrt{b_1^2 - 4b_2}}{2} \qquad (20.4)$$

Here, A_1 and A_2 are arbitrary constants, and $b_1^2 \neq 4b_2$. r_1 and r_2 are referred to as *characteristic roots*, and (*20.4*) is the solution to the *characteristic* or *auxiliary equation*: $r^2 + b_1 r + b_2 = 0$. See Examples 1 to 4 and Problems 20.1 to 20.11, 21.9, 21.10, 21.13, 21.14 and 21.16 to 21.20.

EXAMPLE 1. The particular integral for each of the following equations

$$(1) \quad y''(t) - 5y'(t) + 4y(t) = 2 \qquad (2) \quad y''(t) + 3y'(t) = 12 \qquad (3) \quad y''(t) = 16$$

is found as shown below.

For (1), using (*20.2*), $\qquad\qquad\qquad y_p = \frac{2}{4} = \frac{1}{2} \qquad (20.5)$

For (2), using (*20.2a*), $\qquad\qquad\qquad y_p = \frac{12}{3} t = 4t \qquad (20.5a)$

For (3), using (*20.2b*), $\qquad\qquad\qquad y_p = \frac{16}{2} t^2 = 8t^2 \qquad (20.5b)$

EXAMPLE 2. The complementary functions for equations (1) and (2) in Example 1 are calculated below. Equation (3) will be treated in Example 9.

For (1), from (*20.4*),

$$r_1, r_2 = \frac{+5 \pm \sqrt{(-5)^2 - 4(4)}}{2} = \frac{5 \pm 3}{2} = 1, 4$$

Substituting in (20.3a) and (20.3b), and finally in (20.3),

$$y_c = A_1 e^t + A_2 e^{4t} \tag{20.6}$$

For (2),
$$r_1, r_2 = \frac{-3 \pm \sqrt{(3)^2 - 4(0)}}{2} = \frac{-3 \pm 3}{2} = 0, -3$$

Thus,
$$y_c = A_1 e^0 + A_2 e^{-3t} = A_1 + A_2 e^{-3t} \tag{20.6a}$$

EXAMPLE 3.   The general solution of a differential equation is composed of the complementary function and the particular integral (Section 18.2), that is, $y(t) = y_c + y_p$. As applied to the equations in Example 1,

For (1), from (20.6) and (20.5), $y(t) = A_1 e^t + A_2 e^{4t} + \frac{1}{2}$ \hfill (20.7)

For (2), from (20.6a) and (20.5a), $y(t) = A_1 + A_2 e^{-3t} + 4t$ \hfill (20.7a)

EXAMPLE 4.   The definite solution for (1) in Example 3 is calculated below. Assume $y(0) = 5\frac{1}{2}$ and $y'(0) = 11$.
From (20.7),

$$y(t) = A_1 e^t + A_2 e^{4t} + \frac{1}{2} \tag{20.8}$$

Thus,
$$y'(t) = A_1 e^t + 4A_2 e^{4t} \tag{20.8a}$$

Evaluating (20.8) and (20.8a) at $t = 0$, and setting $y(0) = 5\frac{1}{2}$ and $y'(0) = 11$ from the initial conditions,

$$y(0) = A_1 e^0 + A_2 e^{4(0)} + \frac{1}{2} = 5\frac{1}{2} \quad \text{thus} \quad A_1 + A_2 = 5$$
$$y'(0) = A_1 e^0 + 4A_2 e^{4(0)} = 11 \quad \text{thus} \quad A_1 + 4A_2 = 11$$

Solving simultaneously, $A_1 = 3$ and $A_2 = 2$. Substituting in (20.7),

$$y(t) = 3e^t + 2e^{4t} + \frac{1}{2} \tag{20.9}$$

To check this solution, from (20.9),

$$y(t) = 3e^t + 2e^{4t} + \frac{1}{2}$$

Thus,
$$y'(t) = 3e^t + 8e^{4t} \qquad y''(t) = 3e^t + 32e^{4t}$$

Substituting in the original equation [(1) in Example 1],

$$(3e^t + 32e^{4t}) - 5(3e^t + 8e^{4t}) + 4(3e^t + 2e^{4t} + \tfrac{1}{2}) = 2$$

20.2   SECOND-ORDER DIFFERENCE EQUATIONS

The general solution of a second-order difference equation is composed of a complementary function and a particular solution: $y(t) = y_c + y_p$. Given the second-order linear difference equation

$$y_t + b_1 y_{t-1} + b_2 y_{t-2} = a \tag{20.10}$$

where b_1, b_2, and a are constants, the particular solution is

$$y_p = \frac{a}{1 + b_1 + b_2} \qquad b_1 + b_2 \neq -1 \tag{20.11}$$

$$y_p = \frac{a}{2 + b_1} t \qquad b_1 + b_2 = -1 \qquad b_1 \neq -2 \tag{20.11a}$$

$$y_p = \frac{a}{2} t^2 \qquad b_1 + b_2 = -1 \qquad b_1 = -2 \tag{20.11b}$$

The complementary function is

$$y_c = A_1 r_1^t + A_2 r_2^t \tag{20.12}$$

where A_1 and A_2 are arbitrary constants and the characteristic roots r_1 and r_2 are found by using (20.4), assuming $b_1^2 \neq 4b_2$. See Examples 5 to 8 and Problems 20.12 to 20.20.

EXAMPLE 5.   The particular solution for each of the following equations:

(1) $y_t - 10y_{t-1} + 16y_{t-2} = 14$ (2) $y_t - 6y_{t-1} + 5y_{t-2} = 12$ (3) $y_t - 2y_{t-1} + y_{t-2} = 8$

is found as shown below.

For (1), using (20.11),
$$y_p = \frac{14}{1 - 10 + 16} = 2 \tag{20.13}$$

For (2), using (20.11a),
$$y_p = \frac{12}{2 - 6} t = -3t \tag{20.13a}$$

For (3), using (20.11b),
$$y_p = \tfrac{8}{2} t^2 = 4t^2 \tag{20.13b}$$

EXAMPLE 6.   From Example 5, the complementary functions for (1) and (2) are calculated below. For (3), see Example 9.

For (1), using (20.4) and then substituting in (20.12),
$$r_1, r_2 = \frac{10 \pm \sqrt{100 - 4(16)}}{2} = \frac{10 \pm 6}{2} = 2, 8$$

Thus,
$$y_c = A_1(2)^t + A_2(8)^t \tag{20.14}$$

For (2),
$$r_1, r_2 = \frac{6 \pm \sqrt{36 - 4(5)}}{2} = \frac{6 \pm 4}{2} = 1, 5$$

Thus,
$$y_c = A_1(1)^t + A_2(5)^t = A_1 + A_2(5)^t \tag{20.14a}$$

EXAMPLE 7.   The general solutions for (1) and (2) from Example 5 are calculated below.

For (1), $y(t) = y_c + y_p$. From (20.14) and (20.13),
$$y(t) = A_1(2)^t + A_2(8)^t + 2 \tag{20.15}$$

For (2), from (20.14a) and (20.13a),
$$y(t) = A_1 + A_2(5)^t - 3t \tag{20.15a}$$

EXAMPLE 8.   Given $y(0) = 10$ and $y(1) = 36$, the definite solution for (1) in Example 7 is calculated as follows:
Letting $t = 0$ and $t = 1$ successively in (20.15),
$$y(0) = A_1(2)^0 + A_2(8)^0 + 2 = A_1 + A_2 + 2 \qquad y(1) = A_1(2) + A_2(8) + 2 = 2A_1 + 8A_2 + 2$$

Setting $y(0) = 10$ and $y(1) = 36$ from the initial conditions,
$$A_1 + A_2 + 2 = 10$$
$$2A_1 + 8A_2 + 2 = 36$$

Solving simultaneously, $A_1 = 5$ and $A_2 = 3$. Finally, substituting in (20.15),
$$y(t) = 5(2)^t + 3(8)^t + 2 \tag{20.16}$$

This answer is checked by evaluating (20.16) at $t = 0$, $t = 1$, and $t = 2$,
$$y(0) = 5 + 3 + 2 = 10 \qquad y(1) = 10 + 24 + 2 = 36 \qquad y(2) = 20 + 192 + 2 = 214$$

Substituting $y(2)$ for y_t, $y(1)$ for y_{t-1}, and $y(0)$ for y_{t-2} in $y_t - 10y_{t-1} + 16y_{t-2} = 14$ of Equation (1) in Example 5,
$214 - 10(36) + 16(10) = 14$.

20.3   CHARACTERISTIC ROOTS

A characteristic equation can have three different types of roots.

1. *Distinct real roots.* If $b_1^2 > 4b_2$, the square root in (20.4) will be a real number, and r_1 and r_2 will be distinct real numbers as in (20.6) and (20.6a).
2. *Repeated real roots.* If $b_1^2 = 4b_2$, the square root in (20.4) will vanish, and r_1 and r_2 will equal the same real number. In the case of repeated real roots, the formulas for y_c in (20.3) and (20.12) must be changed to
$$y_c = A_1 e^{rt} + A_2 t e^{rt} \tag{20.17}$$
$$y_c = A_1 r^t + A_2 t r^t \tag{20.18}$$

3. *Complex roots.* If $b_1^2 < 4b_2$, (20.4) contains the square root of a negative number, which is called an *imaginary number*. In this case r_1 and r_2 are complex numbers. A *complex number* contains a real part and an imaginary part; for example, $(12 + i)$ where $i = \sqrt{-1}$.

[As a simple test to check your answers when using (20.4), assuming the coefficient of the $y''(t)$ term is 1, $r_1 + r_2$ must equal $-b_1$; $r_1 \times r_2$ must equal b_2.]

EXAMPLE 9. The complementary function for Equation (3) in Example 1, where $y''(t) = 16$, is found as follows: From (20.4),

$$r_1, r_2 = \frac{0 \pm \sqrt{0 - 4(0)}}{2} = 0$$

Using (20.17) since $r_1 = r_2 = 0$, which is a case of repeated real roots, $y_c = A_1 e^0 + A_2 t e^0 = A_1 + A_2 t$.

In Equation (3) of Example 5, $y_t - 2y_{t-1} + y_{t-2} = 8$. Solving for the complementary function, from (20.4),

$$r_1, r_2 = \frac{2 \pm \sqrt{4 - 4(1)}}{2} = \frac{2 \pm 0}{2} = 1$$

Using (20.18) because $r_1 = r_2 = 1$, $y_c = A_1(1)^t + A_2 t(1)^t = A_1 + A_2 t$.

20.4 CONJUGATE COMPLEX NUMBERS

If $b_1^2 < 4b_2$ in (20.4), factoring out $\sqrt{-1}$ gives

$$r_1, r_2 = \frac{-b_1 \pm \sqrt{-1}\sqrt{4b_2 - b_1^2}}{2} = \frac{-b_1 \pm i\sqrt{4b_2 - b_1^2}}{2}$$

Put more succinctly, $r_1, r_2 = g \pm hi$

where $g = -\tfrac{1}{2}b_1$ and $h = \tfrac{1}{2}\sqrt{4b_2 - b_1^2}$ (20.19)

$g \pm hi$ are called *conjugate* complex numbers because they always appear together. Substituting (20.19) in (20.3) and (20.12) to find y_c for cases of complex roots,

$$y_c = A_1 e^{(g+hi)t} + A_2 e^{(g-hi)t} = e^{gt}(A_1 e^{hit} + A_2 e^{-hit})$$ (20.20)
$$y_c = A_1(g + hi)^t + A_2(g - hi)^t$$ (20.21)

See Example 10 and Problems 20.28 to 20.35, 21.11 and 21.12.

EXAMPLE 10. The complementary function for $y''(t) + 2y'(t) + 5y(t) = 18$ is calculated as shown below. Using (20.19) since $b_1^2 < 4b_2$,

$$g = -\tfrac{1}{2}(2) = -1 \qquad h = \tfrac{1}{2}\sqrt{4(5) - (2)^2} = \tfrac{1}{2}(4) = 2$$

Thus, $r_1, r_2 = -1 \pm 2i$. Substituting in (20.20), $y_c = e^{-t}(A_1 e^{2it} + A_2 e^{-2it})$.

20.5 TRIGONOMETRIC FUNCTIONS

Trigonometric functions are often used in connection with complex numbers. Given the angle θ in Fig. 20-1, which is at the center of a circle of radius k and measured counterclockwise, the trigonometric functions of θ are

$$\text{sine (sin) } \theta = \frac{h}{k} \qquad\qquad \text{cosine (cos) } \theta = \frac{g}{k}$$

$$\text{tangent (tan) } \theta = \frac{h}{g} \qquad\qquad \text{cotangent (cot) } \theta = \frac{g}{h}$$

$$\text{secant (sec) } \theta = \frac{k}{g} \qquad\qquad \text{cosecant (csc) } \theta = \frac{k}{h}$$

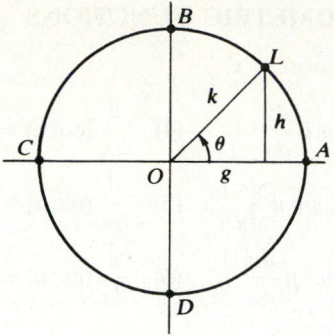

Fig. 20-1

The signs of the trigonometric functions in each of the four quadrants are

$$
\begin{array}{c|c}
+ & + \\
\hline
- & -
\end{array}
\qquad
\begin{array}{c|c}
- & + \\
\hline
- & +
\end{array}
\qquad
\begin{array}{c|c}
- & + \\
\hline
+ & -
\end{array}
$$

sin, csc   cos, sec   tan, cot

The angle θ is frequently measured in *radians*. Since there are 2π radians in a circle, $1° = \pi/180$ radian. Thus $360° = 2\pi$ radians, $180° = \pi$ radians, $90° = \pi/2$ radians, and $45° = \pi/4$ radian.

EXAMPLE 11.   If the radius OL in Fig. 20-1 starts at A and moves counterclockwise $360°$, $\sin\theta = h/k$ goes from 0 at A, to 1 at B, to 0 at C, to -1 at D, and back to 0 at A. Cosine $\theta = g/k$ goes from 1 at A, to 0 at B, to -1 at C, to 0 at D, and back to 1 at A. This is summarized in Table 20-1 and graphed in Fig. 20-2. Notice that both functions are *periodic* with a *period* of 2π (i.e., they repeat themselves every $360°$ or 2π radians). Both have an *amplitude* of fluctuation of 1 and differ only in *phase* or location of their peaks.

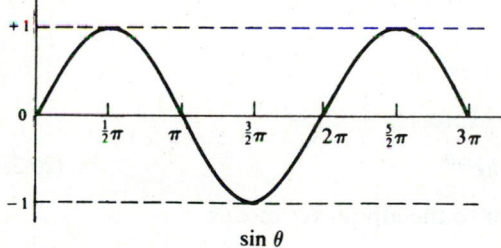

Fig. 20-2

Table 20-1

Degrees	0	90	180	270	360
Radians	0	$\dfrac{\pi}{2}$	π	$\dfrac{3}{2}\pi$	2π
$\sin\theta$	0	1	0	-1	0
$\cos\theta$	1	0	-1	0	1

20.6 DERIVATIVES OF TRIGONOMETRIC FUNCTIONS

Given that u is a differentiable function of x,

(1) $\dfrac{d}{dx}(\sin u) = \cos u \, \dfrac{du}{dx}$ (4) $\dfrac{d}{dx}(\cot u) = -\csc^2 u \, \dfrac{du}{dx}$

(2) $\dfrac{d}{dx}(\cos u) = -\sin u \, \dfrac{du}{dx}$ (5) $\dfrac{d}{dx}(\sec u) = \sec u \tan u \, \dfrac{du}{dx}$

(3) $\dfrac{d}{dx}(\tan u) = \sec^2 u \, \dfrac{du}{dx}$ (6) $\dfrac{d}{dx}(\csc u) = -\csc u \cot u \, \dfrac{du}{dx}$

See Example 12 and Problems 20.21 to 20.27.

EXAMPLE 12. The derivatives for the trigonometric functions

     (1) $y = \sin(3x^2 + 6)$ (2) $y = 4\cos 2x$ (3) $y = (1 + \tan x)^2$

are calculated as follows:

     (1) $\dfrac{dy}{dx} = 6x \cos(3x^2 + 6)$ (2) $\dfrac{dy}{dx} = -8\sin 2x$ (3) $\dfrac{dy}{dx} = 2(1 + \tan x)(\sec^2 x) = 2\sec^2 x \,(1 + \tan x)$

20.7 TRANSFORMATION OF IMAGINARY AND COMPLEX NUMBERS

Three rules are helpful in transforming imaginary and complex numbers to trigonometric functions.

1. g and h in Fig. 20-1, which are *Cartesian coordinates*, can be expressed in terms of θ and k, which are called *polar coordinates*, by the simple formula

$$g = k\cos\theta \qquad h = k\sin\theta \qquad k > 0$$

Thus for the conjugate complex number $(g \pm hi)$,

$$g \pm hi = k\cos\theta \pm ik\sin\theta = k(\cos\theta \pm i\sin\theta) \tag{20.22}$$

2.   By what are called *Euler relations*,

$$e^{\pm i\theta} = \cos\theta \pm i\sin\theta \tag{20.23}$$

Thus, by substituting (20.23) in (20.22) we can also express $(g \pm hi)$ as

$$g \pm hi = ke^{\pm i\theta} \tag{20.23a}$$

3.   From $(20.23a)$, raising a conjugate complex number to the nth power means

$$(g \pm hi)^n = (ke^{\pm i\theta})^n = k^n e^{\pm in\theta} \tag{20.24}$$

Or, by making use of (20.23) and noting that $n\theta$ replaces θ, we have *De Moivre's theorem*:

$$(g \pm hi)^n = k^n(\cos n\theta \pm i\sin n\theta) \tag{20.25}$$

See Examples 13 to 15 and Problems 20.28 to 20.35, 21.11 and 21.12.

EXAMPLE 13. The value of the imaginary exponential function $e^{2i\pi}$ is found as follows. Using (20.23), where $\theta = 2\pi$,

$$e^{2i\pi} = \cos 2\pi + i\sin 2\pi$$

From Table 20-1, $\cos 2\pi = 1$ and $\sin 2\pi = 0$. Thus, $e^{2i\pi} = 1 + i(0) = 1$.

EXAMPLE 14. The imaginary exponential expressions in (20.20) and (20.21) are transformed to trigonometric functions as shown below.

From (20.20), $y_c = e^{gt}(A_1 e^{hit} + A_2 e^{-hit})$. Using (20.23) where $\theta = ht$,

$$y_c = e^{gt}[A_1(\cos ht + i \sin ht) + A_2(\cos ht - i \sin ht)]$$
$$= e^{gt}[(A_1 + A_2)\cos ht + (A_1 - A_2)i \sin ht]$$
$$= e^{gt}(B_1 \cos ht + B_2 \sin ht) \tag{20.26}$$

where $B_1 = A_1 + A_2$ and $B_2 = (A_1 - A_2)i$.

From (20.21), $y_c = A_1(g + hi)^t + A_2(g - hi)^t$. Using (20.25) and substituting t for n,

$$y_c = A_1 k^t (\cos t\theta + i \sin t\theta) + A_2 k^t (\cos t\theta - i \sin t\theta)$$
$$= k^t[(A_1 + A_2)\cos t\theta + (A_1 - A_2)i \sin t\theta]$$
$$= k^t(B_1 \cos t\theta + B_2 \sin t\theta) \tag{20.27}$$

where $B_1 = A_1 + A_2$ and $B_2 = (A_1 - A_2)i$.

EXAMPLE 15. The time paths of (20.26) and (20.27) are evaluated as follows: Examining each term in (20.26),

1. Here $B_1 \cos ht$ is a cosine function of t, as in Fig. 20-2, with period $2\pi/h$ instead of 2π and amplitude of the multiplicative constant B_1 instead of 1.

2. Likewise $B_2 \sin ht$ is a sine function of t with period $2\pi/h$ and amplitude of B_2.

3. With the first two terms constantly fluctuating, stability depends on e^{gt}:

   If $g > 0$, e^{gt} gets increasingly larger as t increases. This increases the amplitude and leads to explosive fluctuations of y_c, precluding convergence.

   If $g = 0$, $e^{gt} = 1$ and y_c displays uniform fluctuations determined by the sine and cosine functions. This also precludes convergence.

   If $g < 0$, e^{gt} approaches zero as t increases. This diminishes the amplitude, produces damped fluctuations, and leads to convergence. See Fig. 20-3.

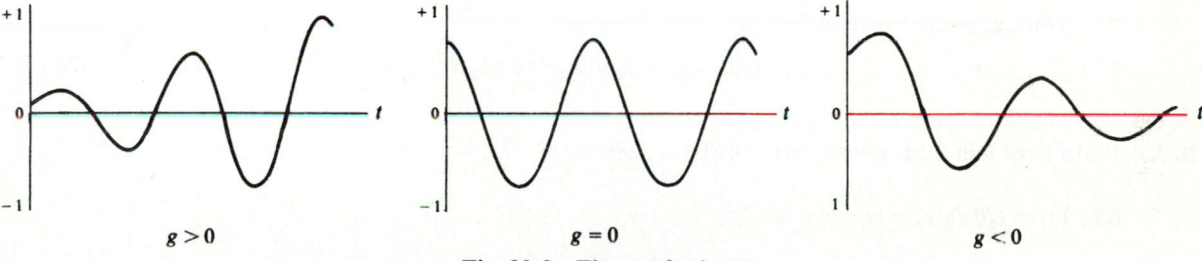

Fig. 20-3   Time path of $y_c(t)$.

Since (20.27) concerns a difference equation in which t can only change at discrete intervals, y_c is a step function rather than a continuous function (see Fig. 19-1). Like (20.26), it will fluctuate, and stability will depend on k^t. If $|k| < 1$, y_c will converge. See Problems 20.8 to 20.11, 20.18 to 20.20, and 20.31 to 20.35.

20.8 STABILITY CONDITIONS

For a second-order linear differential equation with distinct or repeated real roots, both roots must be negative for convergence. If one of the roots is positive, the exponential term with the positive root approaches infinity as t approaches infinity, thereby precluding convergence. See Problems 20.8 to 20.11. In the case of complex roots, g in e^{gt} of (20.26) must be negative, as illustrated in Example 15.

For a second-order linear difference equation with distinct or repeated real roots, the root with the largest absolute value is called the *dominant root* because it dominates the time path. For convergence, the absolute value of the dominant root must be less than 1. See Problems 20.18 to 20.20. In the case of complex roots, the absolute value of k in (20.27) must be less than 1, as explained in Example 15. For economic applications, see Problems 20.36 and 20.37.

Solved Problems

SECOND-ORDER LINEAR DIFFERENTIAL EQUATIONS

Distinct Real Roots

20.1. For the following equation, find (a) the particular integral y_p, (b) the complementary function y_c, and (c) the general solution $y(t)$.

$$y''(t) + 9y'(t) + 14y(t) = 7$$

(a) Using (20.2), $y_p = \frac{7}{14} = \frac{1}{2}$.

(b) Using (20.4),

$$r_1, r_2 = \frac{-9 \pm \sqrt{81 - 4(14)}}{2} = \frac{-9 \pm 5}{2} = -2, -7$$

Substituting in (20.3), $y_c = A_1 e^{-2t} + A_2 e^{-7t}$.

(c) $$y(t) = y_c + y_p = A_1 e^{-2t} + A_2 e^{-7t} + \tfrac{1}{2} \qquad\qquad (20.28)$$

20.2. Redo Problem 20.1, given $y''(t) - 12y'(t) + 20y(t) = -100$.

(a) From (20.2), $y_p = -\frac{100}{20} = -5$.

(b) From (20.4),

$$r_1, r_2 = \frac{12 \pm \sqrt{144 - 4(20)}}{2} = \frac{12 \pm 8}{2} = 2, 10$$

Thus, $y_c = A_1 e^{2t} + A_2 e^{10t}$.

(c) $$y(t) = y_c + y_p = A_1 e^{2t} + A_2 e^{10t} - 5 \qquad\qquad (20.29)$$

20.3. Redo Problem 20.1, given $y''(t) - 4y'(t) - 5y(t) = 35$.

(a) From (20.2), $y_p = \frac{35}{-5} = -7$.

(b) From (20.4)

$$r_1, r_2 = \frac{4 \pm \sqrt{16 - 4(-5)}}{2} = \frac{4 \pm 6}{2} = 5, -1$$

Thus, $y_c = A_1 e^{5t} + A_2 e^{-t}$.

(c) $$y(t) = A_1 e^{5t} + A_2 e^{-t} - 7 \qquad\qquad (20.30)$$

20.4. Redo Problem 20.1, given $y''(t) + 7y'(t) = 28$.

(a) Using (20.2a), $y_p = \frac{28}{7}t = 4t$.

(b) From (20.4),

$$r_1, r_2 = \frac{-7 \pm \sqrt{49 - 4(0)}}{2} = \frac{-7 \pm 7}{2} = 0, -7$$

Thus, $y_c = A_1 e^{(0)t} + A_2 e^{-7t} = A_1 + A_2 e^{-7t}$.

(c) $$y(t) = A_1 + A_2 e^{-7t} + 4t \qquad\qquad (20.31)$$

20.5. Redo Problem 20.1, given $y''(t) - \frac{1}{2}y'(t) = 13$.

(a) From (20.2a), $y_p = \dfrac{13}{-\frac{1}{2}} t = -26t$.

(b) $$r_1, r_2 = \frac{\frac{1}{2} \pm \sqrt{\frac{1}{4} - 4(0)}}{2} = \frac{\frac{1}{2} \pm \frac{1}{2}}{2} = 0, \frac{1}{2}$$

Thus, $y_c = A_1 + A_2 e^{(1/2)t}$.

(c) $$y(t) = A_1 + A_2 e^{(1/2)t} - 26t \qquad (20.32)$$

Repeated Real Roots

20.6. Find (a) the particular integral y_p, (b) the complementary function y_c, and (c) the general solution $y(t)$, given $y''(t) - 12y'(t) + 36y(t) = 108$.

(a) $$y_p = \tfrac{108}{36} = 3$$

(b) $$r_1, r_2 = \frac{12 \pm \sqrt{144 - 4(36)}}{2} = \frac{12 \pm 0}{2} = 6$$

Using (20.17) since $r_1 = r_2 = 6$, $y_c = A_1 e^{6t} + A_2 t e^{6t}$.

(c) $$y(t) = A_1 e^{6t} + A_2 t e^{6t} + 3 \qquad (20.33)$$

20.7. Redo Problem 20.6, given $y''(t) + y'(t) + \frac{1}{4}y(t) = 9$.

(a) $$y_p = \frac{9}{\frac{1}{4}} = 36$$

(b) $$r_1, r_2 = \frac{-1 \pm \sqrt{1 - 4(\frac{1}{4})}}{2} = \frac{-1 \pm 0}{2} = -\frac{1}{2}$$

Using (20.17) since $r_1 = r_2 = -\frac{1}{2}$, $y_c = A_1 e^{-(1/2)t} + A_2 t e^{-(1/2)t}$.

(c) $$y(t) = A_1 e^{-(1/2)t} + A_2 t e^{-(1/2)t} + 36 \qquad (20.34)$$

DEFINITE SOLUTIONS AND STABILITY CONDITIONS

20.8. Find (a) the definite solution for the following equation, (b) check your answer, and (c) comment on the dynamic stability of the time path, given $y''(t) + 9y'(t) + 14y(t) = 7$, $y(0) = -2\frac{1}{2}$, and $y'(0) = 31$.

(a) From (20.28),
$$y(t) = A_1 e^{-2t} + A_2 e^{-7t} + \tfrac{1}{2} \qquad (20.35)$$
Thus,
$$y'(t) = -2A_1 e^{-2t} - 7A_2 e^{-7t} \qquad (20.35a)$$

Evaluating (20.35) and (20.35a) at $t = 0$,
$$y(0) = A_1 + A_2 + \tfrac{1}{2} \qquad y'(0) = -2A_1 - 7A_2$$

Setting $y(0) = -2\frac{1}{2}$ and $y'(0) = 31$ from the initial conditions,
$$A_1 + A_2 + \tfrac{1}{2} = -2\tfrac{1}{2}$$
$$-2A_1 - 7A_2 = 31$$

Solving simultaneously, $A_1 = 2$ and $A_2 = -5$, which when substituted in (20.35) gives
$$y(t) = 2e^{-2t} - 5e^{-7t} + \tfrac{1}{2} \qquad (20.36)$$

(b) From (20.36), $y(t) = 2e^{-2t} - 5e^{-7t} + \frac{1}{2}$. Thus,
$$y'(t) = -4e^{-2t} + 35e^{-7t} \qquad y''(t) = 8e^{-2t} - 245e^{-7t}$$

Substituting these values in the original problem, where $y'' + 9y'(t) + 14y(t) = 7$,

$$8e^{-2t} - 245e^{-7t} + 9(-4e^{-2t} + 35e^{-7t}) + 14(2e^{-2t} - 5e^{-7t} + \tfrac{1}{2}) = 7$$

(c) With both characteristic roots negative, (20.36) will approach $\tfrac{1}{2}$ as $t \to \infty$. Therefore $y(t)$ is convergent. Any time both characteristic roots are negative, the time path will converge.

20.9. Redo Problem 20.8, given $y''(t) - 4y'(t) - 5y(t) = 35$, $y(0) = 5$, and $y'(0) = 6$.

(a) From (20.30),

$$y(t) = A_1 e^{5t} + A_2 e^{-t} - 7 \qquad (20.37)$$

Thus,
$$y'(t) = 5A_1 e^{5t} - A_2 e^{-t} \qquad (20.37a)$$

Evaluating (20.37) and $(20.37a)$ at $t = 0$ and setting them equal to the initial conditions where $y(0) = 5$ and $y'(0) = 6$,

$$y(0) = A_1 + A_2 - 7 = 5 \qquad \text{thus} \qquad A_1 + A_2 = 12$$
$$y'(0) = 5A_1 - A_2 = 6$$

Solving simultaneously, $A_1 = 3$ and $A_2 = 9$, which when substituted in (20.37) gives

$$y(t) = 3e^{5t} + 9e^{-t} - 7 \qquad (20.38)$$

(b) From (20.38), $y(t) = 3e^{5t} + 9e^{-t} - 7$. Thus, $y'(t) = 15e^{5t} - 9e^{-t}$ and $y''(t) = 75e^{5t} + 9e^{-t}$.
Substituting these values in the original problem, where $y''(t) - 4y'(t) - 5y(t) = 35$,

$$75e^{5t} + 9e^{-t} - 4(15e^{5t} - 9e^{-t}) - 5(3e^{5t} + 9e^{-t} - 7) = 35$$

(c) With one characteristic root positive and the other negative, the time path is divergent. The positive root dominates the negative root independently of their relative absolute values because as $t \to \infty$, the positive root $\to \infty$ and the negative root $\to 0$.

20.10. Redo Problem 20.8, given $y''(t) - \tfrac{1}{2}y'(t) = 13$, $y(0) = 17$, and $y'(0) = -19\tfrac{1}{2}$.

(a) From (20.32),

$$y(t) = A_1 + A_2 e^{(1/2)t} - 26t \qquad (20.39)$$

Thus,
$$y'(t) = \tfrac{1}{2}A_2 e^{(1/2)t} - 26 \qquad (20.39a)$$

Evaluating (20.39) and $(20.39a)$ at $t = 0$ and setting them equal to the initial conditions,

$$y(0) = A_1 + A_2 = 17$$
$$y'(0) = \tfrac{1}{2}A_2 - 26 = -19\tfrac{1}{2} \qquad A_2 = 13$$

With $A_2 = 13$, $A_1 = 4$. Substituting in (20.39) and rearranging terms,

$$y(t) = 13e^{(1/2)t} - 26t + 4 \qquad (20.40)$$

(b) From (20.40), $y(t) = 13e^{(1/2)t} - 26t + 4$. Thus,

$$y'(t) = 6.5e^{(1/2)t} - 26 \qquad y''(t) = 3.25e^{(1/2)t}$$

Substituting these values in the original equation,

$$3.25e^{(1/2)t} - \tfrac{1}{2}(6.5e^{(1/2)t} - 26) = 13$$

(c) With both characteristic roots positive, the time path will diverge.

20.11. Redo Problem 20.8, given $y''(t) + y'(t) + \tfrac{1}{4}y(t) = 9$, $y(0) = 30$, and $y'(0) = 15$.

(a) From (20.34),

$$y(t) = A_1 e^{-(1/2)t} + A_2 t e^{-(1/2)t} + 36 \qquad (20.41)$$

Using the product rule for the derivative of the second term,

$$y'(t) = -\tfrac{1}{2}A_1 e^{-(1/2)t} - \tfrac{1}{2}A_2\, te^{-(1/2)t} + A_2 e^{-(1/2)t} \tag{20.41a}$$

Evaluating (20.41) and $(20.41a)$ at $t = 0$ and equating to the initial conditions,

$$y(0) = A_1 + 36 = 30 \qquad A_1 = -6$$
$$y'(0) = -\tfrac{1}{2}A_1 + A_2 = 15$$

With $A_1 = -6$, $A_2 = 12$. Substituting in (20.41),

$$y(t) = 12te^{-(1/2)t} - 6e^{-(1/2)t} + 36 \tag{20.42}$$

(b)   From (20.42), $y(t) = 12te^{-(1/2)t} - 6e^{-(1/2)t} + 36$. By the product rule,

$$y'(t) = -6te^{-(1/2)t} + 12e^{-(1/2)t} + 3e^{-(1/2)t}$$
$$y''(t) = 3te^{-(1/2)t} - 6e^{-(1/2)t} - 6e^{-(1/2)t} - 1.5e^{-(1/2)t} = 3te^{-(1/2)t} - 13.5e^{-(1/2)t}$$

Substituting in the original equation,

$$(3te^{-(1/2)t} - 13.5e^{-(1/2)t}) + (-6te^{-(1/2)t} + 15e^{-(1/2)t}) + \tfrac{1}{4}(12te^{-(1/2)t} - 6e^{-(1/2)t} + 36) = 9$$

(c)   With the repeated characteristic roots negative, the time path will converge since te^{rt} follows basically the same time path as e^{rt}.

SECOND-ORDER LINEAR DIFFERENCE EQUATIONS

Distinct Real Roots

20.12.   Find (a) the particular solution, (b) the complementary function, and (c) the general solution, given $y_t + 7y_{t-1} + 6y_{t-2} = 42$.

(a)   From (20.11),
$$y_p = \frac{42}{1 + 7 + 6} = 3$$

(b)   From (20.4),
$$r_1, r_2 = \frac{-7 \pm \sqrt{49 - 4(6)}}{2} = \frac{-7 \pm 5}{2} = -1, -6$$

From (20.12),
$$y_c = A_1(-1)^t + A_2(-6)^t$$

(c)
$$y(t) = y_c + y_p = A_1(-1)^t + A_2(-6)^t + 3 \tag{20.43}$$

20.13.   Redo Problem 20.12, given $y_t + 12y_{t-1} + 11y_{t-2} = 6$.

(a)   From (20.11),
$$y_p = \frac{6}{1 + 12 + 11} = \frac{1}{4}$$

(b)
$$r_1, r_2 = \frac{-12 \pm \sqrt{144 - 4(11)}}{2} = \frac{-12 \pm 10}{2} = -1, -11$$

Thus,
$$y_c = A_1(-1)^t + A_2(-11)^t$$

(c)
$$y(t) = A_1(-1)^t + A_2(-11)^t + \tfrac{1}{4} \tag{20.44}$$

20.14.   Redo Problem 20.12, given $y_{t+2} - 11y_{t+1} + 10y_t = 27$.

(a)   Shifting the time periods back 2 to conform with (20.10), $y_t - 11y_{t-1} + 10y_{t-2} = 27$. Then from $(20.11a)$,

$$y_p = \frac{27}{2 - 11}\, t = -3t$$

(b)
$$r_1, r_2 = \frac{11 \pm \sqrt{121 - 4(10)}}{2} = \frac{11 \pm 9}{2} = 1, 10$$

$$y_c = A_1 + A_2(10)^t$$

(c)
$$y(t) = A_1 + A_2(10)^t - 3t \qquad (20.45)$$

20.15. Redo Problem 20.12, given $y_t + 7y_{t-1} - 8y_{t-2} = 45$.

(a) From (20.11a),
$$y_p = \frac{45}{2 + 7} t = 5t$$

(b)
$$r_1, r_2 = \frac{-7 \pm \sqrt{49 - 4(-8)}}{2} = \frac{-7 \pm 9}{2} = 1, -8$$

$$y_c = A_1 + A_2(-8)^t$$

(c)
$$y(t) = A_1 + A_2(-8)^t + 5t \qquad (20.46)$$

Repeated Real Roots

20.16. Redo Problem 20.12, given $y_t - 10y_{t-1} + 25y_{t-2} = 8$.

(a)
$$y_p = \frac{8}{1 - 10 + 25} = \frac{1}{2}$$

(b)
$$r_1, r_2 = \frac{10 \pm \sqrt{100 - 4(25)}}{2} = \frac{10 \pm 0}{2} = 5$$

Using (20.18) because $r_1 = r_2 = 5$, $y_c = A_1(5)^t + A_2 t(5)^t$.

(c)
$$y(t) = A_1(5)^t + A_2 t(5)^t + \tfrac{1}{2} \qquad (20.47)$$

20.17. Redo Problem 20.12, given $y_t + 14y_{t-1} + 49y_{t-2} = 128$.

(a)
$$y_p = \frac{128}{1 + 14 + 49} = 2$$

(b)
$$r_1, r_2 = \frac{-14 \pm \sqrt{196 - 4(49)}}{2} = \frac{-14 \pm 0}{2} = -7$$

From (20.18), $y_c = A_1(-7)^t + A_2 t(-7)^t$.

(c)
$$y(t) = A_1(-7)^t + A_2 t(-7)^t + 2 \qquad (20.48)$$

DEFINITE SOLUTIONS AND STABILITY CONDITIONS

20.18. (a) Find the definite solution, (b) check the answer, and (c) comment on dynamic stability, given $y_t + 7y_{t-1} + 6y_{t-2} = 42$, $y(0) = 16$, and $y(1) = -35$.

(a) From (20.43),
$$y(t) = A_1(-1)^t + A_2(-6)^t + 3 \qquad (20.49)$$

Letting $t = 0$ and $t = 1$ successively in (20.49) and making use of the initial conditions,

$$y(0) = A_1 + A_2 + 3 = 16 \qquad y(1) = -A_1 - 6A_2 + 3 = -35$$

Solving simultaneously, $A_1 = 8$ and $A_2 = 5$. Substituting in (20.49),

$$y(t) = 8(-1)^t + 5(-6)^t + 3 \qquad (20.50)$$

(b) Evaluating (20.50) at $t = 0$, $t = 1$, and $t = 2$ to check this answer,

$$y(0) = 8 + 5 + 3 = 16 \qquad y(1) = -8 - 30 + 3 = -35 \qquad y(2) = 8 + 180 + 3 = 191$$

Substituting in the initial equation with

$$y(2) = y_t \qquad y(1) = y_{t-1} \qquad y(0) = y_{t-2} \qquad 191 + 7(-35) + 6(16) = 42$$

(c) The characteristic roots are -1 and -6. The characteristic root with the largest absolute value is called the *dominant root* because it dominates the time path. For convergence, the absolute value of the dominant root must be less than 1. Since $|-6| > |-1|$ and $|-6| > 1$, the time path is divergent.

20.19. (a) Find the definite solution and (b) comment on dynamic stability, given

$$y_{t+2} - 11y_{t+1} + 10y_t = 27 \qquad y(0) = 2 \qquad y(1) = 53$$

(a) From (20.45), $\qquad\qquad\qquad y(t) = A_1 + A_2(10)^t - 3t \qquad\qquad\qquad (20.51)$

Letting $t = 0$ and $t = 1$, and using the initial conditions,

$$y(0) = A_1 + A_2 = 2 \qquad y(1) = A_1 + 10A_2 - 3 = 53$$

Solving simultaneously, $A_1 = -4$ and $A_2 = 6$. Substituting in (20.51),

$$y(t) = 6(10)^t - 3t - 4$$

(b) The time path is divergent because the dominant root 10 is greater than 1.

20.20. Redo Problem 20.19, given $y_t - 10y_{t-1} + 25y_{t-2} = 8$, $y(0) = 1$, and $y(1) = 5$.

(a) From (20.47),

$$y(t) = A_1(5)^t + A_2 t(5)^t + \tfrac{1}{2} \qquad\qquad\qquad (20.52)$$

Letting $t = 0$ and $t = 1$, and using the initial conditions,

$$y(0) = A_1 + \tfrac{1}{2} = 1 \qquad A_1 = \tfrac{1}{2}$$
$$y(1) = 5A_1 + 5A_2 + \tfrac{1}{2} = 5$$

With $A_1 = \tfrac{1}{2}$, $A_2 = \tfrac{2}{5}$. Substituting in (20.52),

$$y(t) = \tfrac{1}{2}(5)^t + \tfrac{2}{5}t(5)^t + \tfrac{1}{2} \qquad\qquad\qquad (20.53)$$

(b) Convergence in the case of repeated real roots likewise depends on $|r| < 1$ since the effect of r^t dominates the effect of t in the second term $A_2 t r^t$. Here with $r = 5 > 1$, the time path is divergent.

DERIVATIVES OF TRIGONOMETRIC FUNCTIONS

20.21. Find the first-order derivative for the following trigonometric functions. Note that they are also called *circular functions* or *sinusoidal functions*.

(a) $y = \sin 7x$

$$\frac{dy}{dx} = 7\cos 7x$$

(b) $y = \cos(5x + 2)$

$$\frac{dy}{dx} = -5\sin(5x + 2)$$

(c) $y = \tan 11x$

$$\frac{dy}{dx} = 11\sec^2 11x$$

(d) $y = \csc(8x + 3)$

$$\frac{dy}{dx} = -8[\csc(8x + 3)\cot(8x + 3)]$$

(e) $y = \sin(3 - x^2)$

$$\frac{dy}{dx} = -2x\cos(3 - x^2)$$

(f) $y = \sin(5 - x)^2$

$$\frac{dy}{dx} = -2(5 - x)\cos(5 - x)^2 \qquad \text{(chain rule)}$$

20.22. Redo Problem 20.21, given $y = x^2 \tan x$.

By the product rule, $\dfrac{dy}{dx} = x^2 (\sec^2 x) + (\tan x)(2x) = x^2 \sec^2 x + 2x \tan x$

20.23. Redo Problem 20.21, given $y = x^3 \sin x$.

$$\frac{dy}{dx} = x^3 (\cos x) + (\sin x)(3x^2) = x^3 \cos x + 3x^2 \sin x$$

20.24. Redo Problem 20.21, given $y = (1 + \cos x)^2$.

By the chain rule, $\dfrac{dy}{dx} = 2(1 + \cos x)(-\sin x) = (-2 \sin x)(1 + \cos x)$

20.25. Redo Problem 20.21, given $y = (\sin x + \cos x)^2$.

$$\frac{dy}{dx} = 2(\sin x + \cos x)(\cos x - \sin x) = 2(\cos^2 x - \sin^2 x)$$

20.26. Redo Problem 20.21, given $y = \sin^2 5x$, where $\sin^2 5x = (\sin 5x)^2$.

By the chain rule, $\dfrac{dy}{dx} = 2 \sin 5x \cos 5x(5) = 10 \sin 5x \cos 5x$

20.27. Redo Problem 20.21, given $y = \csc^2 12x$.

$$\frac{dy}{dx} = (2 \csc 12x)[-\csc 12x \cot 12x (12)] = -24 \csc^2 12x \cot 12x$$

COMPLEX ROOTS IN SECOND-ORDER DIFFERENTIAL EQUATIONS

20.28. Find (a) the particular integral, (b) the complementary function, and (c) the general solution, given the second-order linear differential equation $y''(t) + 2y'(t) + 10y(t) = 80$.

(a) From (20.2), $\qquad\qquad\qquad\qquad\qquad y_p = \frac{80}{10} = 8$

(b) Using (20.19) since $b_1^2 < 4b_2$, that is, $(2)^2 < 4(10)$,

$$g = -\tfrac{1}{2}(2) = -1 \qquad h = \tfrac{1}{2}\sqrt{4(10) - (2)^2} = 3$$

Thus, $r_1, r_2 = -1 \pm 3i$. Substituting g and h in (20.26),

$$y_c = e^{-t}(B_1 \cos 3t + B_2 \sin 3t)$$

(c) $\qquad\qquad y(t) = y_c + y_p = e^{-t}(B_1 \cos 3t + B_2 \sin 3t) + 8 \qquad\qquad\qquad (20.54)$

20.29. Redo Problem 20.28, given $y''(t) - 6y'(t) + 25y(t) = 150$.

(a) $\qquad\qquad\qquad\qquad\qquad\qquad y_p = \frac{150}{25} = 6$

(b) From (20.19), $g = -\tfrac{1}{2}(-6) = 3$ and $h = \tfrac{1}{2}\sqrt{4(25) - (-6)^2} = 4$. Substituting in (20.26),

$$y_c = e^{3t}(B_1 \cos 4t + B_2 \sin 4t)$$

(c) $\qquad\qquad y(t) = e^{3t}(B_1 \cos 4t + B_2 \sin 4t) + 6 \qquad\qquad\qquad\qquad (20.55)$

20.30. Redo Problem 20.28, given $y''(t) + 4y'(t) + 40y(t) = 10$.

(a)
$$y_p = \tfrac{10}{40} = \tfrac{1}{4}$$

(b)   From (20.19), $g = -2$ and $h = \tfrac{1}{2}\sqrt{160 - 16} = 6$. Thus, $y_c = e^{-2t}(B_1 \cos 6t + B_2 \sin 6t)$.

(c)
$$y(t) = e^{-2t}(B_1 \cos 6t + B_2 \sin 6t) + \tfrac{1}{4} \qquad (20.56)$$

20.31. (a) Find the definite solution for the following data. (b) Comment on the dynamic stability.

$$y''(t) + 2y'(t) + 10y(t) = 80 \qquad y(0) = 10 \qquad y'(0) = 13$$

(a)   From (20.54),
$$y(t) = e^{-t}(B_1 \cos 3t + B_2 \sin 3t) + 8 \qquad (20.57)$$

By the product rule,

$$\begin{aligned} y'(t) &= e^{-t}(-3B_1 \sin 3t + 3B_2 \cos 3t) + (B_1 \cos 3t + B_2 \sin 3t)(-e^{-t}) \\ &= e^{-t}(3B_2 \cos 3t - 3B_1 \sin 3t) - e^{-t}(B_1 \cos 3t + B_2 \sin 3t) \end{aligned} \qquad (20.57a)$$

Evaluating (20.57) and (20.57a) at $t = 0$ and equating them to the initial conditions,

$$y(0) = e^0(B_1 \cos 0 + B_2 \sin 0) + 8 = 10$$

From Table 20-1, $\cos 0 = 1$ and $\sin 0 = 0$. Thus,

$$y(0) = B_1 + 0 + 8 = 10 \qquad B_1 = 2$$

Similarly, $y'(0) = e^0(3B_2 \cos 0 - 3B_1 \sin 0) - e^0(B_1 \cos 0 + B_2 \sin 0) = 13$.

$$y'(0) = 3B_2 - B_1 = 13$$

Since $B_1 = 2$ from above, $B_2 = 5$. Finally, substituting in (20.57),

$$y(t) = e^{-t}(2 \cos 3t + 5 \sin 3t) + 8$$

(b)   With $g = -1$, the time path converges, as it does in Fig. 20-3 (see Example 15).

20.32. Redo Problem 20.31, given $y''(t) - 6y'(t) + 25y(t) = 150$, $y(0) = 13$, and $y'(0) = 25$.

(a)   From (20.55),
$$y(t) = e^{3t}(B_1 \cos 4t + B_2 \sin 4t) + 6 \qquad (20.58)$$

Thus,
$$y'(t) = e^{3t}(-4B_1 \sin 4t + 4B_2 \cos 4t) + 3e^{3t}(B_1 \cos 4t + B_2 \sin 4t) \qquad (20.58a)$$

Evaluating (20.58) and (20.58a) at $t = 0$ and equating them to the initial conditions,

$$y(0) = e^0(B_1 \cos 0 + B_2 \sin 0) + 6 = 13$$
$$y(0) = B_1 + 0 + 6 = 13 \qquad B_1 = 7$$

and $y'(0) = e^0(-4B_1 \sin 0 + 4B_2 \cos 0) + 3e^0(B_1 \cos 0 + B_2 \sin 0)$.

$$y'(0) = 4B_2 + 3B_1 = 25 \qquad B_2 = 1$$

Substituting in (20.58), $y(t) = e^{3t}(7 \cos 4t + \sin 4t) + 6$.

(b)   With $g = 3$, the time path is divergent.

20.33. Redo Problem 20.31, given $y''(t) + 4y'(t) + 40y(t) = 10$, $y(0) = \tfrac{1}{2}$, and $y'(0) = 2\tfrac{1}{2}$.

(a)   From (20.56),
$$y(t) = e^{-2t}(B_1 \cos 6t + B_2 \sin 6t) + \tfrac{1}{4} \qquad (20.59)$$

Thus,
$$y'(t) = e^{-2t}(-6B_1 \sin 6t + 6B_2 \cos 6t) - 2e^{-2t}(B_1 \cos 6t + B_2 \sin 6t) \qquad (20.59a)$$

Evaluating (20.59) and (20.59a) at $t = 0$ and equating them to the initial conditions,

$$y(0) = B_1 + \tfrac{1}{4} = \tfrac{1}{2} \qquad B_1 = \tfrac{1}{4}$$
$$y'(0) = 6B_2 - 2B_1 = 2\tfrac{1}{2} \qquad B_2 = \tfrac{1}{2}$$

Thus, $y(t) = e^{-2t}(\tfrac{1}{4} \cos 6t + \tfrac{1}{2} \sin 6t) + \tfrac{1}{4} = \tfrac{1}{4}e^{-2t}(\cos 6t + 2 \sin 6t) + \tfrac{1}{4}$.

(b)   With $g = -2$, the time path is convergent.

COMPLEX ROOTS IN SECOND-ORDER DIFFERENCE EQUATIONS

20.34. Find (a) the particular solution, (b) the complementary function, (c) the general solution, and (d) the definite solution. (e) Comment on the dynamic stability of the following second-order linear difference equation:

$$y_t + 4y_{t-2} = 15 \qquad y(0) = 12 \qquad y(1) = 11$$

(a) From (20.11),
$$y_p = \frac{15}{1 + 0 + 4} = 3$$

(b) From (20.19), $g = -\frac{1}{2}(0) = 0$ and $h = \frac{1}{2}\sqrt{4(4) - 0} = 2$. For second-order difference equations we now need k and θ. Applying the Pythagorean theorem to Fig. 20-1,

$$k^2 = g^2 + h^2 \qquad k = \sqrt{g^2 + h^2}$$

Substituting with the parameters of (20.19) for greater generality,

$$k = \sqrt{\frac{b_1^2 + 4b_2 - b_1^2}{4}} = \sqrt{b_2} \qquad (20.60)$$

Thus, $k = \sqrt{4} = 2$. From the definitions of Section 20.5,

$$\sin\theta = \frac{h}{k} \qquad \cos\theta = \frac{g}{k} \qquad (20.61)$$

Substituting the values from the present problem,

$$\sin\theta = \tfrac{2}{2} = 1 \qquad \cos\theta = \tfrac{0}{2} = 0$$

From Table 20-1, the angle with $\sin\theta = 1$ and $\cos\theta = 0$ is $\pi/2$. Thus, $\theta = \pi/2$. Substituting in (20.27),

$$y_c = 2^t\left[B_1\cos\left(\frac{\pi}{2}t\right) + B_2\sin\left(\frac{\pi}{2}t\right)\right]$$

(c)
$$y(t) = 2^t\left[B_1\cos\left(\frac{\pi}{2}t\right) + B_2\sin\left(\frac{\pi}{2}t\right)\right] + 3 \qquad (20.62)$$

(d) Using Table 20-1 to evaluate (20.62) at $t = 0$ and $t = 1$ from the initial conditions,

$$y(0) = (B_1 + 0) + 3 = 12 \qquad B_1 = 9$$
$$y(1) = 2(0 + B_2) + 3 = 11 \qquad B_2 = 4$$

Thus,
$$y(t) = 2^t\left(9\cos\frac{\pi}{2}t + 4\sin\frac{\pi}{2}t\right) + 3$$

(e) With $k = 2$, the time path is divergent, as explained in Example 15.

20.35. Redo Problem 20.34, given $y_t + 2y_{t-2} = 24$, $y(0) = 11$, and $y(1) = 18$.

(a) From (20.11),
$$y_p = \frac{24}{1 + 0 + 2} = 8$$

(b) From (20.60), $k = \sqrt{b_2} = \sqrt{2}$. From (20.19)

$$g = -\tfrac{1}{2}(0) = 0 \qquad h = \tfrac{1}{2}\sqrt{4(2) - 0} = \sqrt{2}$$

From (20.61),
$$\sin\theta = \frac{\sqrt{2}}{\sqrt{2}} = 1 \qquad \cos\theta = 0$$

From Table 20-1, $\theta = \pi/2$. Substituting in (20.27),

$$y_c = (\sqrt{2})^t \left[B_1 \cos\left(\frac{\pi}{2}t\right) + B_2 \sin\left(\frac{\pi}{2}t\right) \right]$$

(c)
$$y(t) = (\sqrt{2})^t \left[B_1 \cos\left(\frac{\pi}{2}t\right) + B_2 \sin\left(\frac{\pi}{2}t\right) \right] + 8 \qquad (20.63)$$

(d)
$$y(0) = B_1 + 8 = 11 \qquad B_1 = 3$$
$$y(1) = \sqrt{2}B_2 + 8 = 18 \qquad B_2 = 7.07$$

Thus,
$$y(t) = (\sqrt{2})^t \left(3 \cos\frac{\pi}{2}t + 7.07 \sin\frac{\pi}{2}t \right) + 8$$

(e) With $k = \sqrt{2} > 1$, the time path is divergent.

ECONOMIC APPLICATIONS

20.36. In many markets supply and demand are influenced by current prices and price trends (i.e., whether prices are rising or falling and whether they are rising or falling at an increasing or decreasing rate). The economist, therefore, needs to know the current price $P(t)$, the first derivative $dP(t)/dt$, and the second derivative $d^2P(t)/dt^2$. Assume

$$Q_s = c_1 + w_1 P + u_1 P' + v_1 P'' \qquad Q_d = c_2 + w_2 P + u_2 P' + v_2 P'' \qquad (20.64)$$

Comment on the dynamic stability of the market if price clears the market at each point in time.

In equilibrium, $Q_s = Q_d$. Therefore,

$$c_1 + w_1 P + u_1 P' + v_1 P'' = c_2 + w_2 P + u_2 P' + v_2 P''$$
$$(v_1 - v_2)P'' + (u_1 - u_2)P' + (w_1 - w_2)P = -(c_1 - c_2)$$

Letting $v = v_1 - v_2$, $u = u_1 - u_2$, $w = w_1 - w_2$, $c = c_1 - c_2$, and dividing through by v to conform to (20.1),

$$P'' + \frac{u}{v}P' + \frac{w}{v}P = -\frac{c}{v} \qquad (20.65)$$

Using (20.2) to find the particular integral, which will be the intertemporal equilibrium price $\bar{P}$,

$$\bar{P} = P_p = \frac{-c/v}{w/v} = -\frac{c}{w}$$

Since $c = c_1 - c_2$ and $w = w_1 - w_2$ where under ordinary supply conditions, $c_1 < 0$, $w_1 > 0$, and under ordinary demand conditions, $c_2 > 0$, $w_2 < 0$, $-c/w > 0$, as is necessary for $\bar{P}$. Using (20.4) to find the characteristic roots for the complementary function,

$$r_1, r_2 = \frac{-u/v \pm \sqrt{(u/v)^2 - 4w/v}}{2} \qquad (20.66)$$

which can assume three different types of solutions, depending on the specification of w, u, and v:

1. If $(u/v)^2 > 4w/v$, r_1 and r_2 will be *distinct real roots* solvable in terms of (20.66); and $P(t) = A_1 e^{r_1 t} + A_2 e^{r_2 t} - c/w$.
2. If $(u/v)^2 = 4w/v$, r_1 and r_2 will be *repeated real roots*. Thus, (20.66) reduces to $-(u/v)/2$ or $-u/2v$. Then from (20.17), $P(t) = A_1 e^{-(u/2v)t} + A_2 t e^{-(u/2v)t} - c/w$.
3. If $(u/v)^2 < 4w/v$, r_1 and r_2 will be *complex roots* and from (20.26), $P(t) = e^{gt}(B_1 \cos ht + B_2 \sin ht) - c/w$, where from (20.19), $g = -u/(2v)$ and $h = \frac{1}{2}\sqrt{4w/v - (u/v)^2}$.

Specification of w, u, v depends on expectations. If people are bothered by inflationary psychology and expect prices to keep rising, u_2 in (20.64) will be positive; if they expect prices to ultimately fall and hold off buying because of that expectation, u_2 will be negative; and so forth.

20.37. In a model similar to Samuelson's interaction model between the multiplier and the accelerator, assume

$$Y_t = C_t + I_t + G_t \tag{20.67}$$
$$C_t = C_0 + cY_{t-1} \tag{20.68}$$
$$I_t = I_0 + w(C_t - C_{t-1}) \tag{20.69}$$

where $0 < c < 1$, $w > 0$, and $G_t = G_0$. (a) Find the time path $Y(t)$ of national income and (b) comment on the stability conditions.

(a)   Substituting (20.68) in (20.69),

$$I_t = I_0 + cw(Y_{t-1} - Y_{t-2}) \tag{20.70}$$

Substituting $G_t = G_0$, (20.70), and (20.68) into (20.67), and then rearranging to conform with (20.10),

$$Y_t = C_0 + cY_{t-1} + I_0 + cw(Y_{t-1} - Y_{t-2}) + G_0$$
$$Y_t - c(1 + w)Y_{t-1} + cwY_{t-2} = C_0 + I_0 + G_0 \tag{20.71}$$

Using (20.11) for the particular solution,

$$Y_p = \frac{C_0 + I_0 + G_0}{1 - c(1 + w) + cw} = \frac{C_0 + I_0 + G_0}{1 - c}$$

which is the intertemporal equilibrium level of income $\bar{Y}$. Using (20.4) to find the characteristic roots for the complementary function,

$$r_1, r_2 = \frac{c(1 + w) \pm \sqrt{[-c(1 + w)]^2 - 4cw}}{2} \tag{20.72}$$

which can assume three different types of solutions depending on the values assigned to c and w:

1.   If $c^2(1 + w)^2 > 4cw$, or equivalently, if $c(1 + w)^2 > 4w$, r_1 and r_2 will be *distinct real roots* solvable in terms of (20.72) and

$$Y(t) = A_1 r_1^t + A_2 r_2^t + \frac{C_0 + I_0 + G_0}{1 - c}$$

2.   If $c(1 + w)^2 = 4w$, r_1 and r_2 will be *repeated real roots*, and from (20.72) and (20.18),

$$Y(t) = A_1 \left[\frac{1}{2} c(1 + w) \right]^t + A_2 t \left[\frac{1}{2} c(1 + w) \right]^t + \frac{C_0 + I_0 + G_0}{1 - c}$$

3.   If $c(1 + w)^2 < 4w$, r_1 and r_2 will be *complex roots*; from (20.27),

$$Y(t) = k^t(B_1 \cos t\theta + B_2 \sin t\theta) + \frac{C_0 + I_0 + G_0}{1 - c}$$

where from (20.60), $k = \sqrt{cw}$, and from (20.61) θ must be such that

$$\sin \theta = \frac{h}{k} \qquad \cos \theta = \frac{g}{k}$$

where from (20.19), $g = \frac{1}{2}c(1 + w)$ and $h = \frac{1}{2}\sqrt{4cw - c^2(1 + w)^2}$.

(b)   For stability in the model under all possible initial conditions, the necessary and sufficient conditions are (1) $c < 1$ and (2) $cw < 1$. Since $c = $ MPC with respect to the previous year's income, c will be less than 1; for $cw < 1$, the product of the MPC and the marginal capital-output ratio must also be less than 1. If the characteristic roots are conjugate complex, the time path will oscillate.

Chapter 21

The Calculus of Variations

21.1 DYNAMIC OPTIMIZATION

In the *static* optimization problems studied earlier in Chapters 4 and 5, we sought a *point* or *points* that would maximize or minimize a given function at a particular point or period of time. Given a function $y = y(x)$, the first-order condition for an optimal point x^* is simply $y'(x^*) = 0$. In *dynamic optimization* we seek a *curve* $x^*(t)$ which will maximize or minimize a given integral expression. The integral to be optimized typically defines the area under a curve F which is a function of the independent variable t, the function $x(t)$, and its derivative dx/dt. In brief, assuming a time period from $t_0 = 0$ to $t_1 = T$ and introducing a new symbol $\dot{x}$ for the derivative dx/dt, we seek to maximize or minimize

$$\int_0^T F[t, x(t), \dot{x}(t)] \, dt \qquad (21.1)$$

where F is assumed continuous for t, $x(t)$, and $\dot{x}(t)$ and to have continuous partial derivatives with respect to x and $\dot{x}$. An integral such as (21.1) which assumes a numerical value for each of the class of functions $x(t)$ is called a *functional*. A curve that maximizes or minimizes the value of a functional is called an *extremal*. Acceptable candidates for an extremal are the class of functions $x(t)$ which are continuously differentiable on the defined interval and which typically satisfy some fixed endpoint conditions. To compute extremals, we use the calculus of variations.

EXAMPLE 1. A firm wishing to maximize profits π from time $t_0 = 0$ to $t_1 = T$ finds that demand for its product depends on not only the price p of the product but also the rate of change of the price with respect to time dp/dt. By assuming that costs are fixed and that both p and dp/dt are functions of time, and employing the new symbol $\dot{p}$ for dp/dt, the firm's objective can be expressed mathematically as

$$\max \int_0^T \pi[t, p(t), \dot{p}(t)] \, dt$$

A second firm has found that its total cost C depends on the level of production $x(t)$ and the rate of change of production $dx/dt = \dot{x}$, due to start-up and tapering-off costs. Assuming that the firm wishes to minimize costs and that x and $\dot{x}$ are functions of time, the firm's objective might be written

$$\min \int_{t_0}^{t_1} C[t, x(t), \dot{x}(t)] \, dt$$

subject to $\qquad x(t_0) = x_0 \qquad$ and $\qquad x(t_1) = x_1$

These initial and terminal constraints are known as *endpoint conditions*.

21.2 DISTANCE BETWEEN TWO POINTS ON A PLANE

The length S of any nonlinear curve connecting two points on a plane, such as the curve connecting the points (t_0, x_0) and (t_1, x_1) in Fig. 21-1(a), can be approximated mathematically as follows. Subdivide the curve mentally into subintervals, as in Fig. 21-1(b), and recall from the Pythagorean theorem that the square of the length of the hypotenuse of a right triangle equals the sum of the squares of the lengths

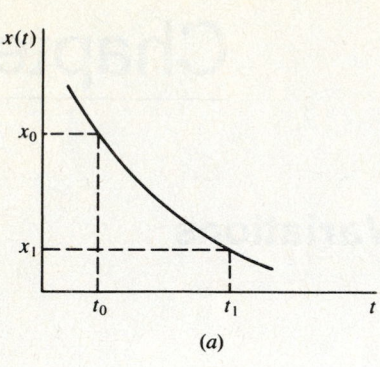 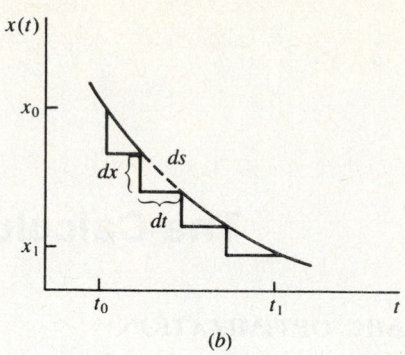

$$(a) \qquad\qquad\qquad (b)$$

Fig. 21-1

of the other two sides. Accordingly, the length of an individual subsegment ds is

$$(ds)^2 = (dt)^2 + (dx)^2$$

Simplifying mathematically,

$$ds = \sqrt{(dt)^2 + (dx)^2}$$

Dividing, then multiplying, both sides by $\sqrt{(dt)^2}$, or simply dt,

$$\frac{ds}{dt} = \sqrt{1 + \left(\frac{dx}{dt}\right)^2}$$

$$ds = \sqrt{1 + \left(\frac{dx}{dt}\right)^2}\, dt$$

or, using the more compact symbol,

$$ds = \sqrt{1 + (\dot{x})^2}\, dt$$

from which the length of the total curve S from t_0 to t_1 can be estimated by simple integration to get

$$S = \int_{t_0}^{t_1} \sqrt{1 + (\dot{x})^2}\, dt$$

See Problems 21.1 to 21.3.

21.3 EULER'S EQUATION AND CONDITIONS FOR DYNAMIC OPTIMIZATION

For a curve $X^* = x^*(t)$ connecting points (t_0, x_0) and (t_1, x_1) to be an extremal for (i.e., to optimize) the functional

$$\int_{t_0}^{t_1} F[t, x(t), \dot{x}(t)]\, dt$$

a necessary, though not sufficient, condition is that

$$\frac{\partial F}{\partial x} = \frac{d}{dt}\left(\frac{\partial F}{\partial \dot{x}}\right) \tag{21.2a}$$

This necessary condition for dynamic optimization is called *Euler's equation*. It is a second-order differential equation which is perhaps more easily understood in terms of different notation. Using subscripts to denote partial derivatives and listing the arguments of the derivatives, which are themselves functions, we can express Euler's equation in $(21.2a)$ as

$$F_x(t, x, \dot{x}) = \frac{d}{dt} [F_{\dot{x}}(t, x, \dot{x})] \tag{21.2b}$$

Then using the chain rule to take the derivative of $F_{\dot{x}}$ with respect to t and omitting the arguments for simplicity, we get

$$F_x = F_{\dot{x}t} + F_{\dot{x}x}(\dot{x}) + F_{\dot{x}\dot{x}}(\ddot{x}) \tag{21.2c}$$

where $\ddot{x} = d^2x/dt^2$.

Proof that Euler's equation is a necessary condition for an extremal in dynamic optimization is offered in Example 2. See also Problems 21.23 to 21.30.

EXAMPLE 2. To prove that Euler's equation in $(21.2a)$ is a necessary condition for an extremal, let $X^* = x^*(t)$ be the curve connecting points (t_0, x_0) and (t_1, x_1) in Fig. 21-2 which optimizes the functional (i.e., posits the optimizing function for)

$$\int_{t_0}^{t_1} F[t, x(t), \dot{x}(t)] \, dt \tag{21.3}$$

Let $\hat{X} = x^*(t) + mh(t)$ be a neighboring curve joining these points, where m is an arbitrary constant and $h(t)$ is an

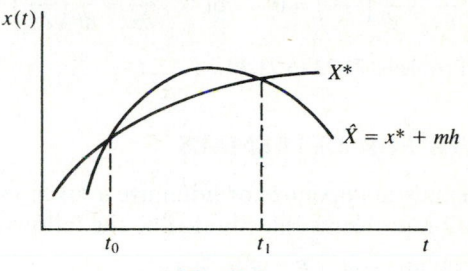

Fig. 21-2

arbitrary function. In order for the curve $\hat{X}$ to also pass through the points (t_0, x_0) and (t_1, x_1), that is, for $\hat{X}$ to also satisfy the endpoint conditions, it is necessary that

$$h(t_0) = 0 \quad \text{and} \quad h(t_1) = 0 \tag{21.4}$$

By holding both $x^*(t)$ and $h(t)$ fixed, the value of the integral becomes a function of m alone and can be written

$$g(m) = \int_{t_0}^{t_1} F[t, x^*(t) + mh(t), \dot{x}^*(t) + m\dot{h}(t)] \, dt \tag{21.5}$$

Since $x^*(t)$ by definition optimizes the functional in (21.3), the function $g(m)$ in (21.5) can be optimized only when $m = 0$ and

$$\frac{dg}{dm}\bigg|_{m=0} = 0 \tag{21.6}$$

To differentiate under the integral sign in (21.5), we use *Leibnitz's rule* which states that given

$$g(m) = \int_{t_0}^{t_1} f(t, m) \, dt$$

where t_0 and t_1 are differentiable functions of m,

$$\frac{dg}{dm} = \int_{t_0}^{t_1} \frac{\partial F}{\partial m} \, dt + f(t_1, m) \frac{\partial t_1}{\partial m} - f(t_0, m) \frac{\partial t_0}{\partial m} \tag{21.7}$$

Since the boundaries of integration t_0 and t_1 are fixed in the present example, $\partial t_0/\partial m = \partial t_1/\partial m = 0$, and we have to consider only the first term in Leibnitz's rule. Applying the chain rule to (21.5) to find $\partial F/\partial m$, because F is a function of x and $\dot{x}$, which in turn are functions of m, and substituting in (21.7), we have

$$\frac{dg}{dm} = \int_{t_0}^{t_1} \left[\frac{\partial F}{\partial x} \frac{\partial(x^* + mh)}{\partial m} + \frac{\partial F}{\partial \dot{x}} \frac{\partial(\dot{x}^* + m\dot{h})}{\partial m} \right] dt$$

With $\partial(x^* + mh)/\partial m = h$ and $\partial(\dot{x}^* + m\dot{h})/\partial m = \dot{h}$, and using (21.6),

$$\frac{dg}{dm}\bigg|_{m=0} = \int_{t_0}^{t_1} \left[\frac{\partial F}{\partial x} h(t) + \frac{\partial F}{\partial \dot{x}} \dot{h}(t) \right] dt = 0 \tag{21.8}$$

Leaving the first term in the brackets in (21.8) untouched and integrating the second term by means of parts,

$$\frac{dg}{dm}\bigg|_{m=0} = \int_{t_0}^{t_1} \frac{\partial F}{\partial x} h(t)\, dt + \left[\frac{\partial F}{\partial \dot{x}} h(t) \right]_{t_0}^{t_1} - \int_{t_0}^{t_1} \frac{d}{dt}\left(\frac{\partial F}{\partial \dot{x}} \right) h(t)\, dt = 0$$

With $h(t_0) = h(t_1) = 0$ from (21.4), the second term above drops out. Combining the other two terms and rearranging,

$$\frac{dg}{dm}\bigg|_{m=0} = \int_{t_0}^{t_1} \left[\frac{\partial F}{\partial x} - \frac{d}{dt}\left(\frac{\partial F}{\partial \dot{x}} \right) \right] h(t)\, dt = 0 \tag{21.9}$$

Since $h(t)$ is an arbitrary function that need not equal zero, it follows that a necessary condition for an extremal is that the integrand within the brackets equal zero, namely,

$$\frac{\partial F}{\partial x} - \frac{d}{dt}\left(\frac{\partial F}{\partial \dot{x}} \right) = 0 \qquad \text{or} \qquad \frac{\partial F}{\partial x} = \frac{d}{dt}\left(\frac{\partial F}{\partial \dot{x}} \right)$$

which is Euler's equation. See also Problems 21.23 to 21.30.

21.4   FINDING CANDIDATES FOR EXTREMALS

Finding candidates for extremals to maximize or minimize a given integral subject to fixed endpoint conditions in dynamic optimization problems is facilitated by the following five steps:

1. Let the integrand equal F. Normally $F = F(t, x, \dot{x})$.
2. Take the partial derivatives of F with respect to x and $\dot{x}$ to find $\partial F/\partial x = F_x$ and $\partial F/\partial \dot{x} = F_{\dot{x}}$.
3. Substitute in Euler's equation from (21.2a) or (21.2b).
4. Take the derivative with respect to t of $F_{\dot{x}}$, recalling that the chain rule may be necessary because $F_{\dot{x}}$ can be a function of t, x, and $\dot{x}$, and x and $\dot{x}$ are functions of t.
5. If there are no derivative terms ($\dot{x}$ or $\ddot{x}$), solve immediately for x; if there are $\dot{x}$ or $\ddot{x}$ terms, integrate until all the derivatives are gone and then solve for x.

Illustrations of this technique are provided in Examples 3 and 4 and Problems 21.4 to 21.15.

EXAMPLE 3.   Given

$$\int_0^T (6x^2 e^{3t} + 4t\dot{x})\, dt$$

the functional is optimized by using the procedure outlined in Section 21.4 and the notation from (21.2a), as follows:

1. Let
$$F = 6x^2 e^{3t} + 4t\dot{x}$$

2. Then
$$\frac{\partial F}{\partial x} = 12xe^{3t} \qquad \text{and} \qquad \frac{\partial F}{\partial \dot{x}} = 4t$$

3. Substituting in Euler's equation from (21.2a),
$$12xe^{3t} = \frac{d}{dt}(4t)$$

4. But $d(4t)/dt = 4$. Substituting above,
$$12xe^{3t} = 4$$

5. Solving for x directly since there are no $\dot{x}$ or $\ddot{x}$ terms, and expressing the solution as $x(t)$,

$$x(t) = \tfrac{1}{3}e^{-3t}$$

Note that since Euler's equation is a necessary but not a sufficient condition for dynamic optimization, the above solution is merely a candidate for an extremal. There are second-order conditions for dynamic optimization problems analogous to the second-order conditions for static optimization problems to help us distinguish between and guarantee a relative maximum or minimum, but further analysis beyond the scope of this book is required.

EXAMPLE 4. The functional

$$\int_0^2 (4\dot{x}^2 + 12xt - 5t)\, dt$$

subject to
$$x(0) = 1 \qquad x(2) = 4$$

is optimized as above, but now with the notation from (21.2b).

1. Let
$$F = 4\dot{x}^2 + 12xt - 5t$$

2. Then
$$F_x = 12t \qquad \text{and} \qquad F_{\dot{x}} = 8\dot{x}$$

3. Substituting in Euler's equation from (21.2b),

$$12t = \frac{d}{dt}(8\dot{x})$$

4. Recalling that $\dot{x} = \dfrac{dx}{dt}$ and that $\dfrac{d}{dt}\left(\dfrac{dx}{dt}\right) = \dfrac{d^2x}{dt^2} = \ddot{x}$,

$$12t = 8\ddot{x}$$

5. Since an $\ddot{x}$ term remains, integrate both sides of the equation successively twice, using only one constant of integration term at each step.

$$\int 12t\, dt = \int 8\ddot{x}\, dt$$
$$6t^2 + c_1 = 8\dot{x}$$

Integrating again,

$$\int (6t^2 + c_1)\, dt = \int 8\dot{x}\, dt$$
$$2t^3 + c_1 t + c_2 = 8x$$

Solving for x,

$$x(t) = \frac{1}{4}t^3 + \frac{c_1}{8}t + \frac{c_2}{8}$$

Applying the boundary conditions,

$$x(0) = \frac{c_2}{8} = 1 \qquad c_2 = 8$$
$$x(2) = \tfrac{1}{4}(2)^3 + \tfrac{1}{8}(2)c_1 + 1 = 4 \qquad c_1 = 4$$

Substituting,
$$x(t) = \tfrac{1}{4}t^3 + \tfrac{1}{2}t + 1$$

21.5 DYNAMIC OPTIMIZATION SUBJECT TO FUNCTIONAL CONSTRAINTS

To find an extremal that maximizes or minimizes a given integral

$$\int_0^T F[t,\, x(t),\, \dot{x}(t)]\, dt \qquad\qquad (21.10)$$

under a constraint that keeps the integral

$$\int_0^T G[t, x(t), \dot{x}(t)] \, dt = k \tag{21.11}$$

where k is a constant, the Lagrangian multiplier method may be used. Multiply the constraint in (21.11) by λ, and add it to the objective function from (21.10) to form the Lagrangian function:

$$\int_0^T (F + \lambda G) \, dt \tag{21.12}$$

The necessary, but not sufficient, condition to have an extremal for dynamic optimization is the Euler equation

$$\frac{\partial H}{\partial x} = \frac{d}{dt}\left(\frac{\partial H}{\partial \dot{x}}\right) \qquad \text{where} \quad H = F + \lambda G \tag{21.13}$$

See Example 5 and Problem 21.22.

EXAMPLE 5. Constrained optimization of functionals is commonly used in problems to determine a curve with a given perimeter that encloses the largest area. Such problems are called *isoperimetric problems* and are usually expressed in the functional notation of $y(x)$ rather than $x(t)$. Adjusting for this notation, to find the curve Y of given length k which encloses a maximum area A, where

$$A = \frac{1}{2}\int (x\dot{y} - y) \, dx$$

and the length of the curve is

$$\int_{x_0}^{x_1} \sqrt{1 + \dot{y}^2} \, dx = k$$

set up the Lagrangian function, as explained in Section 21.5.

$$\int_{x_0}^{x_1} \left[\tfrac{1}{2}(x\dot{y} - y) + \lambda\sqrt{1 + \dot{y}^2}\right] dx \tag{21.14}$$

Letting H equal the integrand in (21.14), the Euler equation is

$$\frac{\partial H}{\partial y} = \frac{d}{dx}\left(\frac{\partial H}{\partial \dot{y}}\right)$$

where from (21.14),

$$\frac{\partial H}{\partial y} = -\frac{1}{2} \qquad \text{and} \qquad \frac{\partial H}{\partial \dot{y}} = \frac{1}{2}x + \frac{\lambda\dot{y}}{\sqrt{1 + \dot{y}^2}}$$

Substituting in Euler's equation,

$$-\frac{1}{2} = \frac{d}{dx}\left(\frac{1}{2}x + \frac{\lambda\dot{y}}{\sqrt{1 + \dot{y}^2}}\right)$$

$$-\frac{1}{2} = \frac{1}{2} + \frac{d}{dx}\left(\frac{\lambda\dot{y}}{\sqrt{1 + \dot{y}^2}}\right)$$

$$-1 = \frac{d}{dx}\left(\frac{\lambda\dot{y}}{\sqrt{1 + \dot{y}^2}}\right)$$

Integrating both sides directly and rearranging,

$$\frac{\lambda\dot{y}}{\sqrt{1 + \dot{y}^2}} = -(x - c_1)$$

Squaring both sides of the equation and solving algebraically for $\dot{y}$,

$$\lambda^2 \dot{y}^2 = (x - c_1)^2(1 + \dot{y}^2)$$
$$\lambda^2 \dot{y}^2 - (x - c_1)^2\dot{y}^2 = (x - c_1)^2$$
$$\dot{y}^2 = \frac{(x - c_1)^2}{\lambda^2 - (x - c_1)^2}$$
$$\dot{y} = \pm \frac{x - c_1}{\sqrt{\lambda^2 - (x - c_1)^2}}$$

Integrating both sides, using integration by substitution on the right, gives

$$y - c_2 = \pm\sqrt{\lambda^2 - (x - c_1)^2}$$

which, by squaring both sides and rearranging, can be expressed as a circle

$$(x - c_1)^2 + (y - c_2)^2 = \lambda^2$$

where c_1, c_2, and λ are determined by x_0, x_1, and k.

21.6 VARIATIONAL NOTATION

A special symbol δ is used in the calculus of variations which has properties similar to the differential d in differential calculus.

Given a function $F[t, x(t), \dot{x}(t)]$ and considering t as constant, let

$$\Delta F = F[t, x(t) + mh(t), \dot{x}(t) + m\dot{h}(t)] - F[t, x(t), \dot{x}(t)] \qquad (21.15)$$

where m is an arbitrary constant, $h(t)$ is an arbitrary function as in Example 2, and the arguments are frequently omitted for succinctness. Using the *Taylor expansion* which approximates a function such as $x(t)$ by taking successive derivatives and summing them in ordered sequence to get

$$x(t) = x(t_0) + \dot{x}(t_0)(t - t_0) + \frac{\ddot{x}(t_0)(t - t_0)^2}{2!} + \cdots$$

we have

$$F(t, x + mh, \dot{x} + m\dot{h}) = F(t, x, \dot{x}) + \frac{\partial F}{\partial x}mh + \frac{\partial F}{\partial \dot{x}}m\dot{h} + \cdots \qquad (21.16)$$

Substituting (21.16) in (21.15) and subtracting as indicated,

$$\Delta F = \frac{\partial F}{\partial x}mh + \frac{\partial F}{\partial \dot{x}}m\dot{h} + \cdots \qquad (21.17)$$

where the sum of the first two terms in (21.17) is called the *variation* of F and is denoted by δF. Thus,

$$\delta F = \frac{\partial F}{\partial x}mh + \frac{\partial F}{\partial \dot{x}}m\dot{h} \qquad (21.18)$$

From (21.18) it is readily seen that if $F = x$, by substituting x for F, we have

$$\delta x = mh \qquad (21.19)$$

Similarly, if $F = \dot{x}$,

$$\delta \dot{x} = m\dot{h} \qquad (21.20)$$

Hence an alternative expression for (21.18) is

$$\delta F = \frac{\partial F}{\partial x}\delta x + \frac{\partial F}{\partial \dot{x}}\delta \dot{x} \qquad (21.21)$$

and the necessary condition for finding an extremal in dynamic optimization can also be expressed as

$$\delta \int_{t_0}^{t_1} F[t, x(t), \dot{x}(t)] \, dt = 0$$

For proof, see Problems 21.31 and 21.32.

21.7 APPLICATIONS TO ECONOMICS

A firm wishes to minimize the present value at discount rate i of an order of N units to be delivered at time t_1. The firm's costs consist of production costs $a[\dot{x}(t)]^2$ and inventory costs $bx(t)$, where a and b are positive constants; $x(t)$ is the accumulated inventory by time t; the rate of change of inventory is the production rate $\dot{x}(t)$, where $\dot{x}(t) \geq 0$; and $a\dot{x}(t)$ is the per unit cost of production. Assuming $x(t_0) = 0$ and the firm wishes to achieve $x(t_1) = N$, in terms of the calculus of variations the firm must

$$\min \int_{t_0}^{t_1} e^{-it}(a\dot{x}^2 + bx) \, dt$$

subject to
$$x(t_0) = 0 \qquad x(t_1) = N$$

To find a candidate for the extremal that will minimize the firm's cost, let

$$F[t, x(t), \dot{x}(t)] = e^{-it}(a\dot{x}^2 + bx)$$

then
$$F_x = be^{-it} \qquad \text{and} \qquad F_{\dot{x}} = 2ae^{-it}\dot{x}$$

Substituting in Euler's equation from $(21.2b)$,

$$be^{-it} = \frac{d}{dt}(2ae^{-it}\dot{x})$$

Using the product rule and the chain rule to take the derivative on the right since $\dot{x}$ is a function of t, we have

$$be^{-it} = 2ae^{-it}(\ddot{x}) + \dot{x}(-i2ae^{-it})$$
$$= 2ae^{-it}\ddot{x} - 2aie^{-it}\dot{x}$$

Canceling the e^{-it} terms and rearranging to solve for $\ddot{x}$,

$$\ddot{x}(t) - i\dot{x}(t) = \frac{b}{2a} \tag{21.22}$$

With $\ddot{x}(t) = i\dot{x}(t) + b/(2a)$ from (21.22) and $\dot{x}(t) \geq 0$ by assumption, $\ddot{x}(t)$ in (21.22) must be positive, indicating that the firm should maintain a strictly increasing rate of production over time.

Equation (21.22) is a second-order linear differential equation which can be solved with the method outlined in Section 20.1. Using Equation $(20.2a)$ to find the particular integral, since in terms of (20.1) $b_1 = -i$, $b_2 = 0$, and $a = b/2a$, and adjusting the functional notation from $y = y(t)$ to $x = x(t)$, we have

$$x_p = \frac{b/2a}{-i} t = -\frac{b}{2ai} t$$

Using (20.4) to find r_1 and r_2 for the complementary function,

$$r_1, r_2 = \frac{-(-i) \pm \sqrt{(-i)^2 - 4(0)}}{2} = \frac{i \pm i}{2}$$
$$r_1 = i \qquad r_2 = 0$$

Substituting in (20.3) to find x_c and adding to x_p,

$$x(t) = A_1 e^{it} + A_2 - \frac{b}{2ai} t \qquad (21.23)$$

Letting $t_0 = 0$ and $t_1 = T$, from the boundary conditions we have

$$x(0) = A_1 + A_2 = 0 \qquad A_2 = -A_1$$

$$x(T) = A_1 e^{iT} + (-A_1) - \frac{b}{2ai} T = N$$

Solving $x(T)$ for A_1,

$$A_1(e^{iT} - 1) = N + \frac{b}{2ai} T$$

$$A_1 = \frac{N + [b/(2ai)]T}{e^{iT} - 1} \qquad (21.24)$$

Finally, substituting in (21.23), and recalling that $A_2 = -A_1$, we have as a candidate for an extremal:

$$x(t) = \left(\frac{N + [b/(2ai)]T}{e^{iT} - 1}\right) e^{it} - \left(\frac{N + [b/(2ai)]T}{e^{iT} - 1}\right) - \frac{b}{2ai} t$$

$$x(t) = \left(N + \frac{b}{2ai} T\right) \frac{e^{it} - 1}{e^{iT} - 1} - \frac{b}{2ai} t \qquad 0 \le t \le T$$

But further testing is required to prove it represents a minimum. For economic applications, see Problems 21.16 to 21.21.

Solved Problems

DISTANCE BETWEEN TWO POINTS ON A PLANE

21.1. Minimize the length of a curve S connecting the points (t_0, x_0) and (t_1, x_1) in Fig. 21-1 from Section 21.2, i.e.,

$$\min \int_{t_0}^{t_1} \sqrt{1 + \dot{x}^2} \, dt$$

subject to $\qquad x(t_0) = x_0 \qquad x(t_1) = x_1$

Using the procedure outlined in Section 21.4 to find a candidate for an extremal to minimize the functional,

1. Let $\qquad F = \sqrt{1 + \dot{x}^2} = (1 + \dot{x}^2)^{1/2}$

2. Take the partial derivatives F_x and $F_{\dot{x}}$, noting that there is no x term in F, only an $\dot{x}$ term, and that the chain rule or generalized power function rule is necessary for $F_{\dot{x}}$.

$$F_x = 0 \qquad F_{\dot{x}} = \frac{1}{2}(1 + \dot{x}^2)^{-1/2} \cdot 2\dot{x} = \frac{\dot{x}}{\sqrt{1 + \dot{x}^2}}$$

3. Substitute in Euler's equation.

$$0 = \frac{d}{dt}\left(\frac{\dot{x}}{\sqrt{1 + \dot{x}^2}}\right)$$

4. Since there are no variables on the left-hand side, integrate both sides immediately with respect to t. Integrating the derivative on the right-hand side will produce the original function. With

$\int 0\, dt = c$, a constant, we have

$$c = \frac{\dot{x}}{\sqrt{1 + \dot{x}^2}}$$

Squaring both sides and rearranging to solve for $\dot{x}$,

$$c^2(1 + \dot{x}^2) = \dot{x}^2$$
$$c^2 = \dot{x}^2 - c^2\dot{x}^2 = (1 - c^2)\dot{x}^2$$
$$\dot{x} = \sqrt{\frac{c^2}{1 - c^2}} = k_1 \qquad \text{a constant}$$

5.   With an $\dot{x}$ term remaining, integrate again to get

$$x(t) = k_1 t + k_2 \qquad\qquad (21.25)$$

which is a linear equation, indicating that the shortest distance between two points is a straight line. The parameters k_1 (slope) and k_2 (vertical intercept) are uniquely determined by the boundary conditions, as is illustrated in Problem 21.2.

21.2. Minimize

$$\int_0^2 \sqrt{1 + \dot{x}^2}\, dt$$

subject to $x(0) = 3 \qquad x(2) = 8$

From (21.25), $x(t) = k_1 t + k_2$

Applying the boundary conditions,

$$x(0) = k_1(0) + k_2 = 3 \qquad k_2 = 3$$
$$x(2) = k_1(2) + 3 = 8 \qquad k_1 = 2.5$$

Substituting,

$$x(t) = 2.5t + 3$$

21.3. (a) Estimate the distance between the points (t_0, x_0) and (t_1, x_1) from Problem 21.2, using the functional; (b) draw a graph and check your answer geometrically.

(a)   Given

$$\int_0^2 \sqrt{1 + \dot{x}^2}\, dt \qquad \text{and} \qquad x(t) = 2.5t + 3$$

by taking the derivative $\dot{x}(t) = 2.5$ and substituting, we have

$$\int_0^2 \sqrt{1 + (2.5)^2}\, dt = \int_0^2 \sqrt{7.25}\, dt = \sqrt{7.25}\, t \Big|_0^2$$
$$= 2.69258(2) - 2.69258(0) = 5.385$$

(b)   Applying the Pythagorean theorem to Fig. 21-3,

$$x^2 = 5^2 + 2^2$$
$$x = \sqrt{29} = 5.385$$

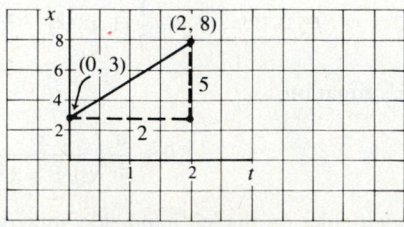

Fig. 21-3

FINDING CANDIDATES FOR EXTREMALS

21.4. Find extremals for

$$\int_{t_0}^{t_1} (2\dot{x}^2 - 42xt + 11t)\, dt$$

subject to

$$x(t_0) = x_0 \qquad x(t_1) = x_1$$

Using the now familiar five steps to find a candidate for an extremal,

1. $$F = 2\dot{x}^2 - 42xt + 11t$$

2. $$F_x = -42t \qquad F_{\dot{x}} = 4\dot{x}$$

3. Substituting in Euler's equation,

$$-42t = \frac{d}{dt}(4\dot{x})$$

$$-42t = 4\ddot{x}$$

4. Integrating both sides to eliminate the $\ddot{x}$ term and using only one constant of integration term at each step throughout,

$$-21t^2 + c_1 = 4\dot{x}$$

Integrating again to eliminate the $\dot{x}$ term,

$$-7t^3 + c_1 t + c_2 = 4x$$

5. Solving for x,

$$x(t) = -1.75t^3 + 0.25c_1 t + 0.25c_2$$

Remember that $x(t)$ here, as in subsequent problems, is only a candidate for a maximum or minimum. Further testing is required to be sure.

21.5. Find extremals for

$$\int_{t_0}^{t_1} (\dot{x}^2 + 60t^3 x)\, dt$$

subject to

$$x(t_0) = x_0 \qquad x(t_1) = x_1$$

1. $$F = \dot{x}^2 + 60t^3 x$$

2. $$F_x = 60t^3 \qquad F_{\dot{x}} = 2\dot{x}$$

3. Substituting in Euler's equation,

$$60t^3 = \frac{d}{dt}(2\dot{x})$$

$$60t^3 = 2\ddot{x}$$

4. Integrating both sides and combining constants of integration for each step,

$$15t^4 + c_1 = 2\dot{x}$$

Integrating again and solving for x,

$$3t^5 + c_1 t + c_2 = 2x$$

5. $$x(t) = 1.5t^5 + 0.5c_1 t + 0.5c_2$$

21.6. Find extremals for

$$\int_{t_0}^{t_1} (3x^2 e^{5t} + 4t^3 \dot{x}) \, dt$$

subject to $\qquad x(t_0) = x_0 \qquad x(t_1) = x_1$

1. $\qquad\qquad\qquad F = 3x^2 e^{5t} + 4t^3 \dot{x}$

2. $\qquad\qquad\qquad F_x = 6x e^{5t} \qquad F_{\dot{x}} = 4t^3$

3. Substituting in Euler's equation,

$$6x e^{5t} = \frac{d}{dt}(4t^3)$$

4. $\qquad\qquad\qquad 6x e^{5t} = 12t^2$

5. With no $\dot{x}$ terms left, simply solve for x algebraically.

$$x(t) = 2t^2 e^{-5t}$$

21.7. Find extremals for

$$\int_{t_0}^{t_1} \frac{3\dot{x}^2}{8t^3} \, dt$$

subject to $\qquad x(t_0) = x_0 \qquad x(t_1) = x_1$

1. $$F = \frac{3\dot{x}^2}{8t^3}$$

2. $$F_x = 0 \qquad F_{\dot{x}} = \frac{6\dot{x}}{8t^3} = \frac{3\dot{x}}{4t^3}$$

3. Substituting in Euler's equation,

$$0 = \frac{d}{dt}\left(\frac{3\dot{x}}{4t^3}\right)$$

4. With $F_x = 0$, integrate immediately.

$$c_1 = \frac{3\dot{x}}{4t^3}$$

$$3\dot{x} = 4c_1 t^3$$

With an $\dot{x}$ still remaining, integrate again.

$$3x = c_1 t^4 + c_2$$

5. $$x(t) = \frac{c_1}{3} t^4 + \frac{c_2}{3}$$

$$= k_1 t^4 + k_2 \qquad \text{where} \quad k_1 = \frac{c_1}{3} \qquad k_2 = \frac{c_2}{3}$$

21.8. Find extremals for

$$\int_{t_0}^{t_1} (7t^2 + 2\dot{x}^2 t) \, dt$$

subject to $\qquad x(t_0) = x_0 \qquad x(t_1) = x_1$

1. $$F = 7t^2 + 2\dot{x}^2 t$$

2. $$F_x = 0 \qquad F_{\dot{x}} = 4\dot{x}t$$

3. $$0 = \frac{d}{dt}(4\dot{x}t)$$

4. Integrating immediately,

$$c_1 = 4\dot{x}t \qquad \dot{x} = \frac{c_1}{4t}$$

Integrating again,

$$x = \frac{c_1}{4}\ln t + c_2$$

5. $$x(t) = k_1 \ln t + k_2 \qquad \text{where} \quad k_1 = \frac{c_1}{4} \qquad k_2 = c_2$$

21.9. Find extremals for

$$\int_{t_0}^{t_1} (15x^2 - 132x + 19x\dot{x} + 12\dot{x}^2)\, dt$$

subject to

$$x(t_0) = x_0 \qquad x(t_1) = x_1$$

1. $$F = 15x^2 - 132x + 19x\dot{x} + 12\dot{x}^2$$

2. $$F_x = 30x - 132 + 19\dot{x} \qquad F_{\dot{x}} = 19x + 24\dot{x}$$

3. $$30x - 132 + 19\dot{x} = \frac{d}{dt}(19x + 24\dot{x})$$

4. $$30x - 132 + 19\dot{x} = 19\dot{x} + 24\ddot{x}$$

Solving algebraically,

$$\ddot{x} - 1.25x = -5.5 \tag{21.26}$$

5. Equation (21.26) is a second-order differential equation which can be solved with the techniques of Section 21.7. Using Equation (20.2) to find the particular integral x_p, where $b_1 = 0$, $b_2 = -1.25$, and $a = -5.5$,

$$x_p = \frac{a}{b_2} = \frac{-5.5}{-1.25} = 4.4$$

Then using (20.4) to find the characteristic roots,

$$r_1, r_2 = \frac{0 \pm \sqrt{0 - 4(-1.25)}}{2} = \pm\sqrt{1.25}$$

and substituting in (20.3) to find the complementary function x_c,

$$x_c = A_1 e^{\sqrt{1.25}\,t} + A_2 e^{-\sqrt{1.25}\,t}$$

Finally, by adding x_c and x_p, we have

$$x(t) = A_1 e^{\sqrt{1.25}\,t} + A_2 e^{-\sqrt{1.25}\,t} + 4.4$$

21.10. Find extremals for

$$\int_{t_0}^{t_1} (16x^2 + 9x\dot{x} + 8\dot{x}^2)\, dt$$

subject to
$$x(t_0) = x_0 \qquad x(t_1) = x_1$$

1.
$$F = 16x^2 + 9x\dot{x} + 8\dot{x}^2$$

2.
$$F_x = 32x + 9\dot{x} \qquad F_{\dot{x}} = 9x + 16\dot{x}$$

3.
$$32x + 9\dot{x} = \frac{d}{dt}(9x + 16\dot{x})$$

4.
$$32x + 9\dot{x} = 9\dot{x} + 16\ddot{x}$$
$$\ddot{x} - 2x = 0$$

5. Using (20.2) where $b_1 = 0$, $b_2 = -2$, and $a = 0$ to find x_p,

$$x_p = \frac{a}{b_2} = \frac{0}{-2} = 0$$

Using (20.4) to find r_1 and r_2,

$$r_1, r_2 = \frac{\pm\sqrt{-4(-2)}}{2} = \pm\sqrt{2}$$

and substituting in (20.3) to find x_c,

$$x_c = A_1 e^{\sqrt{2}t} + A_2 e^{-\sqrt{2}t}$$

Then since $x_p = 0$,

$$x(t) = x_c = A_1 e^{\sqrt{2}t} + A_2 e^{-\sqrt{2}t}$$

21.11. Find extremals for

$$\int_{t_0}^{t_1} (7\dot{x}^2 + 4x\dot{x} - 63x^2)\, dt$$

subject to
$$x(t_0) = x_0 \qquad x(t_1) = x_1$$

1.
$$F = 7\dot{x}^2 + 4x\dot{x} - 63x^2$$

2.
$$F_x = 4\dot{x} - 126x \qquad F_{\dot{x}} = 14\dot{x} + 4x$$

3.
$$4\dot{x} - 126x = \frac{d}{dt}(14\dot{x} + 4x)$$

4.
$$4\dot{x} - 126x = 14\ddot{x} + 4\dot{x}$$
$$\ddot{x} + 9x = 0$$

where in terms of (20.1), $b_1 = 0$, $b_2 = 9$, and $a = 0$.

5. Using (20.2) for x_p,
$$x_p = \frac{0}{9} = 0$$

Using (20.19) since $b_1^2 < 4b_2$, $\qquad r_1, r_2 = g \pm hi$

where $\qquad g = -\tfrac{1}{2}b_1 = -\tfrac{1}{2}(0) = 0 \qquad h = \tfrac{1}{2}\sqrt{4b_2 - b_1^2} = \tfrac{1}{2}\sqrt{36} = 3$

and $\qquad r_1, r_2 = 0 \pm 3i = \pm 3i$

Substituting in (20.26),

$$x_c = B_1 \cos 3t + B_2 \sin 3t$$

With $x_p = 0$,

$$x(t) = B_1 \cos 3t + B_2 \sin 3t$$

21.12. Find extremals for

$$\int_{t_0}^{t_1} (5x^2 + 27x - 8x\dot{x} - \dot{x}^2)\, dt$$

subject to
$$x(t_0) = x_0 \qquad x(t_1) = x_1$$

1.
$$F = 5x^2 + 27x - 8x\dot{x} - \dot{x}^2$$

2.
$$F_x = 10x + 27 - 8\dot{x} \qquad F_{\dot{x}} = -8x - 2\dot{x}$$

3.
$$10x + 27 - 8\dot{x} = \frac{d}{dt}(-8x - 2\dot{x})$$

4.
$$10x + 27 - 8\dot{x} = -8\dot{x} - 2\ddot{x}$$
$$\ddot{x} + 5x = -13.5$$

5. Using (20.2),
$$x_p = \frac{-13.5}{5} = -2.7$$

Using (20.19),
$$g = -\tfrac{1}{2}(0) = 0 \qquad h = \tfrac{1}{2}\sqrt{4(5)} = \sqrt{5}$$
$$r_1, r_2 = 0 \pm \sqrt{5}i = \pm\sqrt{5}i$$

Substituting in (20.26),
$$x_c = B_1 \cos\sqrt{5}t + B_2 \sin\sqrt{5}t$$

and
$$x(t) = B_1 \cos\sqrt{5}t + B_2 \sin\sqrt{5}t - 2.7$$

21.13. Find extremals for

$$\int_{t_0}^{t_1} e^{0.12t}(5\dot{x}^2 - 18x)\, dt$$

subject to
$$x(t_0) = x_0 \qquad x(t_1) = x_1$$

1.
$$F = e^{0.12t}(5\dot{x}^2 - 18x)$$

2.
$$F_x = -18e^{0.12t} \qquad F_{\dot{x}} = 10\dot{x}e^{0.12t}$$

3.
$$-18e^{0.12t} = \frac{d}{dt}(10\dot{x}e^{0.12t})$$

4. Using the product rule,
$$-18e^{0.12t} = 10\dot{x}(0.12e^{0.12t}) + e^{0.12t}(10\ddot{x})$$

Canceling the $e^{0.12t}$ terms and rearranging algebraically,
$$\ddot{x} + 0.12\dot{x} = -1.8$$

5. Using (20.2a) and (20.4),

$$x_p = \left(\frac{-1.8}{0.12}\right)t = -15t$$
$$r_1, r_2 = \frac{-0.12 \pm \sqrt{(0.12)^2 - 0}}{2} = -0.12, 0$$
$$x_c = A_1 e^{-0.12t} + A_2$$

and
$$x(t) = A_1 e^{-0.12t} + A_2 - 15t$$

21.14. Find extremals for

$$\int_{t_0}^{t_1} e^{-0.05t}(4\dot{x}^2 + 15x)\, dt$$

subject to $\quad\quad x(t_0) = x_0 \quad\quad x(t_1) = x_1$

1. $\quad\quad F = e^{-0.05t}(4\dot{x}^2 + 15x)$

2. $\quad\quad F_x = 15e^{-0.05t} \quad\quad F_{\dot{x}} = 8\dot{x}e^{-0.05t}$

3. $\quad\quad 15e^{-0.05t} = \dfrac{d}{dt}(8\dot{x}e^{-0.05t})$

4. $\quad\quad 15e^{-0.05t} = 8\dot{x}(-0.05e^{-0.05t}) + e^{-0.05t}(8\ddot{x})$

Canceling the $e^{-0.05t}$ terms and rearranging,

$$\ddot{x} - 0.05\dot{x} = 1.875$$

5. Using (*20.2a*) and (*20.4*),

$$x_p = \left(\frac{1.875}{-0.05}\right)t = -37.5t$$

$$r_1, r_2 = \frac{-(-0.05) \pm \sqrt{(-0.05)^2 - 0}}{2} = 0.05,\, 0$$

$$x_c = A_1 e^{0.05t} + A_2$$

and $\quad\quad x(t) = A_1 e^{0.05t} + A_2 - 37.5t$

21.15. Find the curve connecting (t_0, x_0) and (t_1, x_1) which will generate the surface of minimal area when revolved around the t axis, as in Fig. 21-4. That is,

$$\text{Minimize} \quad 2\pi \int_{t_0}^{t_1} x(1 + \dot{x}^2)^{1/2}\, dt$$

subject to $\quad\quad x(t_0) = x_0 \quad\quad x(t_1) = x_1$

1. $\quad\quad F = x(1 + \dot{x}^2)^{1/2}$

2. Using the chain rule for $F_{\dot{x}}$,

$$F_x = (1 + \dot{x}^2)^{1/2} \quad\quad F_{\dot{x}} = x\dot{x}(1 + \dot{x}^2)^{-1/2}$$

3. $\quad\quad (1 + \dot{x}^2)^{1/2} = \dfrac{d}{dt}\left[x\dot{x}(1 + \dot{x}^2)^{-1/2}\right]$

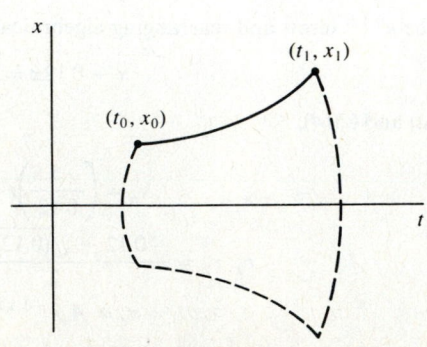

Fig. 21-4

4. Using the product rule and the chain rule,

$$(1 + \dot{x}^2)^{1/2} = x\dot{x}[-\tfrac{1}{2}(1 + \dot{x}^2)^{-3/2} \cdot 2\dot{x}\ddot{x}] + (1 + \dot{x}^2)^{-1/2}(x\ddot{x} + \dot{x}\dot{x})$$
$$= -x\dot{x}^2\ddot{x}(1 + \dot{x}^2)^{-3/2} + (x\ddot{x} + \dot{x}^2)(1 + \dot{x}^2)^{-1/2}$$

Multiplying both sides by $(1 + \dot{x}^2)^{3/2}$,

$$(1 + \dot{x}^2)^2 = -x\dot{x}^2\ddot{x} + (x\ddot{x} + \dot{x}^2)(1 + \dot{x}^2)$$
$$1 + 2\dot{x}^2 + \dot{x}^4 = -x\dot{x}^2\ddot{x} + x\ddot{x} + \dot{x}^2 + x\dot{x}^2\ddot{x} + \dot{x}^4$$

$$\ddot{x} - \frac{\dot{x}^2}{x} = \frac{1}{x} \tag{21.27}$$

5. Let $\dot{x} = u = dx/dt$, then

$$\ddot{x} = \dot{u} = \frac{du}{dt} = \frac{du}{dx} \cdot \frac{dx}{dt} = \frac{du}{dx} \cdot u = u\frac{du}{dx}$$

Substituting in (21.27),

$$u\frac{du}{dx} - \frac{u^2}{x} = \frac{1}{x}$$

Separating the variables and integrating,

$$u\frac{du}{dx} = \frac{1}{x}(1 + u^2)$$
$$\int \frac{u}{1 + u^2}\, du = \int \frac{1}{x}\, dx$$
$$\tfrac{1}{2}\ln(1 + u^2) + c_1 = \ln x$$

Solving for u,

$$e^{\ln\sqrt{1 + u^2} + c_1} = e^{\ln x}$$
$$c_2\sqrt{1 + u^2} = x$$

where $c_2 = e^{c_1}$. Squaring both sides and rearranging algebraically,

$$1 + u^2 = \frac{x^2}{c_2^2}$$
$$u = \frac{\sqrt{x^2 - c_2^2}}{c_2} = \frac{dx}{dt}$$

Separating variables again and integrating,

$$\int \frac{dx}{\sqrt{x^2 - c_2^2}} = \int \frac{dt}{c_2} \tag{21.28}$$

Using integral tables for the left-hand side,

$$\ln(x + \sqrt{x^2 - c_2^2}) = \frac{t + c_3}{c_2} \tag{21.29}$$

or by applying trigonometric substitution directly to (21.28),

$$\cosh^{-1}\frac{x}{c_2} = \frac{t + c_3}{c_2}$$

$$x(t) = c_2 \cosh\frac{t + c_3}{c_2} \tag{21.30}$$

The curve in (21.30) is called a *catenary* from the Latin word for chain because it depicts the shape a chain would assume if hung from points (t_0, x_0) and (t_1, x_1). The constants c_2 and c_3 can be found from either (21.29) or (21.30) by using the initial conditions $x(t_0) = x_0$ and $x(t_1) = x_1$.

ECONOMIC APPLICATIONS

21.16. The demand for a monopolist's product in terms of the number of units $x(t)$ she or he can sell depends on both the price $p(t)$ of the good and the rate of change of price $\dot{p}(t)$:

$$x(t) = ap(t) + b\dot{p}(t) + c \qquad (21.31)$$

Production costs $z(x)$ at rate of production x are

$$z(x) = mx^2 + nx + k \qquad (21.32)$$

Assuming $p(0) = p_0$ and the desired price at time T is $p(T) = p_1$, find the pricing policy to maximize profits over $0 \le t \le T$. That is,

$$\text{Maximize} \quad \int_0^T [p(t)x(t) - z(x)] \, dt$$

Substituting from (21.31) and (21.32),

$$\int_0^T [p(t)x(t) - z(x)] \, dt = \int_0^T [p(ap + b\dot{p} + c) - (mx^2 + nx + k)] \, dt$$

Substituting from (21.31) again,

$$\begin{aligned}
\int_0^T [p(t)x(t) - z(x)] \, dt &= \int_0^T [ap^2 + bp\dot{p} + cp - m(ap + b\dot{p} + c)^2 - n(ap + b\dot{p} + c) - k] \, dt \\
&= \int_0^T (ap^2 + bp\dot{p} + cp - ma^2p^2 - mabp\dot{p} - macp - mabp\dot{p} - mb^2\dot{p}^2 \\
&\quad - mbc\dot{p} - macp - mbc\dot{p} - mc^2 - nap - nb\dot{p} - nc - k) \, dt \\
&= \int_0^T [a(1 - ma)p^2 + (c - 2mac - na)p + (b - 2mab)p\dot{p} \\
&\quad - (2mbc + nb)\dot{p} - mb^2\dot{p}^2 - mc^2 - nc - k] \, dt \qquad (21.33)
\end{aligned}$$

Letting F = the integrand in (21.33),

$$F_p = 2a(1 - ma)p + c - 2mac - na + (b - 2mab)\dot{p}$$

and

$$F_{\dot{p}} = (b - 2mab)p - 2mbc - nb - 2mb^2\dot{p}$$

Using the Euler equation,

$$2a(1 - ma)p + c - 2mac - na + (b - 2mab)\dot{p} = \frac{d}{dt}[(b - 2mab)p - 2mbc - nb - 2mb^2\dot{p}]$$

$$2a(1 - ma)p + c - 2mac - na + (b - 2mab)\dot{p} = (b - 2mab)\dot{p} - 2mb^2\ddot{p}$$

Rearranging algebraically,

$$2mb^2\ddot{p} + 2a(1 - ma)p = 2mac + na - c$$

$$\ddot{p} + \left[\frac{a(1 - ma)}{mb^2}\right]p = \frac{2mac + na - c}{2mb^2}$$

Using (20.2) and (20.4),

$$p_p = \frac{(2mac + na - c)/(2mb^2)}{a(1 - ma)/(mb^2)} = \frac{2mac + na - c}{2a(1 - ma)}$$

$$r_1, r_2 = \frac{0 \pm \sqrt{0 - 4a(1 - ma)/(mb^2)}}{2} = \pm\sqrt{\frac{a(ma - 1)}{mb^2}}$$

Thus,

$$p(t) = A_1 \exp\left(\sqrt{\frac{a(ma - 1)}{mb^2}}\right)t + A_2 \exp-\left(\sqrt{\frac{a(ma - 1)}{mb^2}}\right)t + \frac{2mac + na - c}{2a(1 - ma)}$$

If $a < 0$ and $m > 0$, as one would expect from economic theory, independently of the sign for b, $\sqrt{a(ma - 1)/(mb^2)} > 0$ and the time path $p(t)$ will have distinct real roots of equal magnitude and opposite signs.

Note: This is a classic case that has appeared in one form or another in the economic literature over the decades.

21.17. Maximize the stream of instantaneous utility $U(t)$ from the flow of consumption $C(t)$ where

$$
\begin{array}{ccccc}
C(t) & = & G[K(t)] & - & \dot{K}(t) \\
\downarrow & & \downarrow & & \downarrow \\
\text{Flow of consumption} & = & \text{production} & - & \text{investment}
\end{array}
\qquad (21.34)
$$

and the endpoints are fixed at $K(0) = K_0$, $K(T) = K_T$. That is,

$$
\text{Maximize} \int_0^T U[C(t)]\, dt = \int_0^T U\{G[K(t)] - \dot{K}(t)\}\, dt
$$

subject to

$$
K(0) = K_0 \qquad K(T) = K_T
$$

Letting $F = U\{G[K(t)] - \dot{K}(t)\}$, $U' = dU/dC$, and $G' = dG/dK$,

$$
F_K = U'[C(t)]G'[K(t)] \qquad F_{\dot{K}} = -U'[C(t)]
$$

Substituting in Euler's equation,

$$
U'[C(t)]G'[K(t)] = \frac{d}{dt}\{-U'[C(t)]\}
$$
$$
= -U''[C(t)] \cdot \dot{C}
$$

where, upon using the chain rule on (21.34),

$$
\dot{C} = \frac{dC}{dt} = G'[K(t)] \cdot \dot{K} - \ddot{K}
$$

Substituting above,

$$
U'[C(t)]G'[K(t)] = -U''[C(t)] \cdot (G'[K(t)] \cdot \dot{K} - \ddot{K})
$$

The Euler equation thus yields a second-order ordinary differential equation, the solution of which maximizes the given extremal.

21.18. Maximize the discounted stream of utility from consumption $C(t)$ over $0 \le t \le T$, that is,

$$
\text{Maximize} \int_0^T \{e^{-it}U[C(t)]\}\, dt
\qquad (21.35)
$$

where $C(t) = G[K(t)] - \dot{K}(t) - bK(t)$, $0 \le b \le 1$, $G[K(t)]$ is the rate of production, $\dot{K}(t) + bK(t)$ is investment, and b is a constant rate of capital depreciation.

Substituting in (21.35), we seek to maximize

$$
\int_0^T (e^{-it}U\{G[K(t)] - \dot{K}(t) - bK(t)\})\, dt
$$

With

$$
F = e^{-it}U\{G[K(t)] - \dot{K}(t) - bK(t)\}
$$

and letting $U' = dU/dC$ and $G' = dG/dK$, while retaining $\dot{K} = dK/dt$,

$$
F_K = e^{-it}U'\{G[K(t)] - \dot{K}(t) - bK(t)\} \cdot \{G'[K(t)] - b\}
$$
$$
F_{\dot{K}} = -e^{-it}U'\{G[K(t)] - \dot{K}(t) - bK(t)\}
$$

Substituting in Euler's equation and simplifying notation,

$$e^{-it}[U' \cdot (G' - b)] = \frac{d}{dt}(-e^{-it}U') \qquad (21.36)$$

Using the product and chain rules for the derivative on the right,

$$e^{-it}[U' \cdot (G' - b)] = -e^{-it}U'' \cdot (G'\dot{K} - \ddot{K} - b\dot{K}) + U'ie^{-it}$$

and canceling the e^{-it} terms,

$$U' \cdot (G' - b) = -U'' \cdot (G'\dot{K} - \ddot{K} - b\dot{K}) + U'i$$

With $U\{G[K(t)]\}$ unspecified, we cannot proceed further. Going back to (21.36) and using general notation for the derivative on the right, however, we see that

$$e^{-it}[U' \cdot (G' - b)] = -e^{-it}\frac{d}{dt}(U') + U'(ie^{-it})$$

Canceling the e^{-it} terms and rearranging,

$$\frac{d}{dt}(U') = U'i - U' \cdot (G' - b)$$

$$\frac{d(U')/dt}{U'} = i + b - G'$$

where the term on the left, the rate of change of the marginal utility, equals the discount rate plus the depreciation rate minus the marginal product of capital. In brief, if we consider the term on the left as capital gains, the optimal time path suggests that if capital gains are greater than the discount rate plus the depreciation rate minus the marginal product of capital, then more capital and hence more consumption should be forthcoming. If it is less, capital accumulation and consumption should be scaled back.

21.19. Maximize the discounted stream of utility from consumption $C(t)$ over $0 \le t < T$, that is,

$$\text{Maximize} \quad \int_0^T e^{-it}U[C(t)]\, dt \qquad (21.37)$$

given (a) $\qquad\qquad U[C(t)] = [C(t)]^n \qquad \text{where} \quad 0 \le n \le 1$

(b) $\qquad\qquad\qquad C(t) \quad = \quad G[K(t)] \quad - \quad I(t)$
$$\qquad\qquad\qquad\qquad \downarrow \qquad\qquad\quad \downarrow \qquad\quad \downarrow$$

$$\text{Flow of consumption} = \text{production} - \text{investment}$$

where $G[K(t)] = aK(t)$, a linear production function with $a > 0$ and

(c) $\qquad\qquad I(t) = \dot{K}(t) + B + bK(t) \qquad 0 \le b \le 1 \qquad B > 0$

derived from

$$\dot{K}(t) \quad = \quad I(t) \quad - \quad [B + bK(t)]$$
$$\downarrow \qquad\quad \downarrow \qquad\qquad\quad \downarrow$$

$$\Delta \text{ in } K \text{ stock} = \text{investment} - \text{linear depreciation}$$

Substituting in (21.37), we wish to maximize

$$\int_0^T e^{-it}[aK(t) - \dot{K}(t) - B - bK(t)]^n\, dt$$

which by rearranging and omitting the arguments for simplicity becomes

$$\int_0^T e^{-it}(mK - \dot{K} - B)^n\, dt$$

where $m = a - b$. Letting $F = e^{-it}(mK - \dot{K} - B)^n$,

$$F_K = mne^{-it}(mK - \dot{K} - B)^{n-1} \qquad F_{\dot{K}} = -ne^{-it}(mK - \dot{K} - B)^{n-1}$$

Using Euler's equation,

$$mne^{-it}(mK - \dot{K} - B)^{n-1} = \frac{d}{dt}\left[-ne^{-it}(mK - \dot{K} - B)^{n-1}\right]$$

Using the product rule and the chain rule on the right,

$$mne^{-it}(mK - \dot{K} - B)^{n-1} = -ne^{-it}(n-1)(mK - \dot{K} - B)^{n-2}(m\dot{K} - \ddot{K}) + (mK - \dot{K} - B)^{n-1}(ine^{-it})$$

Dividing both sides by $ne^{-it}(mK - \dot{K} - B)^{n-1}$,

$$m = -(n-1)(mK - \dot{K} - B)^{-1}(m\dot{K} - \ddot{K}) + i$$

$$m - i = \frac{(1-n)(m\dot{K} - \ddot{K})}{mK - \dot{K} - B}$$

Cross-multiplying and simplifying,

$$(1-n)\ddot{K} + (i + mn - 2m)\dot{K} + (m^2 - im)K = (m-i)B$$

$$\ddot{K} + \frac{i + mn - 2m}{1-n}\dot{K} + \frac{m^2 - im}{1-n}K = \frac{m-i}{1-n}B \tag{21.38}$$

Letting

$$Z_1 = \frac{i + mn - 2m}{1-n} \qquad Z_2 = \frac{m^2 - im}{1-n} \qquad Z_3 = \frac{m-i}{1-n}B$$

$$K_p = \frac{Z_3}{Z_2} = \frac{B(m-i)/(1-n)}{(m^2 - im)/(1-n)} = \frac{(m-i)B}{m(m-i)} = \frac{1}{m}B$$

where $m = a - b$, a is the marginal product of capital ($dG/dK = a$), and b is the constant rate of depreciation.

$$K_c = A_1 e^{r_1 t} + A_2 e^{r_2 t}$$

where

$$r_1, r_2 = \frac{-Z_1 \pm \sqrt{Z_1^2 - 4Z_2}}{2}$$

and A_1 and A_2 can be computed from the boundary conditions.

21.20. Maximize

$$\int_0^T e^{-it}U[C(t)]\, dt$$

given the discount rate $i = 0.12$, the endpoints $K(0) = 320$ and $K(5) = 480$, and the utility function $U[C(t)] = [C(t)]^{0.5}$, where

$$C(t) = G[K(t)] - I(t)$$

$$G[K(t)] = 0.25K \qquad I(t) = \dot{K} + 60 + 0.05K(t)$$

Substituting in the given functional, we seek to maximize

$$\int_0^5 e^{-0.12t}[0.25K(t) - \dot{K}(t) - 60 - 0.05K(t)]^{0.5}\, dt$$

Rearranging and omitting the arguments for simplicity,

$$\int_0^5 e^{-0.12t}(0.2K - \dot{K} - 60)^{0.5}\, dt$$

Letting

$$F = e^{-0.12t}(0.2K - \dot{K} - 60)^{0.5}$$

and using the chain rule or the generalized power function rule,

$$F_K = 0.1e^{-0.12t}(0.2K - \dot{K} - 60)^{-0.5} \qquad F_{\dot{K}} = -0.5e^{-0.12t}(0.2K - \dot{K} - 60)^{-0.5}$$

Substituting in Euler's equation, then using the product rule and the chain rule,

$$0.1e^{-0.12t}(0.2K - \dot{K} - 60)^{-0.5} = \frac{d}{dt}\left[-0.5e^{-0.12t}(0.2K - \dot{K} - 60)^{-0.5}\right]$$

$$= -0.5e^{-0.12t}\left[-0.5(0.2K - \dot{K} - 60)^{-1.5}(0.2\dot{K} - \ddot{K})\right]$$
$$+ (0.2K - \dot{K} - 60)^{-0.5}(0.06e^{-0.12t})$$

Dividing both sides by $0.5e^{-0.12t}(0.2K - \dot{K} - 60)^{-0.5}$ and rearranging,

$$0.2 = \frac{0.5(0.2\dot{K} - \ddot{K})}{0.2K - \dot{K} - 60} + 0.12$$

$$0.08(0.2K - \dot{K} - 60) = 0.1\dot{K} - 0.5\ddot{K}$$

$$\ddot{K} - 0.36\dot{K} + 0.032K = 9.6 \qquad (21.39)$$

Using (20.2) and (20.4),

$$K_p = \frac{9.6}{0.032} = 300$$

$$r_1, r_2 = \frac{-(-0.36) \pm \sqrt{(-0.36)^2 - 4(0.032)}}{2} = \frac{0.36 \pm \sqrt{0.0016}}{2}$$

$$r_1 = 0.2 \qquad r_2 = 0.16$$

Thus,
$$K(t) = A_1 e^{0.2t} + A_2 e^{0.16t} + 300$$

Applying the endpoint conditions,

$$K(0) = A_1 + A_2 + 300 = 320 \qquad A_2 = 20 - A_1$$
$$K(5) = A_1 e^{0.2(5)} + (20 - A_1)e^{0.16(5)} + 300 = 480$$
$$A_1(2.71828) + (20 - A_1)(2.22554) = 180$$
$$A_1 = 274.97 \approx 275 \qquad A_2 = 20 - 275 = -255$$

Substituting,

$$K(t) = 275\,e^{0.2t} - 255\,e^{0.16t} + 300$$

21.21. Since Problem 21.20 is a specific application of Problem 21.19, check the accuracy of the answer in Problem 21.20 by substituting the given values of $a = 0.25$, $b = 0.05$, $B = 60$, $i = 0.12$, $m = 0.2$, and $n = 0.5$ in Equation (21.38) to make sure it yields the same answer as Equation (21.39).

Substituting the specific values in (21.38),

$$\ddot{K} + \left[\frac{0.12 + (0.2)(0.5) - 2(0.2)}{1 - 0.5}\right]\dot{K} + \left[\frac{(0.2)^2 - (0.12)(0.2)}{1 - 0.5}\right]K = \left(\frac{0.2 - 0.12}{1 - 0.5}\right)60$$

$$\ddot{K} - 0.36\dot{K} + 0.032K = 9.6$$

On your own, check the values of r_1, r_2, K_c, and $K(t)$ by substituting the specific values in the equations immediately following (21.38) in Problem 21.19 and comparing them with the solutions found in Problem 21.20.

CONSTRAINED OPTIMIZATION

21.22. Minimize
$$\int_{t_0}^{t_1} e^{-it}(a\dot{x}^2 + bx)\,dt$$

subject to
$$\int_{t_0}^{t_1} \dot{x}(t)\,dt = N$$

where
$$x(t_0) = 0 \qquad \text{and} \qquad x(t_1) = N$$

Setting up the Lagrangian function, as in Section 21.5,

$$\int_{t_0}^{t_1} [e^{-it}(a\dot{x}^2 + bx) + \lambda\dot{x}] \, dt$$

Letting H equal the integrand, the Euler equation is

$$\frac{\partial H}{\partial x} = \frac{d}{dt}\left(\frac{\partial H}{\partial \dot{x}}\right)$$

Taking the needed partial derivatives,

$$H_x = be^{-it} \qquad H_{\dot{x}} = 2a\dot{x}e^{-it} + \lambda$$

Substituting in Euler's equation,

$$be^{-it} = \frac{d}{dt}(2a\dot{x}e^{-it} + \lambda)$$

Using the product and generalized power function rules,

$$be^{-it} = -2ai\dot{x}e^{-it} + 2a\ddot{x}e^{-it}$$

Canceling the e^{-it} terms and rearranging,

$$\ddot{x} - i\dot{x} = \frac{b}{2a}$$

which is identical to what we found in (21.22) without using constrained dynamic optimization. This is another example of an isoperimetric problem, and it can be solved as it was in Section 21.7.

PROOFS AND DEMONSTRATIONS

21.23. In seeking an extremal for

$$\int_{t_0}^{t_1} F(t, x, \dot{x}) \, dt$$

show that Euler's equation can also be expressed as

$$\frac{d}{dt}\left(F - \dot{x}\frac{\partial F}{\partial \dot{x}}\right) - \frac{\partial F}{\partial t} = 0 \tag{21.40}$$

Taking the derivative with respect to t of each term within the parentheses and using the chain rule,

$$\frac{dF}{dt} = \frac{\partial F}{\partial t} + \frac{\partial F}{\partial x}\frac{dx}{dt} + \frac{\partial F}{\partial \dot{x}}\frac{d\dot{x}}{dt} = \frac{\partial F}{\partial t} + \frac{\partial F}{\partial x}\dot{x} + \frac{\partial F}{\partial \dot{x}}\ddot{x}$$

$$\frac{d}{dt}\left(\dot{x}\frac{\partial F}{\partial \dot{x}}\right) = \dot{x}\frac{d}{dt}\left(\frac{\partial F}{\partial \dot{x}}\right) + \frac{\partial F}{\partial \dot{x}}\ddot{x}$$

and substituting in (21.40),

$$\frac{\partial F}{\partial t} + \frac{\partial F}{\partial x}\dot{x} + \frac{\partial F}{\partial \dot{x}}\ddot{x} - \left[\dot{x}\frac{d}{dt}\left(\frac{\partial F}{\partial \dot{x}}\right) + \frac{\partial F}{\partial \dot{x}}\ddot{x}\right] - \frac{\partial F}{\partial t} = 0$$

$$\dot{x}\left[\frac{\partial F}{\partial x} - \frac{d}{dt}\left(\frac{\partial F}{\partial \dot{x}}\right)\right] = 0$$

$$\frac{\partial F}{\partial x} = \frac{d}{dt}\left(\frac{\partial F}{\partial \dot{x}}\right) \qquad \text{or} \qquad F_x = \frac{d}{dt}(F_{\dot{x}})$$

21.24. Show that if F is not an explicit function of t, the Euler equation can be expressed as

$$F - \dot{x}\frac{\partial F}{\partial \dot{x}} = c \qquad \text{a constant}$$

If t is not an explicit argument of F, $\partial F/\partial t = 0$ and Equation (21.40) reduces to

$$\frac{d}{dt}\left(F - \dot{x}\,\frac{\partial F}{\partial \dot{x}}\right) = 0$$

Integrating both sides with respect to t,

$$F - \dot{x}\,\frac{\partial F}{\partial \dot{x}} = c$$

21.25. (a) Show that if $F = F(t, \dot{x})$, with x not one of the arguments, the Euler equation reduces to

$$F_{\dot{x}} = c \qquad \text{a constant}$$

(b) Explain the significance.

(a) With $F = F(t, \dot{x})$

$$F_x = 0 \qquad F_{\dot{x}} = F_{\dot{x}}$$

Substituting in Euler's equation,

$$0 = \frac{d}{dt}\,(F_{\dot{x}})$$

Integrating both sides with respect to t,

$$F_{\dot{x}} = c \qquad\qquad (21.41)$$

(b) Equation (21.41) is a first-order differential equation with arguments of t and $\dot{x}$ alone which, when solved, provides the desired extremal. See Problems 21.7 and 21.8.

21.26. (a) Show that if $F = F(\dot{x})$, that is, a function of $\dot{x}$ alone, the Euler equation reduces to

$$F_{\dot{x}\dot{x}}\,\ddot{x} = 0$$

and (b) explain the significance.

(a) Given

$$F = F(\dot{x})$$

$$F_x = 0 \qquad F_{\dot{x}} = F_{\dot{x}}$$

Using Euler's equation,

$$0 = \frac{d}{dt}\,[F_{\dot{x}}(\dot{x})] = F_{\dot{x}\dot{x}}\,\ddot{x} \qquad\qquad (21.42)$$

(b) From (21.42), either $\ddot{x} = 0$ or $F_{\dot{x}\dot{x}} = 0$. If $\ddot{x} = 0$, integrating twice yields $x(t) = c_1 t + c_2$, which is linear. If $F_{\dot{x}\dot{x}} = 0$, $F_{\dot{x}} = c$, a constant, which means that F is linear in $\dot{x}$. If F is linear in $\dot{x}$, the solution is trivial. See Problems 21.27 and 21.28.

21.27. Find extremals for

$$\int_{t_0}^{t_1} e^{-3\dot{x}^2}\,dt$$

subject to

$$x(t_0) = x_0 \qquad x(t_1) = x_1$$

$$F_x = 0 \qquad F_{\dot{x}} = -6\dot{x}e^{-3\dot{x}^2}$$

$$0 = \frac{d}{dt}\,(-6\dot{x}e^{-3\dot{x}^2})$$

By the product rule,

$$0 = -6\dot{x}(-6\dot{x}e^{-3\dot{x}^2}\ddot{x}) + e^{-3\dot{x}^2}(-6\ddot{x})$$

$$6\ddot{x}e^{-3\dot{x}^2}(6\dot{x}^2 - 1) = 0 \qquad\qquad (21.43)$$

which is a nonlinear second-order differential equation, not easily solved. However, since $\ddot{x}$ in (21.43) must equal zero for the equation to equal zero, from Problem 21.26 we know that the solution must be linear. Thus,

$$x(t) = c_1 t + c_2$$

21.28. Find extremals for

$$\int_{t_0}^{t_1} (27 - 5\dot{x})\, dt$$

subject to

$$x(t_0) = x_0 \qquad x(t_1) = x_1$$
$$F_x = 0 \qquad F_{\dot{x}} = -5$$
$$0 = \frac{d}{dt}(-5) = 0$$

The Euler equation is an identity which any admissible value of x satisfies trivially, as was indicated in Problem 21.26. This becomes clear upon direct integration of the extremal in this problem:

$$\int_{t_0}^{t_1} (27 - 5\dot{x})\, dt = 27(t_1 - t_0) - 5[x(t_1) - x(t_0)]$$

and any x satisfying the endpoint conditions yields the same value for this integrand.

21.29. (a) Show that if $F = F(t, x)$, with $\dot{x}$ not one of the arguments, the Euler equation reduces to

$$F_x = 0$$

(b) Explain the significance.

(a) With $F = F(t, x)$,

$$F_x = F_x \qquad F_{\dot{x}} = 0$$

Substituting in Euler's equation,

$$F_x = \frac{d}{dt}(0) = 0$$

(b) When there is no $\dot{x}$ term in F, the optimization problem is static and not dynamic. The condition for optimization, therefore, is the same as that in static optimization, namely,

$$F_x = 0$$

21.30. Show that if application of Euler's equation results in a second-order differential equation with no x or t terms, the second-order differential equation can be converted to a first-order differential equation and a solution found by means of Equation (18.1). Demonstrate in terms of Equation (21.22) from Section 21.7.

From Equation (21.22),

$$\ddot{x} = i\dot{x} + \frac{b}{2a}$$

Since there are no x or t terms in (21.22), it can be converted to a first-order linear differential equation by letting

$$u = \dot{x} \qquad \text{and} \qquad \dot{u} = \ddot{x}$$

Substituting in (21.22) above and rearranging,

$$\dot{u} - iu = \frac{b}{2a}$$

which can be solved by means of the formula in (18.1). Letting $v = -i$ and $z = b/2a$,

$$u = e^{-\int(-i)\,dt}\left(A + \int \frac{b}{2a}\, e^{\int(-i)\,dt}\, dt\right)$$

$$= e^{it}\left(A + \int \frac{b}{2a}\, e^{-it}\, dt\right)$$

Taking the remaining integral,

$$u = e^{it}\left[A + \left(-\frac{1}{i}\right)\frac{b}{2a}\, e^{-it}\right]$$

$$u = Ae^{it} - \frac{b}{2ai}$$

But $u = \dot{x}(t)$ by definition, so we must integrate once again to find $x(t)$. Replacing A with c_1 for notational consistency with ordinary integration,

$$x(t) = \frac{c_1}{i}\, e^{it} - \frac{b}{2ai}\, t + c_2 \qquad (21.44)$$

Letting $t_0 = 0$ and $t_1 = T$, from the boundary conditions we have

$$x(0) = \frac{c_1}{i} + c_2 = 0 \qquad c_2 = -\frac{c_1}{i}$$

$$x(T) = \frac{c_1}{i}\, e^{iT} - \frac{b}{2ai}\, T + c_2 = N$$

Substituting $c_2 = -c_1/i$ in $x(T)$ and solving for c_1,

$$\frac{c_1}{i}\, e^{iT} - \frac{b}{2ai}\, T - \frac{c_1}{i} = N$$

$$\frac{c_1}{i}\, (e^{iT} - 1) = N + \frac{b}{2ai}\, T$$

$$c_1 = \frac{i\{N + [b/(2ai)]T\}}{e^{iT} - 1} \qquad (21.45)$$

Finally, substituting in (21.44) and noting that the i in (21.45) cancels out the i in the denominator of c_1/i, we have as a candidate for an extremal:

$$x(t) = \frac{N + [b/(2ai)]T}{e^{iT} - 1}\, e^{it} - \frac{b}{2ai}\, t - \frac{N + [b/(2ai)]T}{e^{iT} - 1}$$

$$= \left(N + \frac{b}{2ai}\, T\right)\left(\frac{e^{it} - 1}{e^{iT} - 1}\right) - \frac{b}{2ai}\, t \qquad 0 \le t \le T$$

Compare the work done here with the work done in Section 21.7, and note that conversion of a second-order differential equation to a first-order differential equation before integrating does not necessarily reduce the work involved in finding a solution.

VARIATIONAL NOTATION

21.31. Show that the operators δ and d/dt are commutative, i.e., show that

$$\delta\left(\frac{dx}{dt}\right) = \frac{d}{dt}\, (\delta x)$$

From (21.19) and (21.20),

$$\delta x = mh \qquad \text{and} \qquad \delta \dot{x} = m\dot{h}$$

where m is an arbitrary constant and h is an arbitrary function $h = h(t)$. Substituting dx/dt for $\dot{x}$ above on the right,

$$\delta\left(\frac{dx}{dt}\right) = m\dot{h}$$

Expressing $\dot{h}$ as dh/dt and recalling that m is a constant,

$$\delta\left(\frac{dx}{dt}\right) = \frac{d}{dt}(mh)$$

Then substituting from (21.19),

$$\delta\left(\frac{dx}{dt}\right) = \frac{d}{dt}(\delta x)$$

21.32. Given

$$\int_{t_0}^{t_1} F[t, x(t), \dot{x}(t)]\, dt$$

show that in terms of variational notation a necessary condition for an extremal is

$$\delta \int_{t_0}^{t_1} F[t, x(t), \dot{x}(t)]\, dt = 0$$

Moving δ within the integral sign,

$$\int_{t_0}^{t_1} \delta F[t, x(t), \dot{x}(t)]\, dt = 0$$

From (21.21),

$$\int_{t_0}^{t_1} \left(\frac{\partial F}{\partial x}\,\delta x + \frac{\partial F}{\partial \dot{x}}\,\delta \dot{x}\right) dt = 0$$

Substituting from (21.19) and (21.20) where

$$\delta x = mh \qquad \delta \dot{x} = m\dot{h}$$

$$\int_{t_0}^{t_1} \left(\frac{\partial F}{\partial x}\, mh + \frac{\partial F}{\partial \dot{x}}\, m\dot{h}\right) dt = 0$$

Dividing by m, an arbitrary constant,

$$\int_{t_0}^{t_1} \left(\frac{\partial F}{\partial x}\, h + \frac{\partial F}{\partial \dot{x}}\, \dot{h}\right) dt = 0 \qquad\qquad (21.46)$$

Equation (21.46) is identical to Equation (21.8) in the Euler equation proof from Example 2 and can be concluded in the same manner.

Index

The letter *p* following a page number refers to a Problem.

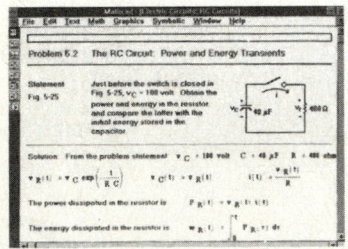